D1432983

# Human Jurisprudence

# Human Jurisprudence

## Public Law as Political Science

Glendon Schubert

Foreword by David J. Danelski

The University Press of Hawaii
Honolulu

*Designed by Penny L. Faron*

**Library of Congress Cataloging in Publication Data**

Schubert, Glendon A
    Human jurisprudence.

    Bibliography: p.
    Includes index.
    1.  Judicial process—United States.  2.  Judicial
process—Australia.  3.  Judicial process—Japan.
I.  Title.
KF8700.S33          347′.73         74-78862
ISBN 0-8248-0294-2

To the memory of

**LEONARD BROWN**

humanist,
scientist,
teacher,
and friend

# Contents

# Figures

# Tables

# Foreword

## David J. Danelski

**Goldwin Smith Professor of Government, Cornell University**

This book provides a rare view of a creative scholar at work during a highly productive phase of his career. It shows him as an innovator, theorist, methodologist, "missionary," critic, and scientist, but he remains, withal, in his fashion, a humanist. He believes that institutions and processes—particularly law, politics, and scholarship—are best understood in human terms. With Holmes, he believes that law is a prediction of what courts will do; hence, to understand law it is necessary to understand judicial behavior. A full explanation of a judge's behavior would take into account his health (both physical and mental), his personality, his culture and society, and his ideology. Glendon Schubert concedes this but focuses primarily on ideology because he believes the other variables are sublimated in it. Therefore, to him, ideology—attitudes toward human values—is the basic explanation of judicial behavior, and jurisprudence is necessarily human.

The genesis of innovative ideas is usually rooted in a dimly remembered past. This is not the case in regard to Professor Schubert's ideas. He remembers clearly his undergraduate days at Syracuse in the late 1930s when he climbed the steps to Leonard Brown's home on "the Hill" to participate in Brown's seminar on literary criticism. The use of Marxian and Freudian paradigms in that seminar to study literary behavior led Schubert some twenty years later to use other paradigms to study judicial behavior. Schubert shares with Brown the humanist-scientist connection, but unlike Brown he was not influenced by the thought of Marx and Freud; indeed he rejected their ideas. Instead, he was influenced by the work of rigorous social and behavioral scientists—C. Herman Pritchett, Louis L. Thurstone, Milton Rokeach, Hans J. Eysenck, Louis L. Guttman, and Clyde H. Coombs.

The studies in this volume are important in the study of judicial behavior, for they broke new ground, and some were forerunners of major books, such as *The Judicial Mind*, which was published in 1965. Each shows Professor Schubert's concern at the time they were written, and taken together they show movement and growth of his ideas and interests.

The first part of the book shows Professor Schubert reaching out to other disciplines, doing missionary work, explaining the importance of research on judicial behavior. Each of the articles is addressed to a different audience—practicing lawyers, law professors, and social scientists. The heading under which these articles appear—"From Legal to Behavioral Realism"—is significant. Legal realists like Jerome Frank had preceded Schubert in proclaiming that judges are human, and judicial behavioralism might be regarded as neo-legal realism. But there is an important difference between legal realism and judicial behavioralism. Legal realism, in Holmes' words, sought to "wash the law in cynical acid"; it destroyed legal myths, it proclaimed that the Emperor had no clothes, but it did not consciously seek to develop empirically verifiable theories that would explain law and its operation in society, nor did it seek to develop research methods. Judicial behavioralism, with Schubert as its chief spokesman, seeks to do both.

The second part of the book presents some of Professor Schubert's most important contributions to understanding judicial behavior. The first article sets forth an ingenious solution to Thurstone and Degan's early factor analysis of Supreme Court voting behavior. Thurstone and Degan showed that judicial voting behavior is susceptible to factor analysis, but they were unable to interpret the positions of the justices in factor space. By positioning scale axes of voting behavior of justices on specific issues—that is, political and economic liberalism—Schubert was able to show that their positions in factor space were closely related to their positions on the scale axes, strongly suggesting that the principal dimensions in the factor analysis measured ideological components of voting behavior. In the same article Schubert developed his theory of judicial voting behavior and methods he later used to test it. In the next article he tested the theory using data from a single Supreme Court term, and later, in *The Judicial Mind*, he expanded the study to cover sixteen terms. Schubert's study of Justice Jackson deals with a question raised in the previous studies, namely, does correspondence of the justices' positions on a Guttman scale with their positions in factor space mean that attitudes underlie votes? In the case of Jackson, at least, Schubert offers persuasive proof that the answer is yes, for Jackson's values, which were ascertained by content analysis of his opinions, were significantly related to his voting behavior. Professor Schubert's study of Australian High Court behavior reflects his interest in comparative judicial behavior and illustrates his ability to adapt his approach and methods to study a court that operates somewhat differently than the American Supreme Court. Yet his concern remains the same throughout, and it is to show that the law, whether in the United States or Australia, is a manifestation of human behavior. His Jackson study was the basis of a book entitled *Dispassionate Justice: A Synthesis of the Judicial Opinions of Robert H. Jackson*. When asked about the title, Professor Schubert acknowledged that it was an intentional pun. "Several of the opinions that I have included," he said, "reecho the phrase 'dispassionate justice,' an ideal that Jackson delighted in positing for other persons (such as colleagues, including Black and Murphy, whom he particularly disliked). My wish is to present Jackson as a very human judge, whose writings as a Supreme Court justice reflect directly the human values that he cherished most dearly. Hence, his passionate defense of these values; and hence it seems fitting to suggest the antonym as a most suitable epitaph for his literary testament."

In the third part of the book, Professor Schubert's concern goes beyond judicial ideology. In his article on ideological distance, he compares cross-culturally the attitudes of judges and non-judges. And in the two preceding articles he deals with academic ideology. If the behavior of judges is greatly influenced by ideology, so too, says Schubert, is the behavior of scholars who study judges. But he does more than make a statement; he gives proof. The article on academic ideology and the study of adjudication when published was bitterly criticized by some and dismissed by others, but it raises serious questions about objectivity in research and commentary about research. My proximity to Schubert in ideological space, as shown in that article, is, of course, related to my view of his work. That should be taken into account in reading this Foreword. But that is precisely Schubert's point—ideology is important in explaining all human behavior. Indeed, when I read the article originally, I thought it was imaginative pedagogy, an attempt to teach two things: (1) the importance of the relationship between ideology and behavior, including scholarly behavior; and (2) the appropriateness of the methods like factor analysis and smallest space analysis to show ideological proximity. If Professor Schubert was unsuccessful in teaching these lessons, he may have taught another lesson, namely, certain beliefs may be so strongly held by some persons that even empirical proof will not convince them.

The fourth part of the book is firmly rooted in the preceding pages, yet it goes beyond them and in a sense makes a full circle. "Three Models of Constitutional Change," "Future Stress," and "Justice and Reasoning" provide a series of paradigms for understanding judicial behavior and a great deal more. It is in this part of the book that the influence of Leonard Brown shows. Professor Schubert, reflecting on his careful empirical studies, generalizes and discusses models of constitutional change, future stress in the constitutional system, and a model of judicial reasoning. In all of Professor Schubert's work there is discernible progression; one study suggests and anticipates the next. In the final article of this book, Professor Schubert's current research interest is suggested—the biological basis of political behavior.

In places in *Human Jurisprudence*, the human side of Glendon Schubert shows. Much of the work presented in the book was and is controversial. It has been criticized and even attacked, and when it was, Professor Schubert unhesitatingly entered the polemical lists and argued forcibly in defense of his ideas and findings. Like Robert H. Jackson of whom he wrote, he is not a dispassionate man. His most remarkable quality is his passion for honesty in research and everything else. To the extent that his publishers have permitted him, he has published his data so that others can replicate his work and if possible disprove his findings. He has never covered his tracks, and that has been indeed fortunate for the scholars who have followed his lead.

# Preface

In the early autumn of 1939, I was fortunate in associating myself with the work of what without doubt was the most challenging, and to me the most interesting, course in which I enrolled as a university student. This was Leonard Brown's seminar in literary criticism, at Syracuse University.[1] There was a group of about twenty persons, mostly senior majors or graduate students in English or American literature, but with a scattering minority of others whose major work lay in disciplines ranging from forestry to physics. In at least this respect I was a quite typical member of the seminar, working in it first as an undergraduate English major and then as a graduate student (otherwise) in political science, for a total of two full years until the advent of World War II brought an abrupt hiatus of several years in my academic activities. When I knew it the class used to meet weekly, for the evening, in the L-shaped living-and-dining room of Brown's modest residence, perched on a crag (at least fifty or sixty almost vertical steps above the sidewalk) near the crest of one of the drumlins which surround, to the south and east, a campus that is itself referred to locally as "the Hill."

Brown's approach to literary criticism involved an endeavor to guide his students to an understanding of what he believed to be the most intellectually significant interpretations of human experience that were predominant

---

1. Leonard Stanley Brown (1904–1960) was born in Belvidere, Nebraska, and he was a graduate of Cotner College (B.A., 1924) and the University of Nebraska (M.A., 1925). He taught on the faculty of the English Department of Syracuse University from 1925 until his death almost thirty-five years later, with the exception of a year of resident graduate work at the University of Chicago. According to a colleague and friend who knew him well, "He was a marvellous teacher [with] an original and highly stimulating mind. The best things he did, academically, were to vitalize the teaching of criticism and to bring the twentieth century into a curriculum that had previously stopped short with, say, Thomas Hardy. His course in criticism (which well may be the one of the greatest duration around, for it has been continued since his death) was a remarkable achievement indeed, bringing students into close touch with ideas, old and new, in a way that animated their own thinking. . . . To me Leonard's greatest quality was a kind of intellectual charm—and I think he practiced this on his classes. Without committing himself beyond a point, he could get one engaged, animated, extending himself." Brown was the editor of and a contributor to a literary magazine, *Avenue* (c. 1934–1935); the editor (1929, 1947) or coeditor (Brown and Perrin 1935) of three anthologies; the author of a collection of stories and verse (1928) in addition to other verse (1935a) and fiction (1944); and the author of five critical articles or notes (1933a, 1933b, 1934a, 1934b, 1935b).

in the America of the middle decades of the twentieth century—and so our models included such figures as Karl Marx and Sigmund Freud. We would then use the Marxist (cf. L. Brown 1935b; or the Freudian, or some other) paradigm as a guide to both theoretical and methodological approaches to the investigation of a problem posed by some aggregation of empirical phenomena—which for him typically would be an endeavor to correlate a person's writings with the personal, social, and cultural experiences which the writer sought to interpret through his art. Hence writing was best conceptualized as art; while criticism of it was best conceptualized as science, and to be more explicit, as a particular kind of social science. And what Brown had in mind was what we would refer to today as the life sciences. So my own socialization into the scientific temper came virtually not at all from my graduate education per se in political science after World War II,[2] but stems instead from my education in English before the war.

The group worked collectively, allocating an entire semester or more to such an important writer as Thomas Mann or Ernest Hemingway. Our method was to read everything that had been published by, and about, our literary subject; then we would bring to bear in our analysis of this writer both theories and methods that had been developed in what we would today call the behavioral sciences, as well as borrowing our theories of criticism from such leading exponents as Malcolm Cowley and Kenneth Burke. A seminar paper might, for example, seek to explain some aspect of an author's work by relating changes in the content or style of his writing to changes in his life experiences (e.g., Hemingway's adolescent physicalism and death-wish fantasies, and his guilt over his father's suicide: one paper based on the Freudian metaphor predicted, and over a score of years before the event, the ultimate suicide of the man who by his middle years had acquired the appropriate cognomen of "Papa"—the latter was not predicted, but it certainly fits the analysis.) Another paper was a content analysis of Mann's use of color images (e.g., red was always and only a prelude to direct physical action). Among the group during my own first year were some people whom I recognized to be pretty good, but it was not until somewhat later that I came more fully to appreciate why the competition seemed to be so rough, as well as rewarding. The late Shirley Jackson and Stanley Edgar Hyman were not yet married then, but I believe that the seminar was not unrelated to their subsequent partnership in private life, just as it must have affected their subsequent in-

---

2. Even that was before the "impact of the behavioral revolution" had been felt in the political science department at Syracuse University, with the conspicuous and solitary exception of Herman Carey Beyle, with whom I found it virtually impossible to do graduate work for reasons quite independent of his approach to political science. That was most unfortunate, because Beyle was a product of the "Chicago school" of political science of the twenties—a subject that we shall consider at greater length in the introduction to Part I—and his major published work (1931) was a study in legislative behavior that was methodologically a direct antecedent of what later became one of my own principal interests in judicial behavior, as much of the present volume exemplifies.

dividual careers as (respectively) a gifted writer, whose fiction ranged from domestic comedy to Gothic tales of the psychology of horror,[3] and a distinguished literary critic of the fifties and sixties,[4] who was for many years on the staff of *The New Yorker* magazine and associated with Kenneth Burke on the English faculty at Bennington College.

Brown called his course one in "scientific" literary criticism, and he was himself that rare humanist who, without feeling any need to express the intense defensive feelings that permeate the columns of such parochial journals as *The* [Phi Beta Kappa] *Key Reporter*, embraced both art and science as equally appropriate approaches to guide his own, and his students, understanding of great literature.[5] Because this book owes at least as much to my literary apprenticeship with Leonard Brown as it does to my subsequent training and experience in political science, I have dedicated the volume to his memory.

## A

In applying, for example, the Marxist paradigm (L. Brown 1935*b*) as the basis for critical literary analysis, Brown's seminar not only read and discussed the original sources, but also the secondary literature in which others had attempted to apply that paradigm to criticize art. Of course that secondary literature is enormous (and itself the subject of an extensive tertiary social-scientific critique), so I should like to specify the kind of work that seemed useful for purposes of this literary behavioralism. At a time before most contemporary political radicals had been born, Kenneth Burke was prototyping both their social role and their private life-style for them, by criticizing the conventions and institutions of the society around him while living on a farm in New Jersey with both his then present and his former wives (sisters) and their combined offspring.[6] The fellow-traveling was a phenomenon of the times (cf. Aaron *et al.* 1966), and corresponds to the middle of the

---

3. Shirley Jackson (1919–1965) was the author of (inter alia) *The Lottery* (1949), *The Haunting of Hill House* (1959), as well as *Life among the Savages* (1953), and *Raising Demons* (1957).

4. Stanley Edgar Hyman (1919–1970), whose better known works include *The Armed Vision: A Study in the Methods of Modern Literary Criticism* (1948) and *The Tangled Bank: Darwin, Marx, Frazer, and Freud as Imaginative Writers* (1962), edited (with Barbara Karmiller) two collections of the writing of his colleague Kenneth Burke, *Perspectives by Incongruity* (1964*a*) and *Terms for Order* (1964*b*).

5. Cf. Merle E. Brown's remark (1969:10) that "In contrast to most of the New Critics, Burke would accept the science and technology of his environment and would strive to redeem it with a poetic rhetoric. That, indeed, is what is going on in most of his books."

6. I have never met Burke personally, but Brown knew him well. See Burke's acknowledgement of Brown in the foreword to *The Philosophy of Literary Form* (1941: xiv), in which Burke mentions having delivered a course of lectures to Brown's seminar, shortly after the advent of World War II had brought about my own departure from the campus. Almost twenty years later came another near-miss in my getting an opportunity to become personally acquainted with Burke: he was a Fellow at the Center for Advanced Study in the Behavioral Sciences during 1957–1958, while my own fellowship period there was 1960–1961.

three periods in terms of which Burke's work now has come to be classified.[7] But he never joined the Communist party, and repudiated it after the outbreak of World War II; and during the period since then he has emerged as a leading American man of letters. According to his biographers, "Kenneth Burke is probably the most controversial literary figure of the past fifty years in America," (M. Brown 1969: 5), and now "Burke is the foremost critic of our age, and perhaps the greatest critic since Coleridge" (Hyman and Karmiller 1964a: vi; and cf. A. Frank 1969 and Rueckert 1969).

That part of his work that I found most useful in the seminar was his two-volume *Attitudes toward History* (1937), which stemmed from the middle of his experience with leftism, following on the heels of *Permanence and Change* (1935) and constituting at once a critique of forms of literary art, a politically radical commentary upon then (and still) contemporary modes of social behavior, and an ethical analysis of social attitudes. Burke argued, for example, that the distinction between comedy and tragedy (as art forms) is an essential one to make because, although both "warn against the dangers of pride," in comedy the "emphasis shifts from *crime* to *stupidity*." Thus "Comedy deals with *man in society*, tragedy with the *cosmic man*." And in that sense "The best of Bentham, Marx, and Veblen is high comedy." Burke suggests that the most useful social attitude (or, in his vocabulary, "acceptance frame" for "the charting of human motives") is comic, because "The progress of humane enlightenment can go no further than in picturing people not as *vicious*, but as *mistaken*. When you add that people are *necessarily* mistaken, that *all* people are exposed to situations in which they must act as fools, that *every* insight contains its own special kind of blindness, you complete the comic circle, returning again to the lesson of humility that underlies great tragedy." (1937, vol. 1: 51–53, emphasis in the original.) This is a very different methodology, and approach, to the study of attitudes than one finds in contemporary social psychology (e.g., Jahoda and Warren 1966; Rokeach 1968; and Summers 1970); and because so much of the research presented in the present volume is explicitly concerned with the study of social attitudes (of both judges and academicians), I feel that candor compels the admission that my own introduction to the subject came not from a computer, nor even from the course in the subject that was taught by Floyd Allport[8] during the years of both my undergraduate and graduate education at Syracuse University and which I (not really perversely, but simply out of ignorance) never took. Instead, my baptism into attitudinal analysis came through Kenneth Burke.

---

7. Thus "by 1935 (*Permanence and Change*) Burke's primary interests had shifted from literary to social criticism, and by 1945 (*A Grammar of Motives*) from social criticism to linguistic analysis as a way of confronting the world." Rueckert (1963: viii); cf. Krutch (1935).

8. Floyd was the older brother of the somewhat better known Harvard psychologist Gordon Allport. Among Floyd Allport's major contributions to the study of attitudes were his *Social Psychology* (1924) and *Institutional Behavior* (1933). See also Katz and Allport (1931), a work that he coauthored with one of his graduate students who subsequently became a leading contributor to the field of attitude psychology.

## B

In the present volume I have sought to emphasize four themes in particular, and each of these finds reflection in one of the parts into which the chapters are divided. The first part is concerned with the continuities between legal and political research, and with the extent to which and the ways in which lawyers and political scientists have interacted in the concern—which they clearly do share—to comprehend the processes by which judges make law and the effect of judicial policies upon the society, economy, and polity. All three of these chapters were written to communicate with audiences of lawyers or sociologists of law; hence they assume the standpoint of someone who is inside the profession of political science, looking outside and attempting to explain to outsiders what has been on-going within the field of judicial process and behavior. A few other political scientists have engaged in similar missionary-type activities,[9] and an even smaller number of law professors has attempted to play the role of ethnographer of political science society;[10] but much less has been done by either lawyers or sociologists to interpret their activities to political scientists.[11]

Part 2 shifts focus to several examples of the kind of research that political scientists have been carrying on in their investigations of judicial behavior. The selections that I have chosen to include here are in no sense a representative sample of work during the sixties in the more general field of judicial process and behavior, nor do they purport to accomplish any such purpose. They do constitute, I believe, a fair sampling of the kind of studies that I have done during the past couple of decades. And these chapters do typify what has been a core focus of political science research in constitutional law since before the founding of political science as an academic discipline: the analysis of the policy content of Supreme Court decisions, which generations of distinguished political science forebears have thought important because of the peculiarly influential political role that the Supreme Court has played in the American constitutional polity since the founding of the republic (Schubert 1967c). Beyond that, the empirical focus of these chapters upon the values articulated by Supreme Court judges certainly is consistent with the theme of what has consensually been perceived to be the most important book published in the field of judicial process and behavior, during at least the past three decades—the subtitle of that book was: "A Study in Judicial Politics and Values" (Pritchett 1948). Hence the chapters in Part 2 can properly be viewed as an endeavor, on my own part, to carry on an unbroken tradition that runs through American political science, a line of succession that by no means is limited to but certainly includes at least Frank Goodnow, Charles Grove Haines, Edward Samuel Corwin, Robert Eugene Cushman, Carl Brent Swisher, Rodney Mott, and Charles Herman Pritchett. There is, I believe, a

---

9. For example, Shapiro 1964b; Nagel 1965; and Sheldon 1969.
10. Jones 1963; Miller 1965a; and Lewis 1970.
11. Skolnick 1968; and Jones 1965.

still-strong current of adolescentlike father-rejection[12] running in contemporary political science, a current which finds expression in such behaviors as vying for place in exposing the shortcomings of such former intellectual leaders of the profession as David Truman and Robert Dahl. Having felt slight allegiance to such established figures when they were ascendant, it is perhaps natural that I feel less repugnance (than some of my colleagues seem to) toward them now that they have been deposed. But I do feel appreciative of the contributions of Goodnow, Haines, Corwin, Cushman, Swisher, and Mott, and I do wish explicitly to create this opportunity to acknowledge the very substantial intellectual debt that I owe to them all. (I am also, of course, continuously indebted to a good many of my own contemporaries [including, certainly, Pritchett] and to various of my students; but them I can tell directly and personally.)

In Part 3 the focus shifts again, and this time from values to valuation. It is of course impossible to segregate theory from facts and methods, except for analytical purposes; and it is only in that limited sense that it is possible to describe Part 3 as the most "theoretical" segment of this volume. But there is also a second respect in which its focus is constrained: the theory with which it is concerned is that of attitudes, and in particular of the interrelationships among the sets of attitudes, for both any given individual and for a group of individuals. Moreover, the discussion is deeply concerned with the question of to what extent and how the attitudes of any person (including myself) who undertakes to study the attitudes of judges, wittingly or otherwise, influences what he reports as findings, due to the extent of his own involvement in the research enterprise because of his own attitudes toward the subject studied. Some of the avant-garde among my graduate students and younger colleagues act and talk as though to them alone has been revealed the great secret of analyst bias (possibly as a reward for their loyal subservience to the ideology into which they happen to have been socialized). But policy science was not the issue of any virgin birth; it was proclaimed with all his (very considerable) might by Harold Dwight Lasswell, an exceptionally vocal political scientist and one who thought of himself as a political behavioralist, at a time (Lasswell 1947; Lerner and Lasswell 1951; and Lasswell 1951) when many of those who have just recently heard the good news were suckling their mothers (or were not yet even born). My own rather contrary conviction is that what political science (and other behavioral sciences) today need is less affect and more effect; instead of merely exhibiting our biases proudly we should understand how and why they affect our behavior, whether as scholars or in other of our manifold roles as human actors, so that to the extent that we may wish to do so, we shall be better able to establish statistical (if not psychological, social, or cultural) controls over that particular source of error variance in our research equations. Those who insist that

---

12. Cf. Jerome Frank 1930, part 3, chap. 1.

social life is a blob are almost certain to leave it precisely as they purport to find it.

Part 3 develops also another facet of the study of the integration of values through attitudes and ideologies: their variance across national cultures. That emphasis is perfectly consonant with what became increasingly a major theme of American political science generally during the sixties: the attempt to reconsider the knowledge that had been developed out of studies in America, by subjecting such propositions to the test of cultural variance. My own interests were of course affected by the force of such social currents, which provide the underlying explanation for such more discrete events as a Fulbright year in Scandinavia, or a series of research residences in the explicitly cross-cultural setting of the East-West Center in Hawaii, or a teaching residence of two years in the fratricidal academic atmosphere of Canada, or research residences of half a year each in Switzerland and South Africa, all of which certainly are directly related (both before and after the event) to the development of a cross-cultural dimension to my own work in judicial behavior. One cannot become involved in logomachy with a drunken Norwegian communist, or have a militaristic Swiss James Bond enthusiast snatch one's interview schedule (so that xerox copies can be turned over to the local prosecutor), or have an irate Afrikaner supreme court judge substitute an inquisition for a scheduled interview (with loud accompanying assertions that one is a "phony," challenges to prove that one has any kind of academic degree, and demands that one admit his C.I.A. sponsorship) without becoming impressed with both personal and cultural variation as a phenomenon *within* as well as *between* societies.

The concluding part of the volume brings us back into closer rapport with Leonard Brown's seminar because these closing chapters are largely concerned with an attempt to understand the process of legal-social-political change, by invoking the guidance of selected cosmological paradigms as the basis for interpreting complex empirical phenomena. Three such paradigms are explicitly postulated and discussed; these correspond to points of view according to which social action is analogized to be like unto a (by definition, inanimate) machine, a (by definition, living) organism, or a nuclear system (of which, at least at certain submicroscopic levels, it is difficult to be sure what the difference between life and nonlife can be understood to mean).[13] The first of these concluding chapters undertakes a relatively straightforward exposition of the three points of view, and undertakes to demonstrate how they necessarily lead to differing conclusions about both the meaning of law and the forms that appropriate political action, to change law, should assume. One of the remaining two chapters undertakes to develop, more particularly, the implications of the biological model for predicting change in judicial systems; the other chapter attempts to use the nuclear model to predict how the

---

13. Cf. Monod 1971, which is among the works discussed in my review article (1973*e*).

discipline of political science should be changed the better to meet the needs of the world it will be confronting during the next generation.

# C

The composition of this volume leaves me directly obligated to only a few persons, but indirectly to many more than I can possibly list. My deepest obligation is to David J. Danelski, a friend with whom I have collaborated in regard to other projects and whose advice and suggestions in regard to this one proved most helpful. Danelski shares with two other friends and sometime colleagues of mine, Robert Vance Presthus and Yasumasa Kuroda, and one of my current doctoral candidates, David John Gow, a concern for the significance of what Abraham Kaplan calls the "logic-in-action" (1964, esp. pp. 3–18) of a research inquiry, which entails its placement as a historical event within the context of the personal, social, and cultural fields whose intersection created it. Their continuing affirmation of the importance of this dimension to an adequate social accounting for one's responsibilities in the reporting of research has encouraged me to give prominence to that emphasis, given the fortuity that the situation under which the present publication takes place can tolerate and accommodate to this kind of unorthodoxy far more readily than could the dozen different editors of almost as many different journals whose idiosyncratic policies and requirements tended (to what I felt at the time was a completely unreasonable degree) to determine the form as well as (in respects such as this) the content of the original publication of these papers. Nevertheless I am grateful to those now responsible for the management of these various journalistic enterprises for their kindness in permitting me to reprint material concerning whose use they are, in most instances, the owners of the respective copyrights. To the extent that more explicit expression of that legal indebtedness is appropriate or requisite, signification of it appears on the title page of each chapter.

For more detailed information concerning Leonard Brown's career than I was able to retrieve from either my own memory or the local libraries at my present residence, I am indebted to Donald A. Dike, professor of English at Syracuse University; and for putting me in touch with Professor Dike, I thank a longtime mutual friend of both Leonard Brown and myself, President Frank P. Piskor of Saint Lawrence University.

For the typing of the manuscript I thank my secretary, Mary Grayson, and for their toleration of yet another book (which from their point of view we need like we need another visit by the plague), I thank my family—a social system that is (like judicial systems) much more biological and nuclear than mechanical.

# PART I
# From Legal to Behavioral Realism

THE BEHAVIORAL REVOLUTION in political science—as certain enthusiasts (e.g., Truman 1955) described what seemed to be the central thrust of change in the profession a generation ago—was a misnomer. It was no more (and no less) a revolution for the discipline than adolescence is for an individual person: both are no doubt better understood as natural stages of development. Certainly political behavioralism has neither a beginning nor—at least so far—an ending. It is dubious whether behavioralism ever has defined an ethic acceptable to a majority of the members of the American Political Science Association (APSA); and it is clear that behavioralism always has been, and that it remains today, a minority point of view among those political scientists whose particular interests include constitutions, law, courts, and legal processes. At a time when fashions in academic ideology are such that one-upmanship requires those who value social acceptance to define their position in terms of *post*behavioralism (Baker et al. 1972), the "revolution" interpretation holds a certain attraction because it enables veterans to exhibit their purple hearts and good conduct medals, whilst they close ranks with yearlings who can know of the relevant events only through story and myth, and with whom they can look back with no regrets upon an era that history has foreclosed (and which was, after all, not much worse to have endured than a bad cold). It is attractive, as I say, but like so many other of our most cherished beliefs, it is not true (in the sense that if it *were* true the proposition would find more support than disconfirmation in observations of the empirical events that it purports to denote).

It has been full half a century since Charles Merriam (1925) stated the case for a science of political behavior. Merriam spoke as a founding father and leading member of the profession, as an experienced and skillful academic politician who worked hard to gain support for his views, and as the chairman of a department that from the mid-twenties through the mid-thirties was the first-ranking department of political science in the country.[1] Merriam put before the profession a program and justification for a behavioral approach to the study of politics, and he did this with both an intellectual and a political vigor that no one else has equalled, let alone surpassed, in the intervening decades. But Merriam was a prophet—a prophet with both honor and disciples in his own time, it is true, but not himself among those who lived to experience the promised land. Another generation, and another world war, were to elapse before some of Merriam's students, and more particularly the students of those students, would produce during the fifties the political writings and research literature that tend to be associated with the behavioral approach to the study of politics (Kirkpatrick 1962). Even then it was not until the sixties that it became common for graduate students to be educated in the substantive lore and with the research skills appropriate to the practice of political behavioralism (Luttbeg and Kahn 1968)—that is, with cognate

---

1. Foreword by Barry D. Karl to the 3rd edition of C. Merriam, *New Aspects of Politics*, Chicago: University of Chicago Press, 1970, pp. 1–32. Cf. Gosnell 1971.

study in psychology and anthropology and sociology (instead of history and philosophy and classical economics), and with training in statistics and computer technology (instead of the smattering of French and German that used to suffice). And it has really only been during the seventies that persons trained as behavioralists have taken over the editorship of the *American Political Science Review* (together with at least some of the regional association journals), and that a majority of the articles in those journals have become adorned with tables, charts, and figures of statistical curves and mathematical functions, for the very good reason that the analysis in these articles focuses upon the discussion of relationships that have been measured (and, therefore, quantified). The route from Charles Merriam's presidency of the APSA in 1925 to that of Heinz Eulau in 1972 marks a gradual and continuing (though by no means uniform, complete, nor universal) process of growth and development, whose sources lie in a much more remote past and whose effects are not likely to become obliterated during the lifetimes of those who presently are active in the profession.

## A

Merriam's best-known student, and the most renowned product of the Chicago department during the twenties, was Harold Lasswell, a compleat behavioral scientist who legitimately could claim competence in—and be claimed as a member by—half-a-dozen different life science disciplines, ranging from psychiatry to anthropology, in addition to law and political science (Rogow 1969). But since 1945 his institutional affiliations have remained as a law professor; and Lasswell's impact upon the behavioral study of law has been felt (in company with that of his longtime colleague Myres McDougal) primarily among lawmen (and, especially, other law professors) as an exemplification of a somewhat latter-day legal realism,[2] rather than as a wellspring of behavioral jurisprudence among political scientists. The latter role, that of godfather to the judicial process and behavior movement among political scientists during the fifties and sixties, was played by C. Herman Pritchett, who had been a student of both Merriam and Lasswell at Chicago, and who had taught at Chicago for more than a quarter of a century, much of that time serving also as chairman of the department over which Merriam had reigned as "The Chief." Like Merriam (but unlike Lasswell) Pritchett's career remained anchored in the mainstream of the profession; and taken together, Merriam and Pritchett span the entire life of the APSA, from its earliest days of organization in 1905 up to the present time of writing (some two-thirds of a century later).

---

2. Arens and Lasswell 1964; McDougal 1966. See also the recent remark in an essay by A. S. Miller and D. S. Sastri that "there still has been no sufficient jurisprudential effort in the United States—other than, perhaps, the policy-science or configurative jurisprudence of Lasswell and McDougal—since the legal realists first ripped the facade off the Blackstonian conception of the judicial process several decades ago" (1973:805).

A behavioral science of history must go beyond the doings of kings and generals (Landes and Tilly 1971), and I do not mean to imply that one can adequately discuss the evolution of either political behavior or behavioral jurisprudence by tracing the aspirations and accomplishments of only two or three persons, however great their distinction. I invoke their names, rather, as symbols of the careers of the many other persons—hundreds, in the aggregate—whose activities in professional research, teaching, and communications *do* account for the changes within political science that constitute the objective content of the behavioral approach to the study of politics and law.

## B

At the same time that Merriam was building a behavioral political science at Chicago, and a few other pioneers were similarly occupied elsewhere, the movement that came to be known as "legal realism" erupted in a few law school faculties, of which the main axis developed chronologically from Columbia to Yale to Chicago (Rumble 1964). Legal realism was, like political behavioralism, a completely indigenous American development, and both emerged, as major issues for discussion within their respective professions, at about the same time in the early twenties. But there the similarities end. After a flurry of disputation in the pages of leading law journals, a few seminal books, and a small but promising output of empirical research reports, the legal realist movement had spent its force: some of its protagonists became first administrative adjudicators and then judges, like William O. Douglas (1956) and Jerome Frank (1942); some (like Llewellyn: Llewellyn and Hoebel 1941; Llewellyn 1960; and cf. Hayakawa 1964) changed their interests, and ultimately their mind; and others (like Hutchins) left legal education behind to become pre-occupied with very different kinds of pedagogical experiences. A few, like Underhill Moore, kept on working, but their example failed to induce enough others to follow in their footsteps, so as to stem the advancing tides of legal rationalism.

Legal study in the United States failed to become scientific because of its preemptive fascination with policy and the empirical consequences of such policy having been made; and the changes in legal education that erupted during the sixties involved not so much a change in theory or methodology as a switch in topics deemed meritorious: a generation that grew up during a depression valued economic security for itself, and hence Wall Street firms and corporations and federal taxation and mineral law and things like that; the modern generation of younger lawyers and law professors—persons who have never experienced economic insecurity—worry instead about poverty law and the plight of minorities (however defined) and the representation of indigent criminal defendants rather than (or at least more than) the social objects of criminal behavior.

C

The field of judicial process and behavior within contemporary political science stems, most directly and immediately, from the publication of two books, Pritchett's *The Roosevelt Court* in 1948,[3] and Jack W. Peltason's *Federal Courts in the Political Process* in 1955.[4] Pritchett's book was anticipated and foreshadowed by half-a-dozen articles, as he has recounted;[5] all were strongly empirical in tone and content, although his work was guided explicitly by the theory of attitudes prevalent in psychology at the time he began his studies. Peltason had published a prior article (1953) which, like his monograph, was programmatic in tone and ideological in character: Peltason explicitly repudiated the desirability of interdisciplinary collaboration between political science and other social or behavioral science fields,[6] with the explicit exception of sociology, which supplied the basis for the theory of group interests (and of interest groups) that he recommended to the profession for analyzing the judicial process. Pritchett's work laid the groundwork for the subsequent investigations that employed cumulative scaling, factor analysis, and smallest space analysis of the voting behavior of justices of both the federal and state supreme courts, in the United States and an increasing number of other countries as well. Ironically, there has been an almost perfect but negative correlation between the direction of Pritchett's own research since 1948 and that of the judicial behavioralists who have built upon his beginnings: while research into judicial values and attitudes has grown, both in depth and in scope, Pritchett himself has retreated more and more into the traditional constitutional law work that had constituted virtually the exclusive content of the field at the time he began his own work. Peltason, on the other hand, went on (1961) to carry out an extensive field survey of the attitudes and social backgrounds of all fifty-eight of the federal district judges who were legally responsible for the interpretation and carrying out (or frustration) in the South of the Supreme Court's School Segregation decision. But by that time there were at least a dozen other political scientists actively involved in research, including Schmidhauser and Nagel, who were exploring the social backgrounds of judges; Tanenhaus and Ulmer and Spaeth, who had begun to scale judicial attitudes; Danelski, who was investigating judicial ideology; Kort, who was making content analyses of judicial opinions as a basis for predicting decisions quantitatively; and myself: I was venturing experimental forays in all of those directions, plus a few (such as game theory) for which at least temporarily I established a corner on the political science market in judicial behavior. Out of these eclectic inquiries

---

3. Reprinted in 1969 as a paperback by Quadrangle Books, Chicago. Cf. Wolf 1970.
4. Originally published by Doubleday; subsequently reprinted and distributed by Random House.
5. Pritchett (1970) cites four of these articles.
6. His concluding sentence urged political scientist public lawyers to give up "trying to 'out-history' the historian, 'out-law' the lawyers, or 'out-psychology' the psychologist" (1953:56).

I undertook during the middle fifties came an article (1958e) that was just as programmatic as Peltason's (but with advice in direct opposition to his on virtually all counts save one); a book (1959) that undertook to exemplify (in much greater detail than had been possible in the article) both what to do and how to do it; and a text-casebook (1960a) that was intended to do for teaching what the other book was supposed to do for research—to help other persons with similar (however inchoate) interests to bridge the gap between constitutional law and the study of judicial politics. The one exception upon which Peltason and I could agree was that it had long since become inappropriate for political scientists to continue making legalistic analyses of courts and law: on this point I could and did quote him often, and with approval. We agreed also that the study of law should become "political," but this seeming coincidence in the prescription (as well as in the diagnosis) was quite spurious, because our respective understandings of what "political" should mean remained so very different. To Peltason political meant interest group interaction, following the now classical sociological theory that had been advanced a full half century earlier by Bentley and popularized after World War II by Truman. This was a research perspective that I had then only recently had occasion to examine in some depth, and to criticize in a work on political theory which—for reasons that are extraneous in the present context—I happened to write at about the same time, in the late fifties. To me political meant not abstract institutional fallacies such as "groups," but rather people—discrete, usually identifiable, humans acting in roles that directly affect the making or the carrying out of public policy choices. And to study law from such a perspective required that political scientists get off their ramparts and scale the interfaces separating them from the life sciences: anthropology, psychology, social psychology, and modern sociology; and although I clearly mentioned biology also back at this earlier time, and had indeed by the mid-sixties made it the very core of my paradigm of the behavioral sciences, I should now (cf. my 1973e, 1975a) want to insist upon a much greater emphasis on the necessity for including ethology (and especially primatology), population genetics, ecology, and other major subfields of human biology as essential components of a behavioral approach to the study of politics (including judicial politics).

The difference between Peltason and myself is a fairly important one, not because of anything involving either of us personally, but rather because each of us was then espousing (and still advocates) a perspective that has considerable social importance, because it has served and continues to serve as a focal point for organizing the time and energies of a substantial number of other political scientists. It is evident that what Peltason advocated as the "judicial process" approach finds expression in linkages with legal sociology such as, for example, the *Law and Society Review* under the recent editorship of political scientist Krislov, or sociologist Selznick's administration of the Center for the Study of Law and Society at the University of California,

Berkeley. Three of the twenty-odd individuals who comprise the faculty of the Department of Political Science at the University of Hawaii would be identified by their colleagues with the study of law and courts; and two of these three would certainly be associated by other knowledgeable persons in the field—and would identify themselves—with the judicial process approach, rather than with the judicial behavioralism that I am understood to represent. One convenient objective test of the proposition that I have stated is found in the circumstance that about a dozen years ago Peltason (1968) and I (1968e) were engaged, completely independently of each other, in writing essays that were to appear (when that opus eventually became published) in the revised edition of the *International Encyclopedia of the Social Sciences*; his topic was "Judicial Process" and mine was "Judicial Behavior"; and as I have remarked elsewhere, "the two articles, although they do include some of the same authors, are almost completely independent in the specific works that they cite; the only common references are to Jerome Frank [*Law and the Modern Mind*] and two genuflections, one in which Peltason cites Schubert [*Judicial Policy-Making*] and the other vice versa (citing Peltason [*Federal Courts in the Political Process*]) (1972c:74). An alternative but perhaps equally objective test is found in the circumstance that at the end of the fifties, Peltason was out in the field, conducting an empirical survey of the facts (his study of Southern federal judges [1961]), while I was first off to Scandinavia for a year, studying contemporary legal realism there, and then off to the Center for Advanced Study in the Behavioral Sciences at Stanford, trying to learn something about behavioral science theory and methods.

## D

The three articles that comprise the first part of this book all were written as a direct response to events that arose out of the interrelationships between law and political science as academic disciplines, reflecting in turn the influence of the scenario, of which I have attempted to sketch a few relevant fragments in the preceding paragraphs of this introduction. All three essays are directly concerned with the relationship with law school work that overlaps with that of political science, in particular regard to the analysis of court processes and interactions. All three were written within a period of less than two years, but in different locales (and therefore subject to the impact of differing local academic environments). None of the three is based directly upon empirical research of my own, and I never planned to write any of them—each was, instead, written at the explicit request of another person whom I respected, so that the impetus for the writing was directly social, even if (and it is for others to judge) the product did turn out to be intellectual. All three were published in law journals, which means that none has probably been read by more than a very small minority of either lawyers *or* political scientists—the former because not even a law professor can begin to keep up with the more than a hundred (counting American alone) law journals published from quarterly to monthly, and the latter because only political scientists working in the judicial process/behavior field would be likely to have checked the most directly relevant law journals closely enough to have, perhaps, stumbled across even one of the three essays. Hence part of my motivation in including them herein is to make them accessible to a larger number of political scientists and political science students, as well as to the much larger audience of other life scientists who also are cut off from the law journals for the same reasons.

In several ways, the invocatory essay draws together several of the themes that already have been stated. It began, in a sense, with the establishment of a newsletter by the Special Committee on Electronic Data Retrieval of the American Bar Association (ABA): these were a small group of law librarians, law professors, and practicing lawyers, who shared an interest in the use of computers, most of them for purposes of the storage and retrieval of legal data (e.g., Franz 1967), but some for purposes of legal research (as distinguished from legal search). An early chairman of the committee was Reed C. Lawlor, a Los Angeles patent lawyer whose friendship with political scientist Fred Kort resulted in the production of a considerable amount of experimentation, joining Boolean algebra with computer technology in an attempt to specify the equations and variable weights (under differing sets of empirical circumstances) that describe how courts (and especially the United States Supreme Court) make decisions in regard to particular subjects of public policy. Kort's side of the work led on to his statement of one of the more sophisticated mathematical models of decision-making to appear in the research literature of political science during the sixties (Kort 1963, 1966, 1973); while Lawlor attracted National Science Foundation support for his activities, which had as one by-product a provocative contribution to the theory of stare decisis (Lawlor 1967, 1969). The committee chose as its editor Layman Allen, then a young law professor (and former student, as well as a colleague, of Harold Lasswell) at Yale, whose interests (in a sense, paralleling Lawlor's) lay in developing deontic logical models of legal arguments and norm structures. The newsletter circulated (though rather irregularly) for several years under the title of *M.U.L.L.* (*Modern Uses of Logic in Law*), and was just in the process of becoming converted to a more regular quarterly (under the sponsorship of the American Bar Center, with the new title of *Jurimetrics Journal*, and after a publication hiatus of almost a year) at the time my own article was published in it. I had previously published an article in the second volume of *M.U.L.L.*, and had been a subscriber and reader since its establishment. So when the ABA scheduled its annual main convention in Honolulu during the summer of 1967, at a time when I planned to be in residence there anyhow, and when Reed Lawlor asked me to discuss political science research for the Special Committee on Electronic Data Retrieval, I accepted. But in view of some of the committee members' overweening concentration (as it seemed to me) upon computer technology, as distinguished from what I considered to be the far more important matter of the kind of theory being tested, it seemed to me to be most appropriate to have my remarks focus upon the difference between what I understood to be their concerns, and the typical interest of political scientists in the use of computers—which with some few exceptions was primarily for complex data processing in support of theory testing and building, rather than data storage and retrieval, and the prediction of decisional outcomes. In order to sharpen the point, consideration is given in the article to the possibility— suggested (albeit with tongue in cheek) by Harold Lasswell (1955)—that the Supreme Court of the United States be replaced by a computer, and this leads to an examination of both the pros and cons of such a sociotechnological innovation.

The second article was not prepared for oral delivery, but instead was written in response to the invitation to contribute the Centennial Essay to an issue of the volume commemorating the founding of the George Washington University Law School. The inspiration for that request had come from a member of that university's law faculty, Professor Arthur Selwyn Miller, whose work I then had been reading and admiring for over a dozen years, since his days as a faculty advisor to the fledgling *Journal of Public Law.* Miller is something of a latter-day legal realist himself, echoing in his work an iconoclasm that one finds in such well-known New Deal lawyer-authors as A. A. Berle and Thurman Arnold. Hence Miller has been what Jerome Frank called a "rule skeptic," with a strong orientation toward progressivism in matters of socioeconomic policy and national programming. Clearly he was preeminent among a very tiny number of law professors (or, at least, of contemporary legal writers) who have made a special effort to familiarize themselves with not only welfare economics, but also the judicial process-and-behavior literature in political science, and his own prolific essays on political economy reflected a much broader base, in both social science theory and data, than the usual rehash of appellate court language that continues to adorn the pages of most law journals. Ironically, Miller was already by the mid-sixties starting to mend his ideological fences, by repudiating (1967) his then still-recent mesalliance with judicial behavioralism (1965a), in response to the riptide of humanistic antiscientism which (to paraphrase Cardozo [see p. 45 n]) does not pass professors by, but sweeps them along in its currents together with other men. There were some who chose to swim against the current (e.g., Kort 1972), and I happened to be one of them (Schubert 1969f); but awareness of the extent to which my relationship with Miller could no longer be symbiotic came somewhat later.[7] It is noteworthy however, that Miller's movement toward increasing radicalism— including both the explicit rejection of science and the preoccupation with

---

7. Cf. his article with D. S. Sastri (Miller and Sastri 1973) and my comment (Schubert 1973c).

the instrumental use of policy analysis to subserve goals of social reform—
was strictly in phase with changes that took place in the ideological line of
the modal group of "judicial process" workers (Peltason's heirs at public law,
whom I shall describe as the "conventional" group in Part 2 of this book).

In view of the circumstance that Miller himself a few years earlier had
authored an article in which he had examined the place of public law in
American law school curricula at the end of the fifties, and incidentally had
urged a closer liaison between law school and political science work in adjudication processes, I thought it would be most appropriate to investigate
in the essay a most neglected subject: the history of public law within political science, its relationship to the legal realist movement in American law
faculties, and the subsequent developments (from the early thirties onward)
in both law and political science. And given my opinion that public law in
political science was about as healthy as the Cardiff giant (cf. Somit and
Tanenhaus 1964:chap. 6, esp. Tables 7 and 8 at pp. 54 and 56; Dixon 1971;
Schubert 1972b), it is understandable that, once the outline of the subject
had been decided, the model of Dickens' *Christmas Carol* came irresistibly
to mind as the most appropriate poetic paradigm in which to envelope my
essay. My doctoral dissertation had been written under a man who had
himself been a student of Ernst Freund, and Freund was one of the founding
fathers, not only of American political science (having been the eleventh president of APSA), but also of the subfield of administrative law (within public
law). Yet it was apparent, only a few years after I had left graduate school,
that many aspects of public law (as it had been taught to me) already were
disappearing from political science curricula. This subjective impression was
confirmed, at least in regard to administrative law, by survey data (Schubert
1958b); and in regard to constitutional law, I have done my share in helping
to convert the observation into a self-fulfilling prophecy (cf. Shapiro 1972a
and Schubert 1973a).

But I had long been puzzled by the neglect visited by legal and political
science writers alike upon the question of the common roots and entangled
destinies of the two disciplines. Writers on jurisprudence generally have ignored political science completely (as though they were afraid they might
catch something noxious).[8] The eminent Julius Stone did unburden himself
of a polemical attack on behavioral jurisprudence (1964b), as the fruit of his
own fellowship experience at the Center for Advanced Study in the Behavioral Sciences; but such activity on his part certainly was more affective than
effective in helping to satisfy the lament, which he expressed elsewhere at
about the same time (and indeed, through an alternative publication outlet
of the same university), over the dearth of awareness, as between jurisprudes
and "behavioural scientists specialising in law," concerning the substance of

---

8. There are three conspicuous exceptions: Ingersoll 1966; and Kawashima and Ishimura
1964; and Lloyd 1972.

their respective work.[9] The only two books, authored by political scientists and directly in point, that have appeared thus far since the end of World War II have little or nothing to say concerning the impact of legal realism upon political science. It happens that the first book I ever reviewed professionally (1952b) was one of these two, and it ignores the subject; the other (Rumble 1968:169–179) devoted a few pages to describing contemporary developments in behavioral jurisprudence within political science, but it relies upon my own previous assertions concerning the linkages (e.g., Schubert 1964a:9–13). Evidently thě matter was wide open for closer and more sustained scrutiny; and that is what I endeavored to provide in the ensuing essay.

The third article was a by-product of the Shambaugh Conference on Judicial Research which was convened at the University of Iowa in October 1967. The purpose of this conference was to bring together well over a score of persons active in judicial research, most of whom were American political scientists but who included also a few law professors from Canada and Japan, plus several American law professors, social scientists from disciplines other than political science, and political scientists identified primarily with subfields other than judicial research. Among the conferees was Richard D. Schwartz, then a professor of sociology at Northwestern University and the incumbent editor of *Law and Society Review* (and now the first nonlawyer to serve as dean of a major American law school, the State University of New York at Buffalo); and at a breakfast meeting he asked me to prepare for his journal an article that would discuss recent theoretical developments in political science research into judicial behavior, and also to attempt to forecast the trend of research developments in the field during the short-run future of the succeeding five to ten years. By now, of course, the near end of that future already is at hand, so the door is open for any knowledgeable reader to determine his own verdict on the merits of the question of the goodness of fit between the future that I describe in the essay and the present that we can observe. Although I am not above auditing my own earlier predictions, when the latter have been so quantified and the test of the stated hypotheses

---

9. In reporting a survey of "Innovators in the Study of the Legal Process," Alfred de Grazia and Charles L. Ruttenberg had suggested, as a possible explanation for the unexpectedly low level of familiarity with each other's work on the part of those deemed to be innovators, that "Perhaps they are like the avant garde poets who read Shakespeare but not each other" (1963:50). Evidently the suggestion struck a responsive chord in Stone, who intruded a contextually quite gratuitous footnote to misquote the above remark—Professor Stone brands as a "conclusion" what the authors of the survey were themselves careful to state as an hypothesis, since their evidence was inferential rather than empirical—and to raise the query "whether many of [the 120 leading 'innovators' (Stone's quotes) in work on law as a behavioral science] could name a commonly-recognized 'Shakespeare' [also Stone's quotes] for law" (Stone 1966b:26n. 53a). In the survey, Professor Stone is listed neither among the 10 persons deemed "most innovative" nor among the 120 persons who were considered by the authors of the survey to be leading innovators; instead his name appears in a list of 134 "other innovators." Nevertheless, his preeminence in the field of *jurisprudence* is beyond cavil, and one can only wonder whom he may possibly have had in mind as an appropriate Shakespeare for law? It is, after all, his question.

is so objective that analyst bias would be exceptionally difficult (either to engineer or to allege), the predictions of the present essay are stated in such verbal terms that I think it unseemly for me to say more than that I can reread the closing pages of the essay without experiencing future shock. To the extent that I feel disappointment, it is because the *rate* of change, in the directions indicated, has been slower than I had thought probable, certainly slower than I had hoped.

The original title of this essay for *Law and Society Review*, at the time I wrote it, was "Human Jurisprudence," a concept that I initially had thought appropriate not only because it invokes the remembrance of one of the great manifestos of legal realism (Jerome Frank 1931), but also, and more importantly, because it directly analogizes the study of legal theory to the perspective provided by the life sciences. Such an ascription would of course have been a signpost pointing to the future, whereas "behavioral jurisprudence" would be much more a road map charting the present. For reasons that no longer impress me as very persuasive, I decided that it would be more useful, at that time and in the context of the particular forum in which the essay was scheduled to appear, to invoke a title that would be unambiguously descriptive of its contents. But I'm glad that I made the change, because the prescriptiveness of "human jurisprudence" strikes just the tone that I now want to symbolize the present collection of my past work: not a record of what happens to have been done, but rather an invitation to join in the construction of a theoretical edifice that remains to be built.

# 1

# On a
# Computer Court

A major influence upon modern political science has been the impact of the behavioral sciences, particularly that of sociology and social psychology. The resulting mode of political inquiry has become known as the political behavior approach (Eulau 1963, 1966). The behavioral movement has recast into a more scientific posture the work in all fields of political science, but the timing and the rate of change have been different for the various subfields of the discipline (Kirkpatrick 1962). Those to cling longest to the work ways of the past were the subfields of political philosophy and public law, and their intransigence is reflected in the judgment of their colleagues who rated philosophy and law as the subfields of least importance to the contemporary study of political science (Somit and Tanenhaus 1964). But the yeast of behavioralism already had begun to ferment within the oak staves of traditional doctrine encapsulating—from each other, as well as from the rest of political science—both political philosophy and public law; and, at least within public law, the reformulation of research orientations (Schubert 1967b, 1967a) to bring them into line with the rest of the discipline already was well advanced at the time of the survey upon which the ratings were based (Schubert 1963f).

It is possible to denote seeds of potential change that had been sown at an earlier time, but these were cast upon barren ground and remained infertile: The time was not yet ripe for other political scientists to respond to

This chapter was originally published, in slightly different form, as "The Importance of Computer Technology to Political Science Research in Judicial Behavior" in *Jurimetrics Journal* 8 (March 1968):56–63. It was earlier presented in oral form at a meeting of the American Bar Association's Special Committee on Electronic Data Retrieval on August 6, 1967, in Honolulu, Hawaii.

the intellectual leadership of such isolated pioneers as Charles Grove Haines (1922) and Rodney Mott (Mott et al. 1933; Mott 1936). (At about the same time, lawyers were turning equally deaf ears to the importunities of Underhill Moore [Moore and Sussman 1932], Edward S. Robinson [1935], and Felix Cohen [1935].) It was not until after World War II and the appearance of C. Herman Pritchett's book on *The Roosevelt Court* (1948),[1] to be followed after a gap of more than half-a-dozen years by Jack W. Peltason's monograph on the federal judiciary (1955), that public lawyers, at least among political scientists, began to pay serious attention to theoretical and methodological approaches to the study of courts and judges (alternative to the traditional approaches of history, law, and philosophy) such as those provided by small-group and interest-group analyses—the former proposed by Pritchett, the latter by Peltason. Even then, sustained and continuous activity by several persons, working largely independently but simultaneously, did not begin until about the time that Joseph Tanenhaus ventured a preliminary report to the profession on his exploratory quantitative studies under a grant from the Social Science Research Council (1956).[2] Although to some extent parallel modifications have been on-going in the orientations of some law professors to the study of law (Mayo and Jones 1964; Miller 1965a), the impression gained by an outside observer is that behavioral jurisprudence has thus far secured a much more tenuous beachhead in the law schools than in political science faculties (Schubert 1966a; and cf. Ralph Brown 1963).

Readers of this journal are quite familiar with the uses of computer technology for such purposes as document retrieval and the logical analysis of norm concepts in the content analysis of such documents; here I wish to direct attention, instead, to the quite different function that computers have been assigned by political scientists working in the field of behavioral jurisprudence. The difference is symbolized, indeed, by the disparate degrees of sympathy and antipathy that lawyers and political scientists have shown toward describing their respective activities by invoking the rubric which distinguishes this journal: "jurimetrics." Jurimetrics is a lawyers' concept, and the reasons which explain why it has come into vogue in the legal, but not in the political science, profession lie deep in the roots of the two academic cultures. Put most simply and perhaps crudely, lawyers are (at least some of them) interested in the measurement of law; *political scientists are not*. Public law scholars in political science do not want to measure *anything*; they are practitioners of an ancient and long-respected art. Judicial process proponents want to describe court systems, within the context of larger political, social, and economic systems. As long, at least, as quantification remains relatively unsophisticated and does not begin to dominate the structure of the design of empirical research projects (to say nothing of the design of re-

---

1. Subtitled: *A Study in Judicial Politics and Values, 1937–1947.*
2. The changes that occurred in the following decades can conveniently be observed by comparing two articles of mine: 1958e and 1968a.

search theory and hypotheses), advocates of the process approach are amenable to the use of measurement in the study of *politics*. But for these political scientists law is policy, and they are much more interested in trying to measure its sources and consequences in the form of social action than in measuring policy as substantive content. This leaves the political behavioralists, and, although they are the most supportive (among these three subgroups of political scientists) to the systematic measurement of data, they reject the implication that the study of law is the object of their inquiry. They want to understand human behavior in the context of sociopolitical situations that involve the professional roles of lawyers, and they are much more interested in understanding such political behavior at the level of systematic theory than they are in the empirical description—even the quantified description—of the same class of events. For students of behavioral jurisprudence, "jurimetrics" gives too much emphasis to law (instead of to behavior) and to measurement (instead of theory).

In political science of the modern, computerized era—that is to say, in the political science of the last half-dozen years or so—computer technology has been important primarily as an instrument to facilitate the processing and statistical analysis of data for purposes of research. The primary function of computers has been to generate new information, rather than to try to keep track of (or even to gain access to) information that previously has been or currently is being produced. I do not wish to seem to demean the latter task or its intrinsic importance, particularly in relation to the very different professional needs and practices of law from those of political science; rather, I seek to make the point that the use of computers in political science to facilitate research is a quite different emphasis than appears to have been given to the use of computers thus far in legal work.

The difference in the instrumental application of computers in behavioral jurisprudence reflects the characteristics of the behavioral approach as a scientific mode of inquiry: (1) The behavioral approach seeks to develop systematic theoretical knowledge, relying upon the use of controlled methods of observation, operationalized concepts, and the testing of hypotheses that are formulated before data are collected. Such an approach stands in contradistinction to one, frequently found in legal research, in which data are collected and analyzed and then post hoc "explanations" offered as possible interpretations of the relationships denoted (e.g., Nagel 1963b). (2) The behavioral approach is interdisciplinary and cross-cultural in the scope of its affiliations and interests; it seeks to focus upon and to understand what is common in human action, transactions, and interaction across both space and time. Adjudicative behavior is of interest precisely to the extent that the understanding of judiciallike decision-making can contribute to more general decision-making theory. But this stands in sharp contrast to the typically intradisciplinary, subcultural (viz., parochial) focus of legal method. As Loevinger (1966–1967) has pointed out, "the dialectic method of law stands as a formal, flexible, clinical approach to data gathering which is suitable to the investigation of individual cases but not to group or mass phenomena." (3) The behavioral approach is empirical in its orientation toward data; the reality in which it is interested consists of the consensual perceptions of equivalently trained observers. Its "facts," that is to say, are functions of interpersonal agreement. Legal study, to the contrary, seems much less concerned with what people do than with statements about what some persons think others ought to do, and the "facts" with which it is concerned are determined (also contrariwise) as functions of interpersonal *dis*agreement. But it is nonetheless in its emphasis upon empiricism (as distinguished from ideational sources of data) that the behavioral approach finds its closest link with legal method, in the research activities of American legal realists. (4) The behavioral approach seeks to quantify its data: The goal is theoretical statements in mathematical form, and empirical statements in statistical form. (There is no need to belabor the point that the legal approach shares neither of these aspirations.) The reason for quantification has been well expressed by an English historian of physical science:

> I shall distinguish first between quantified procedures and quantified concepts, and I shall take a quantified procedure in science to be one that aims at measurement, that is, any procedure that assigns numbers in a scale. To be complete such a procedure must comprise both mathematical techniques for operating the scale theoretically and measuring techniques for using it to explore the world. Technology need contain little more than procedures of these kinds, which provide for the measurements and calculations with which it is concerned. But most sciences aim beyond these at providing explanations by means of a system of theory. So *a quantified science, as distinct from quantified technology, comprises not only quantified procedures but also quantified explanatory concepts, each applicable to the other within a theoretical system.* The development of a science then takes place through a dialogue between its theories and its procedures, the former offering an exploration of the expected world through predictions and explanations made by means of the technical procedures, and the latter confronting these theoretical expectations with the test of quantified data.
>
> A dialogue of this kind requires that both sides should speak the same language. We are so familiar with the close and precise adaptation of conceptual and procedural language to each other in modern physics that it may come as a surprise to find authentic scientific systems in which this is not the case. Yet we do not have to look very far to find examples. In the contemporary social sciences and in psychology, they are notorious. We do not have to go many decades back in the history of modern genetics to find a very incomplete and interrupted dialogue between theories and procedures. Somewhat earlier, in the eighteenth century, we find the same situation in chemistry. The main interest of medieval physics in this context seems to me to be that it provides the earliest example in the development of modern science in which we can study the state of affairs when the dialogue between concepts and procedures was incomplete or absent. Then we can study the difference it made when clear and exact communication was opened, as it was in the seventeenth century. (Crombie 1961, emphasis added)

The implication of the last sentence—that the *birth* of Albert Einstein remained two full centuries away, as a possible (but certainly improbable) event of a remote and uncertain future, even at that point in space and time when isomorphism developed between physical theory and method—may bring some slight comfort to the many contemporary observers who purport to experience dismay (and whether with positive or with negative affect matters not) over the crudity of current efforts at quantification in the behavioral sciences. As Felix Cohen remarked, apropos of earlier attempts to infuse the behavioral approach into legal pedagogy, "The first steps taken are clumsy and evoke smiles of sympathy or roars of laughter from critics of diverse temperaments. The will to walk persists." (1935:834.)

The computer is a useful instrument in research in behavioral jurisprudence because (1) It facilitates inquiry by reducing time costs, thus freeing the investigator for less routine operations. (Anyone who has ever calculated a forty variable correlation matrix, which contains 380 different coefficients, by means of pencil and paper, or with a mechanically operated desk machine—to say nothing of factor analyzing such a matrix using the same procedures—will readily appreciate the difference that computers make in this regard.) (2) It makes feasible many types of inquiry that could not have been undertaken heretofore. (See, e.g., Somit, Tanenhaus, and Wilke 1960, a recent study of judicial sentencing behavior, in which a set of samples of about 150,000 cases was drawn from a universe of about 2,000,000 cases.) (3) And it provides, increasingly, better data (in the sense of empirical observations that have been transformed by the researcher into quantified units suitable for measurement manipulations [Coombs 1964:chap. 1]) by making feasible a greatly expanded repertoire of alternative modes of analysis. (Antecomputer factor analysis, for example, was largely confined to such relatively gross and approximate procedures as those of the complete centroid method, with relatively few iterations and—usually—graphical procedures for rotation; principal axes factor analysis is now routine, coupled with extensive iterations, a choice among various orthogonal and oblique rotational solutions, and with a plotting subroutine for whatever output one may choose to specify.)

But the computer, notwithstanding these manifest advantages, is not without its limitations: Among others, the computer (1) asks no questions; (2) provides no answers; and (3) solves no problems—and it is a disservice to scientific inquiry to tout the contrary, as some enthusiasts appear to have done. In order to explore the implications of these dogmatically phrased assertions, I should like to discuss an example gleaned from an article by Harold Lasswell (1955) published at the very threshhold of the technological revolution that the computer was to bring to behavioral (along with other branches of) science. Lasswell might seem to be an appropriate choice as a spokesman, for present purposes, because he is one of the world's most renowned behavioral scientists, he is one of the few political scientists who is a member of a faculty of law, and in this article he explicitly is concerned with the development of creativity in a society whose decision-making processes will become increasingly computerized. Lasswell explicitly raises the question, in this article, that the time might soon be at hand when engineers could construct a "bench of judicial robots"—as Professor Lasswell, characteristically, chose to express it, juxtaposing a novel idea with rather old-fashioned words. The Supreme Court, he suggested (1955:398), might be an appropriate object for simulation (cf. Schubert 1972*f*). But after a suitable period of experimentation, during which the engineering problems would be resolved and techniques perfected, the community would be given an opportunity "to develop a rational consensus on whether to use [the judicial] robots or not"—that is, by the substitution of a computer for the Supreme Court.

From the standpoint of 1967 the proposal seems to be at least as antiquarian as it is audacious. Note that the metaphor "bench of judicial robots" is, like its second substantive (*robots*), explicitly anthropomorphic. But robots had had it, even by 1955, except for purposes of entertainment (as in Bob Cummings' "living doll") rather than for those of science. Manlike machines were displaced by less romantic, but more functional, models. As one of the few persons who, at least thus far, has been disanthropomorphized and depersonalized into the image of a computer (by an evidently unhappy and doubtless misanthropic lawyer [Rosenthal 1966]), I feel that it is important to make a clear distinction between people and computers. I have argued elsewhere, incidentally, my opinion that both humans and computers have their strong and weak points and that, in a more rational world, efforts would be made so to structure decision-making processes—including research investigations—as to maximize the strengths and to minimize the weaknesses of both computers and their human masters (Schubert 1963*e*).

It may well be that, as one student of Professor Lasswell's work has suggested to me, in this particular passage of the article the author was merely indulging some free association, and with tongue in cheek at that. Doubtless this is the correct interpretation to make, particularly in view of the evident thrust of the rest of the article in favor of creativity rather than of automation. Even so, there are plenty of others around who would not blink at the proposal, once the technology can be demonstrated to be adequate to the task. I intend, therefore, to take the proposition at face value and to consider the question of feasibility from a more extensive and behavioral point of view that goes beyond its merely engineering and technological aspects.

It certainly seems correct that already, within a dozen years from Lasswell's writing, a fairly good start could be made in the programming of judicial values (Lawlor 1963; Schubert 1965*c*). (Note that I do not speak of "feeding" these values to the computer, as appears to be the mode of discourse among many contemporary commentators who write about interactions between humans and machines. For one thing, my sensitive nature is appalled by the thought of pushing too far the explicit analogizing of computers to the alimentary canal; for another, my reading several years ago of a particularly seminal article by Martin Landau (1961) has made me skeptical of the degree of intellectual clarity that is to be gained by the maladroit mixing of biological with mechanical metaphors.

Certainly there are available on today's market several different computers that would probably be adequate to store and manipulate the requisite data. Merely documentary judicial inputs such as briefs and records of lower court proceedings evidently could be filed, with the Computer Court, as tapes. Oral argument should present not much greater challenge than does the programming of teaching machines. And a number of advantages can readily be visualized.

"Delay in the court," a problem which lawyers have found troublesome (at a somewhat earlier time, in the Supreme Court itself; and in most metropolitan civil courts today), could be cut to the few hours that might be required for "turnaround time" in making as many runs as might be necessary—and usually only one would suffice—to produce a decision in a case. Actual decision time would be a few seconds, or a few minutes at the most, and quite possibly microseconds would suffice for the more routine decisions as the technology improves. And the Computer Court could tremendously expand the number of decisions made on the merits each year; perhaps there would need to be only a single decision day per year instead of the twenty to twenty-five now required, and the costs of administration for the Court could be greatly reduced. The Computer Court could, for example, be completely installed in a small room, approximately of the same dimensions as the one in the basement of the old Capitol building in which the Supreme Court used to meet under John Marshall, thus obviating the need for maintaining the opulent Marble Palace which houses the present Court and its (superfluous) accouterments. Contrary to the present state of uncertainty which is associated with at least a portion of the work of the Court, predictability of the decisions of the Computer Court would be perfect—for those privy to the programming and data inputs, of course. Not least, the decision-making procedure that was established for the Computer Court could readily be generalized, with only slight technical modifications, to include at the very least all of the United States Courts of Appeals as well as the Supreme Court, with consequent bigger savings in the federal budgetary allocations for both judicial personnel and housekeeping (since the same machine could probably be required to perform this somewhat expanded task, and without moving it from whatever basement room had been established for its domicile).

Regrettably, there would be a few undesirable side effects, most of which can be traced directly to the Computer Court's inhuman characteristics. Indeed, a mere listing of some of the most obvious of these side effects impels one to the conclusion that, however successful the Computer Court might be from a legal point of view, the results of its establishment would be politically disastrous. To start with some that seem relatively innocuous, we might note that however unphotogenic one might deem the annual opening-of-the-term portraits of the Supreme Court that are published in the *New York Times*, ones of the Computer Court are not likely to be perceived by most readers to be more attractive. After all, the Computer Court cannot be constructed as a mobile, and there may be a psychological problem for readers who discover that, as they grow older, the Court will be—and will seem to be—newer in its aspect (as technological innovation proceeds) with each year that passes. The Computer Court's decision-making process will not enjoy the prestige of the present Court; it seems improbable that thousands of high school seniors from throughout the land will pass—even in single file—through the basement door to observe the quiet efficiency of the console in operation. The Computer Court, even if constructed in literal accord with Lasswell's metaphor, would lack something in the way of human interest for the masses: it could, of course, produce articles on the side for popular magazines, and be listed on the letterheads of various organizations, but on the other hand it would never climb mountains, or fall off horses, or take brides. It will be easy to provide for minority interest representation in the Computer Court, but difficult to symbolize that this has been done, as some think may be the effect of the visible presence of justices such as Thurgood Marshall, Abe Fortas, and William Brennan.

The Computer Court would have limited value as a scapegoat target in political billboard advertizing, although its impeachment and removal from office would remain open as a technical possibility. The odds are, however, that most Computer Courts would be replaced on grounds of technological, rather than of political, obsolescence. We could not expect the Computer Court to be creative, in its political leadership role, in quite the same way in which we sometimes observe creativity in the decision-making of the present justices—in the redefining of situations, that is to say, by the posing of novel alternative possibilities for the solution of conflicts—but the programming of random components in the decision-making process (which would be easy to do) might to some degree function as a substitute for human creativity (Aubert 1959; Lasswell 1955:387, 398). At the same time, such a modification would entail the disadvantage of precluding perfect prediction of the Court's decisional outcomes. It might well be argued, however, that the achievement of perfect predictability would be not an unmitigated virtue, but rather the Computer Court's greatest flaw, and that the greatest defect of a tested and perfected bench of judicial robots, whether in anthropomorphic or in the more conventional console form, would be its *lack of uncertainty*. Indeed, our examination of the implications of the Computer Court suggests the hypothesis that *the ideal of certainty in law is tolerable only in the context of an empirical world in which forces inducing change are so manifold that the attainment of the goal is never possible.*

Lasswell concluded his article with the suggestion that the development of an expanded computer technology posed no threat to, but rather increased the need for, human creativity. The events of the past dozen years in political science research in behavioral jurisprudence certainly confirm his expectations.

# 2

# The Future
# of Public Law

To speak of the future of "public law" is to trace out the denouement of
an anachronism. To be sure, public law has a past, one that extends back
almost a century in American intellectual life among academicians and lawyers. But it has an uninteresting present, and no future—or at least, not as
public law. Under these circumstances, an attempt at postdiction seems to
be a psychological (as well as a chronological) prerequisite to any sensible
venture in prediction about the subject. Those who are ignorant of the past
are not doomed to repeat it; they are just doomed to ignorance. That fate
alone, however, is sad enough to justify some inquiry into the developmental
relationship between public law and the professions of law and of political
science, before we turn to the Ghosts of Public Law Present and of Public
Law Yet to Come.

## I. THE GHOST OF PUBLIC LAW PAST

### In the Beginning

Public law is not even an American legal concept, let alone one derived
from the common law; it was imported from the Continent in the postbellum
decades when the German university circuit was having its maximal impact
upon the men who were to shape and direct higher education in the United

Reprinted in slightly different form from *The George Washington Law Review* 34 (May
1966): 593–614. Copyright 1966 *The George Washington Law Review*. This article was the
Centennial Essay of the issue.

States during the closing decades of the nineteenth century.[1] The alien concept soon was engrafted upon American legal and political thinking; no doubt one encouraging factor was the widespread emphasis, following the crisis of the Civil War, upon instruction in the Constitution in order to inculcate civic loyalty. Indeed, there is deep irony in the circumstance that it was exaggerated demands for super civic loyalty during the First World War—by then directed, however, *against* Germanophiles—which catalyzed Charles A. Beard's resignation from the first department of public law to be established at any American university.[2] As John Millet has pointed out, the first great change in that department (since its establishment in 1887) had come with Beard's appointment in 1907.[3]

The establishment of the Department of Public Law and Jurisprudence at Columbia University represented a stage of structural differentiation in an institutional movement that began with the appointment of John W. Burgess to the faculty of law at Columbia in 1876. Although the incumbent (and long-time) dean of Columbia's then quasi-proprietary School of Law, Theodore Dwight, had abetted the recruitment of Burgess from Amherst, the two men soon became, and remained, in fundamental disagreement over precisely this question: What is the appropriate place of public law instruction in a law school curriculum? Dwight wanted to, and did, provide what was for its day considered to be successful and high quality vocational training. Burgess wanted to add a compulsory third year to the law school curriculum, to consist of public law courses taught by men who were trained broadly in the social sciences.[4] Eventually, both were forced to accept a compromise that neither wanted: Columbia established in 1880 a School of Political Science, which in another decade differentiated into the nuclei of several social science departments, including Public Law and Jurisprudence. Throughout the period 1890–1910, the four leading members of that department were Burgess, Munroe Smith, Frank Goodnow, and John Bassett Moore. All held joint appointments in the law school, and their courses were taken both by law students and candidates for advanced degrees in political science. Indeed, "Students in the School of Law could take courses in constitutional law, administrative law, Roman law, and international law *only* from professors of the Department of Public Law and Jurisprudence" (Hoxie 1955:258, emphasis added). These courses, plus those in criminal law and in comparative juris-

---

1. Austin (1869) 1:69–71 and 2:770–787; Walz 1934. Neither Austin (of course) nor Walz, a German professor at the University of Marburg, had anything to say about public law in the United States. In sharp contrast on just about all relevant dimensions stands the article on American public law by David Danelski, a political scientist at Yale University (1968).

2. Beard resigned for reasons of academic freedom; there was never any question raised concerning his personal support of the war. See Hoxie 1955:106–108.

3. As quoted by Hoxie (1955:264).

4. "The two-year course offered in the School of Law furnished an excellent preparation for the practice of private law; but, in Burgess' eyes, as a school of jurisprudence, to impart knowledge and develop law as a science based on history, economics, sociology, ethics, and philosophy, it left much to be desired" (Haddow 1939:178–179n. 25). Cf. Hoxie 1955:8–19.

prudence, were intended to supplement the courses in history and economics offered by other departments of the School of Political Science "and 'to give with them a complete system of political science'" (Haddow 1939:181n. 32). In practice, however, it was Dwight's rather than Burgess' vision that became a reality. Burgess, Smith, Goodnow, and Moore all were broad-gauged law-yers,[5] who continued throughout their careers to teach law to law students and at the same time had a hand—and particularly was this true of Burgess and Goodnow—in shaping the early development of political science as a discipline. But their successors were increasingly oriented toward law rather than toward political science; and after the pioneers had retired and the de-partment in 1926 had moved out of the law school building (Kent Hall) into quarters of its own, the identification of "public law" with the law faculty became so complete that only a handful of law professors (Joseph Chamber-lain, Hyde, Jessup) offered a few courses (legislation and international law) that were taken by political science as well as by law students.[6] In 1937, at least a generation after the change in symbols would have been appropriate, the name of the department was changed from Public Law and Comparative Jurisprudence to Public Law and Government; and it remains the latter today, a designation that evidently pays more respect to sentiment than to accurate description.

The golden years at Columbia spawned the Golden Age of American public law. But to encounter a vigorous discipline of public law of which we might speak (with at least metaphorical validity) as being in the prime of intellectual life, it is necessary to go back that far, a full half century, to the era before World War I. In 1905, Frank Goodnow became the first president of the American Political Science Association (APSA). Various of his students

---

5. The first three had followed graduation from Amherst with Continental tours before going to Columbia. Burgess studied law for a year (1867–1868); Smith and Goodnow received LL.B. degrees from Columbia Law School; and Moore, though self-taught in law, was the first great American scholar of international law and a judge of the Permanent Court of International Justice at The Hague.

6. As noted above, Dwight had helped to recruit Burgess, but the two men divided over the question of how broad legal education should be just as soon as they came to understand the extent of the difference in their ideological standpoints. Similarly, and although Goodnow had been his student and early protege, Burgess refused upon his retirement to recommend Goodnow as Burgess' own successor to the Ruggles Professorship of Political Science and Con-stitutional Law, and explicitly on the ground that Goodnow was much too deeply oriented toward political science, and too little toward law and constitutional history. As a consequence, Goodnow resigned in 1914 to become president of Johns Hopkins University, and he was re-placed by one of his own students, Howard Lee McBain, whose degrees and training and interests lay in political science rather than in law. However,

> McBain's death in 1936 had interrupted the unbroken [sic] line of instruction in con-stitutional law which had started with Burgess sixty years before. An adequate replace-ment could not be found, and thereafter for nearly twenty years the Department relied for instruction in this field upon Noel T. Downing, Harlan Fiske Stone Professor of Con-stitutional Law in the School of Law, who was given a seat in the Faculty of Political Science in 1937. We may note here that in the same year Walter Gellhorn of the Law School faculty also became a member of the Faculty of Political Science in recognition of his work in providing instruction in administrative law for graduate students. (Hoxie 1955:278).

attained equal eminence as public lawyers and as political scientists: of particular note were Ernst Freund, Thomas Reed Powell, and Charles Grove Haines.[7] Each of these three emphasized in his own work a different aspect of the subject; but collectively (administrative law, constitutional law, constitutional history) they replicated the central understanding of public law, as this was taught in the department in which they were trained.

Of course, Columbia was not the only university in which political science developed out of an extension of public law; nor did political science by any means derive exclusively from public law (Haddow 1939). But it is the public law strand that is of crucial relevance to the present paper; and it was at Columbia that the most important roles were being played in the parturition of political science from public law. As an example of a parallel but alternative form of development, let us consider briefly what happened at a neighboring university. Perhaps the most important fact of relevance is that Princeton does not now have, and never has had, a law school. For reasons that are no doubt equally as sentimental as Columbia's, but with ties to a very different pattern of remembrance, Princeton continues to call its department of political science a Department of Politics. The courses offered by the department in 1890–1892 were in two groups: the first group, taught by Professor of History and Political Science William Sloane, included Constitutional and Political History of England, American Political History, History of Political Theories, and Contrasts between Parliamentary and Congressional Governments; the second group, taught by Professor of Jurisprudence and Political Economy Woodrow Wilson, included Public Law, General Jurisprudence, American Constitutional Law, International Law, Administration, and English Common Law (Haddow 1939:184–185). Wilson, it may be recalled, had failed to complete the law course at the University of Virginia and had failed in his subsequent attempt to practice law in Atlanta, before undertaking the Ph.D. in history and political science, which he completed at Johns Hopkins in 1886. His early writings, ranging from his precocious essay on public administration (1887) through his dissertation on the

---

7. Ernst Freund received his Ph.D. from Columbia in 1897 and taught there as acting professor of administrative law during 1892–1894, after which he taught until 1932 on the Chicago political science and law faculties. Freund stepped into the shoes of his former colleague, Goodnow, as the leading American scholar of administrative law; and he served as the association's eleventh president in 1915. Thomas Reed Powell (Harvard, LL.B., 1904; Columbia, Ph.D., 1913), the thirty-second president of the APSA in 1937, was sufficiently more under the aegis of Burgess to be appointed to the Ruggles Professorship that was denied to Goodnow. He taught constitutional law at Columbia from 1907 to 1925, and then returned to his alma mater to become lion of the Harvard law faculty until his retirement in 1949—and in saying this I am not unmindful of the fox who served as his sometime colleague for over a dozen years. (For an appraisal of the latter's nonacademic contributions to public law, see Grant 1965.) Charles Grove Haines (Columbia, Ph.D., 1909), a leading constitutional historian, was the thirty-fourth president of the association; he taught as a political scientist at several colleges and universities during the two decades before he joined the political science department of U.C.L.A. in 1925, where he remained until his death in 1948. [See Kraines 1974.]

legislative process (1885) and his pioneering text on comparative government (1889), all are characterized not by legalism, but rather by the evolutionary *Zeitgeist* of the natural science that predominated during his era. He taught courses in public law, but to students of social science rather than to students of law. A professor of jurisprudence teaching nonlaw students in a department of politics acts in a very different environment than does a professor of public law teaching law and nonlaw students together in a school of law; and this was the difference between Princeton and Columbia in the 1890s. Before leaving Princeton, Wilson recruited his successor to the McCormick Professorship of Jurisprudence and Politics, Edward S. Corwin, who for most of the forty years after his appointment in 1905 was recognized as the doyen of American public law scholars. Corwin's Ph.D. was in history, from the University of Pennsylvania. He followed Wilson (after some two decades) in the association presidency, but he confined the interests of the McCormick chair within much more recognizably "public law" bounds than had Wilson, specializing in the political history of the Supreme Court and of the Presidency and in constitutional law (Mason and Garvey 1964). In 1947, Corwin was succeeded, in the McCormick Chair of Jurisprudence, by Alpheus Thomas Mason (Princeton, Ph.D., 1923), who had been first Corwin's student and then for over twenty years his colleague. Mason has been a leading contributor to judicial biography (Brandeis, Stone, and Taft), as well as to constitutional law and the modern political history of the Supreme Court.[8] Clearly, public law at Princeton developed along very different lines than did public law at Columbia, where it was captured back by the law school to become basically certain courses in a program of vocational education. Princeton, having no law school to compete (or to deal) with, has instead continued the Wilsonian tradition of public law defined as political history and political jurisprudence.

These sketches of the public law orientations of two leading American universities are relevant to our present concern primarily because of the extent to which they symbolize more general movements in law and in political science during the past half century. In the days of Burgess, Goodnow, and Wilson, law and political science and history were joined in a secular trinity—and their unity was called public law. That unity was already gone by 1914 (with Burgess retired, Goodnow moving up to academic administration, and Wilson having accepted an even higher calling); and the second generation of public law scholars (Freund, Corwin, Haines, Powell) showed a distinct proclivity for greater specialization than had the pioneers. It is true that a third generation (William Anderson, Minnesota; Robert Cushman, Cornell; Carl Swisher, Johns Hopkins; and Mason) already has reached the age of retirement; but however distinguished they are—and they are distinguished—personally, the definition of public law that they symbolize constitutes "the

---

8. See the *Festchrift* volume (Dietze 1965) presented to Mason by his students.

last long-drawn-out gasp of a dying tradition."[9] All of these men (but most particularly the pioneers) were great public lawyers, renowned as scholars, as teachers, and as counselors on the public policy issues that loomed large during their lifetime. It is literally true that none has emerged to fill their shoes, in either the political science or the law faculties of the present generation; and one does not need to be a romantic to observe that we shall know their like no more. The reason is not hard to discover. Great men tend to be attracted to great causes (or vice versa); and public law has not been a noble subject, let alone a great one, in the academic hierarchy of values for a long time.

## In the Law Schools

In considering what has become of public law during the past half century, there are really two quite distinct histories to relate because law and political science followed separate and diverging paths after the brief but spectacular period of their partnership around the turn of the century. It is true that men trained as lawyers continued to teach political science courses (and especially such "public law" courses as constitutional law and administrative law), sometimes with, but often without, any formal training in political science. Usually, those with both a law degree and a doctorate in political science chose to teach as members of political science faculties; and usually such persons acquired their law degree first. Sometimes practicing lawyers, resident in or near a college community, taught as adjunct lecturers political science courses in public law; and sometimes law faculty members offered such courses as a "service" for political science departments—even such a major university (and political science department) as Yale gave up such a practice only a couple of years ago. But these arrangements by no means should be interpreted to have implied a happy symbiosis between law and political science. Quite to the contrary, to the extent such arrangements existed, they meant that the political science departments had completely given up the attempt to integrate the "public law" subfield with the rest of the discipline; and having concluded that the subjects concerned were exotic and technical, these departments handled the problem by fencing off the public law work in isolation from what otherwise constituted their major concerns and interests. And the almost unthinkable reciprocal relationship—that is, to expose law students to instruction by a person who had had no formal legal socialization, but merely a political science background—simply never happened. Or rather, it happened only once,[10] in the very special case of Harold Lasswell's cooptation by the Yale Law School at the end of World War II.

---

9. Paraphrasing Felix Cohen's characterization of the American Law Institute's attempts to "restate" the principles of the common law (Cohen 1935:833).

10. Conceivably twice, if one were to include Walter F. Dodd, who preceded Lasswell at Yale. It was expected that Dodd, who was a Chicago Ph.D. in political science, would broaden the content of instruction due to his interest in comparative government. Instead, Dodd became the very model of a modern legal gentleman.

The history of public law instruction in the law schools, since about 1915, is pretty much a story of rigor mortis. The law casebook already had achieved its classic form in the decade following that date; and one need only compare, say, the fifth with the first edition of Dodd (1932) to observe how miniscule have been the subsequent changes in conceptualization and in approach during the thirties, forties, and fifties. Constitutional law is still today defined, by the typical law casebook on the subject, as an extensive form of the constitutional document, with practically all of the extension consisting of some writer's (either the editor's or that of some essayist whom he reprints) impressions of what the justices of the Supreme Court say in their opinions about the Constitution.[11] Administrative law remains basically what it was in Freund's day: the study of how courts keep administrators in line; and what some legal writers like Davis call "informal" administrative processes reflect a crude mode of structural description that had become passé in political science study of public administration over a generation ago.[12] (The principal reason why the legal experts on administrative law failed to recognize how stodgy their "new" revelations were,[13] one suspects, is that they could not or would not read the modern research literature in such subjects as decision-making theory.)[14] It seems almost certain that a better political education might have helped to avert some of the more egregious blunders, such as those (revealed in his own confessional) of one professor of administrative law who made the mistake of attempting to put his theories to the test of personal practice (Schwartz 1959).

Let us consider the advice of a research manual on the subject how to investigate an aspect of administrative law:

> When you, a student, wish to become familiar with some phase of governmental activity—let us take, as an example, the Interstate Commerce Commission—you have two ways of acquiring this information. The first and most generally used method is to go to the library and secure a book which describes the Interstate Commerce Commission. This plan has several serious defects. For

---

11. See Schwartz 1963. "If the Supreme Court Justices are the high priesthood of the Constitution, then the Founding Fathers . . . are the saints in America's hagiology. We worship our ancestors as well as the Document. The analogy can be pressed further. The law clerks of the Justices are the altar boys; the lawyers are the acolytes. Law professors (and some political scientists) are the Pharisees. The high priests, aided by the altar boys, produce exegesis on the sacred text. The acolytes pay respectful court (though sometimes not so respectful), while the Pharisees grind out heavily footnoted critiques of what the high priests have said." (Miller 1965c: 155).

12. See, e.g., Lepawsky 1949; Simon 1947; Simon, Smithburg, and Thompson 1950.

13. See Davis 1953. Cf. the subsequent exchange of views between Davis, Gellhorn, and various political scientists (Symposium 1954a, b). Evidently Professor Davis did not profit much from that encounter, as was exemplified by the subsequent exchange: Grundstein 1964; and Davis 1964.

14. See, e.g. March 1965; March & Simon 1958; Presthus 1962; Simon 1957. Cf. Wasserman & Silander 1958; 1964; Thomas Jefferson Center for Studies in Political Economy 1964. There have always been a few exceptions, such as Walter Gellhorn and Ralph Fuchs, among law school professors of administrative law, just as men like John P. Frank and Arthur Selwyn Miller would be exceptions to an equivalent generalization about law school instruction in constitutional law, and Thomas A. Cowan would be for jurisprudence.

one thing, it limits your investigations to those matters about which books have been written. Then, too, the value of knowledge acquired in this manner is limited by the author's familiarity with his subject, his ability to express his thoughts, his desire to tell the truth, and the number of words his publisher would accept.

The other way to secure information about the Interstate Commerce Commission is more cumbersome, but much more accurate and complete. It involves finding and reading the act which created the Commission, and examining the debates in Congress concerning it. It also includes an inspection of the Interstate Commerce Commission's rulings and reports, and of court decisions affecting its powers. These laws, administrative reports, legislative debates, judicial decisions, and similar documents are known as original sources, because they form the basis for all investigations. (Macdonald 1928:1–2)

The above advice comes from a political scientist, but almost forty years ago. It is almost inconceivable that any political scientist who could obtain a professional audience would recommend such an approach today; and if he did so before an audience of political science graduate students at any of our leading universities, he would almost certainly be laughed at.[15] But this is the very approach that law school instruction in administrative law still considers, apparently, to be highly relevant to the acquisition of important knowledge about the subject. To be perfectly blunt, legal research remains today at the primitive level of development, as a science, that generally characterized political science one or two generations ago. By and large, legal method is no more in phase with modern science than it was in the days of Austin, or (better) Aquinas, or (best) Aristotle, all of the talk about "legal science" and computerized methods of retrieving legal data to the contrary notwithstanding.

It might be objected that the legal realists of the 1920s and 1930s were—as many of them claimed to be—legal scientists; but such an objection misconceives both the requirements of science and the accomplishments of the realists. Science requires both theoretical models from which operationalized hypotheses can be inferred and methods for testing such hypotheses with data derived from empirical observations. The realists, with rare exceptions, such as Walter Wheeler Cook and Underhill Moore, had neither theory nor methods; Llewellynisms about "getting at" facts and "polishing them" until they "shone" were nothing more than advocacy of barefoot empiricism. The contribution of the realists lay in the mood they created, through the attention attracted by the iconoclastic essays that several of them wrote (e.g., Jerome Frank 1930, 1931; Cohen 1935; Loevinger 1949); but lacking the technical training to do scientific research, they rarely followed through with the substantive findings to confirm (or refute) their often provocative, and sometimes brilliant, cues and hunches (Rumble 1964, 1965; Hayakawa 1964). Most of their work remained at the verbal level, in perfect harmony with the traditions of the profession of which they were a part.

---

15. See the series of Handbooks for Research in Political Behavior which Northwestern University Press began to publish in 1963, including Backstrom and Hirsch 1963; Janda 1965; and North 1963. Cf. Rummell 1970.

If we disregard, for the moment, the few political scientists (such as Haines and Powell) who sometimes have been classified among the realists, none of them was primarily interested, in any event, in the reform of public law sectors of law school instruction. On the contrary, the law professors who were identified with public law teaching were proponents of the sociological school of jurisprudence; and it seems appropriate, for present purposes, to accept the distinction between sociological and realist approaches that spokesmen for both insisted upon. Sociological jurisprudence really made no pretense of being either sociological or scientific.[16] Pound and Frankfurter taught and wrote prolifically about public law subjects, but their approach was that of the humanities, not that of modern social science.

One aspect of the realist movement does merit our attention, however. This is the endeavor, and most conspicuously that of Robert M. Hutchins during his brief dynamic tenure as dean of the Yale Law School about forty years ago, to reform the law school curriculum by deliberately building into the faculty the kinds of competencies which, though essential if law were to become a science, were so conspicuously lacking in the training of law school teachers.[17] Thus, if law professors were not trained as economists, sociologists, statisticians, historians, psychologists, or as political scientists, the way to get such points of view into the law curriculum would be to employ such nonlegal specialists to teach in the law school. How this idea would work in practice we can only guess, because it has never really been tried. When only one or two such persons are put into a group of a score or more of law professors, the principal effect of interaction seems to be for the majority to socialize the minority, so that (as one experienced observer has put it) the "outsiders" become even more legalistic, in their point of view and approach, than are the law professors. But even such token integration of social scientists with law faculties has taken place in only a very few instances. To take an almost contemporary example, we might consider the widely publicized program in "Law and Behavioral Sciences" at the University of Chicago Law School. The 1964–1965 catalogue lists three social scientists (out of a regular faculty of twenty-seven)—two economists plus Hans Zeisel; and Zeisel, consistently with the view expressed above, has been just as rabid a critic of behavioral research as his legally educated public law colleague Kurland (which is saying a great deal). The behaviorally trained and oriented persons "on the law faculty" (such as Strodtbeck and Haggard) have been used as consultants or adjunct research personnel in conjunction with such specific research program areas as the jury project and the arbitration project. And the published results of such cooperative research, although of high interest, are to date of such limited quantity that their impact upon the legal profession, in the context of the copious outpourings of traditional legal writing, remains small.

---

16. Ehrlich is a possible exception. See Cahill 1952: chap. 4.
17. Much of the information in this paragraph is based upon, or was confirmed in, an interview with Robert M. Hutchins, February 23, 1966.

The underlying problem with which Hutchins was concerned is, of course, the same issue that divided Dwight and Burgess fifty years before Hutchins became dean at Yale: Should training in the law be vocational or educational? One possible solution is to broaden the law curriculum; and in this endeavor Columbia probably went much further (relatively speaking) from the 1870s to World War I than did Yale from the 1920s to World War II. The other solution is to give up on the law school and establish a separate school of jurisprudence; and having failed to reach the first solution at Yale, Hutchins tried at Chicago to achieve the second alternative, but again without success. In fact, John W. Burgess' School of Political Science probably went as far in the direction of such a jurisprudence school as American experience has produced.

If it had proved possible for any of several things to have happened that did not—if the realists had produced something other than discrete facts and unverified hypotheses; if law professors themselves could have been educated as social scientists; or if social scientists could have been imported into law teaching and research in sufficiently large numbers that it might have been possible for them to have established, and to have maintained, some intellectual beachheads—then it is not inconceivable that law school instruction in public law courses also might have been affected and forced as it were out of the tried and true familiar grooves in which it has been running for so many years. Lacking such rejuvenation from the larger setting in which it was produced, law school public law has remained in the same old rut.

## In Political Science

While law school instruction in public law remained in rigor mortis after the Burgesses and the Goodnows passed from the teaching scene, political science work in public law went through a long period of degeneration, in which the gains achieved by the preeminence of a few outstanding figures (e.g., Corwin, Cushman, Haines, Mason, and Swisher) could not compensate for the bland mediocrity that characterized the field generally. Most of the persons who taught political science courses in public law during the long period spanned by the two world wars either were themselves lawyers or (which was often worse) were imitators of lawyers whose pedagogical ideal was the stereotyped law-school-type course in public law, of which they offered a watered-down version for political science undergraduate students. Such persons did little research, and what little they did was in the legal tradition and was published mostly in law rather than in political science journals. No wonder other political scientists ignored their public law colleagues. No wonder that, as recently as 1951, an official committee of the APSA, which had been appointed at the end of World War II to take stock, complained:

> We recommend that the profession work toward a balanced development
> of the field and avoid the recurring enthusiasms which lead to new emphases and
> the neglect of old ones. We are convinced, for example, that political science

suffered untold harm during the period in which public law was neglected. Any outsider [lawyers? who else?] knows that public law is [NB: read "ought to be"] one of the strongest areas of proficiency within the field of political science; we overlooked this fact for a while, and we are only now taking steps to restore the balance. (Dimock 1951:128–129)

No one knows what specific steps to restore the balance Chairman Dimock and his distinguished colleagues on the committee may have had in mind, for they suggested none, and the restorative step that took place in fact— the emergence of the behavioral approach toward the study of public law (cf. Schubert 1963*d:*1–3)—was doubtless the last kind of emphasis that they would have favored.[18]

It is not that the political science profession was unaware of the source of the problem. Almost two decades earlier, William Anderson had focused attention directly upon the effects and the implication of relying upon lawyers to teach political science courses:

> To what extent does the training now offered in American law schools for the LL.B. degree fit men for their responsibilities as teachers and research workers in the field of political science? . . . It is not "law in action" or the work of the courts that is studied, but rather the law as crystallized in rules and principles by judges in the highest courts who have rendered past decisions. . . . The stress in legal education must of necessity be on the preparation of private practitioners, men who are to advise and represent private clients. The purpose is not to train teachers of government. It is probably not unfair to say, therefore, that in most cases even the courses in public law are taught with an eye to the needs of the practicing lawyer. Everyone at all familiar with the subject knows how differently courses in constitutional law, for example, can be taught by teachers having essentially different purposes. Because most constitutional cases encountered in private practice will deal with the due process, contract, and commerce clauses, it is not surprising to find these topics strongly emphasized in law school courses in constitutional law. One teaching the same subject for the purpose of giving students some understanding of government will give emphasis to very different topics.
>
> Other dangers in an exclusively legal education for the teacher of political science are not hard to indicate. The main subjects of a modern political science curriculum are not covered in the law school. . . . There is danger, also, in a merely juristic approach to the study of government. All the new developments in the study of politics are going toward the enrichment and the rounding-out of the whole subject, not toward the narrowing of it, and particularly not toward further emphasis upon the legal phases. History, economics, psychology, anthropology, and other disciplines offer just as interesting and fruitful approaches to the study of politics as does the law.
>
> There is, finally, another characteristic of the present-day training of legal practitioners which makes it inadequate as a training for research and teaching in political science. The most commonly employed research method is that of

18. It hardly seems possible today that an official committee of the American Political Science Association could have produced, a scant fifteen years ago, a report of over three hundred pages in length which barely mentions, and devotes less than a single page to, the discussion of political behavior, but Dimock's group succeeded in such a tour de force. See Dimock 1951: 139.

looking up cases in point, finding the principles embedded in them, and testing these principles by logic or "dialectic techniques." There is no time or demand for training in other research methods, no urge to apply statistical and other techniques to the materials, and often no desire to go outside of the decisions in order to test the results of the operation of legal rules on social or economic life, or on personal conduct. (1934:740–742)

Except in some very small departments that were run or dominated by senior men whose training was exclusively as lawyers, the lawyers-acting-as-political scientists always were a minority in any department, and the trend definitely was toward reducing their influence in relation to the rest of political science. There was an important difference between political science and law school faculties, however: the former were relatively much more heterogeneous, and consequently much less effective agencies for socializing lawyers to conform with the diversified group norms of political science, than were the law schools for remolding social scientists into law professors.

Over the course of the past half century, there have been five surveys of the political science profession, four official ones (in 1914, 1923, 1930, and 1950) and one unofficial inquest in 1964. We can trace the decline of public law through the eyes of these observers of and for the profession.

The first audit was made by a committee whose chairman was Charles Grove Haines. We have already noted Haines' preeminence in and identification with the field of public law; and it seems plausible to assume that, if his committee's report showed any bias, it was in favor of public law. The Haines committee classified the political science of its day into four fields, saying that one of these consisted of

the work offered in constitutional law, administrative law, commercial law, Roman law, elements of law, and jurisprudence. These courses mark the dividing line where the technical phases of law merge into the realm of public policy, ethics and custom and thus constitute a common vicinage in which the departments of law and political science are equally interested and involved. It is in this latter type of course that the question arises whether they should not be offered primarily as law courses to which advanced undergraduates might be admitted instead of being offered under departments of political science and admitting law students. (Haines 1915:372)

Among the list of "queries relative to instruction" that the committee thought it important to raise for discussion were several concerning "law and law courses," including the following:

Should Roman law and jurisprudence be offered in the law school rather than in the college department?
Should administrative law and administrative methods be given more attention in elementary courses?
Is it necessary to omit judicial procedure from elementary courses because of the technical nature of the subject?
Is it advisable to offer commercial law in undergraduate departments of political science? (Haines 1915:373)

By and large, the report provides substantial evidence of the continuing importance of public law at that time; but it also contains many suggestions that public law already was on the way out as a core area of political science (Haines 1915:356–357, 366, 371–373). In the polite phrasing of the Dimock Committee, who began their own report with a commentary upon their predecessors, "The [Haines] report also shows the extent to which political science ha[d] broadened since outgrowing its public law beginnings inherited from Europe and since the establishment of the Association in 1906" (Dimock 1951:8).

Although less than a decade separated the Haines report from that authored primarily by Charles E. Merriam in 1923, at least two generations of professional work and development lie between the two conceptions of political science articulated in them. The Haines report was a workmanlike description of the then status quo, while the Merriam committee filed a statement of aspirations so deviant from the reality of the political science of the early twenties that, after the lapse of forty-three years, his ideals finally were beginning to describe the activities of a substantial minority of the profession. But Merriam's report, according to Dimock, did correctly predict the course along which future development of the profession lay:

> it pointed out how the field of political science, which originally consisted almost entirely of constitutional and administrative law, had developed new emphases and new absorptive capacities extending in the direction of economics, statistics, history, sociology, anthropology, psychology, and geography. . . . In his list of ten prominent trends Merriam drew particular attention to the tendency toward more general use of quantitative measurement of political phenomena and toward a decided emphasis on social psychology as one of the foundations of an expanding political science. (1951:9)

Merriam's euphoric prelude to the study of political behavior, however sound strategically as a prescription, seems in retrospect to have been somewhat— thirty years somewhat—premature as a description. For the same reason, his report's intimations of the demise of public law doubtless were slightly exaggerated. But the committee's recommendations did lead directly to the establishment of the Social Science Research Council and hence to the creation of an institutional godfather to foster the growth and development of the interdisciplinary definition of political science that Merriam anticipated.

By 1930, in sharp contrast to the Haines report of 1914, there was not only no separate report on public law (as there were for other fields deemed by the Reed committee to be of greater importance to the profession); the Reed report (1930) gave little or no consideration to public law as a subject that might be of interest to political scientists. Twenty years later, however, the Dimock report recognized public law as one-and-a-half units of the "eight subdivisions of political science," which it considered to be a listing "apparently still acceptable to the profession" (1951:xv, 18–19). Constitutional and administrative law were together counted as one unit; and international law as half of another unit described as international law and relations. The Dimock committee also noted that to obtain a "background for law" was the primary reason why students (according to the professorial respondents who spoke for their students) major in political science, although the committee felt it important to point out that "law has long been a steppingstone to politics" (1951:27–28).

The most recent report, in 1964, suggests that, if it remains true that the primary reason why students major in political science is to prepare for law school, such prelaw students must be making their preparations in some other fields of political science than public law. Analysis of the 1961 *Biographical Directory* of the American Political Science Association showed that, for the six fields recognized by this classification of almost all of the members of the association, public law was listed by far the fewest persons as a field in which they worked (Somit and Tanenhaus 1964:54). Similarly, of seven fields that were listed in a questionnaire administered to a sample of several hundred political scientists, public law was chosen by the fewest respondents as the field with which they identified themselves (Somit and Tanenhaus 1964: 52). Another question used in the same survey asked the respondents to identify the fields of political science in which they felt that the most and the least significant work was being done. The replies showed that

> In the esteem of the profession, comparative government and general politics almost tie for first place. International relations, public administration, and American government and politics constitute, in that order, a middle group. The bottom of the ranking almost replicates the top, with public law and political [philosophy] running neck and neck—if this is the appropriate figure of speech—for last place.
> A comparison of the actual scores earned by the several fields is even more revealing. The ratio of favorable to unfavorable mentions for the two top fields runs about 300 per cent higher than for the middle group and almost 1,000 per cent greater than for public law. (Somit and Tanenhaus 1964:55–56, and cf. p. 58)

It might seem surprising, in view of the glum perceptions one receives from the 1923 and 1930 reports about the foreboding lack of any future for public law as a field of political science, that public law was still around to be counted as a field in 1951 and 1964—even though the best the Dimock committee could say about public law was to lament its neglect, and Somit and Tanenhaus were compelled to report how low its status is compared to other fields. There is, however, a ready explanation why public law survived into the second half of the twentieth century instead of quietly disappearing from view in the midst of the doldrums into which it had drifted. In the first place, administrative law has (as we shall note below) disappeared from political science curricula; and international law seems rapidly to be following suit. What saved constitutional law from a similar fate, more than anything else, was the constitutional crisis of 1937 and the high degree of public attention generated in the Nine Old Men, the Court-packing episode, and its aftermath. No political scientist could really ignore the key role of the Supreme Court as a national policy-maker, particularly in regard to such sweeping issues as racial integration during the fifties and legislative reapportionment during the sixties. Political scientists and their students may not have been terribly interested in constitutional *law*, but they were vitally interested in constitutional *politics;* and the most convenient way to work consideration of such issues into existing curricula was through the available courses in constitutional law. Not only that: the neglected political science professors of constitutional law were thereby enabled to enjoy the heady experience of being looked up to as experts of a kind, about a subject of some importance. So the United States Supreme Court gave the political scientist public lawyers a shot in the arm, which kept them in business for another decade or so, until about a dozen years ago when other and more exciting approaches to the study of adjudicatory decision-making processes began to command the attention of the profession. In recent years, the burden of work increasingly has shifted from traditional public law work to the conventional and behavioral orientations, for reasons to which we shall now turn.

## II. THE GHOST OF PUBLIC LAW PRESENT

The contemporary understanding of public law is, understandably, not the same in law schools as in political science departments. There would be agreement upon constitutional law and (in principle, if not in practice) upon international law and administrative law. Beyond that, political scientists probably would concede the relevance of constitutional history; but those who did so would doubtless also assume that this is a major aspect of the subject subsumed by the course in constitutional law. The law schools, however, entertain a much more expansive notion concerning the metes and bounds of public law as a field. One law school, for example, listed twenty-one courses in the subgroup of public law, including one or more of the following "public law" subjects: administrative law, civil liberties and civil rights, constitutional law, criminal law and procedure, federal jurisdiction, federal taxation, international economic relations, international law, labor relations and law, military law, regulated industries, urban renewal, social legislation, state and local government, trade regulation, workmen's compensation, and world law. An examination of the course descriptions typically associated, in law school catalogues, with courses such as these suggests two conclusions. In general, it appears that the arguments stated over a century ago by Austin, against the usefulness of a conceptual distinction between public law and private law, continue to be pertinent. Turning more particularly to the "core" courses in constitutional, international, and administrative law, one would have to conclude that, if any important changes have occurred during the past half century in the type of content and in the approach used in teaching these courses, it is impossible to infer this from their description in the catalogues.

In the light of the discussion to follow, concerning political science developments, it is relevant to note that what is both literally unprecedented and exceptionally rare, in contemporary law school curricula, are behaviorally oriented courses such as Thomas A. Cowan's seminar in Decision Theory at Rutgers or the University of Denver College of Law's seminar in Law and Behavioral Sciences.

The only public law course that is really standard in political science curricula today is constitutional law. Frequently, such courses include a substantial amount of material on constitutional history, particularly as supplementary reading. Otherwise, constitutional history courses, as such, are taught by history departments and rarely by political scientists. International law courses are taught in the larger colleges and universities, but they are less common than the constitutional law courses; and it seems probable that courses in international law are less common today than they were twenty years ago. Courses in international law are almost always taught by different persons from those who teach constitutional law; and one apparent reason why the international law course is less popular today is that political scientists identified with the international relations field have shown increasing interest, during the past couple of decades, in international organization and international politics; courses in these latter subjects have tended to take the place of the earlier emphasis upon international law. Administrative law has largely disappeared from the contemporary political science curriculum. A survey conducted in the late fifties (Schubert 1958b) showed that many departments that had formerly offered the course during the thirties and forties had dropped it because of "lack of student interest" (i.e., low enrollments); even those departments that continued to teach it did so to small classes averaging (then) thirteen to fourteen students and in almost half of the instances on an alternate year basis. Political scientists who taught the course identified more with public administration than with public law. There is no evidence to suggest that the status of administrative law within political science has improved in recent years. In the political science department with which the author of this article is affiliated, for instance, a full-year course in administrative law was taught every year a decade ago. It is now a one-quarter course that has been offered once in the last five years. None of the political scientists in the department is interested in teaching the course; and so far as is known, no students wish to take the course in any event. Certainly none has protested its being dropped or asked that it be offered again. To some extent, courses in governmental regulation, in regulatory administration, and in public policy have been substituted for the former courses in administrative law. But a much more important development has been the increasing tendency to introduce into the political science curriculum new courses in the judicial process, in the Supreme Court as a political (or as a decision-making) institution, and in judicial behavior. Usually, these new courses coexist with courses that continue to be called constitutional law, although it seems likely that the content of the latter is changing, too, in response to the same influences that are responsible for the establishment of the new courses. In fact, political science now has reached a stage of development such that, in considering political change, the focus of attention is upon policy analysis in the context of decision-making groups (including, but by no means typified by, the Supreme Court and other clusters of judges and the persons with whom they interact in the functioning of adjudicative processes [Schubert 1965*d*]). To get discussion focused on the Constitution as a central element in political change today, it is necessary to leave the mainstream of significant academic inquiry and enter the arena of political debate about current issues of public policy. It is doubtless true, however, that in many departments of political science, the courses in constitutional law are still taught by persons who use their classes as havens for constitutional doctrinal disputation. But the point is that, yesterday, there was no alternative to such an approach, while today there is (Schubert 1965*d*:158–165; 1967*a*; 1967*b*; 1967*d*).

The older alternative, in the context of modern political science, is the traditional approach that remains committed to the study of constitutional law, doctrine, and history. The public law men in political science are uninterested in either systematic theory, quantitative methods of research, statistical measurement of data, or observations of courts and judges—pursuits that would make it possible to study adjudication in the context of the larger political process. Their own intellectual roots lie in the humanities rather than in the social or behavioral sciences; the cognate academic disciplines with which they empathize are law, history, and philosophy. The focus of inquiry in their writing—because it is not research in any rigorous or scientific sense—consists of generalizations about verbal statements in normative form: i.e., law. Persons of this orientation probably predominate, if we take as our reference group all political science teachers of courses about courts, judges, and adjudication, but they are clearly a minority among the active leaders of the field today.

Beginning about the early fifties, the approach that is now conventional in political science emerged, initially as a protest against and as a critique of the formalism, the lack of realism, and the lack of relevance (to the rest of political science) of the traditional approach and its scholarly fruits. Conventionalists seek to emphasize courts as political institutions and judges as political actors, enmeshed in the same struggle among conflicting group interests as are legislators, administrators, presidents, ward heelers, and so forth (Jacob and Vines 1962; Peltason 1955). Courts (i.e., institutional groups) are the proper object of inquiry; but courts are viewed as being in the midst of the political process, and it is insisted that courts should be studied in the same manner that political scientists investigate other political phenomena (Shapiro 1964*b*, 1965). The conventional approach articulates with the social sciences rather than with the humanities; the cognate academic disciplines that are perceived to be closest are sociology, economics, and, of course, the rest of political science. Conventional spokesmen exhort their colleagues to give up their ivory towers in favor of excursions out into the field where political life can be observed in action and described. Scorn is manifested with perfect impartiality for traditional and behavioral rivals alike, since both are perceived as cloistered visionaries who prefer to dally (with their law reports and quill pens, or cumulative scales and Hollerith punch cards, respectively) rather than to enlist in the phalanxes of the group struggle. These enthusiasts for political jurisprudence now constitute the plurality position in the field that they would rather call "the judicial process" than public law; and since their point of view is isomorphic with that which predominates in political science generally today, it seems appropriate to call this the conventional approach.

The behavioral approach to the field is scarcely a decade old. It is true that Pritchett's pioneering work, and major contribution, came in the forties (Pritchett 1941, 1942, 1943a, 1943b, 1945a, 1945b, 1946, 1948); but it was the middle fifties before other and younger men began to argue in behalf of a point of view that Pritchett himself (by this time) no longer was interested in asserting (Tanenhaus 1956; Kort 1957; Schubert 1958e). The most relevant cognate fields are social psychology, psychology, biology, anthropology, and statistics. Behavioralists focus their inquiry upon judges (rather than upon "courts" or "law") as well as upon lawyers and other actors in socially defined roles as decision-makers; and although behavioralism accepts both the norms of the traditional approach and the empirical observations of political action of the conventional approach, it is interested in these instrumentally, as data that may help to contribute to more valid, more reliable, and more widely applicable generalizations about how and why humans act as they do when cast in adjudicatory roles (Eulau 1963). Judicial behavioralists remain a minority voice; but already they include about the same number of persons from among the leaders of the field as do the traditionalists. Two considerations have tended to make the behavioral approach much more influential than the traditional has been in shaping the development of the profession in recent years. The behavioral position is much closer to the conventional than either is to the traditional one, and this has tended to make the traditional spokesmen appear to be aligned in dissent against a majority of their (visible) colleagues, at convention panels, in the professional journals, and in the books in the field published by political scientists during the sixties. Moreover, the behavioralists, due perhaps in part to their age and in part to their (necessarily) iconoclastic writing, have pre-empted considerably more than equal time in the forums of the discipline in recent years.

Naturally, the behavioral work provoked rebuttal from both the traditional (Roche 1958; Berns 1963) and the conventional (Becker 1964; Shapiro 1964a) camps. There has even begun what might be described as the preface to a serious debate about the possible contribution that the behavioral approach might make to the study of law by lawyers. Some of the lawyers who have entered this discussion have argued the affimative (Hayakawa 1964; Mayo and Jones 1964; Miller 1965a; Nagel 1965), others, the negative (Blawie and

Blawie 1965; Stone 1964*b*; Weiner 1962); and at least one first-round bout has occurred, in regard to administrative law.[19] Perhaps the present article will contribute, in some modest way, to the acceleration of the debate of the more general question.

## III. THE GHOST OF PUBLIC LAW YET TO COME

Public law, in political science, is a rapidly dying tradition; and it seems certain that, no matter what happens in the law schools, students of politics increasingly are going to study the judicial process and judicial behavior instead of constitutional doctrine. It is by no means certain, at this time, what direction legal study will choose, although the prognosis cannot be very favorable, if one is to judge in the light of the governing precedents of the past half-dozen decades. On the other hand, if we answer the question:

> Are these the shadows of the things that Will be,
>
> or,
>
> are they the shadows of things that May be, only?

then it is clear that the shape of the future of public law, in American law schools, remains undetermined. The outcome may well depend upon what kind of a job the universities do in educating the next generation of law school professors, before they ever get to law school.

One or two explicit suggestions seem pertinent to both the theme of this essay and the setting in which it appears. Law schools might well consider the important contribution that could be made if instruction in public law were given up, by leaping a generation ahead and remodeling in the image of a school of political jurisprudence and legal behavior. Yale, with the help of a very few persons, still projects the image of legal realism and political liberalism that reflect the impetus of Hutchins' deanship forty years ago; the Yale Law School dared to be different. If law schools were to adopt the dynamic orientation proposed, it would surely be controversial, but controversial because they had assumed a role of leadership in the never-ending task of bringing legal research and pedagogy into closer correspondence with an even more dynamic criterion: the human life that supplies both the sole and the sufficient justification for the existence of law schools and legal study.

Groundwork already has been laid for the kind of studies that most fruitfully could be followed up in the program for teaching and research in the kind of school of political jurisprudence and legal behavior that has been

---

19. See Davis 1964 and Grundstein 1964. In regard to this exchange between Grundstein and Davis, it is hardly surprising to discover that the professor of public administration is on the opposite side of the dispute from the professor of law; or that the latter, having by far the larger interest vested in the status quo of law school pedagogy in his subject, should have elected to defend his stake.

proposed.[20] It is only in the context of an instructional program that maximizes the integration of legal study with the social and behavioral sciences that there is any justification for a law school being a part of a great university.[21] Vocational training in how to practice law, or how to pass bar examinations, has no need for a university—nor does the university either need, or have an excuse for supporting, that kind of law school.

Understandably many law schools will continue to exploit their proximity to the various law-making processes. Very properly, however, this kind of emphasis should not exclude—and has not excluded—concern for the even broader study of law in transnational and cross-cultural terms; and one assumes that courses in comparative law, Russian law, and Chinese law are intended to contribute to the realization of these broader goals. It happens, however, that the most interesting kinds of developments, from the point of view of building a comparative dimension into the work of the proposed schools of political jurisprudence and legal behavior, have not necessarily taken place in the countries that have been, or that are, most significant from the very different point of view of international politics. Neither in France, the United Kingdom, the Soviet Union, nor the People's Republic of China is there any interesting work going on that contributes to the scientific study of law-making processes. But there is in several of the Scandinavian countries (Aubert et al 1952; Eckhoff and Jacobson 1960; Aubert 1963*a*; Eckhoff 1960, 1965; Torgersen 1963; Blegvad 1966) and in Japan (Kawashima and Ishimara 1964; Hayakawa 1962; Kawashima 1968*b*); and increasing attention should be given to the comparative political sociology of law, as schools reshape their own programs. The kind of law school program that has been proposed would seek for leadership on a global, as well as on a national, basis.

It should not be assumed, however, that, even if these proposals should successfully be carried into effect, a solution will have been found for the problem that has provided the theme of this essay. Society has need for both generalists and technicians, and no doubt there is a need for both legal generalists and legal technicians. At the present time, when so much of legal education seems (from a modern perspective) to be so narrowly vocational, there is little room for doubt that the direction in which blows for change ought

---

20. Arthur Selwyn Miller of the Graduate School of Public Law of the George Washington University Law School has attempted to relate legal study to the social studies generally, and to political science in particular, in a series of articles that range deeply into the interrelationships between legal study and the political process, the other social sciences, and behavioral research in law. See particularly the following articles by Professor Miller: 1958, 1962, 1963, 1964, 1965*b*, 1965*c*; Miller and Howell 1960.

21. See Miller 1965*a*. His earlier article (1960) argues persuasively in behalf of a major theme of the present essay—a closer rapprochement between legal and political science study of adjudication processes. A casual reader might perceive contradiction between Miller's advocacy of an expanded concept of public law (which would pretty much gobble up private law in the process of being extended conceptually) and the emphasis of the present essay upon doing away with public law *as a concept*. It is submitted, however, that the disagreement is at a semantic rather than at a substantive level, and relates to strategies rather than to goals. [Postscript: I was wrong about this: cf. Miller and Sastri 1973, and Schubert 1973*c*.]

to be struck is toward the education of more, and of more general, generalists. This will not solve the conflict between the humanities and behavioral science because these are points on a shifting continuum in a moving field of space; and hence the gap—and the tension—between them always is relative to time and place. Nonetheless, the time may be ripe for quite a bit more of Burgess, and a little less of Dwight. If that were to happen, the public law yet to come, for American law schools, might be considerably less ghastly.

# 3

# Behavioral
# Jurisprudence

$\mathbf{F}$or over two thousand years, the science of law has been a dull esoteric subject, with traditional logic its long suit and syllogism its ace in the hole (Pound 1932). The erudite tended to empathize with Socrates, who could define justice only in metaphysical terms, and to scorn the occasional iconoclasts in the Thrasymachian tradition, who would have operationalized the concept of justice on the basis of political interrelationships of power and influence. Throughout these two millennia, jurisprudence was a "science" only in the sense of "moral science," that is to say, it was a branch of philosophy. It was concerned with prescriptive norms rather than with descriptions of human action, and therefore it dealt almost exclusively with ideals for, rather than with the realities of, the behavior of judges, lawyers, jurors, and litigants.

The emergence of social science during the nineteenth century was both the precursor and the cause of significant changes in the "scientific" component of legal science. Particularly under the influence of the historical approach then dominating legal study on the Continent, and the indigenous American pragmatic philosophy developed by Charles S. Peirce and William James, a new approach—now termed legal realism—arose in the latter part of the century. The pioneers of the realist approach included the Boston lawyer-scholar Oliver Wendell Holmes, Jr., and political scientist Frank Goodnow at Columbia. At its height during the twenties and early thirties the realist movement included primarily law professors, along with a few lawyers, politi-

Reprinted in slightly different form from *Law and Society Review* 2 (June 1968):407–428. The *Law and Society Review* is the official publication of the Law and Society Association. The author thanks the Institute for Research in Social Science of the University of North Carolina at Chapel Hill, and the Social Science Research Institute of the University of Hawaii, for the typing of various drafts of this article.

cal scientists, and historians; associated with the movement are such names as Karl Llewellyn, Jerome Frank, Underhill Moore, Robert Maynard Hutchins, Charles Grove Haines, and Felix S. Cohen.

The realist movement in American jurisprudence, like the social science of its day, was highly pragmatic and empirical in its orientation, but not overly burdened or concerned with the development of systematic theory.[1] More recently, as one of the fruits of the shift in emphasis (and in scope) that is involved in the difference between social and behavioral science, a really new approach to jurisprudence has evolved (Handy and Kurtz 1964). In political science, where much of the new work has been done, it has tended to be identified as the study of judicial behavior (Schubert 1963a, 1968e) or as "political jurisprudence" (Shapiro 1964b), while lawyers with analogous interests have tended to use the rubric "jurimetrics" (Loevinger 1949, 1961, 1963) to describe their work. Among both lawyers and political scientists, there have been some whose primary interest lies in the endeavor to work toward a cumulative and systematic body of theoretical knowledge, based upon and guiding further inquiry through empirical studies (Danelski 1964). Others, in the tradition of legal realism, have been more concerned with an attempt to provide case studies which offer a realistic political description of facets of the decision-making of courts and lawyers (Pritchett and Westin 1963; Murphy 1965). Still others have been particularly interested in collecting data which would lend themselves readily to quantification and to research designs amenable to computer processing and analysis (Lawlor 1963). All have agreed, however, that the proper subject of study is not "law" in the classical sense of verbal statements purporting to rationalize the content of constitutional and statutory documents, or appellate court opinions (Stone 1964a). Inquiry has instead focused on what human beings, cast in socially defined roles in certain characteristic types of decision-making sequences which traditionally have been identified as "legal," do in their interactions and transactions with each other (Murphy 1964a; Eulau and Sprague 1964).

The new human (i.e., behavioral) jurisprudence has had an important influence in redirecting research, publication, and teaching in political science. It has, however, had much less effect thus far upon work in the law schools (R. Brown 1963; Miller 1960; Schubert 1966a; Loevinger 1966–1967); and candor compels the admission that the older mechanical jurisprudence (Haines 1922) remains the overwhelmingly dominant metaphor among judges themselves, practicing lawyers, journalists, and the public. Among the many dimensions useful in distinguishing between the approaches, four are of particular importance: their respective stand-points toward theory, toward data, toward the object of inquiry, and toward the importance of culture.[2]

---

1. For a more sanguine appraisal of the methodological sophistication of the realists, see Rumble 1966.

2. I recognize, of course, that other dimensions, such as those representing methodology and quantification, might also be deemed of equal significance as differentiating characteristics. See Schubert 1967a.

The new approach seeks to relate what we think we know, and what we can learn, about how persons behave in adjudicatory roles and institutional relationships, to a general body of theory about human decision-making behavior (March 1956). The traditional approach emphasizes, quite to the contrary, what are considered to be the unique and indeed the idiosyncratic aspects that are said to characterize "law," "courts," and the decisions of judges; and the objective therefore is to build a segregated theory of adjudication which will distinguish judicial from other forms of human behavior (Becker 1963a).

The new approach defines its data on the basis of observations of what kinds of factors influence adjudicatory decisions, what kinds of values are preferred in such decisions, and how the decisions affect the behavior of other people (Danelski 1966). The old approach defines as its data the verbal statements of opinions that are written to justify the decisions of appellate court majorities, and seeks to discover the effect of such opinions upon a metaphysical essence which is called "the law" (Wasserstrom 1961).

The new approach focuses upon humans who act in adjudicatory roles, and is interested in understanding judges as people—or, better put, people as judges (Schubert 1969b). The old approach studies institutions which it calls courts, and what courts do purports to be the objective of investigation.[3]

The new approach is very much concerned with understanding the effect that cultural—and subcultural—differences have upon adjudicatory behavior (Schubert 1967c). The old approach recognizes that cultural variation results in institutional differences among courts, but it is not concerned with cross-cultural analysis as the basis for identifying both the communalities and the differences that can be observed to obtain among courts in differing cultures (Abraham 1968:chaps. 2, 6).

The traditional approach has undoubtedly contributed many important insights into the nature of judicial institutions, and the relationships of these institutions among themselves and with other sets of institutions in the American polity. But the theories of judicial decision-making that have been associated with this approach have not led to any new understanding, or even generated any new hypotheses, for a very long time. The highly formal, abstruse images suggested by the traditional approach are descriptive of a static universe of political organs in which human beings appear to play a relatively insignificant part.[4] Nevertheless, the traditional theoretical structures continue to provide the basis for almost all teaching about courts and law, in courses taught by both political scientists and other academic specialists.

In the discussion that follows, I should like to present, in rudimentary form, the outline of a behavioral model of adjudicatory decision-making. It

---

3. See, e.g., Kurland 1964a, 1964b, and the various annual volumes of the *Supreme Court Review*, which Kurland has edited, beginning in 1960. Cf. Kommers 1966.
4. For discussion of the implications of premising analyses upon mechanical, biological, and configurational jurisprudential models, see Landau 1961, 1965b, 1968; Schubert 1967d.

will then be possible to specify the kinds of data that we would need in order to be able to discuss the questions which the model suggests as important. This will permit us to appraise the major trends in contemporary research and probable future developments in relation to what we shall need to do if we are to construct an empirically based theory of adjudication, which articulates with the findings and theories of the rest of behavioral science (Berelson and Steiner 1964).

## I. A BEHAVIORAL VIEW OF THE JUDICIAL SYSTEM

Figure 1 depicts in an elementary way the kinds of structures, functions, and interrelationships that from a behavioral standpoint are important to the understanding of the judicial system, and indeed, to any other kind of political system. The concepts which denote the important variables are sufficiently general so that the figure bears no particular relation to judges and courts. It should therefore be at least equally relevant to the analysis of other political roles. Indeed, if it were not so, then we ought to question whether it is sufficiently general to be of much help in constructing the kind of theory I have postulated as desirable. As Cardozo pointed out almost fifty years ago[5] and as Jerome Frank insisted, judges really *are* human, and inescapably subject to all the ills (as well as the satisfactions) to which flesh is heir. It must therefore be assumed that for judges and others active in the adjudicatory process, as well as for people in general, each human biological subsystem establishes parameters within which personality may function, and which affects how it will function within those bounds (Ulmer 1969). Three major psychological functions of a personality subsystem are perception, cognition, and choice-making.

Relationships among other persons with whom an individual comes into contact constitute the social system. Without intending to adopt his complete schema, I shall borrow from Gabriel Almond (Almond and Coleman 1960: 17; Almond and Powell 1966:chaps. 4, 5, 7) certain concepts which I shall designate as input functions: interaction and communication, and interest

---

5. I have spoken of the forces of which judges avowedly avail to shape the form and content of their judgments. Even these forces are seldom fully in consciousness. They lie so near the surface, however, that their existence and influence are not likely to be disclaimed. But . . . deep below consciousness are other forces, the likes and the dislikes, the predilections and the prejudices, the complex of instincts and emotions and habits and convictions, which make the man, whether he be litigant or judge. . . . There has been a certain lack of candor in much of the discussion of the theme, or rather perhaps in the refusal to discuss it, as if judges must lose respect and confidence by the reminder that they are subject to human limitations. I do not doubt the grandeur of the conception which lifts them into the realm of pure reason, above and beyond the sweep of perturbing and deflecting forces. None the less, if there is anything of reality in my analysis of the judicial process, they do not stand aloof on these chill and distant heights; and we shall not help the cause of truth by acting and speaking as if they do. The great tides and currents which engulf the rest of men do not turn aside in their course and pass the judges by. (Cardozo 1921:167–168)

Cf. Jerome Frank 1930, 1931.

articulation and aggregation. These are represented by the residual social space "C." The cultural system represents widely accepted patternings of beliefs and social values, such as myths, customs, and law. The content of this system is ideational rather than any directly observable activity.

The sociopsychological segment (2), which represents the overlap between the personality system and the social system, is concerned with the individual's socialization and recruitment, and with his attributes and attitudes; the psychocultural segment (3), where the personality and cultural

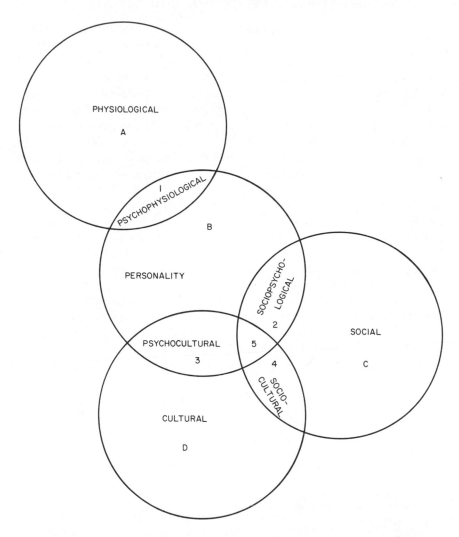

Figure 1. A Behavioral View of the Subsystems of any Political
(including any Judicial) System

systems overlap, represents the individual's conception of his role(s), and the ideologies which he accepts. The sociocultural segment (4) of overlap between the social and cultural systems represents the patterning of institutional roles, and the output functions of accommodation and regulation of the behavior of others.

An individual's physiological system will affect his political relationships with other persons and their ideas only indirectly, through the functioning of his personality. Therefore, only the three subsystems, personality, social, and cultural, share a space of mutual intersection (which is also, necessarily, the area of mutual intersection among the three joint segments of sociopsychological, psychocultural, and sociocultural functions). This central space, segment 5, represents the individual's decision-making, that is, his choices among political alternatives.

One can infer from Figure 1 that when any individual is cast in a political role, his choices among alternative possibilities for action will depend upon complex (and doubtless shifting, through time) interdependencies among several different sets of variables. In order to understand, and perhaps ultimately to be able to predict with some accuracy, how any individual acts or is likely to act in such a role, it is necessary that we observe and examine data which bear upon operations involving each of the relevant variables. It should be emphasized, however, that each of the concepts denoted in the figure (e.g., "attributes" and "institutional roles") is itself a complex configuration of subvariables. Anyone who has ever attempted to do either field or experimental research involving an attempt to measure the effect of any *one* of these subvariables upon behavior is well aware of the magnitude, complexity, and long-range implications of the research task that Figure 1 implies.[6] The designated segments and residual spaces correspond to areas of our fragmentary knowledge and substantial ignorance.

The process of decision-making may be understood as taking place within the context of certain input structures (components of the personality system usually associated with an ego), input functions (certain facets and effects of interactions with others), and conversion functions (psychological processes of the ego). Table 1 suggests that an individual's socialization and recruitment into his political role will provide the basis for the articulation and aggregation of his interests, which in turn will set limits for his interaction and communication with others. The counterpart input structures, to these functions, are the individual's attributes (or his "social background characteristics"), his ideologies, and his attitudes; the table indicates that his attitudes are influenced by his ideologies, which in turn are influenced by his

---

6. As Cardozo pointed out in his introductory apologia to what remains a brilliant qualitative analysis of the subject, "We must apply to the study of judge-made law that method of quantitative analysis which Mr. [Graham] Wallas has applied with such fine results [in his *Human Nature in Politics*] to the study of politics. A richer scholarship than mine is requisite to do the work aright [, however]." (1921:13)

attributes. The individual's perception, cognition, and choice-making are psychological conversion functions. His perceptions are the basis for his cognitions, which he then integrates, in relation to his attitudes, in making choices among decisional alternatives. Perceptions are also influenced by his attributes, which in turn are affected by his socialization experiences. Similarly, an individual's "social expression" of his interests (interest articulation and aggregation) affects his ideologies, and what he "knows"—his cognitions—depends upon what he believes as well as upon what he perceives. There is an equivalent lateral linkage between interaction and communication, attitudes, and choice-making; likewise his attitudes are affected jointly by his social interactions with other people, and by his beliefs.

In Table 1 the relationships of interdependence among the variables become increasingly complex as we trace paths from the upper left to the lower right corner of the table. It should be noted, also, that in terms of the conceptualization that lawyers traditionally have utilized to discuss decision-making, the column of "conversion functions" delineates the route by means of which "facts" enter into human choice-making, while the bottom row traces the path by which "values" are admitted. In the older terminology also, decision-making is an integration of facts and values; but the significant differences are that Table 1 implies that both facts and values are defined in terms of analytical concepts that can be (and have been) operationalized (Kort 1966; Danelski 1966), so that empirical study of how and why and when "facts" integrate with "values" becomes possible (Tanenhaus et al. 1963; Schubert 1962c). We do not (and need not) speak of *legal* facts and *legal* values, thereby letting the adjective suggest a mystique which is beyond analysis—at least, by nonexperts (i.e., by nonlawyers), and which both explains and justifies the necessity for leaving the actual processes of choice-making unexamined,

**Table 1. The Processing of Inputs of Choice**

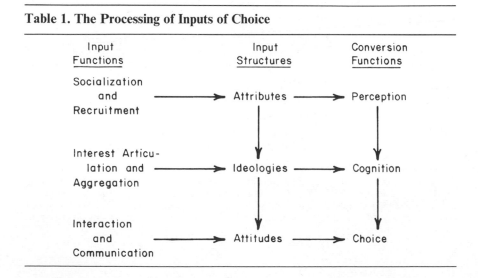

## Table 2. Some Behavioral Parameters of Outputs

| Standpoint | Role Concepts | Output Functions | Output Structures | Feedback Concepts |
|---|---|---|---|---|
| *Psychological* | Individual | Decision-making | Votes and opinions | Commitment |
| *Sociological* | Group | Accommodation and regulation | Decisions | Reinforcement |
| *Cultural* | Institutional | Policy-making | Policies | Norms |

except at the formal level of what institutions (rather than humans) do.[7]

Table 2 presents three alternative modes of conceptualizing some of the more important outputs of individual choice-making, from the varying points of view of focus upon the individual, upon groups of individuals, and upon institutions. From the point of view of psychology, the individual makes decisions, which are in the structural form of his votes and opinions, and which entail for him the feedback effect of *commitment*. From a sociological point of view, a group undertakes to accommodate and to regulate conflicting interests by making decisions, the feedback effect of which, for the group, is *reinforcement*. From the cultural point of view, institutions sponsor policies which provide feedback, for persons living in a particular culture, in the form of *norms*.

We are now in a position to return to Figure 1, and to examine the circular order among the major system variables. These are the sequence of alternating residual and overlapping spaces which surround the central space which symbolizes decision-making. Table 3 suggests that this circular relationship among the behavioral spaces can be interpreted from the points of view of three differing concepts of rationality: logical, psychological, and non-logical. The concepts denoted in the column for *logical* rationality correspond very closely to the traditional wisdom: judges are persons who, as the result of *legal training*, acquire special *skills* which they apply to the analysis of socially determined *facts*, and acting under the procedural decision-making norm of stare decisis, they dispense *justice* between the parties and reaffirm the *law* which is supposed to control the behavior of all persons in the society (Howard and Summers 1965). From a perhaps equally extreme point of view at the other tail of the postulated continuum of rationality, judges are ordinary humans who are controlled by their neuroses; they therefore react to social *stress* by displacing their inner anxieties upon outer (viz., social) objects (Lasswell 1948). This *displacement* is a process of *rationalization*, which judges articulate in conventionally acceptable arguments, or "*rationales*," in order to attempt to bring about *homeostasis* in the balance of their own inner lives (i.e., tensions).

---

7. Cf. Becker: "The judicial process is verily a vehicle by which revealed truth is discovered through skill in logic" (1964:11).

## Table 3. Three Types of Rationality in Adjudicative Decision-Making

| System variables | Logical | Psychological | Nonlogical |
|---|---|---|---|
| Social | Facts | Interest articulation and aggregation Interaction and communication | Stress |
| Sociopsychological | Legal training | Socialization and recruitment Attributes Attitudes | Neuroses |
| Personality | Skill | Perception Cognition Choice | Displacement |
| Psychocultural | Stare decisis | Ideologies Individual roles | Rationalization |
| Cultural | Justice | Norms | Rationales |
| Sociocultural | Law | Accommodation Regulation | Homeostasis |

Psychological rationality is in a modal position between the other two types of rationality. According to this theory, judges receive certain information concerning cases they are expected to decide, as a consequence of social input functions of interest articulation and aggregation, and of interaction and communication. (These correspond to argument between counsel, the examination of witnesses in trials, and the sequence of interim decisions, by the judge, on questions of procedure that arise during the course of the trial, or also, in appellate courts, to briefs filed by counsel and to discussions among the judges.) To be distinguished from this proximate information about the pending case is the more stable and enduring kind of information which the judge has accepted, at earlier stages of his career, as the result of his socialization and recruitment experience.[8] Sociopsychological structures such as a judge's attributes and his attitudes are causally related to, and dependent upon, the input functions of socialization and recruitment. Both kinds of information—the proximate data about the case, and his predisposition or bias toward the kind of policy question that it raises for decision—are of critical importance to the choice that he will make, and both kinds of information are produced primarily as the result of his interaction with other people (Murphy 1966).

---

8. As Almond and Coleman have noted,

> political socialization produces the basic attitudes in a society toward the political system, [and the] political recruitment function takes ... members of the society out of particular subcultures ... and inducts them into the specialized roles of the political system, trains them in the appropriate skills, provides them with political cognitive maps, values, expectations, and affects. (1960:31)

Cf. Almond and Powell 1966:Chap. 3.

Perception, cognition, and choice-making are personality function concepts which purport to distinguish sequential states in a continuous and continuing process. Their utility is for purposes of analysis. For example, both the logical and the nonlogical types of rationality also assume—although usually with no discussion of the matter—that perception takes place before, in the first instance, skill can be exercised or, in the second instance, displacement can occur. But neither cognition nor choice-making are necessary elements in the logical, or in the nonlogical, theories of personality. The personality structures which will affect one's choice-making are ideology and role. The former is his pattern of beliefs, expectations, obligations, and related knowledge about life and the world, and the latter is his understanding of others' expectations, and his own expectations, concerning how he shall make his choices and what they should be (Herndon 1964; Jaros and Mendelsohn 1967; Vines 1969; and generally, see Biddle and Thomas 1966). The latter point in particular—the psychocultural concept of role, in comparison to the logical concept of stare decisis, and the nonlogical concept of rationalization—illustrates the advantages that the psychological theory offers, even if we speak for the moment only in terms of greater flexibility. There is nothing to preclude either stare decisis or rationalization from supplying the content for the concept of role, for any particular judge or group of justices; but both stare decisis and rationalization are limiting cases, and the psychological theory does not require that *either* of these provide a monistic definition of judicial role.

The output functions of a judge's decisions are, from a cultural point of view, the policy norms associated with his choices, and, from a sociological point of view, output functions include the accommodation and regulation of the interests of the litigants, and of other persons directly affected (Dolbeare 1967a, 1969).

No doubt, the psychologically rational approach to judicial decision-making involves considerable oversimplification of the multidimensionality of empirical reality, but the circular two-dimensional ordering does offer a much more complex model than does either of the alternative linear schemes (Guttman 1954). It seems likely, moreover, that it may also offer some promise of affording a better fit to the relevant empirical data than does either of the other two alternatives. The present difficulty in testing the utility of the model is that most of the relevant empirical data remain to be observed, analyzed, and reported. But, however inadequate it might prove to be when data become available to appraise its "goodness of fit," the theory of psychological rationality may in the meantime be of some use in guiding the very research efforts which can result in its disconfirmation. At least, it offers two considerable advantages over the conventional wisdom about judges: it is not fettered with the idiosyncratic parameters of the American politicolegal culture; and it offers some promise of forging a theory about judges and courts which can articulate with what otherwise is known scientifically about human behavior.

## II. BEYOND THE FRONTIERS OF JUDICIAL RESEARCH

What are the implications of the standpoint of behavioral jurisprudence for the development of research in judicial process and systems? The answer to that question depends in part upon what are the present trends in this subfield, in political science as an academic discipline, and in the behavioral sciences generally. One can make certain inferences about present trends on the basis of a recent national conference which focused on the frontiers of judicial research.[9] Four emphases in particular were explicit in the papers and discussions there:

(1) Transnational comparison;

(2) Inquiry into mass behavior beyond the boundaries of judicial systems, to analyze the inputs that may lead to litigation, and the consequences of judicial policy choices;

(3) Acceptance of quantification as an indispensable component of empirical scientific inquiry; and

(4) Agreement upon the importance of interdisciplinary contributions to theory construction and empirical knowledge.

A fifth point, which was made by C. Herman Pritchett, the keynote speaker at the Shambaugh Conference, and which seems to be amply supported by empirical evidence, is that the field of judicial process and behavior has become (at last) an integral part of political science inquiry. Political scientists in such other fields as legislative behavior, comparative politics, and international behavior take an active interest in what their colleagues in the adjudicative field have to say—and about theory and method as well as about substantive findings. As Professor Pritchett pointed out, the isolation of the field, as an exotic enclave within the discipline, is no more. In choosing the term "political jurisprudence" to refer to the judicial process and behavior approaches, Pritchett was emphasizing the reciprocal *intra*disciplinary contributions that now obtain among political scientists who study judicial systems and decision-making, and political scientists who study other aspects of political behavior.

My own answer to the question takes the form of hypothetical statements in a developmental analysis, projecting into the near future these present trends, in relation to the needs for empirical data relevant to the variables and relationships that I have hypothesized to be important to behavioral jurisprudence. I shall discuss my prospectus in terms of three facets: substantive inquiry, theory, and methods.

Considerably more work will be done on interest aggregation and articulation as inputs to, and at the boundaries of, judicial systems. The studies by Vose (1958, 1959), principally of the NAACP, were products of the fifties;

---

9. The Shambaugh Conference on Judicial Research, convened at the University of Iowa, Iowa City, Iowa, October 5–7, 1967.

and Hakman's occasional interim article reports (1957, 1966, 1969) on his continuing studies of what he calls litigation sponsorship and management, although directly relevant, are by no means sufficient to guide understanding concerning the extent of empirical support for the Bentleyan thesis, as it relates to the judicial process. Early attempts to study the relationship between the background characteristics of judges as gross ideological categories, by means of direct and simple (bivariate) correlation, yielded few significant findings (Bowen 1965; Goldman 1965: chap. 8). This phase is over; instead there will be much greater concern for studying the socialization (Warkov 1965; Lortie 1959) and recruitment (Grossman 1965; Jacob 1964) of judges, and for the use of causal modelling techniques (Alker 1966; Blalock 1967) to investigate hypotheses concerning the relative strength and the direction of relationships among attribute, ideological, attitudinal, and decisional variables (Schubert 1964a, 1969a). Such work on input analysis will take into account such facets of logical rationality as legal training, occupational skills, and stare decisis (though defined in psychocultural terms); and indeed there will be a continuing concern for investigation of such other facets of logical rationality as facts, law, and justice: such efforts will come, however, primarily from nonbehaviorally oriented law professors, from those political scientists who continue to identify their interests as the study of public law, and from normatively oriented sociologists of law (Selznick 1959; Skolnick 1965). But the major focus will be upon work at the boundaries of the social and the biological sciences in investigations of the interplay among the human mind, body, and personality (Tomkins and Izard 1965; Knutson 1965; Campbell 1966) in the conversion processes of decision-making postulated by the models of both psychological rationality and—to the extent that it proves possible to operationalize and to make systematic empirical observations that relate to its key concepts—nonlogical rationality.

Thus, what lawyers call "stare decisis" will be studied not only from the psychocultural point of view of the way in which a judicial actor defines his individual role, stare decisis will be studied also as a function of such psychological variables as commitment and identification, and of such sociopsychological variables as reinforcement and reference group behavior (Schubert 1960a; Lawlor 1963). Considerable attention will focus upon group interaction processes, and upon judicial attitudes as dependent variables influenced by such independent variables as the frequency, affectiveness, and propinquity of interpersonal contacts, in relation to preferences among alternatives of substantive policy content (Ulmer 1965, 1970). There will be inquiry into the differences in individual judicial performance, when the individual is placed in the shifting social context of differing ad hoc decisional subgroups, as in the panels of the national courts of appeals. The description of most trial courts in the United States as "single-judge" institutions for purposes of decision-making will be treated as a hypothesis rather than as a self-evident truth; and studies will be designed to analyze not merely trials—which so evidently are group performances—but also the trial *judge* as the (by institutional role) leading actor in a social system, with various other judgelike actors (referees in bankruptcy, commissioners, clerks) sharing in the accouterments of the judicial office (viz., wearing robes, being addressed as "judge" or "your honor") and participating actively in specialized aspects of the "court's" decision-making function. Also within the American judicial system, there will be emphasis upon comparative (i.e., cross-subcultural) study of the structuring of institutional roles in relation to differences in the sociocultural content of inputs, policy outputs, and the policy effects of judicial decision-making.

Although there have been impact studies of national judicial policy-making, these have tended to be case studies of the responses of individual communities to discrete Supreme Court decisions (Patric 1957; Sorauf 1959; Wasby 1965; Birkby 1966). In the future there will be much more broadly gauged and systematic investigations into the relationships among judicially pronounced policies as stimuli, the response of governmental and other elites who constitute (variously, depending upon the policy content) the Supreme Court's audience, and mass responses either to the Court directly or, as seems much more probable, to the cues provided by the Court's elite audience (Murphy and Tanenhaus 1969). Such studies will involve extensive inquiry into the correlation between judicial manipulation of cultural norms and the extent of change in relevant mass behavior; and these surveys will go beyond correlational to causal analysis. The kinds of questions that will be examined will include: What is the relationship between the Supreme Court's obscenity decisions (beginning in the mid-fifties) and the contemporary liberalization of artistic expression in magazines, books, movies, and supper clubs? What is the relationship between the Supreme Court's postulation of greater procedural rights for defendants in criminal cases and changes in the behaviors of police, criminals, and other populations such as students seeking institutional procedural due process from their universities, or persons who oppose current governmental policy in regard to such matters as the Vietnam war or the regulation of LSD and marijuana? What is the relationship between the new constitutional policy of racial equality and integration and the rise of social movements advocating racial segregation and black power? Judicial policy-making, that is to say, will be viewed as falling within the mainstream of development and change in national social movements and mass behaviors; and it will be studied accordingly.

As Harold Lasswell long has urged ought to be done (1955; and cf. Schubert 1968*d*), the judicial policy-making process will be studied from the perspective of its past and potential contribution to political creativity, that is, to the postulation of new alternatives—and frequently, these will be the very ones that have been screened out of public view, by the legislative and administrative processes—which thereby become possible options of choice for other actors in both the public and private sectors of the society. (Racial integration and reapportionment are recent judicial policies which might be viewed as examples of creative contributions to the redevelopment of American political society.)

The policy output of courts will also be studied from the points of view of institutional differentiation, specialization of function, and the partitioning of local populations into functionally oriented clientele groups. To what extent, for example, do national district courts in metropolitan areas articulate their work with the major national urban policy programs in such areas; and how do the policy decisions of such national district courts relate to those of state courts in regard to the same metropolitan population (Dolbeare 1967b, 1969)?

Feedback, as a response to judicial policy-making and as an aspect of both elite and mass behavior, will be studied in relation to perception ("awareness"), the structure of cognitions, and psychological involvement with judiciaries at all levels of hierarchical differentiation of such judicial systems (Murphy and Tanenhaus 1968a, 1968b; Dolbeare 1967a; Kessel 1966; Dolbeare and Hammond 1968). A by-product of the more widespread recognition that there is an important and continuing interrelationship between judicial process and behavior and such other political science fields as public opinion will be much closer intradisciplinary integration, with the probable consequence that the study of judiciaries will increasingly come to be viewed as one among several facets of the study of domestic politics, as distinguished from comparative ("transnational") politics, or as distinguished from international politics. But there will also be much closer cross-disciplinary integration between political science students of judicial process and scholars in other behavioral disciplines. In part, this will involve the development of new ties with biologists and psychologists, and particularly with scholars in the health sciences: senescence, for example, will no longer continue to be considered merely at the rhetorical level of analysis in studies of the decision-making of (typically) elderly judicial elites. There will, however, be even closer collaboration with the social sciences of anthropology, economics, and sociology.

The current interest in transnational comparison of judiciaries, one of the major emphases of the Shambaugh Conference, will lead to multi-cultural (horizontal) analysis of adjudicative processes and functions, as well as to the development of systematically designed vertical descriptions of the role of judiciaries, in both European and non-Western political systems. One consequence of this development will be that the field of study of adjudicative behavior no longer will remain one which is monopolized by scholars in the United States.[10]

In terms of theory, the major emphasis in the near future—in behavioral jurisprudence as in political science generally—will be various types of systems analysis. Some of these will directly reflect the biological models from

---

10. Already there have been important research contributions by colleagues abroad. See Aubert 1963a, 1963b; Torgersen 1963; Hayakawa 1962; Peck 1967a, 1967b; Samonte 1966. Others will be forthcoming soon. See Schubert and Danelski 1969.

which they are borrowed (Landau 1965a, 1965b); others will be presented in a rhetoric which borrows heavily from the new sciences of information theory, cybernetics, and semiotics, and from computer technology (Deutsch 1963; Ulmer 1969). Even today the systems vernacular has none of the novelty which it presented, at least as applied to the study of judiciaries, as recently as a couple of years ago (Schubert 1965d); and tomorrow systems analysis will be the conventional mode of discourse in the field. Strong emphasis will also be placed, however, upon continuation of the present work in decision-making theory (Robinson and Snyder 1965), role theory (Vines 1969), and transactional theory (Danelski 1964). Game theory, which has seemed to offer such considerable promise for studies of legal decision-making processes, providing as it does a measure of the deviation of empirically observable behaviors, from what would be strictly rational behavior, will receive greater attention now that more political scientists are becoming increasingly familiar with contemporary research in economics.

From the methodological point of view, future work in the adjudicative field will see much greater emphasis upon present predictions of future events (Schubert 1963e:102–108, 137–142; 1964a:575–587); and the effect will be to strengthen tremendously the power of behavioral jurisprudential theory. Accompanying the shift in emphasis to predictive work will be much greater reliance upon experimentation (Becker et al. 1965), simulation (Grunbaum 1969), and field surveys (Becker 1966b) as methods of inquiry than has been evident heretofore. There will also be an acceleration of the present trend away from linear and toward multivariate analysis, in phase with both the longstanding recognition that the questions of interest to the field are better fitted to multidimensional models, and the growing capacity of scholars in the field to take advantage of computer technology in their research (thereby freeing them from the limitations of time and competence imposed by manual routines of statistical analysis). And especially in the latter regard there will be a dramatic change in the standards of literacy in the profession and consequently in what are accepted as the conventional modes of professional practice. Even today the ratio of persons working in the field who have had any mathematical or statistical training beyond the freshman undergraduate level is very small; but graduate students now entering the field are required to have had such training as part of their education as *political scientists*; and the impact of such better education, upon the level of sophistication in the quantitative work to be done in the next several years, will be considerable (Gerard 1961).

The most general projection that one would make, on the basis of present trends, is that beyond the frontiers of judicial research lies the field of behavioral jurisprudence: empirical in its approach toward data collection; quantitative in its methods of data manipulation; eclectic in its intradisciplinary ties within political science; pandisciplinary in its theoretical orientation; and cross-cultural in the scope of its interests.

# PART II
# An Empirical View of Judicial Values

THE FIRST SYSTEMATIC effort to employ quantified decisional data as the basis for discussing differences in the attitudes of Supreme Court justices was undoubtedly that of Pritchett, in his several articles that appeared during World War II (1941, 1942, 1943a, 1943b, 1945a, 1945b, 1946), and in his book (based on the same research) on the Roosevelt Court, which was published in 1948.[1] Pritchett presented basically two types of data in the book. He grouped decisions according to broad policy issues (such as "state regulation of business" and "freedom of speech") and reported the percentage, of the total votes of each justice concerning the issue, that the justices voted in support of the issue. Pritchett didn't exactly describe them as such, but *in effect* for respondents these tables were the columns of marginal frequencies that would have been one parameter of a cumulative scale of the issue—if he had undertaken to construct such an array of his data. Furthermore, presuming that the ordinal relationships in conjoint voting by his respondents were sufficiently transitive (i.e., that the proportion of inconsistent voting was sufficiently low), then a sequencing of the justices according to the percentages of their support of the scale value ought to correspond very well to their rank order in a cumulative scale of the same data. Hence, what he reported in these tables were *potential* scales: he could not know (and he certainly did not say) whether they were scales, but at the same time there was also no reason to assume that they were not. It should be remembered, of course, that the basic reference on the theory and method of cumulative scaling (Stouffer et al. 1950) was not published until two years *after* Pritchett's book, and was therefore not available to him at the time he wrote. The other principal format upon which Pritchett relied for presenting and analyzing his data was the matrix of agreement scores: here he ignored subject matter differences, and aggregated all of the dissensual decisions for a given term of the Court, observing and cumulating votes by dyads. Given dichotomous scoring of decisions, there are four possible ways in which two persons can relate to each other in a given decision; and if we signify a majority vote as ($+$) and a dissent as ($-$), these are $++$, $+-$, $-+$, and $--$. Pritchett was interested primarily in patterns of agreement; hence, he reported as frequencies dyadic term totals for joint dissenting ($--$); and proportions of overall agreement ($++$ plus $--$, divided by the sum of $++$ and $+-$ and $-+$ and $--$) he expressed as percentages. Evidently he had available all of the information that one needed to calculate phi correlation coefficients, a more sophisticated statistic that takes account of patterns of both agreement and disagreement as well as of their totals; and in this instance the procedure was reasonably well known and accessible at the time his work was done (cf. Yule 1912). But as we noted above to have been true in the case of his inchoate scales, so also his matrices were measures that, because of their ad hoc character, were inherently limited in their utility to support other and more sophisticated analyses (such as, for example, factor analysis). At the same time it should

---

1. Reprinted as a paperback by Quadrangle Books (Chicago, 1969).

be noted that, from a public relations point of view, Pritchett's decision to use either simple matrices of raw frequencies or percentages had one great virtue over even such a relatively uncomplicated statistic as a correlation coefficient: persons untrained in statistics could understand (or could at least *feel* that they understood) Pritchett, so that although they were still turned off by his use of numbers, they were not completely shut out.

The audience for whom Pritchett wrote consisted primarily of political scientists, but it included also lawyers, historians, and journalists—none of whom generally were educated, a quarter of a century ago, in statistical methods. (Pritchett's audience included also a few sociologists [e.g., Snyder 1958], and they did of course know factor analysis [Bernard 1955].) As it was, the criticism of his work was not addressed to his substantive findings, which were almost universally accepted and even applauded. Criticism focused instead upon his "boxscores" and was not even concerned with him particularly; rather it was levied against the very idea of quantification in such an arcane context. Much of this criticism was quite indignant, and very self-righteous, and was uttered in the spirit of a letter that I recently received from a sitting judge of the Supreme Court of the Republic of South Africa, who informed me that anyone (like myself) who used the word "vote" to describe what judges do in making decisions would in South Africa be fined for contempt of court, and properly so! So under the circumstances it is doubtless true that Pritchett attracted a good many more flies with his bittersweet honey than a more austere approach, which peddled straight vinegar (however much denatured), would have done.

We have some direct evidence on the latter point, and therefore we do not need to rely upon supposition. Only two years after the appearance of *The Roosevelt Court* there was published a brief, tightly written, erudite, methodologically sophisticated, and conceptually revolutionary factor analytic study of a biennium of the Supreme Court's decisions (Thurstone and Degan 1951). Its senior author was about as competent a person, in the methodology and in the relevant psychometric theory generally, as existed in 1950: he was the American discoverer and proponent of the multiple factor analysis approach, Louis L. Thurstone, the founder and at that time still the head of the Psychometric Laboratory at the University of Chicago, which published the study in its series of occasional technical reports. Of course it is not surprising that few political scientists at that time would have stumbled across the study in such an outlet; but it was also reprinted in the proceedings of the National Academy of Science—though even so, few persons interested in judicial process and behavior (and probably none interested in public law) make systematic and periodic searches of such reference works as *Psychological Abstracts* in order to attempt to avoid the possibility that, if something like the Thurstone and Degan study of the Supreme Court should appear (at a probable frequency of, say, once in a generation), they will not miss seeing it. I believe it is correct to say that I happen to have been the person to bring the Thurstone and Degan study to the attention of the profession, about a decade after it was originally published, and that few other political scientists (at least) or lawyers have seen fit to cite it (to say nothing of to use it) since then. But I can claim no particular acumen in the matter; it was, rather, a social by-product of my more general efforts (at the time) to become better educated in behavioral science. My recollection is that Frank Pinner, who was then my colleague at Michigan State University, had shown or possibly given to me a copy of the original *Psychometric Lab Report*, probably sometime in 1958, but too late for me to do more than footnote it in a book of mine (1959:78n) which was then in press. Pinner had been, as a then quite recent doctoral graduate from the University of California at Berkeley, a member of the initial group—which included also, incidentally, Harold D. Lasswell—at the Center for Advanced Study of the Behavioral Sciences (CASBS), in Palo Alto. Pinner and I had worked together throughout 1956 in a national field survey of local civil defense, the report of which was sufficiently critical of federal policies and procedures that it was promptly classified and suppressed (Schubert, LaPalombara, Pinner, and Presthus 1956). In 1958 he was the director of the Bureau of Social and Political Research at Michigan State; and the report had been brought to his attention by a social psychologist friend in a different department. (Unfortunately, neither Pinner nor I understood factor analysis at that time.) So I put the Thurstone and Degan study aside for several years, while I went off to Norway for cross-cultural education on a Fulbright appointment, and then to Palo Alto for further interdisciplinary education at the CASBS. It was while I was at the latter center, engaged in a research project that was designed explicitly to (inter alia) articulate with and update Pritchett's *The Roosevelt Court*, and incidentally learning factor analysis, that I experienced a genuine (if unexpected) need for Thurstone and Degan. Then, of course, I did read it with care, and put it to use.

The need arose because my principal goal at the center was to develop a multidimensional psychometric model of the Court that would combine cumulative scaling, factor analysis, and the theory of psychological choice that had been developed by Clyde Coombs (a former student of Thurstone, and my then colleague at the center who was engaged in the writing of the book that expounded his theory [Coombs 1964]). I probably never would have constructed the model under other circumstances (of either time or space); but a combination of environmental and personal vectors coalesced and coaligned sufficiently to thrust me almost irrevocably into the enterprise. (Another colleague, William Riker, wrote his *Theory of Political Coalitions* [1962] in the same fellowship year; and yet another, Abraham Kaplan, was in at least the early stages of work upon what became his *Conduct of Inquiry* [1964]; and I have never entertained the slightest doubt that I acted properly, when I dedicated "To the Fellows of 'the Class of '61' and to the Staff of the Center for Advanced Study in the Behavioral Sciences" the book that I wrote based on my own research that year [1965c:v.].) But constructing the model was one thing; believing in it—that is to say, establishing an empirical basis for sufficient confidence in its probable validity to justify one in committing substantial resources of time and energy to its use in guiding further research—was quite another matter. I attempted to satisfy myself by several procedures, of which two are worth mentioning here. First, I ran a comprehensive experimental test of the procedures, simulating a set of decisions for a hypothesized term of the Court by plotting on graph paper the positions of both cases and justices; then I observed the geometric relationships among both types of points, as the basis for calculating a set of cumulative scales and also a correlation matrix; factor analyzed the correlation matrix to recover the two-dimensional configuration of points for the justices; and finally I compared the plot of factorial positions of judges with their known (i.e., predetermined) positions on the initial graph (Schubert 1965c:chap. 4: "An Experimental Factor Analysis of Simulated Data"). This experiment convinced me that the technique would faithfully reproduce the kind of relationships that I hypothesized to obtain in real life; it did not and could not, of course, provide any assurance that such relationships did, in fact, obtain (in the minds of the relevant justices). A different kind of (thus far, indirect) proof would be required for the latter validation. But I wanted also to assure myself that my claim of continuity with *The Roosevelt Court* could not be impeached—that is to say, I wished to prove that, notwithstanding the greater complexity of my methods and the more precise articulation of the theory that I had invoked, Pritchett had studied exactly the same kind of relationships in his book, and his findings could therefore be assimilated as an approximate statement of what would also be found by using my model, if my empirical data were projected backward in time for an additional sixteen years. (My own data were not immediately deposited in a data bank, but they were on punch cards and I did make them available to several individuals upon request during the next several years until 1969. By then I had updated them [to include the period September 1946 through June 1969] and extended them [to include unanimous decisions as well as nonunanimous] and made them available for general public use on either magnetic tape or cards [through the Survey Research Archive of the Inter-University Consortium for Political Research located at the University of Michigan].[2]

Neither the data banks nor the practice of exchanging data for reanalysis had yet been established in political science when Pritchett wrote; and I guess I just assumed that his data were not on cards—although I never asked him, and I still don't know for sure. It would have been a little easier, and somewhat more accurate, to have had access to his coding sheets; but there was one distinct advantage in *not* having such access. What I proposed to do, as a further test of my own model, was to combine Thurstone and Degan's factorial data with Pritchett's scaling data for the corresponding terms, and

---

2. P. O. Box 1248, Ann Arbor, Michigan, 48106. See also Ryan and Tate 1974.

to use the scales derived from Pritchett's data as the basis for providing the substantive interpretation of the factors which Thurstone and Degan had reported, but had been unable to explain in substantive terms. I thought then that this would provide an unimpeachably objective test of my own theory, because both studies upon which I planned to rely were entirely independent of each other; both had been published over a decade earlier, and therefore there was no way in which (whatever anyone might wish to assume concerning my research ethics) I could possibly fudge in the employment of either half of the data. Another full decade elapsed before I learned, through correspondence with Pritchett, that it was indeed *his* data for the 1943–1944 terms that Degan (as it also turned out) had factor analyzed. Consequently, I was correct about the *methodological* independence of the two studies, which was really the point of importance so far as concerns assuring the objectivity of my own test; but I was wrong in the presumption that Degan had coded his decisional data directly from the *United States Reports*. It was, I suppose, a fortunate mistake, because the use of Pritchett's data assured that the observations which generated the scales and the factor configurations would be, although methodologically independent, made of the *same* universe of decisions. If a psychologist, relatively unsophisticated in the empirical characteristics of the decisional sources, *had* made the observations upon which the factor analysis was based, it is entirely possible that I would have been forced to conclude that the test of my model by interpreting Degan's factors with Pritchett's scales had failed—and for the quite spurious reason that not only the observations of them, but the data sets themselves, might then have been based upon partially independent samples of decisions.

The initial essay in this part is my report of the experiment that demonstrated that the factors which Thurstone and Degan had left uninterpreted were functions of Pritchett's scales, and vice versa. Stated otherwise, what the model stipulates is that if matrices of agreement scores are analyzed by some method (such as factor analysis) which partitions the variance among one or more dimensions, and if the resulting dimensions are used as reference dimensions to locate the configuration of points representing the judges in the space (of whatever dimensionality) they define, then that same space will be transected by the set of cumulative scales among which the decisions have been apportioned according to the substantive content of the scale variables. Stated alternatively, the decisions are classified into nonoverlapping subsets according to their subject matter; each of these subsets of decisions is scaled linearly; and the set of these linear scales will then provide an extrinsic criterion for oblique rotation of the reference dimensions of the space generated by the pooling of all decisions and by their classification according to no substantive (subject matter) criterion at all, but rather according to the procedural criterion of participation/nonparticipation in the majority that determines the outcome of each decision. The theory states that if what has been

---

3. His letter to me is dated November 14, 1971.

described can be done (as measured by some appropriate statistical test of goodness-of-fit), then it must be because the agreement and disagreement of judges in their decisions is due to their attitudinal differences, as measured by the linear cumulative scales. The crux of the argument rests upon an insight—which certainly was not my own, but rather was gleaned from one of Coombs' lectures at the center—concerning what seem prima facie to be two completely different techniques for data manipulation and representation, Guttman's method of linear cumulative scaling and Thurstone's method of multiple factor analysis. The former of these originated out of efforts by army management to comprehend the psychology of soldiers confronting combat experience, while the other developed out of efforts by educational psychologists to discover what was cognitively common among various tests designed to measure imputed mental "traits" and skills. Coombs had demonstrated (1964:23, and chaps. 11, 12) that cumulative scaling and factor analysis—whatever their historic and superficial differences—both are alternative ways of measuring the same fundamental psychometric relationship; and once I could assume that, I could and did put the rest of the model together.

Because the model purported to deal *only* with psychological relationships, it was evidently suitable to provide the basis for only a partial explanation of Supreme Court decision-making; and I never thought of it as more than that (see chapter 3, above). The imputed cause for both factorial and scale positions was not only psychological, but also limited to a very special aspect of psychology: that aspect, of belief systems about public policy issues, that I have called ideological. To the extent that judges are also influenced by such matters as bellyaches or high blood pressure, or the infidelity of loved (or hated) ones, or social considerations arising out of their interaction with each other or with other persons in their bureaucratic entourage, or by aspects of their professional ideology functioning as role constraints such as belief in stare decisis, we ought to expect that such other independent variables will over a sufficient period of time affect a *set* of cumulative scale variables either in a constant or else in a random fashion, so that their overall effect will be to either cancel or wash out. This is not the same thing as saying that these other variables (of health, affection, and social interaction) are unimportant to the determination of the outcome of decisions; but it is to say that however important these other variables may be, that does not preclude us from examining the effect of the psychological variables that do purport to measure ideological differences. If A always votes with B on a particular issue, or on all issues, not because he shares whatever opinion B may have, but because he does not want to seem to disagree with B, then it is perfectly true that scaling will attribute to A beliefs about public policy that he does not entertain. The observation of what men are willing to do (including their formal speech) for public consumption cannot assure what is in either their conscious or their subconscious minds. Scaling tells us not what judges believe, but what they are prepared to say they believe. To get at the effects of genetic special fortune or disability, or physiological disturbances serious enough to entail psychic consequences, or role distraints,[4] or other social interaction effects (such as, to put it most crudely and in terms of what may be a frequently inappropriate legislative analogy, logrolling votes), one must design and carry out research that will measure the effects of these other phenomena; and my ambition, back in 1960, was not to solve simultaneously (as some critics seem to have felt I should have done) all possible problems involved in the modeling of Supreme Court decisions, but rather to attempt to isolate and to focus upon one aspect, that seemed to me to be important to clarify, of the more complex general situation.

The model is explicated briefly in chapter 4, but the weight of the discussion there is upon the accommodation of two sets of empirical data. It is rather chapter 5, which deals with what was (at the time of its publication) the most recently completed term of the Warren Court, that provides a more detailed and discursive exposition of the theory and model. Chapter 5 also provides (as the Thurstone-Degan paper does not) a discussion of both the phi correlation statistic and the method of factor analysis, so that it can function as an introduction to those subjects for readers who may not previously have encountered them. Chapter 5 presents also, in extensive form (as, again, chapter 4 does not) the set of linear cumulative scales for the term.

The scales are in the basic format that has become conventional in the field, stemming from the initial paper that brought the method to the attention of the political science profession (Tanenhaus 1956). There followed a period of exploration, during which several political scientists employed the method of judicial scaling to investigate a variety of different kinds of hypotheses. The initial forays dealt with hypothesized variables that were narrowly defined but that nevertheless related to postulated *political* concepts and tended to cut across the orthodox legal categories under which the cases, attributed to the scale, would have been classified (e.g., Schubert 1959:chap. 5, "Scalogram Analysis"). In order to get samples of adequate size it was necessary to extend the scope of the analysis chronologically over several terms of the Court, thereby paying the side cost of increasing respondent nonparticipation (and therefore scale indeterminancy) due to personnel changes. All of the scaling studies made during the late fifties and early sixties continued to deal exclusively with the United States Supreme Court, although at least one of these skipped a century and focused imaginatively upon the Taney Court in the antebellum period that produced the Dred Scott catastrophe (Schmidhauser 1961); and this study, which interrelates political party and sectional differences to judicial attitudes toward the major policy issues of the time (slavery and industrialization), remains the only behavioral study of the Supreme Court during the 19th century. Then, beginning in 1960, Sidney

---

4. See the recounting of how Frankfurter conned Frank Murphy into suppressing his intended dissent in *Hirabayashi* v. *United States*, purportedly in the name of enhancing the reputation of the Supreme Court—but with what was clearly, in fact, the opposite effect (Murphy and Tanenhaus 1972:157–158).

Ulmer published the first article which combined all of the civil liberties cases decided by the Court during a single term (1960). This was an important advance, because it identified what has proved to be the most important single attitudinal scale in the decision-making of the United States Supreme Court, term in and term out for the past third of a century (at least). Shortly thereafter Harold Spaeth published a scale of the labor decisions of the first six terms of the Warren Court; and when I learned that he was also collecting data on the business regulation decisions for the same period, I suggested that he combine the labor and business regulation scales into a combined E scale (Spaeth 1963b: 82–83). It was apparent that the pooled data would have to scale acceptably, because I already had completed scaling E for sixteen individual terms, from 1946 through and including the 1961 term.[5] Since then linear scaling of these and other variables has been extended to subsequent terms of the United States Supreme Court (Schubert 1974b); to the United States Courts of Appeals (Atkins 1972); to several state supreme courts (Brown and Haddad 1966–1967; Beatty 1970; Ulmer 1966; Feeley 1971; Fair 1967); and to the supreme courts of several other countries, including Australia (Schubert 1969d; Blackshield 1972), Canada (Peck 1967b, 1969; Fouts 1969; Slayton 1971), India (Gadbois 1970a, 1970b), Japan (Hayakawa 1962), and the Philippines (Samonte 1969; Tate 1973).

Chapter 6 stemmed from a different and prior research project, which began in the early fifties when Robert Jackson was on the United States Supreme Court. I was then teaching constitutional law, and Jackson interested me (as he has likewise several other persons) because of the exceptional felicity of his style and mode of self-expression. I began work on the Jackson project at a time when I knew that I was dissatisfied with traditional public law as an approach to either teaching or research, but when the implications of behavioralism for work on the judicial process remained undefined. Jack Peltason had not yet come forth with his call for a sociological (interest-group process) jurisprudence; and Fred Kort's initial foray into mathematical prediction of the Supreme Court's right-to-counsel decisions (Kort 1957) was then itself an even less predictable event than Peltason's brochure. I looked upon the Jackson project as both a learning experience for myself and as a bridge to a possibly more satisfying research future. What I planned to do was to read all of his opinions as a judge, and to analyze systematically their value content (as normative rather than empirical propositions). I intended also to classify the voting decisions of Jackson, which his opinions were intended to justify, on the basis of the same content categories that would be used to analyze his associated opinions. Hence, it would be possible to correlate his value articulations, not only with each other, but also with his voting behavior, so as to ascertain to what extent his verbal (opinion) behavior was consistent with his decisional (voting) behavior, both in any given decision

---

5. The E scale for the 1960 Term is reported in chapter 5 below.

(and for any specified period of time) and also dynamically (that is, longitudinally throughout his baker's dozen years of service as an associate justice of the Supreme Court). Such results could of course be reported statistically; but I aspired from the very beginning of my conceptualization of the project to do much more than report the quantified results of an extensive exercise in content analysis. I wanted to report the opinion evidence *in context*, which would have to be discursively; and in view of the consensual opinion (which I shared) that Jackson was well worth reading for his style alone, I wanted to select a sample of his opinions that could go both ways—the same opinions would exemplify typical articulations of his key value assertions, and they would also constitute his best judicial writing from a strictly literary point of view.

Execution of this idea entailed certain modifications, invariably in the direction of complicating my procedures and adding to my costs (in terms of both time and data processing). As a graduate student, I had had no training in content analysis, statistics, computer programming, or any of the other skills that proved to be important to carrying out the proposed analysis; so things like these I had to learn as I went along, during the decade and a half that separates the inception of work and the publication of the book that presents Jackson's opinions. I soon learned, for example, that there was a problem of reliability, concerning the data that would denote Jackson's expressed values, if I were to attempt to rely exclusively upon my own reading of the opinions (of which there were about three hundred at the time I began reading them all for purposes of the project); so it became necessary to fund, recruit, train, and work with several academic generations of graduate student assistants, who comprised the membership of the panels of three other persons who also read and independently evaluated Jackson's opinions and votes.

Jackson died during the early stages of the project, of a heart attack at the age of sixty-two (and quite contrary to the prediction that one would have made, based on mortality tables, in the previous year). One reader for The University of Chicago Press, to which I subsequently (in the late fifties) submitted for consideration in regard to publication the book manuscript which at that time was the fruit of the project, objected to my statistical approach and deplored my failure to undertake a lawyerlike case-by-case discussion of the opinions of all of the participating justices in the decisions I had analyzed, instead of attempting to quantify Jackson's opinions alone (cf. Kommers 1966). Such a focus would have resulted in a very different book than that I had in mind, and it would not have taken into account my own particular interest in Jackson, the individual, as a literary stylist. Frankfurter, for example, voted most frequently like Jackson (and vice versa) during the last eight of the terms that they were together on the Court; but no one who had ever read many of their respective opinions would ever suggest that Frankfurter's legal needlepoint could serve as an adequate substitute for

Jackson's "trenchant, concrete, Saxon vigor (Bar and Officers of the Supreme Court 1955:xxxv; Schubert 1969b:6–10)."

I was about the only person privy to my original manuscript on Jackson who liked the mixing of the behavioral and humanist components of the book. Another reader for The University of Chicago Press advised me to separate the quantified, statistical analysis of Jackson's votes and values and publish that independently from whatever I might do with his opinions. This I was reluctant to do; but I felt that there were other, technical, problems involving the statistical analysis, so I put the manuscript aside for a couple of years, while I went on leave, first in Norway, and then at the CASBS at Stanford. Near the end of my fellowship year at the center I retrieved the manuscript and made plans for a reanalysis of the data, in view of the fact that by then I had begun to acquire a better grasp of the multivariate research methods necessary to a more appropriate (and sophisticated) analysis than I had initially undertaken. This work was carried out after I returned to Michigan State University in the fall of 1961; and I then wasted another couple of years in a fruitless endeavor to publish the rather long resulting article in any of several outlets sponsored by the American Psychological Association. They didn't like the design, and were even more troubled by the fact that I wrote like a political scientist instead of a psychologist; they advised me to send it off to a political science journal. So eventually I sent it to the *American Political Science Review*, which did publish it, and that is the article that appears as chapter 6, below.

After the article had been out for the better part of a year, I raised with a publisher the question of bringing out the opinions as a strictly literary book, with no numbers at all; so on the basis of a contract with him I then went ahead and completed the work that seemed necessary to round out the enterprise. Primarily that consisted of reading the not inconsiderable corpus of Jackson's nonjudicial writings, plus the literature that had appeared during the previous thirty years about him; theretofore, I had read much, but by no means all of this related literature, because it was not essential to the content analysis work that I had been doing. The upshot is a book that presents some fifty-odd of his best opinions, in each instance with an introduction that explains the decision of the rest of the Court and appraises its political and social significance. I attempted also, in introductory and concluding chapters, to place Jackson himself in the context of his political and social times, and to evaluate his significance as a legal spokesman. A variety of additional delays (including, but by no means limited to, a neurotic copyeditor [who unbeknown to me was working on contract, rather than on salary, with the publisher] who disappeared for several months with the manuscript of my book—she didn't like the first chapter of it at all) forestalled actual publication until late in 1969 (1969b), by which time I was living abroad again. It had been sixteen years since I began; and I suppose a dispassionate observer would have to conclude that the ultimate publication of the article and the book were a greater tribute to perseverance than to prudence. But I still wish they had been published together; the disjunction in their format seems to me an excellent symbolization of much of what has been wrong with *both* the social sciences and the humanities. Jackson's behavior, in the form of both his policy and his linguistic choices, was unified in life, and I think it would have been better if they could have become joined in my discussion of their interrelationships.

The seventh chapter also is drawn from a large, long, and complex (though different) project, which began in the summer of 1962 when I commenced a luckless correspondence with Geoffrey Sawer, research professor at Australian National University in Canberra and the doyen of public lawyers in Australia. Sawer upholds the spirit of legal realism in his country, and he has written a very good book on legal sociology (1965), plus frequent commentaries upon the High Court and its justices, generally from a political perspective that would place him in this country in the conventional camp (as I shall call it in Part 3, below). What soon became clear was that we differed about methodology: he is a legal humanist, with a considerable vested interest in his status as the authoritative expositor of judicial behavior on the High Court. He became very much opposed to the idea of having anybody undertake to interview Australian judges, or to collect systematic information about their social and political backgrounds, and most particularly to have such data classified and analyzed statistically; and he professed to be strongly opposed to having me come to Australia to undertake such study, because of his certainty that any such research would be infeasible (because of the lack of judicial cooperation), doomed to failure (because of inherent defects in the method), and fruitless (because of the impossibility that it could lead to meaningful results). This did not all become clear immediately, but rather over a period of several years, in the course of which it also became clear that without his cooperation there was no suitable means of funding field research in Australia, during the early sixties when I was interested in undertaking such research. So I didn't do it.

Instead, I limited the inquiry to the library research (that I had intended originally to be preliminary to the field research), supplemented by a none-too-successful endeavor to collect social background data (unavailable in the United States) on High Court justices. The consequence was distinctly another compromise, and a settling for second (or third) best; but at the end of a decade there was something (where before there had been virtually nothing; but cf. Playford 1961) in the way of behavioral research on Australian judges.

During the same decade social science inquiry into the judicial process was also beginning to take place in Canada, Japan, India, and the Philippines. My own interest in undertaking cross-cultural research in judicial behavior stemmed from my Fulbright year in Norway (1959–1960); and so once the project on the United States Supreme Court was substantially completed at the CASBS the following year, and research on the American judicial process seemed well underway (1963f), I chose Australia in preference to Canada (on the basis of theoretical criteria, which I have articulated elsewhere [1966b]) as the best place to begin a program of research in comparative judicial behavior. As it turned out, I was wrong—at least from a pragmatic point of view—because the Canadian academic culture was much more receptive, during the sixties, to research in judicial behavior. (The irony of life is exemplified, again, by my own experience: at the close of the fifties I had been forced into debt by the Fulbright-sabbatical combination, and during the early sixties, when I would have welcomed an opportunity to do field research in Australia on a shoestring budget, I was unable to arrange even that; but by the end of the sixties, I rejected the offer of a very large grant to do field research in Canadian judicial behavior, because by that time my interests and priorities had shifted and I preferred, instead, to undertake similar work but in Switzerland and South Africa—even though it meant going back to a shoestring budget once again.)

I selected Australia first because it seemed to present a minimum of cultural variance from the United States, and therefore an opportunity to undertake research in judicial behavior similar to that which had been and was being done in the United States under circumstances in which one could expect to have relatively good control over research comparisons. I decided to begin by reading and coding a sample of the then most recent decade of the decisions of the High Court of Australia. For reasons that are discussed in chapter 7, it soon became apparent that differences in both the style of voting and opinion behavior, and in the content of policy issues, were going to necessitate changes in certain aspects of the research design that seemed appropriate for the United States. The High Court, for example, acted mostly through committees, and rarely decided issues as a group; opinions were customarily given individually, if with great collective redundancy; and virtually no civil liberties claims were considered. Samples of votes were, consequently, relatively much smaller than for the Supreme Court, and there were forbidding problems of missing data (from the points of view of either cumulative scaling or correlational analyses). It was also necessary to acquire access to an at least partial set of the case reports, none of which was available initially at or near either of the universities where I was resident when I began work on this project. Neither was there even sketchy biographical information available for the nine judges who were members of the High Court during the period covered by my proposed study; and although a projected national biographical dictionary was in process during the sixties, that publication never became available in time to do me any good. Contrary to the situation in the United States, where judicial biographies and autobiographies were plentiful (and in some instances, rife) for Supreme Court justices, a counterpart literature for Australia was virtually nonexistent (see Pannam 1961; the only apparent exception is Cowen 1967). But by the time my need seemed pressing, I had established communication with quite a few Australian academics besides Geoff Sawer; and one of them, Professor Henry Mayer, very kindly offered to engage and supervise a research assistant to attempt to collect such information on my behalf. The resulting data were not ample, but they were adequate to my then limited, and relatively crude, purposes. But no foreigner could expect, on the basis of having read a few books, to avoid mistakes in judgment in the interpretation of indices to social status in an alien culture, as I was only too well aware; so I felt no particular chagrin at the fact that in the use of these biographical data I did make a couple of judgments that Australians were quick to pounce upon as mistakes (e.g., Vinson 1968, reprinted here as an addendum to chap. 7). These I corrected at the first opportunity (1969d), and went on with the other aspects of the work.

As the research proceeded, I planned to write a series of some half-dozen reports upon it. As originally projected, these included (1) an initial preliminary, summary, and general discussion, the first draft of which was presented to a meeting of the fellows at the East-West Center and a subsequent draft to a panel session of the American Political Science Association (1966b); (2) an article[6] which presents and analyzes in detail the cumulative scales that were derived—by inductive rather than the customary deductive categorization; (3) a factor analysis of the same voting data from which the scales were derived, and a discussion of the ideological dimensions defined by the scales (1968g); (4) the analysis of opinion behavior and social deference that is reprinted here as chapter 7; (5) a comparative factor analysis of both voting and opinion data, demonstrating that the same ideological dimensions were defined by either votes or opinions, and that votes and opinions are alternative modes of behavioral response representing the same underlying value choices (1969a); and (6) a causal analysis of the relationships among background characteristics, decisional participation, attitudes toward policy issues, and (as the dependent variable) opinions—I chose opinions rather than votes for the dependent variable because they provide a better sample for statistical analysis (1969g). I also wrote two cross-cultural studies, one com-

---

6. Schubert 1969d. This paper became the last (instead of, as I had intended, the first) to be published, due to a manifestation of Australian humor. One T. B. J. Steele, a person purporting to be the literary editor of the *Summons*, a law journal at Melbourne University, and writing to me from the law school there, stated that a copy of the article had "come into [his] hands"—which seemed plausible, because I had previously submitted it to the *Melbourne University Law Review*—and that he would be grateful if I would give him permission to publish it in his journal, which he described as "a magazine which circulates to practitioners and law graduates as well as to students within the University of Melbourne." So I sent him the manuscript of what I supposed would be the initially published article, on scale analysis of the Dixon Court's decisions. It took many months to confirm that the person who had written to me, and to whom I had sent the freshly revised and retyped ribbon copy of my manuscript, was, purportedly, unknown at the University of Melbourne. I never did retrieve the manuscript that I had sent to Melbourne; and the episode delayed publication of the article by almost two years. It was obviously a great practical joke.

paring the political leadership role of the High Court of Australia with that of the Supreme Courts of Japan, the Philippines, and the United States (1967c), and the other the importance of institutional role concepts in the Philippines compared to that of the state of Hawaii (Flango and Schubert 1969); but both of these were by-products of the research, rather than a part of the original design. Evidently, the latter pair were among the earliest studies of the judicial process to rely upon systematic empirical analysis, employing a common design, of data for more than a single country; at least these are the only two that Murphy and Tanenhaus (1972:216n.) could find to cite as examples of such an approach.

By 1969 when the last of my own reports on the High Court was published, the initiative already had passed (as I had expected and hoped) into the hands of Australian scholars, drawn from political science and law faculties alike (R. Douglas 1968; Gow 1971; Neumann 1971; Blackshield 1972). These scholars, who were personally products of the legal and political cultures about which they wrote, were in a far better position than I to make valid and sensible judgments about judicial behavior in Australia. The initial work continued to focus, like my own had done, upon the High Court; but this indulgence in what some American critics have called the "supreme court fallacy" has been an invariable characteristic of judicial process and behavior research in every country concerning which such work has been done during the past two decades; and it reflects, I have long been convinced, not some perverse or willful blindness, but rather a natural expediency, with pioneers in the behavioral approach turning first to the same institutional subject that had been featured in traditional research. This initial preoccupation with the country's supreme court is followed by a broadening of focus to include the courts at the next level below, which interact with the supreme court; and then inquiry is extended to trial and specialized courts and adjudicative processes in other agencies. It is most likely that this is what will happen in Australia during the seventies. So chapter 7 here should be viewed as a relatively crude enterprise in cross-cultural research, by a foreigner who lacked both substantive insight and access to data that alike were needed to support a more sophisticated study; but at the same time the article succeeded, I believe, in directing the attention of Australians to a line of inquiry which they had theretofore neglected. (There was then, after all, no English model of this sort that they might have followed.)

As an illustration of how the publication of my article called attention to what was for its Australian legal readers a novel approach (and for its Australian sociological readers a novel subject for sociological investigation), I have appended to chapter 7 the comment by an Australian that appeared in the same volume of the same journal later in the same year. Evidently, among the many other American customs that Australians do not follow is that of inviting an author to reply to such entailed critique of his work, because I first learned of the Vinson comment when a friend sent me a copy of the published version of it. But all questions of courtesy aside, there isn't much I could (or should) have said other than to thank Mr. Vinson for his interest. Beyond the additional details that he provides concerning certain judges and their families, Vinson corrects two of my mistakes about matters of attribute classification, at least one of which, involving Justice Kitto, affected my findings and interpretations. I agree that where a judge was born is far less important than where he grew up and became socialized; and I had blundered in my classification of Kitto according to domicile, because of inadequate information about him. But for the other mistake I cannot even plead ignorance: my own, however limited, data show (Schubert 1969*d*) that there is no justification for inserting the qualifier "lower" to modify the middle-class origins that I attributed to the High Court judges. The phrasing and choice of adverb suggest that I may have been humming tunes from *My Fair Lady* to myself, and became carried away by that muse instead of the one that I purported to be following. Who knows? Certainly I no longer do, so I'm not even sure that the adjective was ever *consciously* employed. On the other hand, Vinson is a bit hyperbolic himself when in one sentence he concedes my use of the adverb "typically", and in the next he asserts that my use of "lower" "appears to refer to all nine justices covered in the study." At least in American usage, "typically" implies "for the most part" or "generally speaking." It is notable also that Vinson provides social-class information about only a bare majority—five—of the judges. Given his assertion that my use of "lower" applies to all nine justices, one might think his discussion would have been more complete—as well as more fair—if he had reported the corresponding social class-origin information for Webb, Williams, Taylor, and—not least—McTiernan, whose father was a policeman.

One other point should be made about chapter 7. I was at least as interested in its methodological as in its substantive implications. There had been a great deal more talk than action in the United States about analysis of opinions and the related social interaction, and apparently the only relevant prior work was that of Ulmer on the Michigan Supreme Court (1963). The relative abundance of opinion as compared to voting data, for the Australian High Court, made possible an analysis of functional in comparison to formal leadership, in relation to the social characteristics of the judges; and this study of opinion behavior was prerequisite to the subsequent test of the hypothesis that—contrary to the intuitive expectations of many American commentators—opinion and voting behavior do in fact function as alternative sides of the same decisional coin (Schubert 1969*a*). And in this latter respect, chapter 7 constitutes an extension, both to a larger group of judges and to a foreign setting, of the equivalent concern which from its inception had informed also the Jackson project.

# 4

# A Factorial Model of the Roosevelt Court

Over a decade has elapsed since Thurstone and Degan (1951) published what remains the only attempt to use factor psychology (Guilford 1961) and factor analytic methods in a study of the United States Supreme Court. This pilot research in the application of factor analysis to official voting data has been summarized in a textbook (Fruchter 1954) as an example of obverse (Q-technique) factor analysis, but its usefulness to psychologists, political scientists, sociologists, or lawyers has been limited by the inability of the original authors to interpret the factorial resolution that they deemed appropriate to the data (Thurstone and Degan 1951:4). The purpose of this article is to demonstrate that these same data are amenable to an intuitively plausible interpretation by the employment of a specific psychometric model of the Supreme Court. The proposed model utilizes, but is not limited to, factor psychology for the interpretation of the relationship between stimulus and response points in what Coombs (1964:chap. 1) calls a joint multidimensional psychological space.

This chapter was originally published, in slightly different form, as "A Solution to the Indeterminate Factorial Resolution of Thurstone and Degan's Study of the Supreme Court" in *Behavioral Science* 7 (October 1962):448–458.

This article was prepared with the very substantial aid and assistance of the Center for Advanced Study in the Behavioral Sciences. In particular, I wish to acknowledge my indebtedness to John Gilbert, staff statistician, and to my colleague of the fellowship year 1960–1961, Professor Clyde Coombs of the Department of Psychology of the University of Michigan.

A very brief description of the Thurstone and Degan study will be followed by a description of the proposed alternative model, and a proposed solution to the problem of indeterminancy in accounting for the variance in the Supreme Court's decision-making in the set of decisions that comprise the raw data.

## I. THE THURSTONE-DEGAN STUDY

Because of the brevity with which the authors described their universe of raw data, it is impossible to be certain precisely what they observed in the *United States Reports*, since there are serious empirical problems of classification of judicial opinions and votes (cf. Schubert 1959:164–166) concerning which there is as yet no consensus among lawyers and political scientists who are specialists in the study of judicial behavior and/or the Supreme Court. However, they did observe, generally speaking, decisions in which from two to four justices disagreed with the majority during the period from October 1943 through June 1945; and their sample included a set of 115 subsets of votes of the justices, classified dichotomously as either in agreement (+) or in disagreement (−) with the majority who controlled the disposition of cases in specific decisions. Phi coefficients were then computed from fourfold tables for each pair of justices; and the resulting 9 × 9, symmetric correlation matrix was factored by the complete centroid method. The orthogonal factor matrix was then rotated obliquely to simple structure (Table 2, from Thurstone and Degan 1951:5), thus yielding the configuration of points and the factorial resolution depicted in Figure 2 (from Thurstone and Degan 1951: 6–7).

The authors' conclusion with regard to Figure 2 was that "The entire configuration of nine vectors might be thought of as representing actually five distinct attitudes or points of view which . . . would then be represented by [five groups of] the judges as follows, namely, (1) Reed and Stone, (2) Murphy and Rutledge, (3) Black and Douglas, (4) Frankfurter and Roberts, and (5) Jackson and, to a lesser degree, Frankfurter" (Thurstone and Degan 1951:3). Consultations by the authors with colleagues in the political science and law faculties proved to be inconclusive, since these experts were unable to agree upon any common interpretation of the "groupings of attitudes" that were associated with the oblique rotated factors. As an alternative, it was suggested (p. 4) that by a reexamination of the raw data "with grouping according to the votes of the judges it should be possible to clarify more objectively just what the factors are that are common to the cases," although the authors thought that such further work should be done by subject matter specialists rather than by psychologists. Such further work is the basis for the present paper, on the premise that the Thurstone and Degan study constitutes an imaginative and highly suggestive demonstration of the potential utility of factor psychology for the investigation of political attitudes and the study of political behavior.

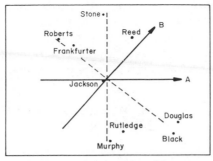

Figure 2a: Axes A and B

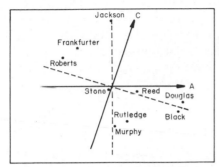

Figure 2b: Axes A and C

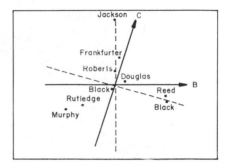

Figure 2c: Axes B and C

Figure 2. The Judicial Point Configuration after Oblique Rotation of the Reference Axes to Simple Structure

The authors of the original study suggest that they would expect the factors to represent attitudes toward such general issues as civil rights and economic liberalism, but they do not explain how and why a correlation matrix representing dyadic agreement with the Court's majorities changes to sets of individual correlations with *substantively* defined variables. It will be recalled that the raw data observed consisted of votes that were classified so that + was defined to mean "voted in agreement with the majority whose decision controlled the disposition of a case" and − was defined to mean disagreement with the majority; neither + nor − was defined in terms of the subject matter of the cases decided, and a computer is given no information about the substantive variables involved in the decisions of the cases to which assenting and dissenting votes relate. If, as Thurstone and Degan speculated, a high correlation of an individual justice with a particular factor is to be interpreted to mean (for example) an attitude of considerable sympathy for freedom of speech as a constitutional right, then the votes to which such a correlation coefficient relates have been reclassified, at least implicitly, so that + now means "relatively considerable sympathy for free speech" and − means a lesser degree of such sympathy.

Such a reclassification of the meaning attributed to judicial votes implies a discussion of the relationship of judicial cases (as a source of raw data) to the ideal-points of the justices. Indeed, the basic stimulus-response model which Thurstone and Degan assumed implies that *both* kinds of points are located somewhere in the same psychological space, since each stimulus-response dyad symbolizes different aspects—perception and response—of the behavior of the same organism in the empirical world.

## II. A PSYCHOLOGICAL MODEL OF SUPREME COURT DECISION-MAKING

An obvious strategy, therefore, for one who would seek to bridge the gap between judicial attitudes and judicial votes would be to construct a psychological model of Supreme Court decision-making by using a multi-dimensional generalization of the stimulus-response model to define the psychological space and the underlying measurement relationships (Schubert 1961*a*). The hypothesis to be tested is that the attitudes of each individual justice toward the major variables which define the substantive value content of sets of cases before the Court for decision cause him to react through his voting to the stimuli presented by the cases.

### A Composition Model for the Voting Behavior of the Justices

In his general theory of data, Coombs (1964) classifies the mapping and the analysis of the recorded observations of raw psychological data according to three criteria: whether (1) the observations are of one or two pairs of points; (2) a pair consists of an individual's ideal-point and a stimulus-point, or of two stimulus-points; and (3) the measurement relationship of the pair (or pairs) of points is one of ordinality or proximity. The joint application of these three criteria results, of course, in eight categories, and both factor analysis and cumulative scaling are mapped into the same octant of Coombs' classification chart; both involve ordinal measurement of the relationship between a pair of points drawn from distinct sets (i.e., a pair consists of an individual's ideal-point and a stimulus-point). In other words, at the abstract level of Coombs' theory of data, both metric and nonmetric factor analysis and cumulative scaling are conceptualized as alternative approaches to the same basic measurement problem, which Coombs has defined as:

$$P_{hij} \geqslant 0 < = > i > j. \tag{1}$$

In other words, "if, and only if, at the moment $h$, the point corresponding to the individual $[i]$, dominates the point corresponding to the stimulus $[j]$, the individual responds positively to the stimulus," where $P_{hij}$ is defined as the distance between the pair of points in the joint space of the relevant dimensions, and where $< = >$ signifies "implies and is implied by." (Coombs 1964:chaps. 1–4:Quadrant IIa.)

Coombs and his associates also have worked on methods and models for multidimensional extension of the one-dimensional Guttman model of cumulative scaling, and Coombs and Kao (1960) recently have shown that metric factor analysis and multidimensional cumulative scaling (or, as Coombs prefers to call it, nonmetric factor analysis) may—given suitable data—provide alternative methods of data processing for the recovery of $i$- and $j$-points in the same genotypic space. In his theory of data, Coombs (1964:chap. 12) explicitly considers nonmetric factor analysis to be a multidimensional generalization of Guttman scalogram analysis. Thus, the theoretical equivalence between scaling and factorial measurement of stimulus-response dyadic distances in $r$-dimensional space has been suggested, and established at least to the extent that it does not seem unreasonable to posit such equivalence as a hypothesis in constructing a model of the Court. Although the raw data for Supreme Court decision-making do not provide sufficient information to permit deterministic analysis of voting choices by means of multidimensional scaling techniques, it is useful to borrow a concept developed in the work in multidimensional unfolding, since we shall assume the theoretical equivalence of factor analysis, for which the data are adequate. The relevant concept is that of the *individual compensatory* composition model (Torgerson 1958:345–359; Coombs 1964:chap. 12) according to which (1) it is the individual (rather than the stimulus) who determines the weighting function, which is considered to be constant over all stimuli for the responses of that individual; and (2) it is not essential that the individual exceed the stimulus on all relevant dimensions, since it may be possible for him to compensate for his deficiency on one dimension with an excess on other dimensions—depending upon the precise location of both the $i$-point and the $j$-point, and the number of dimensions, which obviously must be more than one.

## Judicial Votes as Attitudinal Responses

Both cases and justices are conceptualized as sets of vectors in the same psychological space. A case which has been accepted by the Court for decision on its merits raises questions about one or more issues of value (which may be denominated as questions of law, public policy, etc.), in relationship to a particular set of facts which tends to specify more precisely the meaning of these questions of value.

In the simplest circumstance where only one variable is operative in a case, the particular issue perceived by an individual justice defines for him the relevant variable for decision-making in the case, and his response will be determined by the projection of his $i$-point on the scale axis which represents this variable. Cases which raise questions of differing degrees of valuation about the same variable (e.g., sympathy for constitutional claims of the right to counsel in state criminal trials) are located at various points in the space but in an approximate linear relationship to each other; thus, each such point may be conceived of as lying upon or near an axis representing the variable (or variable cluster), which intersects the space. A case which is perceived by the justices to raise a question concerning only one variable is located precisely upon the line of the axis for that variable, at a particular positive or negative distance from the origin corresponding to the degree of valuation of the question. Through the centroid of a set of scale axes, representing a set of civil liberties subvariables, would pass an axis representing a broadly defined heterogeneous variable (such as "all civil liberties" cases for a given term); and this axis would follow the trace of the mean of the projections of all the relevant *j*-points for cases.

The *i*-points also project on the scale axes, and the loci of these respondent-points is determined by the correlations that each has with these scale axes (that is, by the orthogonal projections on each axis from each point). Where a justice "is" in the space, therefore, is a function of his attitudes toward the major decisional variables, as these attitudes have been sampled by his voting responses to questions of valuation raised by particular cases during the specified period of analysis.

If the attitude of the justice is such that he agrees with (accepts, responds positively or affirmatively to) the degree and intensity of valuation which he perceives a case to demand, he votes in support of the variable; otherwise, he rejects or votes against it. How a case will be decided by the Court depends, therefore, upon where the *i*-points of a majority of the justices participating in a decision are located in relationship to their individual perceptions of the locus of the *j*-point representing the case.

## The Relationship between Scaling and Factorial Measurements

The orthogonal factor matrix of Table 4 provides the necessary information, as determined by Thurstone and Degan, to plot the configuration of *i*-points in three dimensions. The orthogonal reference axes need not be rotated, since the analysis and interpretation below, which are based upon the

**Table 4. Centroid and Rotated Oblique Factor Loadings for Supreme Court Justices, 1943 and 1944 Terms**

| | Centroid Matrix | | | Oblique Matrix | | |
|---|---|---|---|---|---|---|
| Justices | I | II* | III* | A | B | C |
| Mu (Murphy) | .67 | .24 | .17 | .02 | −.49 | −.39 |
| Ru (Rutledge) | .64 | .10 | .10 | .14 | −.33 | −.31 |
| Bl (Black) | .80 | −.23 | −.24 | .63 | −.03 | −.05 |
| D (Douglas) | .70 | −.29 | −.31 | .67 | .08 | .05 |
| S (Stone) | −.53 | −.38 | .23 | −.04 | .49 | −.04 |
| Re (Reed) | −.21 | −.45 | .06 | .23 | .48 | .02 |
| F (Frankfurter) | −.57 | .19 | −.08 | −.35 | .04 | .27 |
| J (Jackson) | −.28 | .23 | −.58 | −.02 | −.01 | .64 |
| Ro (Roberts) | −.64 | .23 | .10 | −.49 | −.01 | .12 |

* Reflected (with reversed polarity).

composition model and theory of voting behavior of the justices described in the preceding sections, do not involve the imputation of substantive meaning to the factorial axes. The orthogonal factor axes are statistical constructs which provide a frame of reference for the space in which is located the configuration of $i$-points; although it may be possible to infer appropriate labels for the factors, this is not an essential nor even necessarily a useful step in interpretation under the model of the Court's behavior that is proposed here. What is essential is to pass scale axes through this factor space in such a way that the ordinal rankings of $i$-points on the respective scales correlate positively high, and at an acceptable probability level with the ordinal ranking upon these same scale axes of the projections from the $i$-points; and these latter points already have been determined in a fixed and invariant configuration by the factor measurement. Of course, the substantive content of the scale axes must correspond to the major policy issues decided by the Court during the period of time under analysis; in other words, the set of cumulative scales must include a classification of the same raw data that were used for the factor analysis, although the Guttman procedures will map these data both differently and independently from the factor analysis.

## III. AN EMPIRICAL APPLICATION OF THE MODEL

It would, of course, have been possible to collect the data for the scale analysis directly from the official case reports; but in order to provide an even more rigorous test of the theory, it has been considered preferable to utilize data that have been collected independently, and for quite different purposes, by a third researcher. Pritchett's study of the Roosevelt Court (1948), which was published over a decade ago and prior to the Thurstone and Degan study, appears to be the only available source of data that might be adapted for present purposes. Pritchett does not report his observations of the raw data, but he does report matrices of paired agreement in dissenting votes, by terms of the Court, and other information on the basis of which it is possible to reconstruct a set of fourfold tables which will reproduce a satisfactory approximation of the correlation matrix reported by Thurstone and Degan. (The reproduced correlation for the Douglas-Black dyad, for instance, is .53, while the correlation for this dyad reported by Thurstone and Degan is .59; for the Black-Roberts dyad, the reproduced correlation is −.67, while the correlation reported by Thurstone and Degan for this dyad is −.66; and for the Murphy-Rutledge dyad, the reproduced correlation is .43 as compared to .46 in the original study.) The purpose of making this check is to establish a basis for confidence in the assumption that, although there is no mention in Pritchett's book of either factor analysis or cumulative scaling, he did indeed observe the same raw data as was observed by Thurstone and Degan; and therefore it is reasonable to assume that, since Pritchett also reports measurements in the form of scales, there is some justification for inferring that the ordinal rankings of the justices on Pritchett's scales are at least rough approximations to the set of ordinal rankings that would be derived from cumulative scaling of the same data.

## The Error Variance

Pritchett's scales consist of simple percentage rankings of the justices, according to the proportion of the cases, in a sample relating to a particular value, in which each justice voted in favor of what was defined as the positive direction of the continuum for the value. One source of error, if one is to adapt Pritchett's scales to define the ordinal ranking of the justices on the scale axes, results from the fact that it is only assumed that Pritchett's rankings are about the same as those derivable from cumulative scaling of the same cases. This assumption seems justified because of the success that has been achieved in cumulative scaling for recent terms (Schubert 1962b; Spaeth 1963b; Ulmer 1961b) of many of the same variables that Pritchett defines, although it is not known for certain that Pritchett's scales are based upon universes of data that are scalable in the Guttman sense during the time period that they cover.

A second source of possible error can be attributed to the circumstance that Pritchett's scales are based upon a temporal interval of six years, with the Thurstone-Degan sample for the 1943 and 1944 terms falling in the middle of Pritchett's period, which spans the 1941 through 1946 terms. It seems altogether likely that rankings based upon the 1943 and 1944 terms would not be completely typical of the longer period, although the extent to which they may have deviated and the nature of such deviance are unknown. It is also possible that the variables that Pritchett scaled for the longer period are not precisely the same as one might prefer to work with for cumulative scaling of the shorter period alone.

In addition to these errors that are likely to arise in the adaptation of Pritchett's scales, the present writer has determined experimentally, by the study of a set of hypothetical data for which both $i$- and $j$-points were plotted as observations of imaginary raw data, that the total error variance due to the correlational and factor analysis is about 10 percent. The latter finding confirms the wisdom of Thurstone and Degan's decision to work with three factors, since it seems doubtful that much confidence can be reposed in factors extracted beyond the third, in applying centroid factor analysis to data of this type, considering the characteristically small magnitude of the correlations in the third and subsequent residual matrices. Ordinarily one could assume that error variance arising from the use of cumulative scales with acceptable reproducibility levels would be less than the factor error variance, but in this particular instance it is necessary to be aware of the likelihood that the error variance in the rankings on the scales is at least as great as the error variance in the location of the configuration of $i$-points by the factor routine.

## The Ordinal Scales

Although Pritchett (1948) reports scales of other subvariables that might have been selected for present purposes, the most generalized variables with which he attempted to work were two broad aspects of liberalism as a sociopolitical value: civil liberty and economic liberalism. According to the theory advanced by the present writer, the paravariable of liberalism should appear in the factor space as a centroid axis between the scale axes of civil liberty and economic liberalism, so a general scale of liberalism has been constructed from Pritchett's data for the civil liberty and economic liberalism variables. Moreover, the theory also stipulates that both the civil liberty and economic liberalism variables will appear in the factor space as the centroids of sets of scale axes representing subvariables. In order to demonstrate this relationship, "support of labor's claims and interests" has been selected as a characteristic subvariable of economic liberalism, and "support of workmen's compensation claims" has been selected as a characteristic sub-subvariable of the prolabor subvariable. The five scales presented in Table 5 represent, therefore, four different levels of generalization, and two categories of substantive differentiation, of liberalism as a sociopolitical value.

Pritchett's tables report, for each justice, the percentage of votes in support of the variable. These percentages have been converted to scores ranging from $+1$ to $-1$ by use of the formula,

$$s = \frac{2P - 100}{100}, \tag{2}$$

where $s$ is the score shown in Table 5, and $P$ is the percentage reported by

**Table 5. Scales of the Liberalism Variable and Subvariables for the Stone Court (1941–1946 Terms)**

| | Scale Variables | | | | |
|---|---|---|---|---|---|
| Justices | L (Liberalism) 1 | CL (Civil liberty) 2 | EL (Economic liberalism) 3 | EL-L (Prolabor) 4 | EL-L-WC (Workmen's compensation) 5 |
| Mu | .72 | .88 | .64 | .88 | 1.00 |
| Ru | .54 | .66 | .50 | .76 | 1.00 |
| Bl | .62 | .32 | .76 | .86 | 1.00 |
| D | .54 | .26 | .64 | .72 | 1.00 |
| S | −.27 | −.14 | −.32 | −.36 | −.60 |
| Re | −.10 | −.44 | .04 | .32 | .08 |
| F | −.28 | −.32 | −.22 | −.12 | −.16 |
| J | −.26 | −.40 | −.24 | .04 | .10 |
| Ro | −.66 | −.42 | −.76 | −.90 | −.88 |
| Page references in Pritchett (1948) | 254, 257 | 254 | 257 | 208, 257 | 208 |

**Table 6. Reference Axis Coordinates, Coefficients, and Cosines for Scale Axes**

| Coordinates/ coefficients | Scale Axes | | | | |
|---|---|---|---|---|---|
| | L 1 | CL 2 | EL 3 | EL-L 4 | EL-L-WC 5 |
| I/α | 1.00 | .90 | 1.00 | 1.00 | 1.00 |
| II*/β | −.10 | .40 | −.10 | .10 | .20 |
| III*/γ | .40 | 1.00 | .10 | .00 | .10 |
| *Cosines* | | | | | |
| Figure 2a | −06° | 24° | −06° | 06° | 11° |
| Figure 2b | 22° | 48° | 06° | 00° | 06° |
| Figure 2c | 104° | 68° | 135° | 00° | 26.5° |

\* Reflected (with reversed polarity).

Pritchett. Scale 1 is based upon a set of average percentages calculated from the totals columns of Pritchett's summary tables.

## The Scale Axes

Table 6 gives the reference axis coordinates and the corresponding cosines, which have been used to plot the scale variables as scale axes in the factor space defined by the centroid reference axes reported by Thurstone and Degan (Table 4). Since the direction of orthogonal axes extracted by the complete centroid method is arbitrary, reference axes II* and III* have been reflected, as noted in the footnote to Table 6, in order to reverse the signs of factor loadings reported by Thurstone and Degan, so that the point configuration and scale axes can be shown in positions that are characteristic. These characteristic positions for the justices and the liberalism scale axes have been determined by research on subsequent terms of the Court by the present writer. The scale axes have been positioned in the factor space so as to maximize the positive correlation between judicial rankings on Pritchett's scales and on the scale axes. In order to determine the latter set of rankings, it is necessary to ascertain the orthogonal projections from the $i$-points on each scale axis, in the various possible positions that it might assume. The distance from the origin to the point which is closest to a given $i$-point, on any scale axis, is computed by use of a standard formula from analytical geometry,

$$d = \frac{\alpha x + \beta y + \gamma z}{(\alpha^2 + \beta^2 + \gamma^2)^{1/2}} \tag{3}$$

where $d$ is the distance from the origin to the point on the scale axis where it is orthogonal to the projection from the $i$-point; $x$, $y$, and $z$ are coordinates on the centroid factor axes for the $i$-point; and $\alpha$, $\beta$, and $\gamma$ are the coefficients which determine the position of the scale axis in the three-dimensional factor space. Alpha, beta, and gamma are derived by trial and error, working with the factor matrix. A reasonably close first approximation for the values of these weights is suggested by an examination of two-dimensional plots (viz., as in Figure 3) of the configuration of $i$-points in the factor space. It should be noted that the same coefficients are also the reference axis coordinates for the positive terminus of the scale axes in Figure 3. It is not assumed that the positions in which the scale axes have been placed constitute a uniquely "best" fit to the configuration of $i$-points; but it is assumed that the positions defined in Table 6, as computed by the use of Equation (3) and shown in Figure 3, are an appropriate and approximately correct solution. One way to conceptualize this question is to think of a cone which intercepts a small circular area on the surface of a unit sphere; all axes lying within the cone are so positioned that the coefficients, which determine the position of each axis, will array along the axis the projections from $i$-points so as to produce the same set of rankings of the justices as will be produced by any other axis within the cone.

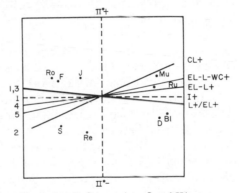

Figure 3a: Reference Axes I and II*

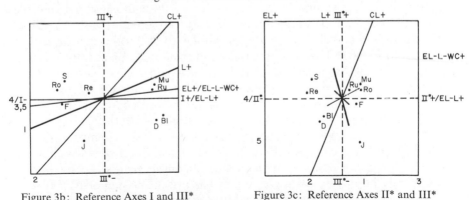

Figure 3b: Reference Axes I and III*     Figure 3c: Reference Axes II* and III*

Figure 3. Scale Axes and the Judicial Point Configuration in the
Orthogonal Factor Space

**Table 7. Judicial Correlations with Scale Axes**

| Justices | Scale Axes | | | | |
| | L 1 | CL 2 | EL 3 | EL-L 4 | EL-L-WC 5 |
|---|---|---|---|---|---|
| Mu | .66 | .62 | .66 | .69 | .72 |
| Ru | .62 | .51 | .63 | .65 | .65 |
| Bl | .67 | .32 | .79 | .77 | .71 |
| D | .56 | .15 | .69 | .67 | .60 |
| S | −.37 | −.28 | −.46 | −.57 | −.57 |
| Re | −.13 | −.30 | −.16 | −.25 | −.29 |
| F | −.57 | −.37 | −.59 | −.55 | −.53 |
| J | −.49 | −.53 | −.36 | −.26 | −.28 |
| Ro | −.58 | −.27 | −.65 | −.61 | −.57 |

Figure 3 shows the set of two-dimensional plots of the five scale axes in relationship to the point configuration determined for the centroid factor space. The orthogonal projections on the scale axes from the points, in the three-dimensional space, are given in Table 7 as distances from the origin on the scale axes. In Figure 3a, the L axis is almost parallel to reference axis I; and in these two dimensions, the first centroid factor is a good approximation of the liberalism axis. The L and EL axes coincide in the first two dimensions, and the subvariables of EL (EL-L and EL-L-WC) lie between EL and CL. In Figure 3b, the CL axis lies almost equally spaced between reference axes I and III*, while EL is again almost parallel to I, and L now appears as the centroid between CL and EL. In these first and third dimensions, EL-L coincides with I, while EL-L-WC coincides with EL. Since our three dimensions define a space corresponding to a cube, Figure 3c shows the "end-on" view, and confirms the impressions that one gets from the top view of Figure 3a and the side view of Figure 3b. In accordance with our theory, the L axis should be positioned as the three-dimensional centroid of the CL and the EL axes, and this is clearly seen to be the case. The EL-L and EL-L-WC axes should be almost parallel to each other and in such a relation to EL that, if other subvariables of economic liberalism were identified and plotted as scale axes, the EL axis would appear as the centroid of the set of such axes; the relationship among the three EL axes shown certainly is consistent with such an interpretation. Moreoever, the EL-L-WC axis is the closest of the three economic liberalism axes to the CL axis, which is tantamount to saying that the issue raised by claims to compensation by injured workers is closer to the general set of civil liberties issues than are the rights of labor or issues of economic liberalism generally. This finding is not only intuitively plausible, but it has also been supported by other research which suggests that judicial attitudes toward workmen's compensation claims are an excellent index to more generalized attitudes toward liberalism (Schubert 1959: 129–142).

The most striking finding suggested by Table 7 is that this set of Supreme Court justices was clearly partitioned into liberal and conservative subsets: Murphy, Rutledge, Black, and Douglas are positively correlated, and the remaining justices are negatively correlated, with all five of the scale axes. Murphy and Rutledge evince the greatest sympathy for claims of civil liberty, while Black and Douglas are the strongest supporters of economic liberalism. Black is the justice most favorable to the claims of labor and economic liberalism generally, while Murphy is most favorable to civil liberties. Among the conservative justices, Reed is the most favorable on the EL scales, while Roberts is the most conservative justice in his attitudes toward issues of economic liberalism. All of these findings correspond very well to Pritchett's findings (Table 5). If Pritchett's scales are used as norms, most justices are appropriately spaced on the scale axes although the mean absolute variance is least for the L axis, slightly greater and equal for the CL and EL axes, and considerably larger for the two axes which represent subvariables of EL. The correspondence between paired rankings, however, is much closer.

## A Correlational Test of the Theory

Table 8 shows the rank correlations for the five pairs of scales and scale axes. Of the total of seven inconsistencies, two are in the ranks on the L axis, because of the Murphy-Black and Jackson-Stone reversals. These are trivial, however, because Murphy and Black are almost tied on the L axis, and Jackson and Stone are almost tied on the L scale. Murphy and Black are again reversed, as are Rutledge and Douglas, on the labor axis, although

**Table 8.  Correlation of Judicial Ranks on Scales and Scale Axes**

| Variables | L 1 | | CL 2 | | EL 3 | | EL-L 4 | | EL-L WC 5 | |
|---|---|---|---|---|---|---|---|---|---|---|
| Rankings based on table | 2 | 4 | 2 | 4 | 2 | 4 | 2 | 4 | 2 | 4 |
| *Justices* | | | | | | | | | | |
| Mu | 1 | 2* | 1 | 1 | 2.5 | 3 | 1 | 2* | 2.5 | 1 |
| Ru | 3.5 | 3 | 2 | 2 | 4 | 4 | 3 | 4* | 2.5 | 3 |
| Bl | 2 | 1 | 3 | 3 | 1 | 1 | 2 | 1 | 2.5 | 2 |
| D | 3.5 | 4 | 4 | 4 | 2.5 | 3 | 4 | 3 | 2.5 | 4 |
| S | 7 | 6 | 5 | 6 | 8 | 7 | 8 | 8 | 8 | 8 |
| Re | 5 | 5 | 9 | 7* | 5 | 5 | 5 | 5 | 6 | 6 |
| F | 8 | 8 | 6 | 8 | 6 | 8* | 7 | 7 | 7 | 7 |
| J | 6 | 7* | 7 | 9 | 7 | 6 | 6 | 6 | 5 | 5 |
| Ro | 9 | 9 | 8 | 5* | 9 | 9 | 9 | 9 | 9 | 9 |
| Rank correlation coefficient (tau) | .873 | | .722 | | .873 | | .889 | | .913 | |
| Significance level, 1-tailed (p) | <.00043 | | .00290 | | <.00043 | | .00012 | | .00043 | |

* Inconsistent rankings.

these are also trivial inconsistencies, since Murphy and Black are practically tied on the labor scale, and Rutledge and Douglas are almost tied on both the scale and the axis. Both Reed and Roberts are inconsistently ranked on the CL axis, because of their relatively low negative loadings; and Frankfurter's rank on the EL axis is inconsistent because of his high negative loading. Otherwise, the rankings on the axes are all consistent with the rankings on the corresponding scales.

The correlations are remarkably high, ranging from .72 to .91; and the probabilities associated with these coefficients are all less than three chances in a thousand. In other words, if one were to plot Pritchett's scales against $i$-point configurations in three dimensions, the coordinates for which were drawn from tables of random numbers, he would have to repeat the experiment hundreds of times before he could expect to encounter as high a positive correlation for any one pair of rankings; and of course, the odds against replicating by chance as good a fit for all five pairs of rankings are considerably higher.

It seemed preferable to avoid tied ranks; consequently Table 8 shows no ties in the axis ranks, and there are only the few that Pritchett reported in the scale ranks. However, it is obvious that the error variance in either set of measurements is sufficiently large so that one might reasonably consider all close scores in Tables 5 and 7 to be tied in rank. Defining "close" as a difference of less than .05, ten additional tied doubles and five tied triples are produced in the scale and axis rankings. The resulting rank correlations, however, are just as high as those reported above, ranging from .82 to .93, with the highest significance level being .002; so the error variance in both sets of rankings appears to be unsystematic. As a further check, Spearman rank correlation coefficients were also computed, for the pair rankings shown in Table 8; rho was higher than tau for CL (.817), and it was also higher for the other four sets of rankings, ranging from .94 to .97, with a significance level of .0041 for the CL coefficient and of less than .001 for the others.

It seems quite clear that the scales and their corresponding axes are very highly correlated, and it makes little difference which method of rank correlation is preferred for the measurement of the relationship. Moreover, the level of significance seems to be well within the limits of confidence usually accepted for attitudinal measurement. It seems reasonable to conclude that the justices voted as they did in the set of cases under examination because of their respective individual attitudes toward the liberal values that the cases evoked for decision. The centroid factor routine locates the $i$-points of justices as it does in the factor space primarily because of the differentials in the attitudes of the justices toward different aspects of liberalism. Of course, it is altogether likely, and related research in more recent terms of the Court (Schubert 1962b) confirms, that other values than those of liberalism are raised in cases for decision by the Court. But the liberalism values so predominated, in a quantitative as well as a qualitative sense, that they can well account for all but a small portion of the variance in the voting behavior of the justices during the two terms examined in this paper.

## IV. CONCLUSIONS

The purpose of this paper has been to suggest a theory of the voting behavior of Supreme Court justices, and to describe a method which can be used to provide a test of the theory. It is believed that the application of the theory and method to sets of factor data provided by Thurstone and Degan and attitudinal data provided by Pritchett has made possible a plausible solution to the problem of factorial interpretation that was left unresolved by the earlier study of Thurstone and Degan. It is also possible that the proposed combination of factor analysis and cumulative scaling, within a multidimensional composition model suggested by Coombs' theory of data, may prove to be of general interest to psychologists who are concerned with the empirical problem of measuring attitudinal differences among a small number of respondents who are presented with a large number of stimuli, under circumstances such that the group decision-making process is highly stylized and quite routine, and it is reasonable to suspect that the stimuli raise questions about a limited number of basic values toward which the respondents' attitudes are functions of consistently high levels of cognition.

# 5

# A Psychological Analysis of the Warren Court

**M**uch recent research in the decision-making of the United States Supreme Court has been characterized by a pronounced emphasis upon the invocation of sociopsychological theory (Spaeth 1961; Ulmer 1961a, 1961b) and statistical methods of data processing (Fisher 1960; Kort 1960b; Nagel 1960; Tanenhaus 1960) in lieu of exclusive reliance upon the legal-historical theory and methods typical of most research in this field of study. Symbolic of this development is the increasing tendency of political scientists to consider constitutional law as an aspect of political behavior as well as a branch of law, and correspondingly, to study the subject matter as judicial behavior. Naturally, this recent work has evinced a preoccupation with unidimensional analysis, since it is less complicated to work with one variable than with many, and the experience so gained no doubt is a prerequisite to multivariate study. Nevertheless, students who remain committed to the more traditional workways in constitutional law are quite right in insisting, as they do, that most Supreme Court cases raise what at least appear prima facie to be many issues for decision, and that their more subjective and impressionistic mode

This chapter was originally published, in slightly different form, as "The 1960 Term of the Supreme Court: a Psychological Analysis" in *American Political Science Review* 56 (March 1962): 90–107.

This article was prepared with the very substantial aid and assistance of the Center for Advanced Study in the Behavioral Sciences. In particular, I wish to acknowledge my indebtedness to John Gilbert, staff statistician, and to my colleague of the fellowship year 1960–1961, Professor Clyde Coombs of the Department of Psychology of the University of Michigan.

of analysis retains the great virtue of not oversimplifying the rich complexity of many Supreme Court cases to the extent that inescapably seems to be required by the newer theories and methods. Clearly, further advances in the behavioral study of Supreme Court decision-making depend upon the development of multidimensional models of Court action, which will make possible the observation and measurement of interrelationships among the significant major variables that in combination provide the basis for an adequate explanation of the manifest differences in the voting and opinion behavior of the justices.

The purpose of this article is to describe one such multidimensional model of the Court, and to explain its theory and application to the empirical data of the most recent session of the United States Supreme Court, which terminated only a month prior to the time when this was written. Substantively, the purpose is to demonstrate that the psychological approach to be proposed leads to more significant, more comprehensible, and more valid insights into the political behavior of the Supreme Court than seem to be provided by the case-by-case approach—an approach that attempts to realize the same ends by the quite different means of a series of précis upon what are inevitably (since there must be some space limitations in professional journals) a fraction of the hundred-odd cases that the Court decides nonunanimously on the merits each term. The specific hypothesis to be tested is that most of the *variance* in the voting behavior of the justices can be accounted for by the differences in their individual attitudes toward a small number of fundamental issues of public policy. These public policy issues constitute the variables of this study.

## I. A BRIEF DESCRIPTION OF THE MODEL

Since both a general statement of the theory (Schubert 1961$a$, 1962$d$) and a technical description of the method (Schubert 1962$a$) have been published elsewhere, only the essentials needed for comprehension of the substantive findings will be presented here. In accordance with modern psychometric theory (Coombs 1964: chaps. 1, 11, 12; Coombs and Kao 1960; Guilford 1961), which generalizes the basic stimulus-response point relationship, Supreme Court cases are treated as raw psychological data which embody the choices of the individual justices among a variety of stimuli. Each case before the Court for decision is conceptualized as being represented by a stimulus ($j$) point, which is located somewhere in a psychological space of the relevant dimensions, depending upon the number and intensity of issues that it raises. The combination of the attitudes of each justice toward these same issues also may be represented by an ideal ($i$) point, located in the same psychological space. In each decision of the Court, what is observed is the relationship between the $i$-point of each justice and the $j$-point for the case. The relationship that is measured is one of dominance; that is, whether the position of the $i$-point in the dimensions that define the space equals or exceeds, or is less than, the position of the $j$-point in these dimensions. Technically, an individual-compensatory composition model (Torgersen 1958:352–359; Coombs 1964:chap. 12) is assumed: for an $i$-point to dominate a $j$-point, it is not essential that the individual equal or exceed the stimulus on *all* of the relevant dimensions, since an individual may (in appropriate instances) be able to compensate for his deficiency on one (or more) dimensions by an excess on other dimensions. To take a specific example, let us assume a simple two-dimensional space, where the relevant dimensions are judicial attitudes toward "civilian control over the military" and "stare decisis." A justice like Clark, whose attitude toward the civilian control variable was relatively negative or unsympathetic, might nevertheless be induced to vote in support of this value in a particular decision, because his relatively positive attitude toward stare decisis might lead him to follow a recent precedent, even though he had disagreed with the decision establishing it. Thus, his deficiency (in relationship to the degree of support for civil liberties demanded by the later case) might be compensated for by his strongly pro-stare decisis views. Conversely, a justice like Frankfurter, whose attitude toward civilian control was more positive than Clark's, might nevertheless vote against this value because of his slight regard for the value of stare decisis.[1]

Next let us consider the conjoint relationship between the $i$-points of all nine justices, assuming full participation in the decision, and a particular $j$-point. Obviously, how the case will be decided will depend upon whether a majority or a minority of the $i$-points dominate the $j$-point. If a majority of $i$-points dominate, then the value or values raised by the case will be upheld or supported by the decision "of the Court"; and if, to the contrary, the $j$-point dominates a majority of the $i$-points, then the value or values raised by the case will be rejected—"the Court" will refuse to support them. To take a concrete example, let us assume the general value "civil liberty," and the specific question whether "the Fourteenth Amendment requires" the Supreme Court to reverse a state court conviction of a criminal defendant, based in part upon evidence procured as the result of an unreasonable search or seizure. According to the theory proposed, it would be assumed that the $i$-points of no more than three justices dominated the $j$-point representing this issue at the time of the decision in *Wolf* v. *Colorado*, and that no more than four did so throughout the following decade. As a consequence of Stewart's appointment and of Black's explicitly avowed shift in attitude toward this issue, a majority of $i$-points did dominate when the issue arose once again for disposition in *Mapp* v. *Ohio*, a decision announced on the closing decision day of the 1960 Term; and consequently, *Wolf* v. *Colorado* was overruled. Actually, the voting division in *Mapp* v. *Ohio* was 6–3, with Clark both supplying the extra favorable vote and writing the opinion of the Court; Clark's position should

---

1. See *Kinsella* v. *Singleton*, *Grisham* v. *Hagan*, *McElroy* v. *Guagliardo*, and *Wilson* v. *Bohlender*, all decided January 18, 1960. Cf. Schubert 1963c.

have occasioned no surprise, however, because it was in precise accord with the intention that he had announced seven years earlier when concurring in *Irvine* v. *California*. Clark considered himself bound by the *Wolf* precedent unless and until a majority could be formed that would agree to overrule that decision—an event that was forestalled for several more years, apparently, by Black's idiosyncratic blind spot for the Fourth Amendment.

We can now consider an operational definition of the Court's decision-making. In one dimension, the voting division of the Court is precisely determined by the intersection of the *j*-point with a line along which are arrayed the *i*-points of the justices. (This definition, it should be noted, is the one which applies for cumulative [or Guttman] scaling of Supreme Court cases.) In two dimensions, a decision is determined by the line orthogonal to the *j*-point vector; all justices whose *i*-points fall on the orthogonal line, or beyond it (in the positive direction of the variable) will vote in support of the value, and the remaining justices whose *i*-points lie on the negative side of the line will vote to reject it; while unanimous decisions occur, of course, when all *i*-points lie on, or on the positive side of, the orthogonal line, or else when all *i*-points lie on the negative side of this line. In three dimensions, the decision is determined by the plane which intersects the space orthogonally to the *j*-point vector; and more generally, in *r*-dimensions by a hyperplane of $r - 1$ dimensionality which intersects the *r*-dimensional space in a similar manner.

Thus, we conceive of both *i*-points representing the composite attitudes of individual justices, and *j*-points, representing the composite issues raised by individual cases, as sets of vectors terminating in points, each with a unique position in the same psychological space. Hereinafter we shall assume that this space is three-dimensional, since we shall work in three-space in the empirical application which follows. Cases in a set which raises questions of differing degrees of valuation about the same variable (e.g., sympathy for the constitutional claims of the right to counsel in state criminal trials) are located at various points in the space, but in an approximately linear relationship to each other; thus, each such point may be conceived of as lying upon or near a scale axis, representing the subvariable, which transects the space. Through the centroid of a set of scale axes, representing a set of civil liberties subvariables, would pass an axis representing a broadly defined heterogeneous major variable (such as "all civil liberties" issues for a given term); and this scale axis would follow the trace of the mean of the projections from all of the relevant *j*-points. But the *i*-points also project upon any scale axis; and therefore, a one-dimensional solution for the Court's decision-making function may be achieved by measuring the relationship between the projections from *j*-points and from *i*-points upon a scale axis representing any variable that is of interest. This, in effect, is precisely what is happening, in theory, when an analyst constructs a cumulative scale of a set of decisions that are postulated as pertaining to a single dominant variable, and positions the scale as an axis in the space. It is apparent that if the model is adapted for analysis invoking this particular definition of the decision-making function, as we shall do in the discussion which follows, the Court's decision-making is still being measured in unidimensional terms. But the model itself is multidimensional and, as we shall demonstrate, makes possible measurement of the interrelationship among several variables within a common frame of reference; and moreover, there is every reason to suppose that further research, and subsequent work with the model, will lead to the development of mathematical refinements corresponding to the multidimensional conceptions of the decision-making function given in the operational definition above.

In order to utilize the model that has been described, what we require are procedures to locate both $i$-points and $j$-points in three-dimensional space, and to measure the dominance relationship for any dyad, with each dyad consisting of a $j$-point and an $i$-point. Factor analysis affords a readily available technique for locating the set of $i$-points for a given set of decisions, such as a term of the Court, in a fixed spatial configuration. But the raw data come in a form that preclude the use of factor analysis, at least in the same manner, in order to locate the $j$-points. The reason for this is that, in a typical recent term, the Court divides in about a hundred decisions on the merits. Consequently it is possible to make a relatively large number of observations— about one hundred—of the location of a relatively small number of $i$-points— never more than nine. But more than nine observations of the location of any specific $j$-point are never possible, because there are never more than nine votes recorded in a single case. One hundred observations are ample to locate the $i$-points, by factor analytic techniques, with considerable precision; but nine observations are far too few to permit the same thing to be done for $j$-points. As we shall exemplify presently, factor analysis is essentially a statistical method for breaking down a correlation matrix into its principal component elements; and it can never be more reliable than the matrix upon which it works. No single Supreme Court decision contains enough votes to allow the computation of reliable correlation coefficients. If we had a hundred justices participating in the decision of each of, say, a dozen cases in the typical term, factor analysis could serve very well to locate a configuration of $j$-points, but it would then be incapable of locating the $i$-points. If there were a hundred justices participating in the decision of a hundred or more cases in each term, factor analysis could be used to locate both types of points with what ought to be good precision. This implies that the model here described may very well find application for study of the attitudes of United States senators or for state legislators, as well as for other smaller decision-making groups like the Supreme Court.

Although it is not possible to locate $j$-points in the space as precisely as $i$-points, at least by factor analysis, it is possible to locate *sets* of $j$-points in the same space with the $i$-points. This is done by cumulative scaling of sets of cases. Each cumulative scale measures the one-dimensional alignment of the

attitudes of the justices toward a single variable. If most of the Court's decisions can be associated with a set of cumulative scales, and if the set of scales
can be passed through the space as axes in such a way that the projections
from the *i*-points on the scale axes are consistent with the alignments of the
justices on the cumulative scales, then it will be assumed that the scale axes
are indeed the counterparts of their analogue cumulative scales; and that the
variance in the voting behavior of the justices is adequately accounted for by
the manifest differences in the attitudes of the justices toward the cumulative
scale variables. The procedure for fitting scales in the factor space will be
explained in greater detail in connection with specific empirical data, in a
later section of this article.

## II. THE UNIVERSE OF RAW DATA

The sample of decisions to be analyzed consists of all cases in which the
Supreme Court divided on the merits during the period of the 1960 Term,
which extended from October 10, 1960, through June 19, 1961. Both formal
and per curiam decisions accordingly are included, but unanimous and jurisdictional decisions were excluded. As Table 9 indicates, almost three-fourths
of the Court's formal decisions were reached over the disagreement of one or
more justices, while this was true of less than one-fourth of the per curiam
decisions. These results were in line with previous experience. It has not been
unusual either, in recent years, for the justices to disagree in a majority of their
decisions on the merits, as they did during the 1960 Term. The average annual
number of split decisions over the past fifteen terms was 97, and the average
number of unanimous decisions on the merits was 79; in this respect, the
1960 Term was quite typical.

### Table 9. Summary of Decisions on the Merits, 1960 Term

| Decision | Formal | Per curiam | Totals |
|----------|--------|------------|--------|
| Split | 87 | 12 | 99 |
| Unanimous | 34 | 41 | 75 |
| Totals | 121 | 53 | 174 |

For purposes of this study, each *case*, to which the Court had assigned a
unique docket number and for which the Court had made a disposition on
the merits, was a unit for voting analysis. As a unit of content, the docketed
case offers the advantages of being specifically and uniquely identifiable, and
of providing what with very rare exceptions is an unambiguous basis for
voting attribution which can readily be replicated by other analysts. (Those
familiar with earlier studies of judicial voting behavior will recognize that
some scholars have worked with less explicit units of measurement, such as

the "opinion of the Court" or the "decision" of the Court.) There are also disadvantages to the use of the case as a unit, but none relevant to the empirical data with which we presently are concerned.

For each case, one set of nine votes was counted. In each of eleven cases, one justice did not participate in the decision on the merits; and in one other, two justices did not. There were also two Federal Employers' Liability Act evidentiary cases and one Jones Act case in which Frankfurter, according to his custom (Schubert 1962c), persisted in jurisdictional dissent at the time when his colleagues voted on the merits; these three jurisdictional dissents were classified as nonparticipations, for purposes of the present analysis. Eight votes could not be specified, in one case in which the Court divided equally, without opinion. After these nonparticipations and unspecifiable votes were deducted, a total of 867 votes remained; they constituted the basis for the factor analysis and the cumulative scaling.

## III. THE FACTOR ANALYSIS

### Computation of the Correlation Matrix

The initial task in any factor analysis is the construction of a correlation matrix. In the present study, the correlation matrix was based upon a set of fourfold tables which, in turn, were constructed directly from the 867 votes just described. These votes were tabulated to show the totals of agreement and disagreement with the majority, in the decision of each case, for every pair of justices. For any such pair, each case holds five possibilities: (1) both may agree in the majority; (2) both may agree in dissent; (3) the first member of the pair may vote with the majority, while the second dissents; (4) the second member of the pair may vote with the majority, while the first dissents; or (5) either or both members may fail to participate, in which event there is no score for the pair for that case. In the tabulation of votes for the factor analysis, no attention is paid to the substantive variables to which the decisions relate; the sole criterion for the attribution of votes in each case is agreement or disagreement with the majority.

It is most convenient to arrange the summary tabulation of agreement-disagreement, for each judicial dyad, in the form of a fourfold table such as Table 10. The table shows that Black and Douglas dissented together 29 times; this dis/dis $(-/-)$ cell is the one that contains the kind of information utilized in some earlier studies (Pritchett 1948; Schubert 1959) of "dissenting blocs" of the Court. Similarly, Black and Douglas agreed in 70 of these 98 sets of votes; this is the sum of the major or positive diagonal (i.e., the $+/+$ and the $-/-$ cells), and this is the kind of information that was the basis for the "interagreement" bloc analysis of the studies just cited. The weakness of these earlier approaches was that, by concentrating upon the *agreement* between pairs of justices, the analysts ignored what is at least an equally important

**Table 10. Fourfold Table of Agreement-Disagreement, Douglas-Black, 1960 Term**

| | | Black | | |
|---|---|---|---|---|
| | | + | − | *Totals* |
| Douglas | + | 41 | 5 | 46 |
| | − | 23 | 29 | 52 |
| Totals | | 64 | 34 | 98 |

NOTE. The total of joint votes counted for this dyad is 98 rather than 99, although both Black and Douglas participated in all split decisions on the merits during this term, because of the lack of any objective basis for identifying the partition of the votes in the one case, already noted, in which the Court divided equally.

aspect of judicial voting behavior, that is, the *ways in which justices disagree.* Table 10, for instance, shows that not only did Douglas and Black disagree in over a fourth of these decisions, they tended to disagree in a particular way. In over 80 percent of these instances of disagreement, it was Douglas who dissented while Black adhered to the majority. This finding certainly suggests that Douglas was more extreme in his dissenting behavior than Black (or, as we shall observe presently in Table 11, than any other member of the Court during this term). Moreover, the correlation coefficients, which are computed from the fourfold tables, are very sensitive to how votes are partitioned between the two cells of a diagonal, as well as to differences between the diagonals.

In order to measure precisely the relationship among the four cells of a fourfold table, phi correlation coefficients are computed.[2] In the correlation

2. The phi coefficient is an approximation of the Pearsonian *r* correlation coefficient, and is appropriate to use when, as here, the two distributions to be correlated reflect a genuine dichotomy. The phi coefficient is relatively simple to compute: it is the ratio of the difference of the cross-products of the diagonals of a fourfold table, to the square root of the product of the marginals. For the data of Table 10,

$$r_\phi = \frac{(41 \cdot 29) - (23 \cdot 5)}{[(46) \cdot (52) \cdot (64) \cdot (34)]^{1/2}}$$
$$= \frac{1189 - 115}{(5204992)^{1/2}} \qquad (1)$$
$$= + \frac{1074}{2281.445} = + .471.$$

Evidently, the sign of the coefficient depends upon which diagonal cross-product is the larger; or, in other words, upon whether or not a pair of justices agree more often than they disagree, and *also* upon whether they agree both in assent and in dissent, i.e. whether their disagreement is divided equally or disproportionately between the cells of the diagonals. The maximum range of the phi coefficient is from +1 to −1; but these limits rarely are attained empirically, since the maximum size of phi is a function of the distribution of the marginals, and can be ± 1 only when all four marginal frequencies are equal. See Cureton 1959:89–91.

maxtrix shown in Table 11, phi ranges from +.745 (for Harlan and Frank-furter) to −.602 (for Douglas and Harlan). Harlan, therefore, was the most extreme justice in the range of his agreement and disagreement; and he voted most frequently the same as Frankfurter, and least often in agreement with Douglas.

Since there are nine justices on the Court, there are fourfold tables and correlation coefficients for each of thirty-six dyads.[3] For purposes of this study, all data were placed on punch cards, and both the computation of phi coefficients and the factor analysis were programmed for computer analysis.[4] Since both matrices are symmetrical, and in order to conserve space, Table 11 presents the fourfold tables above the major diagonal, and the correlation coefficients below.

Before turning to the results of the factor analysis of the correlation matrix, some interesting findings may be observed from a mere inspection of Table 11. The most obvious is the sharp demarcation of the justices into what appear to be two opposing blocs. Douglas, Black, Warren, and Brennan all correlate positively with each other, and negatively with the five remaining justices. With the exception of Stewart's marginally negative correlation with Clark, these remaining five justices—Frankfurter, Harlan, Whittaker, Clark, and Stewart—all correlate positively with each other, and negatively with the first group. Stewart clearly was the most independent member of the Court in his voting behavior: his highest correlation with any other justice, in either direction, was less than .35; and his voting was almost perfectly inde-pendent, statistically, from what are otherwise the most marginal members of each group, since his correlation was approximately −.03 with both Brennan and Clark. As the fourfold tables indicate, Black and Warren often dissented together, as did Frankfurter and Harlan also; but neither Black nor Warren ever joined either Frankfurter or Harlan in dissent. It is obvious that these two pairs of justices, and the respective groups with which each tended to associate, were in pretty sharp and basic disagreement over something; and unless we are prepared to accept the somewhat fatuous notion that they couldn't get together over the meaning or application of the principle of stare decisis, as some students of the Court seem to believe (Kort 1960a), then it may not be implausible to entertain the hypothesis that these groups may

---

3. When factor analysis is performed by hand use of a calculator instead of utilizing a com-puter program, it is necessary to arrange the correlation coefficients in the form of a square sym-metrical matrix, with the major diagonal filled with the estimates of the highest communality for each justice. For the techniques of factor analysis the interested reader is referred to any of the several standard works on this subject, e.g. Fruchter 1954; Cattell 1952; Thurstone 1947.

4. I am indebted to John P. Gilbert for developing a program for the computation of the phi coefficients, and also one for the computation of the factorial distances discussed in the final section of this paper. The computer program for the IBM 650 utilized was *Centroid Factor Anal-ysis*, Ident. No. SU-4524, written by Jonathan E. Robbins (April 1957), developed and tested by the Watson Scientific Computing Laboratory, Columbia University, and modified by Mr. Gilbert, Center for Advanced Study in the Behavioral Sciences, Stanford (multilithed).

## Table 11. Fourfold Tables and Phi Correlation Matrix, 1960 Term

| | D | Bl ( + − ) | Wa ( + − ) | Br ( + − ) | S ( + − ) | C ( + − ) | Wh ( + − ) | F ( + − ) | H ( + ) |
|---|---|---|---|---|---|---|---|---|---|
| D | | +41 5 / −23 29 | 42 4 / 31 21 | 44 2 / 33 19 | 31 14 / 43 6 | 23 22 / 51 1 | 20 26 / 45 7 | 16 23 / 47 3 | 20 25 / 50 1 |
| Bl | .471 | | +61 3 / −12 22 | 58 6 / 19 15 | 41 19 / 33 1 | 40 23 / 34 0 | 32 32 / 33 1 | 31 26 / 32 0 | 37 26 / 33 0 |
| Wa | .363 | .655 | | +69 4 / − 8 17 | 51 18 / 23 2 | 50 22 / 24 1 | 41 32 / 24 1 | 39 26 / 24 0 | 45 26 / 25 0 |
| Br | .392 | .403 | .664 | | +57 16 / −17 4 | 55 21 / 19 2 | 45 32 / 20 1 | 44 25 / 19 1 | 49 26 / 21 0 |
| S | −.230 | −.337 | −.195 | −.029 | | +56 18 / −15 4 | 52 22 / 11 9 | 51 15 / 10 9 | 56 17 / 11 8 |
| C | −.551 | −.410 | −.273 | −.175 | .031 | | +56 18 / − 9 14 | 55 14 / 8 11 | 59 14 / 11 12 |
| Wh | −.455 | −.474 | −.367 | −.319 | .133 | .331 | | +51 12 / −12 14 | 53 11 / 17 15 |
| F | −.578 | −.481 | −.390 | −.287 | .228 | .343 | .348 | | +58 5 / − 4 20 |
| H | −.602 | −.441 | −.362 | −.322 | .171 | .317 | .315 | .745 | |

NOTE: The justices are coded as follows: D (Douglas), Bl (Black), Wa (Warren), Br (Brennan), S (Stewart), C (Clark), Wh (Whittaker), F (Frankfurter), H (Harlan).

have been in disagreement about the social, economic, and political values that the Court upholds in its decisions.

### The Factor Loadings

The initial product of a factor analysis is a set of derived correlations (or "loadings," as they customarily are called) which purport to measure the extent to which each element, of whatever has been associated in the correlation matrix, is related to the components or dimensions into which the basic correlation matrix has been broken down. In the present study, the elements are the justices, and the factor loadings purport to express the correlation of each justice with the basic underlying dimensions of the phi matrix. Although it is technically possible to extract as many factors as there are elements intercorrelated in the phi matrix—nine, in the instant case—only six factors actually were computed, and of these, only three will be used for purposes of testing the principal hypothesis. The reason for so limiting the number of factors is twofold: (1) the residual matrix, representing the amount of variance unaccounted for by the first three factors, was very small, and less, indeed, than the estimated error variance; and (2) most readers of the *American Political Science Review* are accustomed to thinking in terms of three-dimensional space, and three factors can be given a Euclidean graphical representation with accords with the spatial intuitions, and therefore the comprehension, of most readers.

The usual procedure in factor analysis is to rotate the orthogonal factor axes, which are the direct product of a complete centroid routine, to oblique positions that are presumed to correspond to some criterion related to empirical reality, and thus to make possible a more meaningful psychological interpretation than would usually be possible if the orthogonal axes were retained.[5] The orthogonal axes have not been rotated in the present study, but for the reason that, contrary to the usual procedure, no reliance is placed upon the association of substantive meaning with the factors. Substantive meaning is associated, instead, with the scale axes which are passed through the space defined by the orthogonal factor axes; and thus the scale axes— which are oblique—perform the same function, for purposes of interpretation, that is usually accomplished by rotation of the orthogonal axes. The orthogonal axes are used, therefore, only as a set of reference axes to define the three-dimensional space in which the $i$-points of the justices and the $j$-points of the cases are located. And the factor loadings, shown in Table 12, function as Cartesian coordinates which locate the $i$-points of the justices in the factor space.

Factor loadings can vary, in principle, from $+1$ to $-1$; in practice, their variance is bounded by the extremity of the correlation coefficients upon which they are based. It will be observed that, on the average, the highest loadings (both positive and negative) are on the first factor, and that the mean magnitude of the third factor loadings is smallest. This is inherent in the centroid routine, which assumes that the first factor, to which the largest portion of the variance is attributed, is the most important factor, and so on. The loadings on the first factor range from a high of approximately $+.77$, for Black, to a low of $-.74$, for Frankfurter. Evidently, the justices are partitioned on the first factor into the same two groups that were manifest in the phi matrix; but evidently also the groupings on the second and third factors are quite different. Mere inspection of the factor matrix of Table 12 suggests that the multidimensional relationships among the justices are going to be

---

5. Perhaps it should be noted, for the benefit of readers not familiar with the method, that orthogonal axes are statistically independent, while oblique axes are correlated with each other; therefore, making a factor interpretation based directly upon a system of orthogonal axes implies an assumption that there is no relationship among the factors, which must be conceived to be independent of each other. Applied to the present data, this would involve the assumption that there was no relationship, at least in the minds of the justices, among the major issues of public policy toward which they responded in their voting.

**Table 12. Factor Loadings for Judicial Ideal-Points, 1960 Term**

| Justices | Factors | | |
|:---:|:---:|:---:|:---:|
| | I | II | III |
| D | .754 | .283 | .170 |
| Bl | .769 | −.259 | −.130 |
| Wa | .699 | −.456 | .089 |
| Br | .578 | −.298 | .291 |
| S | −.289 | .126 | .363 |
| Wh | −.571 | .065 | −.108 |
| H | −.714 | −.373 | .226 |
| F | −.736 | −.338 | .270 |
| C | −.519 | −.245 | −.309 |

somewhat different, and certainly more complex, than the simple bifurcation of a single dimension which will account for much, but not enough, of the variance in the voting behavior of the justices. For a fuller understanding than a single dimension—even when it is overwhelmingly the most important one—can afford, we must turn to an examination of relationships made possible by work with the three-dimensional factor space.

## IV. THE CUMULATIVE SCALES

Cumulative scaling is a research operation completely independent of the factor analysis, and so may be undertaken before, at the same time, or after the factor analysis is completed. In cumulative (or Guttman) scaling, the same universe of raw data is used as for the factor analysis. But instead of tabulating votes by dyads and in terms of agreement with the majority, for scaling purposes votes are tabulated by cases, and are classified as being either in support of, or in opposition to, certain defined scale variables. The variables employed here were identified on the basis of experimental work in previous terms of the Warren Court. The basic procedures for cumulative scaling have been discussed elsewhere (Schubert 1959:270–290), although the format of Figures 4–6, below, differs somewhat in the presentation of results.

Consistent votes in support of the scale variable are denoted by the symbol x, and inconsistent positive votes by x. A blank space indicates a consistent negative vote, and the symbol − is used to signify an inconsistent negative vote. An asterisk signifies nonparticipation. Scale scores are simple functions of scale positions, and a justice's scale position is defined as being fixed by his last consistent positive vote. Where one or more nonparticipations separate a justice's consistent positive and negative votes, his scale position is assumed to be at the midpoint of the nonparticipation or nonparticipations, since it cannot be determined how he might have voted. A justice's scale score is computed by the formula:

$$s = \frac{2p}{n} - 1, \tag{2}$$

where $s$ is his score, $p$ his scale position, and $n$ equals the number of cases in the scale. Scale scores, like correlation coefficients and factor loadings, can range in value from $+1$ to $-1$, with the significant difference in practice that

### 1960 Term, C Scale

*Justices*

| Cases | D | Bl | Wa | Br | S | Wh | F | H | C | Totals |
|-------|---|----|----|----|----|----|----|----|----|--------|
| 5/762 | x | | | | | | | | | 1–8 |
| 6/308 | x | | | | | | | | | 1–8 |
| 6/420 | x | | | | | | | | | 1–8 |
| 6/582 | x | | | | | | | | | 1–8 |
| 4778 : 200 | x | x | | | | | | | | 2–7 |
| 5/265 | x | x | | | | | | * | | 2–6 |
| 4/507 | — | x | x | | | | | | | 2–7 |
| 4/611 | — | x | x | | | | | | | 2–7 |
| 5/458 | x | — | x | | | | | | | 2–7 |
| 4/388 | x | x | x | | | | | | | 3–6 |
| 3370 : 685 | x | x | x | | | | | | | 3–6 |
| 4839 : 122 | x | x | x | | | | | | | 3–6 |
| 5/381 | x | — | x | x | | | | | | 3–6 |
| 4/372 | x | x | x | x | | | | | | 4–5 |
| 4/426 | x | x | x | x | | | | | | 4–5 |
| 5/43 | x | x | x | x | | | | | | 4–5 |
| 5/301 : 70 | x | x | x | x | | | | | | 4–5 |
| 5/301 : 179 | x | x | x | x | | | | | | 4–5 |
| 5/399 | x | x | x | x | | | | | | 4–5 |
| 5/431 | x | x | x | x | | | | | | 4–5 |
| 6/36 | x | x | x | x | | | | | | 4–5 |
| 6/82 | x | x | x | x | | | | | | 4–5 |
| 6/117 | x | x | x | x | | | | | | 4–5 |
| 4581 : 1 | x | x | x | x | | | | | | 4–5 |
| 4623 : 12 | x | x | x | x | | | | | | 4–5 |
| 4719 : 486 | x | x | x | x | | | | | | 4–5 |
| 6/617 | x | — | — | x | x | | | | | 3–6 |
| 6/599 | x | — | — | x | x | | X | | | 4–5 |
| 4/587 | x | x | x | — | x | | | | | 4–5 |
| 4/479 : 14 | x | x | x | x | x | | | | | 5–4 |
| 4/479 : 83 | x | x | x | x | x | | | | | 5–4 |
| 5/85 | x | x | x | x | x | | | | | 5–4 |
| 5/551 | x | x | x | x | x | | | | | 5–4 |
| 6/1 | x | x | x | x | x | | | | | 5–4 |
| 4694 : 233 | x | x | x | x | x | | | | | 5–4 |
| 4842 : 161 | x | x | x | x | x | | X | | | 6–3 |
| 5/715 | x | x | x | x | x | | | | X | 6–3 |
| 4798 : 236 | x | x | x | x | x | | | | X | 6–3 |
| 4/631 | x | x | x | x | x | x | | | | 6–3 |
| 5/312 | x | x | x | x | x | x | | | | 6–3 |
| 6/213 | x | x | x | x | x | x | | | | 6–3 |
| 6/418 | x | x | x | x | * | x | | | | 5–3 |
| 4703 : 238 | x | x | x | x | — | x | | | | 5–4 |

**1960 Term, C Scale (*cont.*)**

*Justices*

| Cases | D | Bl | Wa | Br | S | Wh | F | H | C | Totals |
|-------|---|----|----|----|----|----|----|----|----|--------|
| 4754 : 4 | x | x | x | x | x | x | | | x | 7–2 |
| 4577 : 669 | x | x | x | x | − | x | | | x | 6–3 |
| 4/350 | x | x | x | x | − | − | x | x | | 6–3 |
| 5/534 | x | x | x | x | − | x | x | x | | 7–2 |
| 4/454 | x | x | x | x | x | − | x | x | | 7–2 |
| 4687 : 181 | x | x | x | x | x | − | x | x | | 7–2 |
| 5/610 | x | x | x | x | x | x | x | x | | 8–1 |
| 5/167 | x | x | x | x | x | x | − | x | x | 8–1 |

|  |  |  |  |  |  |  |  |  |  | 221–236 |
|---|---|---|---|---|---|---|---|---|---|---------|
| Totals |  |  |  |  |  |  |  |  |  |  |
| Pros | 49 | 43 | 43 | 38 | 20 | 10 | 7 | 6 | 5 | 221 |
| Cons | 2 | 8 | 8 | 13 | 30 | 41 | 44 | 44 | 46 | 236 |
| Scale positions | 51 | 47 | 45 | 39 | 25 | 13 | 6 | 6 | 1 | |
| Scale scores | 1.00 | .84 | .76 | .53 | −.02 | −.49 | −.76 | −.76 | −.96 | |

$$R = 1 - \frac{22}{403} = .945 \qquad S = 1 - \frac{23}{79} = .709$$

---

NOTE: In Figures 4–6, cases are cited in either of two ways. Those decided prior to June 1961 are cited to the official *United States Reports:* the digit preceding the slash bar is the third digit of the volume number, and should be read as though preceded, in each case, by the digits 36; the number following the slash bar is the page cite; and if more than one case begins on the same page, a docket number follows the page cite, separated from it by a colon. Official citations are not available, at the time this is written, for cases decided during the final three weeks of the term; such cases are cited to Volume 29 of *United States Law Week, Supreme Court Section*, with a four-digit page number followed by the docket number.

Two coefficients appear at the bottom of each scale; they purport to measure the degree of consistency in the set of votes being scaled. R is Guttman's coefficient of reproducibility; .900 or better is conventionally accepted as evidence to support the hypothesis that a single dominant variable has motivated the voting behavior of the justices in the set of cases comprising the sample. S is Menzel's coefficient of scalability; it provides a more rigid standard than R, because S (unlike R) does not capitalize upon the spurious contribution to consistency that arises from the inclusion in the scale of either cases or justices with extreme marginal distributions. Menzel has suggested that the appropriate level of acceptance for S is "somewhere between .60 and .65"; the scales presented in Figures 4–6 are well above the suggested minimal levels of acceptability for both R and S. See Menzel (1953).

---

Figure 4. Judicial Attitudes toward Civil Liberties, 1960 Term

scale scores frequently attain these extreme values, reflecting the extremity of attitude of several of the justices in each of the scales shown in Figures 4–6.

## The C Scale

Figure 4 is a cumulative scale of the fifty-one civil liberties cases that the Court decided by divided votes on the merits during the 1960 Term. In content, the *C* variable was defined broadly to include all cases in which the primary issue involved a conflict between personal rights and claims to liberty, and governmental authority. The number of cases included in the scale—over half of the total—was somewhat larger than in other recent terms; but the ranking of justices on the scale was very similar to that of the 1959 Term, and precisely the same as in 1958, which was Stewart's first term on the Court.

The scale accords with common knowledge that Douglas, Black, Warren, and Brennan are more sympathetic to civil liberties claims than the other members of the present Court. But there are definite gradations among the attitudes of these four "libertarian" justices toward the civil liberties claims of this term, and the scale distance separating Douglas and Brennan is just as great as the scale distance separating Whittaker and Clark. The mean rate of support for civil liberties claims of the four justices with high positive scale scores (the liberals on this issue) is 85 percent; the mean rate of opposition for the four justices with high negative scale scores (the conservatives on this issue) is 86 percent. This differentiation of the Warren Court into a set of liberal justices and a much more conservative group agrees with Pritchett's findings (1954:227) for the Vinson Court, except that Frankfurter now appears as a conservative rather than as an exponent of "libertarian restraint."

It is certainly noteworthy that Douglas, over a wide range of specific issues, supported civil liberties claims in all except two out of fifty-one cases. His two inconsistent (and $C-$) votes both came in cases that raised technical questions of procedure relating to the statutory rights of federal criminal defendants, in cases where another variable ($J-$: Supreme Court deference to lower courts) also was present. Douglas was the only justice to dissent alone against $C-$ decisions of the Court; and his four solitary $C+$ dissents identify him as the justice most sympathetic to civil liberties claims. At the opposite extreme was Clark, who found only five civil liberties claims, out of the total of fifty-one, sufficiently persuasive to gain his vote. Moreover, four of Clark's five $C+$ votes were inconsistencies, suggesting that in these cases he may have been motivated by his attitudes toward other variables than $C$; there is, of course, little empirical basis for assuming that all justices perceive all issues raised by cases in the same way, or that any justice's voting behavior will be perfectly consistent. The Guttman model assumes that if in a particular scale most respondents are highly consistent most of the time, it is reasonable to infer that they are predominately motivated by their differential attachments to a common value. And it is in precise accord with the assumptions of the "individual-compensatory composition model," mentioned earlier, that a justice may, in some decisions, compensate for his lack of sympathy for, say, civil liberties by his strong attachment to other appropriate values that he may perceive to be present in the decisions. This theory seems to provide a plausible explanation for Clark's inconsistencies. His most inconsistent votes, for instance, came in two cases, Burton v. *Wilmington Parking Authority* and *Mapp*. v. *Ohio*, where he joined $C+$ majorities against the dissents of Harlan, Frankfurter, and Whittaker. The first case involved racial discrimination in a restaurant in a publicly owned building; and the second was the decision, already mentioned, which overruled *Wolf* v. *Colorado*. In both cases, Clark's strong attachment to stare decisis appeared to overcome his basically C— attitude sufficiently to cause him to support the majority, although such a consideration obviously did not forestall the more activist conservatives from voting as dictated by their convictions about libertarian claims.

The key decision-maker in C cases during the 1960 Term, however, was Stewart, whose propensity to function as the swing man in an otherwise well-balanced Court was sufficiently obvious to attract journalistic comment (*Time* 1961). Although Stewart tied with Clark for inconsistency with four such votes, he nevertheless voted consistently over 90 percent of the time, and his scale score of −.02 indicates the close balance of his voting on civil liberties issues. Stewart was in the majority far more often than any of his colleagues, dissenting in only seven of the fifty cases in which he participated; and in nineteen 5–4 decisions, Stewart's vote was determinative. Slightly less than half (43 percent) of the cases on the scale were decided C+, but the failure of the cases to break evenly cannot be attributed to Stewart. The division between C plus and minus decisions would have corresponded precisely to Stewart's scale position, except for the inconsistent negative votes of Black, Warren, and Brennan, in the bottom three C— cases near the middle of the scale. Brennan's inconsistency's is of no particular interest; it occurred in a routine case of statutory interpretation involving the imposition of multiple sentences upon a federal criminal defendant. But the Black and Warren inconsistencies appeared in two of the "Sunday Closing Law Cases," *Gallagher* v. *Crown Kosher Super Market* and *Braunfeld* v. *Brown*, both decided on May 29, 1961. Many dispassionate observers will agree that the Black and Warren votes in these cases to uphold the constitutionality of the Massachusetts and Pennsylvania "blue laws," which upheld the principle of majority transgression of both the religious and the economic claims of the defendants, were clearly illiberal; and the fact that such votes appear as inconsistencies in the C scale should enhance confidence in the proposition that the C scale provides an adequate general measure of the civil libertarian sympathies of the justices.

## The E Scale

One finding, which has resulted from applying the research approach of this paper to a much longer period—fifteen terms—has been that political scientists have been living with a somewhat distorted image of the Court during the past two decades. The pronounced emphasis upon the Court's civil liberties decisions,[6] reflecting, perhaps, the no-doubt laudable bias with

---

6. This emphasis is reflected, for example, in Pritchett 1954: viii, and in McCloskey 1962: 71–89. In his series of annual survey articles on constitutional law, published in the *American Political Science Review* during the decade 1952–1961, David Fellman allocates three-fourths of the approximate 370 pages, in which he discussed civil liberties, economic, and taxation issues, to what are here denominated C scale cases, and the remaining one-fourth to E and F scale cases.

which students of the Court approached their subject, has tended to obscure the significance of the Court's decisions relating to *economic* liberalism. The usual impression that one receives from reading the literature is that the traumatic events of 1937 resolved the problems of economic liberalism for our generation; and that since that time, the economic liberalism of the New Deal has motivated at least a clear majority of successively later Courts in supplanting the economically conservative precedents established by a majority of the "Nine Old Men" and their predecessors of the Taft Court. The real issues of public policy on the Court, it has seemed, have related to civil rights and liberties. But a careful and systematic examination of all of the Court's decisions on the merits contradicts the impressions that the Court is preoccupied with questions of constitutional interpretation, and that statutory interpretation—which the economic cases characteristically involve—is a policy-making function of lesser importance to the Court.

Taking the decade of the 1950s as the most relevant recent sample, there were more cases on the E scale than on the C scale in half of the terms. Specifically, there were more E than C cases in both the 1958 and 1959 Terms, so the clear preponderance of C cases in the 1960 Term is atypical. Counting, of course, is no substitute for thinking; and a quantitative measure of the relative importance of the Court's decision-making on the issues of civil liberty and economic liberalism does not foreclose a qualitative judgment on this question. But the mere assumption that constitutional questions are qualitatively more important than statutory questions is no proof; and absent acceptable criteria in terms of which it can be demonstrated that the Court's civil liberties questions generally—not just the School Segregation Cases— have had a greater impact upon American society during the past two decades than have the Court's decisions involving economic issues, it does not seem too unreasonable to accept at least tentatively findings based upon quantitative criteria.

In content, the E scale is just as broadly and heterogeneously defined as the C scale. The basic value that permeates the issues of economic liberalism is that of favoring claims of underpriviledged economic interests as against those of affluence and monopoly power. Thus, E+ is prolabor in union-management conflicts, pro-small business as against big business, procompetition and antioligopoly, pro-governmental economic regulation "in the public interest" of special, "private" economic interests, and, most characteristically, economic liberalism means to favor the claims of injured railroad workers and seamen against their corporate employers and insurers.

As Figure 5 shows, the four justices who are civil libertarians are also the ones who score highest on the E scale. But the remaining five members of the Court vote quite differently upon the two kinds of issues. Clark, who was least sympathetic to civil liberties, appears in the role of an economic liberal, scoring only slightly lower than Warren and Brennan, and definitely emerging as the fulcrum of the Court on E issues. Nor is this a matter of recent con-

## 1960 Term, E Scale

*Justices*

| Cases | D | Bl | Wa | Br | C | H | S | F | Wh | Totals |
|---|---|---|---|---|---|---|---|---|---|---|
| 6/169 | x | | | | | | | | | 1–8 |
| 5/320 | x | x | | | | | | | | 2–7 |
| 4/441 | x | x | | | | | | * | | 2–6 |
| 4614 : 284 | x | x | | | | | | | | 2–7 |
| 4618 : 306 | x | x | | | | | | | | 2–7 |
| 4618 : 307 | x | x | | | | | | | | 2–7 |
| 4713 : 392 | x | x | | | | | | | | 2–7 |
| 4743 : 97 | x | x | x | x | | | | | | 4–5 |
| 5/705 | x | x | x | x | | | | * | | 4–4 |
| 4/325 | x | x | x | x | x | | | * | | 5–3 |
| 4/520 | x | x | x | x | x | | | X | | 6–3 |
| 5/1 : 45 | x | x | x | x | x | | | | X | 6–3 |
| 5/1 : 46 | x | x | x | x | x | | | | X | 6–3 |
| 5/336 | x | x | x | x | x | | | | X | 6–3 |
| 6/316 | x | x | x | x | * | * | | | | 4–3 |
| 6/276 | — | x | x | x | x | x | | | | 5–4 |
| 5/731 | x | x | x | x | x | x | | | | 6–3 |
| 4/642 | — | x | x | x | x | x | * | | | 5–3 |
| 5/160 | x | x | x | x | x | — | x | * | | 6–2 |
| 5/667 : 64 | x | x | x | x | — | x | x | * | | 6–2 |
| 5/667 : 85 | x | x | x | x | — | x | x | * | | 6–2 |
| 5/695 | x | x | x | x | — | x | x | * | | 6–2 |
| 5/705 | x | x | x | x | — | x | x | * | | 6–2 |
| 5/651 | x | x | x | x | x | x | x | * | | 7–1 |
| 6/28 | x | x | x | — | x | x | — | x | | 6–3 |

113–100

| | D | Bl | Wa | Br | C | H | S | F | Wh | |
|---|---|---|---|---|---|---|---|---|---|---|
| **Totals** | | | | | | | | | | |
| Pros | 23 | 24 | 18 | 17 | 11 | 9 | 6 | 2 | 3 | 113 |
| Cons | 2 | 1 | 7 | 8 | 13 | 15 | 18 | 14 | 22 | 100 |
| Scale positions | 25 | 24 | 18 | 18 | 16 | 10.5 | 7.5 | 4 | 0 | |
| Scale scores | 1.00 | .92 | .44 | .44 | .28 | −.16 | −.40 | −.68 | −.100 | |

$$R = 1 - \frac{13}{196} = .934 \qquad S = 1 - \frac{13}{49} = .735$$

Figure 5.  Judicial Attitudes toward Economic Liberalism, 1960 Term

version; Clark also ranked fifth (and again, after Douglas, Black, Warren, and Brennan) on the E scales for both the 1958 and 1959 Terms. Neither fact should be surprising; Clark's judicial voting record is quite consistent with the political position of the Texas "Fair Dealer" who served as Truman's Attorney General at the time of his appointment to the Court.

Stewart scores much lower on the E scale than on C; and Whittaker, who was the most moderate of the four C− conservatives, is identified as the anchor man of the Court in terms of his economic conservativism. Of particular interest is the fact that Frankfurter, who was tied with Harlan at the next to the bottom rank on C, also is in the second lowest rank on E. If we consider, as may seem intuitively justifiable, that the C and E scales taken together provide a good test of liberalism as a generalized range of attitudes, then it seems quite clear that Frankfurter was the most illiberal justice in the 1960 Term: he voted only nine out of sixty-seven times in support of the liberal position. The necessary inference that one would draw, on the basis of cumulative scaling theory, from Frankfurter's low scale scores of −.76 on C and of −.68 on E is that he voted conservatively because of his conservative attitudes. Any inference must be evaluated, however, in the light of Mr. Justice Frankfurter's own explanations, frequently proffered, which contradict the assumption that, for him at least, these two scales each involve a single dominant variable. According to Frankfurter, who often has admitted his passionate personal sympathy for the down-trodden and oppressed among the Court's litigants, many of his illiberal votes in these cases must be attributed to his deference to federalism or to judicial restraint, or to the wise judges who sit on lower courts of the present or the Supreme Court of the past.

## The F Scale

The third most important variable, in recent terms, has been the F scale, which deals with monetary conflicts of interest between private individuals and government. Thus, F+ means to uphold the position of the government (national, state, or local) in tax and eminent domain cases, and in other matters where fiscal claims are at issue. In a sense, therefore, F is a closer analogue to C than is E, since C also is concerned with conflicts of interest between private individuals and governmental authority. But an examination of the voting and opinion behavior of the justices makes it apparent that for *most* of them, the issues of the F scale are more closely related to issues of economic liberalism than of civil liberties. This is hardly surprising, since F is differentiable from E primarily in terms of the parties whose interests are in conflict. Yet this difference in the identity of the parties may make a considerable difference to particular justices, depending upon how far they regard the government as a fiscal trustee acting in the "public interest" of the commonwealth, or as the largest single combination of monopolistic economic power.

The F variable was discovered in the process of empirically examining the voting patterns in several preceding terms. Several justices, and in particular Douglas, voted differently in some cases to which the government was a party from their behavior in most other cases involving economic issues. As Figure 6 shows, Douglas and Black, who ranked first and second on both of the liberalism scales, are at opposite ends of the F scale. In all fourteen cases which comprise the scale for this term, Black voted to uphold the position of the government, while Douglas voted in the opposite way in all

**1960 Term, F Scale**

*Justices*

| Cases | Bl | Wa | C | Br | F | H | S | Wh | D | Totals |
|---|---|---|---|---|---|---|---|---|---|---|
| 4/443 | x | | | | | | | | | 1–8 |
| 5/624 | x | x | | | | | | x | | 3–6 |
| 4811 : 288 | x | x | x | x | x | | | | | 5–4 |
| 4/361 | x | x | x | x | x | x | | | | 6–3 |
| 5/467 | x | x | x | x | x | x | * | | | 6–2 |
| 4/310 | x | x | x | x | x | x | x | | | 7–2 |
| 4469 : 533 | x | x | x | x | x | x | * | x | | 7–1 |
| 4/289 | x | x | x | x | x | x | x | x | | 8–1 |
| 4/446 | x | x | x | x | x | x | x | x | | 8–1 |
| 5/753 | x | x | x | x | x | x | x | x | | 8–1 |
| 3381 : 629 | x | x | x | x | x | x | x | x | | 8–1 |
| 3381 : 843 | x | x | x | x | x | x | x | x | | 8–1 |
| 4/410 | x | x | – | – | x | x | x | x | | 6–3 |
| 6/99 | x | x | x | x | x | – | x | x | x | 8–1 |
| | | | | | | | | | | 89–35 |
| Totals | | | | | | | | | | |
| Pros | 14 | 13 | 11 | 11 | 12 | 10 | 8 | 9 | 1 | 89 |
| Cons | 0 | 1 | 3 | 3 | 2 | 4 | 4 | 5 | 13 | 35 |
| Scale positions | 14 | 13 | 12 | 12 | 12 | 11 | 9.5 | 8 | 1 | |
| Scale scores | 1.00 | .86 | .71 | .71 | .71 | .57 | .36 | .14 | −.89 | |

$$R = 1 - \frac{3}{53} = .943 \qquad S = 1 - \frac{4}{23} = .826$$

Figure 6. Judicial Attitudes toward Governmental Fiscal Claims, 1960 Term

except one case—which would have been decided unanimously, and thus would not have appeared upon the scale, if it had not been for Harlan's inconsistent vote. On the other hand, Frankfurter, who ranked near the bottom of the Court on the C and E scales, is tied with Brennan and Clark for the fourth rank on the F scale. Clearly, the ranking of the justices on F is different from their rankings on either C or E. Moreover, the government won twelve of these fourteen cases, and Douglas was the only member of the Court who did not vote to support the position of the government in at least a majority of the cases.

In terms of content, six of these cases raised questions of national taxation; four were state or local tax cases; and the remaining four were concerned with fiscal claims against the national government: one in eminent domain, one in tort, and two others. It is convenient to postpone, until the next section of this paper where it can be discussed in the context of Figure 7, the question *why* Douglas voted more often in the company of Whittaker and Stewart, than with Black and Warren, on the issues comprising the F scale.

This scale does not meet one of the recommended minimal standards for a Guttman scale, in that fewer than ten of the cases include two or more dissenting votes (Torgerson 1958:324). But this requirement of Guttman scaling was established in order to avoid the spurious inflation of the coefficient R; and, as previously noted, the coefficient S is computed in a way that precludes that possibility. Since the value of S is quite high (.83, or about .20 above the acceptability level), and the ranking of the justices is similar to those of the immediately preceding terms, it seems justifiable to consider F to be scalable for this term, and to accept the scale.

## The Minor Scale Variables

In addition to the three major variables so far discussed, three other minor variables have been tentatively identified on the basis of similar research in other recent terms of the Court. These include A (judicial activism in reviewing the decisions of the Congress, the president, and administrative agencies); N (federalism, and conflict between the national and state governments); and J (the supervisory authority of the Supreme Court over the decision-making of lower courts). Too few cases have been associated with any of these variables in recent years, to permit scaling them. In the 1960 Term there were four cases on A, two on N, two on J, besides the one 4–4 decision in which the votes were not identified. Therefore, ninety-one of the ninety-nine split decisions of the 1960 Term are included on the scales of the three major variables; and together, the C, E, and F scales account for the variance in the voting behavior of the justices in 91 percent of the decisions of the Term.

## V. SCALE AXES IN THE FACTOR SPACE

The next step is to position the scale axes, which are considered to be the psychological analogues of the cumulative scales, in the space defined by the factorial reference axes. It will be recalled that the configuration of $i$-points for the justices is uniquely determined by the set of factor loadings given in Table 12. The problem now is to determine whether it is possible to pass a set of axes through the factor space in such a manner that the rankings of the projections, from the $i$-points onto the axes, are equivalent, in a statistically acceptable sense, to the rankings of the justices on the scale axes. What is required mathematically in order to accomplish this are sets of weights which will determine the position of the axes in the space, and the points on each axis where the projections from the $i$-points fall. Given such data, it will then be possible to compare the rankings of the justices, on the cumulative scales, with the rankings of the projections from their $i$-points on the counterpart scale axes.

It is helpful to prepare a set of two-dimensional plots of the $i$-points against the reference axes, similar to Figure 7 but without the scale axes. Initial estimates of weights can be made from an examination of such two-dimensional plots. More precise determination of a set of acceptable weights requires mathematical analysis of the factor matrix of Table 12, and the use of a calculating machine. The distance from the origin of the factor space to the point which is closest to a given $i$-point, on any scale axis, is computed by the formula,[7]

$$d = \frac{\alpha x + \beta y + \gamma z}{(\alpha^2 + \beta^2 + \gamma^2)^{1/2}}, \tag{3}$$

where $d$ is the distance from the origin to the point on the scale axis where it is orthogonal to the projection from the $i$-point; $x$, $y$, and $z$ are coordinates of the factorial reference axes for the $i$-point; and $\alpha$, $\beta$, and $\gamma$ are the coefficients which determine the position of the scale axis in the three-dimensional factor space. The same set of coefficients also provides the reference axis coordinates for the positive terminus of the scale axis.

The positions in which the scale axes have been placed in Figure 7 do not necessarily constitute a uniquely "best" fit to the configuration of $i$-points; but it is assumed that as defined in Table 13 and shown in Figure 7 they furnish an appropriate and approximately correct solution. One way to visualize this solution is to think of a cone intercepting a relatively quite small circular area on the surface of a unit sphere; any axis lying within the cone will array the projections from $i$-points so as to produce the same set of rankings of the justices as will be produced by any other axis within the cone.

The three plots of Figure 7 may be thought of as three views of a cube: Figure 7a is a top view, Figure 7b is a side view and Figure 7c is an end view. With relationship to reference axis I, the C scale axis enters from the lower right octant of the cube, passes through the origin, and emerges at the end through the upper left octant. The E scale axis passes downward and to the right of I. Reference axis I, it should be noted, is approximately the centroid, or arithmetic mean, of the C and E scale axes. The C axis clearly passes closest to Douglas, who also appears to have the most extreme projection on the positive segment of the axis. (Such a projection would correspond to Douglas' position with the highest score on the C cumulative scale.) Black, Warren, and Brennan project upon the positive segment of the C axis too, but we cannot be certain from an examination of Figure 7 precisely what the sequence of their rankings will be. Stewart clearly will project upon the C axis somewhere near the origin, which means that his "loading" on the axis will be close to zero. And the remaining four justices all will project upon the negative segment of the C axis, corresponding to their negative scores on the C cumulative scale.

Douglas, Black, Warren, and Brennan all will project positively upon the E axis, although it looks as though Douglas will rank lower on the axis

---

7. The use of this formula was kindly suggested by John P. Gilbert [and at that time, in 1960, I needed the advice].

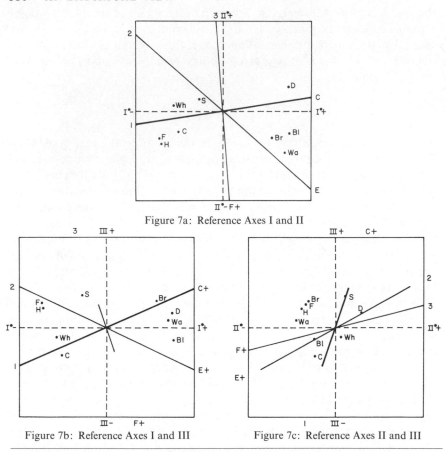

Figure 7a: Reference Axes I and II

Figure 7b: Reference Axes I and III          Figure 7c: Reference Axes II and III

---

NOTE: In figure 7a, the direction of orthogonal factor axes extracted by the complete centroid method is arbitrary; the asterisks following the identifying numbers for the first and second axes (i.e., I* and II*) signify that the polarity of these two axes was reversed to facilitate uniformity in inter-term comparisons in the larger study to which this article relates.

---

Figure 7. Scale Axes and the Judicial Point Configuration in the
Orthogonal Factor Space

than he does on the cumulative scale. Clark, who ranked fifth on the E cumulative scale, also will project to the fifth position on the E axis; and the remaining justices will project negatively, corresponding to their negative scale scores for this variable.

Douglas is somewhat separated from the other three so-called libertarians, and the reason for this becomes apparent when we consider the F scale axis, which cuts across the center of the space to emerge through the front face, with only slight deviation toward the end (at I+) and downward. Particularly in Figure 7a, which includes the two most important dimensions, it can be seen that the relationship of the F axis to the C and E axes is such that the justices who project upon the negative segment of F are Stewart and

Table 13. Reference Axis Coordinates, Coefficients, and Cosines for Scale Axes

| Scale axes | C 1 | E 2 | F 3 |
|---|---|---|---|
| Coordinates/ coefficients: | | | |
| I/$\alpha$ | 1.00 | 1.00 | .08 |
| II/$\beta$ | .15 | −.86 | −1.00 |
| III/$\gamma$ | .43 | −.47 | −.25 |
| Cosines | | | |
| Figure 4a | +08$\frac{1}{2}$° | −40$\frac{1}{2}$° | −85$\frac{1}{2}$° |
| Figure 4b | +23$\frac{1}{2}$° | −25° | −72° |
| Figure 4c | +71° | −151$\frac{1}{2}$° | −166° |

Whittaker, who have the most negative projections on E, and Douglas, who has the most positive loading on C, in these two dimensions. This suggests that F presents issues that pull together the justices who project at opposite extremes on the two liberalism scales. Douglas, in other words, might vote in opposition to governmental fiscal claims because of a strong and generalized antagonism to governmental regulation and control; this could help to explain the extremity of his support for civil liberties claims, which are also claims of private persons in opposition to governmental regulation and control. Whittaker and Stewart, on the other hand, might vote F− because of their strong economic conservativism, and their corresponding sympathy for "free enterprise" and antipathy for public fiscal controls. The converse argument would explain why the remaining justices all would project positively on the F axis. Economic liberalism, as understood by Black, Warren, and Brennan, frequently involves support of governmental regulation and control "in the public interest"; and both liberals and conservatives agree that taxation is necessary to support positive programs of governmental regulation of the economy. Douglas' action appears to have been reciprocated by Frankfurter, Harlan, and Clark, whose support of the government against claims of personal right seems to carry over to the support of the government against claims of private fiscal right. In any event, the position of the F axis in Figure 7 is such that, from a statistical and geometric point of view, F appears to be essentially orthogonal to—that is independent of—the C axis, and moderately correlated positively with the E scale. The suggested psychological explanation is at least not inconsistent with the mathematical relationships that are evident in the data.

## VI. A TEST OF THE BASIC HYPOTHESIS

The principal hypothesis underlying this study is that differences in the attitudes of the justices toward the basic issues raised by the cases that the

Court decides account for the differences in their voting. In short, Supreme Court justices vote as they do because of their attitudes toward the public policy issues that come before them. We are now in a position to make a statistical test of this hypothesis.

The $i$-points of the justices are separated in the factor space because of variance in the extent of majority participation of individual justices; but the factor analysis routine knows absolutely nothing about the subject matter of the values to which the decisions relate. The relative degrees of support by the justices of the key substantive issues can be determined by cumulative scaling; but cumulative scaling is a unidimensional measurement device, and each such scale is based upon a different universe of content, and is quite independent *methodologically* (as distinguished from psychologically) from every other scale. Moreover, the cumulative scale data are inadequate to permit the recovery of the configuration of the $i$-points in multidimensional space (Coombs 1964:chap. 12; Coombs and Kao 1960: 230). We shall assume, therefore, that if the cumulative scales can be reconstituted as a set of scale axes whose position is consistent with the configuration of $i$-points in the factor space, then the attitudinal differences of the justices on the cumulative scales account for the variance in the voting behavior of the justices, which is represented by the spatial separation of their ideal-points in the multidimensional factor space. If the correspondence between the set of cumulative scales and their scale axis analogues can be established in accordance with accepted procedures of statistical proof, then we shall have proved, in a mathematical sense, that the justices of the Supreme Court vary in their voting behavior according to the differences in their attitudes toward the scale variables.

Table 14 presents a comparison of the cumulative scale scores, and the distances along the counterpart scale axes at which the $i$-points project (as determined by formula 3), together with the corresponding sets of rankings, for all justices on each of the three major variables. Although both scale scores and axis loadings range in value, in principle, from $+1$ to $-1$, so that some meaning can be attached to direct comparisons of pairs of corresponding scores and loadings, it will be recalled that, for mathematical reasons relating to the marginal distributions of the fourfold tables, the intervals on the two types of continua are not genuinely commensurable. Moreover, it has been determined experimentally that the error variance in the factor analysis routine is usually around 10 percent; while the error variance in the cumulative scales is only slightly less; and there are other sources of error variance implicit in the general method. Therefore, it seems reasonable to employ the nonparametric rank correlation test for the purpose of making the comparison. In spite of the seeming precision of coefficients carried to the third decimal place, it would be fatuous to pretend that the measurement employed in this study can hope to be more than a rough approximation of empirical reality.

As Table 14 indicates, there are no inconsistencies in the two sets of

## Table 14. Correlation of Judicial Ranks on Scales and Scale Axes

| C | | | E | | | F | | |
|---|---|---|---|---|---|---|---|---|
| Axis | Ranks | Scale | Axis | Ranks | Scale | Axis | Ranks | Scale |
| .791 | 1 D | 1 | 1.00 | .308 | 4* D | 1 | 1.00 | .341 | 2* Bl | 1 | 1.00 |

| C | | | E | | | F | | |
|---|---|---|---|---|---|---|---|---|
| Axis | Ranks | | Scale | Axis | Ranks | | Scale | Axis | Ranks | | Scale |
| .791 | 1 D | 1 | 1.00 | .308 | 4* D | 1 | 1.00 | .341 | 2* Bl | 1 | 1.00 |
| .614 | 2 Bl | 2 | .84 | .752 | 1 Bl | 2 | .92 | .474 | 1* Wa | 2 | .86 |
| .609 | 3 Wa | 3 | .76 | .749 | 2 Wa | 3½ | .44 | .272 | 3 C | 4 | .71 |
| .599 | 4 Br | 4 | .53 | .498 | 3 Br | 3½ | .44 | .263 | 4 Br | 4 | .71 |
| −.104 | 5 S | 5 | −.02 | −.116 | 5 C | 5 | .28 | .205 | 6* F | 4 | .71 |
| −.553 | 6 Wh | 6 | −.49 | −.357 | 6 H | 6 | −.16 | .251 | 5* H | 6 | .57 |
| −.610 | 7 F | 7½ | −.76 | −.406 | 7 S | 7 | −.40 | −.232 | 8* S | 7 | .36 |
| −.612 | 8 H | 7½ | −.76 | −.409 | 8 F | 8 | −.68 | −.081 | 7* Wh | 8 | .14 |
| −.627 | 9 C | 9 | −.96 | −.411 | 9 Wh | 9 | −1.00 | −.256 | 9 D | 9 | −.89 |

| | | | | | | | | |
|---|---|---|---|---|---|---|---|---|
| Rank correlation coefficient (tau) | | .986 | | | .901 | | | .870 |
| Significance level, 1-tailed (p) | | <.000025 | | | .00012 | | | .00043 |

*Inconsistent rankings.

rankings for C. The correlation coefficient is less than +1.00 because of the tie in the scale scores of Frankfurter and Harlan, which increased very slightly the probability of perfect agreement with another set of rankings. The correspondence between the two sets of rankings for E also is perfect, except for Douglas, whose loading on the scale axis is much too low to correspond well with his maximal scale score. We can readily observe, from Figure 7, that with the point configuration given by the factor analysis, it would be impossible to position the E axis in such a way as to accommodate both Douglas' position, and those of the remaining justices. It has, therefore, seemed preferable to position the E axis in the way that best reflects the attitudinal alignment of the other eight justices, and to consider Douglas' $i$-point to be located inconsistently with his manifest attitude toward E. There are several possible explanations for Douglas' apparent inconsistency. The problem might be one of error variance, since the factor routine knows nothing of Guttman scale inconsistencies, and Douglas' two E− inconsistencies would tend to pull him below Black, at least, in projection on E, in the attribution of variance by the centroid factor routine; to this we could add the imponderable effect of the error variance inherent in the factor analysis itself. But an alternative psychological explanation might be that the $i$-point configuration is correct, and that it *is* inconsistent for a justice, who is as hostile to governmental fiscal control as Douglas, at the same time to be the Court's strongest supporter of claims of economic liberalism.

The two sets of rankings for F are generally in close accord, since a tau of .87 is considered to be very high. There are three reversed pairs in the axis rankings: Black and Warren, Frankfurter and Harlan, and Stewart and Whittaker. Reference to Figure 6 shows that the reversal, for each of these pairs, was occasioned by the difference of a single vote; and the value of tau was lowered by the triple tie in the scale ranks. It seems quite likely that the F scale, which is marginally acceptable in any event, is based upon too few (and too extreme) cases to constitute an adequate sampling of the attitudes of the justices toward this value; and that a scale based upon twice as many cases might result in a much closer correspondence between the cumulative scale and the point configuration. In other words, it seems most likely that in the case of F, the inconsistency between the two sets of rankings should be attributed to the inadequacies of the scale, rather than to errors in the point configuration. This question could be resolved only by an examination of the justices' voting behavior in a term in which they chose to accept for decision a considerably larger number of cases dealing with the issue of governmental fiscal powers than they have dealt with in recent years; or, as might well be done, by pooling the data for several terms of the Court.

Nevertheless, the correlation between all three sets of rankings is very high, with or without the above explanations. From a statistical point of view, it should be noted that the probabilities shown in Table 14 relate to the probability of producing, by chance alone, the indicated congruence between any *one* scale and the point configuration. The prospect of chance replication of as good a fit for all three scales simultaneously, with the same fixed point configuration, is of course very much more remote; indeed, the joint probability, which is the product of the three discrete probabilities, is a truly astronomical number: $<.0^{11}129$, or approximately one chance in a trillion.[8] It seems warranted, under these circumstances, to accept the hypothesis that the variance in the voting behavior of the justices during the 1960 Term can be adequately accounted for by the differences in their attitudes toward the fundamental issues of civil liberty, economic liberalism, and governmental fiscal authority.

## VII. THE PSYCHOLOGICAL DISTANCE SEPARATING THE JUSTICES

Taking the judicial ideal-points in the factor space as reasonably adequate symbolizations of the respective attitude syndromes of the individual justices, we can use them to examine one final question. Discussion about the justices frequently revolves around such questions as which ones tend to share the "same point of view," and which ones are "furthest apart" in their thinking. The factor space provides a convenient basis for objective measurement of the psychological distance which separates each justice from each of the others.

Since the measurement of these psychological distances is purely mathe-

---

8. [For a contrary opinion, see Gow 1971.]

matical, we shall carry it out in five-dimensional space. This will afford a slightly more accurate basis for measurement than the three-dimensional space depicted in Figure 7, since the fourth and fifth factors will permit us to consider, presumably, the effect of the minor variables (such as A, N, and J) which, although not scalable in the Guttman sense, nevertheless must be considered to be a part of the attitude syndrome of each justice. The psychological distance will be measured on the same scale as that employed for the three-dimensional factor space: along orthogonal reference axes, each of which extends from $-1$ to $+1$. The standard formula for computing the distance between any two points in orthogonal five-space is:

$$d_{(i_1 - i_2)} = [(v_1 - v_2)^2 + (w_1 - w_2)^2 \\ + (x_1 - x_2)^2 + (y_1 - y_2)^2 + (z_1 - z_2)^2]^{1/2}, \quad (4)$$

where $d$ is the distance, $i_1$ and $i_2$ are the ideal-points of a pair of justices, and $v$, $w$, $x$, $y$, and $z$ are the coordinates (or "loadings") of the justices on factors I–V. Much more simply, one can use the computing formula

$$d = 1 - \phi, \quad (5)$$

where phi ($\phi$) is the correlation between the two points.

The result of computations according to formula (4) are shown in Table 15. Harlan and Frankfurter are by far the closest two justices, in terms of their attitudes toward the policy issues that the Court decided in the 1960 Term; they are separated by a distance of only .14 in the five-dimensional factor space. Contrary to what even many close observers of the work of the Court seem to believe, however, it is Warren and Brennan—not Douglas and Black—who are next most similar in attitude, at a distance of .42. In fact, there are five other pairs (Wh-C, .52; Bl-Wa, .53; Wh S, .57; Wh-F, .67; and Wh-H, .70) with "ideational identity" closer than that of Douglas and Black,[9] who are separated by a distance of .75. On the other hand, the greatest difference in attitude is that between Douglas and Black, on the one hand, and Frankfurter and Harlan, on the other; the average distance separating these two pairs of justices is 1.60. Moreover, Douglas, Black, Warren, and Brennan all agree that Frankfurter and Harlan are the justices whose point of view is most different from their own; and, conversely, Harlan, Frankfurter, Whittaker, Clark, and Stewart all agree that Douglas and Black are the justices most distant psychologically from themselves.

If we seek an "average" justice whose point of view best typifies that of the Court as a whole, he is clearly Stewart at an average distance of .98. The variation of Stewart's separation from his colleagues also is confined to the smallest range. Such a finding is perfectly consistent, of course, with the

---

9. In an article devoted to the attitudinal similarities and differences of these two justices, Spaeth has concluded that his data, also, "show significant ideational difference between Black and Douglas" (1961:176).

### Table 15. Attitudinal Distances among Judicial Ideal-Points, 1960 Term

|     | D    | Bl   | Wa   | Br   | S    | C    | Wh   | F    | H    |
|-----|------|------|------|------|------|------|------|------|------|
| D   |      | .75  | .93  | .83  | 1.21 | 1.53 | 1.44 | 1.63 | 1.63 |
| Bl  | .75  |      | .53  | .80  | 1.30 | 1.47 | 1.44 | 1.58 | 1.54 |
| Wa  | .93  | .53  |      | .42  | 1.18 | 1.38 | 1.39 | 1.52 | 1.50 |
| Br  | .83  | .80  | .42  |      | 1.02 | 1.27 | 1.29 | 1.42 | 1.44 |
| S   | 1.21 | 1.30 | 1.18 | 1.02 |      | .93  | .57  | .78  | .82  |
| C   | 1.53 | 1.47 | 1.38 | 1.27 | .93  |      | .52  | .80  | .85  |
| Wh  | 1.44 | 1.44 | 1.39 | 1.29 | .57  | .52  |      | .67  | .70  |
| F   | 1.63 | 1.58 | 1.52 | 1.42 | .78  | .80  | .67  |      | .14  |
| H   | 1.63 | 1.54 | 1.50 | 1.44 | .82  | .85  | .70  | .14  |      |

findings of scale analysis, and with the configuration shown in the three-dimensional space of Figure 7. In similar accord with expectations is the finding that the most atypical justice was Douglas who, separated by an average distance of 1.24 from his colleagues, entertained the most generally extreme views of any of the justices.

Although Stewart and Clark are adjacent to each other in the two-dimensional matrix of Table 15, since the pattern shown is the most generally consistent one, these two justices are not very close to each other in five-space (as a glance at three-dimensional Figure 7 suggests). Stewart and Clark both are closer to Whittaker, Frankfurter, and Harlan than they are to each other. Finally, it is noteworthy that Whittaker—not Frankfurter—is the most typical of the group who, at least in relationship to the C and E variables, are the conservative justices; Whittaker's average distance from the other four justices at the "right wing" of Table 15 was only .62. And it is Warren—not Black—who is the most typical of the four liberal justices, with an average distance of .63 separating him from the other three.

## VIII. SUMMARY

The objective of this paper has been to demonstrate the utility, for a more accurate insight into the basic factors that underlie disagreement among Supreme Court justices, of a more rigorous psychological approach than has been characteristic of most discussion of their attitudes. The attention of scholars always has focused upon the values articulated in the opinions of the justices, and particularly in majority opinions; but much less attention has been given to the possibility that an examination of the voting behavior of the justices might provide a better and more reliable approach to the understanding of their attitudes than the study of opinions. Research during the last two decades has turned increasingly to the analysis of judicial voting records, in addition to opinion language; and reliance understandably has been placed, during what might well be termed the pioneering stages of the development of a science of judicial behavior, upon unidimensional models. These necessarily are limited in their capacity to represent adequately the complex interplay of attitudes in the mind of any human being. The time has now come when it may be appropriate for students of judicial behavior to consider the advantages to be gained by utilization of multidimensional models of the behavior of Supreme Court justices.

One such model, exemplified here, is suggested by recent (and ongoing) research in psychometrics. It proceeds on the premise that a justice reacts in his voting behavior to the stimuli presented by cases before the Court in accordance with his attitudes toward the issues raised for decision. This article has presented what is believed to be persuasive evidence that this is precisely what the justices were doing when they voted in the decisions of the 1960 Term.

# 6

# Jackson's Judicial Philosophy

**R**obert H. Jackson died more than a decade ago, and his departure from the Supreme Court marked the end of an era in American judicial politics, since he left behind as a minority those remaining of the colleagues who had joined with him to compose the so-called Roosevelt Court (Pritchett 1948). He was still very much alive when I interviewed him shortly after the *Steel Seizure* decision in 1952 and subsequently when the initial stages of the present research were designed and carried out. His unanticipated and fatal heart attack had two incidental consequences that are relevant here: it fixed an unavoidable natural closure for the data—his activities—that I was studying, and at the same time imposed an insurmountable foreclosure upon one of my research ambitions, for the best way to validate generalizations about a man's attitudinal predispositions and belief systems is to check them as predictions against his future behavior. Social scientists understandably repose less confidence in findings about hypotheses that can be validated only statistically, and then only by retrospective testing. Perhaps it was an error, therefore, not to have switched from Jackson to some other justice as a subject; but even one who chose a younger justice (such as Arthur Goldberg)

This chapter was originally published, in slightly different form, as "Jackson's Judicial Philosophy: An Exploration in Value Analysis" in *American Political Science Review* 59 (December 1965):940–963.

This research has been assisted by the Penrose Fund of the American Philosophical Society; the Center for Advanced Study in the Behavioral Sciences; the Institute of Advanced Projects of the East-West Center, and the Computer Center, both of the University of Hawaii; and especially by various research facilities of Michigan State University. Individuals to whom special acknowledgment is due include Frank A. Pinner, Frank Sim, and Norman Luttbeg, all formerly associated with the Bureau for Social and Political Research; George Kantrowitz, Steighton J. Watts, and James E. Holton, all formerly graduate students in political science at Michigan State University; and David Danelski of Yale University, who read and commented on the paper.

might have guessed wrongly about his tenure, and Jackson's career did offer several unusual advantages—for reasons that will be explained shortly—which it seemed important to exploit. This is a sector of political research in which relatively little has been done, and it is possible that the theory and methods employed here may be useful to others in the study of political values. The substantive findings are confined to a single individual; but nothing in the theory and methodology bears any unique relationship to Jackson—or to judges, for that matter. They can be used to analyze the attitudes of other types of political decision-makers who make observable choices with which are associated verbal rationales that are or can be systematically recorded in a reproducible form.

The data for this study include all the three-hundred-odd opinions that Robert Jackson wrote as a Supreme Court justice and all his votes in the more than a thousand formal nonunanimous decisions in which he participated. His opinions have been classified by type and analyzed for their value content, using correlational, cluster, and factorial methods; and his votes have been studied by cumulative scaling. These materials, so analyzed, make it possible to test several hypotheses, primarily by intercorrelating his values, and by correlating his values with his votes and the types of opinions in which they were articulated.

There is no dearth of what evidently is impressionistic literature on the subject of judicial attitudes. The law reviews, and to a lesser extent the political science journals, frequently carry discussions of the imputed attitudes of individual judges—and, especially, of justices of the United States Supreme Court. Moreover, these discussions customarily are based upon an analysis of judicial opinions; and Jackson has not been neglected by the legal commentators or the judicial biographers.[1] Some of them—notably Jaffe and Nielson—have purported to discuss the essence of Jackson's philosophy as a judge, but the essences they find are not in agreement. The typical conclusion has been that it is futile to attempt to discover any systematic structuring of attitudes for Jackson. Weidner, for instance, warns:

> The most striking feature of Justice Jackson's judicial philosophy is that it can only with great difficulty be made to conform to any of the neat and currently popular classifications of Supreme Court justices. . . . The way out is to abandon attempts to squeeze the justices into these deceptively precise categories. . . . The classification of Supreme Court justices as advocates of either judicial activism or judicial restraint, and the use of statistical devices to facilitate the process, can be a helpful approach to some problems of constitutional law. But it is inadequate to the task of determining the judicial philosophy of a particular justice. Jackson, for one, cannot be so readily pigeonholed. (1955:593–594)

In similar although less dogmatic vein, Barnett remarks that "in striving to associate Jackson's views with some doctrine or set of doctrines which will neatly explain them all, one is beset with difficulties" (1948:241). And even

---

1. For example, Barnett 1948; Fairman 1955; Frankfurter 1955; Gerhart 1953, 1958; Jaffe 1955; Nielson 1945; Steamer 1954; Symposium 1955; Weidner 1955.

Pritchett—whom Weidner evidently had in mind as the only previous commentator who attempted to make some use of quantification in guiding his appraisal of Jackson—concludes that his own "figures, however, average out a certain unpredictability in Jackson's votes" (1948:261). In a subsequent attempt at a summing up, Pritchett adds that "the rather erratic nature of his opinions ma[kes] it difficult to catalogue him. . . . The unpredictability of Jackson's performance leads one to question whether he has developed any systematic theories about civil liberties or the judicial function" (1954: 18, 228–229).

In this state of our knowledge, Jackson appears to be a particularly appropriate subject for a study by behavioral methods. Perhaps at least in this instance any substantive findings that emerge will not be open to the usual rhetorical charge that all the elaborate paraphernalia serve only to confirm what already is known by prudent men of common sense.

## I. THE DATA AND METHODS OF ANALYSIS

Jackson participated in the decisions of the Supreme Court for a total of twelve terms: 1941–1944 and 1946–1953.[2] During this period, he wrote 138 institutional opinions (for the Court), 51 concurring opinions, and 113 dissenting opinions. He also wrote 4 opinions, consisting either of jurisdictional dissents or of memorandum opinions in his *ex officio* capacity of supervising justice for the Second Circuit, that are included for some purposes in the analysis below. In addition, he wrote 16 opinions that are here scored as nulls, since his discussion is limited to statements of facts without value preferences indicated. Eight other opinions were jointly written by Jackson and various other justices. These 24 opinions have been excluded completely from analysis in the present study.[3] My principal data for present purposes consist, therefore, of the decisions in the cases to which 306 opinions authored by Jackson relate;[4] and my primary focus is upon his opinions and votes in these decisions.

### The Variables

The data were analyzed in terms of four sets of variables, which I shall call "content variables," "opinion variables," "voting variables," and "chronological variables."

---

2. Jackson was on leave of absence from the Court throughout the 1945 Term, acting in the role of United States Chief Counsel in the Nuremberg war crimes trials. See Harris 1954. Only six months before his death, in his introduction to Harris' book, Jackson wrote that "the hard months at Nuremberg were well spent in the most important, enduring and constructive work of my life."

3. For a list of Jackson's opinions, which contains some omissions and duplications but which corresponds closely to the independently compiled list used in the present study, see the *Stanford Law Review* 8 (1955):60–71.

4. Jackson wrote both the majority opinion and a separate concurring opinion in *Wheeling Steel Corp.* v. *Glander.*

The identification of the content variables[5] was based on an analysis of all of Jackson's opinions. A panel of three judges—two graduate students and myself—read and scored independently each opinion for the presence of any of a set of thirty-three substantive categories. I had first constructed a code that defined these content categories on the basis of a preliminary examination of about 20 percent of the total of Jackson's opinions. This code was to some extent modified in the process of analyzing the complete array of cases—which required, of course, reevaluation of some opinions. Any instances of disagreement in scoring were discussed among the panel of judges until a consensual judgment was reached. Subsequent research in political attitudes and ideologies[6] indicates that the attitudinal dimensions relevant to Supreme Court behavior are considerably broader and more heterogeneous—and consequently fewer in number—than I had assumed at the time the present project was begun.

Conceptually, each of these variables represented a continuous attitudinal dimension for Jackson, but the method of classifying the data had the effect of treating each variable as though it were dichotomous. Each variable was directionally defined, and Jackson might make a statement either in affirmation or in negation of the variable; henceforth I shall use the term "value" to refer to either of the two directional meanings (positive or negative) that are associated with each variable.[7] The coding rules required that such statements be in normative form, and not merely factual assertions. (For example, if Jackson said that a defendant in a state criminal case had confessed during a period of extended interrogation while he was being held incommunicado by the police, the content analyst left such a remark unscored, as a factual assertion; but if Jackson said that it was a violation of the Fourteenth Amendment for a state to convict a defendant on the basis of a coerced confession—and irrespective of whether he thought that this had happened on the facts in that particular case—such a statement was scored as agreement with the positive value of the second variable: "freedom from state restraint of civil liberty." It was also possible, and not uncommon, for Jackson to agree with both the affirmative and the negative value of the same variable in a single opinion; in such cases, the variable was scored as ambivalent for that opinion.) Since most variables were not discussed (at least, normatively) in most opinions, scoring as "absent" was most common. It is the joint occurrence of content values (scored as either affirmative or negative) that is of interest in the analysis below.

Some of the initial set of thirty-three content categories turned out to be univalued, and therefore of little help in making correlational analyses;

---

5. For other recent discussions and examples of content analysis, see North et al. 1963; Kort 1963; and Schubert 1963c.

6. For example, H. McClosky 1958; Lane 1962; Schubert 1965c.

7. "Variable" denotes the content category; the name (or symbol, or short title) of the variable in apposition with a valence symbol (+ or −) or phrase ("positive value" or "negative value") denotes the affective meaning of a particular stimulus or response set.

others appeared to have neither a logical nor a psychological bearing upon Jackson's voting behavior. An example of one of the original categories which was both univalued (in effect, with marginals of sixty-seven pro and four con) and non-functional (in relationship to voting) was judicial *candor*, a subject upon which Jackson often exhorted his colleagues in normative terms and criticized them in factual propositions of which the following are typical:

> Justice "X" [frequently Murphy or Black] is not (but should be) candid; the majority in this case are not candid; etc.
> The Supreme Court should not overrule precedents *sub silentio*, but should come right out and say what it is doing.
> The Supreme Court should not proceed by indirection.
> The Supreme Court should not indulge in legal fictions; the Court ought not to sponsor myths concerning judicial behavior.
> Supreme Court justices should articulate their major premises; the Court should practice what it preaches.
> The Court has [deliberately] sublimated the conflict underlying the instant case.
> The lower court in this case was more candid than is the Supreme Court [by pointing out that ghostwriting flourishes in official circles in Washington].

Accordingly, the original list of thirty-three categories was later reduced to thirteen, in part by eliminating from further consideration the merely verbal (as I came to deem them) ones such as candor. Other categories were combined; for example, among the six initial categories ultimately combined to form the variable "Supreme Court policy-making," is *stare decisis*, which for Jackson was markedly bivalent. The positive value characteristically would take this form of utterance:

> A justice should follow a precedent with which he disagrees until a majority of the Court will forthrightly agree to overrule it.
> The Supreme Court does not appear to (but should) follow its precedents.
> The Court should give "full faith and credit" to its own prior decisions.
> The Court should follow *stare decisis*, even when it leads to a wrong result, when Congress has acquiesced in the decision.
> The Court should follow *stare decisis*, except when the proposed new policy *clearly* is preferable to the old one.
> The Court should not make new constitutional law unless the old law is unsound and "works badly in our present day and society."

Jackson affirmed his belief in stare decisis in seventy-four opinions. On the other hand, in twenty-two other opinions he expressed quite opposing views:

> Throughout its history, the Court has been required from time to time to reconsider a precedent decision (and should do so now.)
> The Court should not follow precedents that clearly are blunders.
> The Court should not follow precedents that are not acceptable to a majority of the sitting Court.
> The Court should not follow *stare decisis* when to do so would lead to a wrong decision.
> It is better to create confusion by overruling a precedent than for the Court to adhere to a rule that it cannot and will not respect in application.

The reduced set of content variables consists of the following:

1. National restraint of political (civil) liberty.
2. State restraint of political (civil) liberty.
3. National restraint of economic liberty.
4. State restraint of economic liberty.
5. Monopolistic control of enterprise.
6. Federal (national-state) relationships.
7. Executive or congressional policy-making, or both.
8. Lower court policy-making.
9. Lawyers.
10. Litigants.
11. The public interest.
12. Colleagues (other Supreme Court justices).
13. Supreme Court policy-making.

The opinion variables fell into four categories: institutional, concurring, dissenting, and jurisdictional or memorandum.

There are only two voting variables: C (political liberalism/conservatism, = civil liberty) and E (economic liberalism/conservatism). Most of the data for these variables are available in the recent report of another research project, which analyzes the votes of all justices of the Supreme Court in all decisions on the merits for the period of the 1946–1962 Terms, on the basis of the political and economic policy variables (Schubert 1965c: esp. chap. 5). The coding of Jackson's votes for the cases in which he wrote opinions, beginning with the 1946 Term, was taken directly from this larger pool of voting data. In order to include similar voting data for his first four terms, the relevant decisions of this earlier period were evaluated in relation to the political and economic variables. Each decision was scored as an outcome for the set of participating justices in that case, and Jackson's vote was then scored (just as that of each other justice) in relationship thereto. This voting analysis of the 1941–1944 Terms was carried out half-a-dozen years after the content analysis of opinions was completed, which no doubt tended to minimize further the possibility of analyst bias and to confirm the independence of the two sets of observations.

Like the content variables, the two voting variables were scored dichotomously, but with the differences that no ambivalent category was recognized for either, and the two voting variables could not jointly occur in the same decision. Although Jackson might (and often did) discuss many values in an opinion, or the same value more than once (and perhaps inconsistently), he could vote only once, and in only one way, in any single decision. Consequently, his vote in each decision was coded in one of the following five categories: (a) politically liberal (C+); (b) politically conservative (C−); (c) economically liberal (E+); (d) economically conservative (E−); or (e) other.

The major chronological variable was derived by partitioning all of Jackson's opinions (and their associated votes) into three equal periods of time: the 1941–1944, 1946–1949, and 1950–1953 Terms. In order to test certain of my hypotheses it was also necessary to compare the first period with the latter two combined; or, the last period with the first two combined; and in one instance to use a slightly different breakdown, in order to compare the 1941–1944 and 1946–1948 with the 1949–1953 Terms.

The primary method of analysis consists of a cross-tabulation of the joint occurrences of variables within and between the four sets. Generally speaking, fourfold tables, phi coefficients, and either chi squares or Fisher's exact probability test were computed for each cross-tabulation of a pair of variables.

## The Reduced Content Matrix

In order to define the political and economic content variables consistently with the two corresponding voting variables, the set of content variables was further reduced by combining the first and second variables "freedom from national restraint of civil liberty" and "freedom from state restraint of civil liberty" into paravariable #14 (political liberalism/conservatism); and by combining the third, fourth, and fifth variables, "freedom from national restraint of economic liberty" and "freedom from state restraint of economic liberty" and "monopolistic control of enterprise" all *with reversed polarity*,[8] into paravariable #15 (economic liberalism/conservatism). At one time I planned to study the phi correlation matrix for this revised set of ten variables (#6–15), using cluster and factor analysis in order to isolate the more fundamental latent dimensions of Jackson's attitudes as a judge. For technical reasons, however, it was necessary to eliminate three more variables from the correlation matrix before undertaking these further analyses. The frequency for the ninth variable (lawyers) was so low (18), and the marginal distributions for variables #11 (public interest) and #12 (colleagues) were so extreme (56–1 and 7–154) that useful correlations between these three and the remaining variables could not be obtained. Therefore, the cluster and factor analyses were based upon a seven-variable matrix. Henceforth, short titles for particular values, or symbols as indicated, will be used instead of numbers to designate these variables: N (#6), A (#7), J (#8), X (#10), P (#13), C (#14), and E (#15).

The correlation matrix for the content variables was cluster analyzed by the elementary linkage, hierarchical syndrome, and rank-order typal methods (McQuitty 1957, 1960, 1963). It was factor analyzed by the principal axes method, followed by varimax rotation (Harman 1960:154–191, 301–308).

---

8. Sign reversals were necessary for the economic variables, in order to maintain continuity with other recently published research in judicial attitudes toward economic policy. See Schubert 1965c; Spaeth 1963a:290–311, 1963b:79–108.

The phi coefficients and associated chi squares, and the factor analysis and rotation, were calculated on computers.

## II. THE HYPOTHESES TO BE TESTED

The hypotheses to be tested will be stated, together with the supporting considerations for each.

1. *The values articulated by Jackson in his opinions correlate in clusters that correspond to meaningful attitudinal concepts.*

Particularly during the period since Jackson's death, a body of cumulative knowledge about the social psychology of judicial attitudes has begun to be developed. I assume that my cluster findings ought to articulate with these data; but the clusters of content values will not necessarily coincide with the impressions that a reader sophisticated in the general subject-matter field—namely, the traditionally trained constitutional law scholar—might gain from having read all or a substantial portion of Jackson's opinions. Findings based on the cluster analysis should be more valid, more reliable, and more precise than those based upon purely qualitative opinion analysis, for few subjective opinion analysts attempt to base their findings upon a reading of all of a judge's opinions; and fewer still could claim to make consistent observations, and retain adequate recall to keep them in mind and to make the millions of associations and comparisons involved, when the universe of data comprises over three hundred opinions, many of which are dozens of pages in length. For such a task, computers have inherent advantages, whatever their other limitations. From a statistical point of view, the cluster analysis findings might be thought of as the mean, from which subjective opinion analyses could be expected to deviate.

The clusters ought also to be "meaningful" in the sense that we should not expect to find patent inconsistency in the relationships denoted. The training of a lawyer and the vocation of a writer of judicial opinions are to articulate arguments characterized by at least prima facie rationality. The test by which we shall measure this hypothesis is whether the cluster analysis findings: (a) define attitudes which are consistent with other behavioral research findings about judicial attitudes; and (b) are internally consistent.

2. *The latent attitudinal dimensions revealed by factor analysis of Jackson's opinions will correspond to the latent attitudinal dimensions attributed to the Court as a whole, during the same period, on the basis of scaling and factor analysis of voting data.*

Since cluster analysis deals only with the manifest or surface relationships of the correlation matrix, the attitudinal dimensions yielded by factor analysis can be expected to uncover more complex and subtle interrelationships. The requirement that Jackson's attitudinal factors correspond to those that previous research has identified as common to the decision-making group of which Jackson was a member is premised upon two assumptions: (a) that opinion writing and voting are alternative behavioral modes of response, both of which are determined by a judge's attitudes toward the stimuli presented by cases for decision; and (b) that the variables that Jackson recognized as most important in his judicial decisions—not necessarily his valuation of those variables—did not significantly differ from the consensus of his colleagues concerning which were the most relevant and important content variables. Black and Jackson, for instance, might agree that the political liberalism/conservatism variable (viz., a civil liberties issue) represented the most important question for decision in a case relating to a Communist's claim of the violation of his constitutional right to freedom of speech; but their respective valuations might be very different: Black might argue in his opinion and vote in favor of political liberalism, while Jackson might affirm the negative value of political conservatism.

The confirmation of this hypothesis will depend upon a comparison of the findings from the factor analysis of the content-variable correlation matrix, with findings from scaling and factor analysis of voting data for the whole Court.

3. *Jackson's votes, in relation to the political liberalism value, will correlate positively and significantly with his affirmations of the same value in his opinions; a similar proposition is asserted to obtain between his votes for and against economic liberalism and the economic liberalism content-value.*

The assumption here is the same as the first advanced in support of Hypothesis 2, above: that opinion writing and voting are alternative behavioral modes of response, both of which are determined by a judge's attitudes toward the stimuli presented by cases for decision. If this is true, then Jackson should affirm the political liberalism value in opinions which he wrote to justify pro-civil liberty votes, and he ought consistently to affirm the political liberalism value more than any other content value in such cases; moreover, there should be few (if any) cases in which his opinion negates the civil liberty value although he votes in favor of it. Of course, this assumption is in accordance with intuitive expectations premised upon the presumed relatively high degree of rationality in judicial behavior; but so far as I have been able to discover, no one thus far has attempted to design an experiment which might make possible either proof or disproof of this basic assumption about judicial decision-making.

The test of this hypothesis will be statistical: the stipulated correlation must be positive and significant, at a level of confidence of not less than .05 (one-tailed).

4. *There are no significant differences between Jackson's value assertions in concurring and in dissenting opinions; but there are significant differences between his value assertions in institutional opinions and in either concurring or dissenting opinions, or both.*

It is usually assumed that there are differences between the values a judge asserts when he speaks for the Court and what he says in dissent. As Cardozo put it:

> Comparatively speaking at least, the dissenter is irresponsible. The spokesman of the court is cautious, timid, fearful of the vivid word, the heightened phrase. He dreams of an unworthy brood of scions, the spawn of careless *dicta*, disowned by the *ratio decidendi*, to which all legitimate offspring must be able to trace their lineage. The result is to cramp and paralyze. One fears to say anything when the peril of misunderstanding puts a warning finger to the lips. Not so, however, the dissenter.... For the moment he is the gladiator making a last stand against the lions. The poor man must be forgiven a freedom of expression, tinged at rare moments with a touch of bitterness, which magnanimity as well as caution would reject for one triumphant. (1925:715)

Little or no consideration appears to have been given, however, to the content-value relationship between concurring and other opinions. One might reasonably speculate that a concurring justice should feel no greater sense of responsibility than a dissenting justice. Therefore, one ought to expect to find significant differences between institutional and separate (concurring or dissenting) opinions, but *not* between concurring and dissenting opinions.

A supporting argument might be drawn from small group theory. Since four justices constitute the minimum number necessary to support an institutional opinion,[9] while it is the maximum for either a concurring or a dissenting opinion, Jackson clearly had to compromise his views with a much larger group when he wrote for the Court than otherwise. The extent to which a judicial opinion represents the personal views and language of the author presumably varies inversely with the size of the group which accepts the opinion; and so institutional opinions should tend to be more depersonalized than concurring or dissenting opinions. On both psychological and sociological grounds, therefore, we should expect that if any significant differences in the value content of opinions emerge, they will be in accord with the stated hypothesis, which can be verified statistically in the same manner as Hypothesis 3, except that the test for Hypothesis 4 is two-tailed.

5. *There were significant changes, reflecting certain critical events that occurred on and off the Court, in both Jackson's opinion and voting behavior.*

Let us examine this hypothesis by testing a set of more specific but independent sub-hypotheses:

5.1 *The longer Jackson remained on the Court, the more conservative he became.*

It frequently has been assumed that judges (like other people) become more conservative as they grow older, and remain longer on the bench. Certainly this assumption was the explicit premise of President Roosevelt's charges against the Court in the "Court-packing" episode of 1937; and evidently, Jackson himself agreed with it (R. Jackson 1941:184–188). In order

---

9. In the relatively rare occasion (for the Court) when only six or seven justices participate in a decision.

to test this hypothesis, we can compare the marginal totals for the voting and content variables of civil liberty and economic policy, for the three four-year periods. In order to accept this hypothesis, it is required that changes occur in the stipulated direction, that these changes be progressive from period to period, and that they should be statistically significant at the .05 level of confidence (one-tailed).

5.2 *There was a significant increase in Jackson's dissenting behavior after his failure to succeed Stone as chief justice.*

Jackson's presidential ambitions had been cut short by Roosevelt's third-term decision; and his apparently good chance of succeeding Chief Justice Hughes was foreclosed by the outbreak of World War II (Anonymous 1938; Childs 1940; Corey 1937; McCune 1947; Gerhart 1958:229–231). Evidently, despite Roosevelt's death in 1945, he then had expected to return from his triumph at Nuremberg and assume the center chair on the Supreme Court bench in place of Stone, who died on April 22, 1946, as the war crimes tribunal's work drew to a close. Soon afterward Jackson was told that Hugo Black was lobbying with Truman against his promotion; the upshot was Jackson's long cable from Germany to the judiciary committees of both houses of Congress (*New York Times* 1946; *United States News* 1946), exposing to public view (in confirmation of long-standing Washington gossip) his version of the "feud" between Black and himself which had split the Court.[10] Since Truman already had submitted Fred Vinson's name to the Senate for confirmation, the almost certain effect of Jackson's pronunciamento would be to serve as an epitaph to his political ambitions.

If it is true that Jackson returned to the Court in 1946, bitterly disappointed at the frustration of his ambition to achieve an honor that he (and many others) thought he had earned and deserved—and more specifically, a frustration due to the political chicanery (as he saw it) of his colleague Black, the leader of a "bloc of libertarian judicial activists" (R. Jackson 1955:57) with whom Jackson differed in a struggle for leadership on the Court—then we might reasonably expect Jackson to articulate his disappointment and disagreement by writing more dissenting opinions than he had felt to be necessary or appropriate during his first four terms on the Court. Such behavior would provide an appropriate denouement for the act of political suicide he had committed at Nuremberg; and Jackson was by no means insensitive to the implications of an increase in a judge's propensity to dissent, for he wrote in his valedictory, the undelivered and posthumously published Godkin Lectures that:

> ... there is nothing good, for either the Court or the dissenter, in dissenting *per se*. Each dissenting opinion is a confession of failure to convince the writer's colleagues, and the true test of a judge is his influence in leading, not in opposing, his court. (1955:19)

---

10. Gerhart 1958:258–265; Schlesinger 1947:73–79, 201–212. Gerhart's pro-Jackson account should be compared with John Frank 1949:124–131, which offers a countervailing bias.

A statistical test of this hypothesis would consist of a comparison of the totals for Jackson's majority and dissenting opinions, for the periods before and after his absence from the Court during the 1945 Term. Since an increase in the proportion of Jackson's dissents is predicted, the test will be one-tailed, and as before the confidence level of .05 is posited as the criterion for acceptance or rejection.

5.3 *After his return from his experiences as chief prosecutor at Nuremberg, Jackson became more conservative toward civil liberty, in both his opinion and voting behavior.*

A subjective reading of Jackson's opinions which discuss civil liberty issues leaves one with the impression that his intimate familiarity with the rise of the Nazi movement under the Weimar Republic—a subject which he frequently found occasion to discuss in his extra-judicial writings subsequent to 1946—had convinced him that it was suicidal for a democracy to permit conspiratorial, revolutionary groups to organize, to advocate openly their seditious doctrines, and to contest with rival groups for the control of the streets. Many persons, including many judges, would agree with such a position, without having had the very exceptional sensitization to the threat of fascism that Jackson must have experienced in his role as chief prosecutor. But the hypothesis here is that Jackson's attitude toward "ordered liberty" became more conservative as a consequence of his having had the unique experience that Nuremberg afforded; and that this change in his attitude had a significant effect upon his subsequent behavior as a judge.

A statistical test of this hypothesis is provided by comparing the marginals for the political liberalism/conservatism content and voting variables, for the periods before and after his absence from the Court during the 1945 Term. The test should be one-tailed, since the direction of change is predicted; and the .05 level of confidence is the criterion for decision.

5.4 *After the end of World War II, Jackson became more conservative toward economic policy, in both his opinion and his voting behavior.*

This hypothesis rests upon the assumption that Jackson's fundamental economic orientation was that of a conservative (cf. Berelson et al. 1954:1, 94, 100; McClosky 1958): he was a self-made man and the leading lawyer in a small city, located in an area where traditional and business values were decidedly dominant; and his lifelong friend and early client was the head of a local utility corporation. Jackson liked and lived the life of the upper middle-class gentleman; and most of his friends enjoyed similar socioeconomic status. The fact that he himself was a Democrat, while the community in which he lived and most of his friends (during the first four decades of his life) were staunchly Republican, presents no real contradiction; to the contrary, the traditional basis for Jackson's choice of party is in strict accord with the findings of many investigations of political socialization (H. Hyman 1959:74; Maccoby et al. 1954–1955). His great-grandfather, Elijah Jackson, was described as a "stiff Democrat" and was identified with a group who "were generally intense partisans of General Andrew Jackson"; his grandfather,

Robert R. Jackson, "was a Democrat throughout his life, [who] boasted to young Robert of having voted for Franklin Pierce and for every Democratic candidate for President from that time down to Woodrow Wilson"; and his father, William Eldred Jackson, "remained an outspoken Democrat," in "a community that was intensely and sometimes bitterly Republican (Gerhart 1958:26–28).

Jackson's conversion to the economic liberalism of the New Deal was a necessary function of his career in national politics, but there is no need to assume that his enthusiastic support of the New Deal's economic programs was not perfectly "sincere." Similarly, his attack upon the economic conservatism of the Hughes Court (R. Jackson 1941) is in the style, and has all of the ear-marks, of the partisan advocacy of a brief filed by the president's counsel before the bar of public opinion, Jackson's disclaimer of "dispassionate. . . . consider[ation]" (1941:v) to the contrary notwithstanding. Both the necessity of preserving the image of a "typical New Dealer"—as he was called by journalists in the late 1930s—so long as hope of the chief justiceship (or even of the presidency) remained, and the pressures to uphold the successful prosecution of World War II, provide reinforcing explanations for the assumption that Jackson would write and vote as an economic liberal during his first four terms on the Court. None of these considerations survived after Jackson returned to the Court in 1946, and we might well expect that his acceptance of the end of his political career would be accompanied by an apparent shift to the right that would bring his decision-making behavior in regard to economic issues in closer accord with his personal ideology.

This hypothesis, it should be noted, is not the same as Hypothesis 5.1, to which it might be thought to bear some superficial resemblance. To test it we require that there be a sharp differentiation between the periods before and after the 1945 Term, and—to the contrary of what we stipulated for 5.1— that there be no significant difference between the second and third periods (i.e., 1946–1949 and 1950–1953). Moreover, 5.4 applies only to the economic conservatism value, while 5.1 requires conjoint change for political conservatism as well. Our test for 5.4 will be: (a) that a change takes place in the direction of Jackson's support for both the content and the voting economic variables, from liberalism to conservatism; and (b) that the difference between the sets of marginals be statistically significant at the .05 level of confidence (one-tailed).

5.5 *Jackson's decision-making behavior became more liberal after Murphy and Rutledge left the Court.*

Both Murphy and Rutledge, who frequently voted with Black and Douglas in support of liberal values (Schubert 1965c: 103–105, 129–131), died during the summer vacation between the end of the 1948 Term and the opening of the 1949 Term. I have demonstrated elsewhere the influence that a bloc of four justices can have in forcing the consideration of an issue by the rest of the Court, under the Court's rule that jurisdictional decisions can be made by a minority of four justices (1962c). I have also shown that the effect of the reduction in size of the libertarian bloc to two justices—actually, to only one justice during the 1949 Term, in view of Douglas' absence during most of this term due to a horseback-riding injury—was a drastic change in the character of the stimuli to which the justices were expected to respond, with an almost total elimination of the more extreme libertarian claims that Murphy and Rutledge frequently favored having the Court consider and decide in behalf of the claimants (1965c:226). From a psychological point of view, then, Jackson's responses ought to appear to be relatively more liberal during a period when he was asked to uphold less extreme libertarian claims—claims that he could more readily accept; or, as Guttman might put it, when he was being asked "easier questions."

We require, under this hypothesis, that Jackson give proportionately greater support to the liberal values in both his voting and opinion writing during the later period. The test will be to compare the marginals for the content and voting variables for both the political and economic variables, for the terms before and after the summer of 1949. The direction of change is predicted, so a one-tailed chi square test at a confidence level of .05 provides an appropriate criterion.

## III. A GENERAL DESCRIPTION OF THE FINDINGS

The voting and content variables can be initially described, in a general way, by the observation of their marginal frequencies.[11] For the political variable, Jackson voted 45–40 and for the economic variable 46–71. The slight positive leaning in his civil liberties votes is of course not statistically significant, but his voting preference for economic conservatism is significant at the .03 level.[12] The joint total for both voting variables, 202, indicates that two-thirds of our 306 cases involved what were for the Court decisions relating to these two major attitudinal variables. Analysis of the much larger sample (1643) of all nonunanimous decisions on the merits during the seventeen terms 1946–1962 shows that a third of these decisions (572) involved the political variable and another third (551) the economic variable (Schubert 1965c:148). Comparison of these two samples suggests that although the present sample is quite typical of the period in which Jackson was a member of the Court, in the relative importance of liberalism and conservatism to other attitudinal dimensions, Jackson showed a marked affinity for writing opinions in cases raising the economic issue: the difference between the total of 85 political votes and 117 economic votes is significant at the .001 level.

---

11. In the discussion that follows, the first of each pair of frequencies will be that for the positive value and the second will be for the negative; for the content variables, the frequency for ambivalent scores appears in parentheses between the marginals.

12. This and the subsequent findings in the text at this point are based on the chi-square one-sample test (two-tailed).

His verbal behavior is in sharp contrast to his voting behavior, however. He favored the liberal political value significantly 35–(30)–16, while apportioning his support for the economic content variable with seeming impartiality 42–(24)–38. One might well conclude that Jackson gave verbal support to civil liberty while giving his voting support to economic conservatism.

For Jackson it made a difference, however, whether the civil liberties claimant opposed the national or a state government. The overall marginals for the political content variable disguise the fact that his support for civil liberty claims against the national government, 30–(13)–7, was accompanied by a negative deference toward state civil liberty claimants, 6–(20)–11. If the 2:1 ratio of national to state cases had been reversed, Jackson's verbal support for political liberalism might have appeared to be just as impartial as his support for the economic content variable. In regard to economic content, however, the differences in his support of national, 19–(6)–10, and of state, 21–(14)–5, regulation of business seem less important—although the latter is statistically significant and the former is not—than the opposite direction of his remarks concerning the antimonopoly component of the economic variable: Jackson favored the *negative* value (promonopoly) 14–(7)–30, and some of the most incisive language in his opinions upholds the virtues of free enterprise and denounces the vices of organized labor. So the fact that the most proximate prelude to his Nuremberg manifesto was his thinly veiled public attack upon Black in a labor relations case is doubtless no accident (*Jewell Ridge Coal Co.* v. *Local No. 6167, United Mine Workers of America*; Gerhart 1958:247–253). And the seeming balance of Jackson's verbal support regarding the economic content variable results from the admixture of his generally liberal remarks about both national and state government regulation of business, and his generally conservative views toward labor-management relationships.

On issues of federalism, Jackson tended to favor states' rights (decentralization:N–), but not significantly so, 23–(9)–30. In regard to the three variables which involve the Court's participation in policy-making, however, he gave quite one-sided and significant verbal support to the negative values, favoring restraint in Supreme Court policy-making (P–) 33–(80)–117; deference to lower-court policy-making (J–) 19–(38)–80; and deference to policy-making by the Executive and Congress (A–) 18–(16)–35. He also manifested significantly negative deference toward litigants (X–) 39–(15)–65.

The remaining three variables could not be included in the correlational analysis, for the technical reasons mentioned earlier. Although most of his remarks about lawyers and their role were favorable 13–(2)–5, he discussed this subject so infrequently that the difference between his favorable and unfavorable statements is of only marginal statistical significance. His sympathy for the public interest 56–(1)–1 and his antipathy for his colleagues 7–(6)–154, to the contrary, are both highly significant statistically. Indeed, the extremity of the division of the marginals for the public interest variable suggests that the phrase "the public interest" had no substantive attitudinal content for Jackson, and that, instead, he employed it as a benediction or malediction for any other subject about which he wanted to speak with favor or disfavor (Schubert 1960b). This view finds support in an examination of the fourfold tables for the public interest and other variables, which reveals that his most frequent affirmations of the public interest occurred in opinions in which he urged judicial restraint or was deferential to lower court judges, or nondeferential to litigants or to his colleagues. His zeal for the public interest was most articulate in relationship to his discussion of ideas that he favored and of the behavior of other people with whom he disagreed: ideas that he approved were identified with the public interest, and persons whom he criticized were stigmatized as behaving contrary to the public interest.

Jackson's favorite subjects for discussion in all of his opinions were judicial restraint and his colleagues. This is hardly surprising; we might well expect Supreme Court justices to be introspective about their role, and sensitive to their interpersonal relationships, especially in the context of essays whose function is to establish the rectitude of one's own ideas and the erroneous thinking of one's associates. However, it is customary, for this very reason, for Supreme Court justices (like congressmen) to bend over backwards to observe the formal marks of courtesy; the usual form of address of a justice who is about to impale a colleague is to refer to him as "brother," and to express extreme respect for his views. Jackson rarely bothered to observe such amenities. As we noted earlier, he was a very candid man; and indeed, "candor" and "rationality" were the words he mentioned most frequently when showing negative deference to his colleagues. He combined remarks critical of his colleagues with advocacy of policy restraint in over a fourth of his opinions; this was the highest association for any pair of variables. He also frequently associated anticolleague remarks with affirmations of the public interest and with deference to lower courts.

## The Correlation Matrix

Table 16 shows the fourfold tables and the correlation matrix for the content variables. One weakness that is probably inherent in the use of the method of content analysis, at least with this type of data, is evident in the fourfold tables: the size of the observed frequencies often is small (the numbers in the cells are low), notwithstanding the fact that the observations were based upon a set of over three hundred opinions. This reflects, of course, the circumstance that judicial opinions are written selectively, and the issues raised by discrete cases are so delimited by the screening processes of lower appellate court review and Supreme Court jurisdictional decision-making that no justice finds it necessary or appropriate to discuss all of his attitudes in all of his opinions. In effect, each opinion of a justice defines a subset which includes a sample drawn from the universal set of all his attitudes.

## Table 16. Fourfold Tables and Phi Correlation Matrix

| Variable | Symbol | 6 N+ | 7 A+ − | 7 A+ + | 8 J+ − | 8 J+ + | 10 X+ − | 10 X+ + | 13 P+ − | 13 P+ + | 14 C+ − | 14 C+ + | 15 E+ − | 15 E+ + |
|---|---|---|---|---|---|---|---|---|---|---|---|---|---|---|
| Federal Centralization | N+ | + | 3 | 0 | 4 | 3 | 3 | 0 | 11 | 2 | 2 | 0 | 1 | 5 |
|  |  | − | 3 | 3 | 7 | 5 | 7 | 5 | 8 | 3 | 2 | 4 | 2 | 4 |
| Judicial Review | A+ | −.50 | + |  | 7 | 0 | 6 | 5 | 3 | 0 | 1 | 5 | 2 | 4 |
|  |  |  | − |  | 7 | 0 | 11 | 4 | 13 | 0 | 3 | 3 | 4 | 6 |
| Judicial Centralization | J+ | .01 | .00 |  | + |  | 3 | 3 | 8 | 1 | 0 | 2 | 1 | 2 |
|  |  |  |  |  | − |  | 21 | 6 | 27 | 9 | 3 | 3 | 9 | 7 |
| Pro Litigants | X+ | −.35 | .20 |  | .24 |  | + |  | 20 | 4 | 1 | 7 | 7 | 2 |
|  |  |  |  |  |  |  | − |  | 21 | 5 | 8 | 6 | 4 | 9 |
| Judicial Activism | P+ | −.15 | .00 |  | −.13 |  | −.03 |  | + |  | 1 | 4 | 4 | 3 |
|  |  |  |  |  |  |  |  |  | − |  | 7 | 16 | 16 | 15 |
| Political Liberalism | C+ | −.58 | .35 |  | −.45 |  | .44 |  | .09 |  | + |  | 3 | 1 |
|  |  |  |  |  |  |  |  |  |  |  | − |  | 0 | 4 |
| Economic Liberalism | E+ | .19 | .07 |  | .17 |  | −.46 |  | −.04 |  | −.78 |  |  |  |

As already noted, the marginal distributions for the variables show that Jackson favored the negative (or deference) value for all except the political and economic variables. Hence it might seem convenient to identify these other five variables by short titles which would emphasize their negative values. It happens, however, that almost all of their intercorrelations are negative or zero—of course, the correlation between (A−, J−) is identical to that between (A+, J+)—and the correlation between (C+, E+) also is negative. It seems more important, therefore, to maximize (as Table 17 does) the positive correlations in the matrix in order to facilitate the cluster analysis. That is best accomplished by reversing the polarity of E and N only. And questions of format aside, all the statistical relationships remain unaffected by such a transformation.

The relationships shown by the correlation coefficients are quite compatible with intuitive expectations. Using the short titles given in Table 17, JUDCEN (Judicial Centralization) for instance, is associated with POLIB (Political Liberalism) (support for civil liberties) and PROLIT (Pro Litigants) (sympathy for litigants)—in the latter instance, for the perfectly sensible reason that in most opinions in which he discussed both subjects, Jackson combined deference to the lower court with remarks hostile to the litigant who was seeking to upset its decision. The zero correlation between JUDCEN and JUDREV (Judicial Review) demonstrates that Jackson's attitude toward judicial review of the decision-making of lower courts was perfectly independent of his attitude toward judicial review of the decision-making of Congress and the administration. Similarly, his attitude toward federalism was independent of his attitude toward lower courts, which shows that he discriminated

**Table 17. The Transformed Correlation Matrix**

| Value | | | | | | | | |
|---|---|---|---|---|---|---|---|---|
| Short titles | | JUDCEN | PROLIT | ECONS | POLIB | FEDECEN | JUDREV | JUDACT |
| | Symbol | J+ | X+ | E− | C+ | N− | A+ | P+ |
| *Name* | | | | | | | | |
| Judicial Centralization | J+ | | .24 | −.17 | .45 | * | * | * |
| Pro Litigants | X+ | .24 | | .46 | .44 | .35 | .20 | * |
| Economic Conservatism | E− | −.17 | .46 | | .78 | .19 | * | * |
| Political Liberalism | C+ | .45 | .44 | .78 | | .58 | .35 | * |
| Federal Decentralization | N− | * | .35 | .19 | .58 | | .50 | * |
| Judicial Review | A+ | * | .20 | * | .35 | .50 | | * |
| Judicial Activism | P+ | * | * | * | * | * | * | |

NOTE: Intercorrelations among the four variables in the cluster denoted by Hierarchical Syndrome Analysis are in boldface. * ≤ ±.15.

sharply between what were for him the disparate policy issues of centralization in the government generally, and within the judicial hierarchy; otherwise, we should expect to find a high positive correlation between J+ and N+.

Table 17 shows that the other two content values most closely related to judicial policy-making (A+ and P+) are independent of each other and (like J+) not very closely associated with the remaining four variables, among which intercorrelation tends to be highest. We might well infer from this that Jackson's attitude toward activism and restraint in policy-making by the Supreme Court, although often articulated with intensity and fervor, had very little to do with his attitudes toward the other content variables. This inference suggests that the Supreme Court policy-making variable functioned for him like the public interest and colleagues variables: all of these were useful as verbal symbols that he could manipulate in support of other values to which he attached greater substantive significance, and which were probably much more important in shaping his decision-making.

JUDREV has its highest correlations with FEDECEN (Federal Decentralization) and POLIB. Both of these are intuitively sensible relationships. Jackson never argued in favor of judicial review of presidential or congressional action (or spoke favorably of a litigant) in an opinion in which he also defended centralization of governmental power; and in the civil liberties cases, he urged judicial review most often when upholding the rights of claimants. His attitude toward the constitutional autonomy of the other two branches was substantially independent of his views on economic policy, however, and the very low or zero correlations with the remaining variables suggest that for Jackson the only legitimate justifications for judicial supremacy were in defense of states' rights and civil liberties. POLIB itself correlates at .35 or better with all except one of the other variables; while the economic variable correlates as highly as this *only* with one other variable (PROLIT) besides POLIB.

## The Cluster Analysis

Various methods of cluster analysis confirm what seems obvious from an examination of the face of the correlation matrix (Borgatta 1958–1959). The simplest of these methods, which focuses upon the primary and secondary levels of interrelationships, is McQuitty's Elementary Linkage Analysis (ELA) (1957). ELA shows for each variable which other is most highly correlated with it, as signified by a solid directional arrow in Figure 8; second highest relationships are depicted by broken directional arrows: and reciprocal relationships are portrayed by pairs of apposite half-arrows.

Figure 8 shows that the closest association is between POLIB and ECONS (Economic Conservation); and that PROLIT is most closely related to ECONS, JUDCEN with POLIB; while JUDREV and JUDACT (Judicial Activism) both are functions of FEDECEN, which in turn is most closely related to POLIB.

Observation of the secondary linkages brings out more clearly the principal cluster relationships. There are three important and interlocking clusters: (X+, E−, C+), (E−, C+, N−), and (C+, N−, A+). PROLIT and

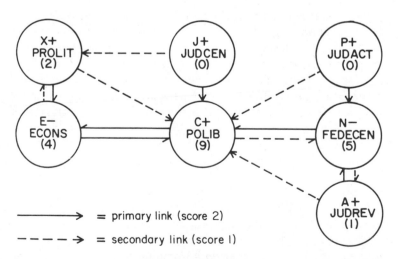

Figure 8. Primary and Secondary Elementary Linkage among Content Values

JUDREV are linked through the (E−, C+) and (C+, N−) pairs, respectively; and the (E−, C+, N−) triple is the central element in the structure. All the other values have either primary or secondary links with POLIB, which serves as the cornerstone. The two least well-integrated values are J+ and P+; judicial review of lower courts is advocated most frequently in conjunction with support for civil liberty and litigant deference, while JUDACT is oriented toward POLIB and FEDECEN.

What the above analysis fails adequately to emphasize is the low level of association between economic conservatism and federal decentralization, which is, however, made quite evident by the alternative methods of Hierarchical Syndrome Analysis (HSA) and Rank Order Typal Analysis (ROTA) (McQuitty 1960, 1963). HSA defines (X+, E−, C+, N−) as the only important quadruple.

ROTA, which is the method most sensitive to intransitivity of relationships, suggest first the (E−, C+) double; next the (X+, E−, C+) triple; and then the (X+, E−, C+, N−) quadruple. The only intransitivity for the triple is a function of the trivial difference between POLIB's correlation of .45 with J+, as compared to its .44 correlation with X+; the only other intransitivity is the previously mentioned low .19 between E− and N−. ROTA confirms that the three policy-making values (J+, A+, and P+) are poorly associated, either with the cluster of four or with each other.

Cluster analysis directs attention to the integrative role of political liberalism in the structure of Jackson's attitudes. The most general finding would be that there is one primary cluster, composed of litigant deference, economic conservatism, political liberalism, and federal decentralization. There are also two overlapping subclusters: JUDREV with POLIB and FEDECEN; and JUDCEN with POLIB and PROLIT. ECONS has important associations *only* with POLIB and PROLIT. The intercorrelations among E−, C+, and X+ are the only ones statistically significant at the .05 level of confidence.

## The Factor Analysis

I have assumed that factor analysis might reveal certain latent relationships among the content variables, but that the latent structure ought, of course, to be consistent with the manifest structure developed by cluster analysis. Six factors were extracted, and 85 percent of the variance was accounted for by the first four axes. Varimax rotation loaded most of the variance on the first two rotated axes, and upon a sixth factor which emphasized the same three variables as did the second. In Table 18 the four principal axes are designated by roman numerals, and the two rotated factors by roman numerals with prime (′) marks; reversed factors are designated by asterisks.

Table 18 shows the first principal axis to be clearly one of political liberalism, and the third to be predominately one of economic conservatism joined with deference to lower courts. The second and fourth axes focus more

**Table 18. Principal Axes and Varimax Factors**

| Factors | I* | II | III* | IV* | I'* | II' |
|---|---|---|---|---|---|---|
| *Values* | | | | | | |
| JUDCEN | .28 | −.56 | .63 | .47 | .00 | .00 |
| PROLIT | .69 | −.24 | .00 | −.11 | .26 | .09 |
| ECONS | .68 | −.27 | −.66 | −.18 | .97 | −.10 |
| POLIB | .94 | −.17 | −.03 | .14 | .82 | .24 |
| FEDECEN | .71 | .49 | .15 | −.04 | .17 | .27 |
| JUDREV | .47 | .58 | .48 | −.23 | .01 | .97 |
| JUDACT | .10 | .47 | −.38 | .77 | .03 | −.01 |

upon the policy-making values: the second pairs judicial review with judicial decentralization, and federal decentralization with judicial activism; while the fourth is mostly concerned with judicial activism and judicial centralization. None of these relationships appears to be illogical or inconsistent. Jackson's attitude toward civil liberty appears strongly related to his states' rights sentiments, his attitude toward civil liberties claimants, and his economic conservatism; the three policy-making values are much less important to his political liberalism. Certainly, as the third axis suggests, it is sensible that at the time when Jackson was on the Court, he should associate economic conservatism with deference to lower-court decision-making. Similarly, it is plausible for the third axis to associate judicial review of executive-legislative policy-making with both judicial activism and the decentralization of judicial policy-making (since the lower federal and state courts then were probably more conservative than the Supreme Court); but of course judicial centralization is also a sensible adjunct to activism in Supreme Court policy-making.

Only two relationships worth mentioning are shown by the fifth and sixth axes (which are not reproduced here). PROLIT correlates −.67, and POLIB .33, with V*, indicating that Jackson by no means sympathized with all claimants even when he wrote and voted in support of their civil liberty claims—and names such as Rosenberg, Beauharnais, and Guy W. Ballard ("alias Saint Germain, Jesus, George Washington, and Godfre Ray King") come readily to mind as examples. On VI, FEDECEN is .49 and JUDREV −.40, suggesting that Jackson frequently advocated judicial restraint toward *state* executive-legislative policy-making.

The varimax factors denote the same two clusters of triples that we observed through cluster analysis: the first (X+, E−, C+) on I', and the second (C+, N−, A+) on II'. Factor I' shows that Jackson's extremely high degree of economic conservatism was associated with a favorable attitude toward civil liberty, a moderate amount of sympathy for litigants, and a lesser degree of states' rights sentiment. Stated otherwise, his liberal attitude toward personal rights was in contradiction to his conservative attitude toward property rights. The inconsistency may lie, however, in contemporary notions of liberalism rather than in Jackson's thinking. To favor civil liberty means to *oppose* governmental control of personal rights, while to favor economic liberalism means to *support* governmental control of property rights. Jackson, therefore, was consistent in his support of both the personal and the property rights of the individual, in opposition to governmental control. He was, in short, more a classic nineteenth-century than a modern twentieth-century liberal (Schubert 1965c:201).

It may seem surprising, at least at first blush, to discover that the author of a book entitled *The Struggle for Judicial Supremacy* (R. Jackson 1941), in which he vigorously attacked his immediate predecessors on the Court for *their* economic conservatism and defense of an out-moded ideology, should become a judge whose most pronounced attitude was one of empathy with John Stuart Mill rather than with John Maynard Keynes. But Jackson the judge did not hesitate to dissociate himself from what he once characterized as "earlier partisan advocacy"; as he remarked in the *Steel Seizure Case*, apropos a policy statement he had issued as attorney general, "a judge cannot accept self-serving press statements of the attorney for one of the interested parties [i.e., the previous, not the then occupant of the office of president of the United States] as authority in answering a constitutional question, even if the advocate was himself" (concurring in *Youngstown Sheet and Tube Co.* v. *Sawyer*). Of course, the correctness of this appraisal rests upon the assumption that Jackson *did* change, in his official behavior, from an economic liberal to an economic conservative, a proposition that we shall test below.

The close correspondence between the cluster and factorial findings is further demonstrated by Figure 9, which depicts the three most important planes in which we can observe the relationships among the content values and between their major clusters.

In the liberalism plane, the first cluster is a prominent substructure in the configuration; and although this cluster includes what clearly appear to be a majority of the values that were most important to him, these are not the values that Jackson seems to emphasize in his valedictory, the Godkin Lectures (1955). There Jackson advocates, instead, primarily political liberalism and the three values aligned with it in the first quadrant of the liberalism plane: federal decentralization, judicial review, and judicial centralization.

Judicial activism is the most extremely positioned value in the policy-making plane, in which the second cluster appears prominently. If JUDCEN were replaced by the negative value for that variable, it (JUDCEN) would appear in the fourth quadrant of the plane, immediately below JUDREV, confirming our earlier observation that in deferring to states rights, Jackson argued that judicial review of state policy-making should be left to the lower courts. But both major clusters are centered around and not far from the origin of the space, which confirms graphically our previous observation that Jackson's advocacy of judicial activism—or restraint—was virtually independent of the crux of his system of values.

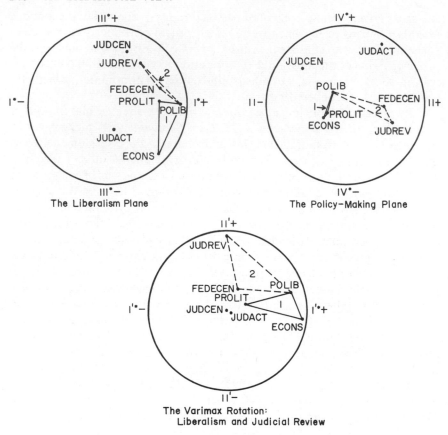

Figure 9. Three Perspectives of the Value Configuration

In the plane defined by the two rotated factors, both major clusters appear in the first quadrant, with the first cluster loaded primarily on the first rotated axis, and the second cluster loaded primarily on the second axis. Here, judicial review is independent of economic conservatism, and political liberalism is the most important correlate for both of them. From this perspective, neither judicial centralization nor judicial activism has any bearing upon the values in the two clusters.

It was anticipated that factor analysis would reveal latent relationships more subtle than those made manifest by cluster analysis. Clearly, the factorial analysis confirms very strongly the cluster findings, while at the same time adding detail, depth, and clarity to the perception of the interrelationships among the values. One additional finding, that cluster analysis did not denote, is most apparent in Figure 9. FEDECEN and PROLIT appear closely associated with each other, as well as with POLIB, in both liberalism planes; and this is also true of the policy-making plane, but with the difference that in the latter perspective, they constitute (with ECONS) the values that are least associated with the function of judicial policy-making.

## IV. THE TESTS OF THE HYPOTHESES

We turn now to an examination of the substantive findings in relation to the set of hypotheses stated earlier.

(1) The cluster analysis findings denoted two overlapping clusters: (X+, E−, C+) and (C+, N−, A+). Other research in Supreme Court voting behavior has identified attitudes toward C and E as the two most basic attitudinal dimensions for the justices as a group (Schubert 1965c: chap. 5). Voting data for the Court as a whole, collected by terms, do not provide sufficient depth to make possible cumulative scaling of all the content variables discussed in the present study, based as it is upon the pooling of opinion data for a dozen terms. However, other evidence suggests that N, A, and J are scalable variables (Schubert 1965c: 146–157). The only cluster element that shows up more importantly in Jackson's opinion writing behavior than in the voting of the justices as a group is the litigant variable.

There is nothing irrational or illogical about the cluster associations. Traditional scholarship discusses and finds much ambiguity in Jackson's views on issues of economic policy, civil liberty, and centralization; but traditional scholarship has little to say about Jackson's views toward judicial review of lower courts, since the usual concern is with "substantive" rather than jurisdictional decision-making; and it has nothing whatever to say about Jackson's attitudes toward litigants, since there is no relevant legal category to encompass this ("bias" means something quite different, in legal parlance, the fiction being that judges' decisions are not affected by their attitudes toward the parties litigant. Our clusters, therefore, seem meaningful; they are internally consistent; and they reveal relationships that transcend the accepted lore about Jackson's "philosophy as a judge." No basis appears for rejecting Hypothesis 1.

(2) Hypothesis 2 states that the latent attitudinal dimensions revealed by factor analysis will correspond to the scaling and factorial attitudinal dimensions that independent research has identified as common for the Court during the period in which Jackson served. The scaling and factor research in the attitudes of the whole Court covers the period of the 1946–1962 Terms, which includes the last eight terms of Jackson's tenure. These data show that Jackson's average rank was between fourth and fifth on C and between eighth and ninth on E (Schubert 1965c: 104–107, 130–133). In relation to the seventeen other justices who were on the Court during the period 1946–1963, Jackson ranked tenth on political liberalism, and seventeenth on economic liberalism (Schubert 1965c: 125, 145). Evidently he was a political moderate but an economic conservative in his attitudes, as one would infer from his voting behavior in relation to his colleagues. Moreover, in that behavior and during that period, Jackson was a moderate on a Court that became more

conservative, as a group, toward civil liberty; and he was a conservative on a Court that became more liberal, as a group, toward economic policy.

The political and the economic variables were the two most important attitudinal scales for the justices as a group, throughout the 1946–1963 period. Many justices are liberals, and some are conservatives, on both scales; but it is precisely because other justices are (like Jackson) more liberal toward political than economic issues—or, like Tom Clark, politically conservative but economically moderate—that two scales are necessary in order adequately to measure the similarities and differences among the justices with regard to the major components of modern liberalism.

Once comparisons are made between his voting in the political and economic cases in which he wrote opinions, and his rank position on the general C and E voting scales, it becomes relevant to inquire whether the votes with opinions constitute a representative sample of the universes of political and economic voting data. Although, as we noted earlier, the sample is representative to the extent that it includes the same ratio of C and E votes, to total votes, as does the universe of voting data, this finding does not inform us concerning the correspondence between the *direction* of those votes, in the sample and in the universe.[13] For the political variables, the ratios of liberal to total votes are .67 for the sample and .34 for the universe, during the period before the 1945 Term; and .50 (sample) and .34 (universe) thereafter. The ratios for the entire period of twelve terms are .53 and .34. For the economic variable, the corresponding ratios are .57 and .43 (before the 1945 Term), .26 and .13 (afterward), and .39 and .26 (overall). Taking into consideration the different frequency sums to which these ratios relate, and using a two-tailed test, the difference is significant (at $< .05$) between all pairs of ratios except for economic voting during the earlier subperiod—and even that difference is significant, if we compare Jackson's voting in cases with opinion with his voting in cases in which he wrote no opinion. Evidently, Jackson voted consistently more liberally on both political and economic issues, in the cases in which he wrote opinions, than when he voted without opinion. This (one might infer) may have been for the very good reason that he chose to write separate opinions, or was assigned the opinion of the Court, in those cases in which he was prepared to take what was for him a relatively liberal position (e.g., concurring in *Edwards* v. *California*, and writing for the majority in *West Virginia State Board of Education* v. *Barnette*). But we must likewise conclude that in his overall decisional behavior, Jackson was even more conservative than he appears to be on the basis of the present analysis of the cases in which he wrote opinions. Jackson also tended to be more liberal in his opinion writing

---

13. The data for voting in decisions with opinion are reported in Table 20; for the marginal distributions for all Jackson's votes in decisions on the merits of the political and economic scale variables, see fn. 15 and 16. A comparison of these two sources shows that for those (non-sample) cases in which he wrote no opinion, the voting marginals (before and after the 1945 Term) are: for C, 11–36 and 37–104; and for E, 40–66 and 8–127.

than in his voting toward either C or E, although these differences are only marginally significant at about .10 (two-tailed). The data are suggestive, therefore, of a consistent scalar relationship for both variables: that Jackson was most liberal in his opinions, that he was relatively moderate in his voting in cases in which he wrote opinions, and that he was most conservative in his voting in the cases in which he wrote no opinions.

Since Jackson's verbal support for civil liberty was *more* extreme than his voting support, while his verbal support for economic conservatism was *less* extreme than his voting support, we should interpret Factor I of Table 18 as indicating for Jackson a more favorable attitude of political liberalism, and a less extreme attitude of economic conservatism, than are suggested by scaling and factor analysis based on observations of his voting behavior. There is certainly nothing inconsistent, however, between the two sets of data; to the contrary they reinforce each other strongly, and the more so once we recognize the apparently consistent differentials between his verbal and his voting behaviors.

Both factors I and I' show Jackson's political and economic attitudes to be functions of a single factor of liberalism. Factor analysis of voting data for the Court shows precisely the same thing, with the difference that observations for a set of nine justices make it possible to relate cumulative scales, representing the C and E variables, to the reference axes in factorial space. Typically, the C and E scales are highly correlated with the first centroid axis, which appears as the mean between the scales (Schubert 1965c: 209–217). As noted above, Jackson in relation to his colleagues was a moderate on civil liberties but the most extreme conservative on the Court on economic issues (although Whittaker, who joined the Court after Jackson's death, was even more extreme in economic conservatism). This attitudinal combination of political moderation and economic conservatism has been identified with the ideological type Pragmatic Conservatism; and among the eighteen justices who served during the seventeen-term period 1946–1963, Jackson ranked thirteenth on liberalism but second on the pragmatism dimension—on which he was exceeded only by Goldberg (for whom only the data of a single term were available) (Schubert 1965c: 262, 266, 271). Pragmatism was there defined as a function of the component ideologies of individualism and libertarianism; and on the individualism factor, Jackson typically ranked very high—in five of the eight terms, 1946–1953, he ranked first (Schubert 1965c: 204, 224).

Jackson can best be characterized, on the basis of his voting in relationship to his colleagues, as ideologically a pragmatic, individualistic conservative; and attitudinally as a political moderate and economic conservative. Nothing revealed by the present study is inconsistent with calling him a conservative judge with a high regard for individualism and pragmatism. These are all qualities which have been stressed as typical of him, by previous commentators upon his philosophy. Barnett concludes that "His general position has been individualistic, pragmatic, hard to predict, middle-of-the-road, and, on balance, conservative."[14] Weidner characterizes his approach to civil liberties as "pragmatic." Jackson himself, incidentally, cited William James in a pro-civil liberty opinion (*United States* v. *Ballard*)—and James is hardly an authority frequently invoked by Supreme Court justices.

It is true that the latent voting-factor ideologies are different from the second, third, and fourth opinion-content factors, which relate to manifest attitudes. On the other hand, we have found significant differences between his verbal behavior and his voting behavior in general; and this destroys any empirical basis for the assumption (underlying Hypothesis 2) that the attitudes revealed by Jackson's opinions necessarily would correspond to the attitudes inferred from his general voting behavior. The manifest opinion factors are a function of the means he employed to proffer a formal rationalization for a small portion of his total votes, and frequently, in direct relationship with small groups (and often, with none) of his colleagues; the latent voting factors are a function of his conjoint relationship with all his colleagues. Neither the strategies nor the tactics nor the processes that govern opinion writing and voting are the same. The opinion factors tell us what was most common in the relationships among Jackson's manifest attitudes in what he chose to write "for the record"; while the voting factors inform us what was most common among the latent ideologies of all the justices— Jackson plus eight colleagues. What we ought reasonably to have expected, in comparing two such sets of factors, was not congruence, but the absence of inconsistency.

The first factor—liberalism—is the same for both sets. The subsequent opinion factors represent attitudes that were important for Jackson in the cases in which he wrote opinions, and which were fundamental components of his personal system of values; but these were not values accepted as the most important criteria for decision by enough of his colleagues, so as to appear as important components of the first three (at least) factors common to the justices as a group in their voting over the period of the past two decades.

We conclude that there is certainly no basis for the complete rejection of Hypothesis 2. It cannot be confirmed in its entirety in the form stated, but the reason lies in the ineptitude of our formulation of the hypothesis rather than in any basic inconsistency in the two sets of factor data. Hypothesis 2 must therefore be partially rejected, but our test of it has not been unfruitful. The present intensive study of the opinions of a single justice and the related extensive studies of the voting behavior of the Court as a group differ in many respects methodologically; yet, to the extent that they may appropriately be compared, they are in very substantial agreement.

---

14. Barnett 1948:241. Cf. the works, all there cited, of the following authors: Fairman 1955:487; Gerhart 1953:969, 971; Jaffe 1955:992–993; Nielson 1945:384, 401–403; and Weidner 1955:593.

(3) Hypothesis 3 assumes a significantly high positive correlation between Jackson's opinions and votes, in support of the political and the economic content variables. Table 19 shows that the correlation between values and votes (1) for political liberalism is positive and moderately high, and (2) for economic liberalism also is positive and slightly higher. Conversely, the cross correlation between political values and economic votes is zero, and between economic values and political votes it is negative and moderately high.

Table 19. Intercorrelations among Values and Votes for the Political and Economic Variables

|  |  | Values | | | |
|---|---|---|---|---|---|
|  |  | E | | C | |
|  |  | − | + | − | + |
| Votes |  |  |  |  |  |
| C | + | 3 | 2 | 2 | 23 |
|  | − | 0 | 3 | 10 | 4 |
|  | $\phi =$ | −.600 | | .659 | |
|  | $X^2 =$ | [Fisher's] | | 16.95 | |
|  | $p$ | $=.179$ | | $<.005$ | |
| E | + | 1 | 23 | 1 | 1 |
|  | − | 23 | 6 | 1 | 1 |
|  | $\phi =$ | .751 | | .000 | |
|  | $X^2 =$ | 29.92 | | [Fisher's] | |
|  | $p$ | $<.0005$ | | $=.833$ | |

These correlations were calculated from only that part of the complete data in which the voting and the content variables were observed to occur together in the same decisions. Table 20 reports the sets of marginals for all votes and content values for both C and E, for each of the three major time periods.

On the basis of the demonstrated relationships between content values and votes, for both variables, I conclude that Hypothesis 3 is confirmed.

(4) Hypothesis 4 supposes no significant differences between Jackson's content values as articulated in concurring and in dissenting opinions, but expects them as between institutional and separate opinions. For purposes of the analysis below, "majority opinions" include both institutional and concurring opinions; "separate opinions" include both concurring and dissenting opinions; and institutional opinions continue to mean opinions for the Court. The data to be discussed are reported in Table 21.

**Table 20. Marginal Frequencies of Values and Votes for the Political and Economic Variables, by Major Periods**

|  | 1941–1944 | | | | 1946–1949 | | | | 1950–1953 | | | |
|---|---|---|---|---|---|---|---|---|---|---|---|---|
|  | C | | E | | C | | E | | C | | E | |
|  | + | − | + | − | + | − | + | − | + | − | + | − |
| Values | 5 | 2 | 19 | 10 | 13 | 6 | 11 | 14 | 17 | 8 | 12 | 14 |
| Votes | 10 | 5 | 28 | 21 | 13 | 15 | 8 | 25 | 22 | 20 | 10 | 25 |

We shall also examine an alternative Hypothesis 4′, which states the orthodox view: that there will be significant differences between majority and dissenting opinions (and, by implication, not otherwise).

In general, the first part of Hypothesis 4—that concurring and dissenting opinions will show no significant differences in content values—cannot be disproved statistically by our data. None of the differences is significant at the .05 level of confidence. For content variable N, the significance level is only slightly greater than .10 (two-tailed), and for P, it is less than .10 but greater than .05; these differences might be considered marginally significant. Jackson distinctly tended to argue for decentralization when he dissented. The difference for P is even more pronounced, however, when majority and dissenting opinions are compared; so the latter interpretation seems the more important one. For none of the variables, then, are differences between concurring and dissenting opinions statistically significant; and one of the two marginal contrasts is less important than another relationship to be considered below.

It is much easier, of course, to *fail* to find significant differences than to find them; so the test for the second part of the hypothesis is much the more important of the two tests. None of the differences between institutional opinions and concurrences is significant. There are significant differences between institutional opinions and dissents for E (and its component subvariables) and for X, and there are marginally significant differences for P; but most of these differences are even greater when majority opinions are compared with dissents, so as before I shall assume that the latter interpretation should be preferred.

Institutional opinions were also compared with separate opinions, but nothing new was revealed by this examination. The frequencies for concurrences are so much lower than for dissents that practically all of the differences that appear must be attributed to the effect of the latter variable; and the differences observed are of the same order as those discussed immediately above. I find no significant differences that properly can be construed as appertaining to a comparison of institutional opinions with concurring or dissenting opinions, let alone both. Consequently, Hypothesis 4 must be rejected.

**Table 21. Associations between Content and Opinion Variables**

| Content<br>Opinion | N<br>+ − | A<br>+ − | J<br>+ − | X<br>+ − | P<br>+ − | C<br>+ − | E<br>+ − | E(3)<br>(National)<br>+ | E(4)<br>(State)<br>+ − | E(5)<br>(Monopoly)<br>+ − |
|---|---|---|---|---|---|---|---|---|---|---|
| Institutional | 12 13 | 5 14 | 8 44 | 13 34 | 17 48 | 9 7 | 25 8 | 10 0 | 13 0 | 10 9 |
| Concurring | 6 3 | 2 7 | 4 12 | 2 8 | 7 14 | 10 5 | 4 2 | 3 2 | 1 0 | 0 0 |
| Dissenting | 5 14 | 10 13 | 7 23 | 23 21 | 8 54 | 15 4 | 13 28 | 6 8 | 7 5 | 4 21 |

Significant differences emerge, however, between majority and dissenting opinions, for economic liberalism and each of its three component variables (freedom from national restraint of economic liberty, freedom from state restraint of economic liberty, and pro business monopoly), at confidence levels ranging from less than .05 to less than .001, two-tailed.

Two other variables also show significant differences. Jackson was anti-litigant in his majority opinions, and ambivalent in dissent; and also significant is his tendency to argue for policy activism in majority more than in dissenting opinions. Thus, almost half of the variables show important differences in Jackson's opinion behavior when he voted with the majority as compared to when he dissented. I conclude that alternative Hypothesis 4′ is partially confirmed by these data; to the extent that significant differences appear in Jackson's opinion behavior, they support the traditional view that a dissenting judge articulates his attitudes more outspokenly than one who votes with the majority. My own hypothesis, which was inferred from socio-psychological theory, is not supported by the evidence of this study.

(5) Hypothesis 5 consists of a set of more specific hypotheses about changes in Jackson's opinion and voting behaviors, in response to what are assumed to have been critical events in his career.

5.1. This hypothesis states that Jackson became increasingly more conservative the longer he remained on the Court; and we have stipulated that, in order to confirm it, the data must provide evidence of progressive change through each of three major time periods. The data to test this hypothesis are contained in Table 20. Our present interest is in a comparison of the marginal distributions, between periods, for each of the four variables (political content values, political votes, economic content values, and economic votes).

For political content values, no significant differences are evident between periods; while for political votes and economic content values change occurs, and in the predicted direction, but only between the first and second periods, and even then it is not significant. For economic votes also, change occurs in the predicted direction between the first and second periods, and it is significant at less than .005; but no significant difference is discernible between the second and third periods. Therefore, the data for none of these four variables confirm the hypothesis; if Jackson became more conservative we must seek some other explanation than aging in office to account for it.

5.2 Was there a significant increase in Jackson's dissenting behavior after his failure to obtain the chief justiceship? Before the 1946 Term, the ratio of Jackson's majority to dissenting opinions was 69:24; thereafter it was 120:89. The difference between the ratios for the two periods is significant at $<.005$ (using $X^2$ and a one-tailed test). The percentage of his dissents was 26 in the earlier period and 43 in the later one. Jackson's rate of dissent increased by two-thirds after the 1945 Term, but was quite stable thereafter: 44 percent for the period of the 1946–1949 Terms, and 42 percent thereafter. Of course, the causal relationship implied by this hypothesis rests upon inference only; it will be no more persuasive than the reasons adduced to support it. The data confirm the descriptive portion of the hypothesis, however, and we cannot reject the hypothesis on the basis of these findings.

5.3. Did Jackson become more conservative in his attitude toward civil liberties, after his experience as chief prosecutor at Nuremberg? Evidently not: when the data for the 1946–1949 and 1950–1953 periods (Table 20) are combined, the direction of change is right for both content values and votes, but $X^2$ is only 0.03 and 1.38, respectively, and neither of these is significant even for a one-tailed test. This hypothesis is not confirmed by these data.[15]

5.4. Did Jackson become more conservative in his attitude toward economic issues after the end of World War II? Again, Table 20 provides the relevant data. The change is in the right direction, for both the content value and voting and it is significant at $<.05$ in both instances—for voting, indeed, $p <.0005$.[16] The relative frequency of his expressions of economic conservatism increased by about two-thirds after the 1945 Term: by 62 percent (from 34 percent to 55 percent) for the content value and by 72 percent (from 43 percent to 74 percent) for voting. The percentages of economic conservatism for the second and third periods are 56 and 54 percent for the content values, and 76 and 71 percent for voting. This shows that both his opinion and his voting behavior were highly stable, in regard to this variable, after his return to the Court in 1946. Since the direction of both his verbal and his voting support was $E+$ during the first period and was $E-$ thereafter, it seems warranted to infer that Jackson was an economic liberal during his first four terms on the Court, and an economic conservative thereafter. As in the case of Hypothesis 5.2, the causal portion of the present hypothesis rests upon inference from biographical data but the objective fact of a significant shift in Jackson's official behavior in relation to economic policy, which coincided

---

15. For all Jackson's votes on the merits (including decisions in which he wrote no opinions), the marginals for the political variable are 21–41 for the period before the 1945 Term, and 72–139 thereafter. $X^2$ for these two ratios is 0.013, which indicates that the goodness of fit is significant at $>.95$. Certainly these data confirm the refutation of this hypothesis.

16. For all Jackson's votes (including decisions in which he wrote no opinions), the marginals for the economic variable are 68–87 for the period before the 1945 Term, and 26–177 thereafter. $X^2$ for these two ratios is 32.5, which indicates that the increase in the conservatism of his voting on economic issues is significant at $<.0005$, irrespective of whether or not he wrote opinions to rationalize his votes.

with the World War II period and its aftermath, seems indisputable. The hypothesis cannot be rejected on the basis of these data and findings.

5.5. Our final hypothesis is obviously in contradiction with the preceding hypotheses 5.1, 5.3, and 5.4, each of which assumed that Jackson became more *conservative* in his attitudes toward either civil liberty or economic issues, or both, during the period following his return to the Court from a year's leave of absence. Hypothesis 5.5 states that Jackson became more *liberal*, in regard to both civil liberty and economic issues, after the deaths of Murphy and Rutledge. The test for this hypothesis requires the partitioning of the data into two sets: the 1941–1944, 1946–1948 Terms; and the 1949–1953 Terms.

Only the political content value changes in the predicted direction; and this change is so minimal that the *goodness of fit* of the two marginal distributions is significant at $>.97$ (with $X^2 < .003$)! Not only are the changes for the other three variables in the wrong direction; economic voting is significantly more conservative although, as we have seen, this change began earlier, as demonstrated by the even higher $X^2$ for change toward economic conservatism after the 1944 Term. But the fact that this hypothesis must so clearly be rejected is not without interest. Jackson's rank in voting in support of civil liberty shifted abruptly from sixth to fourth after Murphy and Rutledge left the Court (Schubert 1965c: 105, 113–115). It would be possible for an analyst working only with the C scale data to interpret this shift in rank as evidence that he changed in his attitude, toward increasing sympathy for civil liberty, during his last five terms on the Court. The present data demonstrate the danger of attempting to make anything other than *relational* inferences, when one is working with ordinal data, for which the underlying metric is unknown and indeed, in terms of such data, incapable of being determined.

### Table 22. Political and Economic Variables, before and after the End of the 1948 Term

| | C | | | | E | | | |
| --- | --- | --- | --- | --- | --- | --- | --- | --- |
| | Values | | Votes | | Values | | Votes | |
| Period | + | − | + | − | + | − | + | − |
| 1941–1944, 1946–1948 | 14 | 7 | 20 | 16 | 27 | 19 | 32 | 37 |
| 1949–1953 | 21 | 9 | 25 | 24 | 15 | 19 | 14 | 34 |

The appropriate inference from Jackson's rise in scale rank after 1948 would be that, in relation to a different (and generally, more conservative) set of colleagues, Jackson *appeared* to be more favorable to civil liberty than a majority of his colleagues. But Table 22 indicates that his own attitude toward civil liberty did not become more favorable; to the contrary, the changes in his opinion and voting behavior toward civil liberty were quite insignificant, and his voting trend was toward greater conservatism.

(6) Table 23 summarizes the decisions that were reached for each of the hypotheses in the tests discussed above.

**Table 23. Summary of Tests of Hypotheses**

| Hypothesis | Subject | Decision |
|---|---|---|
| 1 | Clusters | + |
| 2 | Factors | 0 |
| 3 | Equivalence of liberalism content-values and votes | + |
| 4 | Institutional opinions and separate opinions | − |
| 4' | Majority and dissenting opinions | 0 |
| 5.1 | Increasing conservatism | − |
| 5.2 | Increasing dissent after 1945 Term | + |
| 5.3 | Increasing C—after 1945 Term | − |
| 5.4 | Increasing E—after 1945 Term | + |
| 5.5 | Increasing liberalism after 1948 Term | − |

An examination of Table 23 suggests an additional hypothesis not formulated in advance of the general analysis of the data. The confirmation of Hypotheses 5.2 and 5.4 suggests the question of the relationship between Jackson's economic conservatism and his dissenting behavior. We now know that both his tendency to dissent and his conservatism toward economic policy increased significantly after his return to the Court in 1946; and Tables 19 and 20 both show that his increased economic conservatism during the later period was manifested in both his opinions and his votes. Jackson, in other words, behaved primarily as an economic liberal during the earlier period, and primarily as an economic conservative during the later period; and his switch to conservatism was accompanied by an increasing tendency to dissent. Therefore, it seemed reasonable to infer Hypothesis 6: that there was a significantly high and positive correlation between the economic content-variable and the opinion-variable differences, in that Jackson supported the liberal position in the majority and the conservative position in dissent. To test this hypothesis, let us specify that the stipulated correlation must be observed with both the content and the voting variables during both periods. Thus, the hypothesis would test the relationship between the opinion variable and both the content and voting variables, for Jackson's period of economic liberalism and also for his period of economic conservatism. Confirmation would also establish that the relationship was independent of the *direction* of his support of the economic variable.

It is clear from viewing Table 24 that Hypothesis 6 cannot be rejected. The correlations for both the content value and voting are quite stable, notwithstanding Jackson's metamorphosis from a liberal to a conservative posi-

**Table 24. Economic Liberalism and Conservatism in Majority and Dissenting Opinions, before and after the 1945 Term**

| Period | 1941–1944 | | | | 1946–1953 | | | |
|---|---|---|---|---|---|---|---|---|
| E Variable | Values | | Votes | | Values | | Votes | |
| | − | + | − | + | − | + | − | + |
| Opinions | | | | | | | | |
| Majority | 3 | 15 | 12 | 28 | 7 | 14 | 23 | 15 |
| Dissenting | 7 | 4 | 9 | 0 | 21 | 9 | 27 | 3 |
| $\phi =$ | .480 | | .548 | | .363 | | .332 | |
| $X^2$ | 4.75 | | 11.98 | | 5.31 | | 6.05 | |
| p < | .025 | | .0005 | | .025 | | .01 | |

tion.[17] Of particular interest are the minor diagonals of the fourfold tables, which show that Jackson *argued* in support of economic liberalism in dissenting opinions just as often—indeed, a bit more often—than he supported economic conservatism in majority opinions. In his voting, however, he frequently upheld the conservative position in the majority, while dissenting only thrice in support of economic liberalism during his entire period of service on the Court.[18] The importance of this finding will be apparent presently.

One thing is obvious: the causal parts of Hypotheses 5.2 and 5.4, which were accepted tentatively, must be reconsidered. If Jackson's increasing dissenting behavior and economic conservatism are so highly and consistently correlated, we cannot remain satisfied with independent explanations for each: that his dissenting should be attributed to his disappointment over his failure to become chief justice, while his economic conservatism is attributed to the end of the need for judicial support for the war effort, as well as to the collapse of his political ambitions. In the light of Table 24, it seems preferable to rely upon the broader explanation for both his increasing dissidence and his switch to economic conservatism. "Switch" is probably a very poorly chosen word to describe Jackson's behavior, however, if our interest goes beyond the manifest facts to the latent factors.

As we noted above, Jackson was no more prepared to dissent in behalf of economic liberalism in his "liberal" period than during his "conservative" period. Given his own sophisticated sensitivity to the political implications of dissenting behavior, consider that he was unwilling ever to dissent, *even once*, in support of the position that we can assume would have furthered his political ambitions, during the time when such a display of conspicuous

---

17. The corresponding correlations between political liberalism/conservatism (in either content values or voting) and majority/dissenting opinions, are negative, low, and insignificant. Of course for the entire period of twelve terms, the correlations for the economic variables necessarily are positive and significant: .475 between content values and opinions, and .458 between voting and opinions.

18. All three economically liberal dissents came in the 1952 Term.

economic liberalism might have done him the most good, politically speaking. I attribute his failure so to behave, with such rationality, to a consistency with his own most strongly rooted attitude; and the evidence of the present study strongly indicates that this was economic conservatism. Therefore, Jackson's change in his opinions to greater support for economic conservatism, and his reinforcing dissenting behavior, reflected not a conversion to a new view of political economy, but rather a reversion—at least, at the behavioral level—to the beliefs of his forefathers, his youth, and his manhood prior to his entry into political office.

## V. CONCLUSION

A significant positive correlation exists between Jackson's verbal and voting support for political liberalism, although his overall voting record manifested less sympathy for civil libertarianism than did his opinions; in relation to his colleagues, Jackson consistently was a moderate in his voting on civil liberty issues. He showed a slight but not significant tendency toward greater political conservatism after the end of World War II, which apparently was quite independent of the swings of his colleagues toward greater (1946–1948 Terms) and toward lesser (1949–1953 Terms) political liberalism.

The issue to which Jackson was most deeply attached was economic policy, and a very high and significant correlation shows up between his opinion and voting behavior in this regard. Renowned as an economic liberal at the time of his appointment to the Court, he maintained this image, in both his opinions and his voting, only during his first four terms. After the war, his behavior changed sharply and significantly to strong and consistent support of economic conservatism; and throughout his last eight terms on the Court, he vied with Frankfurter for the bottom position in the cumulative scales of voting in support of economic liberalism. His rate of dissent in behalf of economic conservatism doubled during this later period.

His espousal of economic liberalism and relatively low rate of dissent during the war years were generalized characteristics of his official behavior, in addition to being specifically related to each other. The same was true of his economic conservatism and much higher rate of dissent after the war. My conclusion is that Jackson's economic liberalism was a necessary function of his political career; and that the collapse of his political ambitions for the chief justiceship and even the presidency best explains his reversion to economic conservatism and his increasing dissidence. With life tenure as an associate justice, he had nothing more to lose; and so he wrote and voted in support of the value that was most fundamentally related to his way of life and his career before he went into politics.

# 7

# Opinion Agreement

Sociologists and social psychologists have devoted considerable attention in recent years to the study of small groups (Cartwright and Zander 1960; Collins and Guetzkow 1964; Berelson and Steiner 1964: chap. 8; Olmstead 1959), but relatively little has been done to focus upon appellate courts as a situs for empirical research (Murphy 1966). The data for this paper have been taken from a larger study of High Court decision-making in which I have been engaged for several years.[1] In the present report I shall discuss primarily from a sociometric point of view the question of the relative popularity of judicial opinions among the justices of the High Court, particularly in relation to the participation in decision-making and the background characteristics of the justices. Other papers published elsewhere are concerned with the social attitudes of the justices, as inferred from cumulative scaling of their voting in split decisions of the court (Schubert 1969d), and with the political ideology of the justices in relation to their social attributes, their participation in decision-making, and their voting behavior (Schubert 1968).

The sample for analysis consists of all decisions of the High Court reported in volumes 84–107 of the *Commonwealth Law Reports* for the decade extending from Chief Justice John Latham's de facto retirement, on May 11, 1951, to the appointment of Justice Francis Owen, on September 22, 1961. The only personnel changes occurred during the winter of 1958, when Douglas Menzies (appointed June 12, 1958) replaced William Webb (resigned May 16, 1958), and Victor Windeyer (appointed September 8, 1958) replaced Dudley

This chapter was originally published, in slightly different form, as "Opinion Agreement among High Court Justices in Australia" in *Australian and New Zealand Journal of Sociology* 4 (1968): 2–17, 158–159.

1. For their support of the larger research project, I am indebted to the Institute of Advanced Projects of the East-West Center, and the Social Science Research Institute, both of the University of Hawaii; and to the Asian Studies Center of the Office of International Programs of Michigan State University.

Williams (resigned July 31, 1958). We have therefore two stable subgroups of seven justices each,[2] with one of these groups acting during an earlier and longer period of seven years, and the other group acting during a later and shorter period of three years. Five justices (Dixon, Taylor, Edward McTiernan, Wilfred Fullagar, and Frank Kitto) were members of both groups and participated in the decisions of the Court throughout all (or substantially all) of the entire ten-year period. There is a total, therefore, of nine judges in the sample, and what from a sociological point of view are two different "courts" (Snyder 1958), because of the change in the composition of the decision-making group.

### Table 25. The Sample of High Court Decisional Data

|  | Period 1 (1951–1958) | Period 2 (1958–1961) | Totals |
|---|---|---|---|
| Decisions | 510 | 200 | 710 |
| Opinions* | 2141 | 836 | 2977 |
| Participations | 2321 | 927 | 3248 |

*Opinions in *CLR*, vols. 84–99, are Period 1; those in vols. 101–107 are Period 2; and those in vol. 100 are divided between the two periods.

The frequencies of decisions, participations, and opinions observed in the sample are reported in Table 25, with a breakdown for the two periods. Reference to Table 25 shows that both the ratio of opinions to decisions (4.2) and the mean panel size (4.6) are the same in both periods. The former is a measure of the average number of opinions associated with a decision, and is an institutional characteristic of the court during the period studied; the mean panel size has a more intuitively obvious sociological meaning, because it describes the average size of decision-making groups for the court. The High Court acts through a continuously shifting series of ad hoc committees or panels of two to six members; and it infrequently—11 to 12 percent of the time—utilizes *en banc* (or, as Australian lawyers call it, "full Court") decisions of the entire group of seven justices. Panels of five make a majority of the decisions and panels of three are next in popularity, for the reason (it has been suggested) of avoiding the possibility of an equal division of votes. The ratio of opinions to votes (i.e., participations), which measures change in the relative frequency of individual articulation of opinion, is the same for both periods, .92 and .90. This demonstrates the pronounced extent to which Australian High Court justices do deliver individual opinions. These findings

2. Except that during the initial year of the earlier period, the ailing chief justice took no part in the Court's decision-making, so there was only a six-man group then. The senior "other" justice (cf. Sawer 1957: 488) and the de facto chief during 1951–1952, Owen Dixon, was promoted to chief justice de jure on April 18, 1952, Sir John having formally retired one day earlier; and Alan Taylor was appointed on September 3, 1958, to the position vacated by Sir Owen.

stand in sharp contrast to those for the United States Supreme Court, whose average ratio of participation[3] is much higher, and ratio of opinions to participation[4] is much lower, reflecting the differences in customs and institutional roles that have obtained, for these two courts, at least during the period of their coexistence. During the same ten-year period as that for our High Court sample, the Supreme Court decided on the merits of 1,749 cases, of which 946 (54 percent) were split decisions. Only 187 (26 percent) of the High Court decisions were nonunanimous; so the Supreme Court decided over twice as many cases in absolute terms and it divided in voting twice as often as did the High Court.[5] Voting data provide the more adequate source for the study of the decision-making of the Supreme Court because they provide a larger sample of observations (than do Supreme Court opinions) which discriminate among individual differences in behavior, but for the High Court, opinion data afford a better sample of such observations than do votes.[6] The much higher degree of apparent decisional "unanimity" in the High Court is perhaps another way of saying the much greater tendency to reveal, through individual opinion nuances, sublimated latent voting differences which, given the American institutional ethos, might well have emerged instead as manifest split decisions.

The cultural expectation for the Supreme Court is that, whatever the level of voting disagreement that may obtain, the justices are supposed to minimize the public disclosure of their differences by grouping themselves around the smallest possible number of opinions that can rationalize the outcome:[7] a high social value is placed upon maintaining the illusion of harmony and consensus among the justices.[8] Critics tend to brand as "political" decisions for which the voting division is close, but they are equally disparaging of a multiplicity of opinions, arguing that judges who "knew the law" would be of a single mind on questions of constitutional interpretation. The situation is diametrically reversed for the High Court, for which the cultural expectation is that justices will assume *individual* (rather than collective)

---

3. This is the mean panel size divided by the maximum size of the court, and is .95 for the Supreme Court and .66 for the High Court.

4. Apparently, less than .20. For references to sources, see my paper (1969*d*).

5. Consequently, the corresponding sample of split decisions available for the study of the Supreme Court is five times larger than the present High Court sample.

6. Disregarding for the moment the impact of cultural norms governing disclosure of differences in viewpoint, we can observe that disagreement in opinions is more widespread than that concerning outcomes because dissenters almost without exception disagree with the opinions of justices who vote in the majority, but majority justices are by no means agreed upon their reasons for reaching the same result. For the same reason, opinion differences can be observed also in decisions for which the vote as to outcome is unanimous; and for the High Court such "unanimous" decisions are much more numerous than split decisions.

7. Cf. Walter F. Murphy's discussion of the implications of game theory for Supreme Court behavior (1964*a*): esp. pp. 12–36; and see Bickel 1957.

8. The American practice goes back to the days of John Marshall who used the opinion of the Court, which he usually gave personally and in almost all other cases assigned, as a device for extending his own dominance over his colleagues, and therefore over the policy norms enunciated by the Supreme Court.

responsibility for their votes in the court's decisions, and that one way to enforce this norm is to insist upon individual rationalizations (or critiques) of the collective result. The American Supreme Court best fulfills its institutional role when the nine justices all speak with a single voice to deliver the message behind which they all have united;[9] the High Court remains faithful to its own institutional role[10] when each of the seven justices participating in a full Court decision has his own say, in his own way, even though all say about the same thing. The American approach leads, of course, to a somewhat spurious appearance of monolithism which undoubtedly facilitates the Court's role of political leadership, both in relation to its competitors in national policy-making (the Congress and the administration) and in relation to its control over lower courts. The Australian approach tends to accentuate the public image of High Court justices as a group of competent professional lawyers, although it entails also certain disadvantages of a perhaps minor order, such as inefficiency in the use of the available time, a high level of redundancy in the content of opinions (and this notwithstanding the efforts of court reporters to edit out the repetitious restatements of "the facts" of each case), and what is often substantial difficulty in appraising what "the court" has decided—at least in terms of policy norms for the future.

The number of opinions written by each justice is shown in Table 26. It might be thought that the indicated scale is biased by Taylor's nonparticipation in the first year's decisions, and by the relatively low participation—which does occur—for Taylor during his first year on the court and for Menzies and Windeyer during theirs,[11] but an examination of the data from this point of view does not reveal discrepancies of sufficient importance to justify reporting the details. The decrease in the average number of opinions per justice per volume, from 18.6 in Period 1 to 15.9 in Period 2, is not significant statistically. The order of frequency with which the justices expressed individual opinions is of course highly and positively correlated with the scale of participation ratios,[12] which we shall consider below; and in making

---

9. Note Chief Justice Earl Warren's apparently strenuous efforts to suppress possible dissent (from, among others, Felix Frankfurter) and to present an absolutely united front in the disposition of the *School Segregation Cases* of the early and middle 1950s. See my *Constitutional Politics* (1960a) pp. 487–511.

10. For a description of the High Court's historical development, its organization and procedure and decisional style, and ideological differences among some of the justices as exemplified by their opinions in certain decisions thought by lawyers to be leading cases, see Anonymous 1967.

11. A correction was made by deleting vols. 84–87 and 99–100 from the computations. The court averages are about the same, for each period and for the two periods combined, as they are for the complete data given in Table 26. Taylor does exchange ranks with Fullagar for Period 1, and Taylor's combined total for the twenty volumes (88–107) is second (among the five justices with continuing tenure, of course) only to that of Dixon, reflecting his exceptionally low (and atypical) rate of participation in the decisions reported in the first four volumes for the sample.

12. The rho coefficients are 1.00 for Period 1, .92 for Period 2, and .88 for the composite scales of all nine justices.

**Table 26. Frequency of Opinions by Individual Justices**

| Scale Order | Justice | Period 1 (16.5 vols.)* | Period 2 (7.5 vols.) | Both Periods |
|---|---|---|---|---|
| 1 | Dixon | 435 | 163 | 598 |
| 2 | Menzies | — | 135 | — |
| 3 | Windeyer | — | 129 | — |
| 4 | Kitto | 330 | 110 | 440 |
| 5 | Webb | 316 | — | — |
| 6 | Fullagar | 306 | 108 | 414 |
| 7 | Taylor | 281 | 100 | 381 |
| 8 | Williams | 241 | — | — |
| 9 | McTiernan | 232 | 91 | 323 |
| | Totals | 2141 | 836 | |
| | Average per justice per volume: | 18.6 | 15.9 | |

*Decisions of both the earlier and the later court are reported in volume 100. Hence the opinions of the five justices with continuing tenure have been apportioned, and about half have been tabulated for the earlier and the other half for the later period.

comparisons with measures of background characteristics and opinion agreement, the participation scales will be used.

## I. OPINION AGREEMENT

In order to measure opinion agreement, it is necessary to observe the opinion of each justice, in relation to the opinions of all other participating justices, in each of the 710 decisions of the sample. A set of rules was drawn up to guide the graduate assistant who did the coding of opinion relationships. These rules are reproduced in the Appendix [to this chapter] in order to explain more clearly the concept of agreement that was followed. In general, the coding rules specified that any pair of judges who stated explicitly that they agreed with each other, or who joined in a common opinion, would be scored as in agreement. Judges who wrote separate opinions, and either stated their disagreement or failed to be explicit about agreement, were scored as in disagreement. Relationships are not necessarily symmetrical: it is quite possible (and usual) for Justice B to note his agreement with Justice A, who in turn says nothing about his own attitude toward B's opinion; and under such circumstances A was coded in disagreement with B although B was coded in agreement with A. The index of agreement for a justice, with each other justice, consists of the ratio of the sum of his instances of agreement to the joint sum of both his instances of agreement and of disagreement, for a stipulated period of time. Thus, during Period 1 Fullagar wrote 282 opinions in decisions in which Dixon also participated. Because Dixon agreed with 196, and disagreed with 86, of Fullagar's opinions, the index of Dixon's agreement with Fullagar is 196/282 = .70. The matrices of indices of agreement,

**Table 27. Opinion Agreement**

| | Period 1 (1951–1958) | | | | | | | | Period 2 (1958–1961) | | | | | | | | (1951–1961) | | | | |
|---|---|---|---|---|---|---|---|---|---|---|---|---|---|---|---|---|---|---|---|---|---|
| | D | Wi | T | K | F | We | Mc | | D | K | F | Wn | Mc | T | Me | | D | K | F | T | Mc |
| D | | 68 | 67 | 72 | 72 | 66 | 66 | D | | 57 | 53 | 58 | 58 | 51 | 42 | D | | 68 | 68 | 64 | 64 |
| Wi | 71 | | 61 | 54 | 54 | 67 | 54 | K | 51 | | 34 | 47 | 32 | 44 | 42 | K | 65 | | 56 | 60 | 46 |
| T | 64 | 62 | | 62 | 58 | 56 | 52 | F | 44 | 39 | | 40 | 37 | 41 | 33 | F | 64 | 57 | | 55 | 45 |
| K | 69 | 54 | 64 | | 62 | 55 | 50 | Wn | 48 | 42 | 33 | | 32 | 39 | 29 | T | 60 | 56 | 52 | | 48 |
| F | 70 | 53 | 58 | 62 | | 50 | 48 | Mc | 43 | 27 | 36 | 37 | | 40 | 34 | Mc | 53 | 43 | 47 | 47 | |
| We | 60 | 61 | 52 | 50 | 51 | | 50 | T | 44 | 35 | 26 | 42 | 35 | | 29 | | | | | | |
| Mc | 56 | 49 | 49 | 46 | 51 | 47 | | Me | 38 | 34 | 32 | 34 | 36 | 34 | | | | | | | |

NOTES: All values are two-place decimals; decimal points have been omitted. The justices are coded as follows: D (Dixon), F (Fullagar), K (Kitto), Mc (McTiernan), Me (Menzies), T (Taylor), We (Webb), Wi (Williams), Wn (Windeyer).

for both periods, are reported in Table 27, which should be read *down columns* rather than across rows.

The matrices are of course asymmetrical. They show that during both periods, five of the six associates found themselves consistently in closest agreement with the chief justice, while Williams (Dixon's own first choice) was the consensual second choice during the first period; and after Williams left the group, Kitto emerged as the next best choice during the second period. Conversely, all of his six colleagues were in least agreement with McTiernan during the first period, although he subsequently was displaced by Menzies, who received during the second period even more negative deference than was bestowed upon McTiernan. These first and second order relations, of both positive and negative deference, are illustrated by the elementary linkage analysis (McQuitty 1957) diagrams depicted in Figure 10. It is possible to combine the two sets of linkage relationships, and thereby develop a crude scale of relative agreement, which in effect reduces the variance of each matrix to a single dimension. This is done by assigning weights of $+2$ and $+1$, respectively, to the first and second order levels of agreement, and weights of $-1$ and $-2$ to the fifth and sixth levels of agreement. Table 28 reports the resulting scales, which confirm our previous observations from the face of the matrices, and order all of the justices in a consistent manner along the same dimension, in each period. This table shows that Dixon, Kitto, Fullagar, and McTiernan are in the same rank order in both periods, but Taylor drops three ranks in the second period. The latter difference is not simply contextual, either. It is true that Menzies found himself in agreement with Taylor both absolutely and relatively much less frequently than had Williams; but Fullagar and Kitto and McTiernan also all ranked Taylor lower in the later period than in the earlier one. The columnar sums show that not only was Dixon the consensual choice during both periods (and McTiernan the dissensual one during the first period, and Menzies during the second); these relationships within the group *were* symmetrical, since Dixon has the highest average

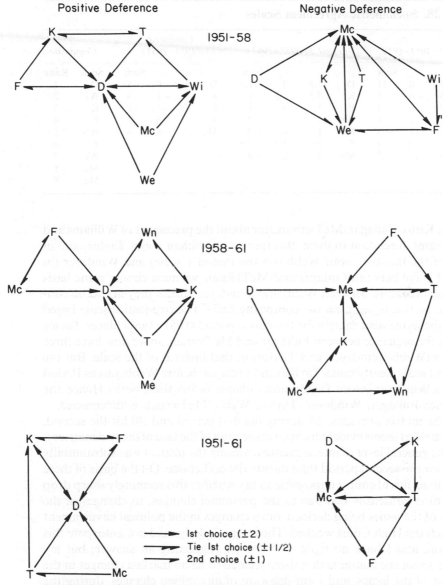

Figure 10. Elementary Linkage in Opinion Deference

level of agreement with all others in both periods, while McTiernan has the lowest average level during the first period and Menzies during the second.

In order to make comparisons with the attribute and participation scales which rank all nine of the justices, it is necessary to construct a composite scale of opinion agreement also. There is no question about the sequence

**Table 28. Sociometric Agreement Scales**

| Period 1 (1951–1958) | | | | Period 2 (1958–1961) | | | | Combined (1951–1961) | | | | Composite | |
|---|---|---|---|---|---|---|---|---|---|---|---|---|---|
| | + | − | Sum | | + | − | Sum | | + | − | Sum | Scale | Rank |
| D | 11 | 0 | 11 | D | 11.5 | 0 | 11.5 | D | 8 | 0 | 8 | D | 1 |
| Wi | 5 | 0 | 5 | K | 5.5 | −1.5 | 4 | K | 4 | −1 | 3 | Wi | 2 |
| T | 2 | 0 | 2 | F | 1 | 0 | 1 | F | 2 | −3 | −1 | K | 3 |
| K | 2 | −1 | 1 | Wn | 2 | −4 | −2 | T | 1 | −3 | −2 | F | 4 |
| F | 1 | −4 | −3 | Mc | 1 | −4 | −3 | Mc | 0 | −8 | −8 | Wn | 5 |
| We | 0 | −4 | −4 | T | 0 | −3.5 | −3.5 | | | | | T | 6 |
| Mc | 0 | −12 | −12 | Me | 0 | −8 | −8 | | | | | We | 7 |
| | | | | | | | | | | | | Mc | 8 |
| | | | | | | | | | | | | Me | 9 |

Dixon, Kitto, Fullagar, McTiernan, nor about the placement of Williams and of Menzies in relation to them. But there is a problem about Taylor; and in view of the fact that both Webb (on the Period 1 scale) and Windeyer (in Period 2) fall between Fullagar and McTiernan, we must choose some basis for discriminating between Webb and Windeyer, unless they are to be considered as tied in rank on the composite scale. The five-justice scale based upon the agreement matrix for the entire period (1951–1961) places Taylor also in the sequence between Fullagar and McTiernan, so we now have three justices (Webb, Windeyer, and Taylor) in that interval of the scale. But the Period 1 scale clearly ranks Taylor (and Fullagar) before Webb, just as Period 2 ranks Windeyer before Taylor (and Fullagar before them both). Hence, the sequence Fullagar, Windeyer, Taylor, Webb, McTiernan is determined.

The matrix averages, .58 during the first period and .40 for the second, confirm what seems evident from an inspection of the face of the two matrices: that the general level of interagreement among the justices was substantially lower for the second period than during the earlier one. On the basis of these data alone, it is of course impossible to say whether this seemingly sharp drop in opinion consensus was due to the personnel changes, to changes in the nature of the issues being decided, or to changes in the political environment in which the High Court worked. The research design did not anticipate this question, and I have no rigorous basis for suggesting an answer; but my feeling about the matter is that there seemed to be no marked changes in the content of the issues, and I am unaware of any milieu changes, during the second period, that would seem likely to have had such an effect upon the court—although I hasten to add that my impressions of the Australian political scene are subject to correction by those more specialized in the subject. The remaining reason—the substitution of Windeyer and Menzies for Webb and Williams—seems to me to be more plausible as an explanation. There is certainly considerable evidence that changes in one or two seats have had a traumatic effect upon the decision-making of the United States Supreme Court; consider Clark and Minton vice Murphy and Rutledge; or Warren and Brennan vice Vinson and Minton. But I am not aware of any studies of opinion agreement in the Supreme Court, which would make possible explicit comparisons with these findings for the High Court.

## II. ATTRIBUTES

There are many possible explanations to account for the fact that the opinions of certain justices are consistently deemed more popular, and those of others less popular, by all of the members of the decision-making group. On the American Supreme Court of the 1920s, for example, William Howard Taft was much more noted for his social than for his task leadership, while the dour McReynolds was notoriously nasty even in his face-to-face behavior toward justices junior to himself whom he disliked (e.g., Brandeis and Clark).[13] One might hypothesize that the two new justices who joined the Court in 1958, Menzies and Windeyer, "fit in" better with the remainder of the group than had the men whom they replaced, Webb and Williams. But "fit in" in what sense? Because their personalities were more pleasing, and deeming the newcomers to be more "sociable" colleagues the others found it easier to agree with them?[14] Providing that data adequate to support discriminations among all of the justices on such a personality variable as sociability could be acquired—and I certainly do not have such information—and scaled, then one might hypothesize that the sociability scale would correlate highly and positively with the opinion agreement scale. Of course, the observation of the predicted correlation would not prove that sociability causes opinion agreement, but the observation of a low or negative correlation certainly would tend to weaken confidence in this particular explanation. Similarly, one might hypothesize that the better explanation lies in differences in the professional legal skill of the justices, and that those with the highest skill enjoy the most (and those with less skill the least) agreement by the other justices with their opinions. Not only is this the conventional explanation that Australian lawyers would proffer—at least, for the benefit of nonlawyers— but a certain prima facie plausibility is immediately suggested by the circumstance that the individual whose opinions were indisputably most popular is none other than Sir Owen Dixon, a man considered by many Australian legal observers to be not only the acknowledged master of analytical positivism but also the "greatest Judge in the English-speaking world."[15] In order to test

---

13. See David J. Danelski's discussion (1961) of "social leadership."

14. Or was it because the two newest justices were (during the brief three years that we observe in the present sample) being wooed by their elders, who sought the neophytes as allies who might tip the scales one way or another in the various differences, both social and ideological, that had tended to harden over the years among the majority of five justices with continuing tenure? See Murphy (1964b), especially "Task Leadership and Social Leadership" at pp. 395–397 and "Social Control through the Glad Hand" at pp. 403–405.

15. The Sydney Morning Herald (April 2, 1964), p. 2; and Sawer: "Dixon is the greatest exponent of the analytic and conceptual type of English common-law thinking in Australian legal history, and probably the greatest living judge in that tradition in any English-speaking country" (1957:497).

this hypothesis, however, it would be necessary to scale the other eight justices as well, and although it seems highly probable that such data could be obtained[16] I do not have them. Other possible hypotheses might predict high positive correlations with scales of seniority on the High Court, or with judicial experience—and Sir Owen would rank first on either of these scales also.[17] Both of these variables are themselves highly correlated with each other and with age, however, and the latter is the one with which I have chosen to work. Rejection of the hypothesis for age would at the same time have the effect of leaving little room for confidence in the likelihood that either of the other two related explanations (seniority and judicial experience) are important.

In addition to age, the background characteristics concerning which I attempted to obtain systematic information for all justices in the sample included: the location, size, and socioeconomic aspects of the community in which each judge was raised; his relatives and family connections; the occupation of his father, father-in-law, and other close male relatives; his ancestry; religion; education; legal, governmental, and other occupational experience; partisan affiliation and political activity, social clubs, and similar group affiliations; military experience; honors and awards; and publications and academic ties. I also sought to acquire systematic information concerning the changing states in the health of the justices, because I hypothesized that both the participation and opinion-writing ratios are directly affected by the biological parameter of relative physical capacity to undertake and to enjoy work. Of course I consulted the published sources available in the United States for the obviously accessible data; what was disappointing was that after having been fortunate in securing the services of a qualified graduate student in Australia, who was able to work in local libraries and interview knowledgeable Australians, the additional yield in terms of usable data was very small. I did not expect to get very far with the inquiry about health, but it was somewhat surprising to learn that it was not possible to complete the inventories, for all nine justices, even with regard to such matters as religious and political party affiliation; such information is readily available about state and lower federal as well as about Supreme Court justices in the United States. (Bowen 1965:chap. 1, and esp. p. 8 no. 1; Nagel 1961*b*, 1962*a*; Goldman 1966).

The limited data available do suggest that the justices of the High Court comprise an exceptionally homogeneous group. All, for example, held uni-

---

16. One obvious procedure would be to conduct an interview survey of High Court barristers. In the United States such peer ratings of the professional competence of lawyers are published on a continuing basis by the *Martindale-Hubbell Law Directory*; and cf. the precocious (at least, for American political science) article by Mott 1936:295–315.

17. Dixon was beginning his career as an undergraduate student at the University of Melbourne when the first session of the High Court convened in 1903; and his personal career in the law, and association with the High Court, spanned almost the entire period of its existence, up to the time of the present study.

versity law degrees; all had been barristers—indeed this particular group had perfect closure on this parameter, because the youngest member (Douglas Menzies) had served as junior barrister to the eldest (Owen Dixon); all belonged to exclusive, upper-class social clubs—reflecting, no doubt, their typically lower-middle-class origins. The two appointees of Labour governments (McTiernan and Webb) also were the only Roman Catholics; Dixon was identified as an agnostic (cf. O. Dixon 1965); and the others were Protestant or were presumably so. There were differences in regard to domicile, with four coming from New South Wales and four from Victoria,[18] and this variable did seem worth examining because of the possibility that differences in what I hypothesized to be the two subcultures might produce, through early socialization and continuing adult reinforcement, differences in the within-group social relations and in the belief systems of the justices. The hypothesis that the subgroup structure of the group would correspond to their domiciliary differences could be investigated by correlating domicile with participation, and we shall examine this relationship presently. The other hypothesis, that differences between the cultures of the two states might be reflected in stable and consistent attitudinal and idealogical differences among the justices, is the subject of other reports (Schubert 1969d, 1968a). My hypothesis about the influence of age upon judicial behavior is not the more usual psychological one that judges (like other humans) experience both biological and social changes as a consequence of the transition from middle age to the status that Americans, with all good will but some perverse side effects, have come to denote as "senior citizenship"; and that as a consequence of the inescapable acceleration of rigidity in personality and soma alike that accompanies advanced aging, there is a corresponding rigidity in attitudes which results in greater conservatism in one's idealogy. Obviously this is not an implausible hypothesis to entertain if one is studying a group whose average age is about that at which most persons expect (and, increasingly, are required) to retire from active employment. I have, however, an alternative hypothesis which I believe to be even more relevant and important: that age is an index to the prevailing pattern of dominant cultural norms during a person's youth, and hence to his socialization and his direct experience of major disturbances affecting his society. A reinforcing consideration is that there are biological correlates of maturation that suggest the likelihood that age-mates are more apt to share social interests than are persons of different generations.

Because age is the only one of the variables which I could use that would permit the establishment of a ratio scale, I had to forgo indulgence in this statistical luxury because the highest level of measurement that could be obtained for most of the variables is ordinal. Indeed, I scaled age nominally, because there were two sharply distinguished subgroups of justices, an older

---

18. Webb, from Queensland, was only the third justice ever to be appointed to the High Court other than from the two leading states; it was necessary, of course, to exclude him from correlations involving the domicile variable.

### Table 29. Attribute Scales

| Justice | Scale Ranks | | |
| --- | --- | --- | --- |
| | Social, Economic, Political Conservatism | Age | Domicile |
| Windeyer | 1 | 7.5 | 6.5 |
| Menzies | 2 | 7.5 | 2.5 |
| Fullager | 3.5 | 3 | 2.5 |
| Williams | 3.5 | 3 | 6.5 |
| Kitto | 5 | 7.5 | 2.5 |
| Dixon | 6.5 | 3 | 2.5 |
| Taylor | 6.5 | 7.5 | 6.5 |
| Webb | 8 | 3 | — |
| McTiernan | 9 | 3 | 6.5 |

NOTE: For age, 3 = older and 7.5 = younger.
For domicile, 2.5 = Victoria and 6.5 = New South Wales.

group all born in the nineteenth century and a younger group. The best I could do with the remaining data was to construct an index scale of social, economic, and political background characteristics, based upon the incomplete information available relating to political party affiliation (Labour, −1; anti-Labour, +1), religious affiliation (Roman Catholic, −1; Anglican or Presbyterian, +1), experience in partisan political office or campaigning (Labour, −1; anti-Labour, +1), partisan character of the government appointing the justice to the High Court (Labour, −1; Bruce–Page, 0 [Dixon]; Sir Robert Menzies' governments, +1), and the familial socioeconomic status of the justice (working class, −1; middle or upper class, +1). Index score sums ranged from +5 (Windeyer) to −4 (McTiernan); Dixon was +1; and Webb, the only other justice with a negative (Labour or non-Conservative) score, was −2. The directionality assigned to this SEP (socioeconomic-political) scale was "Conservative." I have discussed the details of the "Age" and "SEP" scales elsewhere (1969d); these two scales and the one for domicile are reproduced in Table 29.

### III. PARTICIPATION

I have also discussed participation from both a normative and an empirical point of view and in detail but with particular reference to split decisions, in the report cited above, so my remarks here are limited to what is essential for a consideration of participation as it relates to opinion agreement. It is obvious that one constraint upon the volume of a judge's opinions is the relative frequency of his opportunities to write opinions, that is to say, the extent of his participation in both split and unanimous decisions of the court. With regard to the High Court, little is known about the considerations that underlie a chief justice's choices in the staffing of decision-

**Table 30. Participation Scales**

| Justice | Period 1 (1951–1958) | Period 2 (1958–1961) | Combined (1951–1961) | Composite Ranks |
|---|---|---|---|---|
| Dixon | .36 | .31 | .35 | 1 |
| Menzies | — | .06 | — | 2 |
| Windeyer | — | .05 | — | 3 |
| Kitto | .13 | −.01 | .09 | 4 |
| Webb | .02 | — | — | 5 |
| Fullagar | .01 | −.01 | .00 | 6 |
| Taylor | −.05 | −.22 | −.10 | 7 |
| Williams | −.23 | — | — | 8 |
| McTiernan | −.24 | −.19 | −.23 | 9 |

making panels. In Table 30 are shown three participation scales, one for each period and a third for the two periods combined for the five justices with continuing tenure, for the total sample including both split and unanimous decisions.[19] For the five justices who acted during both periods, the product-moment correlation between the two scales is .92, which certainly suggests that there were no important changes in relative participation in the court's decision-making, during the period covered by this analysis. The apparent changes between the two periods are the lower participation of both Kitto and Taylor,[20] and the higher participation of Windeyer than that of the man whom he replaced, Williams. By using the ratios for the combined periods to establish the scale order for the five justices for whom this is possible, the rank positions of the remaining four can be interpolated from their relative positions on the scales for Period 1 and Period 2, respectively. Table 30 reports this composite ordinal scale of participation, in the total decisions of the court, for all nine justices.

## IV. CORRELATIONS AMONG ATTRIBUTES, PARTICIPATION, AND OPINION AGREEMENT

Table 31 shows the correlations among the attribute, participation, and opinion agreement scales, for each period and for the two periods combined.[21] The correlations among the three variables in the submatrix of attribute scales is of course the same whether comparison is made with split or with total decisions; and I have discussed this submatrix elsewhere (1969d).

---

19. I have reported (1969d) the scales for split and for unanimous decisions, separately. The product-moment correlations between this set of scales is .94 (for Period 1) and .75 (for Period 2).

20. The decrease in Taylor's participation is considerably less extreme than the drop in his opinion popularity, noted above.

21. All coefficients in Table 31 are rho rank correlations, except for the three correlations between age and domicile, which are phi coefficients.

### Table 31. Intercorrelations among Scales

| Periods: ₂\¹ | Age | Dom. | SEP | Part. | Opn. |
|---|---|---|---|---|---|
| Age | | .00 | −.08 | −.16 | −.16 |
| Dom. | .17 | | .30 | .88 | .10 |
| SEP | −.51 | .22 | | .11 | .49 |
| Part. | .07 | .58 | .45 | | .39 |
| Opn. | .43 | .43 | −.13 | .32 | |

| | Combined Periods | | | |
|---|---|---|---|---|
| | Dom. | SEP | Part. | Opn. |
| Age | .00 | −.48 | −.34 | .26 |
| Dom. | | .11 | .57 | .22 |
| SEP | | | .40 | .13 |
| Part. | | | | .17 |

NOTE: Scale abbreviations are Dom. (Domicile); SEP (Socio-economic-political); Part. (Participation); Opn. (Opinion).

Attention here will focus instead upon relations involving the participation and the opinion agreement scales. During the first period, there is a very high correlation of .88 between domicile and participation, which shows the extent to which not only Chief Justice Dixon, but also his fellow Victorians, Kitto and Fullagar, tended to dominate the structure of the court's decision-making panels. In the second period, the two new and younger justices joined these activists; and Windeyer's domicile in New South Wales accounts for the .30 drop in the corresponding coefficient. Overall, the participation scale shows only moderate correlations, negative with age and positive with domicile and with SEP, which is to say that (notwithstanding the preeminent exception provided by the chief justice himself) young conservatives from Victoria tended to dominate the court's decision-making.

The opinion popularity scale has moderate positive correlations with participation during both periods, and with conservatism during Period 1; but there is an abrupt shift to higher correlations with age and domicile during Period 2. Dixon, whose opinions were most popular, lowers the correlation between SEP and the opinion scale in both periods because of his relatively liberal rank on the conservatism scale; but the principal reason for the sharp drop in this correlation for the second period is that Menzies, second only to Windeyer in conservatism, wrote the least acceptable opinions. A major cause for the rise in correlation between age and opinion agreement was that Taylor, a younger judge, wrote less popular opinions during the second period; while Webb, an older judge whose opinions were not popular, retired after the first period. The correlation between domicile and opinion agreement rose because Williams, a New South Wales judge whose opinions were popular, retired; and Fullagar, a Victorian whose opinions were unpopular, rose in rank on the scale because of William's retirement and Taylor's drop in popularity—indeed, the coefficient for the second period would be twice as high as it is (i.e., in the plus eighties) were it not for Menzies' inconsistent position, with three of his fellow Victorians in the first three ranks, then the three from New South Wales, and finally Menzies bringing up the rear.

When we examine the correlations for the composite opinion agreement scale, however, we find that all of them—including the relationship with participation—are low, ranging from $+.13$ to $+.26$. Of course, not too great confidence could in any circumstances be placed in rank correlations such as these, based on a very small sample, and so evidently fluctuating depending upon changes in, or changes in the behavior of, one or two justices. Nevertheless, the evidence, such as it is, indicates that none of the hypotheses tested, as possible explanations for the observed consistencies in opinion agreement among these justices, can be supported by these data. We cannot, that is, account for the differences in opinion agreement on the basis of age (whatever our assumption about its direction and substantive significance), or on the basis of differences in the major subcultures from which these men were drawn, or in their conservatism (at least, as I was enabled to measure it), or even (through participation differentials) in their relative degrees of exposure to group esteem.

There would seem to be two ways along which future research into the problems to which this paper has been addressed might usefully be developed. One approach would be to improve upon the defects in design, the adequacy of access to relevant information, and other faults of this exploratory inquiry, and to replicate the research in a sounder manner. A second approach would be to look into some of the alternative hypotheses, such as sociability or legal skill, which proved to be beyond the scope of what I could attempt in this particular project. No matter which of these two approaches were to be pursued, I think it would be highly desirable that the investigation be carried out by an Australian who could hurdle easily many of the roadblocks which are major obstacles for an alien observer, and thereby better focus and concentrate his time and energies upon the substantive problems of decision-making theory toward the solution of which I hope this paper will make some contribution.

# V. APPENDIX

## Coding Rules for Interagreement in Opinions

1. We establish, for each volume, a matrix with columns defined by judges in the role of *initiators*, and rows defined by the same judges in the role of *targets* of agreement or disagreement.

2. The observations which, in each case, we seek to make consist of the extent to which each participating judge agrees with each judge who writes an opinion in the case. We wish to tally each instance of agreement and each instance of disagreement, for each dyadic pair. To record the data, divide each cell of the matrix (except those of

the major diagonal) into two parts. Enter the tallies of agreement in the upper half of the cell, and of disagreement in the lower half.

(a) If Judge A explicitly states that he accepts or joins in Judge B's opinion, then A agrees with B.

(b) If Judge A explicitly states that he rejects or disagrees with Judge B's opinion, then A disagrees with B.

(c) Two or more judges who explicitly reject each other's opinion should be tallied as mutually disagreeing with each other.

(d) If each of two or more judges writes an individual opinion in a case, and there is no explicit language on the part of any of them regarding the acceptance or rejection of other opinions, we shall infer that such judges disagree and tally them accordingly.

(e) The relationship of agreement is not necessarily symmetrical (i.e., reciprocated); similarly, disagreement may be asymmetrical (unidirectional).

(f) Two or more judges who coauthor the same opinion always agree with each other, unless one of them also writes an individual opinion expressing views which the other(s) *explicitly* reject.

(g) Even though two judges (say, A and B) write separate opinions, if A says explicitly that he accepts B's opinion (and wishes merely to add a few words of his own), while B makes no reference to A, tally A as in *agreement* with B, and B as in *disagreement* with A.

(h) A participating judge who writes (or coauthors, in the event of joint opinions) no opinion of his own can agree (or disagree) with a judge who writes an opinion; but none of the other participating judges can either agree or disagree with a judge who neither writes nor coauthors an opinion.

(i) If Judge A, who writes no opinion, expresses agreement with Judge B's opinion, and if B is tallied as being in disagreement with opinions by C and D, then A also should be tallied as disagreeing with C and D.

(j) For cells in the major diagonal, always tally a judge as in agreement with himself if, and only if, he writes or joins in (coauthors) an opinion in the case. (Tally nothing in such a cell, if a judge simply notes that he accepts another judge's opinion in the case.)

3. For example, let us assume a case in which A, B, C, D, and E participate. A, B, and C coauthor an opinion, although C writes an individual opinion expressing additional views of his own. D writes a separate opinion. E writes no opinion, but notes that he agrees with D. None of the opinions included an explicit statement of acceptance or rejection of the other opinions. This case should be coded as shown below. (I have indicated by letter the rule which governs each coding decision.)

|          | *Initiators* | | | | |
| *Targets* | A | B | C | D | E |
|----------|------|------|------|------|------|
| A | $1^j$ | $1/\ ^f$ | $1/\ ^f$ | $/1^d$ | $/1^i$ |
| B | $1/\ ^f$ | $1^j$ | $1/\ ^f$ | $/1^d$ | $/1^i$ |
| C | $1/\ ^f$ | $1/\ ^f$ | $1^j$ | $1/^d$ | $/1^i$ |
| D | $/1^d$ | $/1^f$ | $/1^d$ | $1^j$ | $1/\ ^a$ |
| E | $^{e,h}$ | $^{e,h}$ | $^{e,h}$ | $^{e,h}$ | $^j$ |

[Not relevant to the case: rules (b), (c), and (g)]

4. Transcribe from your work sheet matrix to a summary matrix for each volume, in which the entries for the nondiagonal cells will be fractions in the following form:

$$\frac{\text{sum of agreement tallies}}{\text{sum of agreement tallies plus sum of disagreement tallies}}$$

and the diagonal cells will consist of integers (equal to the number of opinions written or coauthored by each judge). Our example (above) would be transcribed as follows:

|  | | Initiators | | | |
|---|---|---|---|---|---|
| Targets | A | B | C | D | E |
| A | 1 | $\frac{1}{1}$ | $\frac{1}{1}$ | $\frac{0}{1}$ | $\frac{0}{1}$ |
| B | $\frac{1}{1}$ | 1 | $\frac{1}{1}$ | $\frac{0}{1}$ | $\frac{0}{1}$ |
| C | $\frac{1}{1}$ | $\frac{1}{1}$ | 1 | $\frac{0}{1}$ | $\frac{0}{1}$ |
| D | $\frac{0}{1}$ | $\frac{0}{1}$ | $\frac{0}{1}$ | 1 | $\frac{1}{1}$ |
| E | $\frac{0}{0}$ | $\frac{0}{0}$ | $\frac{0}{0}$ | $\frac{0}{0}$ | 0 |

# Comment on "Opinion Agreement among High Court Justices"

by TONY VINSON

G. SCHUBERT HAS INDICATED the difficulties besetting an "alien observer's" attempts to gather reliable background information on High Court Justices in Australia. While wishing to acknowledge these difficulties, it is nevertheless necessary to challenge two points in Schubert's analysis of opinion agreement among the justices. The first of these concerns a question (domicile) which was central to the author's analysis; the second involves his imprecise use of terminology at a time when this appears necessary for the advancement of sociology in Australia.

On page [163] reference is made to the justices' "typically lower-middle class origins". This appears to refer to all nine justices covered in the study and is incorrect by any of the usually accepted criteria of "class" or status. Dixon is the son of a solicitor and was educated at Hawthorn College in Melbourne. Fullagar was educated at Haileybury College in Melbourne and at Ormond College in the University of Melbourne. Kitto's father was the holder of an O.B.E., and Menzies is the son of a clergyman.

Windeyer is the son of a Sydney solicitor and was educated at Sydney Grammar School. To quote from a speech which he made at the Fourteenth Legal Convention of the Law Council of Australia:

> My people were in this country, engaged in the profession or administration of the law, before the Colony of South Australia began; before the Colony of Western Australia began; long before the Port Phillip district became Victoria; long before Moreton Bay district became Queensland, and when Van Diemen's Land had only been for a few years separated from New South Wales.[1]

The Windeyer family was founded in Australia in 1828 by Charles Windeyer who became a magistrate and was appointed first Mayor of Sydney upon its incorporation as a city. His son, Richard, a Sydney barrister, was a

This article was originally published, in slightly different form, in *Australian and New Zealand Journal of Sociology* 4: 158–159, and is here reprinted with the author's kind permission.
1. 41 *Australian Law Journal* 344.

prominent member of the Legislative Council of N.S.W. [New South Wales]. Richard's son, William, was the first graduate of the University of Sydney (B.A. 1856, M.A. 1859). He was for many years a member of the N.S.W. Parliament and was both Solicitor-General and Attorney-General of N.S.W. He was appointed to the Supreme Court of N.S.W. in 1879 and remained a member of that bench until 1896. During that period he was knighted. Sir William Windeyer was the grandfather of the present High Court Judge.

Owen, who was educated at Sydney C.E.G.S., is the son of a N.S.W. Supreme Court Judge, Sir Langer Owen, who was a Judge from 1922 to 1933. Sir Langer was himself the son of another N.S.W. Supreme Court Judge, Sir William Owen, who was on the bench from 1887 to 1908.

On page 163 of the article, reference is also made to variations in domicile and to differences in the two subcultures of New South Wales and Victoria which might produce "through early socialization and continuing adult reinforcement, differences in the within-group social relations and in the belief systems of the justices". Schubert refers to four Judges coming from New South Wales and four from Victoria. He comes back to the same point further in the paper, and on page 166 refers to Kitto as a Victorian. The whole of his mathematics about domicile are based on his belief that Kitto should be regarded as a Victorian. He was born in Victoria, but he attended high school in Sydney, worked in the New South Wales Crown Solicitor's Office and was a member of the New South Wales bar until his appointment to the High Court. He still lives in New South Wales and would in the legal profession be regarded as a "New South Wales" Judge.

There can be no doubt that Dixon and Fullagar were Victorians, having been born there, educated there and practised there at the bar. Menzies was born in Ballarat but attended high schools in Hobart and Devonport, Tasmania. He attended Melbourne University and practised at the Melbourne bar before his appointment. He would be regarded in the legal profession as a "Victorian" Judge.

Windeyer and Owen are from New South Wales. McTiernan and Taylor were born in New South Wales and have spent their legal life in New South Wales.

# PART III
# Quantifying Political Ideology

THE THREE ESSAYS grouped in Part 1 look at the relationship between behavioral jurisprudence and jurisprudence in law; the three in this part examine the relationship between behavioral jurisprudence and the theory of ideology in the rest of political science. There is inevitably a considerable amount of communality in the point of view expressed in all six articles, however, because they all are products of a relatively small period of time (with publication dates ranging from the spring of 1966 through the autumn of 1968). Furthermore, the first two of the articles in this part (chapters 8 and 9) are especially closely related, because the second of the pair was designed to be and functions in fact as an empirical test of a portion of the theory stated in the first and they were published in successive months. The third of these articles (chapter 10) is concerned with an empirical test—though in a much more abstruse and less precise way—of another part of the theory stated in the first article. In its most general form, the theory is concerned with the structure and content of belief systems—with how, that is to say, people organize conceptually their likes and dislikes, their sympathies and antipathies, their biases. In this general form it is therefore a branch of psychology; there is no reason to presume that beliefs about (say) sex or childrearing or religion differ, from a neurophysiological point of view, from beliefs about politics or law (Gluckman 1965; D. Morris 1967); and in any event beliefs about aspects of public policy necessarily deal with questions of sex and childrearing and religion, as well as with politics and law. It is also an aspect of political science, however, because political scientists long have been concerned with the "philosophies" of important political figures, ranging from presidents of the United States to local bosses. The study of the political and social and economic values articulated in the opinions of Supreme Court justices lies close to the core of the traditional interest of constitutional lawyers, whose practice of disguising these policy components by wrapping them in the rhetoric of constitutional conceptualism fooled no one except peasants (the laity); all members of the intelligentsia (lawyers and their acolytes) spoke the same conventional gobbledygook—else what's a law school for?—and therefore understood quite well that conventional references to "due process" and "equal protection" or "commerce among the states" were oblique ways of talking about who could be sent to jail and who not, who could vote and who not, and who must pay his taxes and who need not do so. In its classic form the constitutional law game did not approve that any save a few champions—the Oliver Wendell Holmeses and the Thomas Reed Powells—should speak openly, in front of the (ugh) general public, of constitutional ideologies *as though they were appurtenant to the justices themselves* rather than being functions of the constitutional document. So far as we can tell from what they wrote and taught, there never was a moment when such leading public law scholars as Woodrow Wilson, Frank Goodnow, and Charles Austin Beard, or (to take somewhat more recent figures) Haines, Ford, Cushman, Corwin, Ewing, Mott, and Swisher, to say nothing of such contemporary public law scholars as Mason, Fellman, McCloskey, Mendelson, and Tresolini, ever doubted that, as a then former associate justice of the Supreme Court proclaimed, the Constitution is what the judges say it is.[1]

At least as defined by the political scientists who have almost completely dominated research and writing and graduate instruction in the subject from the beginnings of the profession, the constitutional law game has been a political game, the rules of which specify a very large small group, the members of which are replaced at aperiodic and mostly unpredictable intervals through an indirect process of representational choice. From the perspective of the now almost two centuries of experience with the Court, it seems clear that its membership is continuously but slowly changing: on the average, there is a complete turnover in all nine positions (including that of the chief justice) every sixteen years, which is slightly more often than once every generation. Values, ideas, and beliefs change (and would change, for strictly biological reasons, even if there were not—as there are—other more focused, but not more direct, influences) throughout a person's lifetime, from early infancy until (for most people) virtually the moment of death. But the most intense, pervasive, and enduring stage of enculturation is undoubtedly that of youth, including both the socialization that occurs through the family and that which takes place through more formal educational processes. Consequently the *principal* imprinting of culture is highly correlated with time as well as place; and consequently, the continuous process of replacing the personnel of the Court (or of any court, for that matter) is tantamount to a continuing transformation in the values represented on the Court. At the same time the age at which justices are appointed assures that the cultural configuration that they tend, in the aggregate, to represent, corresponds best *not* to the values typical of the society in which they act, but rather that of the nation *as it was about a generation and a half earlier.* Of course, this statement is an exaggeration, to the extent that Supreme Court justices (either before or after their appointment to the Court) have modified to some extent their views in response to the pressures of the changing environment in which they have continued to live (see Cook 1973). But the fact remains that, at this time of writing (in the winter of 1973), the average age of Americans is thirty-three years, while the average age of incumbent justices is sixty-three— which makes them ideologues of American society during World War II far more than of the time during which they sit in judgment, at least from the point of view of the beliefs into which they were socialized (subject to whatever ideological learning they may have undergone in the interim). The Supreme Court is a system whereby an indeterminate but substantial portion

---

1. There is increasing evidence that a similarly realistic attitude is now coming into acceptance among some legal opinion leaders in other countries whose legal systems derive primarily from the common law: of course, Canada (Weiler 1968); but also South Africa (Dugard 1971); the Mother Country itself (Drewry and Morgan 1969; and Jaffe 1970); and even in Australia (Reid 1972; and Stone 1972).

of the symbols of the national culture are brought into closer correspondence with the modal behaviors of the society; while the generation (-and-a-half) gap in judicial age tends to assure that the meaning of the Constitution will never come into too close a correspondence with that patterning which is most prevalent within the society. So at least among American political scientists the constitutional law game has involved an appraisal of the goodness-of-fit between the image of culture projected by the ideology supported by the Court, in its particular decisions, and the feelings of the commentator about what the needs of contemporary society are, in regard to the policy issues that are the subject of the decisions. And hence, in studying judicial ideology, judicial behavioralists have differed from constitutional lawyers more in research theory and method than in choice of subject.

The differences in research theory and method, however, have been substantial. The theoretical objective of behavioral jurisprudence has been to articulate findings about the belief systems of judges, with the findings of other political scientists about the political valuations of other decision-makers (ranging from such elites as the Congress and office of the president to the mass of citizens). Interest has tended to focus, therefore, upon such questions as the extent to which the views expressed by Supreme Court justices (at any particular time) are typical of other federal judges, and of state or municipal judges; the extent to which the beliefs of judges, in regard to policy issues, are affected by their conceptions of judicial role and by their previous professional socialization and experience, as intervening variables; and the extent to which judicial belief systems are attributable to early enculturation. Another focus of interest has been the effect of *social interaction* upon decision-making. Although alternative paradigms are possible, I prefer to treat social interaction as a set of independent variables that interact with ideology, in a causal model of decision-making. The reason for this is that considerations of strategy, social distance, social deference (or dominance), social exchange, and other aspects of coalition-building (Riker 1962; Atkins 1970) are involved in the process of small group decision-making, whatever may be the ideological or personality similarities and differences among the individual members of the group. It is my view, therefore, that both personality and these social interaction variables must be included in any model of Court decision-making that purports to be more than partial, but that they are best kept analytically distinct from the ideological variables and also from each other. Similarly any comprehensive model of decision-making must make allowance for the effects of the judicial bureaucracy with which the individual justices continuously interact: this bureaucracy includes the law clerks who are assigned to each justice (and who clearly influence his decisions by providing him with both information concerning cases and critique of his proposed decisional choices and rationalizations); the custodians of supporting administrative and controls services (such as the office of the clerk, the librarian, the reporter, and his own secretary); and—particularly for the chief justice—

ancillary bureaucracies concerned with the training, monitoring, and manipulation of lower federal court judges (i.e., the Federal Judicial Center, the Administrative Office of United States Courts, and the Judicial Conference of the United States). I have increasingly come to believe, moreover, that it is of at least equal importance to include in any reasonably adequate comprehensive model certain biological variables, of which health, intelligence, and aging are certainly appropriate examples. So it should be clear that a focus upon the belief systems of individual justices is an avowedly incomplete and partial approach to the analysis of decision-making—but it is a necessary part of (and probably, prelude to) more comprehensive analysis, just as would be also parallel and cognate studies of social interaction among the justices, or analyses of their ecological relationships with supporting bureaucracies, and analysis of their individual biological and personality systems.

The principal methods that have been used to study judicial ideology have been questionnaire and interview surveys, cumulative scaling, cluster analysis, factor analysis, and smallest space analysis. The most extensive use of an attitudinal inventory, according to reports of published research at the time of this writing, remains Stuart Nagel's doctoral dissertation, which was completed over a dozen years ago (1961a). Nagel undertook to make a questionnaire survey of all judges of state supreme courts in the United States; his pooled response data describe no court in particular, but they do tend to characterize in a most general way the ideological differences among American state judges—as of the time when his work was done. The Nagel study was based on the prior research of Eysenck, who had developed the attitudinal inventory from which Nagel drew for the subset of questions that he used. Eysenck (1954) had used it to study the ideological differences among political party supporters—a mass rather than an elite population—in England during the late forties. Neither Eysenck nor Nagel undertook to analyze their response data by cumulative scaling; instead Eysenck moved directly into factor analysis, while Nagel contented himself with reporting percentages of marginal frequencies of responses (1963a). Eysenck had also proposed a theory of the relationship among responses to questionnaire items, scales, and factorial dimensions, and of the corresponding relationships among opinions, attitudes, and ideologies (1954:111–113). Chapter 8 discusses the Eysenck theory of ideology, in particular relation to the theory (and method) of cumulative scaling; while chapter 10 is based upon a reanalysis of the data from three empirical studies (the two mentioned above, by Eysenck and by Nagel; and Dator, 1967).

Chapter 8 originally was written for presentation, in a necessarily somewhat abridged form, as a paper at a panel meeting of the Southern Political Science Association. The panel met in Atlanta in November of 1965, about half-a-dozen years after the inception of the publication of research in judicial behavior in a sustained and continuous way, and at a time when the critical opposition to judicial behavioral research in the United States was peaking.

In a book published in that same year (and, indeed, only a couple of months before the panel meeting), I had ventured an initial attempt at characterizing the critique, and also at rebutting it (1965*d*:chap. 7)—although I relied primarily, for the latter purpose, upon a then recently published article by Martin Shapiro (1964*b*). By then I had been engaged in similar controversy—concerned fundamentally with the propriety of using the scientific approach to study human affairs—for over a decade (cf. Schubert 1954*a*), and it had greeted my own initial article on judicial behavior (1958*e*). It was apparent, by the mid-sixties, that criticism was emanating from three quite different points of view: some critics were public lawmen who simply defended the *status quo ante* (Berns 1963); others were avowedly political and empirical in their professed orientation, but hostile toward quantification and experimental rigor (Peltason 1964*a*); still others were themselves sophisticates in scientific method who deplored the lack of sophistication that, in their view, characterized the initial efforts of judicial behavioralists (Fisher 1958).[2] Corresponding to these points of view I identified three basic approaches to research in the judicial process field: traditional, conventional, and behavioral. In my initial discussion of this typology, I distinguished among them on the grounds of their manifest empirical characteristics, and in the chronological sequence in which they had evolved historically. But a linear model did not seem to fit what I perceived to be significant in the interrelationships between these three points of view. By 1965 my conviction was that the three standpoints were just about equally critical of each other; and if this were true, the mathematical model of their relationship would have to be curvilinear. So one objective of my Atlanta paper was to develop and explain this hypothesis about the structure of positions that defined research postures in the field of judicial process.

A second objective of the paper was to discuss the then recent criticisms of the use of scaling theory and method that had been voiced not by traditional public lawmen but by several research scholars for whom I entertained (then as now) considerable respect, including Samuel Krislov (1966), Martin Shapiro,[3] and Joseph Tanenhaus (1966). I decided that I should attempt a more systematic and comprehensive statement of the *theory* of judicial scaling than anyone had offered theretofore, the previous emphasis having been much more upon technique than upon theory. Consequently, the paper acquired a dual emphasis, with about equal concern for scaling as an approach to the analysis of judicial decisions and as an approach to understanding academic approaches to the study of the judicial process. So the focus was jointly upon judicial and academic attitudes and ideologies.

A third aspect of the paper was not my own idea, but rather reflected the initiative of Joseph Bernd, who organized the panel. As he planned it,

---

2. There were also pseudo-sophisticates, who posed as proscientific critics of judicial behavioralism: e.g., Becker 1963*b*.

3. Martin Shapiro's views were expressed, as I recall, in the form of comments upon the draft of my Atlanta paper.

a paper was to be presented also by Wallace Mendelson, who had emerged by that time as the leading spokesman for the public law ("stand patter") critique of judicial behavioralism (Mendelson 1963). So I wrote the paper under the misapprehension that Mendelson would be present to speak for himself (and to defend himself) in regard to my own remarks; and this explains what otherwise might be considered to be certain somewhat gratuitously *ad hominem* references to Mendelson, in the opening section of the paper. As it turned out, to both my surprise and regret, Professor Mendelson was unable to participate; but that news reached me only after I had arrived in Atlanta, and so I presented the paper as I had written it.

It happened that there was an unusually close relationship, in several respects, between chapters 8 and 9. I left to return to East Lansing on the day after I had presented my paper in Atlanta and when both its content and the response that it had provoked (from discussants and the audience alike) remained uppermost in my mind. By chance I was seated, for the flight to Detroit, next to a person who was conspicuously anxious about air travel – considerably more so even than I. There was a ten-minute wait for clearance to take off, during which time our craft parked with engines idling at the end of a runway; and my fellow passenger was getting me so nervous that I decided to put my mind to something more constructive, so I pulled a tablet out of my brief case and began to consider the question whether, and if so how, it might be possible to make an empirical test of the theory, about the structure of research postures, that I had proposed at the panel on the preceding day. As chapter 8 shows (at p. 187), I had stated the theory as an explicit hypothesis about the ordering of proximity relationships between political science and various cognate fields (of the life and social sciences, and of the humanities). The resulting sequence was a circular ordering, with three equidistant points specifying the loci of the midpoints of segments of the traditional, conventional, and behavioral perspectives. But the empirical content of these segments consisted, according to my theory, of the various political scientists who during the preceding decade had been contributing to research in the judicial process field. Consequently, it should be possible to locate these persons, in at least an ordinal relationship to each other, along that continuum: if my own position (for instance) were in the center of the behavioral segment, then I perceived Peltason (for example) to be in the center of the conventional segment, and Mendelson in the center of the traditional segment. Similarly, I thought I could locate other scholars, with whose work I was familiar, as positions on one or another of the segments. So I proceeded to do that for the thirty or so of the leading contributors to research in the field. That completed the specification and operationalization of the hypothesis; to test it, one could conceivably consult mass opinion (by surveying samples of other political scientists, or of students) or a panel of experts (whose ratings of the subjects could be compared with my own statement in the hypothesis). But I turned instead to what I thought would be an even better test of validity: to ask the subjects themselves where each of them thought he himself should be located, and to ask them also to serve as a panel of experts for rating each other. By the time the flight landed in Detroit an hour later, I had completely worked out the design for the empirical test, including both the detailed statement of the hypothesis and the procedures for testing it. As the Appendix to the article reprinted as chapter 9 shows (p. 247), the questionnaire to collect the empirical data was mailed out two-and-a-half weeks later; and the exigencies of publication happened to work out so that both the Atlanta paper and the empirical validation of one of its major hypotheses were published a year or so later, in different political science journals but in successive months.

Chapter 10 also focuses upon ideological relationships, but with an explicitly cross-cultural design; and it arose out of a very different set of circumstances. An event of considerable importance to the development of the field of judicial process and behavior was the convening in 1963 of a two-week seminar on judicial behavior, at Ann Arbor, Michigan, under the auspices of the Inter-University Consortium for Political Research and at the behest of Warren Miller. Among the fifty-odd faculty members and graduate students who participated in the seminar were several persons who did not then, and do not now, consider themselves to be primarily specialists in judicial behavior; and among such persons was James Dator, whose own field of primary interest was at that time comparative politics. Subsequently he was employed for several years as a faculty member at Rikkyo (St. Paul's) University in Tokyo, and while there he decided to apply a research idea that stemmed from his having attended the 1963 summer seminar in judicial behavior, by carrying out a survey of Japanese high court judges, in replication of Stuart Nagel's questionnaire study of state supreme court judges (discussed earlier). Dator and I began a correspondence concerning his research shortly before the initial report of his research was published in 1967; and we have remained in touch since then, initially in regard to the more extended analysis of his high court data that I had asked him to undertake. His first report had been a straightforward descriptive account of his project; I urged him to obtain a copy of Nagel's data cards, and then factor analyze both his own and Nagel's data, so that it might be possible to discuss comparatively the factorial findings—which, according to the theory of judicial ideology that I had presented in the Atlanta paper, would in substance be a comparison of the ideology of Japanese and American judges. He did carry out the factor analyses, and he undertook to present his findings in a common format, and in relationship to his reappraisal of Eysenck's prior studies, which had employed an extended version of the same questionnaire that was used by both Nagel and Dator, of political party members in several European countries (Eysenck 1953, 1954; Eysenck and Coulter 1972); but Dator chose to direct his own reanalysis to the question of whether the modified Eysenck questionnaire provided an appropriate instrument for investigating the attitudes of Japanese judges. Explicitly, Dator preferred not to undertake a comparative analysis of the substantive findings, about ideological differences, that one might infer to be supported by the respective studies. As Dator's work progressed, it became clear that in order to get at the comparative substantive analysis that I thought important, I would have to do it myself.

Dator's second (and factorial) report (1969) was to be published as a chapter in a book on comparative judicial research, of which I was coeditor; and the completed manuscript of that book (including, of course, Dator's chapter) already had been submitted to the publisher when I was asked to present a paper at an international conference of mathematical theories of voting behavior.[4] I made this the occasion for writing the paper that appears here as chapter 10; I had undertaken the smallest space computer analyses, upon which the analysis rests, during the preceding year, but had put the results aside in the hope that Dator might be willing to carry through with the analysis that I thought ought to be made. Consequently my own paper is strictly a secondary analysis of data collected by several other persons, and I am correspondingly indebted to Eysenck, Nagel, and Dator. The work is also, therefore, an exceptionally clear example of cumulative building in the construction of social science theory: Eysenck had constructed his initial questionnaire on the basis of the pooled items of virtually all of the reported work on political attitudes up through the end of World War II (Eysenck 1947); Nagel adapted what he considered to be the most discriminating items, from Eysenck's questionnaire, for his own work on American judges (Nagel 1963a); and Dator had taken over Nagel's instrument—which of course he had to translate into Japanese, and modify in certain other respects—for his study of Japanese judges. And I started in where Dator left off; but I clearly could not even have conceived of my research design, let alone have carried it out, without the extensive prior labors of the three other scholars, each working in a different country and continent.

Due to another exigency of the publication process—in this instance, the fact that articles normally can be published more rapidly than books—the article that is reprinted here as chapter 10 appeared several months before Dator's second report, upon which it was primarily based. At the time this is written no subsequent studies have as yet been published to carry forward the analysis of ideology presented in chapter 10. But I have been continuing to work along these lines much of the time during the past five years. One such project involved a full year of survey field research, interviewing samples of approximately fifty judges each in Switzerland and in South Africa. One facet of that project was to collect data that would make possible a comparative study of the ideology of supreme court judges in these two countries, which were selected because of the marked extent to which subcultural differentiation is reflected in the representational structure of their judiciaries.

---

4. Organized by Professor Oskar Morgenstern, at the Institute for Advanced Studies, Vienna, Austria, June 26–27, 1968.

Hence the data will support comparative analysis of ideologies within each country, as well as between them. The interviews included both probing open-ended questions, the replies to which were taped, and an extensive schedule which subsumed scales of political, economic, psychological, and social content. Some of the items for the schedule were taken from those used by Dator and Nagel; others were taken directly from Eysenck (because Nagel had not selected them); and still others were taken from a variety of sources, including works by Adorno et al. (1950), Rokeach (1960), and McClosky (1958), and from the handbook on political attitudes published by the Survey Research Center (Robinson, Rusk, and Head 1969). An initial report that discussed primarily the design of this research was presented as a paper at a panel of the Ninth World Congress of the International Political Science Association (Schubert 1973d, and cf. Gow 1974), but the bulk of the coding, computer work, and analysis, still remained to be done then. Another project was not cross-cultural, and indeed was limited in its focus to the United States Supreme Court; but it did involve comparative *methodological* analysis of judicial ideologies (Schubert 1974a). One facet of this project, the data for which covered the periods of the Vinson and Warren Courts, involved an investigation of the differences in substantive findings required by interpretations based upon, respectively, principal component factor analysis, oblique factor analysis, and smallest space analysis (with the dimensionality of the smallest spaces varying from one to four). Another facet of this project that constitutes an extension of the chapters reprinted herein is the construction of a set of physical models of the ideological configurations for three-dimensional smallest space—and certainly from the point of view of reader apprehension, these physical models represent a step forward from the topographical mappings reported in chapter 10.[5]

---

5. It has been suggested to me that the smallest space topography portrayed in chapter 10 is markedly reminiscent of the paintings of Jean Dubuffet, such as his *Amplification of the Tap* (1965).

# 8

# Ideologies and Attitudes

## I. THE CRITICAL FUNCTION

**M**any of those academicians who are most vehement in their disputation of the relevance of attitudinal analysis to political science argue from premises that are patently ideological in character (Becker 1964:3, and chap. 1; Mendelson 1963). Typically such persons are unlettered in the alien academic disciplines of contemporary anthropology, psychology, and sociology, to say nothing of mathematics, statistics, or computer technology. But they know what they like, and also what they dislike; and the vigor with which a growing list of de Maistres of public law (to borrow John Roche's apt phrase) have ridden off to joust in defense of the *ancien régime* demonstrates their conviction that it is far better to fluster in a just cause than to yield to Mephistopheles. The problem has been that this Faustian drama, though frequently advertised, rarely gets into production, primarily because each of the leading would-be protagonists insists upon appearing on stage horsed on a nag, clad in tin armour, and fitted with the accounterments of the White Knight (in *Through the Looking-Glass*). It is difficult to join in combat with champions who keep falling off on their heads into ditches, because they refuse to do their homework. Instead, the Dons Quixote of public law indulge in rhetorical argument, in the heightened phrase, in violet (as well as violent) prose which

This chapter was originally published, in slightly different form, as "Ideologies and Attitudes, Academic and Judicial" in *The Journal of Politics* 29 (February 1967):3–40. Copyright 1967 *The Journal of Politics*.

An earlier draft of this article was presented as a paper, "Academic Ideologies, Judicial Attitudes, and Social Change," at the 37th Annual Meeting of the Southern Political Science Association on November 4, 1965. The author thanks Martin Shapiro, Joseph L. Bernd, David Hughes, and Stephen Whittaker for their comments on the paper.

is intended to appeal to the passions rather than to the intellect of the audience.

It might be of mild interest to answer in the same vein what has been to date the public-law *literary* critique of research in judicial behavior. Wallace Mendelson perforce persists in his own common-sense intuitions, stated in an idiom that is high in emotive content and moralistic exhortation and scholastic allusion but low in observable empirical referents, substituting for behavioral concepts words that have little recognizable semantic correlation with those used by judicial behavioralists to describe their work (1964); while Theodore Becker reiterates repetitious ruminations of straw men.[1] A rose is a rose is a rose, perhaps; and it may be that at some level of abstraction a scale is a scale is a scale. But among behavioral scientists do-re-mi is not Osgood's semantic differential; and neither is Guttman's simplex. It is not possible to join issue at a technical level with persons who insist upon their right to bypass knowledge of the basic research that has been done in such fields as (for example) the social psychology of attitudes.

Consider Mendelson's assertion that "neo-behavioralism has been over-influenced by the judicial activists" and that "behavioralism is a by-product of libertarian activism." This peroration reaches its apogee when Mendelson proclaims that "The knight errantry of judicial activism has bred in the neo-behavioralists (among others) an iconoclasm toward law and the judicial process that goes beyond the bounds of reason. What should be charged to a few judges is chalked up against the legal system" (1963:603). On the merits, the fancy that judicial conservatives like Frankfurter are value-free[2] while the "libertarian activists" (to employ, as Mendelson does, Pritchett's concept) indulge in judicial behavior is simply preposterous. To argue that all judges are, or ought to be, value-free in their official behavior makes some

---

1. Cf. Theodore L. Becker, "[Behavioralists assume] that various *personal* factors located in the judge's mind can *completely* explain his decisions. Put another way, these scholars assume that the judge's own personal predispositions regarding the subject matter before him are the *single* causative factor effecting [*sic*] judicial decision-making patterns. These predispositions, it is believed, are immune from *any* other influences, for example, judicial role (the requirement of objectivity and impartiality) . . . [and] modern researchers have chosen to avoid this factor as even being worthy of consideration and research. . . ." (Becker 1966a:13–14. Emphasis added to "completely"; other italicizations are Becker's.) Neither here nor in anything that he has published to date has Becker cited any behavioral literature to exemplify his charges.

2. "[As] I have just suggested: among his colleagues, such a judge must be the least prejudiced by liberal or anti-liberal bias; in this sense, then, the freest to consider each case on its own merits—our closest approximation of the non-partisan magistrate. The judge in question is Felix Frankfurter." (Mendelson 1963:598). But cf. the evaluation by another scholar who, though familiar with Mendelson's views, has been a student of what he calls "Frankfurterweise" for a much longer time: "It has been said of Holmes that he survived into his own generation. It may yet be written of Frankfurter that he was appointed as his was passing into history. He came to the Court beautifully equipped to carry on the Holmes-Brandeis opposition to judicial activism in the economic field. In twenty-three years on the bench, he had occasion to write just one such opinion. He came totally ill-equipped, emotionally as well as from his sense of values, to meet the challenge of a new era. Although he came from Vienna rather than from Paris, in a way his history is so French. For France, it will be recalled, on the eve of World War II was so beautifully prepared for World War I." (Grant 1965:1042).

sense—not to everyone, to be sure, but to a great many people; and to hypothesize that judges are affected, to a greater or lesser extent, by their beliefs and attitudes, has seemed a proposition worth testing to a great many other persons, going back at least as far as Plato. But the notion that good (nonactivist) judges are value-free, while bad (libertarian activist) judges alone indulge their personal biases, seems to be idiosyncratic to Professor Mendelson. Of course, Mendelson's fancy is closely related to the metaphysic of an analytical jurisprudence which posits an antiseptic judiciary of legal technicians whose exclusive function, interest, and expertise is procedural. But the fervor with which Mendelson sketches the scenario for his morality play—good old Felix, and bad old Hugo—brands his advocacy as a polemic which, however suitable for argumentation in a lawyer's brief, cannot be taken seriously as academic scholarship, even under the looser canons deemed appropriate for nonbehavioral research in political science.

The range of the differences among us in the extent to which we seek to be either "political" or "scientific" in our own work makes it difficult for persons at the antipodes of these two continua to engage in effective communication with each other, let alone to find a level of discourse at which they profitably can debate each other's work. It may, therefore, be of greater benefit to the profession if we eschew logomachy—a game that both behavioralists and their critics can play without generating much light—in favor of an attempt to answer the question why political scientists do divide so sharply in their perceptions of others', as well as of their own, work. The major underlying cause, we might hypothesize, lies in these persons' divergent ideological orientations toward their professional work. A first step toward better common understanding may well consist of a clearer delineation of the relevant academic ideologies; and in an attempt to take that first step, I have suggested that among political scientists today, the three most important orientations toward study of law and courts are the *traditional*, the *conventional*, and the *behavioral*.[3]

## II. ACADEMIC IDEOLOGIES

The traditional approach among political scientists is that of the public lawyer, who is content to define his subject matter as constitutional law (see chap. 2). Even at the organizing meeting (convened at the American Political Science Association annual meeting in September 1965) of the political science section of the Law and Society Association—which may very well have been perceived by many persons as an avant-garde group, in view of its ties with the American Sociological Association—the preponderant majority of those present identified their field interest as either "public law"

---

3. This was first proposed as a hypothesis in my *Judicial Policy-Making* (1965d:158–185). Part II of this chapter ("Academic Ideologies," *infra*) expounds and illustrates the hypothesis in somewhat greater detail. For an empirical test of the hypothesis, see chap. 9.

or "constitutional law." There can be little doubt that most political scientists who have a primary interest in courts embrace the traditional ideology.

The conventional ideology is aptly so called because it corresponds to the modal, or political process, approach among political scientists today—when their subject matter is anything other than courts and law. The characteristic point of view is that courts are political institutions and judges are political decision-makers, and therefore that political scientists ought to study them in the same way that they would seek to understand any other political phenomena. The classic statement of this orientation is found in remarks made by Jack Peltason (1953, 1955).

Judicial behavioralism is an attempt to construct a systematic theory about human behavior, analyzing data about judges and adjudicatory processes of decision-making by using theories and methods from all of the behavioral sciences, according to their relevance to the particular inquiry at hand.

The relationship among these three academic ideologies is suggested by Figure 11. The figure portrays a circular relationship, with three points partitioning the curve into three segments. In this paradigm, the points correspond to the ideological positions, and the segments correspond to movements that have been so labeled (although not, of course, in this context) by other writers. With the objective of further clarifying the idea which the figure is intended to symbolize, let us consider a few more examples, starting with the traditional position and proceeding in a clockwise direction. In addition to the works by Mendelson already cited, Abraham (1968) provides an excellent illustration of the traditional orientation. The judicial process approach, which links the traditional and the conventional points of view, is well exemplified by two recent books: Shapiro (1964a) and Jacob (1965). The conventional ideology is articulated by Pritchett and Westin (1963), and in Krislov (1965). Danelski (1964) and Murphy (1964a) are examples of what Shapiro (1964b) calls "political jurisprudence," spanning the conventional and the behavioral positions. Recent articles by Walter Murphy (1966) and by Joseph Tanenhaus (1966) are characteristically behavioral studies. Probably there would be relatively few disagreements concerning the validity of this classification of the recent literature in the field, at least thus far. Some persons may find much more disturbing the suggestion that the circle appropriately can be closed via the "jurimetrics"[4] segment which links the behav-

---

4. The portmanteau is Lee Loevinger's; I personally dislike the term because it tends to overemphasize measurement and methodology. Loevinger seeks, of course, to draw a sharp contrast with "jurisprudence"; but it seems to me that political scientists have no such obligation. "Judicial behavior" is probably too narrow in scope; perhaps social-scientifically oriented law professors, political scientists, and sociologists all might agree upon the potential usefulness of the concept of "adjudicatory behavior," which implies a relationship to political behavior and the behavioral sciences generally, and invokes the image of human beings rather than of numerical manipulations. Figure 11 recognizes this distinction by attributing differing (though overlapping) content-meanings to the "jurimetrics" and "behavioral" approaches.

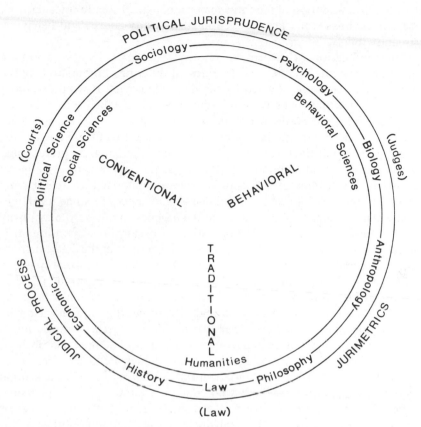

Figure 11. Academic Ideologies toward Adjudication

ioral with the traditional position. The work in jurimetrics often has been relatively spectacular, since it has tended to focus upon the prediction of decisional outcomes (as in much of the recent writing of Stuart Nagel, Fred Kort, and Reed Lawlor).

The points denoting the ideologies can be viewed, alternatively, as the midpoints of segments which correspond to the humanities, the social sciences, and the behavioral sciences, respectively. The resulting sequence of academic disciplines (ranging from law through history, economics, political science, sociology, psychology, biology, anthropology, philosophy, and thus back to law) is of course schematic, but it may have some heuristic value in suggesting the ordinal relationship of the modal tendencies for the frequency distributions of ideological standpoints in these fields. Thus the humanities tend to be concerned with what we might call the letter of the law; the social sciences, with legal institutions and political groups; and the behavioral sciences, with the personality of legal decision-makers. Accordingly, the characteristic focus of attention of the three major ideological standpoints has been that traditionalists study law, conventionalists study courts, and behavioralists study judges.

The implication of the circle, however, is that it defines an infinite continuum of points of view, which represent differing combinations of the bench-mark orientations defined by the three ideologies. It would be more realistic still to define the figure as two-dimensional, in which event we could identify positions within the perimeter, and thus speak of varying combinations of adjacent ideological positions (and cf. Figure 16, infra). Nevertheless, for an initial step in the direction of better comprehending the professional perspectives which differentiate—and at the same time integrate—political scientists, it may be more useful to confine this discussion to the circle, leaving spheres and more complicated multidimensional spaces to some future occasion when the quality of our data and the urgency of our need may justify greater complexity. As it is, the suggestion of a curvilinear continuum is upsetting enough to those colleagues whose conceptions of the field can more readily be accommodated to a straight line. The circle suggests, also, why a person who identifies with any of the three benchmark positions tends to reject both of the other two: from his perspective, they are equally far away from where he perceives himself (ideologically) to be; this explains also why such a person often lumps the other two positions together—even though one who identifies with either of the other two finds his and the other position to be quite different. Thus, for example, we find Jack Peltason recently remarking that "It is difficult to understand the intensity of the attack upon [behavioralist] research by those who champion [traditional] scholarship, for there is not much difference between the basic assumptions and goals underlying the two approaches. . . . They have the same nonpolitical orientation toward judicial decision-making . . ." (1964a). According to our figure, this is precisely the way a conventional theorist ought to feel; and as Peltason had remarked over a decade earlier, we political scientists should "turn our attention to the judiciary as a facet in the group struggle and relate the activities of judges to that of other groups," leaving history to the historians, law to the lawyers, and psychology to the psychologists (1953:56). Similarly, Martin Shapiro is critical of both law-professor exponents of "neutral principles of constitutional adjudication" and of the "behavioral wing of political jurisprudence" (1964a: chap. 1). Public law types, on the other hand, tend to view conventional and behavioral research as equally risqué; while behavioralists consider the case study approach (other than as a possible source of data and hypotheses) to be just as innocent of scientific potential as is the legal case method of analysis.

It is hardly surprising that behavioral research into the attitudes of judges has met with considerable skepticism, much discounting, and more than a little just plain disbelief. Given the value predispositions of most of the relevant professional audience, it could not have been otherwise.

## III. ACADEMIC ATTITUDES

Academic ideologies tend to determine academic attitudes toward the study of judicial attitudes. Attitudinal differences imply differing choices among such core components of academic attitudes as modes of discourse, logic, statistical literacy, rationality, empiricism, methodology, and scientism. We shall now examine some of the differences in academic attitudes toward attitudinal research, in regard to each of these facets.

### 1. *Concepts*

From the traditionalist point of view, a judge's decisions are determined in part by an authoritative structure of norms (the law), in the manipulation of which he is skilled, and in part by what is called the judge's "philosophy." By judicial philosophy, public law scholars mean the judge's views on questions of public policy, which usually are related to a broadly defined linear continuum of liberalism and conservatism.

From the conventional point of view, judicial decision-making is the product of interaction among social groups; and the judge functions as a transmission belt for the articulation of group (social) interests. But group interests are equated to particular positions in regard to proposed dispositions of questions of public policy.

Hence concepts analogous to the behavioral concept of "attitude" are central to both the traditional approach and the conventional approach. This might suggest the facile conclusion that the problem of conflicting academic ideologies is primarily a matter of words,[5] and that "philosophy," "group interests," and judicial "attitudes" are synonymous. There may be more truth in this observation than has been recognized, but there remain important differences in weighting. Behavioralists assign a predominant weight to judicial personality as a source of substantive decisional norms; traditionalists assign a subordinate weight, looking to the law as the more important and more usual source of norms; while conventionalists assign a

---

5. Samuel Krislov, for example, recently has debunked efforts to use systems theory as the basis for analysis of judicial institutions and behavior as principally involving the substitution of "new nomenclature for familiar facts," saying (e.g.) that "little of moment results from referring to the Department of Justice as a 'subsystem'" (1966:1577). Krislov also denigrates as "*post hoc*" reasoning a recent attempt to take advantage of five years of accumulated empirical work in scaling judicial attitudes and in analyzing judicial attributes, by the statement of a hypothesis about the degree of correlation among classes of cultural, attribute, and attitudinal variables (1966:1581). The criticism seems inconsistent with his plea, earlier in the same article, for progress in theory building, by movement "from theory to empirical data and back to theory" (p. 1573). Presumably, Krislov's "from theory" means a priori reasoning, and his "back to theory" means *post hoc* reasoning. *Ergo propter hoc?*

minimal—usually zero—weight to the judge's personal values (as distinguished from his social role). It is not surprising, therefore, that most of the critique of so-called attitudinal-statistical analysis has come from conventionally oriented rather than from traditionally oriented scholars. Moreover, the conventional critique of scale analysis of judicial attitudes has been couched in what purports to be a dispassionate, and even a technical, correction of behavioralist blunders, by real experts in the theory and methods of social psychology. It seems appropriate, therefore, to examine the core arguments of the critique of attitudinal analysis, since this offers some promise of constituting a subject upon which a more scientific debate might be possible.

## 2. *Logic*

One of the charges most frequently levied against studies of judicial attitudes, particularly when the method of cumulative scaling has been employed, is that the findings are based upon a circular process of reasoning. Thus, Mendelson asks: "Could it be that scale analysis is tautological or circular, that the meaning it yields is the meaning one puts into it?" (1963:597). Shapiro makes the point more explicit: ". . . there is a kind of basic circularity in statistical approaches to the problem of judicial attitudes. Consistency in voting behavior is used to infer the attitude, and then the attitude is used to explain the consistency." (1964a:14) And Becker makes it verbose:

> . . . Professor [Q] misuses the data of judicial votes and opinions in relationship to psychological explanatory concepts (including and in addition to attitude). . . . In Hullian fashion, he sets up the stimulus-response bond scheme with the case (the facts within the judicial opinion itself) as the stimulus (S) and the vote (the decision of the court) as the response (R). The former is the independent variable and the latter, of course, the dependent variable. The intervening variable is the judge himself, or his attitude or attitude universe. The conceptual difficulty in this scheme is that these facts, as gleaned from the opinion verbiage, are not a stimulus at all. Are the facts as they are stated in the judicial opinion the same facts presented to the court for decision? No, they are not. The case opinion itself was not that which confronted the perceiving organisms (the judges) at the argument. That set of facts (presented in the opinion) was not the same which, after perception, filtered through the attitude net (behavioral predisposition set) and triggered the response. The case opinion itself represents a *distillation* of the stimulus, which was the actual factual situation presented to the court. Hasn't Professor [Q] utilized the response itself as a stimulus? So it seems. (1964:14)

Have behavioralists attempted to square the circle (or vice versa)? On this question, at least, all three critics seem to be in substantial agreement; and since there appears to be some superficial plausibility in what they say, a reply seems justifiable. Let us start with Becker, and work backwards.

All of the talk about Hull, behaviorist psychology, stimulus-response bonds, and judges being intervening variables is Becker's gloss, not anything that Q ever has said. To the contrary, both Q and other behavioralists have emphasized opinion behavior and voting behavior as alternative forms of decisional response; and the question that they have thought to be of interest is not whether opinion rationales are "stimuli" but rather the extent to which they are correlated with votes (see, e.g., Schubert 1960*a*:516, 1963*c*:62, and esp. 1965*b*). Out of the entire situation (including the record, briefs, oral argument, conversation with colleagues, newspaper and television commentary, law review articles, the competence of his clerk, the current state of mental and physical health of himself and his family, perhaps the war news from Vietnam, et cetera, ad infinitum, plus the remembered and the sublimated historical antecedents of all of these events) a judge defines the issue to which he will react in his decision. Much of his training as a lawyer, and of his socialization as a judge, combine with the customs and institutional procedures for judicial decision-making to provide maximal (within the range of possible variation for human beings) assurance that his cognition of the situation will be highly structured, especially when he defines the question for decision. Unless there were high communality in perception of the issues deemed relevant, consensus on the Supreme Court (for example) would be considerably lower than the present level—which many observers already consider to be deplorable.

In order for rational decision-making to take place, it is not necessary that all justices be in precise agreement concerning the "facts of the case," as these might be inferred from the record. It *is* essential that they be in substantial agreement concerning what issue they are going to decide; and most of the time they are in such agreement. To the extent that agreement is lacking, clues usually are provided by separate opinions and by *jurisdictional* dissents. When their disagreement is sufficiently important (notwithstanding the milieu of consensus-pointing norms in which they work) to lead them to be willing to signify it in the articulate form of opinion language or a minority vote, Supreme Court justices typically disagree about *how* the issue should be decided—not about what issue the case presents. Since those justices who join in it have agreed to accept the common opinion of the Court, in addition to voting the same way in the disposition of the case, it is reasonable to accept what they say there as evidence concerning the issue(s) to which their decision relates.[6] Of course, not all justices are agreed upon

---

6. The principal justifications for inferring stimuli content from judicial opinions admittedly are: (1) convenience and accessibility; and (2) parsimony in research costs. But there is no reason why a researcher could not substitute content analysis of case records (including lower court action, briefs, and what transcripts of oral argument he could get at) if he is concerned that opinions of judges are so unrelated to the questions being decided that they mislead him even in regard to the major issue(s) to which the decision relates. Alternatively, one who fears that the analyst's bias will lead him to substitute his own for the judges' perceptions of the issue(s) in a case might agree to use the categorizations of some putatively neutral classifier (such as the West Key Number System). Moreover, interview and questionnaire data can be correlated with imputed decisional values in order to test the validity of the content of judicial scales. But these are all empirical matters; whether judicial opinions are or are not appropriate as sources of data, for the classification of decisions according to issues, raises no *theoretical* question.

consensual definitions of the issues in all cases; and to the extent that they are not in agreement, this is one (among several) of the sources of error variance. However, if this were a major difficulty, it ought to result in fewer and poorer, not more and better, acceptable cumulative scales. The procedure tests the hypothesis that all justices are responding to the same issue, in each set of votes (decision) of the scale. The only possible effect that can be produced by empirical deviations from the hypothesis is to *lower* the consistency apparent in the scale. We ought to expect that a set of judges, each responding individually to a different item in a miscellany of issues, will vote in random, not in consistent, patterns.

## 3. *Statistical Literacy*

(Un)critical references to "attitudinal-statistical" work tend to create the quite false impression that cumulative scaling is a statistical technique. A scalogram is an ordering of empirical data into a pattern, according to predetermined rules; it is neither a statistic nor the result of statistical analysis. Any claim to the contrary hardly rises above the vulgar linguistic practices whereby "statistics" are used as a substitute for "data," or the latter are used to refer to a single item. Once a scale—the ordering of empirical data in a particular pattern—has been constructed, the question then arises whether (and if so to what extent) the contrived pattern differs from a chance ordering of the same data, or from the least consistent pattern possible for these particular data, given such empirical parameters as the number of participants in each decision and the number of decisions participated in by each respondent. The researcher can use his own judgment in this matter, just as one might examine a painting, by staring at the scale and thereby arriving at a subjective judgment concerning how consistently the justices voted in the cases that comprise the scale. Or the researcher might undertake to contrive some ad hoc index to help guide his judgment; this procedure would at least tend to assure greater consistency in the researcher's *own* judgments concerning a set of different scales than if he were to rely exclusively upon his intuitions and impressions. The difficulty with both of these procedures is that no two researchers are likely to come up with either the same subjective judgments or the same ad hoc indices; and even if they should happen to arrive at identical judgments, there is no precise way in which they can communicate this information to each other.

A third alternative open to the researcher might be to use a conventional statistic to test the consistency manifest in the scalar pattern. However, as has recently been pointed out in a book which reports several dozen empirical scales, "One of the weaknesses of cumulative scaling, from a statistical point of view, is the lack of any really uniform criterion for testing significance" (Schubert 1965c: 78). And even when the available indices indicate that a scale meets conventional levels of consistency, the scale may not satisfy other nonstatistical criteria of scalability (Torgerson 1958:324; Green 1954:356; Schubert 1959:271–280; Lingoes 1963). Only the naive will assume that the use of statistical tests can substitute for the ultimate judgment of the analyst as a responsible scholar. The statistical tests simply make it more likely that several responsible scholars, of equal competence and experience, will reach similar judgments concerning the same scale or set of scales.

So if there is circularity in the use of cumulative scales of judicial votes as a basis for making inferences concerning judicial attitudes, this has nothing to do with statistics. Nor does Shapiro's labeling judicial attitudes as a "problem" (cf. Beard 1948:216) in itself pose any problem, unless it gives rise to other difficulties. This brings us to Shapiro's claim that "Consistency in voting behavior is used to infer the attitude, and then the attitude is used to explain the consistency." According to Guttman's theory, when the questions are arranged in a sequence of increasing difficulty, and a group of respondents answers the questions consistently, then it can be inferred that the responses are evidence of the differences, among the respondents, toward whatever attitudinal dimension the questions have in common. Some error is to be anticipated in empirical investigations, due to faulty observations and classifications of the data and failure of the theoretical model to fit the data; moreover there are computational errors inherent in the measurement techniques themselves. The statistical coefficients are supposed to direct the attention of the analyst to the first two types of error; and he is supposed to keep in mind the possible degree of influence, upon his observed statistical scores, of the third type of error.

## 4. Rationality

There ought to be a rational relationship between the sample of cases being scaled, and the attitudinal dimension that is hypothesized as being related to them. If one were to draw a sample of Supreme Court decisions consisting of all cases for which decisions were announced on even-numbered days of the month, then it would probably be unreasonable for an analyst to claim that he could make an inference about the attitudes, of Supreme Court justices, toward civil liberties—unless there is some nonobvious association between civil liberties decisions and the calendar.[7] It might be reasonable to hypothesize that, with such a sample, one might investigate the attitudes of Supreme Court justices toward announcing decisions on even-numbered days, *providing* that there is some plausible basis (either in theory, or from previous empirical observations) for assuming a functional

---

7. Since the above was written, Tanenhaus has published what appears to be a somewhat similar claim: that by following what are (from the point of view of judicial rationality) non-rational procedures of item selection, he can nevertheless observe a marginally "acceptable" coefficient of scalability (1966:1593). For discussion of this claim, see pp. 196–199.

relationship between the calendar and judicial perceptions of public policy. On the other hand, there *is* some reasonable basis, in the previous research findings of scholars in the humanities, the social sciences, and the behavioral sciences (to say nothing of the explicit earlier work of such students of the Supreme Court as Robert E. Cushman and C. Herman Pritchett) for hypothesizing that Supreme Court justices may, in those cases in which civil liberties issues are predominant, decide on the basis of the attitudes of the justices toward civil liberties.

Many scholars also think it reasonable to hypothesize, for the same or indeed for any other sample of cases, that the more relevant attitudinal dimension to test is stare decisis. Both Becker (1963a:265) and Shapiro (1964a:35–38) have raised this question; but thus far, neither has seen fit to face up to the possible difficulties that might arise, particularly if one were to attempt to do what they recommend: take a sample of cases selected because the predominant issue posed (according to the participating majorities of justices) is some aspect of civil liberties, and use those cases to test the hypothesis that the justices decided them as they did because of their respective degrees of belief in stare decisis. Off hand, one suspects that it might be difficult, even using the traditional methods of legal case research that these authors recommend, to order the cases according to the strength of the relevant precedents for each case—since the cases in the sample have not been selected on the basis of their supposed relationship to precedential decisions (strong or weak, clear or ambiguous). Neither Becker nor Shapiro has even hinted as to how he would operationalize the idea of stare decisis, so that a meaningful test of this hypothesis might be possible, using a sample of decisions drawn on the basis of other parametric characteristics, and using cumulative scaling as a method of analysis (Becker 1965, 1966a; Shapiro 1965). Off-the-cuff suggestions that stare decisis may be the real reason why nine Supreme Court justices voted consistently 402 out of 419 times in a set of 56 civil liberties decisions are not going to convince anybody who understands how a cumulative scale of such cases is constructed. Perhaps it may be also significant that to date, neither Becker nor Mendelson nor Shaprio (nor any other of the traditionalist or conventionalist critics of "attitudinal-statistical" research) has reported a scale of stare decisis—or of anything else, for that matter. There are, on the other hand, several reports of behavioral research in which the possible influence of stare decisis has been investigated (Ulmer 1959; Schmidhauser 1962b; Schubert 1963c, 1965c; Kort 1963; and cf. Becker 1964: chaps. 3–5). In these investigations samples were selected so as to maximize the probability that if stare decisis were an important influence in judicial decision-making, this would show up in the analyses.

## 5. *Empiricism*

There is nothing circular about stating a hypothesis, drawing a sample of data, observing and classifying the data, and then making an analytical judgment concerning the extent to which the observed data support the hypothesis. This is what one does in cumulative scaling, and this is what ordinarily is done in scientific research. Humanists and many social scientists get an idea, collect some data that they think may bear upon the idea, select that portion of the data that seems relevant (or, worse, substantiative) and throw the rest away, and then offer some generalization about the portion of the data that has been selected as relevant. This is what is *really* circular, or in Mendelson's words, a "self-proving hypothesis."

How much confidence one may be willing to repose in the results of a scale analysis is another matter. Traditionalists typically generalize their legal principles on the basis of the observation of individual cases, as discrete items; indeed, they often insist that this is the only legitimate way to analyze cases. But a behavioralist has minimal confidence in an inference generalized from a single case; and with a set of respondents the size of the Supreme Court, one cannot construct a cumulative scale with less than ten items, and usually at least twice that many are required to justify even minimal confidence in a scale. On the basis of a single scale with high apparent consistency in voting behavior, one might feel justified in making the further investment in time, money, and other precious resources necessary to examine other samples, selected so as to articulate with the initial sample, and employing the same research design. This is how, for example, Ulmer (1960) proceeded when undertaking his exploratory investigation of civil liberties as a possible attitudinal variable of importance in Supreme Court decision-making. Suppose one then finds, upon examining cases whose content is *not* civil liberties, that other samples of decisions can be related to different but equally consistent voting patterns for the justices; that in combination a few such scale variables substantially exhaust the universe of the Supreme Court's decision-making on the merits; and that such variables scale term after term, for a changing group of justices totaling almost a score, and over the course of almost two decades (Schubert 1965c: chap. 5). Perhaps one may then be warranted in drawing some tentative inferences about the possible importance to decision-making of attitudinal differences among the Supreme Court justices, at least during the period that he has studied. No behavioralist is clever enough to superimpose or inject enough of his own meaning, as an analyst, into that many (over 1,500) decisions, so that he can get the meaning back out again in the form of consistent patterns of voting.

If the critics actually were to attempt to check upon what the behavioralists have done, then they also are going to have to learn how to do (inter alia) cumulative scaling; and most behavioralists doubtless would welcome such a development in the profession. At the same time it is readily understandable that many traditionally or conventionally oriented political scientists might not feel that it would be worth the effort; but the role of a critic is more difficult, and the time for soothsaying is about over. Critics of judicial scaling ought to be willing to get their hands dirty (with empirical, perhaps even quantitative, labor), and come to grips with errors in the use of scaling at an operational and not merely a metaphysical level. One critic, who has done precisely that, is Joseph Tanenhaus, himself a behavioralist and, indeed, the person who, in a paper which he read at the 1956 Annual Meeting of the American Political Science Association, introduced the method of cumulative scaling of judicial decisions to the political science profession. But like Dr. Frankenstein, Professor Tanenhaus has for some time harbored doubts concerning his monster running amok;[8] and recently he has made public some of his reservations concerning the use and abuse of cumulative scaling to study judicial attitudes.[9]

## 6. *Methodology and Scientism*

Tanenhaus mentions half-a-dozen or so reasons for his skepticism:

(1) He questions the overly rigid procedures, which I once suggested, for ordering cases (1966:1590). (And so have I.) In 1959 these procedures were tentatively proposed in the first published work by a political scientist attempting to use the method to study judicial decisions.[10] The procedures were then advertized as a possible substitute for analyst subjectivity during what explicitly was stated (and presumed) to be an exploratory, experimental (and temporary) period while political scientists were becoming more familiar with the use of the new method. By 1960, less than a year after the suggested procedures had appeared in print, I personally had given them up,[11] because greater familiarity with the sociopsychological literature convinced me that several of these restrictions are unwarranted in theory, and further experience had demonstrated that they provide what is empirically too conservative a criterion. Tanenhaus seems to think that these procedures encourage the production of spurious scales of judicial voting; but the opposite is true of both my intent in proposing them and my observation of their effect in practice.[12]

---

8. I happen to know this from personal correspondence extending back to 1959; and see Tanenhaus 1961.

9. "There is serious doubt," he says, "whether what now passes for the cumulative scaling of judicial decisions is in any strict sense cumulative scaling at all" (1966:1588). Louis Guttman, the innovator of the method, thinks that the use of his techniques to analyze judicial decisions, in the manner that Tanenhaus criticizes, *is* cumulative scaling (personal conversation, when Professor Guttman was my sometime colleague as Visiting Professor at Michigan State University, during the fall term of 1962).

10. An earlier article (1958e) was based directly upon the book *Quantitative Analysis of Judicial Behavior* (1959), which was then in process.

11. See the scales in Schubert 1962b, 1963a, 1963e, 1965c.

12. Tanenhaus was codirector of a summer seminar in judicial behavior convened under the auspices of the Inter-University Consortium for Political Research, at the Survey Research Center of the University of Michigan in 1963, when this question of procedures for ordering cases explicitly was discussed. At that time I argued against rigid adherence to the procedures which I had proposed five years earlier; I urged that instead they be viewed as a guide for beginners to learn how to construct a first approximation of a scale of judicial votes. The intervening development of computer programs, which now provide such an initial approximation, has the effect of making obsolete procedures for manual scale construction (including those at issue here) except for the purpose of instruction as distinguished from research; see, e.g., BMD05S, "Guttman Scale # 1," in W. Dixon (1964 ed.), pp. 390–398.

(2) The basis of the suggested procedures for ordering items was the assumption of a perfect scale as the theoretical model—not, as Tanenhaus thinks, because of an assumption about the "intensity of issues." (Except for purposes of poetic rather than of scientific discourse, I think it is nonsensical even to speak about the intensity of issues; people may feel intense about issues, but intensity is a function of human perception.) It is not even clear to me exactly what Tanenhaus means by "intensity" since he offers no definition; for my attempt at an operational definition and for further discussion of intensity, see Figure 13 and the accompanying discussion of it, in Part "V. Judicial Attitudes," of this article, infra.

(3) Tanenhaus refers to certain assumptions which he attributes to "Those committed to cumulative scaling." I shall presently dispute his assertion that political scientists who have used cumulative scaling to study judicial decisions have assumed that the observation of a CR of .90 (or of a CS of .65) "proves" the existence of some postulated dimension; but I should like first to take issue with the implications of Tanenhaus' charge of commitment. He does not name any particular individual as an example of such commitment; but since my name appears in the adjacent footnotes more than that of anyone else, I don't wish to be presumed guilty by association. In everything that I have ever written on the subject of cumulative scaling (in some dozen or so places during the past eight or nine years), I have emphasized scale analysis as one among several methods that might be worthy of experimentation; I have stressed the desirability of eclecticism in research perspectives; and I have both advocated and worked toward the construction of more open, multidimensional models (as distinguished from exclusive reliance upon determinate, unidimensional models such as that of linear cumulative scaling.) Certainly I, for one, am not committed to cumulative scaling, or to factor analysis, or game theory, or any other method or technique.

(4) Tanenhaus is concerned that judicial scales are not completely determinate. But the difficulty here lies in the inadequacy of the data, not in any defect inherent in the use of the method. With no missing data (i.e., with full participation) and with a sample that includes n ( = the size of the court) + 1 decisions (each with a different voting division, and with no inconsistent votes) one could always (for example) scale the United States Supreme Court with only ten observations. Alas, this ideal rarely is encountered in empirical samples of data. It is quite true that many scales have been reported with multiple observations of voting divisions (i.e., with sets of cases tied in rank order). Since it is possible to get only a single observation of any case, such ties cannot be broken—by the use of cumulative scaling. But we can obtain many observations of respondents; and usually ties in judicial rank can be broken by expanding the analysis temporally to include a more adequate sample (for illustrations, see Schubert 1965c:chap.5). The question is not, as Tanenhaus' discussion seems to indicate, *whether* indeterminacy in empirical scales invalidates recourse to the method. The question rather is: at what point does indeterminacy become so relatively large, and one's corresponding

confidence in the resulting findings so small, that the use of the method of cumulative scaling, to analyze a particular sample of data, must be considered inappropriate?

(5) Indeterminacy in empirical judicial scales stems mostly from either or both of two causes: (a) nonparticipation; and (b) inconsistency in voting patterns. Indeterminacy caused by nonparticipation is, in my experience, the major difficulty which undermines (or ought to undermine) confidence in judicial scales. Tanenhaus discusses, however, only the second cause: "errors" or inconsistent voting. His point seems to be that a statistical measure of consistency in the voting pattern, which meets some conventional threshold criterion level, is a necessary but not a sufficient condition for guiding an analyst in his conclusion whether or not to accept or to reject the hypothesis that he is testing, about judicial attitudes, through the construction of the scale. If this were all, one would merely shrug at what appears to be a super-fluous observation; but it is not all. Tanenhaus states that it is *now* widely recognized that Guttman's coefficient is spuriously high if the marginals of the items in the sample tend to be biased toward the tails of the distribution. But all such standard references as Torgerson (1958), Green (1954), Schubert (1959), and Lingoes (1963), make this same point—and the article by Bert Green in the widely used Lindzey *Handbook* was a dozen years old in 1966. Unless Tanenhaus intends to imply that the persons whose work he criticizes were ignorant concerning the limitations of the coefficients of reproducibility and of scalability, at the time they were doing their judicial scaling, then the relevance of this cookbook information, to his critique of the research that he discusses, escapes me.

(6) From a discussion of the possibility that analysts may not recognize bias and inadequacies in the samples that they draw—again, his concern about the coefficients is directed at possible abuse by users, rather than at inherent defects in cumulative scaling procedures—Tanenhaus turns to the suggestion that an irrational scholar might make irrational inferences from a scale of judicial voting. He makes his point in the form of what he himself calls an "esoteric illustration":

> If one takes all the cases in Volume 355 of the United States Reports handed down on days of the month divisible by three, and then classifies them so that a favorable vote is assigned when a Justice supported petitioners (or appellants) with even docket numbers or opposed those with odd docket numbers, and a negative vote for the reverse behavior, one obtains an S of .62. (1966; 1593)

Such an outcome does not trouble me, and I really do not understand why it seems to strike Tanenhaus as so alarming. The situation is analogous to filling an urn with a thousand balls, two-thirds black and one-third white, mixing them thoroughly, and then expressing amazement when a ball-gum machine shovel, manipulated by a blindfolded operator, picks out sixty-two black balls in the first hundred tries. I first pointed out almost five years ago, and repeated several times in the interim before Tanenhaus published the remark quoted above (Schubert 1962b:98, 100, 102; 1963e:122; 1963a:443n. 74; 1965c:97–98), the explanation for the exceptionally high level of overall voting consistency in divided decisions of the Supreme Court during the 1957 term (which includes 355 *U.S. Reports.*). In the 1957 Term, as has been true generally during the period since the end of World War II, about two-thirds of the Court's decisions related either to the political scale or to the economic scale; and these two scales are positively correlated (at a moderately high level) with each other. Since each scale independently is internally consistent (with CRs of .96 and .99 and CSs of .84 and .90), and, more importantly, since the MMR—the pattern of maximal *in*consistency, given the observed distributions of marginals for voting divisions in these decisions—was .79 for the political scale and .81 for the economic scale (that include the 1957 Term) there is a substantial underlying basis of consistency in the voting of Supreme Court justices *irrespective of the issues.* Stated otherwise, the relevant question in interpreting sets of Supreme Court votes, which have been arranged in patterns of scales, is not "Does it surpass the minima for CR and/or for CS?" but rather is "How much does the scalar pattern improve upon MMR?" If Tanenhaus had reported that his vol. 355 experiment had resulted in a CR of over .90—and I assume it must have been much less, else he would have reported it—constituting a .15 to .20 improvement over the MMR for his data, one would be much more impressed with the implications of his experiment.

(7) Tanenhaus speaks of the establishment of "the existence of a unidimensional continuum" (1966:1594) as though this is the Holy Grail for which cumulative scalers are in quest. It is possible, judging from their published statements on this subject, that several of the persons, who are named by Tanenhaus on the same page where occurs the quoted remark, may conceptualize their efforts in terms of a search for unidimensionality. But I should like to dissociate myself from any such notions. As I have attempted to explain at some length, in a book which Tanenhaus cites (also on the same page), my view is that "unidimensionality" is useful as a concept only if we remain quite clear that it is a possible characteristic of our theoretical model—and *not* repeat NOT of the empirical data themselves. It always has seemed to me preposterous to speak, even figuratively, of *any* set of decisions of the United States Supreme Court as though their empirical content could be "unidimensional."

## IV. JUDICIAL IDEOLOGIES

In the study of judicial decision-making, policy attitudinal analysis is a necessary but by no means a sufficient condition for the development of comprehensive and systematic theory. Even a cursory knowledge of such earlier work as Beveridge's life of Marshall or of Cardozo's lectures on "The Nature of the Judicial Process" suggests the probably critical relevance of sociometric analysis of intragroup relationships, and of biological parameters, to the task of constructing more general models. The study of judicial attitudes toward public policy issues focuses upon the sector of *cultural* parameters for judicial decision-making, since the belief systems of individual justices necessarily reflect the socialization effects of a lifetime of exposure both as a youth and as a professional, usually within the milieu of the same (at least, taking the nation as the universe) system of values. (Frankfurter, for example, became a chauvinistic exponent of the Anglo-American legal systems, although he was born an alien and has said that he never heard English spoken until he reached adolescence [Phillips 1960:4].) It is not necessary to assume that knowledge about judicial attitudes will explain everything about the decisions that (for example) the Supreme Court makes; it is enough to be warranted in assuming that a focus upon the attitudes of the justices toward policy issues will explain part of what we do not yet fully understand. Attempts to illuminate this one sector (among the several others) of our ignorance may also be of value in delineating the boundaries between cultural, social, psychological, and biological subsystems of the judicial decision-making process (Schubert 1968a).

As an initial step in the direction of laying the groundwork for discussing several theoretical criticisms that have been raised against substantive findings about judicial policy attitudes, let us consider the outline of a hierarchical theory of the relationships among judicial decisions, attitudes, and ideologies. Figure 12 is based directly upon a more general hypothesis concerning the structure of social attitudes, suggested by the English factor psychologist Hans J. Eysenck.[13] Figure 12 shows that ideologies are the broadest constructs, and that each ideology is a function of several macroattitudes. Each macroattitude is a function of several microattitudes; and microattitudes are functions of decisional responses. As the figure suggests, there are relatively few concepts at the ideological level, while there will be, even for a single court, hundreds of decisional responses within a relatively short span of time. From one point of view, we might say that particular combinations of ideologies determine attitudinal dimensions, and that decisional responses are determined by the correlations of individual decision-makers with the attitudinal dimensions. This is a statement about how we would infer, on the basis of this model, that decisions are determined by ideologies; and to the extent that in real life judicial decisions are affected by nonideological determinants, then there should be error in attempts to fit sets of empirical data to the model. Conversely, in attempting to reconstruct ideologies from decisional behaviors, attitudes are logical inferences from sets of decisional responses, and ideologies are inferences from sets of attitudes.

Translated into operational terms, decisional responses consist of judicial opinions and votes in individual cases; attitudes are cumulative scales

---

13. For further discussion of Eysenck's theory, and of his relationship to American psychologists, see Schubert 1965c:191–193.

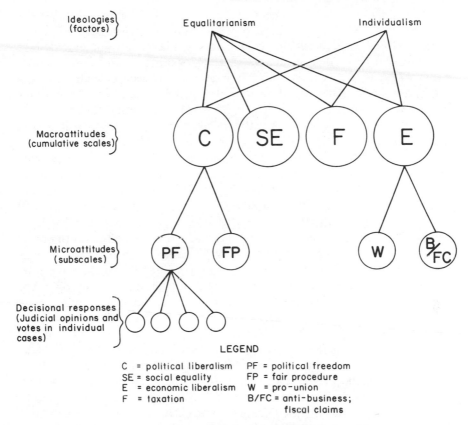

Figure 12. A Hierarchical Model of the Interrelationships among
Ideologies, Attitudes, and Decisions

and subscales; and ideologies are factorial dimensions. From a substantive
point of view, the two ideologies designated in Figure 12 are EQU (Equal-
itarianism/Traditionalism) and IND (Individualism/Collectivism). The four
macroattitudes are C (political liberalism), E (economic liberalism), SE (social
equality), and F (taxation). Of the microattitudes, PF (political freedom) and
FP (fair procedure) are subscales of C; W (prounion) and B/FC (antibusiness;
fiscal claims) are subscales of E. No subscales are indicated for either SE or F.
The relationship between scales and subscales has been discussed elsewhere,
with empirical examples.[14]

Table 32 reports the rankings, upon the two major scales, of all the
justices who were members of the Supreme Court from October 1946 through
June 1963. These scales purport to summarize, therefore, the relative degrees

---

14. Schubert 1965c:chap. 6. For an example of the specification of decisional responses
in relation to a microattitude, see Spaeth's article (1963a) on the prounion subscale.

of political and of economic liberalism, respectively, of eighteen justices over a period of seventeen terms. Evidently, these justices did not all participate together; for some of them (such as Douglas and Black) the number and range of possible observations was maximal, while for others it was less: for Goldberg, only a single term. However, the cumulative scale provides a model on the basis of which it is possible to link together, within a common frame of reference, even respondents who have never participated together in the decision-making of the Court. An attempt has been made to explain elsewhere and at some length both the procedures whereby these scales were constructed, and the explicit judgments on the basis of specific empirical data upon which the validity of these scales rests; that discussion also emphasizes the possibility of error that may have resulted from the inescapable (and not insubstantial) lacunae in the response data.[15] These errors, however, are of a probable magnitude of the following range: it is entirely possible that Jackson and his successor Harlan should not be denoted as tied on both scales; perhaps if we had some kind of data on the basis of which we could make direct comparisons between them, we might conclude that one should rank higher than the other on either or both scales. Even data of the same type relied upon, but for all three of Goldberg's terms on the Court, might result in his appearing a couple of ranks higher on the political scale—in confirmation of an earlier prediction.[16] But it is highly improbable that the errors are of a magnitude such that Douglas is misclassified as a political liberal, because his "true" rank is thirteenth instead of third; or that Frankfurter is misclassified on the economic scale because (as many of his supporters doubtless will continue to argue) his "true rank"—the one which reflects what he "really" believed as a private citizen who happened to be cast in the confining role of a justice—was first instead of sixteenth. In the absence of other evidence to the contrary, we may be warranted in reposing sufficient confidence in the rankings of these two scales, at least tentatively, to use them as the basis for apportioning the justices into a rough classification of scale types.

Table 32 shows that since the end of World War II, the Supreme Court has been divided primarily into three types of justices: (1) "liberals" who have ranked high on both scales; (2) "economic conservatives," who occupy the middle ranks on the political scale and the bottom ranks on the economic scale; and (3) "political conservatives," who have middle ranks on the economic scale but low ranks on the political scale. Only one justice, Harold Burton, appears to have been consistently conservative, and to about the same relative extent, on both scales; and Byron White is the only consistent moderate, judging on the basis of this evidence.

---

15. Schubert 1965c:97–146. Table 32 in this paper is based upon tables reported in ibid., pp. 125, 145.

16. See Schubert 1964a:577, 582. For data on Goldberg's second and third years, during which his average rank, among incumbent justices, was third on six scales, see Schubert 1972f.

**Table 32. Rankings of Supreme Court Justices on General Scales of Political Liberalism and of Economic Liberalism, 1946–1963**

| Justices | Political | Economic | Scale Types |
|----------|-----------|----------|-------------|
| Murphy | 1 | 1 | |
| Rutledge | 2 | 4 | |
| Douglas | 3 | 2.5 | LIBERAL |
| Black | 4 | 2.5 | |
| Warren | 5 | 5 | |
| Brennan | 6 | 6 | |
| White | 8 | 9 | MODERATE |
| Goldberg | 7 | 10 | |
| Stewart | 9 | 13 | |
| Frankfurter | 10 | 16 | ECONOMIC |
| Jackson | 11.5 | 16 | CONSERVATIVE |
| Harlan | 11.5 | 16 | |
| Whittaker | 13 | 18 | |
| Burton | 14 | 14 | CONSERVATIVE |
| Clark | 15 | 8 | |
| Vinson | 16 | 7 | POLITICAL |
| Minton | 17 | 11 | CONSERVATIVE |
| Reed | 18 | 12 | |

## V. JUDICIAL ATTITUDES

The data in Table 32 help to explain, at least in part, some of the aspects of cumulative scaling of judicial voting behavior that appear to have been particularly troublesome for the conventionalist critics. We shall focus particularly upon scalar consistency and attitudinal change, the intensity of attitudes, and the meaning of moderation in scale ranks. For a typical criticism, let us take Martin Shapiro's syllogism (1964a:37):

> "Where attitudes are divined on the basis of membership in a group, the attitudes of the very Justices who decide the Court are least amenable to divination. Scalograms also typically show [MAJOR PREMISE:] Justices with the most uniform votes ranged on opposite ends of the scale, with the decisive votes cast by those Justices in the middle. Even if the votes of the middle Justices are consistent in terms of the scale, [MINOR PREMISE:] their position in the middle indicates that they hold the attitude measured by the scale less strongly than do the other Justices. [CONCLUSION:] Those Justices who actually control the Court's decision are, by the terms of the scale itself, the least influenced by the attitudes that the scaler is using to explain the behavior of the Justices. (1964a;37)

The *American College Dictionary* defines "divine," when used as a transitive verb and in a sense other than prophecy, to mean "to have perception by intuition or insight"; and it is submitted that the purpose of employing the procedures of cumulative scaling is precisely to minimize the extent to which the analyst must rely upon his exclusively subjective appraisal of a set of data. It seems much more in keeping with normal English word usage to describe as "divination" the process by means of which Shapiro undertakes to attribute motivation to the Court as an institution, on the basis of nothing more objective than the most traditional doctrinal analysis, in the succeeding chapters of his book in which he discusses the decisions of the Warren Court in five fields of substantive public policy.

## 1. Consistency

It is not true, empirically, that justices with extreme scale scores show exceptional consistency in their responses; and on the basis of scale theory, one should say that what is decisive is the location of the stimulus-point (representing the issue to be decided) in relation to the set of points representing the justices, assuming that all lie on the same continuum. There is nothing about a moderate scale rank that warrants the *a priori* conclusion that respondents may not be *intense in their moderation* when they are asked to decide relatively extreme questions. Hence, putting to one side the question which justices "actually control the Court's decision," it certainly is not correct to say that moderate justices necessarily are the ones "least influenced" by the attitude measured by the scale. Let us consider why.

Turning first to the questions of attitudinal consistency and change, it is important to distinguish among at least three different levels of analysis: (1) the sociological level of analysis of consistency and change in the institutional attitudes of the Court; (2) sociopsychological analysis of subgroups of the justices; and (3) psychological analysis of individual justices.

Coefficients of reproducibility and of scalability are designed to measure the consistency in the response patterns of the entire group of respondents included in a particular scale; and judging on the basis of this kind of evidence, the *consistency* of the attitudes of the Vinson and Warren Courts, toward issues of political and economic liberalism, was fairly high, with inconsistent responses averaging about five percent (Schubert 1965c:80). On the other hand, the Court certainly did change "its" attitude toward both issues, as a consequence of both (a) changes in the composition of the group, and hence of the values programmed for its decision-making; and (b) changes in the stimuli, reflecting such environmental changes as the rise and fall of Senator McCarthy, the activities of the N.A.A.C.P. and associated groups, the rise of the civil rights movement, and the congressional movement of 1958–1959 to "curb the Court." Both the Jenner Bill and its legislative satellites, and Harry Truman's appointments of Clark and Minton as successors to Murphy and Rutledge, resulted in temporary "civil liberties recessions" in terms of both the quantity and the quality of the Court's outputs regarding political liberalism (Schubert 1965c:109–111, 114–116, 226).

All three of the major scale types denoted in Table 32 (liberals, political conservatives, and economic conservatives) were consistent, in the sense that the same individuals fit the types term after term; and although there were a few instances in which justices moved from moderate positions into one or another of the major types, there were no instances of transfer from one type to another. There were, of course, changes in the composition of the types, as some individuals joined and others left the Court (Schubert 1965c: 244). Thus, there were four liberals during the 1946–1948 Terms, only two for the next half-dozen years, three during 1955 and then four again following Brennan's appointment in 1956. Initially, there were two political conservatives, who expanded to a dominant plurality of four during the 1949–1952 Terms; but because no new appointments of justices of this type were made after 1949, attrition reduced the group to two by 1956, and since then there has been only Clark. During the first ten terms there were two economic conservatives (Frankfurter, and first Jackson and later Harlan), who were joined by Whittaker temporarily, Stewart, and then Goldberg; but only three remained in 1962. Meantime, the ideological structure of the court, as well as its attitudinal structure, was continuously changing as a result of these changes in the relative size of the three major types: it made a very considerable difference whether the Court consisted of two liberals, one conservative, four political conservatives, and two economic conservatives, as in 1952, or whether it consisted of four liberals, one political conservative, and three economic conservatives, plus one relatively moderate justice who did not fit the types, as in 1962.

Generally speaking, the individual justices must appear to be consistent in their voting behavior, and therefore presumably in their attitudes, or else it is not possible for the Court to seem consistent. But there were variations from one individual to another. Douglas, for example, voted consistently—and incidentally, to uphold the value of political liberalism—in 149 out of a total of 150 C scale decisions during the 1955–1958 Terms; while Clark, who participated in the same decisions, had ten inconsistencies and voted liberally only 16 times (Schubert 1965c:108–110). Similarly, in the 203 E scale decisions of the 1954–1959 Terms, Douglas voted both consistently and liberally in 201; while Frankfurter, participating in 180 of the same decisions, had 13 inconsistencies and voted liberally only 36 times (Schubert 1965c:134–136). So individual inconsistency ranged from virtually none to about 7 percent, although individual consistency varied within this range from one period of time to another. None of the justices was exceptionally inconsistent in his voting behavior, as measured by either of the scales, throughout his tenure on the Court. Neither was there any significant relationship between scale rank order and individual consistency; to the contrary, the correlation between rank order and number of inconsistent votes is probably very close to zero. Nor is there any evidence which indicates that any individual changed his attitude, in relation to either of the major scales, with the solitary exception of Chief Justice Warren, who did appear to change from a conservative to a liberal position, in regard to the political scale, during his first two terms on the Court (Schubert 1965c:118–276).

It was concluded, after a detailed review of the evidence relating to attitudinal consistency and change on the Court, and from the points of view of all three levels of analysis, that:

> [A]ttitudes and ideologies appear to be most dynamic when viewed from the perspective of the sociological level of analysis; and they appear to be most consistent when seen from the psychological level of analysis. But . . . [s]ubgroup study links psychological constructs, statistical measurements, and individual behavior. This middle level of socio-psychological analysis is the key to the understanding of the attitudes and ideologies of Supreme Court justices. (Schubert 1965c: 276–277)

## 2. Intensity

The other principle question raised by Shapiro's syllogism relates to his minor premise: whether justices with medial ranks are less intense in their attitude toward the scale variable than justices with either low or high ranks. In the first place, ordinal positions on a scale, or on a set of scales, are strictly relative indices. When Frankfurter, for example, changed from the fifth rank on the 1947 and 1948 C scales, to third during 1949–1954, and then to fourth in 1955, back to fifth in 1956–1957, and then to seventh in 1958–1960, retiring from the Court ranking eighth (out of ten) for the 1961 Term, this does not indicate *any change whatsoever* in his attitude toward political liberalism. Quite to the contrary, he "moved up to" third place because Murphy and Rutledge vacated the first two ranks, and Douglas and Black—who had been third and fourth—then became first and second. Beginning in 1955, Frankfurter seemed to "move" further and further toward the right end of the scale simply because, whatever may have been the range of the interval gap between him and Black, corresponding to the difference between the second and third ranks on the scale, this segment was successively occupied by relatively more liberal judges than he, such as Warren, Brennan, Stewart, and White (Schubert 1965c:104–111, 121, 283–284). There is no apparent reason to assume that Frankfurter was more intense in his attitude toward civil liberties, during the height of McCarthyism (1949–1954) and during the civil liberties backlash symbolized by the Jenner Bill (1958–1960) than when he happened to occupy the fifth rank, as in 1947–1948 and 1956–1957. To the contrary, what evidence there is points in the opposition direction (Schubert 1960a:636–638).

The justice in the middle scale rank may be the central decision-maker, but empirical studies of political behavior show that this tends to make him the most—not the least—involved member of the group, in regard to whatever the policy issue may be. And this goes for involvement of his own belief system, as well as in terms of his interactions with other members of the group; for other members do not hesitate to appeal for his support on an ideological level—as well as on various other bases, depending upon the character of the group. Certainly in the instance of the Supreme Court, where the entire milieu is structured so as to reinforce ideological competition (see John Frank 1958; Shapiro 1964a: chap. 1; Danelski 1964), a justice in the middle of the scale inescapably is involved in the same attitudinal matrix with his colleagues. Shapiro's confusion stems from his failure to distinguish between "intensity" as a relative concept and as an absolute concept. When he speaks of a justice with a middle rank as being "least influenced by the attitude" it is clear that he is talking about intensity in some absolute sense; but it just makes no sense to attribute any kind of absolute meaning to what are defined as being strictly relative measurements and relationships.

Shapiro seems to assume that if a respondent has a moderate rank, he must therefore also have a "moderate" attitude, and be moderately influenced by it—because moderate means moderate and no nonsense about it. Conversely, Shapiro assumes that respondents with extreme ranks (those at the tails of the scale) will also be ones who, in common parlance, might be described as having an "extreme attitude" on the subject; and who therefore are extremely influenced by their extreme attitudes. But this confuses a member's social relationship to the group (scale ranks) with his psychological relationship to the substance of the attitudinal content. A scale rank is (at least, in the scaling that has been done thus far of Supreme Court justices) strictly a social index, a measure of how one person relates to others in responding to some selected set of items. Whether, and to what extent, any of the respondents in a group experience affect as a dimension of (i.e., feel intense about) their responses depends upon the relationship between the respondents and the questions.

Shapiro's commonsensical notion of judges being "influenced" by attitudes begs the question of perception of the relevance of a criterion, and confuses the very different question of perception of the degree of value attributed to an item in relation to a criterion deemed relevant. If a respondent does not recognize a question as bearing upon a particular attitudinal scale (i.e., if the item is not on the scale, for him), then he will not be "influenced" at all by that attitude. If he does accept the dimension as relevant, then he will be influenced to an extent that will depend upon the *intensity* of his response, which is a measure of the relationship between his position and that of the item, both on the same scale.

Figure 13 illustrates, in a schematic manner, the distance relationships among respondents (justices) and stimuli (cases) on a continuum symbolizing an attitudinal scale variable.[17] In working with empirical data, we can assume that it will be highly improbable that we shall ever encounter the situation in which the attitudinal differences between each adjacent pair of respondents

---

17. Cf. the figure, "Deviations Expressed in Percentages," in Pritchett 1941:894.

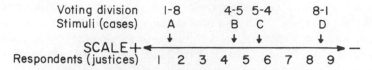

Figure 13. A Psychometric Model of an Attitudinal Scale

is the same distance interval. But a cumulative scale is not an interval scale, irrespective of whether respondent differences are reported as ranks or as scores; and therefore the equal spacing of Figure 13 corresponds to the imperfect information that we are entitled to infer from such a scale. If we assume that each respondent point on the scale identifies the position that best describes the attitudinal position of a judge—where he "is" on the scale— and that the left end of the scale identifies the positive direction of the attitudinal variable, then a judge ought to be most uncertain about his response to stimulus points that are very close to his own position. That is to say, since our model is a dominance rather than a proximity model (Coombs 1964:7–12), a respondent's position on the line is, speaking loosely, *his* point of indecision; more precisely, his position defines the maximum of his acceptance of issues relating to the scale: he will reject (vote against) all claims that correspond to stimulus points to his left (i.e., more positive than he) on the scale; and he will accept (vote to support) all claims whose points he dominates. The further away from his own position a stimulus lies, the easier it is for him to be certain that he favors or disfavors it; and consequently, the "intensity" of his attitude will be strictly a function of the scalar distance between cases and justices. With ordinal measurements only, the best we can do is to estimate distances—and therefore attitudinal intensity—on the basis of rank differences. To invoke a crude hypothetical example, a person who is opposed to capital punishment in any form is going to be more intense in his attitude of disapproval of euthanasia than will be somebody who favors the electric chair as a more humane instrument than the scaffold; but we should note that Agent 007 may well be just as intense in his approval of euthanasia as our liberal humanitarian is intense in his disapproval.

## 3. *Modality*

Returning to Figure 13, we are now able to infer that medial justice R5 (Respondent # 5) will be just about as intense in his approval of D as he will be intense in his disapproval of A, since each of the cases (A and D) is three ranks removed from his position. Note also, however, that we should attribute precisely the same degree of intensity to R1 in his approval of B, or R2 in his approval of C, or R9 in his disapproval of C. In short, justices at the "opposite ends of the scale" may be no more intense than the justice "in the middle," depending upon the issues they are asked to decide; and they may be more intense, or they may be less intense, depending, again, upon the decisional situation. Thus, R6–9 will be more intense in their disapproval of A than R5 will be, although R5 will favor D more strongly than will R6–8. R1–4, however, will favor D even more strongly than will R5. On the other hand, all (R1–9) may feel about the same intensity in unanimous decision, either rejecting an extreme claim far off the scale to the left, or accepting an exceptionally "easy" one (in Guttman's phrasing) far off the scale to the right; and under such circumstances, we might describe R5 as being "intense in his moderation." (Translated into legalese, we should say that the latter case raises a question about the law regarding a matter which long has been considered to be, and which remains, settled.)

The above discussion should make it clear that in relation to any empirical scale with ordinal data, the model requires us to assume that the relative intensity of the medial justice depends entirely upon the voting-division marginals, that is to say, upon the distribution of the stimuli points on the scale. Let us consider Table 33, which summarizes some of the relationships manifest in Figure 13 and thereby operationalizes the concept of attitudinal intensity. If a scale consists of equal numbers of decisions with voting divisions of 1–8, 2–7, 7–2, and 8–1, then R5's intensity will be precisely the same as that for R3, R4, R6, and R7; and it will be the same as that of R2 and R8 in the 1–8 and 8–1 decisions, and only slightly less than that of the extreme respondents otherwise. R4–6 all will be less intense than the other respondents in 3–6 and 6–3 decisions; and only in 4–5 and 5–4 decisions is it correct to say that R5 will be less intense in his attitude than any of the other justices. If a scale is perfectly balanced with equal proportions of decisions of all types (ranging from 1–8 through 8–1), then it is correct to say that to a very slight extent, R5 is less intense in his attitude, as measured by this scale, than any of his colleagues. But a much more meaningful statement, considering the magnitude of the sums of rank differences, would be that the moderate justices

Table 33. Rank Differences as an Index of Respondent Intensity

| | Voting Divisions | | | | | | | | | | | |
| | Split | | | | | | | | | Unanimous | | |
| Respondents | 8–1 | 7–2 | 6–3 | 5–4 | 4–5 | 3–6 | 2–7 | 1–8 | Sum | 9–0 | 0–9 | Sum |
|---|---|---|---|---|---|---|---|---|---|---|---|---|
| 1 | 7 | 6 | 5 | 4 | 3 | 2 | 1 | 0 | 28 | 8 | 0 | 8 |
| 2 | 6 | 5 | 4 | 3 | 2 | 1 | 0 | 0 | 21 | 7 | 1 | 8 |
| 3 | 5 | 4 | 3 | 2 | 1 | 0 | 0 | 1 | 16 | 6 | 2 | 8 |
| 4 | 4 | 3 | 2 | 1 | 0 | 0 | 1 | 2 | 13 | 5 | 3 | 8 |
| 5 | 3 | 2 | 1 | 0 | 0 | 1 | 2 | 3 | 12 | 4 | 4 | 8 |
| 6 | 2 | 1 | 0 | 0 | 1 | 2 | 3 | 4 | 13 | 3 | 5 | 8 |
| 7 | 1 | 0 | 0 | 1 | 2 | 3 | 4 | 5 | 16 | 2 | 6 | 8 |
| 8 | 0 | 0 | 1 | 2 | 3 | 4 | 5 | 6 | 21 | 1 | 7 | 8 |
| 9 | 0 | 1 | 2 | 3 | 4 | 5 | 6 | 7 | 28 | 0 | 8 | 8 |

(ranging from R3–R7) all tend to be less intense in their attitude—if they are presented with such an ideal array of questions—than the more extreme justices at the margins of the scale (R1–2, and R8–9).

Another way of putting this is to say that the medial justice's lesser degree of intensity, to the extent that it arises, is a function *not* of his lesser psychological attachment to the attitude measured by the scale, but rather that this is a function of his *social* position in the group of respondents. Indeed, from a strictly psychological point of view, we might well conclude that the medial justice's own attitudinal position is the most important one to the decision-making of the Court on the issue under consideration, because his relatively moderate view will be closest to the modal position for most decisions and opinions of the Court on that issue, as a consequence of the Court's system of plurality control over which cases it will accept for decision on the merits (Schubert 1962c). So, to the extent that we are interested in the institutional attitude of the Court, that too will best be approximated by the attitude of the medial justice. Conversely, to the extent that any single respondent's position *typifies* the attitude of the Court as a whole, as measured by the scale, it is again that of the medial justice. Therefore, Shapiro's syllogism just doesn't hang together under close scrutiny. His main point, that cumulative scaling fails to measure the attitudes of the respondents with moderate ranks, is contradicted by the theory, the practice, and the empirical studies—including some that *have* made predictions for, and on the basis of, the ranking of medial justices (Schubert 1964a:576–586).

## VI. THE FUNCTION OF CRITICISM

The foregoing analysis of the contemporary critique of judicial scaling should not be construed to imply that behavioral research is not subject to criticism. It is, and for mistakes at all levels and stages of research, from model building to design to the details of empirical analysis of decisional content. And this is a kind of criticism that is much needed. No doubt some behavioralists have hesitated to publish technical criticism of each other's work, because of fears that to do so would give aid and comfort to traditionalist and conventionalist "enemies," who could be expected to seize upon any confessions of error and to exploit them as admissions of guilt. But surely, such a posture is appropriate—if at all—to the toddling stage; and it is out of place now that the question whether the behavioral approach is a passing fancy appears to be settled, and no longer necessary to debate. If behavioral research in adjudication is to improve its capacity to explain the past and to describe the present and to predict the future, it needs criticism from all points of view. Conversely, traditional research and conventional research might profit from behavioral critique.

To be effective, critics must make a much larger effort than has been apparent in the past, to carry on the discussion in the conceptual terms of the *subject* of their criticism—not necessarily those preferred by the critic. This implies that would-be critics must attempt to familiarize themselves with more than one language and level of discourse. Here is where a greater awareness and understanding of the respective points of view characteristic of the three academic ideologies becomes of crucial importance. Then, instead of traditionalists communicating almost exclusively with other traditionalists, conventionalists with conventionalists, and behavioralists with behavioralists, transideological discourse may become possible, and even common. And why not?

The field no longer is public law, but neither is it the judicial process, nor judicial behavior. It is all three of these, and is likely to remain such a combination for some time to come. Neither the traditionalist, the conventionalist, nor the behavioralist has a corner on the market of either wisdom or knowledge about adjudicatory processes; to the contrary, each is specialized in differing emphases upon what is important (or feasible) to study, and how to study it. The time has come when we all should give greater attention to how we can learn from each other, and less to the contemplation of our respective ideological umbilici.

# 9

# Academic Ideology

This paper proposes a theory about the differences in perspective that political scientists bring to bear upon their teaching, research, and writing. It also suggests a method which can be used to study such differences. The particular empirical example discussed relates to only one of the subfields of political science, but this report may encourage parallel investigations into the structure of professional academic values in other component areas of the discipline. Such a result would not merely confirm or refute the applicability of the theory as a generalization about political science; it also would enhance our present meager and unsystematized understanding of the extent to which our professional knowledge is affected by our quasi-professional (personal) biases. The development of such understanding evidently ought to be assigned a high priority in any normative schedule of goals relating to the social ecology of scientific inquiry.

The phenomenon of analyst value predisposition is by no means peculiar to social science, and most certainly it is not idiosyncratic among political scientists. Psychologist Silvan S. Tomkins recently has called attention to the universality of the problem of academic ideology in all scientific work:

> At the growing edge of the frontier of all sciences there necessarily is a maximum of uncertainty, and what is lacking in evidence is filled by passion and faith, and hatred and scorn for the disbelievers. Science will never be free of ideology, though yesterday's ideology is today's fact or fiction.[1]

This chapter was originally published, in slightly different form, as "Academic Ideology and the Study of Adjudication" in *American Political Science Review* 61(March 1967):106–129.

I wish to thank Charles B. Poland, a doctoral candidate in political science at Michigan State University, for his assistance in preparing the data for computer analysis, and in related statistical tasks; and I wish especially to thank the twenty-six political scientists, all of whom are identified in the paper, for their participation in the research described: this is a report of what is in a most real sense our common labor, and I am deeply indebted therefore to these colleagues in the field, whose cooperation made it possible.

1. "Affect and the Psychology of Knowledge," Tomkins and Izard 1965:73, and cf. pp. 75, 97.

This proposition's particular pertinence for political scientists has been pointed out by a law professor, in the context of his evaluation of the legal implications of some recent behavioral research in adjudication theory. Although Arthur S. Miller was writing for an audience of lawyers, the shoe fits us political scientists just as well—and in view of the quotation's personal allusion to me, there can be no doubt of my own implication:

> [I]t is a great fault of behavioral scientists (and lawyers), [to] believe that statements may be made about such very human activities as the official settlement of disputes in adjudication without the intrusion of the biases or prejudices of the observer or commentator. . . . In *Judicial Behavior*, Professor Schubert . . . [says] nothing at all about the mental attitudes and backgrounds of commentators upon the judicial process. Are we to understand that the selection of facts, the organization of data, the construction of theories, and the presentation of conclusions are all value-free? As I have said previously, "the idea that personal values inevitably accompany—and color—research in human affairs (including law) is widely accepted by leading social scientists of the era. In like manner, a 'disinterested legal science' . . . is nonsense. It is unattainable. What this requires, accordingly is avowedly 'facing the valuations' which are present in all commentary" on the judiciary. Another part of the environment in which courts operate is the scholarly community. Those who write about courts and law should "face their valuations" in order to give us as scientific an explication as possible. (1965a:1098)

The present article might well be viewed as an attempt to remedy the deficiency denoted by Miller. Such a rationale is so pat that perhaps I should let it go at that, but the genesis of my inquiry into academic bias was in fact earlier and in response to other stimuli.

## I. THE HYPOTHESIS

From its beginnings following the Civil War until about a dozen years or so ago, the study of public law in American universities was closely linked with law school instruction and research; and the orientation which guided the approach to the acquisition of knowledge about and understanding of the subject, by political science and by law professors alike, was legalistic (Schubert 1966a). Out of the Court-packing episode of 1937 came more than a reform of the Supreme Court, however; the same set of events led also to some modest reforms in theory and method, as well as in the content, of professional discourse about the judiciary. The substantive change, which emphasized the political involvement of courts and the political effects of judicial decisions, came first and soon became the new orthodoxy among most political scientists. The reform in theory and method began with Pritchett's early work (1941, 1948), but it was not until a decade ago that several other persons began to follow the trail that he had blazed (Tanenhaus 1956; Kort 1957; Schubert 1958e, 1963f:1–3). After it had become clear that more than a passing fancy was involved, the various departures from traditional public law pedagogy began to attract rebuttal, and for a while it doubtless seemed to most observers (including participant-observers) that the significant difference in points of view lay between the defenders of the "leading case" approach in public law (and their allies who use the great books approach to political philosophy) and the rest of the political science profession.[2] Such a simplistic rationalization of the conflict seemed adequate to account for the critique that emanated from spokesmen whose point of view readily could be identified with parochial defense of the research modus operandi (or lack thereof) of the humanities (Roche 1958), or with the inculcation of virtue and the promulgation of justice (Berns 1963), or with the retention of Oldspeak as a tactic for helping to embalm preferred aspects of the historical images of selected judicial personalities (Mendelson 1963). But the rationale failed utterly to account for the position assumed by persons whose professed orientation is passionately political, and who purport to see no important difference between the workways and standpoints toward data collection of groups of their colleagues who perceive *each other* as defenders of the *ancien régime* (on the one hand) and as harbingers of a Brave New World of Juridical Robots (on the other hand) (Shapiro 1964*a*: chap. 1; Jacob and Vines 1963; Becker 1963*b*:12).

In an initial attempt to canvass the principal objections that had been raised against behavioral research in legal institutions and processes, I suggested that it might be more useful to conceptualize the academic chorus (or at least those who are performing the adjudication oratorio) as a trio of groups (1965*d*), in lieu of the behavioralist-versus-antibehavioral duet which prior discussion seems to have taken for granted. But if there are three standpoints, how do they relate to each other? The simplest hypothesis, which ought perhaps to be preferred on grounds of parsimony, assumes as a model a linear ideological continuum (ranging from behavioralists through judicial processors to public lawyers). This hypothesis requires, however, not only that students of the judicial process consider themselves to be equivalently distinguished from the other two types, but also that the public lawyers and behavioralists each feel greater affinity for the judicial processors than for each other. The available evidence, consisting of the expression of professional opinion (in books, articles, papers, conversation, panel discussions, and correspondence), seemed to me to support the proposition that most persons in each type consider themselves to be about equally different from persons whom they would identify with either of the other two types. This interpretation suggested the alternative hypothesis that the relationship among the three types is better represented by an equilateral triangle (or the circle on whose perimenter the three points of such a triangle lie) than by a straight line.

---

2. A recent survey of the profession reports that when asked to evaluate the significance of research contributions in seven fields of the discipline, political scientists ranked public law (sixth) and political philosophy (seventh) as "least significant." See Somit and Tanenhaus 1964:56, 58.

The typology, and the hypothesis of a circular ordering of types, provided me with a frame of reference which could be used to guide a more intensive inquiry into some of the more recent criticisms of psychometric research in judicial decision-making, while at the same time supplying an explanation for the affective overtones which typically accompanied the perceptual and cognitive misunderstandings that underlay much of the critique (Schubert 1967b). But the proof of the pudding is in the eating; and anyone who has enough confidence in his theoretical constructions to be willing to publish them ought also to be eager to have them put to the empirical test.[3]

Figure 14 summarizes the set of relationships, among the three ideologies, that was hypothesized.[4] The figure shows the traditional ideology to be centered in the humanities (History—Law—Philosophy) with a focus upon *law*. The conventional ideology centers upon the social sciences (Economics—Political Science—Sociology) and focuses its investigations upon *courts*. The behavioral ideology is centered in the behavioral sciences (Psychology—Biology—Anthropology) and upon the study of *judges*. The three ideological positions divide the perimeter into three segments which designate the overlapping concerns of the major standpoints; thus, the traditional approach merges into the conventional in the *judicial process* segment; the conventional changes into the behavioral in the *political jurisprudence* segment; and the behavioral in turn leads back into the traditional approach in the *jurimetrics* portion of the continuum. The relationship among all three approaches is portrayed as a continuous one, in which an infinite variety of discrete positions can be denoted, indicating particular proportions of emphasis as between any *two* of the ideological standpoints. The figure is completely determinate, it assumes (and indeed suggests) closure, and it precludes the portrayal of ideological syndromes consisting of combinations (in varying proportions) of all three standpoints; but it does afford a theoretical explanation for the tendency, among judicial politics enthusiasts, to view *all* decision-making analysis (whether on logical or psychological grounds) as apolitical.[5] The specification of a circular sequence of ordering for the nine academic disciplines denoted in the figure is intended to be suggestive only, and it is not assumed that such a manifestly oversimplified and overly rigid

---

3. In this instance, the design for the empirical research reported herein was roughed out the day after an oral presentation was made expounding the hypothesis (1965a:esp. 1–8, and Figure 1).

4. Figure 14 here is reproduced from Figure 11 of Chapter 8, and except for the minor modification of changing Economics from third to first in the sequence of Social Sciences is the same as Figure 1 in the paper. For further discussion of the a priori theory of academic ideologies in relation to Figure 14, with examples of writings which exemplify the three standpoints, see Chapter 8.

5. As Harry Stumpf has remarked, "there are a good many scholars who . . . cry out for a political approach to constitutional law while at the same time denouncing most or all behavioral techniques" (n.d.:6 n. 7).

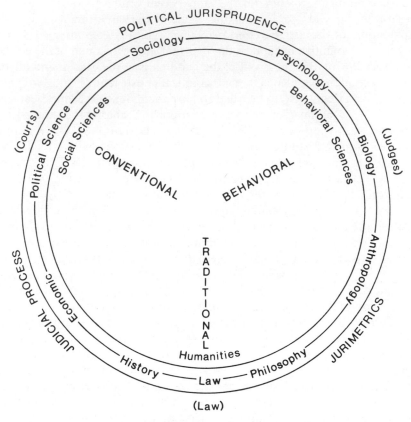

Figure 14. Academic Ideologies toward Adjudication.

rank ordering corresponds, except as a very rough approximation, to empirical reality; but at the same time, the ordering suggests the central tendencies that tend to define the core content, in terms of academic fields, of the major standpoints, and this definition of the modes in relation to the disciplines may have heuristic value.

## II. THE RESEARCH DESIGN

### A. Theory

If anyone (including oneself) were to take seriously the hypothesis implicit in Figure 14, then the obvious next step would be to attempt to test with empirical data the propositions that:

1. Political scientists with a primary interest in the study of adjudication are divided among three distinct groups;
2. Each group consists of persons who identify with one of the three corresponding ideological positions (traditional, conventional, or behavioral, as defined above); and
3. The three groups are equidistant in psychological space (i.e., their position in two-dimensional space defines an equilateral triangle).

A possible way of obtaining empirical data relevant to the above propositions would be to ask some of the political scientists who work in the field of the judiciary where *they* think others are in relation to themselves, and where they would locate themselves in Figure 14.

The answers to the first question might be converted into data in such a form that it would be possible to intercorrelate the responses of the various individuals in the sample; and if this were done, it occurred to me that I might very well be able, in analyzing the correlation matrix, to take advantage of the theory and methods with which I recently had worked in carrying out a study of *judicial* ideology (1965c). If one had any confidence in the interpretation that had been based upon the application of these theories and methods to data collected from official sources in libraries, then one ought to be willing to put them to the test of a design that would involve experimental research, survey-type "field" data, and a bevy of dynamic, "live" respondents who would be in a position to comment critically upon the interpretation made of their replies. Most human sources of data for such reasons as lack of status, ignorance, and inaccessibility to the relevant communication channels, have no chance to correct the mistakes that researchers have made using the data supplied by those sources; and most researchers thereby lose the advantage of exposing their findings to meaningful feedback from their subjects.

The answers to the second question would then make it possible to make a three-way correlational check upon the degree of consistency among several different measures of the cognitive structure attributed to the sociopsychological field of the attitudes of these professionals toward their academic work. First, there would be the researcher's own conception of where the others are, in relation to themselves and to himself. (He would need to generate this information for purposes of drawing the sample of respondents in any event.) Second, there would be the consensual conception of the ideological position of each individual in the sample, in the opinion of the *others*, as derived from the answers to the first question. Finally, there would be the self-conception of each individual of his own position, which the answers to the second question would provide. It would then be possible to examine the relationship among the a priori hypothesis of the researcher, the others' consensual conception of egos, and the egos' individual conceptions about themselves.

## B. Procedures

1. *The Raw Data.* Thirty-two persons were chosen, on the basis of criteria to be discussed below, for a mail survey. Each of these persons was sent the letter and the questionnaire which are reproduced as appendices to this chapter, together with a copy of Figure 14. The letters were individually typed, although their content make it perfectly clear that they were part of a mailing en masse; and the questionnaires were mimeographed. Together the letter and the questionnaire purported to explain to the respondents the objectives of the investigation and the information sought by the two questions; to assure respondents that the raw data for the first question would be kept secret; and to promise them an opportunity to comment critically upon a draft report of the research before the latter was submitted for publication.

Question 1 of the questionnaire asked each respondent to rank all of the other persons listed on the basis of his own perception of how closely they agreed with him in their approach to the field in which, as it was presumed, they had some common interests. The arbitrary assumption was made that each person was in closest agreement with his own point of view. It is recognized that for some types of inquiries and for some types of respondents, the findings would be hopelessly biased by such an assumption. In regard to this particular population of respondents, and the topic under investigation, the assumption of nonschizophrenia seems justified. If cognitive structure in the field of public law-judicial process-judicial behavior (or in any other subfield of political science, for that matter) is so weak that professors have no consistent point of view with which they identify, at least during some reasonably limited span of time, then our whole enterprise as teachers of political science is a kind of madness; and no amount of rational investigation is going to be able to make any sense out of it. So the respondent was asked to rank himself first; the person whom he thought was in closest agreement with him as second; and so on until the individual (among those sampled) with whom his disagreement was maximal was ranked as thirty-second. If the list contained persons with whom the respondent felt that he was insufficiently well-informed to make a decision, the directions specified that ranks of zero were to be assigned to such persons. No particular model of space was specified, nor needed to be specified, as a criterion for respondents in answering the first question. Each could hypothesize a space of any dimensionality and structure that suited him; all that was required of him was that he establish a decision function which would permit him to discriminate degrees of proximity to his own position in the space.

Question 2, to the contrary, specified a circle, upon whose perimeter positions were to be denoted using a clock metric, as a guide to answers. Figure 14 was suggested as one possible hypothesis about the ideological relationships that might be subsumed by a circular model, and respondents were directed to orient themselves in relation to the three major standpoints (at two, six, and ten o'clock, respectively) denoted by Figure 14. It was explicitly pointed out, however, that the positions—and therefore, of course, the sequence—of academic disciplines, as shown in Figure 14, were intended only to suggest one possible theory of the underlying gross associations of the three standpoints; and it was stated that respondents should not choose their own positions because of either their agreement (or disagreement) with the relative positions of the academic fields in the paradigm. The raw data consisted, therefore, of the two types of responses made, and marked on the questionnaires which were returned by the respondents. For the first question, the raw data consisted of the sets of rankings of all or part of the list of names specified by the question. For the second question, the raw data consisted, in each case, of the respondent's specification of a number, ranging from zero to twelve, which would locate a position for him on a circular continuum.

2. *Coding.* Coding was necessary for several purposes: to assure the promised secrecy of the raw data; to correct technical mistakes in the responses; and to transpose the replies to machine-readable cards. The first objective was accomplished by having only the author handle the questionnaire returns, to each of which was assigned a code number which identified the respondent (but only to the author) in subsequent manipulations of the data for the first question. An example of the kind of technical mistake that had to be corrected would be the omission of a rank from those assigned, or the failure to adjust for ties by omitting a corresponding number of intervening ranks between the tied rank and the next to follow in sequence. (Inspection of the returns suggested that a few of the respondents were not very experienced in the use of ordinal measurement; but all managed to indicate their decisions with sufficient clarity to preclude the necessity for eliminating any set of rankings on grounds of ambiguity.)

3. *Measures.* In order to calculate the correlation between each pair of rankings, the coded data were input for computer anaylsis, using both rho and tau rank correlation programs (J. Morris 1966; and cf. Kendall 1955; Siegel 1956:202–223). These coefficients are not directly comparable numerically because at any given level of association, the value of rho will be greater. Either coefficient measures, for any two respondents, the degree of similarity or of difference in their answers to the first question. The theoretical range for both tau and rho is from plus one (indicating perfect agreement) to minus one (indicating perfect disagreement); but the effect of requiring each respondent to rank himself as first was to place an empirical limit upon the positive range. Since this limit is well above +.99 for both coefficients, however, it was concluded that such a trivial difference could have no practical effect upon either the analysis or the resulting interpretation of the data. Either coefficient also can be used to measure the degrees of association among the hypothesized, the consensual, and the autogenous conceptions of the sequential ranking of the respondents on a circular continuum.

4. *Factor Analysis.* Some inferences could be based directly upon visual

inspection of the correlation matrices. But one major objective of the research would be to isolate and to identify the principal dimensions which, while accounting for a major proportion of the variance, would define a space in which points representing the respondents could be located in a psychologically meaningful configuration. This objective implied the use of a statistical procedure for multivariate analysis, such as factor analysis. I decided to use an available computer program for principal axes analysis, and to call for both quartimax and varimax rotation[6] of (successively) the first two through the first ten factors.

## C. Data

1. *The Sample*. The criteria for choosing the sample were visibility, accessibility, and balance. Visibility meant that the persons selected must be sufficiently well known generally *and to each other* that the probability of significant nonresponse due to ignorance would be low. I assumed that persons would know each other primarily, but not exclusively, through their writing; and it would by no means be adequate that persons merely "know who others are" by their names and general reputation. What would be required would be familiarity with other persons' ideas in some depth, and in particular concerning their beliefs about how—in relation to theory, method, and kind of data—it is best to study the subject (adjudication).

Accessibility required that the persons selected know the author personally, so that it could be assumed that they would at least read his letter circulating the survey instrument, and the probability that they would reply would be maximized. Balance required that there be approximately an equal number of persons chosen to represent each of the three hypothesized points of view; and further, that the persons selected be dispersed throughout all segments of the postulated circular continuum.

It might have been possible to restate at least the first of these criteria in a form that would have permitted objective and quantified selection procedures, but I decided to proceed instead upon the basis of what was presumed to be my adequate personal knowledge, resulting from recent bibliographical activities which had required me to survey (and resurvey) the research literature in the field (Schubert 1963a, b; 1964a; 1968e; 1972c). What was sought, after all, was not a random or probability sample, but instead a highly biased (in terms of those statistical concepts) sample which would consist of almost the entire universe of the elite leadership for one subfield of an academic discipline. The design included a check upon the author's bias, however: the extent to which his judgment about the persons selected corresponded with

---

6. The purpose of quartimax rotation is to simplify the variables (respondents), by making the extreme loadings tend toward unity or zero on every factor; the purpose of varimax rotation is to simplify the factors (the columns of the factor matrix) by making all loadings tend toward unity or zero on each factor. Harman 1960:294–308; Rummel 1970:390–393.

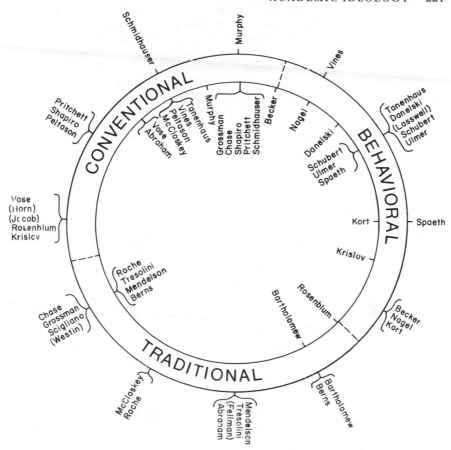

INNER = Self perceptions (Q.2 responses)
OUTER = The sampling assumption

Figure 15. Hypothesized and Autogenous Ideological Positions.

the group's responses. If many persons with poor visibility were included in the sample, the rate of nonresponse would be high. If persons were not accessible, they would not bother to respond at all. If the author's judgment concerning the subgroup (i.e., ideological) identification of persons deviated from either the consensual understanding or their own autogenous judgments, then the correlations between his ranking of the sample and theirs (Figure 15) would be low or even negative.

The advice of colleagues was sought concerning an initial proposed sample of thirty, and as a result one younger person was deleted (for presumed failure to meet the visibility criterion) and three others were added (of whom two turned out to be nonrespondents, presumably because of poor accessibility). The revised and final sample of thirty-two persons is listed in Appendix

**Table 34. Expected and Observed Balance among Ideological Types, in the Sample**

| | Observed[b] | | | | | |
|---|---|---|---|---|---|---|
| *Expected*[a] | Behavioral | Conventional | Traditional | Idiosyncratic | Non-response | Totals |
| Behavioral | 7 | 2 | | | 1 | 10 |
| Conventional | | 7 | | 1 | 2 | 10 |
| Traditional | | 2 | 7 | 1 | 2 | 12 |
| Totals | 7 | 11 | 7 | 2 | 5 | 32 |

[a] See the outer sequence, Figure 15.
[b] See Figure 16.

B. Table 34 shows that it was assumed that the sample would include approximately equal numbers of persons of each major point of view; and the outer circle of Figure 15 shows that it was further assumed that these persons were spread throughout the continuum. The observed distribution of persons among the three types, based upon the responses to the first question and the correlation and factor analyses that we shall presently discuss, indicates that the sample was somewhat biased in favor of the conventional point of view, primarily because two of the persons whom I had assumed to be behavioral in their orientation, and two others whom I had assumed to be traditional, were consensually deemed to be conventional.

It was assumed that although there would be considerable qualitative variation in visibility, any instances of exceptionally low visibility could be handled by "purifying" the sample and deleting relatively "unknown" persons, at least as items, in the generation of the correlation matrix. Accessibility seemed likely in all except three or four instances, although it was recognized that a few persons might be blocked by their own emotional reactions from responding to the intended query, as a consequence of previous professional interaction which had entailed affective side effects for them; but it was assumed that almost all persons in such an elite group of professionals would distinguish between their private and their public attitudes toward the project, at least to the extent that their evaluation of its merits would induce them to respond.

2. *The Survey.* The only person in the sample who refused to acknowledge either the initial letter or subsequent correspondence was also the one person whom the author never had met personally; he was one of those added to the sample on the advice of colleagues. The mailing went out to all persons in the sample on November 22, 1965; and positive responses to Question 1 were received from twenty-five of the thirty-two during the ten-day period

November 29–December 8. Three of the seven who had not responded to the first question, by the latter date, had replied declining to do so; subsequent endeavors to follow up with a second mailing evoked responses from two of the four persons who did not reply to the initial mailing. There were, therefore, a total of twenty-seven replies to the first question. All except three of the persons who answered the first question replied also to the second question; and there were no persons who replied to the second but not to the first. An attempt was made to follow up with the three persons who had answered the first question but declined to answer the second, by directing their attention to that part of the instructions which emphasized that response to the question did not require one to accept the location of academic disciplines that is suggested in Figure 14; and as a result, two of them did answer the question. The twenty-six responses to Question 2 are reported in Figure 15. The rate of response was 84 percent for Question 1, and 81 percent for Question 2.

In addition to the five persons who refused to give any response to the first question, the instructions anticipated that there would be partial nonresponse in the form of omitted rankings, for those persons to whom respondents assigned ranks of zero. Actually, there was much less partial non-response than had been expected. Almost half of the total of forty-eight omitted rankings (out of a possible total of $27 \times 32 = 864$) were due to a single respondent, who ranked only the half-dozen persons with whom he was in closest agreement and the other half-dozen persons with whom he was in least agreement. By thus reporting only the tails of his distribution, he provided a useable reply; his deletion of a score of other persons in the sample was a reflection, no doubt, of the less intense affect, or the less adequate information, that he entertained with regard to them. Five of the respondents were responsible for an additional twenty-five of the omitted ranks; three respondents omitted one each; and the remaining seventeen persons all were able to rank the entire sample. It is noteworthy that 79 percent of the omitted rankings were attributable to four of the seven persons whom we shall, shortly, discuss as affiliates of the traditional viewpoint; the seven behavioralists, on the other hand, made no omissions. One possible inference is that there is a consistent differential in the quality of information input by these two groups of persons: behavioralists seem to think that they are familiar with all of the literature produced in the field, but at least several of the traditionalists appear to be unaware of at least part of the behavioral and conventional research; the pattern of zero ranks, for one traditionalist, is B:4, C:4, T:0; and for another, it is B:3, C:4, T:0.[7] (As one distinguished affiliate

---

7. Walter Murphy suggests as an alternative inference "that behavior[al]ists are acquainted with the work of traditionalists more than vice versa because so many of the behavior[al]ists were trained in a traditional fashion by traditionalists; but few [if any] traditionalists have been trained by behavioralists" (personal communication to the author, May 4, 1966).

of the traditional standpoint remarked at a panel meeting of the American Political Science Association just a decade ago, the then editor of the *American Political Science Review* had asked him to read a manuscript which was about courts and judges but was "full of numbers"; so the eminent reader proceeded to advise the editor, as he jovially remarked to the panel audience, to "send the paper off to some mathematics journal.")

3. *Other Feedback.* Two-thirds of the persons who answered the questions also volunteered comments, ranging from a sentence or two to long letters, in which they discussed their responses and their opinions concerning the utility and probable findings of the survey.[8] Many were skeptical concerning the possibility that anything meaningful would emerge from the study, and often these persons explained in some detail the difficulty that they had experienced in replying to the questions. Typically they pointed out that they perceived themselves to be very complicated persons, with multivariate systems of academic values which could not possibly be projected onto some crude one- or two-dimensional space without gross distortion of their feelings. In replying to these comments, the author attempted to point out that there was no specified dimensionality for response to Question 1; and that the problem, with regard to Question 2, was to find the space with the minimal dimensionality adequate to account for most of the common variance among the respondents. To the extent that they were as idiosyncratic (i.e., unarticulated with the prevailing academic cultural norms) as many believed themselves to be, the question of the dimensionality of the space was irrelevant, since their idiosyncracies could not, by definition, be measured in any common frame of reference. In any event, their answers should make it possible to test the validity of their objections: gross distortion in the enfolding of many *n*-dimensional spaces into the hypothesized circle ought to produce a randomized pattern of autogenous positions for the respondents upon that circle, thus facilitating the rejection of the hypothesis that Question 2 was designed to test. It was also explained that the space selected for Figure 14 was two-dimensional because the effect of attempting to portray or otherwise suggest a space of higher dimensionality would almost certainly be to increase nonresponse to the second question even more than the widespread feeling of vexation at its seeming oversimplification. The two-dimensional model corresponded, of course, to the relevant dimensionality of the physical apparatus (i.e., a piece of Xerox paper) that was employed for purposes of pre-

---

8. In addition, a draft of this report was circulated among some seventy persons, including the twenty-five respondents who had indicated their wish to see a copy (by inserting a check in the query at the close of the questionnaire form, Appendix B). Twelve of the respondents replied in writing, some more than once and some in considerable detail. Three other respondents conveyed their views to the author orally in direct conversation, as also did several of the persons who had commented in writing on the draft. So the views of 60 percent of the respondents were taken into consideration, in revising for publication the draft report. Only one person suggested that it would be better to suppress the report of this research.

sentation; and more importantly, many of the persons in the sample might be assumed, on the basis of their previously published remarks, to entertain little empathy for the extension of a psychological/statistical model to its Euclidean limits of dimensionality (viz., three), let alone going beyond that into conceptions of space that could be perceived only through mathematical intuition. Even if the sample had been limited to persons who would have understood a question keyed to an explicit model of multidimensional space, the explanation of how to operationalize and to execute a decisional function for such a more complicated space would have required a covering letter of considerably more than two pages. Again the greater demands that such a question would have made upon a set of (in)voluntary respondents almost certainly would have entailed significant reduction in the level of response.

Several persons pointed out, in volunteered comments when they returned the survey instrument, that they had found Question 1 to be difficult but Question 2 even more so. This is readily understandable. What the first question requires is some procedure for partitioning the universe of items (persons in the sample) into sets which will be, in turn, successively further subdivided into subsets and subsubsets; it is further necessary that the subsets scale, both internally and in relation to each other, along a linear continuum. Few respondents, doubtless, were able to sit down and ask themselves: "Now, who is closest?" and then, "Who comes next?" and so on, through a list of over thirty names, with a resulting sequence that would represent a very reliable decision for them. Some persons attempted to do this, however, as evidenced by a few answer sheets which were returned with many crossings-out and changes in the initial ranking that was contrived. Doubtless it was naive of me, but I guess I had assumed that responding to Question 1 would not be too difficult, basing my assumption on my own (and my colleagues' apparent) ease in making decisions for departmental elections over the course of the past decade, using a preferential ballot to rank a group of about thirty members. After the survey materials had been put in the mail, however, and I faced the task of explicating my own response to the first question, I better appreciated the extent to which I had become accustomed to relying upon a host of clues and information in depth that were available for the face-to-face group to a much greater extent than for the synthetic one (cf. Collins and Guetzkow 1964:chap. 2). Moreover, the task of ranking persons in order to attempt to assure or to preclude their selection to serve the group in some representative capacity (e.g., as members of a committee) is not the same as the task of evaluating all members of the group in relation to a single selected and highly abstruse criterion. So I fell back upon the "equally noticed difference" (or equal-appearing intervals) method (Thurstone and Chave 1929) to guide my own responses. This involved sorting all thirty-two names (including my own) into three groups (+ [like me], 0 [yes and no], − [different from me]) and then, by the same procedure, dividing each group into three subcategories. This placed each person in a subcategory of three or four persons; the subcategories already were scaled; and the few persons within each subcategory could then be ranked on the basis of man-to-man discriminations.

The first question presumed no structure in particular for a respondent's own psychological space, but the second question clearly demanded that he accept, as the basis for making a response, at least three assumptions of mine. Many of the respondents went out of their way to record in their volunteered comments their disagreement with these assumptions, which were that: (1) persons active in the field today can be classified into one of three positions, or into a combination of any two, but not of all three, of them; (2) the three positions are related to each other in a scalar order; and (3) the scale is a circular (determinate, psychologically closed) continuum rather than a linear (indeterminate, psychologically open) one. It should be clear by now that I did not necessarily "believe in" all three of these assumptions; but I did consider it essential to make them in order to construct the frame of reference within which to ask the question. Evidently some common space would have to be hypothesized if the respondents' self-perceptions were to be denoted and measured in relation to a metric that would permit commensuration. No doubt this question was easy for me, not only because the assumptions were mine but also because I was aware of the limited purposes that they were designed to subserve; it would be much more difficult for other respondents to say, in effect, "this is where I am," particularly if they felt that they were being asked to specify their location in some strange place that they had never visited and did not recognize. But it is doubtful, also, that the differences between traditionalists and behavioralists, and between both of them and certain other persons who rejected either affiliation, was really all that novel a conception for very many of these thirty-odd persons. The sample, it bears repeating, was of what one would have to presume to be the most (not the least) aware members of this field of the profession.

4. *The Data Matrix.* The raw data cannot, because of my explicit prior commitment to the respondents, be divulged; but they certainly can be described. They were coded in the form of two-digit numbers in the cells of a $27 \times 32$ rectangular matrix. Each respondent initially was assigned a two-digit identifying number (from the sequence 01–32); this set of numbers identified the columns of the matrix, and the respondents in their role as *items* to be ranked by others. Those twenty-seven persons who answered the first question also were assigned two-digit identifying numbers (from the sequence 01–27); and this second set of numbers identified the rows of the matrix, and the respondents in their role as *rankers* of the items (other persons). The cell entries in any row include a continuous sequence of numbers ranging from 01 to as many persons as the ranker ranked: all cells in that row contain either a number from that sequence or the entry 00 (signifying that this item was omitted by this ranker). All (and only) entries for self-ranking (the cell identified by a person's columnar number as an item, and by his (other) row

number as a ranker, are unity (01). The only constraints upon the total of entries for any column, of course, are that each includes only one entry of unity, and that other numbers be 00 or else range from 02–32—and either 00 or any particular number within that range may appear several times or not at all.

Either the tau, or the rho, matrix is calculated by comparing the sequences of rankings for any two *rows* of the raw data matrix. In making comparisons between rankers with rankings of different lengths, it is necessary to delete from either sequence any items that are not included in both, and to renumber either or both sequences of rankings accordingly. The rank correlation coefficient (rho or tau) measures the differences, between two sets of rankings, of items common to both. Consequently, the empirical correlations are based upon discrete data pools of differing sizes, depending upon nonresponse; but this entailed no serious problem for the subsequent analyses of the correlation matrices, because of the generally very high proportion of complete or almost complete response. To the slight extent that nonresponse did affect a few of the correlations, this shows up in the testing of their statistical significance, as discussed below. The computer program that was used to calculate the rank correlations evaluated their significance, and it also accommodated nonresponse (i.e., to the differing lengths of row sequences).

## III. THE SOCIOMETRIC RANKINGS

### A. The Correlation Matrices

Table 35 reports the correlation matrix, with rho coefficients below and with tau coefficients above the major diagonal (the self-correlations of unity). It is evident that the rho and tau matrices are equivalent, in the sense that although the values of rho are larger (in both directions), the same patterns of relationships are explicit in both matrices. Either matrix denotes three groups of respondents. The first group includes eight persons, ranging from Kort through Krislov, among whom the correlations are all positive, at a minimal level of .33 for tau (with all intercorrelations significant at less than .005) and of .39 for rho (which is significant at .014; otherwise all are below the .002 significance level). A second group of seven persons, at the opposite end of the major diagonal, ranges from Roche through Mendelson. All correlations among persons in this second group are positive, at a tau minimum of .13 and a rho minimum of .31, and all are significant at less than .07 except for two correlations involving the three individuals who accounted for almost three-fourths of the total nonresponse, so the reduced rankings available for comparison readily explain the lack of statistical significance in the low positive correlations for these two pairs.

The fifty-six intercorrelations between the eight members of the first group and the seven members of the second group all are negative at a minimal

# Table 35. The Rank Correlation Matrices

| | Kort | Nagel | Tanenhaus | Danelski | Ulmer | Schubert | Spaeth | Krislov | Vines | Grossman | Becker | Peltason | Shapiro | Pritchett | Murphy | Chase | Schmidhauser | Rosenblum | Vose | Scigliano | Roche | McCloskey | Bartholomew | Tresolini | Abraham | Berns | Mendelson |
|---|---|---|---|---|---|---|---|---|---|---|---|---|---|---|---|---|---|---|---|---|---|---|---|---|---|---|---|
| Kort | | 46 | 54 | 56 | 59 | 51 | 41 | 44 | 35 | 32 | 25 | 32 | 25 | 30 | 27 | 21 | 26 | 12 | 02 | 06 | 37 | 43 | 29 | 33 | 50 | 62 | 67 |
| Nagel | 65 | | 62 | 57 | 46 | 48 | 33 | 47 | 47 | 54 | 59 | 37 | 34 | 20 | 26 | 16 | 31 | 13 | 03 | 06 | 28 | 55 | 32 | 49 | 51 | 50 | 40 |
| Tanenhaus | 70 | 81 | | 71 | 58 | 48 | 47 | 58 | 44 | 49 | 36 | 36 | 31 | 37 | 30 | 15 | 27 | 07 | 06 | 00 | 21 | 41 | 22 | 49 | 54 | 44 | 58 |
| Danelski | 75 | 78 | 87 | | 67 | 65 | 57 | 58 | 46 | 42 | 36 | 40 | 35 | 33 | 30 | 16 | 21 | 09 | 04 | 08 | 32 | 37 | 25 | 44 | 53 | 53 | 80 |
| Ulmer | 79 | 67 | 77 | 85 | | 59 | 57 | 45 | 42 | 27 | 24 | 33 | 34 | 37 | 31 | 07 | 18 | 02 | 10 | 05 | 26 | 36 | 53 | 43 | 36 | 51 | 58 |
| Schubert | 70 | 67 | 76 | 84 | 79 | | 51 | 47 | 38 | 36 | 38 | 30 | 34 | 46 | 25 | 23 | 12 | 18 | 04 | 05 | 21 | 31 | 32 | 38 | 40 | 39 | 52 |
| Spaeth | 57 | 39 | 58 | 76 | 72 | 71 | | 33 | 30 | 26 | 07 | 30 | 30 | 35 | 31 | 11 | 11 | 05 | 15 | 07 | 15 | 28 | 34 | 31 | 38 | 39 | 48 |
| Krislov | 61 | 68 | 60 | 62 | 66 | 64 | 54 | | 53 | 44 | 46 | 58 | 36 | 43 | 46 | 29 | 25 | 25 | 13 | 03 | 25 | 25 | 36 | 32 | 36 | 36 | 33 |
| Vines | 51 | 64 | 60 | 59 | 60 | 54 | 47 | 70 | | 42 | 52 | 51 | 49 | 49 | 31 | 41 | 29 | 21 | 14 | 03 | 02 | 29 | 25 | 39 | 31 | 42 | 31 |
| Grossman | 49 | 74 | 69 | 59 | 42 | 52 | 36 | 59 | 53 | | 52 | 40 | 23 | 49 | 31 | 30 | 09 | 29 | 08 | 13 | 18 | 22 | 32 | 43 | 38 | 29 | 39 |
| Becker | 46 | 80 | 52 | 51 | 32 | 44 | 24 | 69 | 61 | 67 | | 57 | 53 | 28 | 46 | 32 | 26 | 31 | 22 | 13 | 06 | 12 | 34 | 27 | 29 | 37 | 18 |
| Peltason | 37 | 59 | 53 | 57 | 50 | 47 | 42 | 76 | 80 | 70 | 34 | | 73 | 31 | 39 | 35 | 20 | 28 | 12 | 14 | 03 | 07 | 23 | 12 | 24 | 30 | 30 |
| Shapiro | 41 | 27 | 45 | 46 | 52 | 63 | 51 | 59 | 49 | 37 | 32 | 42 | | 31 | 36 | 29 | 06 | 19 | 22 | 14 | 22 | 09 | 16 | 09 | 17 | 24 | 27 |
| Pritchett | 30 | 20 | 37 | 33 | 37 | 46 | 35 | 43 | 49 | 49 | 28 | 31 | 48 | | 42 | 35 | 12 | 31 | 02 | 02 | 05 | 07 | 08 | 01 | 13 | 18 | 24 |
| Murphy | 27 | 26 | 30 | 30 | 31 | 25 | 31 | 46 | 31 | 31 | 46 | 46 | 36 | 36 | | 30 | 20 | 42 | 31 | 31 | 12 | 17 | 08 | 11 | 10 | 29 | 15 |
| Chase | 36 | 44 | 15 | 16 | 07 | 23 | 11 | 29 | 41 | 30 | 32 | 35 | 29 | 35 | 16 | | 27 | 12 | 06 | 03 | 17 | 13 | 05 | 15 | 15 | 41 | 21 |
| Schmidhauser | 17 | 24 | 27 | 21 | 18 | 12 | 11 | 25 | 29 | 09 | 26 | 20 | 06 | 07 | 44 | 63 | | 18 | 06 | 07 | 12 | 11 | 03 | 10 | 13 | 07 | 03 |
| Rosenblum | 05 | 24 | 10 | 13 | 18 | 24 | 16 | 37 | 18 | 20 | 16 | 31 | 17 | 30 | 49 | 48 | 18 | | 34 | 12 | 03 | 18 | 06 | 18 | 13 | 11 | 09 |
| Vose | 08 | 08 | 04 | 05 | 10 | 04 | 15 | 07 | 05 | 04 | 23 | 12 | 20 | 07 | 07 | 21 | 12 | 49 | | 15 | 07 | 06 | 19 | 01 | 27 | 15 | 30 |
| Scigliano | 08 | 06 | 00 | 08 | 05 | 05 | 07 | 03 | 03 | 13 | 13 | 14 | 14 | 02 | 31 | 03 | 07 | 19 | 15 | | 04 | 12 | 25 | 06 | 01 | 27 | 24 |
| Roche | 45 | 28 | 21 | 32 | 26 | 21 | 15 | 25 | 02 | 18 | 06 | 03 | 22 | 05 | 12 | 17 | 12 | 03 | 07 | 04 | | 75 | 31 | 48 | 55 | 46 | 24 |
| McCloskey | 55 | 59 | 41 | 37 | 36 | 31 | 28 | 25 | 29 | 22 | 12 | 07 | 09 | 07 | 17 | 13 | 11 | 18 | 06 | 12 | 75 | | 77 | 70 | 54 | 41 | 68 |
| Bartholomew | 40 | 29 | 22 | 25 | 53 | 32 | 34 | 36 | 25 | 32 | 34 | 23 | 16 | 08 | 19 | 15 | 06 | 13 | 01 | 10 | 48 | 28 | | 55 | 69 | 27 | 58 |
| Tresolini | 48 | 70 | 68 | 62 | 57 | 53 | 31 | 49 | 41 | 36 | 26 | 23 | 21 | 15 | 19 | 12 | 10 | 17 | 27 | 10 | 55 | 70 | 55 | | 87 | 42 | 67 |
| Abraham | 67 | 71 | 73 | 74 | 67 | 61 | 49 | 54 | 57 | 46 | 46 | 47 | 36 | 26 | 24 | 20 | 21 | 17 | 34 | 27 | 55 | 59 | 69 | 87 | | 84 | 67 |
| Berns | 79 | 71 | 61 | 69 | 67 | 51 | 46 | 53 | 54 | 60 | 40 | 30 | 18 | 15 | 18 | 20 | 07 | 16 | 15 | 24 | 41 | 22 | 36 | 42 | 84 | | 83 |
| Mendelson | 83 | 77 | 79 | 87 | 77 | 72 | 70 | 57 | 55 | 64 | 40 | 49 | 40 | 38 | 18 | 35 | 07 | 20 | 38 | 24 | 81 | 83 | 42 | 75 | 84 | 83 | |

NOTE: The numbers above the major diagonal are tau coefficients; those below are rho. All numbers are two-place decimals; the self-correlations, which have been omitted above, all are 1.00. The italicized correlations are negative.

level of .15 (for tau, with p = .142; and .20 for rho, with p = .168) for Krislov/ Roche. Five other pairs (all involving one of the three persons with high non-response in the second group) also have marginal significance values (.050 to .075 for tau, and .050 to .090 for rho); the remaining fifty correlations all are significant at less than .05, for both coefficients.

The average correlation among the eight persons in the first group is +.53; among the seven persons in the second group it is +.45; and the average correlation, between persons in the first group and persons in the second, is −.40. It seems reasonable to infer that these are two distinct and cohesive groups. Each group consists of persons who are in very substantial agreement with each other, and in very substantial disagreement with persons in the other group.

A third group, adjacent to the Kort-Krislov group, extends from Vines through Chase. All eight of these persons are positively intercorrelated (at a minimal level of .21 on tau, and .32 on rho) and with very few exceptions (three for tau, and two for rho, which have probability values between .04 and .06), all are significant at less than .03. The intercorrelations of this group with persons in the Kort-Krislov group all are positive, but somewhat lower than that group's correlations among its own members; and the intercorrelations of this third group with the Roche-Mendelson group are mostly negative (of the fifty-six correlations, forty-five of the tau, and forty-six of the rho, are negative) but again at a lower level than the negative intercorrelations between the first two groups. These findings suggest that there is a third group which falls in between the first two, but which is more closely aligned with the first than with the second.

The three groups, which together account for twenty-three persons, leave only four individuals who are not clearly aligned with any of the groups. Schmidhauser is positively correlated with everyone in the two groups to his left, and negatively correlated with members of the Roche-Mendelson group; but many of his correlations are weaker, in both directions, than those of persons in the Vines-Chase group: Schmidhauser has one tau correlation of −.41, another of +.31, and nine in the plus twenties, but his other fifteen correlations all are less than ±.20— which means that his common variance with most persons is less than five percent ($\pm .20^2 = .04$). The correlations for Rosenblum and for Vose are no higher, and they tend to agree—but not very enthusiastically—with everybody else; of the fifty-one correlations for them both, only nine are negative, and the highest of their negative correlations is −.10. Unlike Schmidhauser, who seems to lean toward the two groups to his left, the remaining individual, Scigliano, appears to lean toward the group to his right. His highest correlations are +.24 and +.22, with Mendelson and Berns respectively—who are at the right wing of the correlation matrix. Scigliano's correlations with the Kort-Krislov group all are within the ±.08 range, and six are negative; with the Vines-Chase group, the range is ±.14, and half are negative; while with the Roche-Mendelson group, the range is ±.24, and a majority are positive.

In the light of the hypothesis associated with the sampling assumption (Figure 15, outer perimeter), it seems reasonable to note the general correspondence between the composition of these three groups, and the ideological typology that was hypothesized. Although we shall make a more precise test of the relationship in Part IV of this article, it will be convenient henceforth to refer to the Kort-Krislov group as "behavioral," the Vines-Chase group as "conventional," and the Roche-Mendelson group as "traditional." On the basis of only these correlation data, we should have to conclude that the remaining four individuals are not clearly identified with any of the ideologies for which the three groups stand.

## B. Factor Analysis

Initially, a principal axis analysis was made of both matrices. The eigenvalues drop very rapidly after the second: for the rho matrix, the first axis is 12.27 and the second 4.21, the next five range between 1.83 and 1.04, and all factors beyond the seventh have eigenvalues of less than 1.00. Similarly, for the tau matrix, the first axis is 9.18, the second 3.41, the next five range between 1.64 and 1.00, and all factors beyond the seventh have eigenvalues of less than 1.00. It is clear that interpretation ought to be confined to the first two factors.

The research design called for successive output, for both matrices and for both quartimax and varimax rotations, of the first two, then the first three, and so on through the first ten factors. Two-dimensional plots were made of the first four factors, for both rotations based upon both matrices. These plots confirmed that the rotations limited to the first two factors provide the most information with the greatest parsimony. The only notable difference between the rho and the tau plots is that the vectors are longer in the rho configuration (because the correlations are larger). It makes no difference which is chosen; we shall select tau and focus attention upon the two-dimensional rotations shown in Figure 16, the coordinates for which are reported in Table 36.

The varimax rotation is the one which provides the reference axes for the configuration in Figure 16. It is evident that three clusters are discriminated by these two dimensions: a behavioral group consisting of Ulmer, Kort, Danelski, Nagel, Tanenhaus, Spaeth, and Schubert; a conventional group, consisting of Vines, Krislov, Becker, Grossman, Peltason, Shapiro, Pritchett, Murphy, Chase, Rosenblum, and Vose; and a traditional group composed of Roche, McCloskey, Mendelson, Tresolini, Abraham, Berns, and Bartholomew.[9] The first dimension scales these groups in the sequence B, C,

---

9. These groups agree with the clusters apparent in the correlation matrix, except that this factorial configuration shows Krislov to be conventional rather than behavioral, and it also shows two of the four isolates from the correlation clusters (Rosenblum and Vose) to be conventionally oriented.

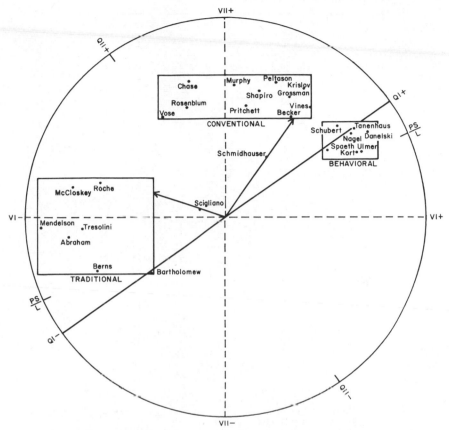

Figure 16. Ideological Positions in Factor Space.

T; the second dimension, in the sequence of C, B, T. All three groups are discriminated without intransitivity on both dimensions. The most cohesive (i.e., tightly clustered) group is the behavioral, next is the conventional, and the least cohesive is the traditional. In other words, the seven behavioralists appear most similar in their point of view, and the seven traditionalists share a distinctive but a much more diversified academic ideology.

Two individuals do not lie in any of the three clusters. Their independent positions imply that their views tend to be idiosyncratic, in the sense that whatever is represented by the two ideological dimensions which are common factors for twenty-five of the twenty-seven respondents, these two individuals tend to conceptualize their respective approaches to the subject in other terms. In a statistical sense, this finding is expressed by their communalities, the sums of the squares of their correlations with the two factorial dimensions, which are much lower for the two isolates than for the other

### Table 36. Factor Loadings

| Variable | Varimax | | Quartimax | | Smallest Space | | |
|---|---|---|---|---|---|---|---|
| | I | II* | I | II* | I* | II | III |
| Abraham | −78 | −10 | −70 | 38 | −82 | 20 | −36 |
| Bartholomew | −37 | −27 | −46 | 00 | −47 | 35 | −66 |
| Becker | 32 | 51 | 55 | 22 | 34 | 24 | 33 |
| Berns | −64 | −27 | −68 | 15 | −81 | −11 | −53 |
| Chase | −19 | 69 | 25 | 67 | −13 | 19 | 17 |
| Danelski | 71 | 43 | 83 | −07 | 52 | −16 | 10 |
| Grossman | 32 | 61 | 62 | 31 | 36 | 14 | 21 |
| Kort | 65 | 33 | 72 | −11 | 56 | −09 | −05 |
| Krislov | 39 | 66 | 70 | 30 | 35 | −11 | 19 |
| McCloskey | −77 | 15 | −53 | 57 | −74 | 04 | −28 |
| Mendelson | −92 | −05 | −77 | 50 | −84 | 10 | −33 |
| Murphy | 04 | 67 | 42 | 52 | 01 | −19 | 26 |
| Nagel | 62 | 42 | 75 | −02 | 55 | 06 | 15 |
| Peltason | 26 | 69 | 61 | 41 | 25 | −02 | 32 |
| Pritchett | 10 | 57 | 42 | 40 | 11 | −37 | −02 |
| Roche | −63 | 17 | −41 | 51 | −68 | −14 | −30 |
| Rosenblum | −22 | 58 | 17 | 60 | −21 | 27 | 28 |
| Schmidhauser | 20 | 29 | 33 | 12 | 34 | 45 | −18 |
| Schubert | 55 | 46 | 71 | 05 | 46 | −23 | 06 |
| Scigliano | −10 | 04 | −05 | 09 | ** | ** | ** |
| Shapiro | 16 | 64 | 50 | 42 | 14 | −11 | 36 |
| Spaeth | 50 | 33 | 61 | −02 | 41 | −41 | −01 |
| Tanenhaus | 64 | 45 | 78 | −01 | 52 | −08 | 09 |
| Tresolini | −72 | −06 | −62 | 37 | −75 | 26 | −38 |
| Ulmer | 68 | 33 | 74 | −13 | 55 | −25 | 03 |
| Vines | 41 | 56 | 66 | 21 | 40 | −02 | 31 |
| Vose | −32 | 51 | 04 | 60 | −43 | −01 | 27 |

NOTE: All numbers are two-place decimals.
*Means the factor has been reflected. All factors except
  smallest space II have been rotated.
**This variable was not included in the smallest space analysis.

respondents. Scigliano's communality is .01, and Schmidhauser's is .13, while the average communality for the twenty-five affiliates of the three groups is .50 (with Mendelson's .85 maximal).

Both the varimax and the quartimax rotations represent orthogonal repositioning of the principal axes, and it is easy to suggest in Figure 16 how the configuration appears in relation to the quartimax rotation. The perimeter points labelled "$QI$" and "$QII$" identify the termini of the quartimax axes. Axis $QI$ separates the configuration as follows: the seven persons whose points are in the traditional cluster, plus Scigliano, all have negative correlations (i.e., are to the left of $QII$) on $QI$, while all others have positive correlations. Thus, the quartimax rotation suggests the best *one*-dimensional array of the ideological differences, along the first quartimax axis, with the traditional ideology distinguished from the conventional and behavioral views entertained by the other persons in the sample; and the 8–to−19 split implies at least a rough index of the relative importance of the traditional approach, in relation to the rest of the field, at the present time. The point configuration remains invariant, of course; it is only the frame of reference (the set of orthogonal axes) that is rotated. Therefore, the apparent gap between the traditional and the conventional groups does not change under any rotation, although it is the quartimax rotation which directs attention to the fact that the conventional group is closer to the behavioral than to the traditional one.

The proportion of the total variance that is accounted for, by the first and second axes, is .466; for varimax, it is .263 (I) plus .203 (II), while for quartimax it is .340 ($QI$) and .126 ($QII$). These data confirm the suggestion above that the first axis on the quartimax rotation (viz., the third data column of Table 36), which accounts for 34 percent of the total variance, provides the best one-dimensional solution of the correlation matrix. (For the rho matrix, the first two factors account for 61 percent of the total variance, and of this 45 percent is attributable to the first quartimax factor.) The rho quartimax two-factor rotation, incidently, is *identical* with the first two principal axes; and for tau it is virtually so—none of the corresponding correlations of any of the respondents on either of the first two axes differ, as between the principal axes and the quartimax factors, by as much as |.015|. The extension of the analysis to include the third and fourth factors did not prove particularly fruitful: the total variance accounted for was increased only by .11 (.14 for rho), and the effect of adding the additional factors was of course to add quite weak factors for quartimax (neither the third nor the fourth factors added as much as 7 percent additional variance, for either rho or tau).

## C. Interpretation

The interpretation of any factorial data involves reliance upon some extrinsic criterion which can be related to the variables in such a way as to provide a basis for defining the substantive content of the factors. In other words, what the factor analysis does is to denote the important patterns of relationships among the variables; the task of interpretation then becomes, on the basis of what are otherwise the known characteristics of the variables, to identify the factors. In the case of our present data, there is one factor which is by far the most important in explaining the observable relationship among the variables. As Figure 16 shows, this is the first factor, which separates over 90 percent of the variables into three clusters. The observed clusters conform so closely to the predicted clusters that we cannot, on the basis of this evidence, reject the working hypothesis, which assumed that the persons in the sample represent three distinctive standpoints.

If the first factor distinguishes between the behavioral and the traditional approaches to the study of adjudication, with a third (conventional) group arrayed between the other two because of its relatively much more moderate correlations with the factor, what does such a dimension stand for? I submit that this factor is one of method, which relates to *how* one studies his subject. Behavioralists advocate a scientific approach with the goal of developing systematic theory out of research that has been carefully designed in advance, that operationalizes the relationships among variables, that employs an articulate methodology, and that relies upon quantification and (so far as possible) statistical measurement. Traditionalists reject all of these goals, in favor of a more subjective, speculative, and literary approach which, in their opinion, avoids the many undesirable by-products that the behavioral approach necessarily entails. This dimension, therefore, posits a continuum with modern "political science" at one extreme, and "political philosophy" at the other. In its most pristine terms, the conflict is that between physics and metaphysics. In the context of the development of the rest of the discipline of political science during the past half century, this is a factor of academic liberalism and conservatism.[10] In terms of the present study, the behavioral group is liberal, and the traditional group conservative, in its academic ideology.

The second factor is one upon which all of the members of the conventional group are strongly loaded. The behavioral group is moderately correlated, in the same direction as the more extreme conventionalists, but the traditionalists are only weakly correlated with the second factor. In the light of the conventionalists' insistence upon the importance of observing and describing political action—the facts of the judicial process in the context of the larger political process—it seems reasonable to identify the second factor as one of theory which is concerned with *what* is to be studied. The conventionalists are empiricists who seek to build a theory of the judicial process out of observations—preferably made in the field or laboratory—of the politics of the judiciary. The negative pole of the second factor represents a rational approach to the study of law. Although our sample includes no persons who can be described as adhering strongly to the ideology of legal rationalism, the behavioral group is less enthusiastically political in its orientation than are the conventionalists, and the traditional group is least so.

We now are in a position to ascribe ideological content to the four quadrants of the space described by Figure 16. Designating them in the usual manner,[11] the first quadrant, which evidently can appropriately be described as the behavioral quadrant, is scientific empiricism, emphasizing the scientific study of political action; and a majority of the conventional group also fall in this quadrant. The second quadrant, the literary study of political action, is much less densely populated than the first, but includes minorities from

---

10. The author is indebted to David Danelski for having pointed out that the first factor also appears to discriminate among the respondents on the basis of age: *all* persons with negative loadings on $VI$ (i.e., to the left of the middle of Figure 16) are (when this is written, in May 1966) over 40 years of age, and the average age of these eleven persons is 46.4 years; while half of the remaining persons (i.e., those with positive loadings on $VI$, to the right of the middle of Figure 16) are under 40, and the average age of these sixteen persons is 39.4 years (personal communication to the author, April 24, 1966).

11. $I+/II+ = 1st$; $I-/II+ = 2nd$; $I-/II- = 3rd$; $I+/II- = 4th$.

both the conventional and traditional groups, plus (weakly) Scigliano. The third quadrant, the literary study of nonpolitical action—or, as we can put it in relation to this particular field, the speculative study of legal norms—is where most of the traditional group falls. The fourth quadrant would, of course, be the scientific study of legal norms; but it is unpopulated in our sample. To summarize: in terms of the typology of academic ideologies that I have attributed to the factorial space of Figure 16, the behavioral group are scientific empiricists; the conventional group are political empiricists; and the traditional group are nonscientific rationalists.

One final aspect of that space warrants consideration. Our hypothesis (Figure 14) requires that we observe a configuration of points that lie, at least roughly, in the pattern of a circle. It is manifest, in Figure 16, that this is not the case; what we do observe is a *semicircle*, extending from Kort and Ulmer on the extreme right through Nagel, Schubert, Vines, Grossman, Shapiro, Murphy, Rosenblum, Vose, Roche, and Tresolini, to Berns at a position diametrically opposed to that of Kort and Ulmer. Figure 16 suggests the positioning of another axis, whose termini on the perimeter of the space are identified by the symbol: PS/L. This axis, whose position was determined by the method of visual (or "graphical") rotation, discriminates almost the entire configuration– everyone except Bartholomew—from the empty space that otherwise lies below the axis. Above this axis, the configuration of our sample arches in a semicircle, with the points representing persons located at least roughly (it would appear) in the sequence that had been hypothesized for them by Figure 15 (the outer perimeter).

We are now in a position to infer why our hypothesis of a circular configuration turned out to be only half right. The position depicted in Figure 14 at six o'clock is for the academic discipline of law. We included no law professors in the sample; and Figure 16 suggests that there is an important difference between even those political scientists who have been designated as traditional in their approach and the law professors. Evidently, the spacing of the academic disciplines is different than Figure 14—in the absence of empirical data—presumed. Political scientists are more closely allied in their ideological range than was assumed; and conversely, the legal approach preempts a much larger segment of the total relevant ideological continuum than was expected. In order to have obtained a circular configuration, it would have been necessary to have included in the sample some law professors— preferably, a dozen or two, so as to maximize confidence in the discriminating power of the factorial analysis—so as to be able to populate the fourth quadrant. Then we might find representation for the rationalist academic ideology, advocacy for the scientific study of legal norms, and allies for those relatively few political scientists who specialize in the speculative study of legal norms. Unfortunately, however, we would have encountered immediate technical problems, which would have precluded the extension of the present study to a broader sample that included a goodly representation of law professors. Neither the sampling criterion of visibility nor that of accessibility could have been satisfied, if a dozen law professors had been added to our sample. Probably something could be done to alleviate, or to correct for, the accessibility problem; but the difficulty in regard to visibility appears to be almost insuperable. Political scientists and law professors simply do not read enough of each other's work for a mixed sample to be able to avoid producing overwhelming quantities of either nonresponse or uninformed response. Given the differences that continue to obtain in the respective socialization experiences of members of the two professions at both the graduate and post-professional-degree levels, it is understandable that the motivation of most political scientists to read the typical writings of law professors should be low, and vice versa. Perhaps, however, an independent replicative study, but using a sample consisting only of law professors, would produce the missing semicircle; and then the two halves might be fitted together.

## D. Smallest Space Analysis

In order to provide an additional perspective of the sociometric relationships implicit in the correlation matrix, I shall report also the results of a Guttman-Lingoes "smallest space" (a nonmetric factor) analysis.[12] This approach might be deemed particularly suitable for our data, since it calculates a set of Euclidean coordinates for points so that the distances among them correspond to the rank order differences among the coefficients in the correlation matrix, which in turn are functions of the intersubjective rankings (of the members of the group) of each other. The two-dimensional solution was computed, but it is not reported here because it is almost identical with the first two factors of the three-dimensional solution, which is much more interesting.

In Table 36, the output values for dimension coordinates have been converted to the usual metric for factorial space (viz., ranging from $+1.00$ to $-1.00$), and the first and third factors have been rotated orthogonally $27.5°$ clockwise with the second factor remaining unrotated and orthogonal to them both. Figure 17 shows the two-dimensional factor plots for $SI/SIII$ and $SII/SIII$. The first and third factor plane shows almost exactly the same configuration as does Figure 16, the only exception worth noting being Pritchett's appearance as an isolate. Just as do the first and second varimax axes, both the first and third small space dimensions discriminate absolutely among the three clusters; and the rotation of the latter two was made so as to bring the dimensions into alignment with the axes.[13] Hence the psychological content

---

12. Lingoes, Kay, and Spear 1965. I am indebted to David J. Peterson, then a graduate student at Michigan State University, for assistance in the use of the program to analyze the rho matrix (with Scigliano omitted because of his exceptionally low communality, as evidenced by the principal axis factor analysis). See also Lingoes 1966a; and Guttman 1968.

13. A counterclockwise rotation of $60°$ produces the quartimax rotation of the principal axes: that is, the traditional cluster then is negative on the first dimension, and everyone else is positive.

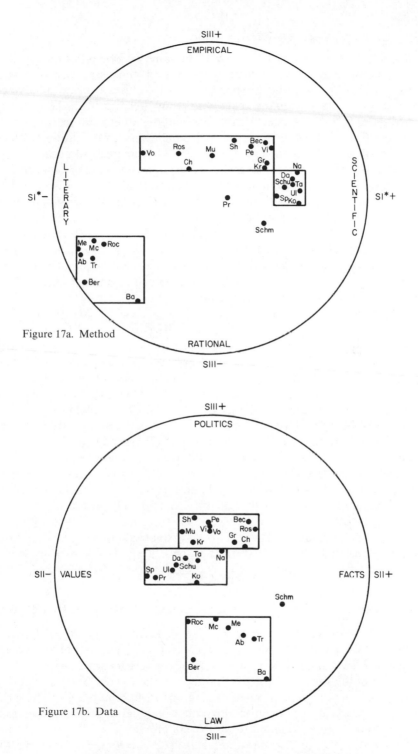

Figure 17a. Method

Figure 17b. Data

Figure 17. Ideological Positions in Small Space.

of $SI$ must be the same as $VI$, and $SIII$ the same as $VII$. What the smallest space analysis adds to the picture is the second dimension, $SII$, on which most of the traditional group are positive, the conventional group are divided about equally, and most of the behavioral group are negative, although there is (as Figure 17b shows) considerable overlapping among groups, unlike the differentiation provided by the other two dimensions. Examination of which members of each group are most positive, and which are most negative, suggests that this is a factor of positivism versus nomism—that is, of a primary concern for the study of what are conceptualized to be facts, as distinguished from a primary concern with values. Such a distinction is quite independent of what may be deemed to be the appropriate substantive content of either facts or values. Thus, we might expect to find some persons preoccupied with political facts and others with legal facts; some with political values and others with legal values. And cross-cutting all of these categories is the question of methodology, since either type of fact or value can be studied scientifically, and it can also be studied belletristically.

$SI$ reveals the latter orientation; and the plane of $SII/SIII$ (Figure 17b) indicates both the predisposition and the relative intensity of persons in our sample toward the dimensions of empiricism/rationalism and of positivism/nomism. Starting in the first quadrant, the persons who emphasize the factual study of judicial politics are Becker, Rosenblum, Chase, and Grossman. The empiricists, who are more concerned with politics than whether it relates to facts or values, are Shapiro, Peltason, Vines, and Vose. Political values is the focus of Murphy, Krislov, Danelski, and Tanenhaus. Spaeth, Pritchett, Ulmer, and Schubert are interested in values, irrespective of whether they relate to political or legal variables. A shift to a concern for legal values characterizes Roche and Kort, while Berns and McCloskey are rationalists whose primary concern is with law. Bartholomew, Tresolini, Abraham, and Mendelson are more concerned with legal facts; and the only positivist, interested in facts whether they be legal or political—although leaning toward the former—is Schmidhauser. The validity of this interpretation can, of course, readily be checked against the content of the writing of these persons, which in most instances is prolific.

## IV. THREE VIEWPOINTS OF THE IDEOLOGICAL STRUCTURE

Figure 16 also can be used to provide a consensual ranking of "others" by "egos." We have noted that the configuration of points lies in a rough semicircle. The semicircle is "rough" because the vectors, which project (from the origin of the space) the points representing the variables, arc of differing length; they vary in length precisely according to the communality differences among the variables. Thus, it is apparent from Figure 16 that if Schmidhauser's vector were extended to double its present length, he would then clearly be a member of the conventional group. Similarly, if Scigliano's vector were quadrupled in length, he would then be in the traditional group. But we can extend all vectors to unit length, in which event all points will be arrayed in sequence along the semicircular perimeter of the factorial space above the PS/L axis. We can then use that sequence of points as a ranking of the variables, assigning the first rank to Ulmer, the second to Kort, and so on until we reach Berns, who will be twenty-sixth, and Bartholomew, twenty-seventh. By so doing, we shall have used the responses to Question 1 in order to provide a consensual ranking of the respondents along a circular continuum which we already have construed to be the empirical equivalent of the continuum depicted in Figure 14. This ranking can then be compared with the rankings which can be inferred from Figure 15, which shows the postulated boundary between the "traditional" and "behavioral" segments to be at about 4:30 o'clock. We can measure both the inner and the outer circles of Figure 15, proceeding in a counterclockwise direction, just as we did in the case of Figure 16. Evidently, we should begin each ranking with the person who appears in the "behavioral" position that is closest to the boundary between the behavioral and the traditional segments. For the inner ring of self-perceptions, Krislov is in the first rank, and Kort is in the second; while for the outer ring of the sampling assumption (the hypothesis to be tested), Kort, Nagel, and Becker all are tied for the initial (and, therefore, for the second) rank. The three rankings are reported in Table 37.

The nonrespondents are (parenthetically) named along with the respondent members of the sample, in the outer ring of Figure 15, since the nonrespondents of course were included in the sampling assumption. It is equally evident that we cannot include the nonrespondents in the autogenous ranking, since they did not supply us with their self-perceptions. It is possible, however, to make a nominal consensual classification of the nonrespondents, by a procedure that will be explained in the next part of this article; so the nonrespondents are classified, in the first two rankings of Table 37, by ideological type rather than by rank.

Inspection of the table suggests that the different rankings are at least roughly similar. In considering the rows—the set of three ranks for each of the twenty-seven respondents—the range of rank differences is four or less for a majority, and the average range is less than five. There are only two really big discrepancies, and both of these involve self-perceptions—those of Krislov and Tanenhaus—which deviate markedly from both the sampling hypothesis and the consensual perception. Reference to Figures 15 and 16 shows that Krislov appears to consider himself to be much more behavioral[14]—while Tanenhaus, conversely, considers himself to be much *less*

---

14. Subsequent to the writing of this sentence, Samuel Krislov has reported that "my self-perception is not so out of line as might appear. . . . I did not then and, alas, still do not, quite understand the clock metric and what I was trying to indicate was that I was at the middle or the right wing of the behavioral group expecting such stalwarts as yourself to be at '5:30' or so" (personal communication to the author, April 7, 1966).

### Table 37. A Priori, Group, and Self-Perceptions of Rankings on the Ideological Continuum

| Variable | Hypothesized[a] | Consensual[b] | Autogenous[c] |
|---|---|---|---|
| Abraham | 24 | 25 | 19.5 |
| Bartholomew | 26.5 | 27 | 25 |
| Becker | 2 | 10 | 8 |
| Berns | 26.5 | 26 | 22.5 |
| Chase | 19 | 17 | 11 |
| Danelski | 6.5 | 3 | 6 |
| Fellman | T | T[d] | NR |
| Grossman | 19 | 19 | 11 |
| Horn | C | T[d] | NR |
| Jacob | C | C[d] | NR |
| Kort | 2 | 2 | 2 |
| Krislov | 16 | 11 | 1 |
| Lasswell | B | B[d] | NR |
| McCloskey | 21.5 | 22 | 16.5 |
| Mendelson | 24 | 24 | 22.5 |
| Murphy | 10 | 16 | 14 |
| Nagel | 2 | 5 | 7 |
| Peltason | 13 | 13 | 16.5 |
| Pritchett | 13 | 15 | 11 |
| Roche | 21.5 | 21 | 22.5 |
| Rosenblum | 16 | 18 | 26 |
| Schmidhauser | 11 | 9 | 11 |
| Schubert | 6.5 | 7 | 4 |
| Scigliano | 19 | 20 | NR |
| Shapiro | 13 | 14 | 11 |
| Spaeth | 4 | 4 | 4 |
| Tanenhaus | 6.5 | 6 | 16.5 |
| Tresolini | 24 | 23 | 22.5 |
| Ulmer | 6.5 | 1 | 4 |
| Vines | 9 | 8 | 16.5 |
| Vose | 16 | 19 | 19.5 |
| Westin | T | T[d] | NR |

[a]See Figure 15 (the sampling assumption).
[b]See Figure 16 (Q. 1 responses).
[c]See Figure 15 (Q. 2 responses).
[d]See Table 41.
NR = No response.

behavioral—than others seem to think. Examination of the inner ring of Figure 15 shows that except for Tanenhaus, the behavioralists are about where they are hypothesized to "belong"; but the conventionalists are bunched together in the narrow segment spanning 11:00 and 12:00 o'clock, and all of the traditionalists except Bartholomew are similarly escalated toward what was hypothesized to be the conventional segment. Of course, this does not indicate that the self-perceptions are inaccurate, but rather it refutes the a priori assumption of equal spacing along the continuum. The bunching of the conventionalists up close to the behavioralists, the gap between the conventionalists and the bulk of the traditionalists, and the latter's self-placement near the boundary between the "traditional" and the "conventional" segments, all of these are precisely in accord with the configuration of points in Figure 16. Hence we should conclude that, in general, it appears that the perceptions of selves by selves, and of selves by others, are in very good agreement.

We can, of course, confirm these intuitive judgments by subjecting the three rankings to the more rigorous statistical test of correlating the pairs of rankings; and the results of this test are reported in Table 38. The rho

**Table 38. Intercorrelations among Hypothesized, Consensual, and Autogenous Rankings of the Ideological Continuum**

| rho / tau | Hypothesized | Consensual | Autogenous |
|---|---|---|---|
| Hypothesized | | .92 | .74 |
| Consensual | .80 | | .78 |
| Autogenous | .57 | .65 | |

coefficient of .92, for the correlation between the hypothesized and the consensual ranking, is exceptionally high; and we should have to conclude, on the basis of this evidence, that the a priori assumptions about the ideological content and structure among political scientists working in this field tend to be strongly supported.[15] The rho coefficient of .78, for the correlation between the autogenous and consensual rankings, is high enough to tend to confirm our subjective judgment that the respondents perceptions of their own ideological positions are in close accord with the perceptions about them that their coworkers in the same field entertain. Incidentally, the feeling of many of the respondents, as articulated in their comments to the author, that their attempts to comply with the author's request, by "forcing" themselves to commit themselves to a single point in two-dimensional space when they felt their positions to be much more complicated than that, should be somewhat assuaged, perhaps, by the results reported above. It seems clear, now at least, that their replies make a lot more—and more consistent—sense than they thought possible. Of course, persons more familiar with psychometric theory would have anticipated the likelihood of such an outcome. The problem is strictly analogous with the one we faced, in interpreting the factorial output, in choosing whether to employ one, two, three, or four or more

15. We can make an equivalent extension to unit length of the vectors in Figure 17a and then observe their rank order. The rho correlations for the smallest space ranking are .97 with the consensual ranking derived from Figure 16, and .88 with the hypothesized ranking of Figure 15. (Pritchett, Scigliano, and Schmidhauser were deleted from the rankings for these computations, because of their low communalities in either or both of the factor spaces from which the rankings were derived.)

factors as a frame of reference. We could have settled for a four-factor, rather than a two-factor, solution of the correlation matrix. This would certainly have afforded a richer, more complicated, and more difficult-to-conceptualize space; and if the payoff, in terms of the quality as well as the quantity of information thereby provided, had justified recourse to a four-dimensional interpretation, then this is what we should have preferred. We found, however, that in fact the dimensions beyond the third were so relatively weak that we passed the point of diminishing returns just as soon as we added a fourth factor. We could also, of course, have settled for the first factor alone, because the first varimax factor did offer a linear solution that arrayed the three groups in sequence. Evidently, however, that would have been oversimplification, because we then would have been foreclosed from studying the second respect, in relation to *what kind* of data should be studied, by which these three groups differ; and we also would have been unable, of course, to say much about the validity of the assumptions about ideological structure that are explicit in Figure 14. This is why, in correspondence with respondents, I attempted to suggest that the question of the dimensionality of the relevant space is an empirical rather than a theoretical question; and that although it might be helpful to formulate a hypothesis about the number of dimensions—as was, in fact, done—that hypothesis should be subjected to the test of the empirical data collected—as we have done.

The third correlation in Table 38, between the inner and the outer ring of Figure 15, is also high enough to support the intuitive judgment that they are in fairly close agreement. Finally, it should be noted that in Table 37 the consensual ranking should be considered to be the norm from which both the hypothesized and the autogenous rankings deviate in varying degrees.

## V. CONCORDANCE AND IDEOLOGICAL AFFINITY

### A. Concordance

The raw data matrix can supply evidence bearing upon another and quite different type of question relating to the responses to Question 1. Given a set of rankings, we might wish to know how consistent are the judgments expressed by the persons making the rankings. Ordinarily, with psychological data, persons are asked to rank some extrinsic objects, and our expectation is that, if their perceptions and judgment are similar, then their rankings ought to be in close agreement. Hence, W, the coefficient of concordance, which ranges between .00 and 1.00, usually is interpreted so that a high score signifies high agreement among the subjects, and a low score poor agreement. With sociometric data, however, the situation is very different. When each subject is evaluating the position of others in relation to himself, the criterion is a shifting rather than a presumably fixed one. If we were to array a dozen persons along the perimeter of a circle, or along a line, and to ask each to rank the others in terms of his perception of their physical proximity to himself, we should anticipate a set of rankings in a very different pattern. If everybody were spaced equally in a circle, and each exercised perfectly consistent perception and judgment, then the sums of the ranks for each column of the data matrix ought to be equal to each other; and the value of a coefficient of concordance, calculated from such data, ought to be .00. Consequently, with our data matrix, we should interpret a low value of W to mean high concordance—that is, that there is very considerable consistency among the persons in our sample, and in their conceptions of their ideological relationship to each other and to the nonrespondents in the sample. A high value of W, to the contrary, could only mean that a considerable number of the persons in the sample all thought that they perceived the others, not only in the same way, but also *from the same base position*—that is, both their conceptions of others, and their self-perceptions, would have to be identical, or at least very similar. In effect, we could anticipate a high W coefficient only if there were a *single* ideological standpoint, which practically all of the respondents shared. We know that, empirically, neither of these conditions obtains; and the coefficient of concordance substantiates our judgment.

The available computer program for W (J. Morris 1966) does not accommodate to, and could not readily be adjusted to, the missing data occasioned by the double zero entries in the raw data matrix. In order to get around this difficulty, the following procedure was adopted in order to calculate a value for W. Ranks were substituted for the correlation coefficients in each row of the correlation matrix—it would not matter whether the rho or the tau matrix were used for this purpose. This provided a complete set of rankings, with no missing data, for a new 27 × 27 matrix. It seems intuitively reasonable to assume that, if the ranks of the raw data express a respondent's judgment of how close another person is to him, then the correlation coefficient for the two persons can be viewed as an expression of their conjoint perception of this relationship. This assumes that a person will feel closest to the person with whom he is most highly (and positively, of course) correlated; and this is, indeed, precisely the assumption that underlies the point configuration of the factor analysis. The value of W calculated by the computer, for the data matrix described above, was .13. It was possible, of course, also to calculate, by hand, the value of W for the complete thirty-two-column raw data matrix; this was done, and the coefficient obtained was .17. Although both of the observed values are low, they doubtless reflect the substantial homogeneity of viewpoint among the behavioralist cluster and among several subclusters of the conventional group.

## B. Classifying the Nonrespondents

Although five persons in the sample did not reply to either question, it was inherent in the research design that these persons nevertheless would remain a part of the project, at least in the status of items whom the respondents ranked along with themselves and each other. As in the calculation of W, we shall use the means of the columns of the raw data matrix for purposes of the present analysis. These average rankings, for each column, are reported in Table 39, which ranks all persons in the sample accordingly from lowest to highest. If one analyzes the upper and lower halves of this ranking, in relation to ideological groupings, then we can observe the relationship shown in Table 40. Persons in the conventional group are "in the middle" (as in Figure 16), and therefore tend to seem closer to persons in both of the other two groups than do the latter to each other. The traditional group, as it appears in Figure 16, is the most isolated, as evidenced by the fact that all seven of its members had average rankings (as items, it will be recalled) in the bottom half of the sample.

Another approach to these data is to consider the rankings, *of* each of the nonrespondents and *by* each of the respondents, by ideological groups. As before, we are precluded from reporting the raw data, but we can report the averages, after describing more precisely how they were derived. A new

### Table 39. Average Rankings

| Rank | Subject | Ranking |
|------|-------------|---------|
| 1 | Danelski | 9.24 |
| 2 | Murphy | 10.00 |
| 3 | Schmidhauser | 10.65 |
| 4 | Grossman | 10.92 |
| 5 | Pritchett | 11.34 |
| 6 | Peltason | 11.50 |
| 7 | Schubert | 12.14 |
| 8 | Krislov | 13.15 |
| 9 | Tanenhaus | 13.24 |
| 10 | Jacob | 13.36 |
| 11 | Vose | 13.68 |
| 12 | Vines | 14.34 |
| 13 | Shapiro | 15.24 |
| 14 | Rosenblum | 15.52 |
| 15 | Westin | 15.55 |
| 16 | Lasswell | 15.60 |
| 17 | Abraham | 15.69 |
| 18 | Ulmer | 15.69 |
| 19 | Nagel | 16.34 |
| 20 | Chase | 16.41 |
| 21 | Spaeth | 17.08 |
| 22 | McCloskey | 17.37 |
| 23 | Scigliano | 17.58 |
| 24 | Becker | 18.20 |
| 25 | Horn | 18.64 |
| 26 | Fellman | 19.55 |
| 27 | Kort | 19.61 |
| 28 | Tresolini | 21.00 |
| 29 | Mendelson | 21.11 |
| 30 | Roche | 21.73 |
| 31 | Bartholomew | 23.08 |
| 32 | Berns | 24.52 |

**Table 40. Rankings according to Ideological Types**

| Types* | Rankings | |
|---|---|---|
| | 1–16 | 17–32 |
| Conventional | 9 | 2 |
| Behavioral | 3 | 4 |
| Traditional | 0 | 7 |

*See Figure 16

data matrix was established, with five columns (one for each of the nonrespondents.) The twenty-five respondents who fit the types then were listed in column to designate the rows of the matrix. The respondents were grouped exactly as they appear in Figure 16: first the seven behavioralists, and an extra row in which to accumulate totals and averages for them; then, similarly, the eleven conventionalists; and then the seven traditionalists. The cell entries were the ranks assigned, in their responses to Question 1, by each respondent to each nonrespondent. Thus, there were a total of 125 cells, grouped into fifteen subcolumns. There were only five double zero entries in the entire matrix, which suggests that the visibility of these five nonrespondents was excellent, albeit their accessibility was poor. These five omitted ranks occasioned no problem for the analysis, which is based upon the average rankings for each of the fifteen subcolumns (i.e., for each nonrespondent by each ideological group). The resulting data are reported in Table 41.

The pattern of consistency seems very high; the only intransitivity in the table is the slight difference by which Horn's average ranking, by the conventional group, exceeds Westin's. The table shows clearly that Fellman is ranked lowest (i.e., perceived as being most exemplary of the type) by the traditionalists, followed by Westin and Horn. Jacob, on the other hand, is clearly preferred by the conventional group, and Lasswell is clearly preferred

**Table 41. Average Rankings of Nonrespondents, by Ideological Types**

| Types* | Nonrespondents | | | | |
|---|---|---|---|---|---|
| | Lasswell | Jacob | Horn | Westin | Fellman |
| Behavioral | 10.9 | 17.7 | 21.8 | 23.4 | 27.4 |
| Conventional | 17.2 | 9.2 | 20.0 | 18.3 | 24.9 |
| Traditional | 20.7 | 19.5 | 12.0 | 5.3 | 4.9 |

*See Figure 16.

by the behavioralists. Indeed, it goes further: Fellman, Westin, and Horn are ranked least by the traditionalists, next by the conventionalists, and highest by (indicating they are perceived as being furthest away from) the behavioralists. This is just what we should expect, on the basis of Figure 16. Similarly, Jacob is ranked least by the conventionalists, next by the behavioralists, and highest by the traditionalists; and Lasswell is preferred most by the behavioralists, next by the conventionalists, and least by the traditionalists. All these findings are in perfect accord with the scale of preferences that we ought to expect from these three groups, for these five persons, assuming that Fellman, Westin, and Horn are consensually perceived *by all three groups* to be traditionalists, that Jacob is consensually perceived to be a conventionalist, and that Lasswell is consensually perceived to be a behavioralist. It does appear to be so; and my sampling assumption, which classified Horn with the conventional group, must be considered to have been erroneous.

## VI. SUMMARY

The purpose of this investigation was to collect and analyze empirical evidence which would make it possible to test my a priori hypothesis about the structure and content of the approaches of different persons in the field of public law-judicial process-judicial behavior, to the study of their subject. The hypothesis is that there are three distinctive ideological standpoints, and that these ideological positions are commonly recognized, to the extent that a sample of persons chosen from the field would correspond to these standpoints.

The major findings are that there are three such ideological groupings: the traditional, the conventional, and the behavioral. Most persons in the sample identified with the latter two groups, which are much closer to each other than to the traditional group. Factor analysis suggested that the three groups are arrayed, in scalar order, upon two dimensions. The first is a major factor of academic liberalism and conservatism, which is concerned with *how* to do research, the scientific versus the philosophical approach. The second factor is empiricism versus rationalism, and it relates to *what* to study, the empirical field data of political action versus legal norms. The interpretation made of the position of the groups, in relation to these two factors, is that the traditional group consists of academic conservatives, who strongly favor the philosophical approach but who take no particular position on the second dimension. The conventional group consists of empiricists who strongly favor political analysis of judicial acts but are much more diverse and moderate in regard to methodology, and who therefore assume a more neutral position on the first dimension. The behavioral group strongly supports a scientific approach with systematic theory and explicitly quantitative methods, and favors, but is less strongly committed than is the conventional group to, the analysis of data based upon field observations. The sample did not include persons who strongly favored the rationalist position of legal norm study, and it was inferred that it would have been necessary to have included law school professors in the sample in order to have been likely to have obtained representation, in the study, for that point of view.

The analysis also showed that there is a close correspondence between persons' self-perceptions, and their perceptions of the ideological positions of others working in the field—and this irrespective of whether the others are persons with whom the persons making the evaluation are in close agreement or in substantial disagreement about the proper approach to the augmentation of knowledge in the field. The close correspondence between the relationships that were hypothesized and those that are observed on the basis of these field data lead to the conclusion that there is a considerable degree of consensual understanding of the standpoints common to the field today; and that, in substantive terms, the conventional academic ideology is the modal one, the behavioral ideology is the most cohesive, and the traditional ideology is the least cohesive and most isolated.

So far as is known, there is no precedent for this study, and therefore no body of related knowledge to which comparisons might be made. It is tantalizing to speculate whether similar ideological groupings of persons—not necessarily, of course, in the same proportions as are suggested by this single sampling of this single field—would be observed in related sub-fields of political science. It would certainly be of interest if the three basic ideological types hold for the political science profession in general, and indeed, conceivably, for other of the social sciences as well. Further scientific research may make it possible either to confirm or to refute such conjectures, and should in either event help us to comprehend better how (and how much) our academic ideologies bias our professional inquiries.

## APPENDIX A

November 22, 1965

Dear —————— ———:

I am writing to you in the hope that you will be willing to aid me in making an exploratory study of academic ideologies toward the study of judicial decision-making. An enclosure to this letter lists the other persons to whom I am writing at this time. I selected this group because of my assumption that (1) all of these persons know each other; (2) they represent collectively a variety of orientations toward adjudication; and (3) they all are sufficiently interested in contemporary pedagogical and research trends, in relation to adjudication processes, to want to participate.

The first enclosure (Fig. 14) suggests one possible hypothesis about the latent structure which underlies our disparate attitudinal similarities and differences. Although it is crude and doubtless much over-simplified, this model might be used as a basis for attempting to scale a set of respondents, or selections from among their writings. By making the present empirical investigation, I propose to substitute, for my own intu-itions about our conjoint relationships in regard to the question of academic ideology, your own replies to the enclosed two questions.

The first question asks you to rank *yourself* as number 1 (indicating that you are in closest agreement with your own point of view), and to rank as last (i.e., # 32, if you rank all) the person whose approach is most different from your own. The others on the list should be ranked from 2–31, depending upon your perception of how closely the view of each toward the subject of adjudication processes is similar or dissimilar to your own. It will be much more helpful if you are able to rank everybody; if you feel that the list includes a person (or persons) whom you simply do not know, assign him (or them) the rank of # 0.

The second question asks you to specify your own relative position on the perimeter of the circle depicted in Fig. 14. Using a clock metric, please specify as closely as you can a point that approximates "where you are." The sequence of academic disciplines which is apparent in the space between the two circles is intended only to be *suggestive* of the content of the three approaches, and *not* to specify directly positions on the pe-rimeter. Therefore, you should orient yourself in relation to the three major approaches: the traditional at 6:00 o'clock, the conventional at 10:00 o'clock, and the behavioral at 2:00 o'clock. The hour hand of the imaginary clock is capable of denoting position to the nearest minute as well as marking the hours, and therefore you should feel free to make your designation either roughly (to the nearest hour) or more precisely as a point between two hour-loci.

It is possible that the replies to the first question could be used in a manner that might prove to be embarrassing to some individuals. There is no way of assuring that respon-dents will remain anonymous to the analyst, for the structure of the answers provides a quick identification. However, I will not publish nor otherwise reveal to any other person the individual responses to the first question; and the sample size is sufficiently small that I can code these raw data myself. We happen to have a recently debugged tau program for our computer, so I shall use it to calculate a matrix of rank correlation coefficients, which will measure the extent to which each pair of respondents agree in their evaluation of the psychological distance separating them from each other and from the other persons in the sample. *Only these correlation coefficients* and measures based upon them (and explicitly *not* the individual sets of rankings) will be used and reported in the pub-lished analysis.

The replies to the second question will, of course, be reported; and I plan to compare the findings with those which result from the analysis of the first question. This will make it possible to compare self-perceptions with others' perceptions. Conclusions based there-on should contribute to a much better common understanding of whatever degree of cognitive structure may obtain in our orientations towards the substantive professional field in which we labor. It will then be possible to base our future discourse upon more valid and reliable knowledge than the idiosyncratic and unsystematized intuitions of individuals (including my own present intuitions).

With luck, I hope to be able to complete the analysis and write the research report early next winter, and then after revision (see below) to submit the ms. for possible publication in the *Law and Society Bulletin*, the new journal of the Law and Society Association, which is perhaps a particularly appropriate forum. At the bottom of the second enclosure you will note a place which you should check if you would like to have me send you a copy of the draft paper, thereby providing you with an opportunity to comment critically upon, and suggest revision in, the ms. before I do submit it for publication.

I have tried to include in the sample persons representing a variety of different points of view. It is of course my hope that everyone replies to both questions, so that the sample available for analysis does not become biased by either the over-representation or the under-representation of persons who represent any of the major perspectives which characterize our field today.

Please use the stamped and addressed envelope that is enclosed for your reply. Now that you have read the letter, only a few more minutes will be required to answer the two questions.

With my sincere appreciation,

Glendon Schubert

# APPENDIX B

PLEASE RETURN THIS SHEET IN THE ENCLOSED REPLY ENVELOPE

QUESTION #1. Rank the following individuals from 1 to 32. Place the number "1" after your own name, the number "2" after the name of the person whose point of view (concerning how to study law, courts, and judges) is most similar to your own, and so on with the person whose viewpoint is most different from yours ranked last.

| | | | | | | | |
|---|---|---|---|---|---|---|---|
| Abraham | ____ | Jacob | ____ | Nagel | ____ | Shapiro | ____ |
| Bartholomew | ____ | Horn | ____ | Peltason | ____ | Spaeth | ____ |
| Becker | ____ | Kort | ____ | Pritchett | ____ | Tanenhaus | ____ |
| Berns | ____ | Krislov | ____ | Roche | ____ | Tresolini | ____ |
| Chase | ____ | Lasswell | ____ | Rosenblum | ____ | Ulmer | ____ |
| Danelski | ____ | McCloseky | ____ | Schmidhauser | ____ | Vines | ____ |
| Fellman | ____ | Mendelson | ____ | Schubert | ____ | Vose | ____ |
| Grossman | ____ | Murphy | ____ | Scigliano | ____ | Westin | ____ |

QUESTION #2. Your own position on the perimeter of Figure [14] is best approximated by a point at about ____:____ o'clock.

Check here ____ if you would like to receive a copy of the draft of the report.

# 10

# Ideological Distance

This is a report of a secondary analysis of data on social and political ideology. The data variously were collected, through field questionnaire surveys, by other scholars who supervised their administration to samples of elite respondents in England, the United States, and Japan. The initial study was made (apparently in the middle 1940s) by an English psychologist, Hans J. Eysenck (1947), with a sample of 750 persons, students and their friends at the University of London. The second study was made in 1960 by an American lawyer-political scientist, Stuart S. Nagel (1963), with a United States sample of state supreme court judges, of whom 101 replied to all questions in such a manner that their answers could be intercorrelated. The third study was made in 1964 by an American political scientist, James Dator (1967)—then a resident of Tokyo—of a national sample of Japanese high courts judges, of whom sixty-eight provided replies that could be used

This chapter was originally published, in slightly different form, as "Ideological Distance: A Smallest Space Analysis across Three Cultures," and is reprinted from *Comparative Political Studies* Vol. 1, No. 3(Oct. 1968) pp. 319–350 by permission of the publisher, Sage Publications, Inc. This article was presented as a paper, to a conference on "Mathematical Theory of Committees and Elections," organized by Professor Oskar Morgenstern and directed by Professor Doctor Ernst F. Winter, at the Institute for Advanced Studies, Vienna, Austria, June 26–27, 1968. Much of the work upon which this report is based stems from two seminars: one in judicial behavior, convened by the Inter-University Consortium for Political Research at Ann Arbor, Michigan, during the summer of 1963; and the other, in comparative judicial behavior, convened by the Institute of Advanced Projects of the Center for Cultural and Technical Interchange between East and West at the University of Hawaii in Honolulu, during the late spring and summer of 1965. For previously unpublished data analyzed herein, I am indebted to James A. Dator of Virginia Polytechnic Institute, and to Stuart S. Nagel of the University of Illinois. All three of us participated in the 1963 conference in Ann Arbor, and Professor Nagel and I were participants in the 1965 conference at the East-West Center. I thank also Dr. Forrest R. Pitts, associate director of the Social Science Research Institute of the University of Hawaii, for making possible computer facilities for the smallest space analyses upon which this paper relies.

in the present analysis. From one point of view, each of these three studies is independent of the others, in that the samples (and their responses) are not in any sense dependent upon each other. However, Nagel (1963:33, Table 2) patterned his study directly upon Eysenck's, utilized a modified version of the Eysenck questionnaire, and undertook explicit comparisons between his findings and those that Eysenck had reported; and Dator, who in turn patterned his work upon Nagel's and employed a modified version (Dator 1967 :422, Table 10) of the Nagel-Eysenck questionnaire, has interpreted his own data in relation to both the Eysenck and Nagel samples described above, and to other attempts (Eysenck 1953; Tanaka and Matsuyama 1954; Dator 1969) to base surveys upon the Eysenck questionnaire, in Germany, Sweden, and Japan. Hence, from the points of view of the structure and content of the survey instrument, and the design of the research, it was the intent of the later investigators to make their inquiries as similar as possible to those that had preceded; and it was their hope that the studies would be substantially the same, to the extent at least that their respective findings would be properly comparable. We shall turn presently to a consideration of certain problems involved in the comparability of the three studies; but, for present purposes, I wish to note the unusual opportunity that the availability of these data presents, to the student of comparative political ideology, to undertake an experimental investigation, utilizing relatively sophisticated theory and methods, of the effect of cultural differences upon the cognitive structure of political thinking.

It is pertinent to observe certain differences in the goals and interests of the three scholars who collected the data. Dr. Eysenck, long an antagonist of both American and Israeli social psychologists,[1] was interested primarily in the use of his data to advance understanding of psychometric theory and techniques, as is suggested by his dedication of one of his books, *The Psychology of Politics*, to his son "in the hope that he will grow up in a society more interested in psychology than politics." Nagel, quite to the contrary, viewed his own study in instrumental terms, and his explicit hope was that his data might serve the social engineering purpose of contributing to the reform of the American judiciary along more "objective" lines by "decreasing the effect of judicial attitudes." And Dator was primarily interested in neither the promotion of psychometry nor judicial reform; as a student of comparative politics, his interest is (like my own) in theory construction about political behavior. Indeed, the only justification for my having undertaken the present study, which is best seen as an extension of Dator's work, lies in the differences in our respective methodologies.

Eysenck based his interpretation of his data upon Burt's "Summation Method" of factor analysis, a desk calculator routine which, appraised by

---

1. See, for example: Eysenck 1951, 1956a, 1956b; Guttman 1951; Christie 1956a, 1956b; Rokeach and Hanley 1956; and Hanley and Rokeach 1956.

contemporary standards of computer technology, could provide only a relatively rough approximation of the findings that one would reach on the basis of a modern principal axes factor analysis. His analysis was limited to two factors. Nagel did not extend his own analysis beyond the observation of percentage differences in response categories. Dator used the BMD principal axes computer program (see W. Dixon 1964 and continuations) to analyze both his own and Nagel's samples of data, but his analysis is restricted to the first two unrotated factors, in each instance; and for comparison with Eysenck, Dator used Eysenck's own factors. In carrying through his comparison of the British, American, and Japanese samples, utilizing a bi-factorial model, Dator (1969) has made what I consider to be an important contribution to the advancement of understanding in comparative politics. In the present study, my objective is to carry the work of Eysenck and Nagel and Dator one step further than any of them has as yet seen fit to take it.

Mathematical psychology is beginning to have a much more important influence upon work in American political science (cf. Kaiser 1968). One of the most exciting developments in contemporary mathematical psychology is the development of a series of computer programs[2] by Louis Guttman, director of the Israeli Institute of Applied Social Research, in Jerusalem, and James Lingoes, professor of Psychology at the University of Michigan, for multivariate analysis of ordinal-level data which fail to meet the strict assumptions (of normally distributed variables that are rectilinearly related to each other and which have been measured at the interval level) that underlie, in principle, the use of factor analysis (see Stephenson 1953 and Guilford 1956). SSA-I, the initial program in the series, is a method for nonparametric "smallest space analysis" which requires no assumptions about the shape of frequency distributions, nor that correlation be linear, nor even that the indices of association be correlation coefficients. Assuming that data have been measured at the ordinal level, smallest space analysis makes interpoint distances embedded in Euclidean space a monotonic function of rank order differences, using a statistical criterion based on Guttman's rank-image principle to determine the smallest possible space. SSA-I is designed for analyzing any complete, real, symmetric matrix of coefficients— which can represent similarities, dissimilarities, proximities, or distances— without solving for communalities.[3] Although factor analysis can be used to support an interpretation in terms of social or psychological distance, it is necessary to standardize factor scores prior to computing distances (Rummel 1970: chap. 22). SSA-I, however, provides a direct distance inter-

---

2. Published and periodically revised in the "Computer Abstracts" section of *Behavioral Sciences* beginning in vol. 10 (1965), and now available on tape in Fortran IV upon application to the Survey Research Center of the University of Michigan. See Torgerson 1965; Lingoes 1967; and Guttman 1968.

3. For an explanation of the algorithm for SSA-I and some examples of its use, see Lingoes 1966a; and Lingoes and Guttman 1967.

pretation of spatial interrelationships, in the sense that points closest together in the smallest space are most alike in terms of the dimensions that define that space. My own previous experience in the use of smallest space analysis indicated that, in addition to the advantage of assuming only the cruder level of observation and measurement[4] that usually is achieved by political scientists, smallest space analysis may identify a third dimension for matrices which would be adjudged two-dimensional when examined by principal axes factor analysis (see Schubert 1966b, 1967b, 1968g). Comparisons of both factor analytic and smallest space solutions for the same matrices, and also of both two- and three-dimensional smallest space solutions for these matrices, indicated that the second factor (or second dimension of a two-dimensional smallest space analysis) is differentiated into the second and third dimensions of a three-dimensional smallest space analysis; and in the latter three-space, it is the *second* dimension which is novel.[5] Of the three earlier studies, Nagel's measurement was at the level of aggregate descriptive statistics of the manifest survey response data, and therefore his interpretation had to be confined to the level of the first dimension. Eysenck and Dator were enabled, by their invocation of factor analytic techniques, to make interpretations at the two-dimensional level. By taking advantage of the recently developed method of smallest space analysis, I sought to investigate the hypothesis that the matrices of attitudinal interagreement, for all three cultures, were of a higher rank (i.e., were more complicated) than two, and therefore a three-dimensional analysis would support findings and an interpretation more appropriate to the cognitive structure of the respondents, to the extent that that phenomenon had been replicated in their responses to the Eysenck-Nagel questionnaire.

In moving from one-space to three-space, there are both advantages and disadvantages, of course. The functions of either psychological or statistical complexity, for such a transition, are harmonic rather than arithmetic. No doubt, crude observations and measurement produce data that are least strained by one-dimensional methods of analysis; and there is no doubt in my own mind that the data analyzed in the present study are subjected to substantial stress by the demands made upon them even by the relatively minimal requirements of smallest space analysis. Neither am I insensitive to the reinforcing strains, superimposed upon at least the Nagel and Dator samples of the data, by both the linguistic and ideological variance that stem from the cross-cultural design of this research. What the satisficing (see Simon 1957:204) social scientist seeks to achieve is that level of analysis which asks neither too much, nor too little, of his data; and one who works within the ethos of a profession which has been, at least until very recently,

---

4. See, especially, the introduction to Lingoes 1967; Baggaley 1964: chap. 1; and Siegel 1956:26.
5. See Schubert 1967a, Fig. 4; 1966b, Fig. 2; and 1968g, Fig. 1.

noteworthy for its characteristic failure better to exploit what might have been learned from the impressive aggregates of empirical observations that it laboriously collected perhaps may be pardoned for committing the error (if such it be) of trying to squeeze too much out of the data available. At least one possible by-product of such endeavors may be a heightened sensitivity to the importance of improving the quality of our empirical observations, and of the measurements that we make of them, so that what are mathematically and statistically more elegant investigations of our data can be justified.[6]

The earlier Japanese replication[7] using the full Eysenck questionnaire could not be included in the present study, because the correlation matrix was not published in the report of the research and attempts to obtain a copy of the matrix through correspondence with the senior author were unsuccessful. If these data had been accessible for smallest space reanalysis, the Tanaka and Matsuyama findings might have (1) helped to clarify how much difference it makes to employ the twenty-four-item (infra) rather than the complete forty-item survey instrument; and (2) made possible an *infra*-cultural longitudinal comparison (with Dator's findings) of different elite groups within Japanese society.

## I. THE SURVEY INSTRUMENTS

According to Eysenck:

> From a total of some 500 items, all those were selected which had been shown to be of importance or relevance in any previous research. When pruned of duplications, it was found that these items did not suffice to make up the minimum [*sic*] number considered requisite, and others were added by random selection until 40 items altogether had been chosen. (1954:121–122)

In adapting this questionnaire (Eysenck 1947: appendix, and 1954:122–124) for purposes of his doctoral research, Nagel reduced the number of items from 40 "to 24 in order to have a less bulky questionnaire and thereby presumably a higher rate of response." Moreover:

> The particular 24 items selected were chosen in such a way that there would be three items for describing each of the eight sub-attitudes [which Nagel inferred to have been identified by sociopsychological research], anticipating that correlations would be made between each sub-attitude and the decisional behavior of the judges (as well as between the over-all attitude of liberalism and their decisional behavior.) The particular three items chosen to represent each sub-attitude were those three items which had the highest correlation with [Eysenck's first] factor [,] of liberalism. (Nagel 1963a:30)

Consequently, the Nagel version might be expected to include the items which would discriminate best between liberal and conservative differences in the attitudes of American, and of Japanese, judges—providing, that is,

---

6. See Coombs 1964; Blalock 1968: chap. 1, and Alker 1965, 1966.
7. See Tanaka and Matsuyama 1954, and the discussion in section IV in Dator 1969.

that American and Japanese judicial concepts of liberalism-conservatism are structured similarly to those of English university students and their friends, and provided further that the judges understood the questions to signify the same meaning as these items conveyed to the Englishmen. On the other hand, and *ceteris paribus* (especially communalities), the price paid for exceptionally high factor loadings on one dimension inescapably is relatively low factor loadings on other dimensions. Of course, Nagel was not thinking in terms of a factorial model when he designed his adaptation, else he might have selected items (as Eysenck *had* attempted to do) so as to be able better to discriminate differences among his respondents in relation to other dimensions than liberalism-conservatism; and Dator, similarly, had no goals of factor (or other multivariate) analysis in view when he coopted the Nagel version of Eysenck's questionnaire.

In using Eysenck's correlation matrix, I abstracted the submatrix which includes intercorrelations among the twenty-four items chosen by Nagel;[8] and this explains, of course, why all twenty-four items load so highly—not, to be sure, why they load relatively higher for the British than for the Americans or the Japanese, but rather why the metric value of the coordinates is high—for the British sample, on the first dimension: Nagel had picked them this way.

The other major innovation that Nagel introduced was his a priori clustering of items, by triads, according to what he considered to be the "sub-attitudes of liberalism." We can treat these eight clusters as a set of subhypotheses concerning the homogeneity and integration of the semantic components[9] of liberalism-conservatism for persons socialized in the *British* culture. If multivariate analysis should indicate that Nagel's a priori clusters do correspond to the empirical clusters that would be denoted for Eysenck's reduced correlation data matrix, then we should expect to observe poorer cohesion within, and differentiation among, these same clusters for either the American or the Japanese data. Indeed, taking into consideration even grossly the relative degrees of affinity among the British, the American, and the Japanese cultures (see Schubert 1967c), we ought to posit the following hypothesis: that the spatial clusters for the item triads[10] are most cohesive and best discriminated for the British data; that the corresponding clusters will be less well defined, in terms of both criteria, for the American data; and that they will be least well defined for the Japanese data. This hypothesis (although not explicitly articulated by Dator) certainly is supported by Dator's two-dimensional factor analysis which includes plots of the following

---

8. The appropriate row and column numbers, which also identify the corresponding items in Eysenck's questionnaire, are denoted parenthetically in Table 42.

9. See Guttman 1954: chaps. 5, 6 at 216, 258; and Schubert 1965c: chaps. 5, 6 at 39–40.

10. Spatial clustering could be measured precisely as the mean interpoint distance for each triad (see Schubert 1963e: 135–137), but the degree of apparent measurement error in the data analyzed here precluded, in my opinion, recourse to such an elegant criterion; instead, I shall rely upon what I presume will be consensual reader visual inference from the figures below, as no close judgments seem to be called for.

samples: Eysenck's British, Eysenck's German, Nagel's American, Tanaka and Matsuyama's Japanese, and Dator's Japanese.[11] We shall test the same hypothesis for our three samples in three-dimensional space.

One further aspect of the format of the survey instruments, as employed by the three investigators, requires comment. One can readily sympathize, of course, with the feeling of an American investigator that questions originally phrased for a British audience need to be rephrased, to some extent, in order to communicate well with an American audience. (I pick deliberately the weaker example; it is hardly necessary to observe that this problem is vastly intensified—and extended—for translation from either the Queen's or American English into the Japanese language, to say nothing of translation into accustomed Japanese modes of thought, for reasons that have been very well stated by Dator [1967, 1969] who is exceptionally well qualified to explicate this syndrome of problems.) But we cannot yield to such temptations, or even felt necessities, with impunity: each bit of tinkering with the language of the original entails the cost, *and to an unspecifiable degree,* of loss in stimulus identity, and therefore in comparability. What is worse, retention of the original language may entail even greater stimulus change than does linguistic variation; this probably happened when Tanaka and Matsuyama proffered to their Japanese subjects a literal translation of Eysenck's first item ("Colored people are innately inferior to white people"), thereby perplexing respondents "who, while vaguely recognizing that they are 'colored,' generally consider themselves to be a superior people" (see Dator 1969). This particular item, on the other hand, doubtless was perceived with at least equal clarity by American as by British respondents. What clearly must be avoided, as entailing not an exchange of value but rather a net loss with no gain, is what we might call "elegant variation" (after Fowler 1965:148–151) in the phrasing of questionnaire items.

Nagel made changes in five of the twenty-four items that he selected from Eysenck, including one reversal in the direction of an item. Dator, in turn, changed the substance of seven items (e.g., as in substituting "Korean" for "colored," and "Japanese" for "white," in term 1) so that these items became different from the versions used by both (or either) Eysenck and Nagel; he retained Eysenck's version of two items, thereby differing from Nagel's; and he retained Nagel's version of two other items (including the one that Nagel reversed), thereby differing from Eysenck's, and accepting Nagel's reversal of the one item. Dator himself reversed another item from the form in which both Eysenck and Nagel had used it.[12] Therefore, in half

---

11. See Dator (1969: Figs. 2–6). In Fig. 7 Dator presents what he designates as the "General Position of the Eight Subcategories of Progressive-Conservative Ideology in Four Countries"; these ideal clusters correspond almost precisely to the observed empirical clusters of Eysenck's British sample, which provide the criterion in terms of which one observes the extent of deviation of the other four samples.

12. Dator (1969: secs. 3–5) comments upon the details of these changes.

of the twenty-four items, Dator used language that differed in substance from that of Eysenck, or Nagel, or both of them.[13] Of course, in all twenty-four items Dator differed from them in that he used the Japanese rather than the English language.

Table 42 is a retranslation from Japanese back into English of the Dator version of the inventory. This table arranges the items in clusters, for the convenience of readers of this paper; as administered to respondents, however, all three versions of the instrument followed Eysenck's original sequence of the items, which proffers an aspect of seeming randomness. Moreover, Eysenck's own forty-item original version was partitioned into what were presumed, on a priori grounds, to be equal numbers of statements that were on the one hand liberal, and on the other conservative, in direction. This balance is preserved in the subsample of twenty-four items selected by Nagel, so that for the present British inventory twelve items were worded in a liberal direction, and twelve in a conservative direction. However, when Nagel reversed the direction of item 7 of Table 42, he changed the balance to eleven liberal and thirteen conservatively worded statements, for his own sample; and when Dator subsequently reversed item 14 also, he created an even more unfavorable balance of ten liberal and fourteen conservative statements, for the Japanese sample. The effect of both changes necessarily was to build response set bias into the interview schedule. The bias becomes, of course, more conservative as we move from the British through the American to the Japanese versions of the instrument; and as we shall soon observe in Table 43 and in the figures the direction of the bias coincides with the observable increase in apparent conservatism in responses, as we move from the British through the American to the Japanese sample. No doubt the degree of this instrument bias is much too small to provide a sufficient explanation for the latter phenomenon. Neither, however, will we be able to give full credence to an explanation keyed to substantive cultural variables, when it is probable that a small but evident and systematic response set error also was operative. An even more serious problem posed by the item reversals, however, is the consideration that agreement with a liberally worded question, and disagreement with a conservatively worded one, readily can be scored as statistically equivalent; but by no means does this assure that they function, in fact, as psychologically equivalent stimuli.

Table 43 reports the average percentage of approval, by the various samples, of the clusters of items. In order to calculate these cluster means, it was of course necessary to reverse the direction of response categories for conservatively worded questions (i.e., the percentage who disagree strongly with a conservative statement was considered to be the same as the percentage who would strongly agree with the statement had its wording been

---

13. For Eysenck's questionnaire, see Eysenck 1954; for Nagel's version, see Nagel 1963a: 52–53; and for Dator's version, see Dator 1967:439.

**Table 42. Back-Translation (from Japanese to English) of the Questionnaire Dator Used for a Sample of Japanese Judges**

SEXUAL FREEDOM
14 (23).    Divorce laws should be altered to make divorce harder [easier]. (C)
17 (29).    Men and women have the right to find out whether they are sexually suited before marriage (e.g., by companionate marriage). (L)
22 (35).    Birth control, except when medically indicated, should be made illegal. (C)

RELIGIOUS FREEDOM
6 (9).    Religious [Sunday] observance is old-fashioned, and should cease to govern our behavior. (L)
11 (16).    Only by going back to religion can civilization hope to survive. (C)
16 (28).    It is right and proper that ethical [religious] education in schools should be compulsory. (C)

ECONOMIC EQUALITY
2 (2).    Present laws favor the rich as against the poor. (L)
9 (12).    Ultimately, private property should be abolished, and complete socialism introduced. (L)
15 (27).    The nationalization of the great industries is likely to lead to inefficiency, bureaucracy, and stagnation. (C)

HUMANITARIANISM
4 (6).    Our treatment of criminals is too harsh; we should try to cure, not to punish them. (L)
18 (30).    The principle "It is bad to pamper your child" [Spare the rod and spoil the child] has much truth in it, and should govern our methods of bringing up children. (C)
23 (36).    The death penalty is barbaric, and should be abolished. (L)

POLITICAL FREEDOM
8 (11).    Unrestricted freedom of discussion on every topic is desirable in the press, in literature, on the stage, etc. (L)
13 (20).    There should be far more controversial and political discussion over the radio and television. (L)
24 (40).    Only people with a definite minimum of intelligence and education should be allowed to vote. (C)

INTERNATIONALISM
3 (3).    War is inherent in human nature. (C)
5 (8).    In the interest of peace, we must give up part of our national sovereignty. (L)
10 (13).    A person who refuses to defend his country cannot be called a patriot. [Conscientious objectors are traitors to their country, and should be treated accordingly.] (C)

ETHNIC EQUALITY
1 (1).    Koreans [colored people] are innately inferior to Japanese [white people]. (C)
12 (17).    Marriages between Japanese [white] and Koreans [colored people] should be strongly discouraged. (C)
20 (33).    Foreigners [the Jews] have too much power and influence in this country. (C)

SEXUAL EQUALITY
7 (10).    It is right [wrong] that men should be permitted greater sexual freedom than women by society. (C)
19 (31).    Women are not the equals of men in intelligence, organizing ability, etc. (C)
21 (34).    Differences in pay between men and women doing the same work should be abolished. (L)

NOTE: The bracketed words are the language of Eysenck's original inventory. The symbols in parentheses, following items, denote their presumed directionality, liberal or conservative. On Item 7, the direction is L for Eysenck; on Item 14, the direction is L for both Eysenck and Nagel.

opposite). It might seem that this procedure immediately raises the very problem to which I just have directed attention, namely, concerning the psychological equivalence of reversed and nonreversed items, as stimuli; but there is an important difference. So long as the statements are aligned in the same direction for all samples, no matter which the direction may be, differences in averages will be uniformly biased for all three samples, which is to say that mean differences will remain meaningful. It is the reversal of an item so that it differs in one sample from its direction in the other two that creates difficulties.

### Table 43. Average Percentage of Liberal Approval, by Attitude Clusters

| Cluster | Sample British | American | Japanese |
|---------|---------|----------|----------|
| Sexual equality | 72 | (80) | 64 |
| Political freedom | (68) | 50 | 44 |
| Internationalism | 62 | (66) | 39 |
| Ethnic equality | 51 | (55) | 49 |
| Sexual freedom | (58) | 39 | 42 |
| Religious freedom | (49) | 38 | 33 |
| Humanitarianism | (51) | 28 | 31 |
| Economic equality | (38) | 12 | 27 |

NOTE: The highest percentage for each row is placed within parentheses; the lowest is underscored.

Examination of the table shows that the British nonjudges tended to respond most liberally on five of the eight clusters, and least so on none; the American judges were most liberal on three clusters, and also least liberal on three; while the Japanese judges were most liberal on none, and least liberal on five. Evidently, the aggregate response data may be interpreted to indicate that the young British academics tended to give more liberal replies than did the elderly judges in either of the other samples; and as between the latter, the Americans expressed more liberal (or, at least, less conservative) sentiments than did the Japanese. But was this because Eysenck's sample was British; or because they were younger; or because they were not judges; or because they were asked in the mid-forties, rather than in the late fifties or mid-sixties? Obviously, there are just too many degrees of freedom among the samples for us ever to have confidence in steps to move beyond the sample differences per se, and in the direction of causal analysis. To do that, it would clearly be necessary to design a project of comparative research which would assure equivalence by stratification of the various country samples in regard to such attributes as age, professional role, sample size, the structure and substance of the survey instrument, measurement procedures, and time of observation, so that everything that possibly could be controlled would be, leaving (presumably) nothing relevant *except* culture to vary. Clearly, that ideal situation is not the one that confronts us in the present secondary analysis.

The American sample differs from the other two in one other respect: the extremes of variation in liberal support, for the differing types of clusters. The range of liberal approval—although at a higher level for the British than for the Japanese—is confined to a difference of only 34 percent in the case of the British and also the Japanese sample; for the Americans, it is 68 percent, exactly twice as great. Only the American sample includes about equal numbers of all three support positions: maximal, modal, and minimal. Moreover, the differences in degrees of support seem to make intuitive sense. The American judges, for example, are well parsed in their cultural heritage: they are most supportive of the ideals of feminism (Momism?), internationalism (*sic semper* the League!), and ethnic egalitarianism (with *Brown* v. *Board of Education* barely a half-dozen years in the past). Conversely, their 12 percent support rate for economic egalitarianism testifies to the extent of their conviction about the virtues of capitalism as a way of life; and their tendency to reject both humanitarianism and sexual freedom bears witness to the continuing vitality of the Puritan ethic among those in whom it is imbued at an early age. Or so, at least, one might infer, reasoning strictly in intuitive terms. Similarly, lack of great support among Japanese judges for such Anglo-American ideas as sexual equality, free speech, pacifism, racial heterogeneity, and functional agnosticism will come as no great surprise even to Western readers whose familiarity with Japanese culture goes little beyond *The Chrysanthemum and the Sword* (Benedict 1946). In the matter of religion, incidentally, it seems doubtful that these Japanese judges were more sanguine about the prospects for social Buddhism than were their American counterpart enthusiasts for a Christian society;[14] they differed much more on item 16, concerning public education, which *for the Japanese sample had nothing to do with religion*. Two-thirds of the British respondents, but only one-third of the American judges, endorsed the proposal for compulsory integration of church and school; 94 percent of the Japanese judges, however, favored a compulsory system of "ethical education" which, as Dator (1967: 429) has pointed out, "was the backbone of Japanese militarism before and during the [Second World] War." If this inference is correct, we ought to expect to find that in the empirical clusters for the responses of the Japanese sample, item 16 should lie closer to the points in the "internationalism" cluster than it does to the other two points in the "religious" cluster. A glance ahead at Figure 20 shows that ethical education consistently is closer to the

---

14. Dator reports that only one of the eight High Court judges in his sample professed membership in the Nichiren Buddhist sect; and none claimed affiliation with the Soka Gakkai, a lay Buddhist organization (with a political wing, the Komei-to) which has been mushrooming in importance during the past five years, both in Japan proper and in overseas concentrates such as the Japanese-American population in Hawaii. See Dator 1967:411, 416–417 and 1966:27; Ward 1967; and J. White 1967.

conscientious objectors' point than it is to the other items which do relate to religion.

One further aspect of Table 43 should be noted. There is a reciprocal relationship between the directionality of the extent of liberal approval, and the extremity of claims to liberal support. In terms of scale theory, the British respondents manifest a higher rate of liberal approval precisely because (as they perceive these issues) the claims raised by the questionnaire statements are less extreme than they seem to be to the Japanese judges. That is to say, it is much easier for a Briton raised on *Areopagitica* to indicate assent to the notion that what his society needs is more controversial discussion over the mass media, than it is for the Japanese whose childhood training emphasized the avoidance of open social conflict and the virtue of acquiesence in what are at least manifestly consensual decision-making processes. Hence, a low rate of liberal support can be interpreted to imply a perception of an extreme liberal claim.

## II. THE CORRELATION MATRICES

The Eysenck correlation matrix (1947:79–80) is not reproduced here because it already has been published. From the vantage points of both the wisdom of hindsight and contemporary statistical opinion, it is unfortunate that Eysenck relied upon tetrachoric correlation coefficients, because tetrachorics tend to provide exaggerated estimates of the magnitude of correlations, particularly when any cell of the contingency table is empty.[15] Dator calculated the Pearsonian correlation[16] matrices for both his own

---

15. See the discussions in Schubert 1965c:67–68; and Guilford 1956:310–311.

16. The calculation of a Pearsonian r from data that have been observed ordinally, and in only the five categories of a Likert scale, results of course in a not inconsiderable amount of measurement error which can be attributed to the (doubtless, false) statistical presumption that intervals between categories on the scale are metrically equal. And the problem is compounded when nonresponsive answers are coded in with the modal ("don't know") Likert category. Dator attempted to minimize the latter defect by eliminating respondents whose sum of NA + DK (i.e., modal category) responses was greater than four (out of the twenty-four items comprising the inventory), thereby incurring the alternative cost of reducing the size of his sample from eighty to sixty-eight. (Eysenck, in calculating his tetrachorics, had simply partitioned his NA/DK answers approximately equally between the two response categories ["agree" and "disagree"] which entered into his correlations, thereby preserving his sample size and avoiding artifactually any computational problems of "missing data," but at the same time impaling himself on the other [measurement error] horn of the dilemma posed by respondents who did not make choices for certain questions.) Dator's only other correlational alternative would have been to calculate phi coefficients; and apart from other problems (e.g., regarding both theoretical assumptions about the data, and empirical restrictions upon the range of correlational variation) that using this would have involved, it is most doubtful that enfolding five categories into two would have done less violence to the data than did treating them as intervals. No doubt it would have been much better if both Eysenck and Dator had used either rho or tau (both of which are explicitly measures of rank) correlation, either of which would have been much more suitable both to their data, and to the assumptions underlying the use of smallest space analysis. Neither did, because both undertook correlation with factor analysis explicitly in prospect. Hopefully, future workers who tread the same path will profit from the example—including what hindsight wisdom indicates to have been the mistakes—of those who blazed the trail.

# Table 44. Correlation Matrices for Samples of American Judges and Japanese Judges

| Variables | 01 | 02 | 03 | 04 | 05 | 06 | 07 | 08 | 09 | 10 | 11 | 12 | 13 | 14 | 15 | 16 | 17 | 18 | 19 | 20 | 21 | 22 | 23 | 24 |
|---|---|---|---|---|---|---|---|---|---|---|---|---|---|---|---|---|---|---|---|---|---|---|---|---|
| 01 |  | -26 | -01 | -08 | -16 | -16 | 12 | -12 | 01 | 28 | 10 | 28 | 03 | -05 | 11 | 18 | -08 | -03 | 28 | 32 | 26 | 01 | -15 | 29 |
| 02 | 07 |  | 02 | 18 | 17 | 05 | 10 | 24 | 37 | -08 | -14 | -16 | 05 | 10 | -19 | 04 | 16 | -07 | 12 | -04 | -09 | -02 | 20 | -29 |
| 03 | 29 | -04 |  | 09 | -17 | 03 | -05 | -01 | -10 | 10 | -03 | -04 | -02 | 03 | 08 | 13 | 11 | 08 | 22 | 16 | -11 | -02 | -03 | 08 |
| 04 | -02 | 12 | -02 |  | 20 | 25 | -06 | -05 | 06 | -13 | -11 | -11 | 17 | 18 | -12 | 09 | 14 | -35 | 10 | -07 | 06 | -07 | 43 | -16 |
| 05 | -02 | 16 | -14 | -13 |  | 13 | -00 | 10 | 03 | -10 | -30 | -19 | 10 | 13 | -18 | -07 | 12 | -08 | -01 | -01 | 06 | -09 | 08 | 00 |
| 06 | 05 | 20 | 08 | 11 | 01 |  | 36 | 21 | 03 | 09 | -38 | -10 | -04 | 21 | 03 | -10 | 22 | 04 | 16 | 14 | -14 | -10 | 22 | 06 |
| 07 | 20 | -33 | 17 | -14 | -16 | 09 |  | 03 | 21 | 22 | -19 | 13 | -13 | 19 | 02 | 02 | 03 | 03 | 13 | 35 | -07 | -13 | -01 | 10 |
| 08 | 14 | 13 | -20 | 03 | 22 | 14 | 09 |  | 15 | -11 | -05 | 05 | 33 | 42 | -02 | -18 | 14 | 12 | -02 | -17 | 12 | -11 | 20 | 05 |
| 09 | -15 | 35 | -09 | 32 | 03 | 03 | -23 | 15 |  | 09 | 15 | 01 | 13 | -15 | -24 | 32 | 02 | 07 | 11 | 09 | 06 | 19 | 10 | 13 |
| 10 | 11 | 00 | -01 | -03 | -10 | 09 | 02 | -11 | 09 |  | 01 | 09 | 09 | 11 | 29 | 37 | -05 | 25 | 10 | 22 | -07 | -05 | -27 | 19 |
| 11 | 06 | -04 | 11 | 02 | -05 | -11 | 00 | -05 | 15 | -05 |  | 07 | -05 | -07 | 14 | 30 | 06 | 19 | 03 | 23 | 18 | -12 | 14 | -06 |
| 12 | 35 | 06 | -01 | -21 | -02 | -10 | 13 | 05 | 01 | 10 | 07 |  | 00 | -02 | 30 | 01 | -09 | 03 | 09 | 05 | -07 | -10 | 17 | -13 |
| 13 | -16 | 03 | -22 | 05 | -30 | -04 | -13 | 33 | 03 | 09 | -04 | 00 |  | 00 | 03 | -30 | 00 | 03 | 20 | 01 | 11 | -21 | 33 | -03 |
| 14 | 19 | 14 | 09 | -06 | -12 | 21 | 19 | 42 | -15 | 13 | 15 | -02 | 00 |  | 24 | 14 | 31 | 25 | 10 | 31 | -04 | 26 | -01 | 12 |
| 15 | 12 | 00 | -01 | -08 | -18 | 03 | 02 | -02 | -24 | 29 | 01 | 30 | 03 | 24 |  | -13 | -04 | 06 | 23 | -07 | -00 | -04 | -01 | -00 |
| 16 | 22 | -04 | 11 | 13 | -07 | -10 | 02 | -18 | 32 | 37 | 05 | 01 | -30 | 14 | -13 |  | 23 | -13 | 10 | 31 | -00 | 26 | 10 | 12 |
| 17 | 35 | -01 | 13 | 07 | 12 | 22 | 03 | 14 | 02 | -05 | 03 | -09 | 00 | 31 | -01 | 02 |  | 05 | 23 | -07 | -12 | -02 | 18 | -03 |
| 18 | 18 | 15 | 09 | 03 | -08 | 04 | 03 | 12 | 07 | 25 | -00 | 03 | 03 | 25 | 34 | 09 | -08 |  | 09 | 18 | -07 | 14 | -02 | 03 |
| 19 | 37 | 13 | -07 | 14 | -01 | 16 | 13 | -02 | 11 | 10 | 13 | 09 | 20 | 15 | 03 | 29 | 02 | 17 |  | 28 | 04 | 20 | 15 | 12 |
| 20 | 31 | 15 | 13 | 18 | -01 | 14 | 35 | -17 | 09 | 22 | 18 | 05 | -07 | 22 | 10 | 10 | 16 | 19 | 30 |  | -03 | -01 | 04 | 17 |
| 21 | -21 | 17 | -33 | -25 | 06 | -14 | -07 | 12 | 06 | -07 | -07 | -07 | -01 | -08 | -21 | -13 | 03 | -03 | -04 | -03 |  | 20 | -10 | 16 |
| 22 | -08 | 03 | -10 | 26 | -09 | -10 | -13 | -11 | 19 | -05 | 07 | -02 | -07 | 22 | -14 | -32 | -14 | -10 | -11 | -01 | 05 |  | 07 | -13 |
| 23 | -19 | -05 | -28 | 26 | 08 | 22 | -01 | 20 | 10 | -27 | 02 | -11 | 03 | -09 | -14 | -32 | 03 | 10 | -21 | -05 | 25 | -11 |  | -31 |
| 24 | 22 | 01 | 20 | 07 | -33 | 06 | -21 | -17 | -21 | 19 | 26 | 19 | -02 | 30 | -19 | 24 | -14 | 16 | 40 | 28 | -28 | -13 | -31 |  |

NOTE: The American sample is above, and the Japanese sample is below, the diagonal space; all entries are rounded Pearsonian correlation coefficients, but decimal points have been omitted. The variables are the items listed in Table 42.

sample and that of Nagel, using the computer facilities of Virginia Poly-technic Institute. Nagel kindly had made available to Dator the response data for his survey of American judges. Neither the Nagel nor the Dator sample matrix has been previously published, so both are reproduced here in Table 44. Observation of that table (cf. Borgatta 1958–1959) indicates that the level of magnitude of neither of these Pearsonian correlation matrices is very high, but they do appear to be rather similar. In fact, the average absolute values are .13 for the American sample, and .14 for the Japanese. The corresponding coefficient for the British sample is, however, .22, about two-thirds higher than for the other two. Hence, when we discuss differences in the smallest space configurational patterns for the three samples, we should keep in mind that at least in part, the more extreme positions that we ob-serve for the British sample are certainly a statistical artifact due to Eysenck's use of tetrachoric correlation.

## III. THE SMALLEST SPACES

Table 45 reports the dimensional coordinates for each of the three sam-ples, in three-space configuration. These coordinates are the data plotted in

**Table 45. Smallest Space Coordinates**

| Sample | | English | | | American | | | Japanese | | |
|---|---|---|---|---|---|---|---|---|---|---|
| Dimensions | | 1 | 2 | 3 | 1 | 2 | 3* | 1* | 2* | 3* |
| Variables | 01* | 75 | −50 | −35 | 35 | −34 | −44 | 41 | −13 | −01 |
| | 02 | 79 | 35 | −12 | 44 | −52 | −25 | 34 | −02 | 29 |
| | 03* | 93 | −61 | −07 | 27 | 44 | −39 | 57 | −44 | −19 |
| | 04 | 93 | −43 | 30 | 37 | −35 | −53 | 27 | 33 | 51 |
| | 05 | 101 | −43 | 08 | 75 | 04 | −34 | 61 | 10 | −36 |
| | 06 | 91 | 35 | 32 | 58 | 01 | 17 | 19 | 63 | 14 |
| | 07 | 31 | −95 | −48 | −29* | −07* | −50* | 47* | −44* | 47* |
| | 08 | 62 | 60 | −46 | 36 | 28 | −35 | 47 | 37 | −31 |
| | 09 | 106 | −09 | 19 | 32 | −52 | 09 | 62 | 40 | 19 |
| | 10* | 69 | 57 | 07 | −01 | 09 | −79 | 48 | 43 | 23 |
| | 11* | 77 | 62 | 53 | 79 | −19 | 37 | 16 | 65 | −04 |
| | 12* | 93 | −23 | −01 | 42 | −56 | 17 | 33 | 14 | −38 |
| | 13 | 76 | −15 | −57 | 10 | 28 | −62 | 31 | −24 | −65 |
| | 14 | 79 | 27 | 40 | 40 | 13 | −27 | 12* | 39* | −10* |
| | 15* | 107 | −04 | −01 | 61 | −40 | 08 | 21 | 01 | 48 |
| | 16* | 101 | 12 | 38 | 46 | 31 | 06 | 55 | 28 | 30 |
| | 17 | 93 | 32 | 42 | 55 | −25 | 01 | −12 | 48 | −25 |
| | 18* | 79 | −48 | 42 | 71 | 06 | 03 | 11 | 26 | −48 |
| | 19* | 45 | −57 | −78 | −08 | 02 | −21 | 46 | 15 | −04 |
| | 20* | 90 | −01 | −38 | 27 | 06 | −37 | 26 | −02 | −32 |
| | 21 | 60 | −54 | −55 | 02 | 72 | −14 | 75 | −13 | 19 |
| | 22* | 81 | 78 | 54 | 48 | 67 | 11 | −49 | 64 | 11 |
| | 23 | 99 | −30 | 20 | 20 | −22 | −52 | 76 | 28 | 08 |
| | 24* | 62 | 51 | −62 | 10 | −49 | −52 | 57 | 29 | −20 |

NOTE: All coordinates are two-placed decimals
*Dimension or variable reversed

Figures 18a–20c, which focus upon the British, American, and Japanese samples, respectively. In these figures a cluster defines a sector of the space that encloses a triad of points representing particular items of the questionnaire. All items have been aligned in what is for the British the liberal direction, and items are individually identified. It must be remembered, however, that these are two-dimensional perspectives of three-dimensional configurations; hence, even points that seem contiguous, as perceived in a plane, can be widely separated on the third dimension—and, therefore, in the space.

In general, our working hypothesis seems to be supported by these data. The clusters of Figures 18a-c are relatively smallest (viz., occupy the least space, on the average) and best differentiated (viz., there tends, on the average, to be greater space *between* clusters);[17] by these same criteria, the clusters of Figures 20a-c clearly are worst. This impression is confirmed by a crude but convenient guide to observation of these planes: for the British configuration, all clusters are differentiated in Figure 18c, all except one (SEX F) are so differentiated in Figure 18a, and all except two (SEX F and ETHNIC) in Figure 18b. The corresponding observations for the other two samples show that their *best* differentiation is, in either instance, no better than the poorest view of differentiation for the British: there are two undifferentiated clusters in Figure 19c, and also on 20a and 20c; in both Figures 19a and 20b, only half of the clusters are separated; and in Figure 19b three clusters are undifferentiated. I interpret this to mean that, even after full allowance has been given to the various sources and degrees of measurement variance already discussed, there remains considerable support for the hypothesis that these questions about liberalism were best understood (as well as, relatively at least, most enthusiastically endorsed) by the British respondents (see Minogue 1964). The simulated cognitive structure of the Eysenck survey instruments had maximal isomorphism with the cognitive structure of respondents who had been socially conditioned and culturally reinforced *to think in these terms*. Of course, such a finding, and at this level of abstraction, is not very surprising. What is surprising is that the Japanese cluster differentiation seems to be at least as good as that of the American.

In the three-dimensional spaces of Figures 18a–20c, liberalism/conservatism is a vector, the position of which is determined (and differently, in the three spaces) by the dimensional parameters. In view of Nagel's procedure for selecting the questionnaire items that were used (subject, of course, to the exceptions noted above) in all three samples, it comes as no surprise to discover that in Figures 18a-c the liberalism vector is fully loaded on all three dimensions, pointing toward the upper right-hand corner of the spatial perspective in each of Figures 18a, 18b, and 18c. The three dimensions are (as

---

17. Those familiar with Guttman's earlier work will recognize this description as a multidimensional generalization of his definition of the first principal component of a simplex matrix, and an application of the least squares principle of minimal point separation within, and maximal separation between, sets (clusters). See Guttman 1954:225.

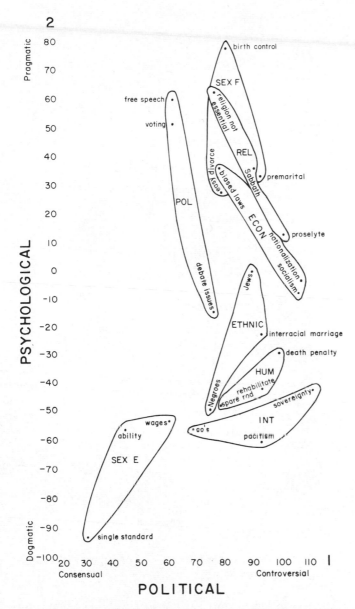

Figure 18a. Political-Psychological Smallest Space Dimensions of Liberal
Ideology (British Sample)

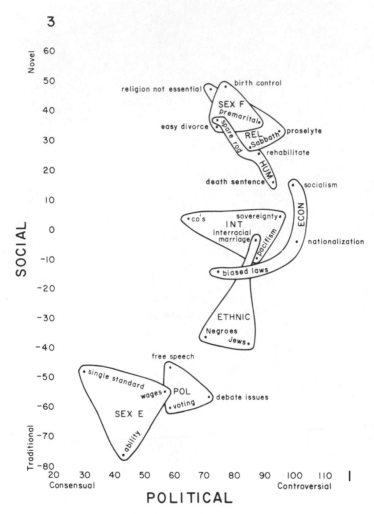

Figure 18b. Social-Political Smallest Space Dimensions of Liberal Ideology
(British Sample)

I hypothesize) political, psychological, and social respectively. The first (political) dimension measures the cultural heterogeneity of the sample, so that
items with a high positive loading have provoked maximal disagreement
among the respondents in the particular sample: such items are designated as
"controversial," while those with lower positive loadings—there being none

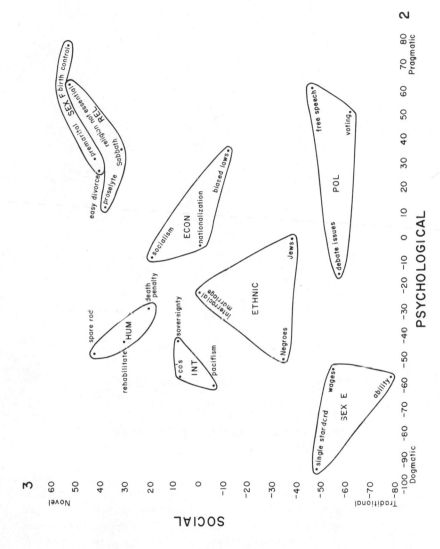

Figure 18c. Social-Psychological Smallest Space Dimensions of Liberal Ideology (British Sample)

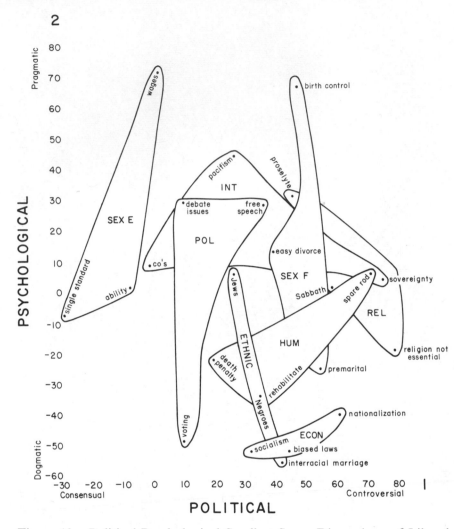

Figure 19a. Political-Psychological Smallest Space Dimensions of Liberal Ideology (American Sample)

with negative coordinates in the British sample—are at least relatively "consensual." For the British respondents, therefore, the most controversial questions were those relating to nationalization of industry, socialism, internationalism, religious instruction in schools, and the elimination of the death penalty. Only 3 percent of the British Tories, but 56 percent of the Laborites, for example, agreed with the socialism item, while 86 percent of the Tories, but only 16 percent of the Laborites, agreed with the nationalization item (in its original conservative direction). In contrast to these ranges of infra-sample differences of 70 percent and 53 percent for items that load high and

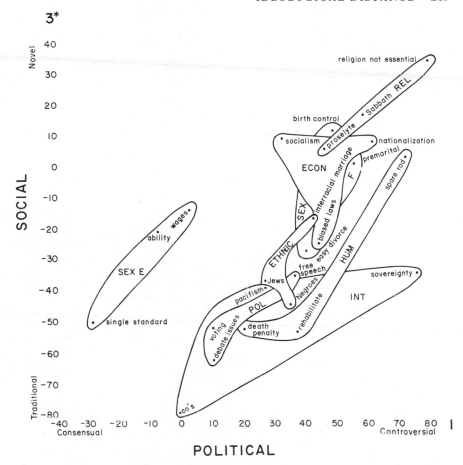

Figure 19b. Social-Political Smallest Space Dimensions of Liberal Ideology
(American Sample)

positive on the first dimension, the equivalent differences for the three items
that comprise the SEX E cluster are 12 percent, 14 percent, and 15 percent.
Clearly, there is much greater homogeneity in the structuring of the attitudes
of the British sample toward questions of sexual equality than there is toward
questions of economic equality.

The second (psychological) dimension is a measure of closure, although
I have attributed that meaning to the negative direction on the dimension.
Items that load highly on the positive direction represent issues in regard
to which the minds of the respondents were (relatively speaking) open to
discussion and counterargument, and to "facts" concerning the consequences
of decisions bearing upon the value in question; conversely, the minds of
respondents were relatively closed in regard to the issues with negative loadings on the second dimension. The pragmatic position implies an open stance

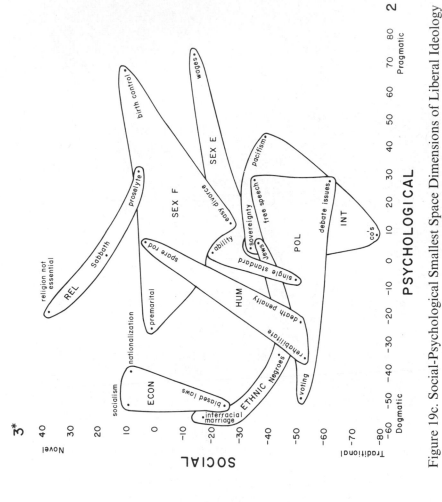

Figure 19c. Social-Psychological Smallest Space Dimensions of Liberal Ideology
(American Sample)

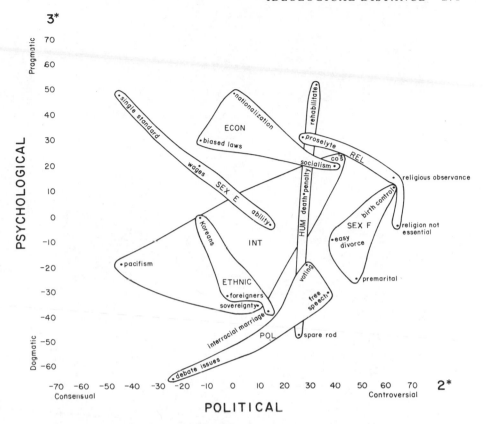

**POLITICAL**

Figure 20a. Political-Psychological Smallest Space Dimensions of Liberal Ideology (Japanese Sample)

toward the merits of birth control, the relevance of religion to *social* salvation, the postulation of an absolute right of freedom of speech, and universal suffrage. Equivalently dogmatic, however, was the orientation of this British sample toward issues of internationalism and sexual equality, and especially noteworthy is the extremely dogmatic attachment, of these British respondents, to the (liberal) "single standard" for sexual promiscuity, as between males and females. In general, the pragmatically perceived issues include sexual, religious, and political freedom; while the dogmatically perceived issues include sexual equality, internationalism, humanitarianism, and ethnic equality.

The third (social) dimension is a measure of the perceived novelty of issues, with the positive direction assigned to contemporary, emerging questions; and the negative to familiar, traditional problems. In relation to British cultural history, the descent of this scale of issues is akin to an archaeological excavation, with the ongoing concerns of British liberalism at the top, and those of an older liberalism (indeed of another century) at the bottom. Stated

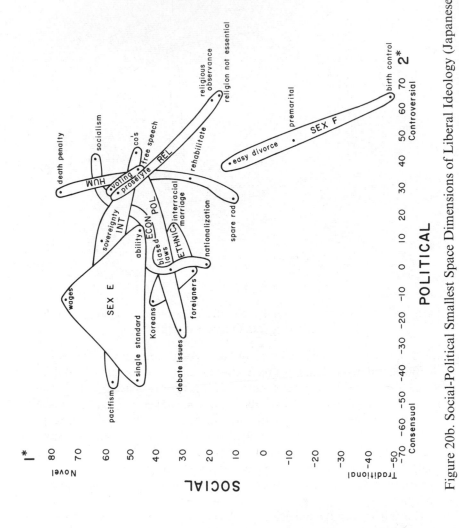

Figure 20b. Social-Political Smallest Space Dimensions of Liberal Ideology (Japanese Sample)

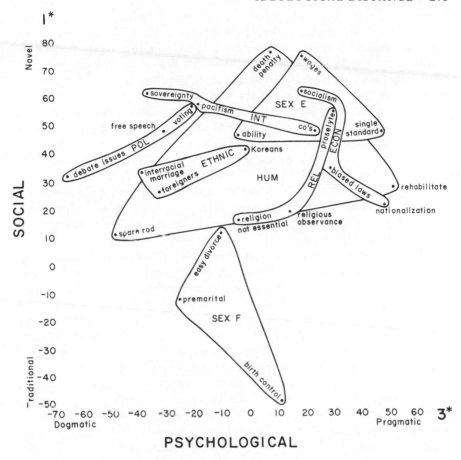

Figure 20c. Social-Psychological Smallest Space Dimensions of Liberal Ideology (Japanese Sample)

otherwise, sexual equality and political freedom were more burning issues in the days of Mills and Bentham; the clusters nearer the middle of the third dimension (internationalism, and economic and ethnic equality) appertain to the turn of the century, and such cultural symbols as the Fabian Society and David Lloyd George; and the more radical issues of post-World War II (when Eysenck collected these data) include those of sexual and religious freedom and of humanitarianism.

Those clusters of issues that are most highly positive on all three dimensions will be most highly and positively loaded on the liberalism vector, and vice versa. An examination of all three perspectives of Figures 18a-c confirms what is most clearly manifest in Figure 18c: that the most extreme liberal issues are those of sexual and religious freedom; followed (descending the major diagonal) by economic, ethnic, and sexual equality, in that order.

Three clusters do not lie on this diagonal: the political cluster is not yet viewed sufficiently dogmatically, considering its cultural age, to lie on the diagonal; and both internationalism and humanitarianism have come (prematurely, we might say) to be viewed *too* dogmatically, considering their relative novelty as articulated issues, to lie on the diagonal. Or we might say, alternatively, that if the political set were perceived to be of *more* (and the humanitarian and internationalism sets of *less*) contemporary relevance, then all three would fall on the diagonal. But this is precisely why, of course, a three-dimensional solution is required. If all items of all issues were aligned upon a common vector, that line would be all we would need to identify; and a unidimensional solution would provide us with a much more parsimonious description of a much simpler pattern of cognitive structure as the liberal ideology of these British respondents. As things stand, it is perhaps noteworthy that five of the eight clusters *do* form, however approximately because of the measurement error, a simplex.

Turning to the American sample, one evident difference in Figure 19a is the relative lack of cohesion that a majority of these clusters show, in comparison to the equivalent ones for the British sample. This tendency toward cognitive diffusion is particularly noteworthy for the internationalism, humanitarianism, sexual equality, political freedom, and religious freedom clusters. The sexual freedom and ethnic equality clusters show about the same cohesion, respectively, as do their British counterparts; and only in regard to the set of issues toward which these American judges were most dogmatically biased—the economic ones—do they appear more cohesive than the Britons. The Americans do not appear to scale the clusters very differently than do the Britons; the difference in the range of the coordinates merits little substantive consideration, because of the correlation and other measurement differences already discussed. More important differences are evident in regard to the second dimension: the Americans are considerably more open-minded toward issues of sexual equality and of internationalism, but considerably more dogmatic on economic questions than are the Britons. On the third dimension, the American scale of issue development roughly agrees with the British in regard to the positioning of the clusters for religious freedom, sexual freedom, ethnic equality, and political freedom; economic issues and those of sexual equality tend to be perceived as more salient by the Americans than the Britons; and only in regard to internationalism do the Americans seem to scale a cluster as more traditional than do the British. A closer look reveals, however, that the latter remark applies actually to only the single item about the tolerance of conscientious objection to compulsory military service; and here we might recall that the British had no experience with nineteenth-century draft riots, as the United States did during the Civil War. So with that exception, we might infer that the American respondents tended to perceive these issues as having either the same, or more contemporary, relevance, than appears to have been true for the British respondents.

The liberalism vector is evident enough in Figure 19b, as the chain of overlapping clusters extending from "COs" up to "religion not essential." The chief differences between this scale, and its British counterpart in 18b, are that the economic and ethnic clusters are perceived by the Americans to be higher on the vector (i.e., to be relatively more liberal), and humanitarianism scales lower (as more conservative). Significantly isolated from the vector is the cluster of sexual equality, and for the reason (as we have inferred) that these American judges viewed feminism as a relatively more contemporary issue than did the British. In Figure 19c, two of the clusters that were off scale in 18c—humanitarianism and political freedom—are on scale for the Americans; and one that was on scale for the British, economic equality, is off scale for the Americans because of their previously remarked highly dogmatic attitude toward this set of values. Sexual equality is on scale for the Americans, but in a considerably more advanced (liberal) position than it occupies for the Britons. The internationalism cluster, which was off scale in 18c, remains off scale in 19c, but for the opposite reason that the American judges were so *open* minded toward these questions. Overall, Figures 19a-c show that the liberalism vector can be identified in all three perspectives, but the patterning of the clusters for the American sample evinces a looser and more complex cognitive structure in comparison to the British sample. Another way to put this might be that these questions about British values make better sense to British than they do to American respondents.

What is perhaps most remarkable about Figures 20a-c is that the patterning of liberal ideology for the Japanese judges is not (contrary to my hypothesis) much more complex than that which we have just observed to obtain for the American judges. The most obvious difference is in the order of the dimensions in Figures 20a-c. Instead of political psychological-social, as it is for both the British and American samples, for the Japanese the first dimension is social, the perceived novelty of these issues. For a culture which has made the transition from the middle ages to a modern industrial society in less than a century, and in which sociopolitical change has been especially rapid since the end of World War II, it is understandable that with a single exception, all of these clusters of issues are perceived to be recent and salient; and the dimension of cultural change itself emerges as the most important dimension, for these (typically elderly) Japanese judges. Only issues of sexual freedom are viewed by them as traditional, when they are asked to evaluate questions that bear upon liberalism as it supposedly is understood in another country and one in which the political, social, and economic revolutions that were midwives to the establishment of most of these liberal ideas occurred over the course of a much longer period of time. For many, if not most, of these Japanese judges, the seven clusters that load positively on the first dimension have become focal questions of public concern only *since* they assumed their professional role as judges!

It is the second dimension in Figure 20 that represents the political component, and therefore corresponds to the first dimension for the British and Americans. Most controversial, as viewed by the Japanese sample, are the issues of sexual freedom and religious freedom. It should be noted that, as Dator has pointed out, the translation of the "birth control" question into Japanese evidently confused many of the respondents who interpreted it to refer to abortion as well as to contraception. If so, it is more understandable that the question was perceived to raise a controversial issue, inasmuch as legal abortions are widespread in Japan, and the conservative direction of the item proposed that *sanji saigen* be made illegal. Notable also is the wide spatial range among items in several of the clusters, along this second dimension; particularly in the case of the internationalism, political, and sexual equality clusters. The sexual equality and ethnic equality clusters are viewed as least controversial; and as Table 19 indicates, these are also the clusters that attracted the highest percentage of liberal approval from the Japanese sample.

The third dimension is the psychological component for the Japanese; and it is apparent that the attitude of these judges was largely openminded toward half of these issues: economic equality, sexual equality, religious equality, and (with the exception of one item) humanitarianism. Apart from the birth control item, however, the respondents were dogmatic in their attitude toward sexual freedom; and except for the conscientious objectors item, they were even slightly more dogmatic toward internationalism. They were particularly dogmatic on the ethnic cluster, and on the question of disciplining children; but most dogmatic of all toward the entire cluster of issues relating to political freedom. This is hardly surprising, however; political democracy has had a very brief existence in Japan, in comparison to either Britain or the United States; and these respondents all were adults during the Tojo military dictatorship before and during World War II. Postwar decisions of the Supreme Court of Japan have been almost without exception hostile to claims of freedom of speech;[18] and 85 percent of this sample responded conservatively on the free speech item. Moreover, the emphasis upon individual acquiescence in consensual decisions was certainly a major element in the socialization of these respondents,[19] which may help to explain why they were most dogmatic of all on the question of whether policy issues ought to be debated publicly in the mass media. Alternatively, as Dator has pointed out, almost a fourth of the respondents chose neither a liberal nor a conservative response to this question, many of them explaining that they did not understand the phrase that was used to attempt to translate "controversy" into the Japanese language. Consequently, the extremely low load-

---

18. In a group of cases chosen to illustrate the typical patterning of values in the Japanese Supreme Court's decisions during 1948–1960, only one (involving a claim of police brutality and coerced confession) out of seventeen civil liberties cases was decided liberally. Of these cases, half dealt with fair procedure, and the other half with political freedom (see Maki 1964).

19. See Kawashima 1968a; Chie 1964; and De Vos 1954.

ing of the "debate issues" item on the third dimension, like the extremely low loading of "birth control" on the first, may be due at least in part to response set error arising out of the linguistic complication.

In general, however, the issues deemed most liberal by these Japanese judges were those raised by the clusters of economic equality, humanitarianism, and religious freedom; these were also the most difficult questions of liberalism, from the points of view of the British and the American samples. The political and internationalism clusters would be in the same position, were it not for the rigid way in which they are viewed by these Japanese, reflecting, perhaps, the authoritarian manner in which the values which these clusters represent were imposed upon Japanese society by means of a process for which these respondents necessarily functioned as participant-observers. The issue of sexual equality raised the least demanding liberal claims, for the Japanese as also for the other two samples. In regard to the ethnic cluster, one can only speculate whether Japanese attitudes toward Koreans and foreigners are properly comparable to Anglo-American attitudes toward Negroes and Jews, respectively; but if they are, then the ethnic cluster raised somewhat less extreme liberal claims for the Japanese than it did for the British and American respondents. Both Britons and Americans perceived the sexual freedom cluster to be in a more advanced liberal position than did the Japanese, but primarily because of the extraordinarily puritanical stance (Dator 1966) adopted by these Japanese judges, in response to any suggestions of extramarital sexual intercourse.

## IV. THE COMPOSITE SPACE

In order to facilitate comparative analysis at an even more general level, one further step was taken in the direction of summarizing the data. Of course, the more refined our analysis, the further removed do we become from the empirical observations; hence the more tenuous are findings which can be supported only by the studies surveyed here. By calculating the simple arithmetic means for each triad, one derives the set of coordinates that are plotted in Figure 21. Because of the mass of overlapping detail that would appear in a single set of planar perspectives for the space including all eight cluster means, each of which would be represented by a triad of points for the three samples, I have chosen instead to present a separate set of perspectives for each cluster mean. It should be understood, however, that there is only one common three-dimensional space which contains, in theory, all eight triads (representing, in each instance, the English, American, and Japanese cluster mean for the attitudinal triad of questionnaire item responses).

Instead of designating the reference dimensions by numbers and semantic content, as was done for Figures 18a–20c, I have identified the dimensions by type—political, psychological, and social. These types correspond, of course, to their referents in the previous figures (e.g., political = controversial = English 1, American 1, Japanese 3; etc.) We can define precisely an ideal cluster: such a cluster would be represented by a single point on the boundary parameter with a vectorial bearing of 45° in all of the plots. This would imply complete agreement among the English, American, and Japanese samples upon a perception of the issue as entailing simultaneously maximal controversiality, pragmatism, and novelty. Such a point, in other words, would be consensually understood, in all three cultures, to involve the most extreme possible liberal demand; such a point would represent the cross-cultural paragon of liberalism. We could hardly expect to observe in our present empirical data a triad that conforms to this ideal, but the ideal point, which is plotted as a small "o" in each subfigure, can serve as a criterion against which to measure the extent of deviation of the empirical triads.

As a matter of fact, the triads for religious freedom appear to come remarkably close to the approximation of our ideal point; and the triads for sexual freedom are not very much worse. These are relatively cohesive sets of points in the three-space, and it should also be noted that the two triads are located quite near each other in that space. This shows that, of all the facets of liberalism measured by the questionnaires, the perception of religious and of sexual freedom was most consensual and most similar; and of course these are also the issues perceived to be most extremely liberal, at least by the English and American samples. On ethnic equality, the Japanese are just as dogmatic as the Westerners, but the Japanese view ethnic issues as at once more novel and controversial than do the Britons and Americans. The triads for economic equality and humanitarianism show less agreement among the three samples; and in both of these triads of what for these data is average cohesion, the Japanese judges are consistently highest on both the social and the psychological dimensions. The issues in regard to which there were least perceptual agreement among the three samples are political freedom, internationalism, and sexual equality. With the conspicuous exception of the virtually identical position taken by the Japanese and the American judges,[20] viewing the issue of sexual equality from a psychological point of view (in which respect they were considerably less dogmatic than the British), the American sample is almost as widely separated from the British on these issues of political freedom and internationalism and sexual equality, as the Japanese sample is separated from both of the other two. Least cohesive of

---

20. There are several other perspectives in which the points for the Japanese and for the American samples are very close; but in only one instance (ethnic equality in the social and psychological plane) are the English and American points close. It is, of course, not without interest that Englishmen and Americans should take what appears to be a similar view of the white man's burden; but we must recall that the closeness of a pair of points on two dimensions does not mean that they are necessarily close together in the three-space. In this instance, the pair of points are not at all close on the first dimension, with the English sample seeing the race issue as a much more controversial one than did these American judges in the mid-fifties. Little did they suspect!

## Table 46. Plotting Coordinates for Figure 21

|        | Political | | | Social | | | Psychological | | |
|--------|-----|-----|-----|-----|-----|-----|-----|-----|-----|
|        | A | E | J | A | E | J | A | E | J |
| REL    | 61 | 90 | 52 | 20 | 41 | 30 | 04 | 36 | 13 |
| SEX F  | 48 | 84 | 50 | −05 | 45 | −16 | 18 | 46 | −08 |
| HUM    | 43 | 90 | 29 | −34 | 31 | 38 | −17 | −40 | 04 |
| ECON   | 46 | 97 | 13 | −03 | 02 | 39 | −48 | 07 | 32 |
| ETHNIC | 35 | 86 | 00 | −33 | −25 | 33 | −28 | −25 | −24 |
| SEX E  | −12 | 45 | −14 | −28 | −60 | 56 | 22 | −69 | 21 |
| POL    | 19 | 67 | 14 | −50 | −55 | 45 | 02 | 32 | −39 |
| INT    | 34 | 88 | 03 | −51 | 03 | 55 | 19 | −54 | −11 |

NOTE: Plotting coordinates for Figures 18a–20c are given in Table 45.

all are sexual equality as measured by the social and psychological dimensions, and internationalism in the context of the political and social dimensions. In addition to looking at the figure from the point of view of the rows (triads), we can do so also from that of the columns (dimensional pairs). The English are the most liberal for all clusters on the political dimension (reflecting, perhaps in part, the effect of those tetrachoric coefficients); the Americans rank second and the Japanese third, for five clusters; and the Americans and Japanese are tied on the other three. It does seem justifiable to infer that in perceptions of these issues of liberalism, the British see them as most controversial, the Americans next so, and the Japanese least so. There is no such clearcut scale for the psychological dimension, however: the English are in the most extreme position for issues of sexual, religious, and political freedom (signifying that they are most pragmatic in their orientation toward these issues); but the Japanese are the most pragmatic toward economic equality and humanitarianism. As previously noted, all three samples were equivalently dogmatic on the ethnic triad; and the Japanese and the American judges were tied in their pragmatic stance toward sexual equality. Only in regard to internationalism do the Americans appear to be the most open-minded of the three sets of respondents. On the social dimension, the Japanese clearly rank highest, perceiving greater novelty than either the British or the Americans in regard to political freedom, internationalism, ethnic equality, sexual equality, and economic equality. Only in regard to sexual freedom and religious freedom are the English the most positive on this dimension; and they and the Japanese are tied concerning issues of humanitarianism. The Americans rank third on this dimension on a majority of the issues, signifying, presumably, that at least in regard to internationalism and humanitarianism—the differences between the Americans and the British being much smaller on the other three cluster means—these are recognized as being older and more familiar as social issues in the American than in the British culture.

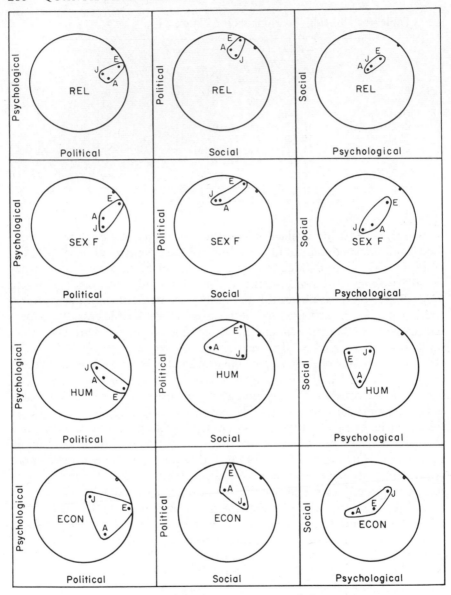

Figure 21. Ideological Distance between Cultures in Smallest Space

## V. CONCLUSIONS

The principal findings of this study relate to the comparison of the distances in multidimensional space separating points that represent the ideological positions of English, American and Japanese respondents, in regard

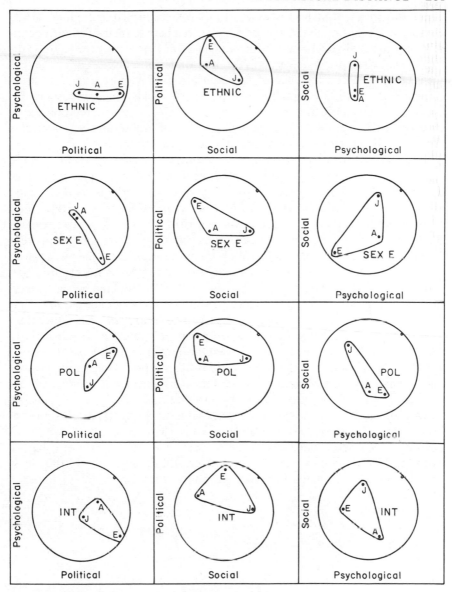

Figure 21 (cont.)

to eight hypothesized semantic components of liberalism/conservatism. Previous research based upon all or part of these data, though cumulative in its objectives and design, had focused upon two-dimensional (or, in the case of Nagel, one-dimensional) analysis. The two dimensions identified in the earlier studies were first a political dimension, and second a psychological dimension; these dimensions were, in general, confirmed as findings of the present study, although the interpretation given here to their substantive content and psychological implications differs from that attributed to these dimensions by the previous writers. The new dimension discussed for the first time here, as a consequence of the invocation of a more complex three-dimensional method of smallest space analysis, is identified as a social dimension which measures the novelty of a set of issues in relation to its emergence as a question of public policy in the cultural setting of a particular country. The empirical evidence clearly supports the finding that the issues of liberalism to which these data relate are most novel in the context of the Japanese culture, which has confronted most of them only since the end of World War II. Somewhat less intuitively obvious, perhaps, is the related finding that most of what were *ex hypothesi* issues of British liberalism tend to be viewed as somewhat more novel by British than by American respondents. Analysis of the issues by regrouping the data, as triads of points representing each of the three cultures on the semantic cluster means, showed that there appeared to be greater homogeneity in the cross-cultural patterning of ideological structures of liberalism than would be anticipated on a priori grounds. The latter conclusion from these data, although so tentative that it is better looked upon as a hypothesis to guide future research rather than as a clearly substantiated finding based upon past research, is particularly impressive when one takes into consideration the considerable degree to which both the data and the computations based upon them, in the present study, evidently were contaminated with measurement error variance of various types. But the effect of such error variance must always be, in general, toward precluding the possibility of discerning meaningful patterns and relationships; the error variance always tends to work in the direction of entropy. With better data, one would expect to discriminate more sharply both the communalities, and the differences, in the patterning of the ideologies of both Western and non-Western political man.

# PART IV

# Toward a Dynamic Jurisprudence of Human Behavior

IN THIS CONCLUDING part, we turn to the theory of legal change, as a function of individual and social behavior and as an aspect of the life sciences. My own thinking along these lines is very greatly indebted to the brilliant theorizing and meticulous craftsmanship of Martin Landau, and most particularly to a series of his essays (1961, 1965b, 1968; and cf. James A. Robinson 1957) that were collected (together with other of his writings) in a volume (Landau 1972) whose purpose is not very dissimilar from my own in the present work. Landau distinguished, with considerable force and clarity, the implications for political theorizing of the acceptance or rejection of the premises underlying two of the principal cosmologies (or, in his words, "metaphors") that presently are invoked—at least, among many social scientists—as a basis for ordering one's comprehension of the universe, life within it, and one's own role in relationship to it. (Landau discusses also the implications for political theory of the [typically, unwitting] mixing of metaphors with consequent ambiguity and confusion; but that is a technical matter that need not concern us here.) The two metaphors that Landau discusses are both based upon systems of meta-scientific logic developed out of human experience in recent but earlier centuries: the mechanical, based on seventeenth-century classical physics; and the organismic, evolving from nineteenth-century biology. There are, of course, other and competing cosmologies that can be traced to leading thinkers besides Newton and Darwin: theological (Aquinas), to take an even earlier example, or one based upon modern twentieth-century biophysics and biochemistry, to take a more recent example. Evidently there are many persons today, including some social scientists, whose cosmology is theological; but Landau does not deal with them for purposes of his own critique of theoretical stances, nor shall I undertake to do so here, other than to note that one who sought to comprehend the establishment of American separatism (and its symbolization in the Declaration of Independence) could hardly afford to ignore the theological model as one (however partial) interpretation of that sequence of events. But neither does Landau undertake to discuss the model that derives from the cosmology of modern science, and in this respect I have attempted to adumbrate some traces of what such a model might be. Consensus long since has come to rest concerning the intellectual significance of classical mechanics, and so the model of law-making and legal change that flows logically from the mechanical metaphor is clear, concise, and indisputable. Similarly, the biological metaphor—which is now clearly dominant in social science theory in the United States—so pervades thinking in the life sciences that it is generally understood at a somatic, if not a semantic, level by judges (see Cardozo 1921, 1924), lawyers, and political scientists today. It is the Einsteinian model that, in its social implications, creates problems for us to comprehend and for me to explicate as a cosmology relevant to understanding law-making processes. Because there is little explicit recognition of its relevance, there is not only a lack of consensus concerning its form and content, there is not even an obvious name that should be used to describe the idea. In what follows below I have vacillated (in denoting it), from "cultural" (in chapter 11) to "configurational" (chapter 13), while in chapter 12 (which was the one most recently written) I avoid calling it anything other than a model based upon "modern physics." Evidently I haven't achieved a personal consensus about it either; but that does not mean that it cannot (or should not) be discussed.

The models themselves are described, together with some of their implications, in the three chapters that follow. Here I should like to explain how and why these papers came to be written. All three of them were originally prepared for oral presentation; all were contributions to symposia organized and defined by other persons, who specified the general topic that (in each case) I agreed to discuss; all three forums were multidisciplinary, with political science playing a distinctly minority role in relation to persons representing such other fields as philosophy and law; and, not least, in each instance my remarks turned out to be sufficiently displeasing to the organizer of the conference that he attempted (in one instance) or succeeded in (in the other two) the repudiation of the agreement, made at the time the invitation to participate was extended, to include the paper in a planned publication of the symposium proceedings. It may well be, therefore, that an iconoclastic stance is common to all three of these chapters; and indeed, it may well be that the attempt to discuss jurisprudential-social relationships from a relativistic-atomic point of view could not be perceived as anything other than a form of radical dissent, by organizers of conferences who had their own (and invariably, conventional) ideas about the most appropriate solutions to the problems that they had posed for discussion.

## A

Naturally I was intrigued when one of FDR's original "brain trusters" asked me to sit in on a colloquium at the Center for the Study of Democratic Institutions on "The Emerging Constitution," and not least because this would entail spending a month or so during the middle of the winter of 1966 in Santa Barbara, California, instead of in East Lansing, Michigan. But I misperceived completely what he was up to: I had presumed, from the title and its prospectus, that we would be concerned with an evolutionary model of constitutional change; and I thought that might be a worthwhile endeavor intellectually. It was with genuine surprise, to say nothing of disbelief, that I confronted upon arrival the shocking truth: that what Rex Tugwell and his patron (Robert Hutchins, who had been dean of the Yale Law School and chancellor of the University of Chicago, during the respective heydays of those institutions) wanted to do was to draft a new and substitute *document* for the Constitution of the United States (see Tugwell 1970*b*; and cf. Crosskey 1953; and Baldwin 1972). Indeed, the role that Tugwell seemed to have in mind for himself was not that of James Madison, but was more akin to that of Moses (Boyd 1971; Davidson 1969)—forcing me, ultimately, to the conclusion that creatorship must be a pretty heady business.

Part of the customary processing of visitors to the Center for Democratic Institutions involves a taped interview, by one of the Center regulars, concerning the subject of one's supposed competence in relation to the topic for which he has been cast as a discussant for the Center. In my case this took the form of Harvey (*Fail-Safe*) Wheeler pressing me to give up my hopelessly conservative posture—which was the gloss that he had put upon my criticism of Tugwell's "new document" approach—and to admit that there was at least *some* part of the Constitution, in its present form, that I would like to see changed; and it was in response to this sort of insistence that I came up with the idea that if something had to go, the Second Amendment would be an excellent place to begin. Nothing that has happened during the past seven years has shaken in the least my confidence that my choice was a good one, and that an armed citizenry has no place in twentieth-century America—or rather, that it defines a place in which no civilized person wants to live.

My remarks at the Center took the form of an analysis of constitution-making and constitution-changing from the points of view of three explicit models: Landau's mechanical and biological models, and the more contemporary atomic model (in the formulation of which I received some help from the work of Karl Deutsch [1951 and 1963]). These models are used also to analyze and interpret three sectors of Constitutional policy-making by the Warren Court: racial, representational, and procedural equality (viz., desegregation, reapportionment, and criminal justice). Finally, the proposal for change in the Second Amendment also is examined from the perspective of all three models, in order to consider the logical implications of each model as a guide to the behavior of persons who might wish to take seriously a plea for civil disarmament.

After having read the extended and documented written version of the paper that I prepared for publication and mailed to him, Tugwell informed me that it had been decided not to publish the symposium on "The Emerging Constitution" after all—with the exception, of course, of his own paper presenting one of the versions of his draft document (Tugwell 1970a). So I sent my paper off to the *Journal of Public Law*, publication in which would assure it much wider dissemination, and among a considerably more relevant academic audience, than would have been the case if Tugwell had carried through with his original publication plans.

## B

Chapter 12 was a by-product of my having joined the faculty of the University of Hawaii. Shortly after my arrival Chief Justice William Richardson of the Supreme Court of Hawaii was engaged in drawing up the agenda for what would be his second quinquennial Citizens' Conference on the Administration of Justice; and because the president of the university had told him that I am supposed to know something about courts and constitutions, Richardson asked me to speak to the conference on such questions as "whether the state system of justice, as structured and operating, was prepared to cope with the future?" and "What is the function, role, and purpose of the judiciary—past, present, and future?" I felt that such a definition of the subject left me free to discuss virtually anything; so I said I'd do it, and what "it" became was an endeavor to take seriously the implications of the biological metaphor, if one invoked that as a model to guide predictions about the probable impact of socioenvironmental change upon the present system of courts in Hawaii. The result of that analysis was sufficiently foreboding that I attempted also, though briefly and at the very end of the lecture, to speculate upon what differing results (if any) might be produced were one to undertake an equivalent analysis with the guidance of the relativistic-atomic model?

A few of the local allusions in the lecture should perhaps be explained. At the time the conference was meeting the state legislature had under consideration a proposal to establish, beginning only a few months later in that same year, a law school to be funded by the state and affiliated with the University of Hawaii. This was a matter in which Chief Justice Richardson and the president of the university and I all had deep interests; and among the questions that remained unresolved at the time I spoke was whether it would be primarily a trade school or an integral part of the university; and consequently, whether it should be located downtown in the Capitol complex or on the main university campus; and whether the law school should build its own relatively autonomous library, or be attached to the main university library, or be integrated with the only existing law library in the entire state—that of the Supreme Court (which was open to use by local lawyers, and by sufferance to a few professors from the university).

James Dator, my by this time colleague at the University of Hawaii had then recently completed starring in a fairly widely viewed (for educational TV) program. That show was sponsored by the extension division of the university and offered as a course for credit. It was on the subject of "Futuristics," and much of its thrust was upon how residents of the state could and should adapt to the increasingly pernicious effects of a rapidly deteriorating environment. (The general approach was that not much could be done about the environment, so humans should increase their satisfactions by redefining their own attitudes in an acquiescent mood—"Love that concrete!" as some wags put it.) Dator's multimedia presentation on the morning of May 25, 1972, was entitled "Dowager in a Hurricane: Law in a Charging Hawaiian Society." The second speaker was Alvin Toffler, whose address was on "The Future of Law and Order." I came after lunch, and was introduced by Mrs. Winona Rubin. My intent in the introductory paragraph of chapter

12 is to refer to Professor Dator's presentation as "Future Shock," and to Mr. Toffler's as "Future Joy." I am not unaware of the titles of Mr. Toffler's recent best sellers.

## C

Chapter 13, the last of these three lectures, was written for a symposium at which I was the political scientist participant, together with several philosophers of law and legal philosophers, including Chaim Perelman, a distinguished Belgian scholar, and Ronald Dworkin, a leading legal positivist who at that time was in the process of leaving Yale in order to replace H. L. A. Hart as Dicey Professor of Jurisprudence at Oxford. The host was the Department of Philosophy of the State University of New York at Buffalo, at whose campus we convened. I decided that the most useful thing for me to do would be to attempt to direct the attention, of the assembled philosophers and law professors, to the body of recent research that defines an *empirical* jurisprudence in contemporary political science. In order to organize this research for purposes of presentation, I sketched a static empirical model of judicial decision-making; and in order to discuss that dynamically, I considered but rejected the possibility of analyzing it through the aegis of the biological metaphor. Instead, I attempted to employ the relativistic-atomic model, which in this lecture I called "configurational." I attempted also to appraise the implications of this analysis, for the appropriate education of persons who would be qualified to carry forward related research in the future. But primarily the article provides an overview of the on-going and recent research in the field of judicial process and behavior, from the perspective of the late sixties, as seen by a behaviorally oriented political scientist.[1] The emphasis that I strove to give in the lecture was not to dwell upon what had been learned in the past, or even what was being learned in the then present; instead, I attempted to use such events as benchmarks which could and should be used primarily as guideposts to what might and needed to be done in the future. And that, it seems to me, is an appropriate note upon which to bring the present discussion to a close.

---

1. For a more detailed exposition, see my bibliography and bibliographical essay (1972c), the concluding chapter of which is also available as an article (1972b).

# 11

# Three Models of Constitutional Change

*"[A]" constitution . . . continually change[s], and . . . conform[s] in every age to the level of culture attained."* (Pargellis 1938:49)

*"The logic of events [i]s always in command of a doctrine headed for parts unknown."* (Hamilton 1938b:168)

## I. MODELS OF CHANGE

The usual American government textbook statement about change in the Constitution of the United States correctly identifies three principal modes of change, but is inverted in its discussion of the relative difficulty and importance of the different types. The typical textbook statement is that the three methods of constitutional change are: (1) formal amendment; (2) interpretation by the Supreme Court, the Congress, and the President; and (3) custom and usage. The method of formal amendment is said to be the least

This chapter was originally published, in slightly different form, as "The Rhetoric of Constitutional Change" in *Journal of Public Law* 16 (Spring 1967): 16–50. Reprinted with permission of the *Journal of Public Law* of Emory University.

I am indebted to Dr. Rexford Tugwell for having invited me to participate in a series of discussions on "The Emerging Constitution," which were sponsored by and convened at the Center for the Study of Democratic Institutions (at Santa Barbara, California) during January and February 1966. I am grateful to the members and to the other (then) guests of the Center for their comments on my oral presentation of an earlier draft of the present paper; much of the revision constitutes a direct response on my own part to the stimulus provided by the discussions that took place at the Center.

The Social Science Research Institute of the University of Hawaii generously aided me in the typing of the revised draft of the paper.

frequently used because it is the most difficult to employ, but also the most fundamental in importance and, at least by implication, in terms of effects. Custom and usage, it is indicated, is in some unspecified sense "easier" to employ, and more common, but of lesser importance because it relates essentially to interstitial matters that are not dealt with in the formal text of the Constitution. In the concluding section of this paper, my analysis of proposed change in the Second Amendment will suggest that the change of the literal language of the Constitution would probably be by far the *easiest* of the three approaches, in the sense that the costs for a protagonist of accomplishing this kind of change would be relatively minimal in terms of time, labor, and money. The same kinds of costs would be maximal in order successfully to bring about the necessary degree of what I shall call cultural change; while the costs of proceeding along a broad array of institutional fronts would be medial, in comparison to the other two approaches. Our analysis also will indicate that cultural change would be most likely to be the most effective, and amendment of the document the least effective, of these three approaches to civil disarmament.[1]

The probable reason why the textbooks scale importance and impact in the reverse direction is that their authors—whose task, after all, is to replicate rather than to create what is accepted as political theory in the profession of political science—orient their own thinking primarily in terms of hierarchical structure and of a *mechanical* model of the Constitution, even though they base substantial portions of other parts of their texts upon analyses keyed to what I shall shortly define as the *biological* model, and even though they increasingly have come to accept some of the implications and findings of research stemming from a *cultural* model of the Constitution.

To begin a discussion of constitutional change with—as usually is proposed—consideration of such constitutional principles as the separation of powers, federalism, and civil liberties drastically delimits the scope and range of possible constitutional change, because of the narrowness and rigidity of the terms of reference that have been accepted—the mechanistic conceptualism of the eighteenth century. From either of the other two points of view (the biological and the cultural), such constitutional principles have no particular claim to sanctity, to say nothing of any preordained right to survival in perpetuity; political concepts such as these are not themselves goals for contemporary political society, and they are relevant to a discussion of constitutional change only insofar as they serve to define the *status quo* to constitute the boundary parameters for decision-making about the Constitution.[2]

The document itself necessarily is a poor description of empirical reality (the on-going political, social, and economic systems), and from a normative

---

1. By "civil disarmament" I mean the negation of the constitutional right to bear arms.
2. These very same political ideas were thought of in instrumental terms by the Founding Fathers, and we might well follow their preeminent example in this regard.

point of view, the document long since has ceased to contain language that bears directly upon more than a small residue of our most pressing contemporary constitutional ideals. Such ideals are posited for us by elite political actors, but only most obliquely by the constitutional text. Consider, for example, the constitutional bases for each of the following aspects of the constitutional culture today:

(1) *private*-institutional due process
(2) the right to privacy
(3) one man, one vote
(4) freedom from want
(5) political equality for blacks
(6) social equality for blacks
(7) economic equality for blacks
(8) a nationalized "bill of rights"
(9) the right to counsel at public expense

It has taken the intermediation of some conspicuously human "constitutional storks" (Lerner 1941:259) to relate any of these ideals to the document, a fact which is inexplicable under the mechanical model, although one that could readily be predicted under either of the other two models.

Constitutions probably are best not conceptualized as "frameworks for governmental systems" or as "blueprints." They are more like dictionaries, recording the standards of political, as well as of linguistic, preference of the generation most recently buried—or, characteristically, of even earlier generations. Proposals to change institutional structures, because of anxiety about possible future contingencies[3] doubtless, for many advocates, stem from notions that constitutional law ought to be a "seamless web," and the related desire to plug up suspected holes. Such a posture readily can be interpreted as a compulsion for premature closure (Rokeach 1960), and it certainly is that from the point of view of either the biological or the cultural model. Concern about the electoral college probably does no good and little harm, except to the extent that it diverts attention from more important matters; and such apprehensive preoccupation with institutional structure can appropriately be viewed as dilettantish escapism, or, alternatively, as a conservative ploy for distracting public attention from alternative possibilities for making significant political changes. From both the biological and the cultural points of view, constitutional structures will be modified as and when they get in the way of significant policy change[4]—that is to say, as functional prerequisites shift or as attitudes change.

---

3. E.g., the twenty-second (anti-third term) amendment, or the suggested direct election of the president.

4. Under the biological model, for example, the states will be abolished only if they have ceased to perform politically (or other) important functions. Even then they may continue for some time as administrative districts because of the custom, of various departments of the national government, of using them for such a purpose. See generally Miller 1963.

From the perspective that is now at least conventional among most political scientists, it is better to use all of the political instruments at hand in order to attempt to bring about a posited policy change. The objects (and the objectives) of such an approach typically are institutional functions: legislation, judicial decisions, administrative regulations, political-party platforms, and interest-group programs. Most political scientists today would think it also of importance to affect public opinion, and in doing that they are accepting the implications of the cultural model.

If, however, preoccupation with the manipulation of the document is to be rejected as the sole, or even as the primary, objective of constitutional change, then we need to distinguish other aspects of constitutionalism which are more appropriate for consideration. A distinction must be made between the constitutional document, constitutional institutions, and the constitutional culture, akin to that suggested by three concentric circles, with the document imbedded in the set of relevant institutions, which in turn are enveloped by the culture. The document is central not because it is most but rather because it is least important, and is a subset of the set of constitutional institutions; similarly, constitutional institutions are a subset of the constitutional culture. Each of these is, in turn, also a subset of the broader series of parallel sets of political documents, political institutions, and political culture.

Even to speak of "the emerging Constitution" is to express a preference among alternative concepts of constitutionalism. From some points of view it is arrant nonsense—that is to say, it is a contradiction of the basic logic of the model of political reality which is assumed by a given point of view—to talk about emergence as a possible attribute of a constitution; from other points of view only a constitution in metamorphosis—one which continuously is in the process of emerging from one state to assume a different relationship of accommodation to another state—makes any sense at all to discuss. The most critical dimension on which we can compare such differing perspectives is that of constitutional change, which has widely varying implications and meaning in relation to different models of constitutionalism. Given the same universe of empirical events, one's perception of "constitutional change," either in descriptive or in normative terms, necessarily will vary with his underlying conception of what a "constitution" is (Hamilton 1938a:vii), and of how "change" takes place in government and society, and the kind of action that this involves.

I have selected for consideration three models which are conceptually isomorphic with the typology: the constitutional document, constitutional institutions, and constitutional culture.[5] Each model is a modal represen-

---

5. Of course, men have guided their political thinking with many other, and with simpler, models than the three upon which our attention will focus in this paper. One such older and simpler model, for example, is the scales (so dear to the unimaginative designers of dust jackets

tation of an important and enduring perspective toward the relationship between mankind and its milieu, including, of course, the political sets of relationships that are involved in notions about constitutions. Associated with each model is a distinctive mode, and vocabulary, of discourse, as Landau has explained:

> Any model, as any theory, is a linguistic system. Accordingly, it has its own grammar and vocabulary and it points its user toward special types of observations, evaluations, and interpretations. The more developed (formal) the language (model), the clearer are its concepts, the more explicit and certain are its rules. Where undeveloped, it is largely metaphorical but even here (if used as a frame of reference) it structures inquiry and establishes relevance. Models and metaphors, thus, are logics: they constitute methodologies—rules by which we analyze, make inferences, and do research. The logic of a model is very strict: it is expressed in the precise vocabulary (operational) of a scientific language. The logic or program of a metaphor is pre-scientific: it retains the relative ambiguity of the natural language in which it is stated. The transformation of a metaphor into a scientific model requires the elimination of this ambiguity, the formulation of an ordered set of rules, and the clarification of its basic properties and relationships: the movement here is from a natural to a scientific language. (1965b:7)

The first of our three models is the mechanical one of classical physics which fits so well the ideas explicit in the document, the Constitution of the United States, constructed and approved by Americans of the late eighteenth century. A second model appeared during the nineteenth century, emphasizing the evolutionary development of organic forms and biological processes, in sharp distinction from the fixed and completely deterministic relationships posited by Newtonian mechanics and optics. The third model is cultural and is that of the network of social communications and decision-making produced by modern social and behavioral science, very largely during the past three decades. Our models are derived, therefore, from the dominant scientific metaphors of the past three centuries, a period that pretty well encompasses American constitutional experience, no matter how it is to be conceptualized.

The purpose of positing any model is, of course, to focus attention upon selected characteristics of some aspects of reality. As Deutsch has explained,

> Men think in terms of models. Their sense organs abstract the events which touch them; their memories store traces of these events as coded symbols; and

---

for books on the subject of law) grasped by a blindfolded but voluptuous female adorned with a free-flowing tunic. Comparing it to the social implications of another primitive but powerful model, the wheel, Deutsch has remarked: "The other of these models is the *balance*, the pair of scales which yields the concept of stable equilibrium, with its implications that the adverse reaction must be the greater, the more the true position of balance has been disturbed. The notion of *dike*, of 'nothing too much,' of the golden mean, and the statue holding the scales of justice in front of many Western lawcourts, all testify to its suggestive power. Both wheel and balance suggest movement which eventually returns to the original position. 'The more it changes, the more it stays the same.'" (1951:233)

they may recall them according to patterns which they learned earlier, or recombine them in patterns that are new. In all this, we may think of our thought as consisting of symbols which are put in relations or sequences according to operating rules. Both symbols and operating rules are acquired, in part directly from interaction with the outside world, and in part from elaboration of this material through internal recombination. Together, a set of symbols and a set of rules may constitute what we may call a calculus, a logic, a game or a model. Whatever we call it, it will have some structure, i.e., some patterns of distribution of relative discontinuities, and some "laws" of operation.

If this pattern and these laws resemble, to any relevant extent, any particular situation or class of situations in the outside world, then, to that extent, these outside situations can be "understood," i.e., predicted—and perhaps even controlled—with the aid of this model. Whether any such resemblance exists cannot be discovered from the model, but only from a physical process of *verification*, that is, physical operations for matching some of the structure of the outside situation—this we might call "taking information off" the outside situation—followed by some *critical process*, i.e., further physical operations which depend in their outcome on the degree of correspondence between the structure proposed from the model and the structure derived from the outside facts. (1951:230)

## Table 47. Attributes of Models

| Attribute | Mechanical Model | Biological Model | Cultural Model |
|---|---|---|---|
| Dominant metaphor | Machine | Organism | Community |
| Century of predominance | 17th-18th[a] | 19th | 20th |
| Subject of constitutional change | The constitutional document | Constitutional institutions | Constitutional culture |
| Jurisprudential orientation | Analytical positivism | Sociological | Realism |
| Branch of science | Physical | Biological | Social |
| Cognate academic discipline | Classical physics | Biology | Anthropology and social psychology |
| Social science research orientation[b] | Traditional | Conventional | Behavioral |
| Animation status of basic particles | Inanimate | Animate wholes | Animate aggregates |
| Social objects of inquiry | Institutions | Groups | Individuals |
| Relationships examined | Interaction | Transactions | Decision-making |
| Processes investigated | Formal[c] | Informal | Internal |
| Concept of change | Obsolescence | Growth | Rejuvenation |
| Effect of change | Negative | Ambivalent | Positive |

[a] I.e., the "Age of Reason" (c. 1650–1790 A.D.) (Deutsch 1951 : 232).
[b] For further discussion of these research orientations, see Schubert 1967a, 1967b.
[c] By "formal," I mean officially sanctioned (legitimate) and organized.

Some of the more important attributes, in terms of which we can distinguish among the three models, are summarized in Table 47. Necessarily, to give emphasis requires that attention be diverted away from other aspects of reality. Consequently, each of the models abstracts from reality and underscores certain differences that can be observed to have occurred in the flow of the relevant manifold of human events over the course of a third of a millennium. But this does not mean that there were not, and are not, many similarities, and broad areas of overlap and intersection, which could be emphasized in the alternative—but with a different set of models—by one entertaining different objectives than mine in this paper. Therefore, for example, the table's indication that the biological model predominated during the nineteenth century does not imply that neither mechanical nor biological models are important today, in which case the present paper would be of interest primarily as a study in history. Neither does the table imply that the cultural model has no empirical referents (at least in terms of attributes) prior to the year 1900, which would ignore the work of social theorists such as Auguste Comte and William James. But Social Darwinism best exemplifies the political and constitutional thinking of the age of enterprise, notwithstanding that some of its better-known legal proponents, such as Oliver Wendell Holmes, Jr., and Roscoe Pound, remained professionally active, and politically visible, well into the middle decades of the present century; note, however, that both Holmes and Pound were nonagenarians, each living to the age of ninety-three years.

Similarly, the table does not suggest that the American Constitution was formerly a machine, then an organism, and that today it is a community. The purpose of a metaphor is to aid in the apprehension of the relationships important to the model; thus, the function of the metaphor is to limit the kinds of questions that are appropriate to ask about constitutional change. If we think of the Constitution *as though it were* a machine, or an organism, or a community, what then? Of course we know and ought to remember that a constitution is none of these, but analogical thinking may help us better to understand both what a constitution is, and what it can become.

The effect of change is necessarily destructive for a machine, since the interaction of all component parts is limited by their respective capacities of strength, durability, and so forth. Assuming that the machine is well designed and constructed, either slow change (obsolescence) or rapid change (breakdown) has the effect, later or sooner, of destroying the machine's capacity to perform its function. If we think of the Constitution as if it is a machine, and if we approve its design and function, we logically ought to assume a conservative position against "tinkering with the machinery of government" and our social task is limited to routine maintenance in order to keep the equipment in operation. For most organisms, orderly and usually slow growth is a requisite of living, but uncontrolled and too rapid growth is pathological and typically results in either impairment of normal function or death of the entire organism. In constitutional terms, this implies that evolutionary—but not revolutionary—adaptation to the shifting requirements of the political environment is to be anticipated, and indeed, encouraged; and there is a correspondingly ambivalent standpoint toward such methods of constitutional change as formal amendments, judicial interpretation, and custom and usage. For a community, however, continuing change is a correlate of the exchange of information, and is therefore a predominant characteristic of the communication process. When the Constitution is viewed as the legal manifestation of a community, there is (relative to the other two models) maximal empathy for change. Indeed, the Constitution, a patterning of the values of many living people, is itself in continuous flux because of the information-producing and -transmitting activities of elites who seek to reinforce or modify the constitutional values of the masses of other persons who comprise the bulk of the community.

Neither is Table 47 intended to suggest that each new model has tended to displace its predecessors; to the contrary, their interrelationship is complementary, since each helps to explain certain phenomena better than its alternatives. The Newtonian universe defines nature as it is ordinarily perceived in human experience; the developmental organisms of Darwinian evolution populate and inhabit the apparent Newtonian environment, but the social relationships among these human organisms are better understood in terms of a more open model of structure and change than either of the older two is capable of providing.

In the social sciences in general, and in political science in particular, most of the classical literature which is accepted as constituting the stockpile of substantive knowledge about the subject of the discipline relates to a society (including a polity) that is molded upon the mechanical model. However, this does not mean that the mechanical approach is the one which dominates inquiry in the social sciences today. Rather, it is the organic concept of society which, after having become established as the prevailing mood in general sociological theory, now appears to have achieved the status of orthodoxy as the conventional temper (under a variety of aliases and in the form of such isotopes as structural-functionalism, transactionalism, systems analysis, etc.) in the political science of the nineteen-sixties. Behavioral theory has made much greater headway in psychology and anthropology than in political science, although this need not preclude us from asking what it might have to offer to us in our attempt to enhance our understanding of development and change in the emerging Constitution in the United States at the present time.

In the discussion that follows, I should like first to sketch more fully each of the three models, as these might relate to constitutional change. Next I shall attempt to exemplify the different kinds of questions which one would deduce as appropriate for investigation under each of the three models, using for empirical data the events associated with three forms of equality which have been important as contemporary issues of constitutional policy. Finally,

I shall discuss the differential implications of the three models for action programs of constitutional change in relation to civil disarmament, an emerging issue of public policy, thereby exploring in greater depth these varying perspectives of the emerging Constitution.

## II. MODES OF DISCOURSE

### A

The United States Constitution necessarily was a by-product of the scientific metaphor of its age,[6] and the science of the eighteenth century was one which hypothesized a determinate world in which all bodies moved inexorably in accordance with the vectorial pressures of universal force. The Constitution is a blueprint for a machine. To be more explicit, and following Landau:

> In physics a system is called mechanical, as with Newton, "if and only if its basic entities are particles that move in orbit." That is, it must be a closed system consisting of discrete bodies, each possessing a specific set of properties (such as mass and position) that act over space and time in accordance with fixed law. The motion of a body is unequivocally determined by the action of other bodies in the system. Changes in position are always and solely a function of the masses of the system members and the distances between them. In such a system there is only lawful behavior: from a definite configuration of particles there will always follow the same results; there are no alternatives, and there is nothing any part of the system can do about it. It is possible, therefore, to build a completely predictable structure. Since the state of the system at any one time determines its state at another, one may predict the future if one knows the present. Hence the method of analysis is to reduce any process to its irreducible elements or parts, and to treat process as the resultant of these separate parts acting externally on one another. (1961:337)

Deutsch has provided an alternative description of the mechanical model:

> The classical concept or model of mechanism implied the notion of a whole which was completely equal to the sum of its parts; which could be run in reverse; and which would behave in exactly identical fashion no matter how often those parts were disassembled and put together again, and irrespective of the sequence in which the disassembling or re-assembling would take place. It implied consequently the notion that the parts were never significantly modified by each other, nor by their own past, and that each part once placed into its appropriate position with its appropriate momentum, would stay exactly there and continue to fulfill its completely and uniquely determined function.
>
> This classical notion of mechanism was a strictly metaphysical concept. No thing completely fulfilling these conditions has ever been on land, or sea, or even, as our cosmologists have told us, among the stars. The more complicated a modern mechanical device becomes in practice, the more important becomes the interdependence and mutual interaction of its parts through wear and friction,

---

6. For a contrary view, see James A. Robinson 1957; for a supporting view, see Pargellis 1938:46.

and the interdependence of all those parts with their environment, as to temperature, moisture, magnetic, and electrical and other influences. The more exacting we make the standards for the performance of a real "mechanism," the less "mechanical" in the classical sense does it become. Even an automobile engine must be "broken in," and a highly accurate timing device depends so much on its environment that it must be assembled in air-conditioned workrooms by workers with dry fingertips. (1951:234)

The fundamental elements of the Constitution are familiar to us all: the national vis-à-vis the individual state governments, and each of the states vis-à-vis each other; the Congress, the president, and the Supreme Court; and in either direct or indirect apposition to these engines, under the federal division and the separation of powers, we the people of the United States are massed. Each of the major elements is subdivided into constituent parts. Thus, the Congress consists of the Senate and the House; the president is distinguished from the executive departments, the principal officers of which must report to him in writing upon his request; and it is presumed that the Supreme Court will review the decisions of inferior courts.[7] The ultimate particles of the Constitution—what a less respectful person than I might call the nuts and bolts of the machine—are the individual incumbents of the public offices for which it provides, such as president, elector, senator, representative, judge, ambassador, juror, and citizen.

The manifest purpose of the Constitution is to define, allocate, and restrain the transmission of power throughout the machinery of government. The president, for example, moves within an orbit defined by the federal division of powers, the separation of powers, and the Bill of Rights. It would be banal to recount the checks and balances that restrain him; I shall instead simply suggest their image by mentioning legislation, appropriations, confirmation of appointments, impeachment, and judicial review. As recently as a generation ago we find an exceptionally sophisticated, as well as articulate, associate justice of the United States Supreme Court invoking the explicitly mechanical metaphor of hydrodynamics first to support[8] and then to restrain[9] the exercise of presidential-congressional power in the heyday of the New Deal. Certainly for most lawyers, and probably also for most political scientists and other commentators upon constitutional change, classical physics continues to provide the orientation, the vocabulary, and the criteria deemed most relevant for analyses—even today as we enter the latter third of the twentieth century—of the meaning of "the contemporary constitutional situation," as well as of prescriptions for its betterment.

---

7. Further compartmentalization into such structural components as legislative committees and subcommittees, or bureaus and offices, although not explicitly mentioned in the document, certainly is consistent with the grosser pattern that is specified.

8. "Discretion is not unconfined and vagrant. It is canalized within banks to keep it from overflowing." Cardozo, dissenting in *Panama Refining Co.* v. *Ryan.*

9. "The delegated power of legislation which has found expression in this code is not canalized within banks that keep if from overflowing. It is unconfined and vagrant. . . . This is delegation running riot." Cardozo, concurring in *Schechter Poultry Co.* v. *United States.*

We find, for example, that traditionally oriented lawyers and political scientists typically propose to bring about changes in function (i.e., in future outcomes which they deem desirable) by accomplishing ad hoc modifications in the machinery of government, such as by changing the structural parts assumed to be the "cause" of the unwanted present outcomes. The shortest way with political dissenters is to require them to confess their crimes by changing the text of the constitutional document[10]; the best way to control a zealous bureacracy is to change the carburetor of the administrative engine from down-draft to up-draft, and add a governor.[11]

The persistence of the mechanistic mode of thought is demonstrated also by the contemporary writings of a leading political theorist, David Easton. In an influential earlier book, Easton defined policy-making, the characteristic and principal task of government, to be "*the authoritative* allocation of values for a society" (Easton 1953 : 129–134, emphasis added). A problem of his continuing attempts to discuss a biological model of political systems is Easton's relentless endeavor to square the circle by retaining his mechanical definition of policy-making as the *deus ex machina* of his biological systems theory.[12] Even if one is going to insist upon the efficacy of biological patterns for the understanding of political action, it may be more efficient, as Landau persuasively has argued (1961:332–333), to eschew mixed metaphors, and to work with an organic rather than a mechanical analogy as one's central concept[13] to explain systemic change.

### B

> One peculiarity of this age [wrote Walter Bagehot a century ago] is the sudden acquisition of much physical knowledge. There is scarcely a department of science or art which is the same, or at all the same, as it was fifty years ago. A new world of inventions . . . has grown up around us which we cannot help seeing; a new world of ideas is in the air and affects us, though we do not see it. A full estimate of these effects would require a great book, and I am sure I could not write it; but I think I may usefully . . . show how . . . the new ideas are modifying two old sciences—politics and political economy. (1908 edition:1)

And only last year, we find a political scientist proclaiming that "we are witnessing the greatest breakthrough in science of all time. Every generation invariably believes that its own time is the most revolutionary, but never in man's history have so many new discoveries in so many fields been made in

---

10. See Mayers 1959. For a contrasting behavioral approach to this problem, see Stouffer 1955.

11. See Abraham 1965. Cf. Edward S. Corwin's proposal to substitute the British for the American cabinet system (1957).

12. Easton 1965*a*:50, 96–97. "[I]ts characteristic mode of behaving as a political system . . . [is] the capacity of the system to allocate values for the society and assure their acceptance" (p. 96). Cf. Easton 1965*b*:349–350. For an earlier but similar endeavor, see McBain 1927.

13. "[The outputs of interest to our analysis] are closely associated with those who hold the positions of authority in the system and thereby set the goals toward which the energies and resources of the system may be directed. This is why I have called them authoritative allocations of values. They are central to our analysis. . . ." (Easton 1965*b*:350)

such a short span of time" (Thorbecke 1965 : 17). Although somewhat widely separated in space and time, these two authors share the objective of urging that biological and, explicitly, evolutionary theory be made the model for political analysis, in both descriptive and normative terms. They differ in that Bagehot was perhaps ahead of his own era and Thorbecke most certainly lags behind ours.

But explicitly what does it mean to suggest that we should pattern political life upon a biological model? Deutsch says that:

> According to the classical view, an "organism" is unanalyzable, at least in part. It cannot be taken apart and put together again without damage. As Wordsworth put it, "We murder to dissect." The parts of a classical organism, in so far as they can be identified at all, not only retain the functions which they have been assigned but in fact cannot be put to any other functions (except within narrow limits of "de-differentiation" which were often ignored), without destroying the organism. The classical organism's behavior is irreversible. It has a significant past and a history—two things which the classical mechanism lacks—but it is only half historical because it was believed to follow its own peculiar "organic law" which governs its birth, maturity, and death, and which cannot be analyzed in terms of clearly identifiable "mechanical" causes.
>
> Attempts have been frequent to apply this classical concept of organism to biology and to human society. On the whole they have been unsuccessful. While "organismic" models might sometimes help to balance the onesidedness of a "mechanical" approach, biologists have failed to derive significant predictions or experiments from the supposed "life force" of nineteenth-century "vitalists," and the inadequacies of organismic theories of society or history have been even more conspicuous. In one aspect organismic notions could be used to draw attention to processes of *growth*: organisms, after all, were supposed to grow before they reached maturity, though not afterwards. (1951:236)

Moreover, as Landau has pointed out:

> A biological system never *is*: it is always happening. It is in continuous interchange with its environment. Accordingly . . . a statement of the biological form "not only relates to the organism but takes in a part of the environment." Which is to state that things and entities, organs and parts are not the essentials of the system: rather, the essentials are specified relationships of a structural-functional nature. Here structure is not a "sum" of the separate parts acting on each other, of the separate organs adding up to a unit, as it is a slow relational process of long duration, the description of which presupposes a stoppage of time and constitutes a momentary glimpse of what is happening. It is only relative to function, a fast process of short duration, that a structure appears constant. Constancy, thus, is not a matter of material substance as it is a matter of form of relationship—relationships that we know as boundary exchanges, mutual interdependence, self-regulation, adaptation to disturbance, approaches to steady states. And by the logic of the system, to speak of one is to "take in" the others. That is, boundary exchange is defined in terms of mutual interdependence which is defined in terms of self-regulation which is defined in terms of adaptation which is defined in terms of steady states. One presupposes the other. The logic of this system is of the order of "transactionalism" as Dewey and Bentley formulated it. What it requires is a close attention to relationship not to things. What it requires is that we minimize nouns. That we see politics as a set of relationships

in a stated environment; that a political leader is not a noun, that a leader is defined in terms of a follower, that it presupposes follower, that you cannot conceive of a leader without a follower, that to speak of one is to speak of the other. That there is no noun federalism but there is a federative relationship such that a statement about the central government is a statement about the states. And so on. The unit of analysis is always a relationship of transactional character and comprehends context and process.[14] (1965b:8–9)

Since the end of World War II, American political science has moved away from the traditional, mechanistic approach to the study of politics to such an extent that the biological metaphor is now the conventional one. We know it, generally, under the rubric "The Political Process" approach; and we associate with it what already has become a classical literature, including such names as Bentley (1955), Herring (1929), and Truman (1951). The shift has been from formal interaction between institutions to informal transactions among groups; and although the political process approach came initially to other sectors of political research, it has now been over a decade since Peltason issued a call for a jurisprudence based upon the group struggle among interest groups.[15] The judicial process approach, as it tends to be called, is now the modal position for research and teaching in American political science today in the field traditionally known as public law.[16]

The biological metaphor requires that we analogize sets of political events to series of life processes. If we are interested in constitutional change, we must seek to observe a vast array of activities that are taking place at and within the boundaries of a manifold of events that we delimit conceptually, for analytical purposes, as the political system (Mitchell 1962). The political system—or polity—is, on the one hand, a subsystem of an even more general social system, while at the same time the political system subsumes a set of subsystems, of which the judicial system is one. Thus conceived, the judicial system includes both federal and state courts as so-called concrete structures, and attention focuses primarily upon functional relationships within the system.[17] In order to discuss constitutional change, however, we must be concerned with the broader field of action encompassed by the political system, since only a part of the relevant activities will be confined in scope to the judicial system.[18] It seems altogether likely that, with regard to any particular policy issue, the findings and conclusions that we might reach about constitutional change, when we have analyzed it in relationship to the political

14. "The application of a biological model to politics," he adds, "is no easy task." (1965b:9)
15. Peltason 1953:51–56. Peltason was anticipated some two decades earlier by the precocious Karl N. Llewellyn, whose "rediscovery" of Bentley (1934) proved to be abortive, since he wrote for the wrong audience (i.e., lawyers).
16. For recent articulations of this point of view, see Jacob 1965; Shapiro 1964a.
17. For a more explicit articulation of structural-functional theory as a conceptual framework for analyzing the judicial process, see Schubert 1965d.
18. For an excellent example of such an analysis, see Danelski 1964, and especially Part Three, in which the author interprets his empirical data in terms of transactional theory.

system, may differ markedly from those that we would derive from an appraisal of constitutional change in the machinery of government.

In the mechanistic model, the Constitution is a blueprint—a design for the construction of institutional structures. The Constitution defines the pattern which determines the structure of the institutions. In the biological model, however, the opposite is true. Change in institutional structure is slow, but it is also inexorable. Nature, not the Constitution, is the cause of institutional evolution; and the function of the Constitution in an organic model of the polity is to maintain a reasonably up-to-date "Restatement" (to borrow a legal concept) of both the contemporary institutional structures of government and of their functional relationships. In the idiom of John Marshall, "the prolixity of a legal code" (*McCulloch* v. *Maryland*, at p. 407) is precisely what is required of the Constitution, as the following sketch of the opening clauses of a draft of the Constitution (but in the organic mode) may suggest:

> Article I.   Section 1.   Legislation is a function which consists of the concurrence of both houses of the Congress in proposals which previously have been agreed to by the Administration.
>
>   2. Administrative participation in legislation is a function of several subprocesses, two of which involve executive clearance of proposals:
>   A. Executive bill clearance.
>     (1) A member of the classified civil service, usually in cooperation with other civil servants and with representatives of various organizations of persons who are not governmental employees, will suggest a proposal.
>     (2) [Administrative review, by the agency, of the proposal]
>     (3) [Consultation with legislative subcommittees and staff]
>     (4) [Consultation with other clientele groups]
>     (5) [Budget Bureau clearance with other agencies]
>   B. Enrolled bill clearance.
>     [Etc.]

The possibility of planned change is not precluded by the biological model, but it becomes a very much more complicated matter than it is for mechanists. Instead of focusing upon linguistic change in the document and letting the institutional chips fall where they may,[19] the social engineer must, under the biological model, make predictions concerning how changes in the practices of one subsystem are likely to affect practices in many other related subsystems. For example, suppose it were proposed that the seniority system for committee assignments and status in Congress ought to be abolished.[20] The biological metaphor requires that to recommend change in the

---

19. Cf. the consequences of the adoption of the Fourteenth Amendment.

20. For a variety of what may seem to most political scientists to be very good reasons: it leads to too much overspecialization among congressmen; it fails to select the best men for positions of functional leadership; it results in overrepresentation of minority segments of the public; it encourages too-detailed congressional surveillance of administration; it fosters the overconcentration of authority in committee chairmen; it gives too much weight to the Southern political culture; etc.

seniority system, it is necessary to attempt to predict at least the range of variation in the processes of a large number of related subsystems.[21] Otherwise there would be no basis for being able to conclude whether the balance of beneficial and of deleterious side effects of the proposed change would be more or less desirable than the anticipated direct benefits expected to result from the abolition of the seniority system.

The biological approach to politics puts flesh upon the endoskeleton of mechanically motivated political structures; but both the conventional and the traditional approaches leave political behavior unexamined at the level of the discrete, individual human being. To the extent that the mechanical approach is concerned with the motivations of individual humans, it imputes these as rational inferences from the natural order—that is to say, as commonsensical rather than as scientific observations. Thus we have the sweeping majesty of the generalizations about human behavior to be found in such relevant sources as *The Federalist* or John Marshall's opinions.[22] In such sources the function of assertions about human behavior is rhetorical, since the operations of the machinery of government depend, not upon what goes on inside individuals, but rather upon the relationships between institutions, "to the end," in the language of Article XXX of the Massachusetts Constitution of 1780, "that it be a government of laws, and not of men."

It is perhaps not surprising that the mechanical orientation tends to define individuals as automata; but we might not have anticipated that a political metaphor which emulates life processes would define political action not as political behavioralism, but rather as Watsonian behaviorism. A leading conventional thinker tells us, for example, that

> Judicial activities are . . . reflections of the legal rules which have the support of the most powerful interests of society. . . .
>
> It is questionable . . . if [the] search for "mind-stuff" is . . . a fruitful endeavor for political scientists.
> . . . [T]he notion [persists] that the extent to which a judge makes policy is an attribute of his personality, that a judge may choose to enter or refrain from entering the group struggle that we call politics. But a judge cannot avoid taking sides. The judiciary is in politics not because of the desire of the individual justice but because it makes decisions. . . .
>
> [I]f we turn our attention to the judiciary as a facet in the group struggle and

---

21. E.g., programmatic and personnel changes in: executive agencies cognate to particular congressional committees and subcommittees; state and local political party organizations; the probable content of policy norms embodied in legislation; the presidency, due to the differing character of the Congress with which presidents will have to interact; the federal district courts, in particular, and judicial patronage; etc.

22. E.g., "That the power to tax involves the power to destroy" in *McCulloch* v. *Maryland*, at p. 431. Nor is it surprising to find, again in the same opinion in the same case, at least an equally famous dictum in the organic mode: "we must never forget that it is a constitution we are expounding," and one which is "intended to endure for ages to come, and consequently, to be adapted to the various crises of human affairs" (pp. 407, 415). Marshall, as usual, was interested in political effect, rather than in the consistency of his metaphors.

relate the activities of judges to that of other groups, we can begin to develop a political science of public law without trying to "out-history" the historian, "out-law" the lawyer, or "out-psychology" the psychologist. (Peltason 1953:53, 55, 56)

We are advised, in short, to confine our attention, as analysts of constitutional (or any other kind of political) change, to empirical descriptions, letting others worry about why we observe what is manifestly there to see.

## C

It is entirely possible, however, to derive from the underlying biological metaphor theories of communication which emphasize human psychology and physiology, and indeed which posit political systems modeled in part upon the biological processes of human beings (Deutsch 1963; Wiener 1954). As explained by Deutsch the model of the communications network integrates selected characteristics of both machines *and* organisms, which results in a much less rigid and more flexible view of reality than is provided by either of the two older models:

> [W]e may derive from them [cybernetics, the science of communication and control], a generalized concept of a *self-modifying communications network* or "learning net."
>
> . . . [C]*ommunications engineering transfers information.* It does not transfer events; *it transfers a patterned relationship between* events. . . .
>
> . . . From the amount of information transmitted as against the information lost, we may derive a measure for the *efficiency* of a channel, as well as of the relative efficiency or *complementarity* of any parts or stages of the channel in relation to the others.
>
> These patterns of information can be measured in quantitative terms, described in mathematical language, analyzed by science, and transmitted or operated on a practical industrial scale.
>
> . . . By a *society* we may designate a group of persons who "have learned to work together," that is, persons tied together by some division of labor, some exchange of goods and services, with only as much communication essential to its functioning as is required to get these goods or services exchanged. By a *community* we mean a group of persons united by their ability to exchange information. A society can carry on economic processes as studied by economics but only a community can carry a culture as studied by cultural anthropology. Society and community, or therefore, society and culture, may or may not coincide for the same set of persons. . . .
>
> The *complementarity* of the parts of any communications channel or system may be defined as their capacity of transmitting information to each other. It can be tested and even measured by suitable operations. This is true not only for the parts of a mechanical or electrical communication system but also of the members of a communications system made up of human beings. We may use, therefore, complementarity as a measure for the unity and inner cohesion of a group.

In particular, we may define therefore a *people* as a larger group of persons linked by complementary habits and facilities of communication, or more briefly, as a community of both internal and social communications equipment. . . .

With the aid of these models, we may recognize a basic pattern which minds, societies, and self-modifying communications networks have in common. Engineers have called this pattern the "feedback."

. . . [B]y feedback is meant a communications network which produces action in response to an input of information and *includes the results of its own action in the new information by which it modifies its subsequent behavior.* . . .

*Values* have material reality in any such communications system: we may think of them as the operating preferences according to which certain messages rather than others are transmitted, or transmitted first. . . .

A "machine" has been defined as an "apparatus for applying mechanical power, having several *parts each with definite function*"; and an organism as a "body with *connected interdependent parts* sharing common life"; and an "organ" as a "part of animal or vegetable body adapted for special vital functions." Both machines and organisms are . . . characterized by a high degree of permanence in the functions assigned to each part, be it a cog in the wheel or an organ grown permanently in its place in the body. Learning nets may conform to these limitations, if they are of mechanical or organic construction, but their functions as learning nets may point beyond these limits, to the different characteristics of societies.

. . . [T]his *possibility of relatively free transfer and recombination*, not only of the symbols treated, but *of the very physical elements* of a *learning net* for the performance of new operations, is the critical property which makes a given learning net into a *society*.

A learning net functions as a society, in this view, to the extent that its constituent physical parts are capable of regrouping themselves into new patterns of activity in response to changes in the net's surroundings, or in response to the internally accumulating results of their own or the net's past.

The twin tests by which we can tell a society from an organism or a machine, on this showing, would be the freedom of its parts to regroup themselves; and the nature of the regroupings, which must imply new coherent patterns of activity—in contrast to the mere wearing of a machine or the aging of an organism, which are marked by relatively few degrees of freedom and by the gradual disappearance of coherent patterns of activity. . . .

The difference between organisms and societies rests, then, in the degree of freedom of their parts, and the degree of effectiveness of their recombinations to new coherent patterns of activity.

This in turn may rest on specific properties of their members: their *capacity for readjustment to new configurations, with renewed complementarity and sustained or removed communication.*

The degree of complementarity between the members of a society may determine its capacity for sustained coherence, while their degree of freedom—and their range of readjustments available without loss of complementarity—may determine the society's capacity for sustained growth. . . . The more complex and readjustable the constituent parts of a society become, the greater the coherence and freedom of each of its subassemblies, the greater should be the society's possibilities of itself achieving greater coherence and freedom in the course of its history. Learning nets and societies do not grow best by simplifying or rigidly subordinating their parts or members, but rather with the complexity and freedom of these members, so long as they succeed in maintaining or increasing communication, both with each other and with the outside world—communication of increasing variety, richness, precision, and freedom for new kinds of intake and new recombinations. (Deutsch 1963:240–252 passim; emphasis in the original)

The model of many contemporary communications systems, such as a modern electronic computer installation or Telstar, suggests not only a world but also a universe in continual flux and with elementary particles of subatomic dimensions. The behavior of these elementary particles is governed to a considerable extent by chance (Aubert 1959; Moore and Sussman 1932), as distinguished from the structure of organic particles, which are affected less conspicuously by chance (through mutation and in reproduction) and in sharp contradistinction from the completely determined behavior of mechanical particles.

From the cultural point of view, the individual is the atom of political action, and the small group is the molecule of political interaction (Pritchett 1948; Schubert 1965c). But behavioral analysis, unlike nuclear physics, inevitably involves working within the framework of the biological metaphor, since these particles of social action and interaction are clusterings of living persons. However, a major difference between the cultural and the organic approaches is that behavioral analysis goes beyond large group theory by viewing social clusters as aggregations of individual behaviors rather than as (e.g., for purposes of sociological analysis) entities having an independent existence.

But what do such physical attributes—indeterminacy, unrestricted growth and development,[23] chance occurrence, and autogenous learning (i.e., feedback)—imply for the modeling of social relationships? These are the very qualities which many social psychologists and other behavioral scientists have stressed as the hallmark of a democratic constitutional polity (Lasswell and Kaplan 1950: esp. xvii–xviii; Rokeach 1960). It may be, therefore, that what we seek is the concept of constitutionalism suggested by the political behavioral point of view, under which what counts most directly in initiating constitutional change is the "political wisdom" (i.e., the values, attitudes, ideologies, information, experience, socialization, and skill in predicting probable consequences for alternative outcome possibilities) of a majority of the incumbent set of most relevant political decision-makers.

From a behavioral point of view, decision-makers such as voters, legislators, judges, administrators, and chief executives act in socially defined roles in relation to policy issues of contemporary importance. Decision-making roles become "socially defined" as a consequence of more or less con-

---

23. And often in response to serendipity (another name for expediency and opportunism) rather than to genetic or vectorial combinations.

sensual expectations about how persons in particular relationships to others ought to act; these norms relate to both the procedures by which they make decisions and the substantive content of such decisions. Issues become recognized as important as a consequence of the attempts of decision-makers to anticipate what are likely to be recognized (either at moderate to high intensity by many sectors of their relevant clientele, or at high intensity by a few sectors) as allocations of goods and values that affect their clientele's needs, wants, goals, beliefs, and so forth. The study of political behavior is therefore the analysis of how, why, and with what effects decisions are made that affect public policy and political action. Public policy consists of patterns of norms which articulate ideals of behavior; political action consists of whatever men do in their attempts to influence either the statement of norms or behavior that is the subject of norms. From this point of view, public policy norms *are* metaphors, in the figurative sense, since they are assertions that people are behaving in ways that they never are *universally* behaving.

Let us consider a few examples of public policy norms:

(1) All men are created free and equal.
(2) We the People of the United States . . . do ordain and establish this Constitution.
(3) No State shall . . . deny to any person within its jurisdiction the equal protection of the laws.
(4) The opportunity for an education is a right available to all on equal terms.
(5) One man, one vote.
(6) Equal justice under law, for rich and poor alike.

One characteristic shared by the above propositions is that they are relatively abstract norms; all are at the level of generality (vacuity) characteristic of constitutional documentary norms. Other more explicit norm statements might be:

(1) Speed limit: 20 m.p.h.
(2) Keep off the grass.
(3) Stop.

But in the case of either the constitutional or the traffic norms, the focus of interest for political analysis is upon: (1) the factors underlying the decisions to establish the norms in their past, present, and probable future form—what Lasswell calls developmental analysis; (2) the degree and causes of the gap between the ideal behaviors posited by the norm and the behaviors that empirically can be observed; and (3) the probable consequences that alternative proposals to restate norms are most likely to have in terms of present and future political behavior. From a cultural (relativistic) point of view, constitutional norms are only a special and limited case of political norms.

They are important because, at least in many parts of the American culture, the Constitution (in either a literal or in an extensive sense of its authoritatively expounded "true" meaning) is invested with an aura of prestige which makes its manipulation in support of or in opposition to preferred political values a question of great political significance.

Lawyers generally, judges more particularly, and the United States Supreme Court *par excellence*, are accepted in most parts of the American culture as the legitimate expositors of constitutional doctrine. In analogical (as distinguished from metaphorical) terms we might say that just as the pope is the infallible expositor of Christian truth for Roman Catholics, so the Supreme Court expounds constitutional truth for the faithful members of the American body politic.[24] The Supreme Court's most important political function is to legitimate (or to *il*legitimate) the decisions of actors in the American political system, and the Court's manipulation of the meaning of the Constitution (e.g., of constitutional doctrine) is a quantitatively lesser but qualitatively major instrument for providing such legitimations and illegitimations (Hamilton 1938b:167–190).

The Court states constitutional norms in opinions that are written to accompany its decisions. But the Court makes decisions through the deliberation and voting and opinion writing of nine individual justices, who act under the procedural norm of majority rule. Therefore, from a behavioral point of view, "the Constitution" is, in a narrow but important sense, whatever at least a majority of the incumbent justices are willing to agree, for purposes of decision-making, that it ought to be said to mean. In the same sense, the Constitution is what the incumbent president (or those who speak in his name) or what various members of Congress (in relation to their sectors of functional expertise) may proclaim by word or by deed. A Harry Truman who recalls a MacArthur or who directs the use of nuclear weapons is, like a Thomas Jefferson purchasing the Louisiana Territory, interpreting the Constitution; but so is an Adam Clayton Powell, who from extraterritorial hideaways presided over both his Harlem fief and the House Education and Labor Committee, in the first instance as an absentee political landlord and in the second as a chairman *in absentia*, all in the name of the combined sacrosanctity of congressional immunity and seniority.

In a broader sense of the cultural standpoint, however, neither the justices of the Supreme Court nor the president nor congressmen nor members of other or affiliated political elites can interpret the Constitution. What these

---

24. It has been barely a dozen or so years since John F. Kennedy, as an American citizen and Catholic layman who was then also a potential president, felt compelled to confess his differentiation between his obligation to the pope and his obligations to the Constitution, and, at least by strong implication, to the justices of the Supreme Court, who are (metaphorically speaking) the vestal virgins of the sacred meaning to be associated with it. By the same metaphor, the Judicial Conference of the United States is the Court's College of Cardinals, and the American judiciary is its hierocracy.

elites can (and do) do is to influence the beliefs and thereby the actions of each other and of their publics; and it is there, in the consensually dominant patterns of values that constitute American political ideologies, that "the Constitution" is to be found. Like the very foremost of the Founding Fathers, the Constitution lives on in the hearts of his countrymen.

## III. FORMS OF EQUALITY

In an attempt further to sharpen the differing implications of our three models of constitutional change, let us consider the kinds of questions that one ought logically to infer, as a means of guiding inquiry into what the model would suggest is significant, about several contemporary issues of constitutional policy. For such exemplification, I have selected three major aspects of the ideological dimension of egalitarianism: racial, representational, and procedural.

### A. Racial Equality

1. TRADITIONAL.[25] In its decision in *Brown* v. *Board of Education*, did the Supreme Court follow stare decisis?

Did the Court substitute social psychology, or the philosophic beliefs of individual justices, for law and legal authority?

Did the Court engage in judicial activism in the *Brown* case?

Was the Court's decision politically irresponsible and subversive of the constitutional separation of powers, since the power to make any such decision rightfully belonged to the Congress?[26]

Is the Court's decision a threat to the maintenance of our federal division of powers by arrogating to the federal government control over public education, a subject which the Constitution has reserved for state control?

Is the pattern of the Court's decisions dealing with racial integration, especially during the decade of the nineteen-fifties, a real threat to civil liberties, since the use of federal troops to enforce individual claims to civil rights creates a dangerous kind of "police state" precedent, which is contrary to the basic premises of our democratic system?

2. CONVENTIONAL. What was the effect upon the recent change in national policy toward racial integration, of the realignment of interest groups in the two major political parties, consequent upon the defeat of both the Dixiecrats and the Progressive party in the 1948 presidential election?

To what extent was the decision in the *Brown* case due to the growth of an urban Negro electorate? To the increasing strength of organized labor?

---

25. Since we are here concerned with orientations toward research, I shall identify each of the sets of questions by the model's corresponding academic ideology (mechanical = traditional; biological = conventional; cultural = behavioral). See Table 47 and note b to Table 47.

26. Cf. Crosskey 1953; Schwartz 1963.

To the activities of the NAACP, the Urban League, the ACLU, the American Jewish Congress? What was the effect upon the development of integration policy, of groups which were fostered by it (i.e., CORE, Black Muslims, White Citizens Councils, the resurgence of the Ku Klux Klan)?

How are the Civil Rights Acts of 1964 and 1965[27] an outgrowth of the continuing interaction between Congress and the Court, and hence related to the Court's earlier interpretation of the Fourteenth Amendment and the Civil Rights Acts of the Reconstruction era?

How is the Court's decision in the *Brown* case related to Franklin Roosevelt's failure to purge the Democratic party, with the consequent resurgence of Southern influence in both houses?

3. BEHAVIORAL. What have been the individual ideologies of Supreme Court Justices since 1937?

What kind of skills, as a lawyer and political organizer, does Thurgood Marshall have? What will be the effect upon future integration policy of his appointment to the Supreme Court?

What role did Howard University play in the socialization of plaintiffs and counsel in the early generation of court cases to raise the issue? In the socialization, at a later time, of Freedom Riders and voting registration assistants? How was the emergence of this issue affected by changes in the international cultural milieu (i.e., the rise of new nations in Africa and Asia)?

How is national integration policy related to urbanization and mass education?

To what extent, and how, was the Court's decision, and its implementation, influenced by the prior establishment of consensus within the scientific community that available evidence required the rejection of deterministic rationales for the justification of racial inequality?

## B. *Representational Equality*

1. TRADITIONAL. Can we reconcile, with the constitutional separation of powers, having federal judges thrust into the activist role of deciding the basis upon which the people will choose their representatives in Congress?

How can the states remain laboratories of socioeconomic experimentation if they no longer are free to experiment?

Does *Baker* v. *Carr* violate the Tenth Amendment?

Is the interference of judges with "politics of the people" incompatible with the basic premises of our democratic system?

Is *Baker* v. *Carr* (like *Swift* v. *Tyson*) an unconstitutional usurpation of power by the national government?

---

27. Civil Rights Act of 1964, 78 Stat. 241 (1964) (codified in scattered sections of 5, 28, 42 U.S.C.); Voting Rights Act of 1965, 79 Stat. 437, 42 U.S.C. §§ 1971, 1973 (Supp. I, 1965).

Does the Supreme Court's reapportionment policy violate the due process clauses of both the Fifth and the Fourteenth amendments by sacrificing, to the overriding interests of merely numerical majorities, minority rights to "liberty" and "property"?

2. CONVENTIONAL.[28] To what extent was the timing of the Supreme Court's announcement of a new policy on legislative reapportionment a function of the increasing urban proportion of the national population?

How is reapportionment related to the finding of the Kestnbaum Commission's Report (1955; and cf. Gottman 1961) that megalopolitan regions—not states—are now the key units in the intergovernmental complex?

How is the persistence of the constitutional structure of federalism related to the extraconstitutional and decentralized structure of the American political party system?

Is *Baker* v. *Carr* leading to centralization of political parties, first at the state and then at the national level? To what extent will the national centralization of political parties (as recommended a decade and a half ago by the American Political Science Association's Committee on Political Parties [1950]) function as a catalyst to hasten the atrophy of the states as units of governmental structure?

Does *Baker* v. *Carr* fulfill the basic function of closing the gap between the political party system and the functional requisites of the American polity in the mid-twentieth century?

How does reapportionment policy relate to the urbanization of state politics?

Has American federalism been important primarily in an instrumental sense by bridging the gap between the autonomous colonies of the Revolutionary era and the nation of today?

3. BEHAVIORAL. Is *Colegrove* v. *Green* best explained on the basis of chance considerations (i.e., Stone's death, Jackson's absence in Europe, Rutledge's concern for idiosyncratic [procedural] aspects of this particular case)?

If *Colegrove* v. *Green* (instead of *Baker* v. *Carr*) had become the instrument for announcing the new reapportionment policy, what effect would this have had upon the Court's capacity to develop a new policy for racial integration?

If *Colegrove* had been the instrument, what would have been the effect upon the structuring of compliance, of the loss of the favorable majority within three years due to the deaths of Murphy and Rutledge? What would have been the effect of having Truman president instead of Eisenhower?

On what bases can we explain Frankfurter's intense opposition to the Court's reapportionment policy, as distinguished from his reluctant acquiescence in the Court's integration policy?

---

28. I am particularly indebted, for the questions in this section, to Landau 1965a.

How was the implementation of *Baker* v. *Carr* affected by President Kennedy's appointment of over a hundred new federal judges (over a fourth of the total federal judiciary) in the same year that the decision was announced?

How is *Baker* v. *Carr* related to the coming of age of the older immigrant classes (i.e., to the ideological and political integration of their children)?[29]

## C. Procedural Equality

1. TRADITIONAL. Do recent changes in the interpretation of the Constitution demonstrate that the elder John Marshall Harlan was correct about the proper construction of the procedural guarantees of the Bill of Rights?

Should the Supreme Court have followed its precedents in *Barron* v. *Baltimore, Betts* v. *Brady,* and *Wolf* v. *Colorado,* instead of disregarding the intent of the framers of the Bill of Rights and the Fourteenth Amendment by distorting the Constitution to make it limit the powers of the states to protect the rights of the majority to life, liberty, and property?

Are the Court's recent decisions in cases such as *Gideon* v. *Wainwright, Mapp* v. *Ohio,* and *Douglas* v. *California* a departure from the concept of "ordered liberty," as enunciated for an almost unanimous Court by Mr. Justice Cardozo nearly thirty years ago?

2. CONVENTIONAL. To what extent are the Court's recent decisions, expanding the right to counsel in both trials and appeals before state courts, consequent upon the efforts of the American Bar Association and related lawyers' organizations to expand the employment opportunities for lawyers? From the point of view of local compliance with the Supreme Court's policy directives, is the recent expansion of the right to counsel possible now only because of the relative affluence today of local communities (i.e., their capacity to pay for the considerable increase in the public costs for providing legal services to indigent defendants)?

How has the Court been influenced in its development of more extensive civil rights and liberties for criminal defendants, by the explicitly relevant activities of the American Civil Liberties Union and similar groups? By the more diffuse political activities of civic action and proselyting carried out by the complex of groups and interests associated with the civil rights movement in recent years? In other words, to what extent has the Court been responsive to feedback from its own racial integration decisions?

Have the Court and the community been, at least to some extent, re-

---

29. We might hypothesize that such persons would be particularly sensitive to the gap between democratic ideology, in relation to representation theory in particular, and prevailing political practices, in view of the high correlation between immigrant concentrations and urban-rural differences.

sponsive to what might be conceptualized as the political demands of an expanded clientele (i.e., growth in the size and political influence of the criminal population)?

To what extent is the redefinition of Fourteenth Amendment due process of law in *Gideon* v. *Wainwright* and *Douglas* v. *California*, to extend the right to counsel for indigent criminal defendants before state courts, a satisfactory accommodation, for the time being, of the conflicting and overlapping interests of lawyers and their vocational development, the civil rights movement, taxpayers, "our convict population" (to borrow the late Mr. Justice Robert Jackson's colorful and characteristic phrase), the general population who are actual or potential victims of criminals, the police, et alia?

3. BEHAVIORAL. Is the most proximate explanation for the recent liberalization of constitutional policy in this field to be found in Kennedy's appointment of Goldberg (and Johnson's of Fortas), thereby providing, for the first time in our history, a solid majority of justices who are sympathetic to civil rights and liberties?

To what extent are the recent policy changes responsive to the influence of the national law schools, which provide the law clerks, supply through their reviews a continuing critical literature, and entertain Supreme Court justices, thereby providing a direct conversational link between them and distinguished members of law faculties?

Are the recent policy changes a reflection of the much better education, both university and legal, that contemporary justices have had, as compared to their predecessors of even a generation ago?

Is the recent expansion of civil liberties (as one sociologist has hypothesized [Snyder 1958:236–238]) a function of the increasingly liberal progression in the thrust of the development of the beliefs and attitudes of Americans?

Are Watts and Hough examples of popular response to the stimulus provided by the Court's decisions in racial and procedural equality cases of the past decade?

## IV. A PROPOSAL FOR CIVIL DISARMAMENT

Let us turn, finally, to the instrumental implications of the three models as a source of strategic and tactical prescriptions for any persons who might be interested, from an engineering point of view, in constitutional reform. What should they do? How can the models guide them?

In order to make the discussion more explicit, we need to assume a particular goal as the object of constitutional change. Both a worthy and a timely objective would be to propose a program of political action that would have the effect not of repealing but of *reversing* the Second Amendment.[30] In favor of such a proposal, on the merits, we may note the following considerations,[31] inter alia:

(1) "A well regulated Militia," armed with privately owned weapons, does not exist in the United States; it has not existed for over a century and a half; and if such a militia did exist in twentieth-century America, its chief political significance almost certainly would be not as a guarantee of the security of the government, but quite to the contrary as a major threat of subversion. It was through the use of such "well regulated Militia" that Hitler came to power in Nazi Germany; and today any organized private body of armed men would have to be viewed, in this country, as an incipient threat of extremist aggression against the presently prevailing constitutional order.

(2) Modern wars, other than civil, do not require the services of militia; neither do the skills of the gunfighter bulk large in the repertoire of expertises of the Defense Department today. (It is even possible that this point is related to the first point, above.)

(3) The Constitution does not include a guarantee of the right to duel (i.e., a guarantee as a civil liberty of the right to conduct private warfare). But this is strictly a matter of timing; duels were becoming illegal as well as unfashionable by the end of the eighteenth century, as Burr's shooting of Hamilton exemplifies. A constitution adopted in 1690 might well have included a constitutional right to duel, just as one adopted in 1890 almost certainly would *not* have contained the second amendment.

(4) Universal civil disarmament is probably a condition precedent to successful disarming of criminals, lunatics, children, and sportsmen.

(a) It seems likely that criminals of all ages will continue to gain access to weapons, both homemade and imported from countries whose citizens live under less enlightened constitutions. Incarcerated criminals get their weapons by these means, and it must be assumed that those with relatively greater freedom of maneuver will not do less. But it will be less convenient than it is now,[32] and considerably more expensive for the average criminal (who is not wealthy) to equip himself with guns.

---

30. "A well regulated Militia, being necessary to the security of a free State, the right of the people to keep and bear Arms, shall not be infringed." *United States Constitution*, amendment II.

31. See also Bakal 1966; Editorial 1966; Buchwald 1966, 1967.

32. According to an Associated Press newswire emanating from New York City in August 1966, the United States Department of Commerce estimated annual domestic production of firearms to be about two million weapons, plus over three-fourths of a million presently legal imports from abroad. For other estimates of the latter datum, see Hearings 1965 and Editorial 1967.

(b) The use of guns by lunatics to assassinate both extraordinary and ordinary targets who happen to fall within the scope of their sights has been particularly noteworthy in recent years. Such names as Lee Harvey Oswald, Jack Ruby, and Charles Whitman come readily to mind; and in each locality there are many other psychotics who fail to achieve national repute only because they kill smaller numbers of ordinary people. In Hawaii, for example, one would think of the Pali hunter, who perched near the spot where Kamehameha I pushed the remnants of the local Oahu militia over a sheer cliff of several hundred feet, one which still affords for tourists a spectacular view of the windward coast. Michael Patrick Moeller, a young man recently in and out of the local mental hospital, and with a previous police and psychiatric record of shooting at people, armed himself with a department store rifle and shot with some little success at tourists and police until he was persuaded to surrender in fear that the police were about to shoot him.

(c) Children, a not inconsiderable number of whom shoot each other, their parents, and friends of the family each year, typically with "unloaded" revolvers found under pillows and in bureau drawers, doubtless can be disarmed once their most convenient source of supply of weapons—in the master bedroom at home—is removed.

(d) This leaves the sportsmen, and they doubtless will constitute the most vocal and best organized opposition to the proposal. Their need for weapons to accomplish their nominal purposes is clear. Among the great areas for hunting is Michigan, a state which grows its deer as a crop, and in which the Department of Conservation manipulates a complex set of regulations in order to assure a harvest of animals that will be within the critical range required for the planned ecological balance. There is also an unplanned—but hardly unanticipated—harvest of humans each autumn, as a veritable army of not very well regulated militiamen march through the woods, fields, and farmyards, shooting at anything that moves. An inevitable consequence of what one might loosely call this shotgun approach to the problem of eradicating wildlife is that many hunters shoot themselves or each other, along with sundry cows, dogs, and other game. An almost equal number die of heart attacks, as middle-aged men whose routine way of life does not include strenuous physical exercise attempt to bring out of the woods the quarries which (or whom) they have bagged. Although social Darwinists will not agree, there is probably a more humane way than this of providing recreational outlets for urban sportsmen; and it is conceivable that a determined elite of opinion-molders might be able to identify, for these imitators of eighteenth-century American food-gathering practices,[33] a set of substitute leisure activities which would be socially acceptable without necessitating the use of weapons.

Undoubtedly there are appealing arguments in support of the status quo (Hearings 1965; Kilpatrick 1967), but they will not be canvassed here, as my purpose is not to weigh the evidence, but rather to suggest a few of the reasons why some persons might favor such a proposal, and some of the arguments which they might advance in support of their position. Instead of debating the merits, let us turn to the question of how our group should proceed to accomplish their goal, which is to negate the constitutional right to bear arms.

The proper course to follow, under the mechanistic model, is easiest to describe: all that is required is another amendment to the Constitution, intruding the prefix "un" before "necessary," and deleting the word "infringed." Such a course of action would have the advantage of keeping *de minimus* the literal modifications of constitutional language, and this in itself is a result that should be pleasing to most lawyers (for technical reasons) and to most political conservatives (for substantive ones). It is, of course, doubtful that such an amendment could be adopted at this time; indeed, it appears doubtful that proposed legislation tied to the commerce clause can get through the Senate judiciary committee, although if by chance the next few years should witness the assassination of more senior senators than of presidents, the odds in favor of the bill getting the approval of the venerable James Eastland of Mississippi might be greatly enhanced.

Assuming that the document has been changed as specified above, it is clear from a normative point of view what the next steps should be. The presumption (under the model) is that Congress and state legislatures will do their duty and enact legislation to back up the prohibition on private arms, and that the Executive and the courts will enforce such legislation. *Quod erat demonstrandum.* But from an empirical point of view, what will happen remains uncertain. A canvass of previous amendments shows that their effects have been quite variable. Most (the first ten, 14th, 15th, 18th, 21st, 22nd) have functioned as *symbolic* resolutions of political conflict with but slight empirical consequences, at least for the disputes from which they emerged. Others (13th, 24th) have *ratified* the terms of political decisions already made by other means. Some (11th, 16th) have *precluded* constitutional change that otherwise already had begun. A few (12th, 20th) have been precursors of *institutional* change in the structure of government. Finally, three (the 17th, 19th, and 23rd) have been *instrumental* in bringing about substantive con-

---

33. Perhaps, as anthropologist John Greenway has suggested, the imitation is of much earlier progenitors: "The bow and arrow was obsolescent as a weapon in the Middle Ages and obsolete in the Renaissance, but it still hangs around as a toy, not only among children, but among adults as well, just as the activity with which it is associated—hunting—is itself a metatactic toy, left over from Paleolithic times, like many of its practitioners" (1964:21).

stitutional change. The most likely outcome for the proposed amendment would be the first category of symbolic resolution of the issue, leaving indeterminate the empirical consequences in terms of the subsequent political behavior of gunlovers.

Under the organic model, proponents of civil disarmament must proceed on a much broader front than is required for modification of the documentary language. They must simultaneously work to get appropriate legislation through Congress and the state legislatures. They will undertake the sponsorship of litigation in order to evoke, at all levels of the judiciary, court decisions which increase the sanctions against private users of weapons. They will attempt to get the Supreme Court to announce a modernizing, liberal[34] interpretation of the Second Amendment which concludes that the right to bear arms, like the privileges and immunities of United States citizenship throughout the past century, is from a *legal* point of view a dead-letter clause of the Constitution.[35] They will lobby with the national administration and also with the hundreds of counterpart administrative authorities at various levels of state and local government, in order to try to suppress access to weapons and familiarization with their use, in such policy program fields as conservation, amusements (shooting galleries), toy manufacturing ("G.I. Joe, complete with bazooka, grenades, and dum-dum bullets"), education (compulsory R.O.T.C. programs in high schools and colleges), and police (auxiliaries). They will organize pressure groups of their own[36] in order to attempt to neutralize the activities of such organizations as The National Rifle Association and the Defense Department's National Board for the Promotion of Rifle Practice. They will work within both political parties, and press for the adoption of planks and individual candidacies committed to the goal of civil disarmament. They will be concerned with amending the document only *after* the policy change already has occurred, since the function of the Constitution, under the organic model, is not to foreshadow or produce changes in the relevant political, social, and economic systems, but rather it is to describe or annotate the current state of the constitutional system. Our past experience, to this extent, tends to support the assumption of the organic model: that it is much easier, and more fruitful in terms of

---

34. "Liberal" in the sense of policy outcome as defined by this sentence, and as distinguished from a liberal or expansive construction of the due process clause of the Fourteenth Amendment. As J. A. C. Grant has pointed out, "it seems fairly certain that the 'full incorporation' asked by four Justices in *Adamson* v. *California* will not be accomplished. At least it is devoutly to be hoped so. . . . [W]e need a liberally construed second amendment as a limitation on the states about as badly as a hole in the head—indeed the two might go together." (1965:1037–1038.)

35. Fortunately, there are no stare decisis problems, because the only relevant precedents all point in the right direction. *United States* v. *Miller*, *Presser* v. *Illinois*, and *United States* v. *Cruikshank* are the only precedent decisions cited in the late Edwin S. Corwin's definitive annotation of the document (1953).

36. In Honolulu, and doubtless in many other communities as well, a group of mothers has formed an organization to combat the widespread indulgence in and propagation of war toys for children.

results, to change first the way of political life, and then to bring the letter of the Constitution up to date, rather than to attempt, as under the mechanical model, to bring political life into accord with the literal text of the Constitution.

The cultural model requires our protagonists to shift their objective from attempts to redesign the structure and functioning of political and other institutions to the even broader task of replacing in part the substantive content of the values consensually shared by the community (in Deutsch's sense of the word).

Evidently, to remap the constitutional culture it is necessary to proselyte with selected audiences in order to influence their beliefs concerning the proposed subject of change. It is necessary, in other words, to change what many Americans presently believe about the wisdom and the feasibility of maintaining other values appropriate to an industrialized, megalopolitan nation, in a populace living in a (privately) armed camp. Images of Dr. Gocbbels and of Orwell's *Goodthink* may spring to mind, but the suggestion here is not that the cultural change deemed desirable by our protagonist group can or will be imposed authoritatively by a totalitarian monopoly of control over the relevant network systems. Quite to the contrary, our group can succeed only by persuading millions of individual Americans that the right of private access to weapons is an anachronism, just as much as the code duello and the wearing of swords as a customary item of dress in public. Most Americans no longer believe in, say, witches, or imprisonment for debt; but the rational arguments in support of our present toleration of semiuniversal private armament have little more, and perhaps less, intellectual compulsion— in relation to the other predominant components in contemporary American culture and mode of life—than did the toleration of beliefs in demonism in seventeenth-century Massachusetts. The task of our protagonist group is, therefore, predominantly one of educational propaganda: to increase the enlightenment of Americans generally on this subject and thereby to induce them to want to change their own behavior. Once the time comes when most Americans believe that civil armament is a vice (i.e., that the human costs of tolerating private access to weapons are, for most people, very much greater than any benefits that can be derived from continuing to permit them), then the relevant changes in political institutions will also be made. Greater tolerance for ambiguity can be expected to accompany greater enlightenment; and although no change necessarily will be made in the document, it may be that there will be circumstances in which it will fortuitously be convenient, or expedient, to modify the constitutional language. Perhaps this will occur when critical stages of decision-making are reached, in order to provide reinforcement for those elites who seek to bring about the necessary institutional changes.

Thus to change public attitudes toward political (including constitutional) values is, ipso facto, to reshape the emerging Constitution of today and tomorrow.

# 12

# Future Stress

**M**rs. Rubin, Mr. Chief Justice, Ladies and Gentlemen:

We have now reached the point in our program where you will be regaled by the last of the three graces of the future. Although I think there was some reversal of roles during the middle hours of the morning, you have already heard from both Future Shock and Future Joy. Now comes Future Sorrow.

Although I am to blame for my own title, I must give the chief justice credit for having suggested the questions to which I am supposed to address my remarks. His very first question asks whether our system of justice, as structured and operating, is prepared to cope with the future? I'm sure you all know how longwinded and theoretical professors are supposed to be, and I'm not likely to disappoint you in either of those expectations; but by the same token we're going to be lucky to get beyond that first question. Of course one way out would be to counter with the gambit: *Which* future? but I am going to take a more forthright stance than that. Instead, I'll say: No, it is not prepared—unless the future is going to be very like what our life was like a generation ago, back at a time when Hawaii was still a territory, Earl Warren was not yet chief justice of the United States, Richard Nixon was not yet cast in the role that in more recent times has been played by Spiro Agnew, and there was still room for doubt (at least in Harry Truman's mind) whether or not General Eisenhower was a Democrat or a Republican. But my negative reply implies no derogation of the Hawaiian judiciary; a similar negative reply would be necessary for any other American judiciary (or indeed, for any other judiciary), or for any other American governmental structure. All complex institutions are organized to solve problems that they no longer confront; and the lag between present capacity and even *present*

This chapter was originally published, in slightly different form, as "Future Stress, Constitutional Strain, and the American Judicial System" in Citizens' Conference on the Administration of Justice, *Proceedings* (Supreme Court of Hawaii, Judiciary Building, Honolulu, Hawaii; February 1973). The speech was delivered orally on May 25, 1972.

needs is always substantial. I cannot imagine how it could be otherwise in a political society that purports to be more or less responsive to popular control, to say nothing of a polity that in fact so functions after a fashion. So the realistic question is not how to avoid lag, but rather it is how to organize processes for institutional change—in this instance, judicial systems reform—so that lag can be subjected to continuing and systematic audit and review.

There are five additional questions, including a few easy ones, such as "What of the function, role and purpose of the judiciary—past, present, and future?" but instead of discussing them now, I'd like to explain to you what I mean by my topic.

To speak of "stress" and "strain" and a "system" is immediately to invoke a particular of view toward the nature of reality; and the metaphor that I have consciously chosen is biological in its overtones and undertones, as well as in its manifest concepts. On the one hand, this has the advantage of putting me on the side of the angels, because biological models have clearly become the predominant basis for theorizing in the field of political science, for more than a generation; and at least at the level of macrotheory, the idea of legal system as an organizing concept for classification purposes has been common throughout this century in the thinking of such influential lawmen as Roscoe Pound—whose doctorate of philosophy and initial university teaching, we might recall, lay in the academic discipline of botany. On the other hand, my invocation of the biological metaphor has the disadvantage of involving us in the mixing of metaphors, and indeed doubly so. Our courts, our constitutional documents, our statutes, and our institutions of government generally reflect a set of theoretical premises that are distinctively and characteristically Newtonian rather than Darwinian; and what little evidence we have indicates that public opinion accepts without question the culturally approved image which analogizes government to an inanimate machine rather than a living organism. But the physical universe in which our social—including political and legal—institutions are so precariously imbedded is neither Newtonian nor Darwinian but Einsteinian: our model of ultimate reality is the atomic nucleus undergoing fission, with matter being converted into energy by means of a process that we can both predict and (at least in one sense) control. I am only proposing that we substitute, at least as an initial step, a nineteenth-century point of view for the seventeenth-century perspective that otherwise would almost certainly serve as our premise in talking about law and social change, either in Hawaii or any place else in the world. I am aware that a twentieth-century model for the analysis of contemporary sociolegal relationships probably proffers an even more appropriate approach; but the hiatus between that kind of theory and our customary ways of thinking about the relevant relationships is so traumatic that I think it may be advisable to stake out a more modest and moderate position, and explore with you what the biological theory forecasts as our constitutional future.

We can be fairly explicit about why it makes a difference, in endeavoring to respond to questions concerning the role of the judiciary in a changing Hawaii, whether our implicit assumption is that courts are part of the machinery of government, or that courts function as a vital organ of the body politic, or that (if I may borrow the title of what I believe to have been Roscoe Pound's last article [1963]) we deal with "Runaway Courts in the Runaway World" in which change is the only constant, truth is a probability statement about culturally shared consensual perceptions, and chance has a greater influence than social purpose does in controlling human behavior. If courts are component parts of some larger mechanism of government, then the implication for judicial reform is clear: let well enough alone. A well-running machine will often benefit from periodic lubrication and occasional first-echelon maintenance, but in general, tinkering is bound to cause more harm than good. Change is either slowly deleterious, in which case it is the consequence of friction and results in the gradual impairment of function due to excessive tolerances, or else it is rapidly destructive in the form of breakdown accompanying either the complete loss of function or else the complete loss of control over functioning.

Change is viewed very differently, if we think of the courts as an organic part of a governmental system that is vitalized by political life. Any organism must undergo continuous, albeit genetically programmed and incremental, change if it is to grow and develop according to its natural potential and the environment in which it dwells. Any organism that is not in the process of changing itself is already dead. But at the same time the organism is a complex combination of interacting subsystems (including various subordinate but independently vital organs), each operating within specific sets of critical limits, and functioning in homeostasis upon which its survival depends. Consequently, either too much change (as in loss of a vital organ, whether by disease or accidental injury) or too rapid change (as in uncontrolled growth) is almost always fatal. The clear implication of such a model is that slow, gradual, planned change—and one would naturally say "evolutionary" change, were it not for the special meaning reserved for the concept of evolution in biological theory—is healthful and a good and desirable thing for the body politic to experience, including its judicial parts; but rapid, drastic, and unscheduled change is inherently dangerous and destructive, and hence to be avoided if possible.

Hence mild stresses are beneficial because they stimulate the organism in ways that make it possible for life to go on; but severe stresses are invariably harmful, because they strain subsystems of the organism beyond the limits that homeostasis can tolerate. The difference between music and a ruptured drum can be measured in decibels, and forecast with acceptable precision for most human ears.

Turning now to the empirical forum provided by the local courts, I'd like to suggest first a couple of examples of mild, beneficial stress that we can expect to experience, I think it is apparent, in the relatively short-run future. The establishment of a law school here in Honolulu is going to be such a stimulating event. At the moment the legal profession in Hawaii can be partitioned into two principal groups: judges and practicing attorneys. The role of law faculty member is different in important ways from either of the two presently entrenched law-roles in the state; and indeed law professors are probably going to act more like other professors than like other local lawyers. One consequence of that orientation is going to be a much greater degree of integration between legal study and the rest of the university (but the social sciences in particular) than prevails in the customary relationship between legal practice (including judicial decision-making) and the practice of the social sciences (i.e., mostly applied sociology, in the form of social work, and applied clinical psychology). Thus the theoretical and methodological—and no longer merely the so-called practical—facets of social and behavioral science are going to impinge, through the institutionalization of the law school, upon legal work in Hawaii, and in novel and unexpected ways. Indeed, it would be possible to interpret my own appearance on your program today, to say nothing of that of my colleague James Dator this morning, as intimations of the kind of cross-fertilization that is apt to become more common in the future.

But the coming of the law school will certainly entail in a variety of ways some strain for the local court and bar systems. One obvious example will be the extension of a continuing, articulate, and by no means necessarily favorable critique of local judicial and other legal work. And even the most open-minded of us enjoy criticism much more in principle than in practice. Another example can be found in the storage and retrieval of legal information. Recent reports indicate that current thinking on this subject tends to focus upon some sort of bootstrapping (or maybe "face-lifting" is a better chosen simile) of the evidently ancient quarters (nestled away in the second-floor Ewa wing of Hale Aliiolani) where the state's only quasi-public law library reposes, so that its lawbook collections can be beefed up to double in buckram, as it were, for law students and faculty alike in addition to its present clientele. (Incidently, these same reports suggest that current thinking would locate the new law school, in precise accord with the tenor of mainland thought prior to the *First* World War, but squarely in the teeth of all relevant mainland experience during the past quarter of a century since the end of the Second World War, downtown where the action is instead of in Manoa where the rest of the relevant part of the University is.) I cannot say whose nest the law school will be feathering if indeed it is put, temporarily or permanently, in a downtown instead of a campus location; although I doubt that such a location will be in the interests of either the university or the law school itself. But I can say a word about current thought regarding the legal information problem: it is on all fours with Thomas Jefferson's ideas for the University of Virginia library that he both planned and founded. My assumption is that within a decade, electronic data storage will have accelerated to such a point that conventional books, which will continue to be used for archival purposes for a while longer, will have been largely displaced for legal search and research concerning then contemporary legal issues and problem-solving. In order to be getting ready for the 1980s a new law school ought to be hiring a computer specialist and legal data-bank expert, to complement the conventional law librarian whose interim services will also be needed; but I have little expectation that what I think wise is likely to happen. Apart from the very slight and transient irritant effect of my having made this remark, the state political system is going to feel unstressed by future law school informational requirements; and feeling no strain, it's going to go right ahead and add a few more books to the present collection. The result, however, is not a favorable example of how the system of justice—of which the law school certainly will become a part—is prepared to cope with future needs.

Another example of educational stress is found in the counterpart development, for the federal judiciary, of the seminars (beginning about a dozen years ago) to socialize new federal judges into their roles, and more recently to provide retraining for more experienced federal judges as well (Fish 1973; Carp and Wheeler 1972; Cook 1971). I shall be surprised if our own Federal District Judge-designate King does not spend a week or two in the District of Columbia, before the present year is out, in attendance at such a seminar. One effect of the seminars is to reinforce the complex of other centralizing and bureaucratizing vectors, already impinging upon what used to be the relatively individualistic role of the federal district judge. Such organizational vectors include circuit conferences, other programs of the Federal Judicial Center, the Administrative Office of United States Courts, and the expansion of federal judicial personnel to the point where virtually *all* federal district benches are occupied by groups of judges—even two years ago there were only four single-judge districts left in the country. As in our experience with similar institutional developments such as judicial councils and state court administrators, a sufficient lag has ensued so that like most other states Hawaii now participates in a variety of counterpart training programs for state judges, in addition to the state's own biennial judicial seminars In the future we can expect such endeavors to involve the cooperation of the law school in interaction with the court and bar systems, including of course the court administrator and judicial council. This may not provide a very good example of the judicial system's capacity to cope with the future, but it at least does suggest a way in which the system is becoming better adapted to cope with the present.

Third, I'll venture a somewhat involuted prediction: that when another conference like the present one is held, perhaps around 1977, it may well meet at (unless the school is then still in temporary downtown quarters), and in any event will be convened under the joint auspices of, the law school. Incidentally, we might well note that the very assembling of a conference such as this is evidence of faith, on the part of at least many of those who planned as well as those who are attending this meeting, in the power and pertinence of the biological model as a theory in terms of which to organize both thought and action about judicial behavior in Hawaii. We meet firm in the conviction that our courts can and should be brought up to date; that rational discussion can and likely will suggest both the direction and the parameter values of desirable modifications; and that the enlightened views of a public-spirited civic group such as this will stimulate an appropriate response from the other relevant subsystems that are (like the judicial system) a part of political life in Hawaii. So we too are an example of mild stress on the local courts.

So much for pleasant stress. You will have observed, no doubt, that the chief reason I was able to keep it relatively pleasant was that the environment to which my remarks related was the supporting legal environment, including such components as the state university and some aspects of the state political system. But once we leave the security of that cozy setting, the prospects for life—including judicial life—are more foreboding.

Let me begin by ticking off a few examples of what I think are inescapably going to be future characteristics of the general environment, the effects of which are going to be experienced by the local courts as painfully stressing. By "inescapably" I mean assuming what I suppose should be called the best: that neither nuclear warfare nor nuclear disease eliminates (I was going to say "liquidates," but I decided that that was just too literal a word to employ when speaking of the more direct and immediate effects of thermonuclear fission upon target populations) some substantial number (and for present purposes, I think a good round number such as a billion will suffice) of human beings during the brief interim between the present and the arrival of my postulated stressing future. One more caveat: most of my examples will be problems that, although global in their incidence, are particularly exacerbated in their application to Hawaii.

Future stress will include (but by no means be limited to):

· crowding (and I speak here in the strict ethological sense);
· competition for air, water, and food (which will soon result in the extermination of all nonhuman animal species);
· mass poisoning from industrial and human waste products (and note that there are already several large civil judgments by courts in Japan, levying monetary damages against chemical polluters of waterways [for mercury and cadmium poisoning of otherwise edible fish that were in fact consumed by a—is the word gullible?—public] and of the atmosphere [thereby causing widespread asthma]);
· competition for space and shelter;
· the disappearance of nonsolar energy sources;
· the deterioration of natural esthetic values (the astronauts who drink their own—and each other's—recycled urine have blazed a trail that the entire species will be following before long);
· plus chronic and worsening breakdowns in transportation, communications, and health/medical facilities.

The principal cause of these conditions is going to be overpopulation, operating both directly, and also through the medium of its two principal helpmeets: industrialization and urbanization.

Overpopulation of *any* species is a result of the more or less temporary occurrence of an environment favorable to its survival and breeding. The tendency for any breeding population is always to expand up to the limits of support (of such essential values as water, food, and security). The human species long since has eliminated serious competition from visible vertebrate competitors, and we are now in the process of selectively exterminating many of the quantitatively most significant of our microscopic predators. Hence some of the natural limits to human overpopulation no longer can nor do operate; and now that we consistently kill many more persons with automobiles than with wars, we must conclude that war also no longer has much effect upon population levels, except in the case of idiosyncratic token or scapegoat subpopulations (like Nigerian Biafrans, or East Pakistani, or Vietnamese on both sides of the 17th parallel).

Of course, the effect of future stress components such as crowding, mass starvation, species poisoning with utterly unpredictable genetic spinoffs, and other universal psychophysical as well as chemically generated stresses on the physiology of surviving human individuals will soon—indeed, already has begun to—inhibit further breeding on anything approaching the scale to which we have become accustomed. But that feedback loop may well take effect too late to prevent irreversibly deleterious effects that will preclude species survival; and even if that does not happen, human life even as we know it now will have become impossible for our own grandchildren; and conversely, what is possible in the early decades of the twenty-first century will probably not be tolerable for any adult human socialized prior to, say— to pick an arbitrary benchmark—1972.

But before we examine some examples of what I think are going to be the consequent strains upon our constitutional system, I think that we should take notice of some of the major component strands of what I'm going to call the "New Egalitarianism," by which I mean a cluster of recently evolved and still evolving rights, none of which counted for or amounted to much, as recently as two decades ago—and I look back now to that same turning point that I mentioned earlier, immediately before so many Americans discovered that they liked Ike. But these same rights, as actualized and potentialized today, have emerged in the span of a single generation as the cutting edge of both legal and social change in our society. In the hands of the Warren Court, which functioned as a principal protagonist in their development,[1]

---

1. Mayor John V. Lindsay bestowed upon Earl Warren, in token recognition of his achievements as chief justice of the United States, the Gold Medal of the City of New York, on Law Day (May 1) 1973, remarking at the time he announced the award that "Justice Warren has become a worldwide symbol for individual liberty, social justice, and human equality." (*Honolulu Star-Bulletin*, April 17, 1973, p. A-5).

326 · TOWARD A DYNAMIC JURISPRUDENCE

the evolving ideology was strictly within the historic confines of nineteenth-century English liberalism, and it in no sense purported to be futuristic in its orientation. In posting national ideals of racial equality, civic equality, and voting equality, the Warren Court was redressing long-standing wrongs and recognizing the legitimacy of legal rights that had been cast in constitutional language for a minimum of eighty years—and that had taken that long or longer to obtain the imprimatur of the Supreme Court of the United States. A fourth right, that of indigent equality, in the courts and under the law, began to gain recognition at about the same time as the other three, but it is still in the process of being formulated (see my Bacon Lectures [Schubert 1970a] for details). But there are at least two other facets of the New Egalitarianism, sexual equality and generational equality, claims in behalf of which are presently being widely pressed throughout our legal system. Sexual and generational equality owe much less to the Supreme Court, partly because their proponents have chosen to push them by relying upon more overtly political approaches than litigation; and it seems unlikely now that either can look forward to getting much support from the Burger Court during the seventies. Furthermore, if we are willing to concede that racial, civic, voting, and indigent equality are liberal rights, then sexual and generational equality are widely perceived to be claims in behalf of radical rights. Partly this may be because they raise the issues that burn more brightly today, but partly it is doubtless due also to the fact that the claims they advance are more fundamental, and therefore more stressing, to the homeostasis that defines (among other things) the status quo of the war between the sexes, and the credibility gap between one generation and another.

Because both are still in process of being worked out, let me specify a few of their explications as components of a newer and more radical aspect of egalitarian ideology. Sexual equality of course involves changes in what are legally recognized to be acceptable sexual (including of course homosexual) behaviors, plus associated rhetoric and other communications about such acts; and the general thrust of consequent legal changes clearly has been in the direction of tolerating a great deal of variance in human behavior that only a decade ago was deemed intolerable. But other explications concerning the variety of modes of cohabitation between and among consenting persons, which are taking their place as alternatives to monogamous marriage, are perhaps more important; and certainly present and prospective changes affecting human reproduction are of considerably greater social significance than the closing of the gap between private sexual practices and their image in public law. There are also associated problems relating to abortion, divorce, and the rearing of children: and you will note that I haven't yet even mentioned women's lib, although I hasten to so now.

Generational equality has perhaps even greater importance for the practice of politics than for the practice of law, although we have hardly begun to start recasting our theories of political behavior so as to bring them to closer accord with empirical changes that are already well advanced. The old civic competence, as I am going to call it, could be pretty well described by what statisticians call a normal (or bell-shaped) curve, with age as the ordinate and the number of persons who are politically competent as the abscissa, although there was some skewness toward old age because the termination of political competence was natural rather than legal; whereas we used to have lots of infants but none who could vote or hold office. The new civic competence looks much more like a rectangle than a bell-shaped curve: we now have a front-end load by having co-opted youths in their late teens, while at the same time, the combined successes of public health, geriatrics, and social security have imposed what we might, for the sake of symmetry if nothing else, call the rear-end load, with a considerable increase in the proportion and absolute number of senior civic participants. Politics is thus no longer a middle-aged man's game to nearly the extent that it used to be; and attempts to appeal to this more heterogeneous electorate will certainly result in further legal changes, involving a constellation of new constitutional rights such as those to which I now turn.

My hypothesis concerning constitutional strain is that the severe environmental stresses (already noted above) are going to continue to receive cultural reinforcement from the expanding ideology of egalitarianism, and that this will result in demands for the recognition of a panoply of novel constitutional rights to facets of the human condition that seemed less precious heretofore, precisely because they were—literally—less precious. The new Bill of Rights will include:

- the right to privacy (which was prototyped by the Warren Court, but with nothing like the critical intensity that it will embody in another twenty years);
- the right to mobility (which also has experienced some judicial encouragement in recent years, but with the sharp difference that it has been claimed mostly by people for whom movement was relatively easy);
- the right to reproduce (in the face of various sorts of limits, which may range from moratoria, selective *non*sterilization, exclusively artificial insemination of stratified samples of females, and more sophisticated controls that geneticists may devise);
- the right to individuality (in the face of crushing pressures, toward stereotyping and behavioral conformity, that will make normal adolescence look like what I understand is now called a good trip);
- the right to physical security (upon which I shall expound in a moment);
- and ultimately, the right to physical survival (which, insofar as concerns individual humans, is apt to come into increasing conflict with claims to the survival rights of particular social groups, and eventually of course with overriding claims advanced in behalf of the species).

I have left the right to physical security for slightly more detailed exposition because it has for so long been such a major preoccupation of judicial work, concerned as it is with what I am loosely going to call the field of criminal law. Everyone here understands, and most of you probably much better than

I, the sweeping changes that are in process in the handling, by courts and associated governmental and private agencies, of persons who at least in recent history have been categorized as criminal offenders. The ideal of punishment has been displaced by the ideal of rehabilitation; and the rejection of punishment as a goal has entailed the repudiation of a host of correlated ethical norms, such as the notion that crime or law-breaking is evil. Indeed, a transposition of roles is evolving so that the previous projection of societal pity for the victims of criminal acts is becoming displaced by feelings of contempt for the socially (or psychologically) inadequate—and therefore, the *really* guilty—victims who are now conceived to *invite* mugging, rape, and even—perhaps especially—murder; while the defendant (that is, the mugger, rapist, or murderer) becomes perceived as the real victim, of society's failure to educate, shelter, love, or otherwise to have supplied whatever he may have lacked; and hence the defendant needs to be neither forgiven nor punished, but rather provided with better information, guidance, emotional releases or satisfactions, or whatever.

If I may suggest a crude scale of vanishing modes of punishment, I would denote first PHYSICAL PUNISHMENT, which has been virtually abolished as a form of punishment awarded in judicial sentences in the United States, although it remains of course common in some countries with similar legal systems (e.g., the Republic of South Africa) and is in general use throughout most of the world today. Second, I would point to CAPITAL PUNISHMENT, which is on the way out in the United States, the United States Supreme Court to the contrary notwithstanding,[2] in accordance with a fairly widespread trend, particularly among the industralized societies of Western Europe. Third comes INSTITUTIONALIZATION, the effects of the elimination of which are just beginning to be felt, as illustrated by California's contemporary embarrassment in having recently completed the construction of two modern custodial institutions (including one that is, as I am told, a maximum security facility) which had become surplus and unneeded during the time between when they were planned and built. Prisons are no longer needed any more than mental hospitals or churches, unless they are to be filled with a continuing supply of—clients (?) [I never could find the right generic to fit here.] (Nor is it difficult to imagine that universities might well become surplus, too, if current tendencies toward antiintellectualism are exacerbated by severe environmental stress, as I fully expect they will be; and so far as that goes, the elimination of prisons may have more than passing consequences for the seeming indispensability of courts.) The prisons grow emptier (while crime rates go up) because of the substitution of out-patient services under circumstances where formerly institutional treatment was deemed essential.

---

2. This comment was, by implication, a failure to anticipate the outcome of *Furman* v. *Georgia*, which the Supreme Court decided five weeks later on June 29, 1972.

And so we come to the fourth point in my scale: GUILT. That, too, is on the way out; sin requires free will as well as choice, and when concepts of social responsibility and community treatment supplant sin, it makes no sense for society's pawns to feel guilty about their victimization. This is clearly how we are headed, and so I ask only the slight additional question: What will be the consequences for individual physical security? In the world—and I mean the physical as well as the social world—of Jeremy Bentham and James Mill, one might conceivably contemplate with equanimity the socialization of antisocial behavior. But by 1984, the institutionalization of persons who continue to commit mugging, rape, and murder, and social condemnation for their acts, alike will have disappeared; and along with them will have gone the cultural ideals which led a more primitive age to socialize such primeval responses to aggression as self- and extended-self-help in the form of direct retaliation, vendettas, blood feuds, tribal warfare, and so forth. But our more civilized modern trend will certainly militate against the already slim chances for mass disarmament of the civilian population, a step that otherwise might be expected to make some contribution to general physical security; and perhaps also by 1984 the Second Amendment will have taken the place of the First in the most preferred position in the liturgy of our federal constitutional rights. But while we await the generalization of Tombstone and Gunsmoke as the American way of life, or to vary somewhat the time and place, the return to conditions under which the skills of a Tybalt are more important than those of a Portia, courts are increasingly going to be confronted with claims to the right to physical security. And since their criminal law function seems likely to atrophy, perhaps ingenious judges will contrive ways to substitute civil remedies for claimants who no longer can expect to receive what used to be thought of as public vindication in the criminal courts.

It is explicitly these emerging claims to constitutional right that seem certain to produce constitutional strain upon the American judicial system, because they are going to be pressed with increasing vigor and vehemence while the possibility of their satisfaction continues to diminish. So what, under these circumstances, are we to do? More specifically, what can and should judges in Hawaii do, if it should be *my* scenario (rather than one of the more pleasing ones with which other speakers have beguiled you) that proves only too true? Even more urgently, what can and should court personnel in Hawaii do to delay, to mitigate, to attenuate, and even conceivably (though I doubt it) to attempt to avoid such a grim constitutional future?

For reasons of both expedience and prudence, I leave the answers to you to deliberate in the workshops to which we shall presently repair. But not without a parting suggestion: The biological model clearly is a prophet of doom, probably because doom is impending, but possibly also because of this model's confinement to controlled gradualism as a means of protecting interests that have already become vested. The third model, based upon modern physics, subsumes (you will recall) among its defining parameters such liberating characteristics as:

- basic entities in continual flux;
- free transfer and recombination among such entities;
- the assignment of a major causative role to chance;
- autogenous learning;
- indeterminism;
- and unrestricted growth and development.

It would seem prima facie that none of these is an apt descriptor of either law or courts as we know them now, and are accustomed to thinking about either. But that may be because we are used to looking at both law and courts with blinders on—the blinders of outmoded theories. Perhaps we should dare to imagine a legal order, including a role for courts, that assigns much more importance to the theory of chaos (cf. Aubert 1959), to which the above factors seem likely to contribute. But that I do leave to your imagination.

And I thank you all for your patience.

# 13

# Justice and Reasoning

*Jesting Pilate*,[1] the title of a recently published collection of the public papers of "the greatest Judge in the English-speaking world,"[2] can serve to remind us of both the normative and the empirical dimensions of inquiry into the effect of justice upon reasoning, and of reasoning upon justice. And if Caesar's magistrate mocked Jesus' claim to bear witness unto the truth, he did so (however unwittingly) with excellent precedent: four centuries earlier (if Plato's Reports are to be credited), Sophists had anticipated sophisticates by scoffing an older martyr's dialectic quest for justice and truth Interest in the trial and judgment of the defendant upon whose cross Pontius Pilate personally had emblazoned—and in three languages—the legend JESUS OF NAZARETH THE KING OF THE JEWS[3] might well focus, of course, upon the normative question whether the decision was just, in relation to the various sets of criteria (the law of God, the law of the Hebrews, and the law of the Romans) that might be deemed relevant to that determination. One

This chapter was originally published, in slightly different form, as "Justice and Reasoning: A Political Science Perspective" in *Rivista Internazionale di Filosofia del Diritto* 46 (October – December 1969):474–496. Reprinted with permission of *Rivista Internazionale di Filosofia del Diritto*.

This paper was presented initially as a lecture at the Symposium on Justice and Reasoning, sponsored by the Department of Philosophy of the State University of New York at Buffalo, 3 December 1968. For their comments upon the lecture, I wish to thank my colleagues in the symposium: Chaim Perelman, professor of Philosophy, University of Brussels; Ronald Dworkin, professor of Jurisprudence, Oxford University; and Thomas Perry, professor of Philosophy, State University of New York at Buffalo. I thank Torstein Eckhoff, professor of Law, University of Oslo, for his advice and assistance.

1. Sir Owen Dixon, quoting Bacon's *Essay on Truth*: "'What is truth?' said jesting Pilate, and would not stay for an answer" (1965:10).

2. *Sydney Morning Herald*, April 2, 1964, p. 2.

3. John 19:19.

might also, or alternatively, be concerned with the empirical questions how and why the decision was made, and with what effects.[4] In this regard, it is notable that although the New Testament tends to be valued for, and evaluated in terms of, its normative content, the interest in the event of the trial, manifested by the four commentators upon whose accounts we largely rely for our knowledge concerning that affair, is strictly empirical. It is notable because it illustrates the extent to which there is no simple one-to-one correspondence between justice and reasoning, on the one hand, and the standpoints of ethics and empiricism, on the other. In adjudicatory decision-making, the effects of justice upon reasoning, and of reasoning upon justice, alike are amenable to inquiry as either normative or empirical questions.

The development of academic disciplines during the present century has resulted, at least in the United States, in certain general tendencies in the specialization of labor, for purposes of allocating research endeavors among (and also within certain of) the fields of social science. By and large, professors of philosophy and of law continue to concentrate their attention upon the normative aspects of judicial decision-making, as a facet of their concern for the extension of wisdom and rationality in the choice of policy alternatives, particularly in regard to issues of contemporary controversiality in the society, economy, and polity (and at all levels—community, state, national, international, regional, and global). To the extent that they have been concerned with the matter, most other social scientists—and I speak here particularly of political scientists, historians, ethnographers, sociologists, and psychologists of the present generation—have concentrated instead upon the empirical side of adjudication. Of course, there have been differences in the degrees of involvement of these various professions, with political scientists and ethnographers relatively most, and with historians and psychologists relatively least, engaged in the study of decision-making by courts and judges. Moreover, there have been at least two countervailing infraprofessional positions, within law and within political science. American legal realism (vide Rumble 1968; Hayakawa 1964; Ingersoll 1966) most certainly has been empirical in its orientation, and it constitutes an important (and conspicuous) albeit minority point of view among academic lawyers, and an exception to the generalizations stated above. Contrariwise, until very recently, hardly more than a dozen years ago, public lawyers in the tradition of Edward S. Corwin, Robert F. Cushman, and Thomas Reed Powell dominated political science inquiry; and for these scholars not only was the subject normative but so also was their own social function, as each sought actively to guide the United States Supreme Court (in particular) along directions of social retrenchment or reform that he deemed beneficial for the body politic. Public law remains the prevailing subject of undergraduate instruction in political science curricula, especially among the large

---

4. Cf. the case studies in Becker 1970. See Winter 1961; and also Cohn 1967.

majority of the profession who teach but undertake little or no research; but clearly it now represents a minority, and a diminishing, influence in graduate instruction and in contemporary scholarship (e.g., see chap. 2, part 2, "The Ghost of Public Law Present"; Schubert 1968b; and Eulau 1969). The focus of political science research today is upon the empirical parameters of adjudicatory decision-making; and it is that perspective that I wish to present in this discussion. In particular, I shall attempt to focus upon a contemporary model of judicial reasoning, as this is hypothesized to relate to observed (or, at least potentially, observable) processes of judicial decision-making.

Judicial reasoning can be understood to signify two very different aspects of the adjudication process. The first, most difficult to observe (even indirectly), and by far the more complicated (and important) meaning of judicial reasoning is *the set of psychological, and of social interaction, processes that configure, for a particular group of individuals during a discrete segment of time in a relatively determinate institutional milieu, to discriminate a preferred choice among a highly stylized subset of culturally approved decisional alternatives.* The empirical questions about this proposition relate to certain events, hypothesized to be relevant, that occur within individuals and within groups (i.e., in the relationships of individuals to each other). These are the kinds of questions with which we shall be concerned in the research to be described below. Beyond these empirical questions lie an even more complicated set of normative questions that relate to the construction of an ideal model of individual, group, and institutional decision-making processes, presumably (in most instances) involving the postulation of severely restricted subsets of behaviors that have been selected from within the range of what can be imagined to be, what can be, or what has been, observed in past and present human experience. Stated otherwise, the range of variation of the variables that interact in the normative model will tend to be much smaller than the range of these same variables in the empirical model; or again, the normative multidimensional space will be a subspace of the empirical multidimensional space. The construction of the normative model can be deemed even more difficult than the empirical task, for two reasons. First, really exhaustive knowledge about the relationships analyzed in the empirical model would seem to be a condition prerequisite to the rational justification of restricting the range of the empirical variables, and particularly in their interaction effects—unless, that is, one is prepared to justify such preferences exclusively on deductive grounds, in either disregard or ignorance of the apparent empirical consequences of such deduced behavioral norms; otherwise deduced norms remain hypotheses unless and until their empirical consequences have been measured. Second, the implementation of even an empirically justified normative model will necessitate the engineering of more or less drastic changes in the behaviors—physiological, psychological, and social—of many (if not, to some extent, *all*) persons in

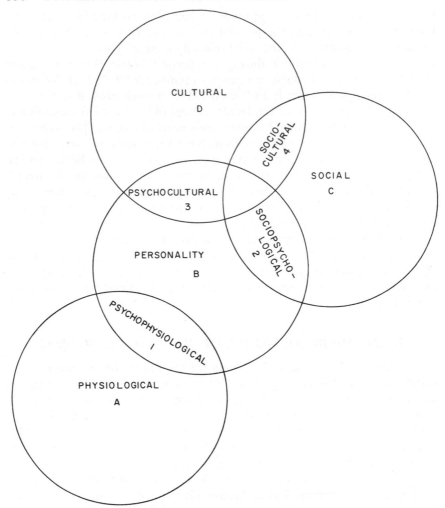

Figure 22. A Behavioral View of the Judicial System.

paradigm specifies only some names for relationships; it remains essential to indicate with greater specificity both the kinds of empirical variables that purport to be subsumed among these analytical categories and processes, and a theory of how these processes interrelate.

The cosmology that continues to supply the philosophical (in the sense of philosophy of science) foundation for the traditional approach of public law (and, more generally, of legal "positivism") is Newtonian: a mechanical set of "power" relationships in which forces act upon and react to each other (Landau 1961; and [contra] J. A. Robinson 1957). Characteristic examples of such thinking are found in contemporary scholarly notions about stare decisis, neutral constitutional principles, judicial activism and restraint, and in proposals to change the language of constitutional documents in order to bring about societal change.[5] A much more radical cosmology, which finds its best expression in American sociological and realist jurisprudence (ranging from Holmes, through Pound, Cardozo, Felix Cohen, Frank, and Llewellyn, to A. S. Miller[6] is the biological approach of Darwinism, which conceptualizes law as the functional result of a subsystem of interdependent processes and institutional structures (Landau 1965b, 1968). It is typical of the realist approach in law, which finds its counterpart in what I have called the conventional approach in political science (Schubert 1967a, 1967b),[7] to conceptualize law as a matrix of social behaviors, which can be understood or explained only in the context of the overlapping social, economic, and political systems with which the legal system interacts. From this point of view, law is a "seamless web"; there is a "living body" of law; law is "in society" and/or it is (like judges)[8] a "vital part" of the political process; and the judicial system converts social, economic, and political inputs into legal outputs, which in turn affect social, economic, and political interests and relationships, which in turn affect judges and courts, and so forth.

From the point of view of historical development in Western civilization, mechanism is a seventeenth- and eighteenth-century cosmology, and organism is a product of the nineteenth century. Much more radical than either of these is, of course, the cosmology that has arisen (at least, in the more developed fields of natural science) during the present century: relativity. Instead of the completely determined relationships of mechanism, or the highly complex functional interrelationships postulated to obtain among the structures of an organism, the cosmology of modern physical science implies a configurational approach to the analysis of social relationships, in which chance operates as a much more important consideration than in either of the older metaphors. The elementary particles of the modern physical universe are in continual flux, in structures that range from the

---

5. For more extended discussion, and for other examples of the legal implications of the Newtonian and of the other two cosmologies discussed in the text, see chap. 11.

6. On the biological premises of Holmes' cosmology of society, see White 1947:chap. 5; and Hofstadter 1944; on that of Pound (whose Ph. D. was in botany) and Cardozo, see Cahill 1952:chap. 4; in regard to the realists see particularly Cohen 1935; Llewellyn 1934; and Miller 1963.

7. For an extended discussion of the realist/conventional approach, in both law and political science, see Weiler 1968.

8. According to Jack Peltason, "When a judge makes a decision he gives his support to one pattern or activity as against another. He becomes . . . an important member of an interest group. . . . Judicial decision-making is one stage, not the only nor necessarily the final one, in the process of determining which of several conflicting activities shall be favored. . . . But a judge cannot avoid taking sides. The judiciary is in politics not because of the desire of the individual justice but because it makes decisions. . . . [W]e [should] turn our attention to the judiciary as a facet in the group struggle and relate the activities of judges to that of other groups. . . ." (1953:51, 55, 56)

relatively stable (such as igneous rock, or a statue) to the relatively unstable (such as the emissions of X-ray photography, or those of a detonating H-bomb). We are compelled to use mathematical and statistical modes of expression to describe and to predict the behavior of such particles, in part because of limits to our capacity to observe them discretely and in part because of the large extent to which what happens to individual particles can best be explained by laws of chance variation. If we ask the question: what is the paradigm for law in the configurational cosmology of relativity, we can only speculate, because the social sciences are still largely engaged in the task of catching up (from the theoretical point of view) with the *nineteenth* century; and none of them, I think it is warranted to say, has as yet progressed to the point such that its fundamental theory is cast in configurational rather than in biological form. (In political science, for example, it is only within the past few years that biological theories of politics—which can readily be traced, of course, back to such progenitors as Woodrow Wilson—have become widely accepted throughout the profession, as exemplified by the current vogue for the writings of Gabriel Almond, the president of the American Political Science Association four years ago, and of David Easton, the president last year.) Moreover, the current mood of reform within the profession is overwhelmingly in the direction of empirical redevelopment—social, psychological, political, and economic—and away from theoretical and methodological work (McCoy and Playford 1967; Haas and Kariel 1970). The prospect seems excellent for an extended period of hostility to the development of scientific method in social science research. So it may be quite a while before it will be possible to speak with any assurance about a configurational theory of law, from an empirical point of view. But it is possible to speculate; and one possible line of development would be to build upon the premises of methodological individualism, according to which the fundamental legal particles of a configurational theory of law would be the discrete behaviors of human individuals.

One set of such behaviors, that would be of particular interest to a more general theory of law, would be the decision-making behaviors of humans acting in the role of judges. Of course, there is no technical reason why many adjudicative tasks could not be allocated for computer determination (Lasswell 1955; Lawlor 1963; Schubert 1968*d*); and certainly it would be possible to program for a much higher degree of rationality than appears to obtain in the processing by human adjudicators of large quantities of stereotyped offenses (such as intoxication, or speeding) that are now tried in magistrate courts (Somit et al. 1960). That is one solution to the problem of judicial reasoning; and just as the maturation of industrial society has witnessed an increasing substitution of administrative for adjudicatory processes of decision-making (Hewart 1929; Jerome Frank 1942), so the atomic age, in whose infancy we dwell, may find it both necessary and desirable to automate judicial reasoning, for the resolution of many types of interest conflict. But before that can be done satisfactorily, we shall doubtless need to acquire a better understanding of how human adjudicators decide such questions.

In the discussion that follows, I shall assume that the cosmology that underlies the paradigm of judicial decision-making portrayed in Figure 22 is neither mechanical nor biological, but that what it suggests represents an endeavor to move in the direction that a configurational approach would imply. Consequently, although any individual judge, whose decision-making (= judicial reasoning) is represented by the paradigm, is himself the embodiment of a living, biological system in the most literal sense, the only part of Figure 22 that is systemic in this organismic sense is A, the set of his relevant physiological characteristics. His personality, set B, includes the universe of his previously experienced and potential dispositions (motor, affective, cognitive, perceptive, and motive) to respond to his environment. The social set, C, includes all of the other individuals with whom our subject judge comes, or might come, into contact; and the sociopsychological space of intersection between his personality set and the social set contains the interactions between him and other persons. The set of cultural elements, D, includes the customs of the social group that comprises the society that includes B and C; the norms, beliefs, and cognitions common to one or more of the individuals in C constitute the content of the segment of sociocultural overlap; and those peculiar to our subject judge define the psychocultural segment of his own area of overlap with D. Our judge's reasoning is defined, therefore, as a configuration of personality components (involving motor responses such as facial expression,[9] voice, hearing, and gesture; also his affective experiences, including physiological feedback processes; his motivations; his cognitions; and his perceptions) that are continuously undergoing actual or potential modification as a consequence of his interactions with other persons and his transactions with the culture that he experiences and in part shares with these other persons. An explicit function of the psychocultural elements is to supply an at least crude system of weights for his evaluation of the relative relevance and importance of both his internalized reactions and his responses to interactions with other persons. But his affective responses to social interactions can also (for example) supply a system of weights for his evaluation of how much relevance and importance to attach to explicit elements of the psychocultural content (such as the norm of stare decisis, in an explicit situational context); only empirical knowledge will inform us which type of personality component tends to dominate what, for whom, when,—and maybe—how.

## II. SOME EXAMPLES OF EMPIRICAL RESEARCH INTO JUDICIAL REASONING

Age, health, race, and sex are examples of the kinds of empirical physiological indicators that have been hypothesized to be relevant to judicial

---

9. Tomkins 1962: esp., vol. 1, *The Positive Affects*, chap. 7, "The Primary Site of the Affects: The Face"; Tomkins and Izard 1965: pt. 6, "Affect and Facial Responses"; and Osgood 1966.

behavior. The hypothesis touted by FDR himself was, as we all know, that advanced age breeds conservatism; and not long after the "court-packing" proposal was rejected one political scientist supplied some relevant descriptive empirical data, with a chapter on "Age Qualifications" in what is one of the first studies to rely upon quantification as an approach to historical generalizations about American judges.[10]

The most comprehensive investigation of the relationship between chronological age and judicial voting behavior is found in Don Bowen's Yale doctoral dissertation (1965). Working with an 89 percent sample of all federal courts of appeals judges and state supreme court judges, for 1960, and a nominal scale for age (with the fulcrum at sixty years), Bowen found that younger judges were consistently and with statistical significance more liberal, on all half-dozen policy scales that he examined (1965:187). However the simple (first-order) correlations tended to be low, and the proportion of variance explained by age, when regression analysis was used to examine the conjoint effect of age in association with other background characteristics, was very small. Bowen's work tends to show that chronological age is causally correlated with judicial decision-making, but in complicated association with other variables and varying in strength as well, according to the kind of policy issue. A contemporaneous Harvard dissertation by Sheldon Goldman (1965), working with a much smaller sample of under a hundred judges (less than a fourth of the size of Bowen's sample), failed to discover statistically significant simple correlations, except in the two instances of labor and fiscal policy; but there are so many differences between the two studies, relating to design and methodology in addition to the matter of sample content and size, that Goldman's findings cannot be said to contradict Bowen's; indeed, they tend, if anything to reinforce one another.

Recent cross-cultural work is suggestive of the widely differing kinds of significance that age can have in various cultures. In the United States Supreme Court, for instance, there is no recognized relationship between age and either formal or informal status. In the Supreme Court of India, however, the combined effect of compulsory retirement at age sixty-five plus a seniority rule for promotion to the chief justiceship makes it possible for any person offered an appointment to the supreme court to calculate the probabilities, subject to the intervention of a variable representing his own and his colleagues' health, of whether and when he would become chief justice himself, if he accepted the appointment (Gadbois 1969:227). Clearly, the system in which age is the better predictor of filling the role of chief justice is also the one in which that role appears to have less institutional and symbolic impor-

---

10. Ewing 1938: chap. 4. For an even earlier quantitative analysis of the attributes of American judges (both state and federal), see Mott et al. 1933; and for the best-known recent study, see Schmidhauser 1959. The best study of age and judicial behavior is Schmidhauser 1962a.

tance as a component affecting policy outcomes, an observation that might lead some critics of quantification to conclude that the better a variable predicts, the less its substantive importance. Moreover, sophisticates might remark that intimations of cultural variation coming rather late in the century *after* the major work of Maine and of Frazer can hardly be looked upon as news. The point, however, is that most of the empirical work that has been done on judicial decision-making (as distinguished from the descriptions of prescriptions, with which comparative law remains preoccupied) *has* been culture-bound; and one possible advantage of the paradigm invoked here is the attention that it focuses upon cultural (and subcultural) variation as a principal component of judicial reasoning.

Both Bowen and Goldman treated age as an indicator of ideology, testing the hypothesis that judges (like, presumably, other humans) become more conservative (in both relative and absolute terms) as they grow older. It is possible, however, to test a very different, and potentially often inconsistent, hypothesis that Danelski has suggested: that age is an indicator of acculturation, and that the degree of liberalism or conservatism that one ought to expect to find correlated with it will be that of the prevailing mood of the political culture at the time a judge is socialized into his civic and professional roles (1969:149). In explicit application to Japanese Supreme Court justices, therefore, Danelski proposed the hypothesis (that had been suggested to him by several retired judges whom he had interviewed) that *older* justices, who had been reared during the relatively liberal era (within domestic Japan) of Taisho democracy (which enveloped the first World War), would be more liberal in their decision-making than younger judges who came of age during the rising tide of militarism during the late twenties and thirties. I have attempted to test a similar hypothesis about justices of the Australian High Court, in a causal analysis of decision-making by that court during the fifties (1969g). My empirical data indicate that the *direction* of liberalism is clearly that specified by my hypothesis, but that the causal paths are very complex, involving both direct and indirect effects upon dependent decisional variables, and in patterns that appear unstable (because they differ for changes in the composition of the court). So the existing empirical studies conclude, though with no very great assurance, that age (as an index to ideology) is weakly but positively linked with liberal policy outputs in the American culture, and somewhat more strongly but negatively linked with similar outputs in the Australian culture. Perhaps the most that one ought to conclude from such findings is that age is an empirical indicator that invites more extensive and intensive study, and in a cross-cultural way, before we can presume to speak with much confidence about its importance as an influence upon judicial reasoning. This may seem, to some, a disappointingly tenuous summary of the product of the admittedly fragmentary empirical work on judicial age that has been reported to date; but it may bear recalling that we toddle (or, perhaps better said, totter) at the threshold of social scientific inquiry, to say nothing of the very tiny domain of behavioral jurisprudence.

We might expect a low negative correlation between the age and health of judges; but whether such a relationship can be observed to obtain is not, so far as I am aware, known, because it has not been investigated. It may come as a mild surprise to be apprised that no systematic research on judicial health appears to have been published, especially when one takes into consideration the considerable effect that the state of health of one person can have upon the work of any really small group. Felix Cohen, the philosopher-of-law son of a philosopher of law, is correct in pointing out that law is more (although I would add, at least, "usually") than "the product of judicial bellyaches"; but in any population whose average age is sixty years, bellyaches of one form or another can be expected to play some part in affecting both the quantity and the quality of judicial decision-making. How much of a part nobody knows. Nonrandomly chosen examples abound; consider the impact, upon the Supreme Court's policy output, of the health component as it affected the lives of Frank Murphy, Wiley Rutledge, and William Douglas, during the brief span of the latter two summer months of 1949: during the following term, the Court's liberal bloc was reduced from four to one (Black), with traumatic consequent effects upon both the selection of the Court's workload (Tanenhaus et al. 1963; Schubert 1962c) and its policy output (Schubert 1965c:210, 226–227. The development of the medical speciality of geriatrics has been accompanied by no corresponding focusing of interest in judicial senescence (but, see Schmidhauser 1962c); so we remain equally ignorant of both the possible physiological and psychological—and, need I add, philosophical?—effects of aging, upon the reasoning processes of elderly judges. After a quarter-century on the Supreme Court, for example, Hugo Black remained a staunch political, social, and economic liberal (Schubert 1965c:112, 138, 217); but since 1963, as the Court's senior associate justice and oldest member has undergone the metamorphosis from septa- to octogenarianism, Black has led the Court in conservative—and many would claim reactionary—opposition to most contemporary claims of civil rights and liberties, ranging from whether librarians ought to feel frightened at the mere presence of well-behaved but black patrons, to his vote to affirm, on June 10, 1968, the second conviction of a robber-murderer. In the latter case Black dissented in company with his latter-day compatriots (Harlan and White), indulging in such now typical statements for him as that "I agree that holdings like this [viz., that of the majority] make it far more difficult to protect society 'against those who have made it impossible to live today in safety'" (Black, dissenting in *Harrison* v. *United States*, at p. 226). Shades of Robert Jackson! Has Hugo Black "changed his mind" in the quite literal sense that synaptic deterioration has changed it for him? Of course, no one knows, and least of all perhaps does Mr. Justice Black; but the issue raised by the question seems sufficiently common to the field of judicial behavior that it warrants scientific investigation. Certainly, the interests, the methodology, and increasingly the language of discourse of environmental and other public health scientists overlap with the concerns of political scientists (Knutson 1965; Rogers and Messinger 1967); and the time may be at hand when we ought to take seriously the hypothesis, that senility may have an important enough effect upon judicial behavior, that we ought to try to understand it better. Conceivably, FDR's attack upon the "nine old men"—the conventional view of which now is that the president was right for the wrong reasons—may have been right for the right reason: that American society has more to gain than to lose, even at the cost of the loss of the services of an occasional Holmes or Brandeis, from a system of compulsory retirement of Supreme Court justices, thereby precluding at least most of the predictable irrationality in judicial reasoning that may result from senescence.[11]

In speaking of race as a physiological indicator that might be deemed relevant to judicial behavior, I select it as one that evidently is important in the structuring of political relationships in the United States today. I assume that, although the manifest basis for classifying individuals on this indicator will be observable physiological characteristics (Nagel 1962a), its relevance to judicial behavior may consist primarily (as in the instance of the socialization hypothesis concerning judicial age) of its function as a discriminator of what many today assert to be major differences between two American cultures, one black and one white, involving of course complex social, psychological, economic, and political components. Presumably one would wish to investigate whether there are any significant differences between the behavior of black judges and of white judges, that can be attributed to the racial (cultural) differences between them. No doubt, any such research in the United States during the proximate future would have to focus (as would, perhaps, be more appropriate in any case) upon local courts in metropolitan areas, because of sampling problems that can be anticipated to rise in attempts to work with federal judges, or with state appellate court judges. Thurgood Marshall's appointment to the United States Supreme Court is both unprecedented and barely two years old.

The other physiological indicator, sex, should perhaps be taken to subsume primarily what *are* physiological differences, with associated psychological and social components. The likelihood that sampling problems would be at least as difficult, in endeavors to discriminate the effect of sex upon judicial behavior (e.g., Lasswell 1930, and 1948:65–88 [on judges X, Y, and Z]). As they will be in efforts to deal with race as either an independent or an intervening variable, suggests that sex still involves—at least in the field of judicial behavior—important political correlates; and this may still be true of its economic implications as well. Indeed, male chauvinists may well assert that any present concern for the sexual implications of judicial behavior—

---

11. For a more extended treatment of this argument and the supporting evidence, see Schubert 1970a: chap. 2.

symbolic or literal—must constitute a fey preoccupation with triviality. But the possibility of sexual differences in judicial behavior can hardly be dismissed as immaterial in other societies that, at least in some respects, are more egalitarian than the American; and from the perspective of democratic ideology, the question of the possible opening up of access to judicial office, irrespective of either race or sex, is not a trivial one. It might, therefore, be relevant for students of judicial behavior to attempt to understand better both the behavior of female judges, and the female behavior of judges. And with regard to the latter matter, I should perhaps point out that none of these physiological indicators needs to be—and perhaps none *should* be—treated as a nominal scale. Age we are accustomed to think of as an interval (indeed as a ratio) scale; health we ordinarily speak of in ordinal terms; and only our cultural bias and empirical ignorance make it possible for any of us to speak of either race or sex as though they constitute natural dichotomies.

I have discussed the physiological indicators at this length, not because I believe they are either the most important causes or the best predictors of judicial behavior, but rather because they clearly have been the most neglected. It is easy to see why this is true; what one might term "orthodox" behavioralism has been demanding enough, with its insistence that students of judicial behavior should become educated as psychologists, sociologists, anthropologists, statisticians, and mathematicians, as well as political scientists, lawyers, historians, economists, and philosophers. Now comes the suggestion that this is by no means enough; the judicial—and really, I believe, political—behavioralist of the next generation ought to be trained also in physiological biology, genetics, mental health, and public health. The prospect may well seem foreboding, and especially so, I should think (now that some of the sociopsychological implications of our noble experiment in mass education at the university level are becoming more obvious) to the adolescent habitués of our undergraduate colleges, many of whom now claim the right to be deemed educated as a consequence of their engagement in informal small group experiments in oral masturbation, thus avoiding the more onerous traditional workways to the acquisition of knowledge. The point seems relevant because these undergraduates are the persons who need to be trained in this broader concept of behavioralism, to include the health sciences as well as both the newer and the older social sciences.[12] Calling themselves "niggers," sucking their thumbs in public orgies of self-pity, and lobbying to define college curricula primarily, if not exclusively, in terms of bull sessions—and I trust that the etymological root of *that* expression will not have been forgotten by the present audience—seem unlikely to imbue in them either the required knowledge and skills or the orientation toward

---

12. The Mental Health Research Institute of the University of Michigan and the National Institutes of Mental Health (Washington, D.C.) are examples of research organizations that do embrace the concept.

scientific inquiry that are needed to get the job done, if such work is ever to be done.

The explicit design and the findings of previous empirical research on the effect of social and of personality components upon judicial reasoning have been reviewed, both by others and by myself, so often and so recently (Pritchett 1968; Shapiro 1964b; Schubert 1963a, 1968e, and 1964a: intro. essay and chap. intros.) that I thought it would be less valuable, for present purposes, to replow those furrows than it might be to discuss, even though speculatively, the possible breaking of new ground. Moreover, the field of judicial behavior has been subjected, throughout the entire period of its existence, to a running cross-fire of critique, emanating particularly from law or philosophy-trained professors of law or of public law (Fisher 1958; Roche 1958; Berns 1963, 1968; Becker 1963a, 1963b, 1964; Mendelson 1963, 1964; Shapiro 1964a: chap. 1; Blawie and Blawie 1965; Krislov 1966; Fuller 1966; Stone 1966a), although there is increasing evidence that the most relevant members of both professions, law and political science, have begun to tire of the logomachy, and to favor allocating a larger share of the field's resources to what I have called giving "greater attention to how we can learn from each other, and less to the contemplation of our respective ideological umbilici"; and for which Herman Pritchett has substituted the more currently fashionable quotation from the chairman, "Let a hundred flowers bloom".[13]

It is fair, I believe, to summarize earlier work in the field by stating that the consistency of judicial voting behavior, by judges in courts at all levels and in a variety of different cultural settings, with consistency measured in relation to a small number of public policy (viz., attitudinal) dimensions, appears to be well established (Schubert 1965c, 1968g; Fair 1967; Gadbois 1969; Hayakawa 1962; Peck, 1967b). Moreover, this research, far from rejecting the possible importance of variables that lawyers tend to call "stare decisis" or "activism versus passivism" or "judicial role," explicitly has attempted to operationalize the legal hypothesis by redefining stare decisis as a psychological variable. In that form, it appears to have an important, but secondary, effect upon judicial reasoning (Schubert 1963c, 1965c:266–272, 1972f; Shapiro 1965, 1972b): most supreme court judges, that is to say, are influenced primarily by their substantive attitudes toward issues of public policy—their policy biases, if you will—and only to a lesser degree by the extent to which their psychological orientation is pragmatic or dogmatic (Eysenck 1954; Schubert 1968c), that is, by the extent to which they have an open or a closed judicial mind (Rokeach 1960). But this research has focused upon the highest courts within the polities examined; whether, as some have hypothesized, the

---

13. Pritchett 1968:509. Cf.: "Letting a hundred flowers blossom and a hundred schools of thought contend is the policy for promoting the progress of the arts and the sciences and a flourishing socialist culture in our land. Different forms and styles in art should develop freely and different schools in science should contend freely." (Schram 1967:174)

psychological dimension of dogmatism is weighted more heavily for lower, and particularly for trial, court judges, remains an open question in the light of the available empirical work, although some recent reports indicate that the importance of policy attitudes is no less for trial, than it is for appellate, court judges (Dolbeare 1967*b*).

There is, moreover, another attitudinal dimension that thus far remains too inadequately explored to permit an appraisal of how relatively important it may be, in relation to the other two dimensions of attitude, policy and institutional, just discussed. The *relations* of judges with each other, in the small groups that appellate courts define, almost certainly produce a sociometric dimension of their *attitudes* toward each other, which also enters into judicial decision-making, and not infrequently into judicial reasoning even in the sense of the manifest content of judicial opinions. Such notorious examples of antipathy as Jackson-Black, Jackson-Murphy, and McReynolds-Brandeis, or of empathy as Taft-Butler, Taft-VanDevanter, and Clark-Vinson, suggest that neither type of relationship is necessarily symmetrical; nor do the voting data which have been used for the study of policy attitudes necessarily provide the most fruitful source of data for studying sociometric attitudes: probably either opinion interagreement (Ulmer 1963; Schubert 1968*f*) or the private papers of judges (Murphy 1966) proffer better bets.

The hypothesis that the beliefs, and therefore the voting and opinion behavior, of judges can be explained substantially on the basis of their social, economic, and political background experiences is as old as the United States Supreme Court—if one is willing to accept Jefferson's letters as evidence on this point (Myers 1912; Haines 1922; Rodell 1955). Several of the earliest quantitative studies of the Supreme Court attempted to assemble descriptive data on the background characteristics of the justices; and more recently several doctoral dissertations and other writings have attempted to test the relationship between background characteristics and decisional behavior (Nagel 1962*b*; Schmidhauser 1962*b*; Bowen 1965; Goldman 1966). The one correlation that does seem to be fairly well established is that between political party affiliation and judicial voting, with Democrats (except in the South) favoring liberal outcomes. Nagel's earlier finding, that the probable scale of liberalism is Jewish-Catholic-Protestant, for justices classified by major religious groupings, was not confirmed by Goldman in a subsequent study (using a differently drawn sample) (Nagel 1962*a*; Goldman 1966); and Bowen found that only a very small amount of variance could be attributed to any single background variable as a decisional predictor, even when the sample size produced statistically significant—although characteristically low—first-order correlations (1965). Of course, none of this suggests that the life experiences of judges have no impact upon their attitudes and decisional behavior. But it does indicate that the relationships involved appear to be too complicated to be discovered by the relatively crude use of simple linear correlation, poorly defined and highly correlated (viz., nonindependent) "independent" variables, and inadequate samples.

Little can or should be said at this time concerning the empirical work on cultural differences, because most of the relevant work with which I am familiar is either just out or else still in press or in process, and appraisal of it at this time would be both premature and presumptuous (Schubert 1967c, 1968c; Grossman and Tanenhaus 1969; Schubert and Danelski 1969).

I should like, however, to make one or two concluding remarks about the importance of guiding future work with a well-developed theoretical model, if not one that builds upon the paradigm of Figure 22, at least (hopefully) one that focuses attention upon the interrelationships among variables likely to be selected for study by scholars working from several different disciplinary orientations, one that directs attention to the possible relevance of physiological dimensions, and one that posits a multidimensional space that can accommodate the variety of empirical findings likely to be generated, over the course of the next decade, by lawyer, sociologist, political scientist, anthropologist, psychologist, and other possible researchers in the field. Such a model should be so constructed as to facilitate its being translated into the scientific dialects of these several disciplines (Cohen 1950), because work upon filling in the interstices of what presently can readily enough be perceived as gaping voids can proceed parsimoniously only to the extent that scholars can become timely aware of, and can more fully understand, each other's contributions. Only in a minimal way do such conditions obtain today, in my opinion. But this very symposium should help to bring about a better common understanding, among philosophers and law professors and political scientists, concerning the present state of our conjoint knowledge concerning judicial reasoning. The Constitution may not be what the justices say it is; but neither can the rest of us, who *do* define the Constitution, project too close an image of what the Supreme Court says it is *not*. To that extent, at least, our quest for justice is confined by judicial reasoning.

# Cases Cited

# Bibliography

Aaron, Daniel (moderator); Kenneth Burke, Malcolm Cowley, Granville Hicks, and William Phillips (participants). 1966. "Thirty Years Later: Memories of the First American Writer's Congress." *American Scholar* 35:495–516.

Abraham, Henry. 1965. "The Need for Ombudsmen in the United States." In *The Ombudsman: Citizen's Defender*, edited by Donald C. Rowat. London: Allen & Unwin.

——. 1968. *The Judicial Process*. Rev. ed. New York: Oxford University Press.

Adorno, Theodore W., et al. 1950. *The Authoritarian Personality*. New York: Harper.

Alker, Hayward R., Jr. 1965. *Mathematics and Politics*. New York: Macmillan Co.

——. 1966. "Causal Inference and Political Analysis." In *Mathematical Applications in Political Science*, vol. 2, edited by Joseph L. Bernd. Dallas: Southern Methodist University Press.

Allport, Floyd. 1924. *Social Psychology*. Boston: Houghton Mifflin Co.

——. 1933. *Institutional Behavior*. Chapel Hill: University of North Carolina Press.

Almond, Gabriel, and James Coleman. 1960. *The Politics of the Developing Areas*. Princeton: Princeton University Press.

Almond, Gabriel, and G. Bingham Powell, Jr. 1966. *Comparative Politics: A Developmental Approach*. Boston: Little, Brown & Co.

*American College Dictionary*. 1964. Rev. ed. New York: Random House.

American Political Science Association, Committee on Political Parties. 1950. "Toward a More Responsible Two-Party System." *American Political Science Review* 44(3): pt. 2 (supplement).

Anderson, William. 1934. "The Teaching Personnel in American Political Science Departments." *American Political Science Review* 28:740–742.

Anonymous. 1938. "Robert H. Jackson." *Fortune* 26:78–80 (March).

Anonymous. 1967. "The High Court." *Current Affairs Bulletin* 40:82–96.

Arens, Richard, and Harold D. Lasswell. 1964. "Toward a General Theory of Sanctions." *Iowa Law Review* 49:233–276.

Atkins, Burton M. 1970. "Some Theoretical Effects of the Decision-making Rules on the United States Court of Appeals." *Jurimetrics Journal* 11 (September 1970): 13–23.

——. 1972. "Decision-Making Rules and Judicial Strategy on the United States Courts of Appeals." *Western Political Quarterly* 25:626–642.

Aubert, Vilhelm. 1959. "Chance in Social Affairs." *Inquiry* 2:1–24.

——. 1963a. "Conscientious Objectors before Norwegian Military Courts." In *Judicial Decision-Making*, edited by Glendon Schubert. New York: The Free Press.

——. 1963b. "Researches in the sociology of law." *American Behavioral Science* 7: 16–20.

Aubert, Vilhelm, Torstein Echoff, and Knut Sveri. 1952. *En lov i søkelyset* [A Law in the Searchlight]. Oslo: Akademisk forlag.

Austin, John. 1869. *Lectures on Jurisprudence*. Edited by Robert Campbell, 3rd ed. London: J. Murray, 2 vols.

Backstrom, Charles, and Gerald Hursch. 1963. *Survey Research*. Evanston: Northwestern University Press.

Bagehot, Walter. 1908. *Physics and Politics; or, Thoughts on the Application of the Principles of "Natural Selection" and "Inheritance" to Political Society*. New York: D. Appleton. (First published in 1872.)

Baggaley, Andrew R. 1964. *Intermediate Correlational Methods*. New York: John Wiley & Sons.

Bakal, Carl. 1966. *The Right to Bear Arms*. New York: McGraw-Hill.

Baker, Kendall L., Sami G. Hajjar, and Alan Evan Schenker. 1972. "A Note on Behavioralists and Post-Behavioralists in Contemporary Political Science." *PS* 5: 271–273.

Baldwin, Leland D. 1972. *Reframing the Constitution: An Imperative for Modern America*. Santa Barbara, California: American Bibliographical Center-CLIO Press.

Bar and Officers of the Supreme Court, The. 1955. "In Memory of Mr. Justice Robert Houghwout Jackson, Proceedings in the Supreme Court of the United States, April 4, 1955." 349 U.S. xxvii–li.

Barnett, Vincent L. 1948. "Mr. Justice Jackson and the Supreme Court." *Western Political Quarterly* 1:233–242.

Beard, Charles A. 1948. "Neglected Aspects of Political Science." *American Political Science Review* 42:211–222.

Beatty, Jerry K. 1970. "Decision-making on the Iowa Supreme Court, 1965–1969." *Drake Law Review* 19:342–367.

Becker, Theodore L. 1963a. "Inquiry into a School of Thought in the Judicial Behavior Movement." *Midwest Journal of Political Science* 7:254–266.

———. 1963b. "On Science, Political Science, and Law." *American Behavioral Scientist* 7(4):11–15.

———. 1964. *Political Behavioralism and Modern Jurisprudence*. Chicago: Rand McNally.

———. 1965. "Judicial Role Variation, Clear Precedents, and Resultant Decisional Tendencies." Honolulu: University of Hawaii, Department of Political Science. Mimeographed.

———. 1966a. "Judicial Structure and Its Political Functioning in Society." Paper read at the Western Political Science Association meeting, Reno, Nevada, March 25, 1966. Mimeographed.

———. 1966b. "Surveys and Judiciaries, or Who's Afraid of the Purple Curtain." *Law and Society Review* 1:133–143.

———. 1970. *The Political Trial: The Use, Abuse, and Misuse of Courts for Political Ends*. Indianapolis: Bobbs-Merrill Co.

Becker, Theodore L., D. C. Hildrum, and K. Bateman. 1965. "The Influence of Jurors' Values on Their Verdicts: A Courts and Politics experiment." *Southwest Social Science Quarterly* 46:132–140.

Benedict, Ruth. 1946. *The Chrysanthemum and the Sword: Patterns of Japanese Culture*. Boston: Houghton Mifflin Co.

Bentley, Arthur Fisher. 1955. *The Process of Government: A Study of Social Pressures*.

4th ed. Bloomington, Indiana: Principia Press. (First published in 1908.)

Berelson, Bernard, Paul F. Lazarsfeld, and William N. McPhee. 1954. *Voting*. Chicago: University of Chicago Press.

Berelson, Bernard, and Gary A. Steiner. 1964. *Human Behavior: An Inventory of Scientific Findings*. New York: Harcourt, Brace and World.

Bernard, Jessie. 1955. "Dimensions and Axes of Supreme Court Decisions: A Study in the Sociology of Conflict." *Social Forces* 34:19–27.

Bernd, Joseph L., ed. 1966. *Mathematical Applications in Political Science*. Charlottesville: University Press of Virginia.

Berns, Walter. 1963. "Law and Behavioral Science." *Law and Contemporary Problems* 28:185–212.

————. 1968. "Behavioral Science and 'Equal Justice under Law.'" A paper delivered at the seminars in the American Political Tradition, Claremont Men's College.

Beyle, Herman C. 1931. *Identification and Analysis of Attribute-Cluster-Blocs*. Chicago: University of Chicago Press.

Bickel, Alexander M. 1957. *The Unpublished Opinions of Mr. Justice Brandeis*. Cambridge: Harvard University Press.

Biddle, Bruce J., and Edwin J. Thomas, eds. 1966. *Role Theory: Concepts and Research*. New York: Wiley.

Birkby, Robert H. 1966. "The Supreme Court and the Bible Belt: Tennessee Reaction to the 'Schempp' decision." *Midwest Journal of Political Science* 10:304–319.

Black, Hugo LaFayette. 1968. *A Constitutional Faith*. New York: Alfred A. Knopf.

Blackshield, Anthony R. 1972. "Quantitative Analysis: The High Court of Australia, 1964–1969." *Lawasia* 3:1–66.

Blalock, Hubert M. 1967. "Causal Inferences, Closed Populations, and Measures of Association." *American Political Science Review* 61:130–136.

————. 1968. "The Measurement Problem: A Gap between the Languages of Theory and Research." In *Methodology in Social Research*, edited by Hubert Blalock and Anne Blalock. New York: McGraw-Hill.

Blawie, James L., and Marilyn J. Blawie. 1965. "The Judicial Decision: A Second Look at Certain Assumptions of Behavioral Research." *Western Political Quarterly* 18:579–593.

Blegvad, Britt-Mari Persson, ed. 1966. "Symposium on Sociology of Law." *Acta Sociologica* 10(1, 2):1–190.

Borgatta, Edgar F. 1958–1959. "On Analyzing Correlation Matrices: Some New Emphases." *Public Opinion Quarterly* 22:516–528.

Bowen, Don Ramsey. 1965. *The Explanation of Judicial Voting Behavior from Sociological Characteristics of Judges*. Ann Arbor, Michigan: University Microfilms #65–15,014. Ph. D. dissertation in Political Science, Yale University.

Boyd, J. D. 1971. "An Extraordinarily Authoritarian Document." *The Center Magazine* (March-April) 4(2):45–47.

Brown, Leonard, ed. 1929. *Modern American and British Short Stories*. New York: Harcourt, Brace. (Second edition, 1937.)

————. 1933a. "The Genesis, Growth, and Meaning of *Endymion*." *Studies in Philology* 30:618–653.

————. 1933b. "On Contemporary Poetry." *Sewanee Review* 41:43–63.

————. 1934a. "Arnold's Succession: 1850–1914." *Sewanee Review* 42:158–179.

————. 1934b. "Poetry as Mimesis." *Sewanee Review* 42:424–435.

————. 1935a. "The Last Angels." *Sewanee Review* 43:159.

————. 1935b. "The Marxist Approach to Literature." *Sewanee Review* 43:378–380.

————. 1944. "The Refrigerator." *The New Yorker* 20 (Dec. 9):53–54.

————, ed. 1947. *Literature for Our Time*. New York: Henry Holt.

Brown, Leonard, A. E. DuBois, E. N. Hooker, M. C. Thomas. 1928. *What Feather: Stories and Verse*. Syracuse, N. Y.: Pendragon Press.

Brown, Leonard, and Porter G. Perrin, eds. 1935. *A Quarto of Modern Literature*. New York: Scribner's. (Second edition, 1940; third edition, 1950).

Brown, Merle E. 1969. *Kenneth Burke*. Minneapolis: University of Minnesota Press.

Brown, Patrick, and William A. Haddad. 1966–1967. "Judicial Decision-making on the Florida Supreme Court: An Introductory Behavioral Study." *University of Florida Law Review* 19:566–590.

Brown, Ralph S., Jr. 1963. "Legal Research: The Resource Base and Traditional Approaches." *American Behavioral Scientist* 7 (December 1963):3–7.

Buchwald, Arthur. 1966. "Gun Lovers, United." Honolulu: *Honolulu Star-Bulletin*, August 6, 1966, p. A–4, cols. 4–5.

————. 1967. "Gun Counter Escalation." Honolulu: *Honolulu Star-Bulletin*, May 27. 1967, p. A–4, col. 3–4.

Burke, Kenneth. 1935. *Permanence and Change: An Anatomy of Purpose*. New York: The New Republic Press.

————. 1937. *Attitudes toward History*. 2 vols. New York: The New Republic Press.

————. 1941. *The Philosophy of Literary Form*. Baton Rouge: Louisiana State University Press.

————. 1945. *A Grammar of Motives*. Englewood Cliffs, N.J.: Prentice-Hall.

Cahill, Fred V., Jr. 1952. *Judicial Legislation: A Study of American Legal Theory*. New York: Ronald Press Co.

Campbell, Bernard. 1966. *Human Evolution: An Introduction to Man's Adaptations*. Chicago: Aldine Publishing Co.

Cardozo, Benjamin N. 1921. *The Nature of the Judicial Process*. New Haven: Yale University Press.

————. 1924. *The Growth of the Law*. New Haven: Yale University Press.

————. 1925. "Law and Literature." *Yale Review* 14:699–718.

Carp, Robert, and Russell Wheeler. 1972. "Sink or Swim: The Socialization of a Federal District Judge." *Journal of Public Law* 22:359–393.

Cartwright, Dorwin, and Alvin Zander, eds. 1960. *Group Dynamics: Research and Theory*. Evanston, Illinois: Row, Peterson.

Cattell, Raymond B. 1952. *Factor Analysis: An Introduction and Manual for the Psychologist and Social Scientist*. New York: Harper.

Chie, Nakane. 1964. "Logic and the Smile: When Japanese Meet Indians." *Japan Quarterly* 11:434–438.

Childs, Marquis W. 1940. "The Man Who Has Always Been a New Dealer." *Forum* 103:148–154.

Christie, Richard. 1956a. "Eysenck's Treatment of the Personality of Communists." *Psychology Bulletin* 53:411–430.

————. 1956b. "Some Abuses of Psychology." *Psychology Bulletin* 53:439–451.

Cohen, Felix S. 1935. "Transcendental Nonsense and the Functional Approach." *Columbia Law Review* 35:809–849.

————. 1950. "Field Theory and Judicial Logic." *Yale Law Journal* 59:238–272.

Cohn, Haim H. 1967. "Reflections on the Trial and Death of Jesus." *Israel Law Review* 3:332–379.

Collins, Barry E., and Harold Guetzkow. 1964. *A Social Psychology of Group Processes for Decision-Making.* New York: John Wiley & Sons.

Cook, Beverly. 1971. "The Socialization of New Federal Judges: Impact on District Court Business." *Washington University Law Quarterly* 1971:253–279.

———. 1973. "Decision-Making by Federal Trial Judges: Reference Groups and Local Culture." New Orleans. Paper presented at 1973 Annual Meeting of the American Political Science Association.

Coombs, Clyde H. 1964. *A Theory of Data.* New York: John Wiley & Sons.

Coombs, Clyde H., and Richard C. Kao. 1960. "On a Connection between Factor Analysis and Multi-Dimensional Unfolding." *Psychometrika* 25:219–231.

Corey, Herbert. 1937. "A Man with a Flexible Future." *Nation's Business* 25 (September): 75–76, 78, 119.

Corning, Peter A. 1971. "The Biological Bases of Behavior and Their Implications for Political Theory." *World Politics* 23:321–370.

Corwin, Edward Samuel. 1953. "The Constitution of the United States of America: Analysis and Interpretation." *Senate Document* No. 170, 82nd Cong., 2nd Sess.

———. 1957. *The President: Office and Powers.* 4th rev. ed. New York: New York University Press.

Cowen, Zelman. 1967. *Isaac Isaacs.* Melbourne: Melbourne University Press.

Crombie, Alistair C. 1961. "Quantification in Medieval Physics." In *Quantification: A History of the Meaning of Measurement in the Natural and Social Sciences,* edited by Harry Woolf. Indianapolis: Bobbs-Merrill Co.

Crosskey, William W. 1953. *Politics and the Constitution in the History of the United States.* 2 vols. Chicago: University of Chicago Press.

Cureton, Edward E. 1959. "Note on $\phi/\phi$max." *Psychometrika* 24:89–91.

Dahl, Robert A. 1961. "The Behavioral Approach." *American Political Science Review* 55:763–772.

Danelski, David J. 1961. "The Influence of the Chief Justice in the Decision Process of the Supreme Court." In *Courts, Judges, and Politics,* edited by Walter F. Murphy and C. Herman Pritchett. New York: Random House.

———. 1964. *A Supreme Court Justice Is Appointed.* New York: Random House.

———. 1966. "Values as Variables in Judicial Decision-making: Notes toward a Theory." *Vanderbilt Law Review* 19:721–740.

———. 1968. "Public Law: The Field." *International Encyclopedia of the Social Sciences.* Vol. 13, pp. 175–183. New York: Macmillan Co.

———. 1969. "The Supreme Court of Japan: An Exploratory Study." In *Comparative Judicial Behavior,* edited by Glendon Schubert and David Danelski. New York: Oxford University Press.

Dator, James. 1966. " 'The Protestant Ethic' in Japan." *Journal of the Developing Areas* 1:23–40.

———. 1967. "The Life History and Attitudes of Japanese High Court Judges." *Western Political Quarterly* 20:408–439.

———. 1969. "Measuring Attitudes across Cultures: A Factor Analysis of the Replies of Japanese Judges to Eysenck's Inventory of Conservative-Progressive Ideology." In *Comparative Judicial Behavior,* edited by Glendon Schubert and David Danelski. New York: Oxford University Press.

Davidson, Leon. 1969. *The Quiet Campaign to Rewrite the Constitution.* White Plains, N.Y.: Blue Book Publishers.

Davies, James C. 1969. "The Psychobiology of Political Behavior: Some Provocative Developments." Paper presented at a panel of 23d annual meeting of the Western Political Science Association in Honolulu.

Davis, Kenneth C. 1953. "Reflections of a Law Professor on Instruction and Research in Public Administration." *American Political Science Review* 47:728–752.

———. 1964. "Behavioral Science and Administrative Law." *Journal of Legal Education* 17:137–154.

de Grazia, Alfred, and Charles L. Ruttenberg. 1963. "Innovators in the Study of the Legal Process." *American Behavioral Scientist* 7 (December 1963):48–52.

Deutsch, Karl. 1951. "Mechanism, Organism, and Society: Some Models in Natural and Social Science." *Philosophy of Science* 18:230–252.

———. 1963. *The Nerves of Government.* New York: The Free Press.

DeVos, George A. 1954. "A Comparison of the Personality Differences in Two Generations of Japanese-Americans by Means of the Rorschach Test." *Nagoya Journal of Medical Science* 17:157–161.

Dietze, Gottfried, ed. 1965. *Essays on the American Constitution: A Commemorative Volume in Honor of Alpheus T. Mason.* Englewood Cliffs, N.J.: Prentice-Hall.

Dimock, Marshall E. 1951. *Goals for Political Science.* New York: William Sloane Associates.

Dixon, Owen, the Rt. Hon. Sir. 1965. *Jesting Pilate, and Other Papers and Addresses,* collected by His Honour Judge Woinarski. Melbourne, Australia: The Law Book Company Ltd.

Dixon, Robert G., Jr. 1971. "Who Is Listening? Political Science Research in Public Law." *PS* 4:19–26.

Dixon, Wilfrid Joseph, ed. 1964. *BMD: Biomedical Computer Programs.* University of California, Los Angeles: School of Medicine, Health Sciences Computing Facility, Department of Preventive Medicine and Public Health.

Dodd, Walter F. 1932. *Cases and Materials on Constitutional Law.* St. Paul: West Publishing Co. (Fifth edition, 1954.)

Dolbeare, Kenneth M. 1967a. "The Public Views the Supreme Court." In *Law, Politics, and the Federal Courts,* edited by Herbert Jacob. Boston: Little, Brown & Co.

———. 1967b. *Trial Courts in Urban Politics: State Court Policy Impact and Functions in a Local Political System.* New York: John Wiley & Sons.

———. 1969. "The Federal District Courts and Urban Public Policy: An Exploratory Study (1960–1967)." In *The Frontiers of Judicial Research,* edited by Joel Grossman and Joseph Tanenhaus. New York: John Wiley & Sons.

Dolbeare, Kenneth M., and Phillip E. Hammond. 1968. "The Political Party Basis of Attitudes toward the United States Supreme Court." *Public Opinion Quarterly* 16:16–30.

Douglas, Roger N. 1968. "Courts in the Political System." *Melbourne Journal of Politics* 1:36–47.

Douglas, William O. 1956. *We the Judges.* Garden City, N.Y.: Doubleday & Co.

Drewry, Gavin, and Jenny Morgan. 1969. "Law Lords as Legislators." *Parliamentary Affairs* 22:226–239.

Dugard, John. 1971. "The Judicial Process and Civil Liberty." *South African Law Journal*

88:181–200.

Easton, David. 1953. *The Political System.* New York: Alfred A. Knopf.

———. 1965a. *A Framework for Political Analysis.* Englewood Cliffs, N.J.: Prentice-Hall.

———. 1965b. *A Systems Analysis of Political Life.* New York: John Wiley & Sons.

Eckhoff, Torstein. 1960. "Sociology of Law in Scandinavia." *Scandinavian Studies in Law* 4:29–58.

———. 1965. "Impartiality, Separation of Powers, and Judicial Independence." *Scandinavian Studies in Law* 9:11–48.

Eckhoff, Torstein, and Knut Jacobson. 1960. *Rationality and Responsibility in Administrative and Judicial Decision-Making.* Copenhagen: Munksgaard.

Edinger, Lewis J., ed. 1967. *Political Leadership in Industrialized Societies: Studies in Comparative Analysis.* New York: John Wiley & Sons.

Editorial. 1966. "Partial Blame for 17,000 Deaths Yearly Laid to Gun Lobby." Honolulu: *Honolulu Star-Bulletin,* August 4, 1966, p. B–4, cols. 1–8.

Editorial. 1967. "Registration Bill Sparks Controversy: Police, Riflemen Split on Gun Law." Honolulu: *Honolulu Star-Bulletin,* April 10, 1967, p. A–12, cols, 4–8.

Endo, O., ed. 1954. *Sengo Nihon Shinrigaku no Tenbo.* Tokyo: Sanitchi Shobo.

Erlenmeyer-Kimling, L., and Lissy F. Jarvik. 1963. "Genetics and Intelligence: A Review." *Science* 142:1477–1479.

Eulau, Heinz. 1963. *The Behavioral Persuasion in Politics.* New York: Random House.

———, ed. 1966. *Political Behavior in America: New Directions.* New York: Random House.

———. 1969. "Quo Vadimus? A Note on the Discipline." *PS* 2(1):12–13.

Eulau, Heinz, and John D. Sprague. 1964. *Lawyers in Politics.* Indianapolis: Bobbs-Merrill Co.

Ewing, Cortez A. M. 1938. *The Judges of the Supreme Court, 1789–1937, A Study of Their Qualifications.* Minneapolis: University of Minnesota Press.

Eysenck, Hans J. 1947. "Primary Social Attitudes: (1). The Organization and Measurement of Social Attitudes." *International Journal of Opinion and Attitude Research* 1(3):39–84.

———. 1951. "Review of Samuel A. Stouffer, Louis Guttman, et al. *Measurement and Prediction*: A Discussion of Vol. 4 of *Studies in Social Psychology* in World War II." *International Journal of Opinion and Attitude Research* 5:95–102.

———. 1953. "Primary Social Attitudes: A Comparison of Attitude Patterns in England, Germany, and Sweden." *Journal of Abnormal and Social Psychology* 48:563–568.

———. 1954. *The Psychology of Politics.* London: Routledge and Kegan Paul.

———. 1956a. "The Psychology of Politics: A Reply." *Psychology Bulletin* 53:177–182.

———. 1956b. "The Psychology of Politics and the Personality Similarities between Fascists and Communists." *Psychology Bulletin* 53:431–438.

Eysenck, Hans J., and Thelma T. Coulter. 1972. "The Personality and Attitudes of Working Class British Communists and Fascists." *Journal of Social Psychology* 87:59–73.

Fair, Daryl. 1967. "An Experimental Application of Scalogram Analysis to State Supreme Court Decisions." *Wisconsin Law Review* 1967:449–467.

Fairman, Charles. 1955. "Robert H. Jackson: Associate Justice of the Supreme Court." *Columbia Law Review* 55:445–487.

Feeley, Malcolm M. 1971. "Another Look at the 'Party Variable' in Judicial Decision-making: An Analysis of the Michigan Supreme Court. *Polity* 4:91–104.

Fish, Peter G. 1973. *The Politics of Federal Judicial Administration.* Princeton: Princeton University Press.

Fisher, Franklin M. 1958. "The Mathematical Analysis of Supreme Court Decisions: The Use and Abuse of Quantitative Methods." *American Political Science Review* 52:321–338.

———. 1960. "On the Existence and Linearity of Perfect Predictors in 'Content Analysis.'" *Modern Uses of Logic in Law* 1 (March 1960):1–9.

Flango, Victor E., and Glendon Schubert. 1969. "Two Surveys of Simulated Judicial Decision-making: Hawaii and the Philippines." In *Comparative Judicial Behavior*, edited by Glendon Schubert and David Danelski. New York: Oxford University Press.

Fouts, Donald E. 1969. "Policy-making in the Supreme Court of Canada, 1950–1960." In *Comparative Judicial Behavior*, edited by Glendon Schubert and David J. Danelski. New York: Oxford University Press.

Fowler, Henry Watson, ed. 1965. *A Dictionary of Modern English Usage.* New York: Oxford University Press.

Frank, Armin Paul. 1969. *Kenneth Burke.* New York: Twayne Publishers.

Frank, Jerome. 1930. *Law and the Modern Mind.* New York: Coward-McCann.

———. 1931. "Are Judges Human?" *University of Pennsylvania Law Review* 80:17–53, 233–267.

———. 1942. *If Men Were Angels.* New York: Harper.

Frank, John P. 1949. *Mr. Justice Black: The Man and His Opinions.* New York: Alfred A. Knopf.

———. 1958. *The Marble Palace.* New York: Alfred A. Knopf.

Frankfurter, Felix. 1955. "Mr. Justice Jackson." *Harvard Law Review* 68:937–939.

Franz, J. Noland. 1967. "Computerized Law Retrieval: Present and Future." *University of Missouri at Kansas City Law Review* 25:219–246.

Fruchter, Benjamin. 1954. *Introduction to Factor Analysis.* New York: Van Nostrand.

Fuller, Lon. 1966. "Science and the Judical Process." *Harvard Law Review* 79:1604–1628.

Gadbois, George H., Jr. 1969. "The Selection, Background Characteristics, and Voting Behavior of Indian Supreme Court Judges, 1950–1959." In *Comparative Judicial Behavior*, edited by Glendon Schubert and David J. Danelski. New York: Oxford University Press.

———. 1970a. "Indian Judicial Behavior." *Economic and Political Weekly* 5:1–11.

———. 1970b. "The Supreme Court of India: A Preliminary Report of an Empirical Study." *Journal of Constitutional and Parliamentary Studies* 4:33–54.

Gerard, Ralph W. 1961. "Quantification in Biology." In *Quantification: A History of the Meaning of Measurement in the Natural and Social Sciences*, edited by Harry Woolf. Indianapolis: Bobbs-Merrill Co.

Gerhart, Eugene C. 1953. "A Decade of Mr. Justice Jackson." *New York University Law Review* 28:927–974.

———. 1958. *America's Advocate: Robert H. Jackson.* Indianapolis: Bobbs-Merrill Co.

Gluckman, Max. 1965. *Politics, Law and Ritual in Tribal Society.* Chicago: Aldine.

Goldman, Sheldon. 1965. *Politics, Judges, and the Administration of Justice: The Backgrounds, Recruitment, and Decisional Tendencies of the Judges on the United States Courts of Appeals, 1961–64.* Ann Arbor, Michigan: University Microfilms No. 65-9924.

———. 1966. "Voting Behavior on the United States Courts of Appeals, 1961–1964." *American Political Science Review* 60:374–383.

Gosnell, Harold. 1971. "The Chicago School of Politics in the 20's and 30's." *PS* 4:1–32.

Gottman, Jean. 1961. *Megalopolis*. New York: Twentieth Century Fund.

Gow, David John. 1971. *Judicial Attitude: A Critique and a Case Study of the High Court of Australia, 1964–1969*. Senior B.A. honours thesis in Government, University of Sydney, Australia.

———. 1974. "Eysenck through Space and Time: INDSCAL Analysis of Political Attitudes." Paper read at the annual meeting of the American Political Science Association, Chicago, August 31. Mimeographed.

Grant, J. A. C. 1965. "Felix Frankfurter: A Dissenting Opinion." *UCLA Law Review* 12:1013–1042.

Green, Bert F. 1954. "Attitude Measurement." In *Handbook of Social Psychology*, vol. 1, edited by Gardner Lindzey. Reading, Mass.: Addison-Wesley Publishing Co.

Greenway, John. 1964. *The Inevitable Americans*. New York: Alfred A. Knopf.

Groennings, Sven, Michael Leiserson, and E. W. Kelley, eds. 1970. *The Study of Coalition Behavior*. New York: Holt, Rinehart and Winston.

Grossman, Joel. 1965. *Lawyers and Judges*. New York: John Wiley & Sons.

Grossman, Joel, and Joseph Tanenhaus, eds. 1969. *The Frontiers of Judicial Research*. New York: John Wiley & Sons.

Grunbaum, Werner F. 1969. "Analytical and Simulation Models for Explaining Judicial Decision-making." In *The Frontiers of Judicial Research*, edited by Joel Grossman and Joseph Tanenhaus. New York: John Wiley & Sons.

Grundstein, Nathan. 1964. "Administrative Law and the Behavioral and Management Sciences." *Journal of Legal Education* 17:121–136.

Guilford, Joy P. 1956. *Fundamental Statistics in Psychology and Education*. New York: McGraw-Hill.

———. 1961. "Factorial Angles in Psychology." *Psychological Review* 68:1–20.

Guttman, Louis. 1951. "II. Scale Analysis, Factor Analysis, and Dr. Eysenck: A Reply." *International Journal of Opinion and Attitude Research* 5(3):103–120.

———. 1954. "A New Approach to Factor Analysis: The Radex." In *Mathematical Thinking in the Social Sciences*, edited by P. Lazarfeld. Glencoe, Ill.: Free Press.

———. 1968. "A General Nonmetric Technique for Finding the Smallest Coordinate Space for a Configuration of Points." *Psychometrika* 33:469–506.

Haas, Michael, and Henry S. Kariel, eds. 1970. *Approaches to the Study of Political Science*. San Francisco: Chandler Publishing Co.

Haber, David, and Julius Cohen, eds. 1968. *The Law School of Tomorrow: The Projection of an Ideal*. New Brunswick: Rutgers University Press.

Haddow, Anna. 1939. *Political Science in American Colleges and Universities*. New York: D. Appleton.

Haines, Charles G. 1915. "Report of the Committee of Seven on Instruction in Colleges and Universities." *American Political Science Review* 9:353–374.

———. 1922. "General Observations on the Effects of Personal, Political and Economic Influences in the Decisions of Judges." *Illinois Law Review* 17:96–116.

Hakman, Nathan. 1957. "Business Influence in the Judicial Process." *Western Business Review* 1:124–130.

———. 1966. "Lobbying the Supreme Court—An Appraisal of 'Political Science Folklore.'" *Fordham Law Review* 35:15–50.

———. 1969. "The Supreme Court's Political Environment: The Sponsorship and

Management of Supreme Court Non-Commercial Litigation." In *The Frontiers of Judicial Research*, edited by Joel Grossman and Joseph Tanenhaus. New York: John Wiley & Sons.

Hamilton, Walton H. 1938a. "1937 to 1787, Dr." In *The Constitution Reconsidered*, edited by Conyers Read. New York: Columbia University Press.

———. 1938b. "The Path of Due Process of Law." In *The Constitution Reconsidered*, edited by Conyers Read. New York: Columbia University Press.

Handy, Rollo, and Paul Kurtz. 1964. *A Current Appraisal of the Behavioral Sciences*, chapter 6: "Jurisprudence." Great Barrington, Mass.: Behavioral Research Council.

Hanley, Charles, and Milton Rokeach. 1956. "Care and Carelessness in Psychology." *Psychology Bulletin* 53:183–186.

Harman, Harry H. 1960. *Modern Factor Analysis*. Chicago: University of Chicago Press.

Harris, Joseph P., and Kenneth C. Davis. 1954. "Reflections of a Law Professor on Instruction and Research in Public Administration: An Exchange." *American Political Science Review* 48:174–185.

Harris, Whitney R. 1954. *Tyranny on Trial*. Dallas: Southern Methodist University Press.

Hayakawa, Takeo. 1962. "Legal Science and Judicial Behavior, with Particular Reference to Civil Liberties in the Japanese Supreme Court." *Kobe University Law Review* 2:1–27.

———. 1964. "Karl N. Llewellyn as a Lawman from Japan Sees Him." *Rutgers Law Review* 18:717–734.

Hearings before the House Committee on Ways and Means. 1965. "Proposed Amendments to Firearms Act." 89th Cong., 1st Sess.: Pt. 1 at pp. 104–105, 119; Pt. 2 at p. 570. Washington, D.C.: Government Printing Office.

Herndon, James. 1964. "The Role of the Judiciary in State Political Systems." In *Judicial Behavior: A Reader in Theory and Research*, edited by Glendon Schubert. Chicago: Rand McNally.

Herring, Edward Pendleton. 1929. *Group Representation before Congress*. Baltimore: Johns Hopkins University Press.

Hewart, Gordon, Lord. 1929. *The New Despotism*. New York: Cosmopolitan.

Hildebrand, James L. 1968. "Soviet International Law: An Exemplar for Optimal Decision Theory Analysis." *Case Western Reserve Law Review* 3:141–250.

Hirsch, Jerry. 1963. "Behavior Genetics and Individuality Understood." *Science* 142: 1436–1442.

Hofstadter, Richard. 1944. *Social Darwinism in American Thought*. Philadelphia: University of Pennsylvania.

Horwitz, Robert. 1962. "Scientific Propaganda: Harold D. Lasswell." In *Essays on the Scientific Study of Politics*, edited by Herbert J. Storing. New York: Holt, Rinehart & Winston.

Howard, Charles G., and Robert S. Summers. 1965. *Law, Its Nature, Functions, and Limits*. Englewood Cliffs, N.J.: Prentice-Hall.

Hoxie, Ralph G. 1955. *A History of the Faculty of Political Science, Columbia University*. New York: Columbia University Press.

Hyman, Herbert. 1959. *Political Socialization*. Glencoe, Ill.: Free Press.

Hyman, Stanley Edgar. 1948. *The Armed Vision: A Study in the Methods of Modern Literary Criticism*. New York: Alfred A. Knopf.

————. 1962. *The Tangled Bank: Darwin, Marx, Frazer, and Freud as Imaginative Writers*. New York: Atherton.

Hyman, Stanley Edgar, and Barbara Karmiller, eds. 1964*a*. *Perspectives by Incongruity*. Bloomington: Indiana University Press.

————, eds. 1964*b*. *Terms for Order*. Bloomington: Indiana University Press.

Ingersoll, David. 1966. "Karl Llewellyn, American Legal Realism, and Contemporary Legal Behavioralism." *Ethics* 76:253–266.

Jackson, Robert H. 1941. *The Struggle for Judicial Supremacy*. New York: Alfred A. Knopf.

————. 1955. *The Supreme Court in the American System of Government*. Cambridge, Mass.: Harvard University Press.

Jackson, Shirley. 1949. *The Lottery*. New York: Farrar Straus.

————. 1953. *Life among the Savages*. New York: Farrar Straus.

————. 1957. *Raising Demons*. New York: Farrar Straus.

————. 1959. *The Haunting of Hill House*. New York: Viking.

Jacob, Herbert. 1964. "The Effect of Institutional Differences in the Recruitment Process: The Case of State Judges." *Journal of Public Law* 13:104–119.

————. 1965. *Justice in America*. Boston: Little, Brown & Co.

————, ed. 1967. *Law, Politics, and the Federal Courts*. Boston: Little, Brown & Co.

Jacob, Herbert, and Kenneth Vines. 1962. *Studies in Judicial Politics*. New Orleans: Tulane University Studies in Political Science.

————. 1963. "The Role of the Judiciary in American State Politics." In *Judicial Decision-Making*, edited by Glendon Schubert. New York: The Free Press.

Jaffe, Louis L. 1955. "Mr. Justice Jackson." *Harvard Law Review* 68:940–948.

————. 1970. *English and American Judges as Lawmakers*. New York: Oxford University Press.

Jahoda, Marie, and Neil Warren. 1966. *Attitudes: Selected Readings*. Baltimore: Penguin Books.

Janda, Kenneth. 1965. *Data Processing: Applications to Political Research*. Evanston, Ill.: Northwestern University Press.

Jaros, Dean, and Robert I. Mendelsohn. 1967. "The Judicial Role and Sentencing Behavior." *Midwest Journal of Political Science* 11:471–488.

Jones, Harry W. 1963. "Law and the Behavioral Sciences: The Case for Partnership." *Journal of the American Judicature Society* 47:109–114.

————. 1965. "A View from the Bridge." *Social Problems* 13 (Supplement) (Summer 1965):39–46.

Kaiser, Henry F. 1968. "A Measure of the Population Quality of Legislative Apportionment." *American Political Science Review* 62:208–215.

Kaplan, Abraham. 1964. *Conduct of Inquiry: Methodology for Behavioral Science*. San Francisco: Chandler Publishing Co.

Karl, Barry D. 1970. Foreword to the 3rd edition of *New Aspects of Politics*, by Charles Merriam. Chicago: University of Chicago Press.

Katz, Daniel, and Floyd Allport. 1931. *Student Attitudes: A Report of the Syracuse University Reaction Study*. New York: Craftsman Press.

Kawashima, Takeyoshi. 1968*a*. "The Notion of Law, Right, and Social Order in Japan." In *The Status of the Individual in East and West*, edited by Charles A. Moore. Honolulu: University of Hawaii Press.

————. 1968*b*. "The Sociology of Law in Japan." In *Norms and Actions: National*

*Reports on Sociology of Law*, edited by Renato Treves and Jan F. Glastra van Loon. The Hague: Martinus Nijhoff.

Kawashima, Takeyoshi, and Zensuke Ishimura. 1964. "Amerika no hoshakai-gaku no myakudo." *Horitsu Jiho* 36 (April):4.

Kelman, Herbert C., ed. 1965. *International Behavior: A Social-Psychological Analysis.* New York: Holt, Rinehart & Winston.

Kendall, Maurice G. 1955. *Rank Correlation Methods.* Rev. ed. London: Charles Griffin.

Kessel, John. 1966. "Public Perceptions of the Supreme Court." *Midwest Journal of Political Science* 10:167–191.

Kestnbaum (The Second Hoover) Commission on Intergovernmental Relations. 1955. *A Report to the President for Transmittal to the Congress.* Washington, D.C.: Government Printing Office.

Kilpatrick, James J. 1967. "Firearms Controversy Revived." *Honolulu Star-Bulletin*, January 20, 1967, p. A–8, cols. 4–6.

Kirkpatrick, Evron M. 1962. "The Impact of the Behavioral Approach on Traditional Political Science." In *Essays on the Behavioral Study of Politics*, edited by Austin Ranney. Urbana: University of Illinois Press.

Knutson, Andie L. 1965. *The Individual, Society, and Health Behavior.* New York: Russell Sage.

Kommers, Donald. 1966. "Professor Kurland, the Supreme Court, and Political Science." *Journal of Public Law* 15:230–250.

Kort, Fred. 1957. "Predicting Supreme Court Decisions Mathematically: A Quantitative Analysis of the 'Right to Counsel' cases." *American Political Science Review* 51:1–12.

———. 1960a. "Letter to the editor." *American Political Science Review* 54:1000.

———. 1960b. "The Quantitative Content Analysis of Judicial Opinions." *Political Research: Organization and Design* (now *American Behavioral Scientist*) 3 (March 1960): 11–14.

———. 1963. "Content Analysis of Judicial Opinions and Rules of Law." In *Judicial Decision-Making*, edited by Glendon Schubert. New York: The Free Press.

———. 1966. "Quantitative Analysis of Fact-Patterns in Cases and Their Impact on Judicial Decisions." *Harvard Law Review* 79:1595–1603.

———. 1972. "The Multiple Dilemma of Political Science." *Modern Age* 1972:15–24.

———. 1973. "Regression Analysis and Discriminant Analysis: An Application of R. A. Fisher's Theorem to Data in Political Science." *American Political Science Review* 67:555–559.

Krislov, Samuel. 1965. *The Supreme Court in the Political Process.* New York: Macmillan Co.

———. 1966. "Theoretical Attempts at Predicting Judicial Behavior." *Harvard Law Review* 79:1573–1582.

Krutch, Joseph R. 1935. "Marx as Metaphor." *Nation* 140:453–454.

Kurland, Philip. 1964a. "The Court of the Union, or Julius Caesar Revisited." *Notre Dame Lawyer* 39:636–643.

———. 1964b. "Foreword: Equal in Origin and Equal in Title to the Legislative and Executive Branches of the Government." *Harvard Law Review* 78:143–176.

Landau, Martin. 1961. "On the Use of Metaphor in Political Analysis." *Social Research* 28:331–353. (Reprinted in Landau 1972.)

——. 1965a. "*Baker* v. *Carr* and the Ghost of Federalism." In *Reapportionment*, edited by Glendon Schubert. New York: Scribners.

——. 1965b. "Due Process of Inquiry." *American Behavioral Scientist* 9(2):4–10. (Reprinted in Landau 1972.)

——. 1968. "On the Use of Functional Analysis in American Political Science." *Social Research* 35:48–75. (Reprinted in Landau 1972.)

——. 1972. *Political Theory and Political Science.* New York: Macmillan Co.

Landes, David S., and Charles Tilly, eds. 1971. *History as Social Science.* Englewood Cliffs, N.J.: Prentice-Hall.

Lane, Robert E. 1962. *Political Ideology.* New York: The Free Press.

Lasswell, Harold D. 1930. *Psychopathology and Politics.* Chicago: University of Chicago Press.

——. 1947. *The Analysis of Political Behavior: An Empirical Approach.* New York: Oxford University Press.

——. 1948. *Power and Personality.* New York: W. W. Norton & Co.

——. 1951. *The World Revolution of Our Time: A Framework for Policy Research.* Stanford: Stanford University Press.

——. 1955. "Current Studies of the Decision Process: Automation versus Creativity." *Western Political Quarterly* 8:381–399.

Lasswell, Harold D., and Abraham Kaplan. 1950. *Power and Society.* New Haven: Yale University Press.

Lawlor, Reed C. 1963. "What Computers Can Do: Analysis and Prediction of Judicial Decisions." *American Bar Association Journal* 49:337–344.

——. 1967. "Personal Stare Decisis." *Southern California Law Review* 41:73–118.

——. 1969. "The Chancellor's Foot: A Modern View." *Houston Law Review* 6:630–664.

Lazarfeld, Paul, ed. 1954. *Mathematical Thinking in the Social Sciences.* Glencoe, Ill.: The Free Press.

Lepawsky, Albert. 1949. *Administration: The Art and Science of Organization and Management.* New York: Alfred A. Knopf.

Lerner, Daniel, and Harold D. Lasswell. 1951. *The Policy Sciences.* Stanford: Stanford University Press.

Lerner, Max. 1941. *Ideas for the Ice Age.* New York: Viking Press.

Lewis, Ovid C. 1970. "Systems Theory and Judicial Behavioralism." *Case Western Reserve Law Review* 21:361–465.

Lindzey, Gardner. 1964. "Genetics and the Social Sciences." *Social Science Research Council Items* 18:29–35.

Lingoes, James C. 1963. "Multiple Scalogram Analysis: A Set-Theoretic Model for Analyzing Dichotomous Items." *Educational and Psychological Measurement* 23:504–510.

——. 1966a. "An IBM-7090 Program for Guttman-Lingoes Smallest Space Analysis—IV." Computer Program Extract. *Behavioral Science* 12:74–75.

——. 1966b. "New Computer Developments in Pattern Analysis and Nonmetric Techniques." In *Proceedings of the 1964 IBM Symposium: Utilization of Computers in Psychological Research.* Blaricum. Paris: Gauthier-Villars.

——. 1967. "Recent Computational Advances in Nonmetric Methodology for the Behavioral Sciences." In *Proceedings of the International Symposium on Mathemat-*

*ical and Computational Methods in Social Sciences.* Rome: International Computation Centre.

Lingoes, James C., Kevin Kay, and Susan Spear. 1965. *Technical Report No. 29.* East Lansing: Michigan State University, Computer Institute for Social Science Research.

Lingoes, James C., and Louis Guttman. 1967. "Nonmetric Factor Analysis: A Rank-Reducing Alternative to Linear Factor Analysis." *Multivariate Behavioral Research* 2:485–505.

Llewellyn, Karl N. 1934. "The Constitution as an Institution." *Columbia Law Review* 34:1–40.

———. 1960. *The Common Law Tradition: Deciding Appeals.* Boston: Little, Brown & Co.

———. 1962. *Jurisprudence: Realism in Theory and Practice.* Chicago: University of Chicago Press.

Llewellyn, Karl N., and E. Adamson Hoebel. 1941. *The Cheyenne Way.* Norman, Okla.: University of Oklahoma Press.

Lloyd, Lord, of Hampstead. 1972. *Introduction to Jurisprudence.* rev. ed. New York: Praeger Publishers. Chap. 7: "American Realism."

Loevinger, Lee. 1949. "Jurimetrics, the Next Step Forward." *Minnesota Law Review* 33:455–493.

———. 1961. "Jurimetrics: Science and Prediction in the Field of Law." *Minnesota Law Review* 46:255–275.

———. 1963. "Jurimetrics: The Methodology of Legal Inquiry." *Law and Contemporary Problems* 28:5–35.

———. 1966–1967. "Law and Science as Rival Systems." *University of Florida Law Review* 19:530–551.

Lortie, Don C. 1959. "Laymen to Lawmen: Law School, Careers, and Professional Socialization." *Harvard Educational Review* 29:352–369.

Luttbeg, Norman R., and Melvin A. Kahn. 1968. "Ph.D. Training in Political Science." *Midwest Journal of Political Science* 12:303–329.

Lyon, J. Noel. 1967. "A Fresh Approach to Constitutional Law: Use of a Policy Science Model." *Canadian Bar Review* 45:554–577.

McBain, Howard Lee. 1927. *The Living Constitution.* New York: Macmillan Co.

McCloskey, Robert. 1962. "Deeds without Doctrines: Civil Rights in the 1960 Term." *American Political Science Review* 56:71–89.

McClosky, Herbert. 1958. "Conservatism and Personality." *American Political Science Review* 52:27–45.

Maccoby, Eleanor E., et al. 1954–1955. "Youth and Political Change." *Public Opinion Quarterly* 18:23–29.

McCoy, Charles A., and John Playford, eds. 1967. *Apolitical Politics: A Critique of Behavioralism.* New York: Crowell.

McCune, Wesley. 1947. *The Nine Young Men.* New York: Harper.

Macdonald, Austin F. 1928. *Elements of Political Science Research: Sources and Methods.* Englewood Cliffs, N.J.: Prentice-Hall.

McDougal, Myres S. 1966. "Jurisprudence for a Free Society." *Georgia Law Review* 1:1–19.

McQuitty, Louis L. 1957. "Elementary Linkage Analysis for Isolating Orthogonal and Oblique Types and Typal Relevancies." *Educational and Psychological Measurement* 17:207–229.

———. 1960. "Hierarchical Syndrome Analysis." *Educational and Psychological Measurement* 20:293–304.

———. 1963. "Rank-Order Typal Analysis." *Educational and Psychological Measurement* 23:55–61.

Maki, John M. 1964. *Court and Constitution in Japan.* Seattle: University of Washington Press.

March, James G. 1956. "Sociological Jurisprudence Revisited, a Review (More or Less) of Max Gluckman." *Stanford Law Review* 8:531–534.

———. 1965. *Handbook of Organizations.* Chicago: Rand McNally.

March, James G., and Herbert Simon. 1958. *Organizations.* New York: John Wiley & Sons.

Mason, Alpheus T., and Gerald Garvey, eds. 1964. *American Constitutional History: Essays by Edward S. Corwin.* New York: Harper and Row.

Mayers, Lewis. 1959. *Shall We Amend the Fifth Amendment.* New York: Harper.

Mayo, Louis, and Ernest Jones. 1964. "Legal-Policy Decision Process: Alternative Thinking and the Predictive Function." *George Washington Law Review* 33:318–456.

Mendelson, Wallace. 1963. "The Neo-Behavioral Approach to the Judicial Process: A Critique." *American Political Science Review* 57:593–603.

———. 1964. "The Untroubled World of Jurimetrics." *Journal of Politics* 26:914–928.

Menzel, Herbert. 1953. "A New Coefficient for Scalogram Analysis." *Public Opinion Quarterly* 17:268–280.

Merriam, Charles. 1925. *New Aspects of Politics.* Chicago: University of Chicago Press.

Merton, Robert, et al. 1959. *Sociology Today.* New York: Basic Books.

Miller, Arthur S. 1958. "The Constitutional Law of the 'Security State.'" *Stanford Law Review* 10:620–671.

———. 1960. "The Impact of Public Law on Legal Education." *Journal of Legal Education* 12:483–502.

———. 1962. "An Affirmative Thrust to Due Process of Law?" *George Washington Law Review* 30:399–428.

———. 1963. "Notes on the Concept of the 'Living' Constitution." *George Washington Law Review* 31:881–918.

———. 1964. "Technology, Social Change, and the Constitution." *George Washington Law Review* 33:17–46.

———. 1965a. "On the Interdependence of Law and the Behavioral Sciences." *Texas Law Review* 43:1094–1101.

———. 1965b. "On the Need for 'Impact Analysis' of Supreme Court Decisions." *Georgia Law Journal* 53:365–401.

———. 1965c. "Some Pervasive Myths about the United States Supreme Court." *St. Louis University Law Journal* 10:153–189.

———. 1967. "Science and Legal Education." *Case Western Law Review* 19:29–39.

Miller, Arthur S., and Ronald F. Howell. 1960. "The Myth of Neutrality in Constitutional Adjudication." *University of Chicago Law Review* 27:661–695.

Miller, Arthur S., and D. S. Sastri. 1973. "Secrecy and the Supreme Court." *Buffalo Law Review* 22 (Spring): 799–823.

Minogue, Kenneth R. 1964. *The Liberal Mind.* New York: Random House.

Mitchell, William. 1962. *The American Polity: A Social and Cultural Interpretation.* New York: The Free Press.

Monod, Jacques. 1971. *Chance and Necessity: An Essay on the Natural Philosophy of Modern Biology*. New York: Alfred A. Knopf.

Moore, Charles A., ed. 1968. *The Status of the Individual in East and West*. Honolulu: University of Hawaii Press.

Moore, Underhill, and Gilbert Sussman. 1932. "The Lawyer's Law." *Yale Law Journal* 41:566–576.

Morris, Desmond. 1967. *The Naked Ape: A Zoologist's Study of the Human Animal*. New York: McGraw-Hill.

Morris, John. 1966. *Technical Report No. 40*. East Lansing: Michigan State University, Computer Institute for Social Science Research.

Moskowitz, David H. 1966. "The American Legal Realists and an Empirical Science of Law." *Villanova Law Review* 11:480–524.

Mott, Rodney L. 1936. "Judicial Influence." *American Political Science Review* 30:295–315.

Mott, Rodney L., Spencer D. Albright, and Helen R. Semmerling. 1933. "Judicial Personnel." *Annals of the American Academy of Political and Social Science* 167:143–155.

Murphy, Walter F. 1964a. *The Elements of Judicial Strategy*. Chicago: University of Chicago Press.

———. 1964b. "Marshaling the Court: Leadership, Bargaining, and the Judicial Process." In *Judicial Behavior: A Reader in Theory and Research*, edited by Glendon Schubert. Chicago: Rand McNally.

———. 1965. *Wiretapping on Trial: A Case Study in the Judicial Process*. New York: Random House.

———. 1966. "Courts as Small Groups." *Harvard Law Review* 79:1565–1572.

Murphy, Walter F., and C. Herman Pritchett, eds. 1961. *Courts, Judges, and Politics*. New York: Random House.

Murphy, Walter F., and Joseph Tanenhaus. 1968a. "Constitutional Courts, Public Opinion, and Political Representation." In *Modern American Democracy: Readings*, edited by Michael N. Danielson and Walter F. Murphy. New York: Holt, Rinehart and Winston. Pp. 341–355.

———. 1968b. "Public Opinion and the Supreme Court: The Goldwater Campaign." *Public Opinion Quarterly* 32:31–50.

———. 1969. "Public Opinion and the United States Supreme Court: A Preliminary Mapping of Some Prerequisites for Court Legitimation of Regime Changes." In *The Frontiers of Judicial Research*, edited by Joel Grossman and Joseph Tanenhaus. New York: John Wiley & Sons.

———. 1972. *The Study of Public Law*. New York: Random House.

Myers, Gustavus. 1912. *History of the Supreme Court of the United States*. Chicago: Kerr.

Nagel, Stuart S. 1960. "Using Simple Calculations to Predict Judicial Decisions." *American Behavioral Scientist* 4(4):24–28.

———. 1961a. "Judicial Characteristics and Judicial Decision-Making." Ph.D. dissertation in political science, Northwestern University.

———. 1961b. "Political Party Affiliation and Judges' Decisions." *American Political Science Review* 55:844–850.

———. 1962a. "Ethnic Affiliations and Judicial Propensities." *Journal of Politics* 24:94–110.

———. 1962b. "Judicial Backgrounds and Criminal Cases." *Journal of Criminal Law, Criminology and Police Science* 53:333–339.

———. 1963a. "Off-the-Bench Judicial Attitudes." In *Judicial Decision-Making: Vol. 4 of the International Yearbook of Political Behavior Research*, edited by Glendon Schubert. New York: The Free Press.

———. 1963b. "Testing Empirical Generalizations in Legal Research." *Journal of Legal Education* 15:365–381.

———. 1965. "Law and the Social Sciences: What Can Social Science Contribute?" *American Bar Association Journal* 51:356–358.

Neumann, Eddy. 1971. *The High Court of Australia: A Collective Portrait, 1903–1970.* Occasional Monograph no. 5. Sydney, Australia: Department of Government and Public Administration, University of Sydney.

*New York Times.* 1946. June 11, p. 2, col. 3–6.

Nielson, James A. 1945. "Robert H. Jackson: The Middle Ground." *Louisiana Law Review* 6:381–405.

North, Robert C., et al. 1963. *Content Analysis.* Evanston: Northwestern University Press.

Olmstead, Michael. 1959. *The Small Group.* New York: Random House.

Osgood, Charles E. 1966. "Dimensionality of the Semantic Space for Communication via Facial Expression." *Scandinavian Journal of Psychology* 7:1–30.

Pannam, C. L. 1961. "Judicial Biography—A Preliminary Obstacle." *University of Queensland Law Journal* 4:57–73.

Pargellis, Stanley. 1938. "The Theory of Balance Government." In *The Constitution Reconsidered*, edited by Conyers Read. New York: Columbia University Press.

Patric, Gordon. 1957. "The Aftermath of a Supreme Court Decision." *Journal of Public Law* 6:455–463.

Paul, Julius. 1968. "The Return of Punitive Sterilization Proposals: Current Attacks on Illegitimacy and the AFDC Program." *Law and Society Review* 3:77–106.

Peck, Sidney R. 1967a. "A Behavioral Approach to the Judicial Process: Scalogram Analysis." *Osgoode Hall Law Journal* 5:1–28.

———. 1967b. "The Supreme Court of Canada, 1958–1966: Search for Policy through Scalogram Analysis." *Canadian Bar Review* 45:666–725.

———. 1969. "A Scalogram Analysis of the Supreme Court of Canada, 1958–1967." In *Comparative Judicial Behavior*, edited by Glendon Schubert and David J. Danelski. New York: Oxford University Press.

Peltason, Jack. 1953. "A Political Science of Public Law." *Southwestern Social Science Quarterly* 34:51–56.

———. 1955. *Federal Courts in the Political Process.* New York: Random House. (Originally published by Doubleday.)

———. 1961. *58 Lonely Men: Southern Federal Judges and School Desegregation.* New York: Harcourt, Brace & Co.

———. 1964a. Book review. *American Political Science Review* 58:675.

———. 1964b. "Supreme Court Biography and the Study of Public Law." In *Essays on the American Constitution: A Commemorative Volume in Honor of Alpheus T. Mason*, edited by Gottfried Dietze. Englewood Cliffs, N.J.: Prentice-Hall.

———. 1968. "Judicial Process." *International Encyclopedia of the Social Sciences* 8:283–291.

Phillips, Harlan B., ed. 1960. *Felix Frankfurter Reminisces.* New York: Reynal.

Playford, John. 1961. "Judges and Politics in Australia." *Australasian Political Studies Association News* 6 (August):1.

Plott, Charles. 1964. "Provisional Bibliography on 'Pure Theory of Collective Decision Processes.'" Thomas Jefferson Center for Studies in Political Economy, Charlottesville, Virginia.

Pound, Roscoe. 1932. "Jurisprudence." *Encyclopedia of Social Science* 8:477–492.

———. 1963. "Runaway Courts in the Runaway World. *UCLA Law Review* 10:729–738.

Presthus, Robert. 1962. *The Organizational Society*. New York: Alfred A. Knopf.

Pritchett, C. Herman. 1941. "Divisions of Opinion among Justices of the U. S. Supreme Court, 1939–1941." *American Political Science Review* 35:890–898.

———. 1942. "The Voting Behavior of the Supreme Court, 1941–1942." *Journal of Politics* 4:491–506.

———. 1943a. "The Coming of the New Dissent: The Supreme Court, 1942–1943." *University of Chicago Law Review* 11:49–61.

———. 1943b. "Ten Years of Supreme Court Voting [1931–1941]." *Southwestern Social Science Quarterly* 24 (June):12–22.

———. 1945a. "Dissent on the Supreme Court, 1943–1944." *American Political Science Review* 39:42–54.

———. 1945b. "The Divided Supreme Court, 1944–1945." *Michigan Law Review* 44:427–442.

———. 1946. "Politics and Value Systems: The Supreme Court, 1945–1946." *Journal of Politics* 8:499–519.

———. 1948. *The Roosevelt Court: A Study in Judicial Politics and Values, 1937–1947*. New York: Macmillan Co. (Reprinted as a paperback by Quadrangle Books, Chicago, 1969.)

———. 1954. *Civil Liberties and the Vinson Court*. Chicago: University of Chicago Press.

———. 1968. "Public Law and Judicial Behavior." *Journal of Politics* 30:480–509.

———. 1970. "'Ten Years of Supreme Court Voting': A Comment in Retrospect." *Social Science Quarterly* 50:983–984.

Pritchett, C. Herman, and A. Westin, eds. 1963. *The Third Branch of Government: 8 Cases in Constitutional Politics*. New York: Harcourt, Brace and World.

Ranney, Austin, ed. 1962. *Essays on the Behavioral Study of Politics*. Urbana: University of Illinois Press.

Read, Conyers, ed. 1938. *The Constitution Reconsidered*. New York: Columbia University Press.

Reed, Thomas H. 1930. "Report of the Committee on Policy of the American Political Science Association. *American Political Science Review* 24: supplement to no. 1 (February 1930).

Reid, Lord. 1972. "The Judge as Law-maker." *Journal of the Society of Public Teachers of Law* (New Series) 12:22–29.

Riker, William. 1962. *Theory of Political Coalitions*. New Haven: Yale University Press.

Robbins, Jonathan E. 1957. *Centroid Factor Analysis*. Ident. No. SU-4524. Developed and tested by Watson Scientific Computing Laboratory, Columbia University, and modified by John P. Gilbert, Center for Advanced Study in the Behavioral Sciences, Stanford. Multilithed.

Robinson, Edward Stevens. 1935. *Law and the Lawyers*. New York: Macmillan Co.

Robinson, James A. 1957. "Newtonianism and the Constitution." *Midwest Journal of Political Science* 1:252–266.

Robinson, James A., and Richard C. Snyder. 1965. "Decision-making in International Politics." In *International Behavior: A Social-Psychological Analysis*, edited by Herbert C. Kelman. New York: Holt, Rinehart & Winston.

Robinson, James Harvey. 1921. *The Mind in the Making: The Relation of Intelligence to Social Reform.* New York: Harper.

Robinson, John P., Jerrold G. Rusk, and Kendra G. Head. 1968. *Measures of Political Attitudes.* Ann Arbor, Mich.: Survey Research Center, Institute for Social Research, University of Michigan. (With Appendix B, 1969.)

Roche, John P. 1958. "Political Science and Science Fiction." *American Political Science Review* 52:1026–1028.

Rodell, Fred. 1955. *Nine Men: A Political History of the Supreme Court of the United States from 1790–1955.* New York: Random House.

Rogers, Edward S., and Harley B. Messinger. 1967. "Human Ecology: Toward a Holistic Method." *Milbank Memorial Fund Quarterly* 45:25–42.

Rogow, Arnold A., ed. 1969. *Politics, Personality, and Social Science in the Twentieth Century.* Chicago: University of Chicago Press.

Rokeach, Milton. 1960. *The Open and Closed Mind.* New York: Basic Books.

———. 1968. *Beliefs, Attitudes, and Values.* San Francisco: Jossey-Boss.

Rokeach, Milton, and Charles Hanley. 1956. "Eysenck's Tender-Mindedness Dimension: A Critique." *Psychological Bulletin* 53:169–176.

Rosenthal, Albert J. 1966. Book review. *Political Science Quarterly* 81:448–451.

Rowat, Donald C. 1965. *The Ombudsman: Citizen's Defender.* London: Allen & Unwin.

Rueckert, William H. 1963. *Kenneth Burke and the Drama of Human Relations.* Minneapolis: University of Minnesota Press.

———. ed. 1969. *Critical Responses to Kenneth Burke, 1924–1966.* Minneapolis: University of Minnesota Press.

Rumble, Wilfrid E., Jr. 1964. "American Legal Realism and the Reduction of Uncertainty." *Journal of Public Law* 13:45–75.

———. 1965. "Legal Realism, Sociological Jurisprudence and Mr. Justice Holmes." *Journal of History of Ideas* 26:547–566.

———. 1966. "Rule-Skepticism and the Role of the Judge: A Study of American Legal Realism." *Journal of Public Law* 15:251–285.

———. 1968. *American Legal Realism: Skepticism, Reform and the Judicial Process.* Ithaca, N.Y.: Cornell University Press.

Rummel, Rudolph J. 1970. *Applied Factor Analysis.* Evanston: Northwestern University Press.

Samonte, Abelardo G. 1966. "The Philippine and American Supreme Courts: A Comparative Study of Judicial Attributes, Attitudes, and Decisions." Paper read at the 62nd Annual Meeting of the American Political Science Association.

———. 1969. "The Philippine Supreme Court: A Study of Judicial Background Characteristics, Attitudes, and Decision-making." In *Comparative Judicial Behavior*, edited by Glendon Schubert and David J. Danelski. New York: Oxford University Press.

Sawer, Geoffrey. 1957. "The Supreme Court and the High Court of Australia." *Journal of Public Law* 6:482–508.

———. 1965. *Law in Society.* New York: Oxford University Press.

Schlesinger, Arthur, Jr. 1947. "The Supreme Court: 1947." *Fortune* 35:73–79.

Schmidhauser, John R. 1959. "The Justices of the Supreme Court: a Collective Portrait." *Midwest Journal of Political Science* 3:1–57.

———. 1961. "Judicial Behavior and the Sectional Crisis of 1837–1860." *Journal of Politics* 23:615–640.

———. 1962a. "Age and Judicial Behavior: American Higher Appellate Judges." In *Politics of Age*, edited by Wilma Donahue and Clark Tibbitts. Ann Arbor: University of Michigan, Division of Gerontology.

———. 1962b. "Stare Decisis, Dissent, and the Background of the Justices of the Supreme Court of the United States." *University of Toronto Law Journal* 14:194–212.

———. 1962c. "When and Why Justices Leave the Supreme Court." In *Politics of Age*, edited by Wilma Donahue and Clark Tibbitts. Ann Arbor: University of Michigan, Division of Gerontology.

Schram, Stuart R., ed. 1967. *Quotations from Chairman Mao Tse-Tung*. New York: Bantam Books.

Schroeder, Theodore. 1918. "The Psychologic Study of Judicial Opinions." *California Law Review* 6:89–113.

Schwartz, Bernard. 1959. *The Professor and the Commissions*. New York: Alfred A. Knopf.

———. 1963. *A Commentary on the Constitution of the United States: The Powers of Government*. Vol. 1. New York: Macmillan Co.

Selznick, Philip. 1959. "The Sociology of Law." In *Sociology Today*, edited by Robert Merton, et al. New York: Basic Books.

Shapiro, Martin. 1964a. *Law and Politics in the Supreme Court: New Approaches to Political Jurisprudence*. New York: The Free Press.

———. 1964b. "Political Jurisprudence." *Kentucky Law Journal* 52:294–345.

———. 1965. "Stability and Change in Judicial Decision-making: Incrementalism or Stare Decisis?" *Law in Transaction Quarterly* 2:134–157.

———. 1972a. "From Public Law to Public Policy, or the 'Public' in 'Public Law.'" *PS* 5:410–418.

———. 1972b. "Toward a Theory of Stare Decisis." *Journal of Legal Studies* 1:125–134.

Sheldon, Charles H. 1969. "Pre-Legal Training, Research and the Judicial Process: A Non-Legal Viewpoint from Non-Legal Sources." *Jurimetrics Journal* 10 (September 1969):1–19.

Siegel, Sidney. 1956. *Nonparametric Statistics for the Behavioral Sciences*. New York: McGraw-Hill.

Simon, Herbert. 1947. *Administrative Behavior*. New York: Macmillan Co.

———. 1957. *Models of Man: Social and Rational*. New York: John Wiley & Sons.

Simon, Herbert, Donald Smithburg, and Victor Thompson. 1950. *Public Administration*. New York: Alfred A. Knopf.

Skolnick, Jerome. 1965. "The Sociology of Law in America: Overview and Trends." *Social Problems* 13 (Supplement) (Summer 1965):4–39.

———. 1968. "The Sociology of Law in America." In *Norms and Actions*, edited by Renato Treves and J. F. Glastra van Loon. The Hague: Martinus Nijhoff.

Slayton, Philip. 1971. "A Critical Comment on Scalogram Analysis of Supreme Court of Canada Cases." *University of Toronto Law Journal* 21:393–401.

Snyder, Eloise C. 1958. "The Supreme Court as a Small Group." *Social Forces* 36:232–238.

Somit, Albert. 1969. "Psychopharmacology and Politics: Potential Problems." Paper presented at a panel of the 23rd Annual Meeting of the Western Political Science Association in Honolulu.

Somit, Albert, and Joseph Tanenhaus. 1964. *American Political Science: A Profile of a Discipline*. New York: Atherton Press.

Somit, Albert, Joseph Tanenhaus, and Walter Wilke. 1960. "Aspects of Judicial Sentencing Behavior." *University of Pittsburgh Law Review* 21:613–621.

Sorauf, Frank J. 1959. "*Zorach* v. *Clauson*: The Impact of a Supreme Court Decision." *American Political Science Review* 53:777–791.

Spaeth, Harold J. 1961. "An Approach to the Study of Attitudinal Differences as an Aspect of Judicial Behavior." *Midwest Journal of Political Science* 5:165–180.

———. 1963a. "An Analysis of Judicial Attitudes in the Labor Relations Decisions of the Warren Court." *Journal of Politics* 25:290–311.

———. 1963b. "Warren Court Attitudes toward Business: The 'B' Scale." In *Judicial Decision-Making*, edited by Glendon Schubert. New York: The Free Press.

Steamer, Robert J. 1954. *The Constitutional Doctrines of Mr. Justice Robert H. Jackson*. Ph.D. dissertation in Political Science, Cornell University. University Microfilms no. 9802.

Stephenson, William. 1953. *The Study of Behavior: Q-Technique and Its Methodology*. Chicago: University of Chicago Press.

Stone, Julius. 1964a. *Legal System and Lawyers' Reasonings*. Stanford: Stanford University Press.

———. 1964b. "Man and Machine in the Search for Justice." *Stanford Law Review* 16:515–560.

———. 1966a. *Law and the Social Sciences*. Minneapolis: University of Minnesota Press.

———. 1966b. *Social Dimensions of Law and Justice*. Stanford: Stanford University Press.

———. 1972. "On the Liberation of Appellate Judges—How Not To Do It!" *Modern Law Review* 35:449–477.

Storing, Herbert J., ed. 1962. *Essays on the Scientific Study of Politics*. New York: Holt, Rinehart & Winston.

Stouffer, Samuel. 1955. *Communism, Conformity, and Civil Liberties*. Garden City, N.Y.: Doubleday & Co.

Stouffer, Samuel, et al. 1950. *The American Soldier: Studies in Social Psychology in World War II. Volume 1: Measurement and Prediction*. Princeton: Princeton University Press.

Stumpf, Harry P., ed. n.d. "The Study of Public Law: A Plea for Consistency." Mimeographed.

Summers, Gene F., ed. 1970. *Attitude Measurement*. Chicago: Rand McNally.

*Sydney* (Australia) *Morning Herald*. 1964. April 2, p. 2.

Symposium. 1954a. "Correspondence Concerning the Treatment of Administrative Law in Public Administration Textbooks." *American Political Science Review* 48: 936–943.

Symposium. 1954b. "'Reflections of a Law Professor on Instruction and Research in Public Administration': An Exchange." *American Political Science Review* 48: 174–185.

Symposium. 1955. "Justice Robert H. Jackson." *Stanford Law Review* 8:1–59.

Tanaka, Kunio, and Yasuo Matsuyama. 1954. "Shakai-teki taido no sotteriron kenkyu."

In *Sengo Nihon Shinrigaku no Tenbo*, edited by O. Endo. Tokyo: Sanitchi Shobo.

Tanenhaus, Joseph. 1956. "The Uses and Limitations of Social Science Methods in Analyzing Judicial Behavior." Paper read at the annual meeting of the American Political Science Association, New York, September 7. Mimeographed.

———. 1960. "Supreme Court Attitudes toward Federal Administrative Agencies." *Journal of Politics* 22:502–524.

———. 1961. Communication to the editor: "On the Scaling of Judicial Decisions." *American Political Science Review* 55:600.

———. 1966. "The Cumulative Scaling of Judicial Decisions." *Harvard Law Review* 79:1583–1594.

Tanenhaus, Joseph, Marvin Schick, Matthew Muraskin, and Daniel Rosen. 1963. "The Supreme Court's Certiorari Jurisdiction: Cue Theory." In *Judicial Decision-Making*, edited by Glendon Schubert. New York: The Free Press.

Tate, C. Neal. 1972. "Social Background and Voting Behavior in the Philippine Supreme Court Justices, 1901–1968." *Lawasia* 3:317–338.

Thomas Jefferson Center for Studies in Political Economy. 1964. *Provisional Biography on Pure Theory of Collective Decision Processes*. Charlottesville, University of Virginia. Rev. ed. Mimeographed.

Thompson, Victor A. 1950. *The Regulatory Process in O.P.A. Rationing*. New York: King's Crown Press.

Thorbecke, Willem. 1965. *A New Dimension in Political Thinking*. Leyden: A. W. Sijthoff; New York: Ocean Publications.

Thurstone, Louis L. 1947. *Multiple-Factor Analysis*. Chicago: University of Chicago Press.

Thurstone, Louis L., and E. J. Chave. 1929. *The Measurement of Attitude*. Chicago: University of Chicago Press.

Thurstone, Louis L., and James W. Degan. 1951. *A Factorial Study of the Supreme Court*. Chicago: University of Chicago Psychometric Lab. No. 64. (Reprinted in *National Academy of Science* 37 (1951):628–635.)

*Time*. 1961. 77 (June 16):18.

Tomkins, Silvan S. 1962. *Affect, Imagery, Consciousness*. New York: Springer. Vol. 1: "The Positive Affects"; Vol. 2: "The Negative Affects" (1963).

———. 1965. "Affect and the Psychology of Knowledge." In *Affect, Cognition, and Personality*, edited by Silvan S. Tomkins and Carroll E. Izard. New York: Springer.

Tomkins, Silvan S., and Carroll E. Izard, eds. 1965. *Affect Cognition, and Personality: Empirical Studies*. New York: Springer.

Torgersen, Ulf. 1963. "The Role of the Supreme Court in the Norwegian Political System." In *Judicial Decision-Making*, edited by Glendon Schubert. New York: The Free Press.

Torgerson, Warren S. 1958. *Theory and Methods of Scaling*. New York: John Wiley & Sons.

———. 1965. "Multidimensional Scaling of Similarity." *Psychometrika* 30:379–393.

Treves, Renato, and J. F. Glastra van Loon. 1968. *Norms and Actions*. The Hague: Martinus Nijhoff.

Truman, David B. 1951. *The Governmental Process*. New York: Alfred A. Knopf.

———. 1955. "The Impact on Political Science of the Revolution in the Behavioral Sciences." In Stephen K. Bailey and others, *Research Frontiers in Politics and Government: Brookings Lectures, 1955*, Washington: Brookings Institution. Pp. 202–232.

Tugwell, Rexford Guy. 1970a. "Constitution for a United Republics of America, Version XXXVII (1970)." *The Center Magazine* 3 (September-October):24–25.

———. 1970b. "Introduction to a Constitution for a United Republics of America." *The Center Magazine* 3 (September-October):10–23.

Ulmer, S. Sidney. 1959. "An Empirical Analysis of Selected Aspects of Law-making in the United States Supreme Court." *Journal of Public Law* 8:414–436.

———. 1960. "Supreme Court Behavior and Civil Rights." *Western Political Quarterly* 13:288–311.

———. 1961a. "Homeostatic Tendencies in the United States Supreme Court." In *Introductory Readings in Political Behavior*, edited by S. Sidney Ulmer. Chicago: Rand McNally.

———. 1961b. "Scaling Judicial Cases: A Methodological Note." *American Behavioral Scientist* 4 (April 1961):31–34.

———. 1963. "Leadership in the Michigan Supreme Court." In *Judicial Decision-Making*, edited by Glendon Schubert. New York: The Free Press.

———. 1965. "Toward a Theory of Sub-Group Formation in the United States Supreme Court." *Journal of Politics* 27:133–152.

———. 1966. "Politics and Procedure in the Michigan Supreme Court." *Southwestern Social Science Quarterly* 46:375–384.

———. 1969. "The Discriminant Function and a Theoretical Context for Its Use in Estimating the Votes of Judges." In *The Frontiers of Judicial Research*, edited by Joel Grossman and Joseph Tanenhaus. New York: John Wiley & Sons.

———. 1970. "Subset Behaviors in the Supreme Court." In *The Study of Coalition Behavior*, edited by Sven Groennings, Michael Leiserson, and E. W. Kelley. New York: Holt, Rinehart & Winston.

*United States News.* 1946. 20 (June 21):81–82. Vines, Kenneth N. 1969. "The Judicial Role in American States: An Exploration." In *The Frontiers of Judicial Research*, edited by Joel Grossman and Joseph Tanenhaus. New York: John Wiley & Sons.

Vinson, Tony. 1968. "Comment on 'Opinion Agreement among High Court Justices.'" *Australian and New Zealand Journal of Sociology* 4:158–159.

Vose, Clement E. 1958. "Litigation as a Form of Pressure Group Activity." *Annals* 319:20–31.

———. 1959. *Caucasians Only: The Supreme Court, the NAACP, and the Restrictive Covenant Cases.* Berkeley: University of California Press.

Wallas, Graham. 1908. *Human Nature in Politics.* Boston: Houghton.

Walz, Gustav Adolf. 1934. "Public Law." *Encyclopedia of the Social Sciences* 12;657–659.

Ward, Robert E. 1967, *Japan's Political System.* Englewood Cliffs, N.J.: Prentice-Hall.

Warkov, Seymour. 1965. *Lawyers in the Making.* Chicago: Aldine Publishing Co.

Wasby, Stephen. 1965. "Public Law, Politics, and the Local Courts: Obscene Literature in Portland." *Journal of Public Law* 14:105–130.

Wasserman, Paul, and Fred S. Silander. 1958. *Decision-Making: An Annotated Bibliography.* Ithaca, N.Y.: Cornell University, Graduate School of Business and Public Administration.

———. 1964. *Decision-Making: An Annotated Bibliography, with Supplement, 1958–1963.* Ithaca, N.Y.: Cornell University, Graduate School of Business and Public Administration.

Wasserstrom, Richard A. 1961. *The Judicial Decision.* Stanford: Stanford University Press.

Watanabe, Tokio, and George Yamamoto, trans. and eds. 1964. *The Pulse of Sociology of Law in America.* Honolulu: East-West Center, Institute of Advanced Projects, Research Translations Series No. 4.

Weidner, Paul A. 1955. "Justice Jackson and the Judicial Function." *Michigan Law Review* 53:567–594.

Weiler, Paul. 1968. "Two Models of Judicial Decision." *Canadian Bar Review* 46:406–471.

White, James W. 1967. "Mass Movement and Democracy. Sokagakkai in Japanese Politics." *American Political Science Review* 61:744–750.

White, Morton. 1947. *Social Thought in America: The Revolt against Formalism.* New York: Viking.

Wiener, Frederick Bernays. 1962. "Decision Prediction by Computers: Nonsense Cubed—and Worse." *American Bar Association Journal* 48:1023–1028.

Wiener, Norbert. 1954. *The Human Use of Human Beings: Cybernetics and Society.* New York: Doubleday.

Wilson, Woodrow. 1885. *Congressional Government, A Study in American Politics.* New York: World Publishing Co., Meridian Book edition 1956.

———. 1887. "The Study of Administration." *Political Science Quarterly* 2:197–222.

———. 1889. *The State.* Boston: D. C. Heath & Co.

Winter, Paul. 1961. *On the Trial of Jesus.* Berlin: Walter de Gruyter.

Wolf, T. Phillip. 1970. "Prelude to a Great Book: A Trailblazer in Public Law." *Social Science Quarterly* 50 (March):969–971.

Woolf, Harry, ed. 1961. *Quantification: A History of the Meaning of Measurement in the Natural and Social Sciences.* Indianapolis: Bobbs-Merrill Co.

Yule, G. U. 1912. "On the Methods of Measuring the Association between Two Attributes." *Journal of the Royal Statistical Society* 75:576–642.

# Publications
# by the Author

1950. "Judicial Review of the Subdelegation of Presidential Power." *Journal of Politics* 12:668–693.

1951*a*. "Judicial Review of Royal Proclamations and Orders in Council." *University of Toronto Law Journal* 9:69–106.

1951*b*. "The Presidential Subdelegation Act of 1950." *Journal of Politics* 13:647–674.

1952*a*. "For Defense or Disaster." *National Municipal Review* 41:294–299.

1952*b*. "A Review of: Fred V. Cahill, Jr. *Judicial Legislation: A Study of American Legal Theory*. New York: Ronald Press, 1952." *American Political Science Review* 46:1180–1182.

1953*a*. "A Review of: Eugene C. Lee. *The Presiding Officer and the Rules Committee in Legislatures in the United States*. Berkeley: University of California, Bureau of Public Administration, Legislative Problems No. 1, 1953." *Western Political Quarterly* 6:205–206.

1953*b*. "The Steel Case: Presidential Responsibility and Judicial Irresponsibility." *Western Political Quarterly* 6:61–77.

1953*c*. "The Twenty-one Day Rule." *Political Science* 5:16–29.

1954*a*. "Letter to the Editor: 'Misinformation about Administrative Law': Some Comments on the Reflections of a Law Professor." *American Political Science Review* 48:941–944.

1954*b*. *The Michigan State Director of Elections*. University, Ala.: University of Alabama Press, Inter-University Case Program, No. 23.

1954*c*. "Politics and the Constitution: The Bricker Amendment during 1953." *Journal of Politics* 16:257–298.

1954*d*. "A Review of: Harry Street. *Governmental Liability: A Comparative Study*. New York: Cambridge University Press, 1953." *Journal of Politics* 16:182–184.

1954*e*. "A Review of: John N. Hazard. *Law and Social Change in the U.S.S.R.* Toronto: Carswell, 1953." *Journal of Politics* 16:364–367.

1955. "The Executive Rule-making Power: Hart and Comer Revisited." *Journal of Public Law* 4:367–421.

---

NOTE: For an appraisal, see Fred Kort, 1974. "The Works of Glendon Schubert." *The Political Science Reviewer* 4 (Fall 1974).

1956. "A Review of: Bernard Schwartz. *French Administrative Law and the Common-Law World.* New York: New York University Press, 1954." *University of Toronto Law Journal* 11:311–313.

1957a. *The Presidency in the Courts.* Minneapolis: University of Minnesota Press.

1957b. "'The Public Interest' in Administrative Decision-making: Theorem, Theosophy or Theory?" *American Political Science Review* 50:346–368.

1957c. "A Review of: Frederick K. Beutel. *Some Potentialities of Experimental Jurisprudence as a New Branch of Social Science.* Lincoln: University of Nebraska Press, 1957." *Administrative Science Quarterly* 2:264–268.

1958a. "Legislative Adjudication of Administrative Legislation." *Journal of Public Law* 7:135–161.

1958b. "Political Science Research and Instruction in Administrative Law." *Journal of Legal Education* 10:294–311.

1958c. "A Review of: Eugene C. Gerhart. *America's Advocate: Robert H. Jackson.* Indianapolis: Bobbs-Merrill, 1958." *American Political Science Review* 52:863–864.

1958d. "A Review of: Roland Young, ed. *Approaches to the Study of Politics.* Evanston: Northwestern University, 1958." *Administrative Science Quarterly* 3:526–529.

1958e. "The Study of Judicial Decision-making as an Aspect of Political Behavior." *American Political Science Review* 52:1007–1025.

1958f. "The Theory of the Public Interest." *Political Research: Organization and Design* 1(5):34–36.

1958g. "The Theory of 'the Public Interest' in Judicial Decision-making." *Midwest Journal of Political Science* 2:1–25.

1959. *Quantitative Analysis of Judicial Behavior.* Glencoe, Ill.: The Free Press.

1960a. *Constitutional Politics: The Political Behavior of Supreme Court Justices and the Constitutional Policies That They Make.* New York: Holt, Rinehart & Winston.

1960b. *The Public Interest.* New York: The Free Press.

1960c. "A Review of: Clement E. Vose. *Caucasians Only: The Supreme Court, the NAACP, and the Restrictive Covenant Cases.* Berkeley and Los Angeles: University of California Press, 1959." *American Political Science Review* 54:533–534.

1961a. "A Psychometric Model of the Supreme Court." *American Behavioral Scientist* 5(3):14–18.

1961b. "A Review of: Henry Kariel. *The Decline of American Pluralism.* Stanford: Stanford University Press, 1961." *American Political Science Review* 55:913–916.

1962a. "Is There a Public Interest Theory?" In *The Public Interest* [NOMOS, The Yearbook of the American Society for Political and Legal Philosophy, vol. 5], edited by Carl J. Friedrich. New York: Atherton Press.

1962b. "The 1960 Term of the Supreme Court: A Psychological Analysis." *American Political Science Review* 56:90–107. (Reprinted as chapter 5 herein)

1962c. "Policy without Law: An Extension of the Certiorari Game." *Stanford Law Review* 14:284–327.

1962d. "Psychometric Research in Judicial Behavior." *Modern Uses of Logic in Law* 2(3):9–18.

1962e. "A Review of: Kenneth N. Vines and Herbert Jacob. *Studies in Judicial Politics.* New Orleans: Tulane University, Tulane Studies in Political Science, Vol. VIII, 1962." *American Political Science Review* 58:138–139.

1962f. "A Review of: Marshall E. Dimock. *The New American Political Economy.* New York: Harper and Row, 1962." *Administrative Science Quarterly* 7:260–263.

1962g. "A Solution to the Indeterminate Factorial Resolution of Thurstone and Degan's

Study of the Supreme Court." *Behavioral Science* 7:448–458. (Reprinted as chapter 4 herein)

1963*a*. "Bibliographical Essay: Behavioral Research in Public Law." *American Political Science Review* 57:433–445.

1963*b*. "Bibliography." In *Judicial Decision-Making*, edited by Glendon Schubert. New York: The Free Press.

1963*c*. "Civilian Control and Stare Decisis in the Warren Court." In *Judicial Decision-Making*, edited by Glendon Schubert. New York: The Free Press.

1963*d*. "From Public Law to Judicial Behavior." In *Judicial Decision-Making*, edited by Glendon Schubert. New York: The Free Press.

1963*e*. "Judicial Attitudes and Voting Behavior: The 1961 Term of the United States Supreme Court." *Law and Contemporary Problems* 28:100–142.

1963*f*. Ed. *Judicial Decision-Making*. New York: The Free Press.

1964*a*. *Judicial Behavior: A Reader in Theory and Research*. Chicago: Rand McNally.

1964*b*. "The Power of Organized Minorities in a Small Group." *Administrative Science Quarterly* 9:133–153.

1965*a*. "Academic Ideologies, Judicial Attitudes, and Social Change." A paper presented at the 37th annual meeting of the Southern Political Science Association, Atlanta, Georgia, November 1965.

1965*b*. "Jackson's Judicial Philosophy: An Exploration in Value Analysis." *American Political Science Review* 59:904–963. (Reprinted as chapter 6 herein)

1965*c*. *The Judicial Mind: The Attitudes and Ideologies of Supreme Court Justices, 1946–1963*. Evanston: Northwestern University Press.

1965*d*. *Judicial Policy-Making: The Political Role of the Courts*. Chicago: Scott, Foresman & Co. (Revised edition 1973.)

1965*e*. Ed. *Reapportionment*. New York: Scribners' Research Anthology.

1965*f*. "A Review of: David J. Danelski. *A Supreme Court Justice Is Appointed*. New York: Random House, 1964." *George Washington Law Review* 33:1167–1170.

1965*g*. "A Review of: Herbert Jacob, *Justice in America: Courts, Lawyers, and the Judicial Process*. Boston: Little, Brown, 1965." *American Political Science Review* 59:1038–1040.

1966*a*. "The Future of Public Law." *George Washington Law Review* 34:593–614. (Reprinted as chapter 2 herein)

1966*b*. "The High Court and the Supreme Court: Two Styles of Judicial Hierocracy." A paper presented at the annual meeting of the American Political Science Association, New York City, September 1966.

1967*a*. "Academic Ideology and the Study of Adjudication." *American Political Science Review* 61:106–129. (Reprinted as chapter 9 herein)

1967*b*. "Ideologies and Attitudes, Academic and Judicial." *Journal of Politics* 29:3–40. (Reprinted as chapter 8 herein)

1967*c*. "Judges and Political Leadership." In *Political Leadership in Industrialized Societies: Studies in Comparative Analysis*, edited by Lewis J. Edinger. New York: John Wiley & Sons.

1967*d*. "The Rhetoric of Constitutional Change." *Journal of Public Law* 16:16–50. (Reprinted as chapter 11 herein)

1968*a*. "Behavioral Jurisprudence." *Law and Society Review* 2:407–428. (Reprinted as chapter 3 herein)

1968*b*. "Directions for Research, Empirical and Non-Empirical." In *The Law School of Tomorrow: The Projection of an Ideal*, edited by David Haber and Julius Cohen.

New Brunswick, N.J.: Rutgers University Press.

1968c. "Ideological Distance: A Smallest Space Analysis across Three Cultures." *Comparative Political Studies* 1:319–349. (Reprinted as chapter 10 herein)

1968d. "The Importance of Computer Technology to Political Science Research in Judicial Behavior." *Jurimetrics Journal* 8:56–63. (Reprinted as chapter 1 herein)

1968e. "Judicial Behavior." *International Encyclopedia of the Social Sciences* 8:307–315.

1968f. "Opinion Agreement among High Court Justices in Australia." *Australian and New Zealand Journal of Sociology* 4:2–17. (Reprinted as chapter 7 herein)

1968g. "Political Ideology on the High Court." *Politics* (The Journal of the Australasian Political Studies Association) 3:21–40.

1969a. "The Dimensions of Decisional Response: Opinion and Voting Behavior of the Australian High Court." In *The Frontiers of Judicial Research*, edited by Joel Grossman and Joseph Tanenhaus. New York: John Wiley & Sons.

1969b. *Dispassionate Justice: A Synthesis of the Judicial Opinions of Robert H. Jackson.* Indianapolis: Bobbs-Merrill Co.

1969c. "From Area Study to Mathematical Theory." In *Comparative Judicial Behavior*, edited by Glendon Schubert and David J. Danelski. New York: Oxford University Press.

1969d. "Judicial Attitudes and Policy-making in the Dixon Court." *Osgoode Hall Law Journal* 7:1–29.

1969e. "Justice and Reasoning: A Political Science Perspective." *Revista Internazionale di filosofia del diritto* 46:474–496. (Reprinted as chapter 13 herein)

1969f. "A Review of: John D. Sprague. *Voting Patterns of the United States Supreme Court: Cases in Federalism, 1889–1959.* Indianapolis: Bobbs-Merrill, 1968." *Journal of American History* 55:879–882.

1969g. "The Third Cla't Theme: Wild in the Corridors." *PS* 2:591–597.

1969h. "Two Causal Models of Decision-making by the High Court of Australia." In *Comparative Judicial Behavior*, edited by Glendon Schubert and David J. Danelski. New York: Oxford University Press.

1970a. *The Constitutional Polity.* Boston: Boston University Press. The Gaspar G. Bacon Lecture on the Constitution of the United States, 1968.

1970b. "The Scope of Interdisciplinary Cooperation." *Osgoode Hall Law Journal* 8:389–391.

1972a. *The Future of the Nixon Court.* Honolulu: University of Hawaii Foundation.

1972b. "Judicial Process and Behavior during the Sixties: A Subfield, Inter-disciplinary, and Crosscultural Overview." *PS* 5:6–15.

1972c. "Judicial Process and Behavior, 1963–1971." *Political Science Annual: An International Review*, vol. 3, edited by James A. Robinson. Indianapolis: Bobbs-Merrill Co. pp. 73–280.

1972d. "A Review of: Virginia Held. *The Public Interest and Individual Interests.* New York: Basic Books, 1970." *American Political Science Review* 66:599–602.

1972e. "The Sentencing Behavior of Ontario Judges: A Methodological Overview." *Osgoode Hall Law Journal* 10:234–257.

1972f. "Simulating the Supreme Court: An Extension of the Tenth Man Game." *Case Western Reserve Law Review* 23:451–500.

1973a. "Letter to the Editor: From Public Law to Public Policy." *PS* 6 (Winter):85–87.

1973b. "Letter to the Editor: In Reply to Krislov's Review of *The Constitutional Polity.*" *American Political Science Review* 67:968–969.

1973c. "One Touch of Adonis: On Ripping the Lid off Pandora's Box." *Buffalo Law*

*Review* 22:849–861.

1973*d*. "Political Culture and Judicial Ideology: Some Cross-and Sub-Cultural Comparisons." Paper presented to the Ninth World Congress of the International Political Science Association, Montreal, August 1973.

1973*e*. "Biopolitical Behavior: The Nature of the Political Animal." *Polity* 6:240–275.

1973*f*. "Future Stress, Constitutional Strain, and the American Judicial System." In *Proceedings* of the Citizens' Conference on the Administration of Justice. Supreme Court of Hawaii, Honolulu, February 1973.

1974*a*. *The Judicial Mind Revisited*. New York: Oxford University Press.

1974*b*. "Letter to the Editor: The Classification of Political Science Doctoral Dissertations." *PS* 7(Fall):449–450.

1975*a*. "Politics as a Life Science: How and Why the Impact of Modern Biology Will Revolutionize the Study of Political Science." Paper read at the Biopolitics Conference, Harry Frank Guggenheim Foundation and the International Political Science Association, Paris, January 1975.

1975*b*. "Sauce for the Gander, or, Putting Political Behavior to Work for Political Science: A Proposal for Implementing the Somit Critique of the Reports of Two Committees of the Social Science Research Council." *PS* 8(Winter):25–27.

Flango, Victor E., and Glendon Schubert. 1969. "Two Surveys of Simulated Judicial Decision-making: Hawaii and the Philippines." In *Comparative Judicial Behavior*, edited by Glendon Schubert and David J. Danelski. New York: Oxford University Press.

Koenig, Louis, Glendon Schubert, Lloyd Musolf, Laurence Radway, and John Fenton. 1971. *American National Government: Policy and Politics*. Glenview, Ill: Scott, Foresman & Co.

Schubert, Glendon, and David J. Danelski, eds. 1969. *Comparative Judicial Behavior: Cross-Cultural Studies in Political Decision-Making in the East and West*. New York: Oxford University Press.

Schubert, Glendon, Joseph LaPalombara, Frank Pinner, and Robert V. Presthus. 1956. *Local Civil Defense*. (A Report to the Federal Civil Defense Administration of a Questionaire Survey and Field Studies, submitted in accordance with the terms of a contract, No. CD-GA-56-104, between Michigan State University and the Federal Civil Defense Administrations; classified; mimeographed, 1,158 pages.)

Schubert, Glendon, and Major R. Marling. 1951*a*. "First Aid and Rescue Squads in Middlesex County." *New Jersey Municipalities* 28:30–32.

———. 1951*b*. "Volunteer Rescuers on Guard." *National Municipal Review* 40:527–532.

Schubert, Glendon, and Donald F. McIntyre. 1953. "Preparing the Michigan State Budget." *Public Administration Review* 13:237–246.

Schubert, Glendon, and Charles Press. 1964*a*. "Measuring Malapportionment." *American Political Science Review* 58:302–327.

———. 1964*b*. "Letter to the Editor: Malapportionment Remeasured." *American Political Science Review* 58:966–970.

Schubert, Glendon, Helenan Sonnenburg, and George Kantrowitz. 1955. *The Michigan Athletic Awards Rule*. University Alabama: University of Alabama Press, Inter-University Case Program No. 29.

# Index

# About the Author

GLENDON SCHUBERT is probably the best-known political scientist working in the field of judicial behavior, and is recognized by his colleagues as a major innovator. He has taught political science at leading universities throughout the United States, and in Canada, and is at present University Professor of political science at the University of Hawaii. An active lecturer, he also has become deeply concerned with biopolitics, and is affiliated with a great diversity of professional societies concerned with political science, sociology, law, and biology.

Dr. Schubert has written numerous books, including *The Constitutional Polity*, published by Boston University Press in 1970; *The Future of the Nixon Court*, University of Hawaii Foundation, 1972; *The Judicial Mind*, Northwestern University Press, 1965; and *The Judicial Mind Revisited*, Oxford University Press, 1974; as well as other research monographs and several textbooks. His articles have appeared in a large selection of leading journals, both American and foreign.